THE
ARTHUR ANDERSEN
EUROPEAN COMMUNITY
SOURCEBOOK

THE
ARTHUR ANDERSEN
EUROPEAN COMMUNITY
SOURCEBOOK

Iain P. A. Stitt
Consulting Editor
Arthur Andersen EC Office
Brussels

John J. McGonagle, Jr.
Research Editor

Triumph Books, Inc.
Chicago

This sourcebook is intended to provide timely, accurate, and authoritative information and resources essential to understanding the Single Market Program of 1992 and its impact on business. It is not intended to represent the rendering of legal, accounting, or other professional advice or services.

It is important for the reader to understand that the Single Market Program is an ongoing, dynamic process that will continue to change as new measures are proposed and legislation is enacted. Consequently, readers should use the sourcebook's extensive listings of contacts and resources as a means of tracking new developments. Due to the complex nature of the issues surrounding 1992, if legal, tax, or other expert assistance is required, the services of a competent professional should be sought.

Every effort has been taken to include the most timely, accurate, and authoritative information and resources that were available at publication time and that met strict selection criteria. However, given the volume of material and breadth of subject matter, some additional sources may have been overlooked. Your suggestions for future editions of the sourcebook are welcome.

Copyright © 1991 by Arthur Andersen & Co. and Triumph Books, Inc. All rights reserved. No part of this publication may be reproduced or transmitted in any form or by any means, electronic or mechanical, including by photocopying, without permission from Triumph Books, Inc., except in the case of brief quotations embodied in critical articles or reviews.

This book is available in quantity at special discounts for your group or organization. For further information contact:

Triumph Books, Inc.
644 South Clark Street
Chicago, IL 60605
(312) 939-3330
Fax (312) 663-3557

Editorial Services: Lynn Brown, Brown Editorial Service
Design and Production: Monica Paxson and Emily Friel, The Print Group
Cover Design: Concialdi Design

Library of Congress Cataloging-in-Publication Data

The Arthur Andersen European community sourcebook; the most comprehensive, authoritative reference guide ever assembled on the European market/Arthur Andersen & Co.; Iain P. A. Stitt, consulting editor; John J. McGonagle, Jr., research editor.

        p. cm.

    Includes bibliographical references and index.

    ISBN 0-9624436-4-6

       1. European Economic Community. 2. Europe 1992. I. Stitt, Iain P. A. II. McGonagle, John J., Jr. III. Arthur Andersen & Co.

  HC241.2.A755 1991
341.24'22--dc20   90-71573
                                                                  CIP

10 9 8 7 6 5 4 3 2 1

Contents

▼ ▼

Preface

For several years, executives throughout the world have been talking about the European Community's Single Market Program, better known as "1992". And yet, despite all the seminars, newsletters, and publicity, many executives still do not really know what 1992 is and what action they should be taking.

The 1992 program has been so well marketed that it has tended to focus attention on the date rather than the single market concept and the underlying principle of removing the barriers to the free movement of goods, services, people, and capital. In reality, 1992 is one point on a continuum—a watershed in an ongoing process of increased economic unity that dates back to the founding of the Common Market in 1957 and that will evolve way beyond 1992.

The Single Market is about competition, opportunities, and challenges. By the end of 1992, sufficient legislative measures will have been implemented by the 12 EC countries to create a single internal market of over 340 million people instead of 12 separate and disparate markets. It will provide new outlets for many products and services, and should lead to increased economies of scale and to decreases in the costs of distribution.

But there will also be real challenges. In particular, competition will increase. Some businesses will want to look outside their home countries and traditional markets—others will have to, if they are to survive. thus, all the implications of the Single Market, positive and negative, will have to be considered. Executives will need to identify those factors that will change quickly and those that will take much longer—there will be significant variations by industry and by product. There will still be 12 separate countries, each with its own characteristics and cultures. Ingrained habits and cultural differences will continue for some time to come.

Executives also need to be aware that the impact of the EC on businesses goes far beyond the Single Market program. There is already a large body of EC law and practice that has to be considered alongside the domestic legislation of each of the 12 Member States.

With so much happening, companies need information to understand and manage the impact of 1992. That's what this book is for—to provide a comprehensive guide to the vast array of alternative sources of information. The secrets to success are knowing where to look, choosing the right source, and making proper use of the information that is obtained. This sourcebook should prove invaluable to executives planning for the future.

Obtaining data and information is only part of the problem; you may also need advice to properly interpret the information and to evaluate the business implications. No organization is better positioned to provide it than the Arthur Andersen Worldwide Organization.

From our inception and throughout our continued growth around the world, we've understood the advantages of unity. With 300 offices, located throughout Europe, the Americas, Asia, Africa, and Australia, we face vastly different market conditions, regulatory environments, and cultural and business climates. Yet we are structured and committed to bringing the most appropriate of our global resources to bear on any issue in any location at any time. Because our European operations always have been a part of a unified practice with a single vision, we are uniquely suited to help your organization understand and react to the challenges and opportunities posed by a single European market—not just in Europe, but around the world. Not just in 1992, but before and beyond.

These are exciting and challenging times for companies doing business in or with the Single Market. The momentum toward unity and its effects are already being felt. And that momentum is accelerating. The changing political climate and the opening of Eastern European markets have already redirected the likely course of events—and made it even less predictable. We hope this sourcebook helps you gain a firmer grasp of what has happened and a better understanding of how it will impact your business.

June 1991
Iain P. A. Stitt
Arthur Andersen
EC Office, Brussels

Acknowledgments

This book has been made possible by the teamwork of dedicated professionals throughout The Arthur Andersen Worldwide Organization. First and foremost, we acknowledge our editors, Iain P. A. Stitt, Managing Partner of the firm's EC Office in Brussels and John J. McGonagle, Jr., of The Helicon Group, Ltd.

We also acknowledge the counsel and assistance of our tax and Single Market Program colleagues throughout Europe who gave their time, skills, and insights:

Hervé Bidaud, Paris
Susanne Braun, Frankfurt
Maria Paula Fins Brites, Lisbon
William T. Cunningham, Lisbon
Allard De Waal, Paris
Jack Favre, Eindhoven
Olivier Ferres, Luxembourg
James R. Gallagher, Dublin
Gabrielle P. Janfils, EC Office, Brussels
Marco Leotta, Rome
Timoleon N. Lizardos, Athens
David N. Marks, London
Michael F. McInerney, Dublin
Wolfgang Oho, Frankfurt
Josê Palacios, Madrid
Michele Paolillo, Milan
Xavier de Sarrau, Paris
Jørgen Skou, Copenhagen
Claus Spangenberg, Copenhagen
Alex Sulkowski, Luxembourg
Marie-Lise Swinne, Brussels
Alberto Esteban Terol, Madrid
Germain J. Vantieghem, Brussels
Rita Winkelmann, Frankfurt

Among the others who provided invaluable support are

Mary L. Leander, Chicago
Brenda Wisniewski, Chicago

Without the encouragement and support of Harry V. Ruffalo, Managing Partner—Tax Practice, the entire project would never have come about.

The editors and publisher would like to acknowledge the continuing assistance of the EC's Office for Official Publications of the European Communities, both in Belgium and in the United States, and the consent of the Commission of the European Communities to reprint or adapt portions from the following materials for use in this sourcebook:

Emile Noel, *Working Together: The Institutions of the European Community* (1988)

Europe Without Frontiers: Completing the Internal Market (1989)

Europe Without Frontiers: A Review Half-Way to 1992 (June-July 1989)

Panorama of EC Industry 1990 (1990)

All are copyrighted by the Commission of the European Communities, and all rights are reserved.

Some of the "highlight" materials in Part III are based on *Europe Without Frontiers: Completing the Internal Market* and *Panorama of EC Industry 1990*. The latter is an annual document and will be republished in the spring of 1991.

Materials in Appendix F are adapted from John J. McGonagle, Jr., and Carolyn M. Vella, *Outsmarting the Competition: Practical Approaches to Finding and Using Competitive Information,* copyright 1990. Reprinted with permission. All rights reserved.

Introduction

SECTIONS IN THIS INTRODUCTION

The Single Market Program of the European Community (EC) is one of the most significant economic and political events to occur in Europe in the last half of the 20th century. It will bring about major changes in the way business is conducted within the EC and will affect most companies worldwide, whether or not they currently do business within any of the 12 countries that make up the European Community.

The program's goal is to create a single, integrated European market free of restrictions on the movements of goods, services, capital, and people. To achieve this goal, the program calls for approval of over 300 measures that together will eliminate the main physical, technical, and fiscal barriers separating the 12 Member States: Belgium, Denmark, France, Germany, Greece, Ireland, Italy, Luxembourg, the Netherlands, Portugal, Spain, and the United Kingdom.

Even if a company doesn't do business in Europe today, it most likely will feel the impact of this Single Market Program, which will make many European companies more competitive in markets throughout the world. And any company doing business there now, or planning to do so in the future, must be prepared to take advantage of the opportunities offered by this new market and must understand the significance of the changes now occurring.

THE SOURCEBOOK AND ITS STRUCTURE

The sourcebook has been developed to serve as a comprehensive guide to the Single Market Program and the vast array of information sources available. In order to manage the impact of 1992 and take full advantage of significant new opportunities, businesses need timely information and a well-thought-out action plan. The sourcebook should help executives in their business decision making and this plan development.

Because the Single Market Program is ongoing, this sourcebook is not intended to give a snapshot of where every Single Market proposal stands today. Rather, the book guides you through the Single Market process and identifies the participants involved in the creation of the largest market in the world. It gives you access to tools needed to understand those aspects of the Single Market Program having critical importance to your specific type of business, but it does not overwhelm you with details in areas that may be of no current interest.

The sourcebook is divided into five major parts, each of which begins with an introduction outlining the contents of the part and ways to use it. An Assistance paragraph directs you to other parts of the sourcebook for additional help.

Part I: Overview of the European Community and the Single Market Program

Chapters 1 and 3 identify key strategic issues relating to the Single Market Program and their potential impact on your business. Chapter 2 provides a range of EC agencies and programs that offer various forms of assistance. Chapter 4 discusses the movement to create economic and monetary union throughout the EC and the use of the European Currency Unit (ECU). For those who want to track developments in the EC and understand the important differences between regulations and directives, Chapter 5 identifies the key institutions and issues involved in the Single Market Program and provides a historical perspective. Chapter 6 describes how Community legislation is developed, adopted, and put into force through specific procedures.

Part II: Summary of the Business Climate in Each EC Member State

Each chapter of Part II, "Profiles of the European Community Member States," follows the same format. Using this feature you can quickly compare specific issues on a country-by-country basis, such as business taxation, exchange controls, or labor laws, and determine which country best meets the needs of your business.

Part III: Data Resources, Associations, and Publications on Broad Economic, Business, and Social Topics

Part III explores sources that cut across industry lines. Each chapter begins with a brief overview of the impact of the Single Market Program on the topics covered. Each chapter then provides specific contact points within the EC and with associations and organizations in the EC that can offer additional specific information on these topics.

Chapter 19 lists many publications prepared by the EC that can provide the capability to track the Single Market Program at almost any level of detail. Most of these publications are nominal in cost; some are free.

Chapter 20 provides sources of EC-wide data on broad topics, such as population and economic growth. Many of these sources also offer information at the country level. As an additional aid, this chapter provides the names and addresses of the statistical offices of the 12 Member States.

Part IV: Data Resources, Associations, and Publications on Broad Economic, Business, and Social Topics

Part IV lists sources that affect specific industrial groups throughout the EC. Each chapter provides contact points within the EC and within associations and organizations in the EC that can offer additional specific information on these industries.

Within both Parts III and IV you will find

- A list of official contact points. These are offices within the Commission of the European Communities committees of the European Parliament directly involved with creating, monitoring, and implementing EC policies. The lowest-level office possible, usually within the subdirectorate, is identified so your inquiries can begin with those EC professionals most intimately associated with an issue.

- Lists of key EC-wide associations involved with the topic or industry in question.
- Lists of data resources and publications produced by the EC itself, plus others from the Organization for Economic Cooperation and Development (OECD), the United Nations, and the General Agreement on Tariffs and Trade (GATT). In many cases, the publications, databases, and periodicals are "recurring." They usually are updated on a regular basis or are published on a regular basis. The goal here is to provide access to the most current official information possible. These are arranged alphabetically within each section.
- Cross-reference notes directing you to other industries or topics of potential interest.

Part V: Supportive and Technical Information and Government Sources

Part V comprises Appendixes A through H and two comprehensive indexes.

Appendix A provides technical information on this sourcebook, including the agencies from which data is available and explanations of telephone number and address presentation. One of the challenges created by the Single Market Program is multilingual communications. EC and association addresses are presented in this sourcebook in the style used in Europe. However, because many word processors and personal computers do not have special character generation capabilities, we have omitted accent marks.

Appendix B features a glossary of business abbreviations and acronyms used in the EC and throughout the sourcebook.

Appendix C lists the designations and abbreviations for the most common forms of businesses used in the EC's Member States, such as "GmbH" and "teo."

Appendix D lists several hundred core titles of Single Market measures, including directives, proposals, and regulations, divided broadly along the same lines as the resource chapters in Parts III and IV.

Appendix E includes a directory of sources of information, government offices, and official distributors from whom resources identified throughout the sourcebook can be acquired. Official outlets and distributors are identified in Canada, Japan, the United States, and the United Kingdom.

Appendix F provides a summary of U.S. government contacts, data resources, and publications on the Single Market.

Appendix G provides a means to reach Single Market contacts in each of the 12 Member States.

Appendix H lists Single Market contacts located in Japan and Canada.

The Index of Organizations lists citations of all the official EC and outside organizations mentioned in the sourcebook.

Finally, the Name and Subject Index is a comprehensive guide to the contents of the sourcebook as a whole.

HOW THE SOURCEBOOK CAN HELP

The information in this sourcebook can assist you in a number of ways. For instance, you can use it to

- Develop major new outlets for your products or services
- Identify new low cost suppliers and methods of distribution
- Understand the intricacies of EC legislation, business regulations, and the complex monetary system
- Locate important new sources of funding and financing
- Find European business partners and joint venture opportunities
- Monitor actions of your competition and address competitive threats
- Evaluate which countries offer the best business climate for your type of organization
- Find and keep a competitive advantage in areas like product development, pricing, cost control, distribution, and customer relations

- Access the impact of the Single Market Program on different segments of your business
- Find and use current market and demographic data needed to make effective marketing decisions about the EC
- Develop a Single Market Program Plan of Action that will track developments in the EC that impact your business

TERMS SPECIFIC TO THE EC

Everyone involved with the EC in any way will need to master a new language that includes its own unique abbreviations and acronyms. The following terms are used throughout the sourcebook and reflect concepts in use throughout the EC:

Approximation. An effort to reduce differences among rules or standards, without actually eliminating them.

Harmonize. A process of bringing different rules or standards into a close, if not perfect, alignment. It is stronger than *approximation*.

Intra-Community. Within the EC.

Member State. Any of the 12 countries that are members of the EC.

Mutual Acceptance or Mutual Recognition. Term used to describe how one Member State permits the actions of another to have some legal effect within its borders. Similar in effect to a reciprocity clause, which provides that "I will do something for you so long as, and to the same extent that, you do it for me."

Rationalize. Term usually applied to significant industrial changes, including reductions in excess capacity and even layoffs.

Restructuring. Term usually applied to a program involving the closing of obsolete facilities, or scaling down older facilities with excess capacity, while engaging in some efforts to modernize remaining facilities.

Subsidiarity. The degree to which policy should be made at the Community level rather than left to the authority of the Member States.

Appendixes B and C list the more common abbreviations and acronyms used in the EC.

DEVELOPING A SINGLE MARKET PROGRAM PLAN OF ACTION

Who Should Have a Plan of Action?

Regardless of size, any of the following types of companies should develop a basic plan of action for dealing with the Single Market Program:

- Companies already buying or selling goods or services anywhere in the EC.
- Companies with operations located in the EC or elsewhere in Europe.
- Companies considering doing any business in Europe, even if it is outside the EC.
- Companies that have actual or potential competitors based in the EC. The Single Market Program could itself create new competitors.

Elements of a Single Market Program Plan of Action

Implementation of a basic plan of action for dealing with the Single Market Program has six key steps:

1. Making a commitment to understanding the EC and the Single Market Program
2. Identifying which Single Market Program measures are relevant to the business
3. Evaluating the business implications of the relevant measures in the Single Market Program
4. Developing strategies and detailed plans
5. Implementing those plans at the right time
6. Performing follow-up reviews and monitoring new proposals

This sourcebook is your key resource for creating and managing this plan.

MAKING A COMMITMENT

First, all members of management must have a proper appreciation of the EC, its institutions, and the Single Market measures. Management should be prepared to review the measures from both a strategic planning and an operational impact perspective. Part I of the sourcebook gives you that understanding.

IDENTIFYING THE RELEVANT PROPOSALS

Identify which of the several hundred Single Market measures are most relevant to your industry, your company, and your business. This means knowing all of the following:

- The purpose of each measure
- How that measure fits into existing EC law
- Whether there is any interaction with other measures
- Expected progress of each proposal, including probable implementation date

Parts III and IV of the sourcebook, as well as Appendix D, can help at this stage. In addition, the government resources listed in Appendixes E and F can provide significant assistance in understanding these issues.

EVALUATING THE BUSINESS IMPLICATIONS

You need to discern the following:

- Which measures, when implemented, will be obligatory and which will be optional
- Which measures are of fundamental importance to your business
- Which measures are beneficial to the business
- When each relevant measure is likely to go into effect

You must consider the interaction of each measure with existing EC and domestic rules. The strategic implications will not be the same as the operational business implications. You will have to make many subjective judgments, and it may not always be possible at this stage to quantify the monetary implications.

Part II will help you understand some of the basic domestic rules dealing with key business decisions.

DEVELOPING STRATEGIES AND DETAILED PLANS

Your strategic decision making will involve how you address many questions, including

- What changes may have to be made in the business
- What changes are likely to be made to any relevant proposal before they are finally adopted at Community level as part of the domestic legislation of each Member State

- How you can influence the details of any relevant proposals
- When those proposals are likely to be enacted

The following are some fundamental issues you need to consider:

- Markets and competition
- Mergers and other strategic alliances
- Your business's legal structure
- Location of different business activities
- Scope for product rationalization
- Sources of finance and banking arrangements
- Personnel policies
- Information technology
- Licensing and other arrangements

The extensive sources included in Parts III and IV can provide critical assistance at this stage and will help you track any relevant Single Market measures and try to influence them.

IMPLEMENTING PLANS AT THE RIGHT TIME

Developing a strategy is not enough. The strategy must be implemented at the right time.

PERFORMING FOLLOW-UP REVIEWS

The development of the Single Market is part of a continuing process. Many of the measures will change or evolve before they become Community law. Others will be modified or supplemented after being in force for a while. New proposals are constantly being introduced. You will need to monitor the progress of any proposals critical to your business. The same parts of this sourcebook that help you identify and evaluate key elements of the Single Market Program can help you monitor this progress.

ASSISTANCE

For additional help on using this sourcebook, refer to the appropriate part introductions.

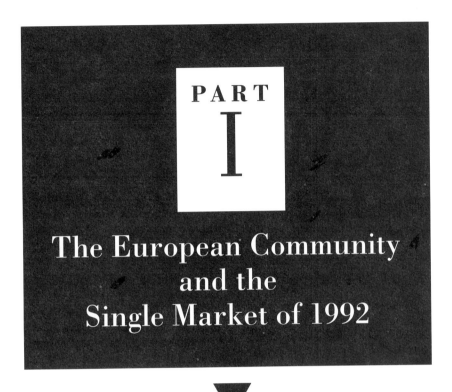

PART

I

The European Community and the Single Market of 1992

INTRODUCTION

This part of the sourcebook presents background information on the EC and the Single Market Program. It comprises six chapters:

1. The Single Market Program: What It Means to Your Business

2. The EC's Efforts to Promote Business Development

3. The Impact of the Single Market Program on Doing Business: Key Strategic Issues

4. Understanding the Evolving European Monetary System

5. The History and Structure of the European Community

6. Community Legislation: Balancing the Needs of the EC and Its 12 Member States

Each chapter contains its own introduction, which explains the importance or relevance of the chapter, briefly indicates the chapter's highlights, and lists  (under the Assistance heading) other places in the book that can help you use these materials.

This part provides you with a good introduction to the European Community and the Single Market Program. It introduces key strategic issues and leads you through the complex structure of the EC and associated legislation and regulations.

Armed with this perspective, you will be positioned to make best use of the comprehensive information and resources included in subsequent parts of the sourcebook—and ultimately take better advantage of the great opportunities presented by the Single Market Program.

ASSISTANCE

For a guide to setting up your own Single Market Program Plan of Action, see the general Introduction. For additional help in understanding and using this part, refer to Appendixes A through H.

The Single Market Program: What It Means to Your Business

1

To fully understand the Single Market Program, you must know where the development of the integrated market now stands and where the program and the EC are heading in the near term.

The Single Market Program will create the largest internal industrial and financial market in the world. The events leading to this integrated market of over 340 million consumers are happening now, and many will be completed by the December 31, 1992, deadline. Companies waiting until 1992 to respond to these events risk losing the opportunity to gain competitive advantage.

This chapter will help you appreciate how the Single Market Program will affect your business in the future.

OVERVIEW

The Single Market Program's proposals are vitally important factors that every business must consider. In many Member States and industries, the directives and other measures will add to, or at least significantly alter, existing national laws. Some of them have already resulted in major changes in the legal and economic environment in which companies operate.

Impact by Industry

Each company seeking to do business with, or in, the EC must appreciate the significance of the EC directives and other measures that specifically apply to its type of business or industry as well as the impact of the more general EC proposals and legislation, such as value added tax (VAT). Part IV of this sourcebook provides sources to help identify EC measures that impact particular types of business and industries.

Impact Across Industry Lines

General proposals, such as corporate (company) law changes and the removal of border controls, as well as the "social dimension" of the Single Market, will affect virtually every kind of business in the EC. Similarly, changes in banking controls and the regulation of other financial services, coupled with the removal of exchange controls in the Member States, will increasingly influence the availability and cost of capital. Part III provides sources to help you identify EC measures of more general impact, including overviews on the progress of the Single Market Program as a whole. These sources also give information on the current and future impact of EC legislation that cuts across industry lines.

Increased Business Opportunities in the EC

The Single Market will offer considerable opportunities and some disadvantages for businesses operating in the EC now and in the future. It will open new markets, allow increased economies of scale, and decrease the costs of distribution. Conversely, some new EC legislation and associated national laws may change and even limit the activities of certain companies.

More Competition from the EC

Even if your business is not intending to compete in the EC, the Single Market Program is important to you. For several reasons, EC-based competitors will begin entering non-EC markets previously ignored:

- In preparation for the Single Market, many EC-based companies have enhanced and will continue to improve internal operating efficiencies.
- The removal of physical, technical, and fiscal barriers will lead to cost savings and economies of scale.

- The EC as a whole is a net exporter and plans to remain in that position.
- The Single Market Program is encouraging cooperative activity among EC businesses, within and outside the EC.

Finally, the Single Market Program should not be considered in isolation. It is one factor (admittedly an important one) to be considered in conjunction with all other factors that affect your company's decision to do business in one particular country or group of countries. In particular, cultural differences will remain an important factor in marketing products in the 12 Member States. Moreover, the Single Market Program is only the "tip of the iceberg"—existing (and new) EC law and practice also need to be considered.

SECTIONS IN THIS CHAPTER

The European Community: The Business Opportunity of the Century

Removing Roadblocks to a Frontier-Free Europe

Monitoring Ongoing EC Legislation

The Future: Changing Relations with Non-EC Countries

ASSISTANCE

Refer to the following units of this book for the information listed:

- Chapter 5, which describes the institutions and historical development of the EC.
- Chapter 6, which explains how the EC adopts Community legislation and how that legislation relates to the laws of the Member States.
- Part III, whose chapters list sources of information on the Single Market Program by broad topic.
- Part IV, whose chapters categorize sources of information on the Single Market Program by broad industrial sector.
- Appendix D, which lists the Single Market directives and other measures keyed to each chapter's scope in this book.

For additional help in using this sourcebook, refer to the Introduction to Part I.

THE EUROPEAN COMMUNITY: THE BUSINESS OPPORTUNITY OF THE CENTURY

The Single Market Program, which is changing the way business is conducted within the EC and affecting most companies worldwide, will create a single European market without restrictions on the movement of goods, services, capital, or people. By eliminating the major physical, technical, and fiscal barriers separating the 12 Member States, the program is bringing into existence the largest single integrated market in the world.

This market will have more than 340 million consumers and will account for more than one-third of the world's imports and exports. Four additional European countries have applied to join the EC; others are considering applying. Discussions have started with a view toward creating a European Economic Area, which would include the balance of Western Europe and will likely encompass Central and Eastern Europe in due course.

Companies throughout Europe are restructuring and repositioning to take advantage of this increased market. In doing so, they are becoming better able to compete in their home countries and throughout the EC and are becoming stronger competitors in the rest of the world. Even if a company doesn't do business in Europe today, it will likely feel the impact of this Single Market Program. Any company doing business in the EC today, or planning to do business there in the future, must understand the significance of the changes now occurring and be prepared to take advantage of them.

The concept of a single European market is not new. Its origins lie in several organizations created by treaties to strengthen the economic well-being of post-World War II Europe.

The principal organization of the past was the European Economic Community (EEC), now subsumed into the EC. The EEC came into being in 1958, following the signing of the Treaty of Rome.

The objective was to create a "common market," principally by eliminating factors that distorted competition.

Although the Community made significant progress in the first 15 years, there was little movement toward this goal during the middle and late 1970s and early 1980s. In 1985, the European Commission issued a White Paper, "Completing the Internal Market"; it was a comprehensive blueprint for achieving the Single Market by the end of 1992. In 1986, the Single European Act was signed.

Together, the 1985 White Paper and the Single European Act rejuvenated and accelerated the effort to eliminate all physical, technical, and fiscal barriers to free trade throughout the EC, and to create a true single market of over 340 million people. The target date for achieving this goal is December 31, 1992. For that reason, the movement toward the Single Market is often referred to as "Europe 92," or simply "1992."

The creation of the Single Market entails the adoption of the 300 measures mentioned in the White Paper, which are designed to remove the barriers to free trade and which will lead to countless changes in the domestic legislation of the 12 Member States. These new measures will be added to the considerable body of EC legislation that already exists.

Additional measures, not initially in the 1985 White Paper, are constantly being proposed. They will facilitate the creation of the Single Market by effecting changes in a broad range of areas, including

- National and regional economic development
- The "Social Dimension," including matters relating to labor, working conditions, and so on
- EC-wide research and development
- The monetary and fiscal policies of the 12 Member States

▼ ▼

REMOVING ROADBLOCKS TO A FRONTIER-FREE EUROPE

The Single Market Program has three key objectives:

- The removal of physical barriers
- The removal of technical barriers
- The removal of fiscal barriers

Removing Physical Barriers

One goal of the 1985 White Paper proposals is the elimination of all national regulations and procedures that create border controls, such as safety checks of vehicles. Such controls hinder the free movement of people and goods throughout the EC:

- *Single Administrative Document.* The EC has adopted the "Single Administrative Document" (SAD). This system eliminates the need for duplicative and overlapping documentation for goods shipped within the EC or into the EC from EFTA. To comply with widely varying national requirements in the past, companies transporting goods from one end of the EC to the other had to produce literally pounds of documents covering the cargo being transported. However, it is anticipated that even the SAD will disappear in 1993, for intra-EC trade.

- *Internal Travel.* The White Paper includes plans to remove all controls for travelers at the internal frontiers of the EC by 1992. This will be accomplished by a progressive relaxation of existing controls. At the same time, the EC and the Member States will implement related measures dealing with terrorism, drug trafficking, crime prevention, and the movement within the EC of nationals of non-Member States.

- *Movement of Agricultural Goods.* The 1985 White Paper calls for increasing the EC's efforts to minimize existing obstacles on the movement of agricultural products throughout the EC. These obstacles often result from different health standards for animals and plants in force in the Member States. One approach to achieving this goal is to establish procedures based on the mutual recognition by Member States of each other's checks, controls, and inspections *prior* to certification at points of departure. These procedures would be coupled with occasional spot-checks on the certification at EC destinations.

- *Hauling Quotas.* The 1985 White Paper proposes directives to reduce national border controls needed to enforce national quotas on hauling goods as well as national laws on safety standards. This objective will be accomplished by replacing national quotas on the number of trips haulers can undertake with an EC quota and by the adoption of common standards for truck safety and enforcement methods throughout the EC.

Removing Technical Barriers

A major barrier to the free movement of goods into and throughout the EC has been the existence of 12 separate sets of industrial standards. When each Member State has a different set of standards, manufacturers and exporters cannot produce goods that can be used throughout the EC. Rather, they must produce goods meeting each set of standards or forgo the ability to sell in every market.

It is expected that EC measures will gradually lead to the development of EC industrial standards acceptable throughout the Community. These common technical standards will increase the EC's international competitiveness.

The types of products covered by the standardization continues to increase. Among those where work has already started are

- Toys
- Chemicals
- Food
- Motor vehicles
- Pharmaceuticals
- Tractors and agricultural machinery

The standardization is not being accomplished by having the EC itself set detailed common standards. Rather, in most cases, the EC establishes essential health and safety requirements; the principle of mutual recognition should then apply, unless a specific EC standard has been established. Under that principle, a product that meets the basic health and safety requirements and meets the standards of country A should be acceptable in all other Member States.

In cases where detailed industrial standards are considered to be necessary and appropriate, the

EC is giving the task of developing and defining them to one of several nongovernmental standards bodies. They are

- CEN (European Committee for Standardization);
- CENELEC (European Committee for Electrotechnical Standardization); and
- ETSI (European Telecommunications Standards Institute).

In cases where there is no EC standard, Member States can adopt their own. However, to prevent the rapid growth of conflicting national standards in areas where the EC has yet to act, the Member States must notify the Commission in advance of all draft agricultural and industrial standards.

CHANGING THE STANDARDS PROCESS

The process of adopting standards is not working as rapidly as the Commission would like. In late 1990, the Commission noted that, to meet the December 31, 1992, target date for the Single Market, a new European industrial standard would have to be created every day. To put this in perspective, during the six-year period from 1984 through 1989, only 814 standards had been adopted.

The delay in adopting standards is not at the national level. The Member States have been establishing minimum standards at what the Commission regards as a satisfactory pace. The problem is at the level where experts develop the resultant detailed technical specifications.

To accelerate the process of adopting final industrial standards, the Commission is seeking to make major changes in the way industrial standards are handled. These changes will include increasing budgets and the formation of a new organization for setting European industrial standards.

TESTS AND CERTIFICATIONS

In a related area, the Commission is developing directives dealing with the mutual recognition of tests and certifications among the Member States. These directives would require each Member State to recognize the adequacy of each other's certification and testing procedures.

OTHER BARRIERS

Other significant technical barriers identified for elimination in the movement toward the Single Market include the following:

- Laws that impede the marketing of food prod-

ucts made in one Member State to the residents of another. This barrier is being removed by establishing EC-wide rules concerning basic consumer protection and safety, such as with additives, preservatives, packaging, and labeling. The Member States can maintain national rules on matters not essential to health and safety. But they *must* permit products from other Member States prepared differently (due to differing national requirements) to be marketed to their own residents, provided those products meet the basic health and safety requirements.

- Elimination of the barriers to employment mobility caused by differing professional and vocational qualification standards in the Member States. This is being accomplished in several different ways. Already, most medical professionals have had their basic training requirements "harmonized" and now have the right to practice in all EC countries.

  However, establishing and agreeing on detailed rules for every profession is a very slow process. Hence, the EC is now establishing a system based upon "mutual recognition." Under it and subject to certain limitations, individuals holding the equivalent qualification from one Member State may practice their field of expertise in another Member State under the same conditions as persons holding the relevant qualification from the other State. In addition, the Commission is working on the mutual acceptance of vocational training qualifications for apprentices.

- Continuing the movement toward a complete liberalization of all financial transactions. This movement includes the creation of a single EC banking "license," based on the principle of mutual recognition of banking supervision standards. It also entails liberalizing cross-border transactions for other financial services, including insurance, investments, and so on.

- Increasing competition in government purchasing by the EC and its Member States. This includes opening procurement activities for both goods and services to non-national firms. Specifically, even third-country bidders would have to receive the same treatment as EC bidders, unless EC bidders are discriminated against in the third country. However, it seems that the final form of directives in this area may still allow some discrimination by Member

States in government purchasing, based on the origin of goods and services offered in a bid within limits set by the GATT. Most other countries operate similar restrictions.

- Opening up all transportation markets to competition by removing protective restrictions applicable to most modes of transportation. Removing these restrictions would in the long term partially or completely deregulate most modes of transportation in the EC.

- Continuing steps toward creating a Europe-wide "audiovisual area." These steps include establishing EC-wide standards for new communications services, in addition to current efforts that have already opened up broadcasting throughout the EC.

- Creation of a single trademark, valid throughout the EC, and registered with an EC Trademark Office. Somewhat similar steps are being taken with regard to patents. The EC is seeking to standardize copyright laws throughout the EC. It is also working on the development of new legal protections for biotechnological inventions.

- Development of a Europe-wide company statute.

- Removing direct tax barriers to cross-border cooperation.

Removing Fiscal Barriers

TAXES

The third set of targets established by the 1985 White Paper deals with the elimination of fiscal barriers, to the extent that they impede cross-border trade within the EC. The 1985 White Paper indicates that two major steps have to be taken to accomplish the removal of significant fiscal barriers:

- Harmonize the value-added taxes (VAT) between countries; and

- Harmonize excise taxes.

The major initiatives must resolve a fundamental political conflict between a European Community without internal frontiers and the desire of the fiscal authorities of each Member State to collect the taxes to which they are entitled. Historically, national fiscal authorities collected these taxes at the border, relying in part on documentation that importers had to provide to bring their goods into the country.

It is important to note that the Commission regards direct tax measures and exchange controls as forming part of the technical—rather than fiscal—barriers to cross-border transactions.

VAT

The very diversity of indirect taxes among the Member Countries of the EC has the effect of distorting competition and producing artificial price differences between the Member States. Thus, even before the Single Market Program, the EC made major progress in removing fiscal barriers. This progress was accomplished primarily through the introduction of VAT, the value-added tax, as the common turnover tax for the EC's Member States. However, even with a common system of VAT and convergence on the scope and coverage of that tax, rates of VAT differ widely among Member States. In addition, there are major differences in the main national excise duties.

In response to this diversity of taxes, the Commission has proposed that variations among the Member States' indirect taxes be reduced but not necessarily eliminated. This reduction would, in turn, mean border controls will no longer be needed to adjust indirect taxes on the import and export of goods. However, one effect of such tax standardization would be to raise prices in countries with relatively lower levels of indirect taxes and to reduce tax revenues in countries with relatively higher indirect tax rates. Because of this impact, some Member States are resisting implementation of these proposals. Indeed, effecting changes in VAT rates and some of the basic principles will be spread over the next five years.

Nevertheless, some progress is being made on VAT. The EC has adopted transitional arrangements for VAT, designed to reduce the burden imposed on businesses and eliminate the need for border checks. The ultimate goal of the Commission is to approximate VAT rates. Each country would set a single standard rate that must not be lower than a minimum level yet to be set (but expected to be 14 percent), a lower rate of between 4 percent and 9 percent for certain goods, and each country would be allowed a zero rate for a restricted range of goods. The highest band of VAT rates, which now can range up to 38 percent on luxury goods in some countries, ultimately would be abolished. Instead of routine border checks, the proposed system would rely on periodic VAT declaration forms and the provision of other detailed information by companies.

The Commission is proposing that after 1992 consumers in the EC be able to buy goods in the EC country of their choice and pay that Member State's VAT. Such purchases would include no controls or tax payments at national borders. However, two classes of items would be exempted from this system: passenger cars and motorcycles, and mail-order sales. They still would be taxed at the purchaser's home-country VAT rate.

The process of removing all fiscal barriers is expected to take several years. Even if all of the Commission's proposals are adopted, the European Community will not have a system of harmonized taxes. It will have a system best described as an "approximation" that will leave to the individual Member States the right to adjust taxes to meet particular national needs and "changes in circumstances."

▼

MONITORING ONGOING EC LEGISLATION

Any assessment of the ultimate effect of the Single Market Program on the EC and its Member States would be distorted if it were limited only to the impact of the proposals included in the 1985 White Paper. To appreciate fully the impact of the Single Market Program, consideration should also be given to EC legislation and actions *beyond* the White Paper's proposals:

- The EC has been enacting, and will continue to enact, legislation on many issues that received only brief, if any, mention in the White Paper, such as competition rules and the social dimension.

- The EC has already established rules on matters that were not specifically referred to in the 1985 White Paper. These include matters such as the use of Structural Funds and the management of the EC's external relations.

- The EC will need to adopt other measures to supplement or modify the White Paper proposals themselves, as well as to change the way in which they are administered.

- The Commission already has the power to act, on its own initiative, on behalf of all Member States in certain areas, including trade policy and competition law.

The topics that fall into these categories are varied. The following illustrate the sweep of the potential actions of the EC in supplemental areas as it moves toward a Single Market:

- *Support for technological research and development.* The EC has put into place a bewildering variety of direct programs, such as Esprit (European Strategic Program for Research and Development in Information Technology) and RACE (Research and Development in Advanced Communications Technology for Europe). It has also established intergovernmental programs like Eureka (European Research Co-ordination Agency). Collectively, these programs should help EC companies take advantage of the large market provided by the Single Market Program as well as respond to external competition.

- *Investment in the transportation infrastructure.* The deregulation of transportation and the liberalization of trade throughout the EC will produce a growing demand for improved transportation to meet this demand. The EC may well have to become actively involved in major work on the infrastructure needed in certain countries.

- *Continued assistance in regional development.* To have the EC and the Single Market provide the maximum benefit to all Member States, the Commission has concluded that it must strengthen internal economic and social cohesion throughout the EC. To do that, the Commission is promoting the development of less-developed regions throughout the EC. It is also helping to redevelop regions suffering economic decline. These activities are being conducted through the EC's Structural Funds. The EC is committed to continued substantial increases in these funds.

- *Broadening of the scope of social policies.* The Commission has stated that one of the EC's goals is to ensure Community-wide economic and social cohesion. To accomplish this, the Commission has targeted four priorities:

  1. Harmonization of rules on health and safety at work

  2. Addition of provisions on workers' rights in any law providing for a European company

3. Adoption of individual measures to implement an EC charter of fundamental social rights for workers

4. Intensification of a "social dialogue" at the European level

• *Formation of an economic and monetary union.* As progress continues toward the free movement of capital and financial services throughout the EC, the need for coordination of the EC's economy becomes increasingly important. Moves toward EMU (economic and monetary union) have already started. This is likely to lead to greater importance for the ECU (the European Currency Unit) and the EMS (European Monetary System). (See Chapter 4 for more information on these topics.)

• *Commercial policies.* As the Single Market nears completion, its growth is expected to benefit companies in the EC as well as companies in the EC's major trading partners by providing a larger market for all of them. This has led to discussions on the creation of a European Economic Area (consisting of the EC Member States and the seven members of EFTA [Austria, Finland, Iceland, Liechtenstein, Norway, Sweden, and Switzerland]) and the negotiation of international trade agreements with the countries of Central and Eastern Europe.

THE FUTURE: CHANGING RELATIONS WITH NON-EC COUNTRIES

The European Free Trade Association

The European Free Trade Association, or EFTA, was established in 1960 to liberalize trade among its members. Within six years after its creation, tariffs between EFTA member countries on most industrial goods had been eliminated.

EFTA's founding members were Austria, Denmark, Norway, Portugal, Sweden, Switzerland, and the United Kingdom. Finland became a member in 1961 and Iceland joined in 1970. In 1973, Denmark and the United Kingdom withdrew from EFTA to join the EC. Portugal transferred to the EC in 1986. Liechtenstein is now a full member of EFTA.

The EC has had a privileged and nurtured relationship with EFTA for decades. For example, in the early 1970s, each EFTA member concluded a bilateral free-trade agreement with the EC, designed to eliminate tariffs on industrial products.

Since an April 1984 meeting between the EC, its Member States, and the EFTA member states, EFTA and the EC have worked closely together to achieve a European Economic Space (EES). It is now usually referred to as the European Economic Area (EEA). The EES/EEA is seen as a way of allowing greater trade between the EC and EFTA than currently exists. If the EES/EEA were put into place today, it could create a market of almost 400 million people.

Increasingly, EFTA members are concerned that the EC's move to complete the Single Market might result in new barriers between EFTA and the EC. This new mood of the EC toward the EES was summed up by a remark from Willy de Clercq, the former EC trade commissioner:

> Let us recognise that there is a difference between the European Economic Space and the internal market and that only [EC] Member States can fully participate in the internal market.

OPTIONS FOR THE EC-EFTA RELATIONSHIP
The EC has established three principles to guide its future relations with EFTA:

• Priority must be given to establishing the Single Market within the EC itself.

• Cooperation with EFTA must not jeopardize the EC's own autonomy.

• There must be a balance of advantages and obligations between the EC and EFTA.

According to the president of the Commission of the EC, currently only two options are available for future relations between the EC and EFTA:

• The EC can maintain its present bilateral relations with EFTA. The ultimate aim would be to create a free trade area, the EES/EEA, encompassing the EC and EFTA.

• The EC can look for a new, more structured partnership with EFTA. One key but highly controversial issue is the question of common decision-making and administrative institutions. This could involve adding a political dimension to EC-EFTA cooperation in the economic, social, financial, and cultural spheres.

From the perspective of EFTA, the long-range choice may well be integration or marginalization.

CURRENT EES/EEA NEGOTIATIONS

In mid-1990, the EC and EFTA began negotiations to create the EES/EEA. The current negotiations would extend the EC's goal of the free movement of goods, capital, services, and people to EFTA. Also, cooperation between the EC and EFTA in such areas as research and development, the environment, and social policy would intensify.

However, some critical differences still exist between the EC and EFTA. Prime among them is a difference in how EC-EFTA decision making would occur. Although EFTA is seeking a voice in decisions that would affect the EEA, the Commission has taken the position that the EC is required to keep complete autonomy over its own decision-making process.

Also, substantial disagreement still exists on the impact of the Single Market legislation. EFTA countries wish to be exempted from a number of specific pieces of legislation they regard as sensitive. EC negotiators, evidently, are willing to consider granting exemptions, but on a much more limited basis than is being sought by EFTA. Basically, the EC position is that any exemptions be limited to areas where "vital national interests" are at stake, and that they exist for a limited time only.

EFTA MEMBERS AND THE EC

An additional factor in relations between the EC and EFTA is the movement of individual EFTA members toward the EC. Austria already has applied for membership ("accession") in the EC. Sweden also has indicated it will make application as well. Norway and Switzerland are examining their positions. The result of these two moves could be the reduction of EFTA to five or even four members. At that time, EFTA's future existence independent of the EC may be problematic.

Central and Eastern Europe

In the past several years, the EC has become increasingly sensitive to, and involved in, events in Central and Eastern Europe.

POLAND AND HUNGARY

In 1989, the EC arranged to provide funds to assist economic reform in Poland and Hungary, in an effort to aid in the restructuring of the economies of these two nations—the PHARE program. This project has now been extended to other Central and Eastern European countries.

GERMAN DEMOCRATIC REPUBLIC

In 1990, the territories that were the German Democratic Republic (GDR) became a part of the Federal Republic of Germany (FRG). As a result, those states automatically became part of the EC. The former GDR had special relationships with many of its Central and Eastern European neighbors, including Poland. Because of these relationships, the FRG is seeking to keep its new borders open to Poles, as the GDR did. However, as the barriers to travel and relocation within the EC fall, this policy could create a potential "back door" for Poles into all of the EC.

SOVIET UNION

In the winter of 1990, the EC offered almost $1 billion in direct aid and trade credits to the U.S.S.R. The assistance was offered to help the Soviet Union obtain needed food and other supplies for its people.

The future role of the EC in the changes sweeping Central and Eastern Europe is as yet unclear. If the trend toward the replacement of state-dominated economies with free-market economies continues, these economies are likely to need various additional assistance from the EC:

- Continuing economic assistance
- Technical and management assistance
- Access to the EC's vast market on a nonprotectionist basis

For the former Eastern bloc to achieve relatively free access to the EC's market, it will, in turn, have to give the EC access to its markets on the same basis. At present, no uniformity in the commercial relations exists between Member Countries of the EC and Central and Eastern European countries. The EC has the goal of establishing an entirely uniform arrangement for products from Central and Eastern Europe.

Conference on Security and Cooperation in Europe

In November 1990, the Conference on Security and Cooperation in Europe (CSCE) was created.

The CSCE is an outgrowth of the European Summit meeting at which NATO and the Warsaw Pact agreed to scrap many of their conventional weapons in Europe. At that meeting, which marked an end to the Cold War, the United States, Canada, and all of the nations of Europe, except Albania, signed the Paris Charter. Among the topics covered by the Charter were

- Respect for the rights of ethnic and cultural minorities
- Recognition of hunger and unemployment problems facing the signatory nations
- Acknowledgment of the desire of an estimated 25 million residents of Central and Eastern Europe to migrate to Western Europe
- Pledges to seek security for all in the context of a United Europe
- Commitments to free elections and market economies throughout Europe

To carry out the commitments made in the Paris Charter, the 34 nations agreed to hold a summit meeting of their heads of state in Helsinki, Finland, in 1992. The foreign ministers of the signatories will meet in Berlin, Germany, in 1991 and annually after that. Senior officials of the signatories will meet more often.

The Paris Charter also created an office, known as the CSCE, in Prague, Czechoslovakia, to administer the process created by the Charter. It also established a Vienna, Austria, center for the prevention of conflict and a Warsaw, Poland, office to monitor free elections.

The Paris Charter and the CSCE are expected to have a major impact on the EC and its relationship with EFTA and Central and Eastern Europe.

The ultimate impact of the CSCE on the Single Market Program is unclear. What is certain is that the CSCE marks another step toward the economic integration of Europe. The long-term result may well be the creation of a trans-European free trade area, including the EC (with a unified Germany), EFTA, and much of Central and Eastern Europe.

The EC's Efforts to Promote Business Development

2

The EC has set up a number of important programs that promote the establishment of new businesses and help existing companies take advantage of the Single Market Program. Understanding the steps taken by the EC to assist businesses can benefit any company wanting to operate within the EC.

OVERVIEW

The EC has already created one new form of business entity, the European Economic Interest Grouping (EEIG), and is currently developing a Community-wide corporation law. It is also refining the way business competition is controlled and is determining what financial assistance the Member States can provide businesses.

Furthermore, the EC has committed itself to helping small and medium-sized businesses exploit the opportunities provided by the Single Market and to helping them increase their competitiveness.

As the Single Market Program progresses, the demand for various types of data needed to make sound business decisions in the EC has been increasing. In response to this demand, the Community institutions, notably the Commission, provide a wide range of useful business data.

SECTIONS IN THIS CHAPTER

Establishing a Business Within the European Community

Funding and Financing Sources Within the EC

Programs of Assistance for Small and Medium-Sized Enterprises (SMEs)

Maintaining a Fair Competitive Environment

Improved Accessibility of Data in the EC

ASSISTANCE

Refer to

- Chapter 21, information on economic and business development (including small and medium-sized businesses)
- Chapter 23, regulation of businesses and competition (including organizing a business)

For additional help in using this sourcebook, refer to the Introduction to Part I.

ESTABLISHING A BUSINESS WITHIN THE EUROPEAN COMMUNITY

To conduct business directly in the EC, companies must open a branch or subsidiary in an EC Member State. Their numerous options for doing this are described in the chapters covering each Member State. Appendix C lists the designations and abbreviations for the Member States' most common forms of business.

New Type of Business Entity: The European Economic Interest Grouping

Once a business has been established in a Member State, it may be able to take advantage of a new type of business entity—the European Economic Interest Grouping (EEIG)—created by the EC. An EEIG is a form of cross-border partnership that has its own legal personality.

The European Economic Interest Grouping is a useful vehicle for companies wanting to form and operate joint activities, such as research and development, sales and distribution, or bidding for public contracts. It is especially useful for small and medium-sized businesses that do not want to merge or form joint venture companies but that wish to carry out some activities in common.

An EEIG is formed by a contract between two or more persons or legal entities from at least two different EC Member States. It is a private matter, so no capital contributions (investments) can be solicited from the public. It is a "legal person," so it can enter into contracts, can sue, and can be sued.

However, an EEIG's members do not have the protection of limited liability, as do shareholders in a corporation. Rather, they have joint and several liability for its debts and other liabilities, as if they were partners. In fact, for five years after their resignation, former members of an EEIG remain liable for any acts that the EEIG committed while they were members.

An EEIG's profits are divided among its members and are taxed under the national laws of relevant Member States.

MEMBERSHIP IN AN EEIG

To be eligible for membership in an EEIG, a person must work in or provide services within the EC. For a legal entity, such as a corporation or partnership, to be eligible for membership, it must be formed under the laws of an EC Member State. At least two of the members of an EEIG must have links with *different* countries within the EC. Thus, an EEIG could be made up of an individual living and working in Spain, together with a Scottish partnership and a Dutch limited liability company.

In addition, subsidiaries of non-EC enterprises are eligible for membership in an EEIG, so long as each member is formed under the laws of an EC Member State.

THE CONTRACT

A valid EEIG contract must contain all of the following:

- The name of the EEIG, followed by the words European Economic Interest Grouping or EEIG

- The registered address of the EEIG
- The object or purpose of the EEIG
- The duration of the EEIG
- The manner in which its profits will be divided
- Basic information on each of its members

REGISTRATION

An EEIG's contract must be registered with a national registry in the EC Member State in which the EEIG has its official address, as well as published in the *Official Journal* of the EC. Future changes in the EEIG's membership, as well as other amendments to the contract, also must be filed in the national registry.

Because there are no specific capital requirements, members of an EEIG can decide the form and amount of their capital contributions.

MANAGEMENT

The management of an EEIG is conducted at two levels:

- The members of an EEIG can act as a group, as if they were shareholders at a meeting; and
- One or more managers can be named in the contract or selected by the members to run an EEIG.

LIMITATIONS

The following are all important limitations on an EEIG and its activities:

- The activity of an EEIG must be "ancillary" to the activities of its members. An EEIG cannot be created and operated in a line of business that has no connection with the activities of its members. Also, an EEIG's operations cannot replace activities carried on by each of its members.
- An EEIG cannot control its members in any way. It cannot own stock in any of its members or exercise any management control and supervision over them.
- Although an EEIG can have employees, it cannot employ more than 500 people.

The creation and operation of an EEIG is subject to the EC regulation that created it. National laws—as well as other EC laws dealing with subjects such as social security, the protection of intellectual property, and the regulation of competition—also apply to its operations, just as they do to the operations of any other business.

The regulation authorizing the creation of the EEIG came into effect on July 1, 1989. Because it is

an EC regulation, the Member States did not have to adopt it as a part of their national laws; the regulation took effect on its own. However, the regulation provided that the Member States were to adopt legislation governing the way in which an EEIG was to be registered (as well as associated fees). Because not all members of the EC have adopted the necessary legislation on registration, EEIGs cannot yet be created and registered in every country.

The taxation of members of EEIGs and their transactions can be complicated. Certain Member States have modified their fiscal laws to address many of the complications.

The European Company Statute

A company formed under the laws of one Member State can establish branches or subsidiaries in any other Member State. In addition, one of the 1985 White Paper proposals involves the creation of a European Company Statute—that is, a company created under EC law rather than the law of any particular country. If this proposed measure is adopted, it is anticipated that an SE (Societas Europa) would be particularly attractive as a means of merging two or more companies that currently are formed under the laws of different countries. It would be available for use by EC companies and the EC subsidiaries of non-EC parent companies.

The final form of the European Company Statute is likely to include some employee participation provisions. *Employee participation* means that employees of the European Company would have a right to participate in the Company's decision-making process on certain identified topics or to be consulted on such matters.

Although employee participation is already a part of the national law in several key EC Member States, notably Germany, not every Member State has such provisions. At present, the scope of employee participation requirements varies widely from Member State to Member State, as shown in Part II.

Harmonizing Business Taxation

The area of taxation poses some of the greatest challenges to the Member States as they move to complete the Single Market. Not only do attempts to harmonize taxation raise sensitive questions of fiscal sovereignty and national budgetary control but the Treaty of Rome still requires that any tax measures must be adopted unanimously.

For the purpose of the 1985 White Paper, a distinction is drawn between differences in indirect taxes and excise duties (which are considered to be fiscal barriers) and direct taxes (which are considered to give rise to technical barriers).

There are no plans for a Community-wide tax system as such. The basic aim is to achieve greater convergence in the different national tax systems, recognizing that the amount of tax that is paid, whether by a business or an individual, depends primarily on

- The type of tax
- The basis for computing taxable income
- The rate of taxation

Value Added Tax

A common system of value added tax (VAT) has been operating in the Member States since 1977, based on the Sixth VAT. The last decade has seen significant progress toward harmonizing the treatment accorded to a large number of goods and services originally allowed diverse treatments by derogations incorporated into previous VAT directives.

Thus, to a large extent, all of the Member States now operate the same type of value added tax, and there is a significant convergence on what goods and services should be subjected to VAT. The 1985 White Paper includes a number of measures designed to continue the process toward achieving a uniform tax base across the Community.

The Commission's initial proposals to achieve greater approximation of tax rates envisaged

- Each country would set a single standard rate of VAT, at a rate between 14 percent and 20 percent.
- Each country would be allowed a single lower rate (between 4 percent and 9 percent) for certain essential goods and services.
- The rate of VAT that would be applied would be that in force in the country of origin of the goods or services, rather than the rate in the country of use/destination (as currently applies).

These proposals were rejected by the Member States. The current proposals, which are likely to apply from January 1993 until the end of 1996, are

- The country of origin principle will apply to goods and services purchased by an individual, with the exception of motor vehicles and mail order business, where the rate of VAT in the country of destination will apply.
- The country of destination principle will apply to goods and services purchased by most businesses.
- Each business in a Member State that exports to other Member States will have to provide certain additional information to the tax authorities in VAT returns it files in its own Member State. Other tax authorities will be able to draw on that information for the purposes of policing the system.

By the end of 1991, the Member States are committed to reach a conclusion on how to achieve greater convergence on rates of VAT. A possible solution in the transitional period to the end of 1996 would involve Member States in

- Working toward a single standard rate of VAT, above a certain floor level (possibly 14 percent), but with no specified ceiling. Many Member States currently have several rates of VAT; hence, consolidation into a single rate would be a major step forward.
- A lower rate for certain specified goods and services.
- A zero rate on a very narrowly defined and carefully controlled range of goods (such as food and children's clothes).

Excise Duties

The 1985 White Paper proposed that there should be a single rate of excise duty (per product) applicable in every Member State for alcohol, tobacco, and mineral oils. That proposal was rejected by the Member States for a variety of reasons, including the impact on revenues, health, and social policies.

The current proposals envisage

- Each Member State would continue to set its own rates of duty, but at or above a specified minimum level.
- Special arrangements will be made to enable goods to move between authorized warehouse keepers under duty-suspension arrangements.

Direct Taxation

The Commission's original plans to have Member States adopt an imputation system of corporate taxation, harmonize their bases for computing taxable income, and adopt corporate tax rates lying within a certain range have been abandoned, or at least suspended, for the time being. Instead, the Commission is now concentrating on measures designed to encourage cross-border transactions and business.

Three measures were adopted in July 1990:

- A directive designed to eliminate the double taxation that arises on payment of a dividend from a subsidiary in one Member State to a parent company in another Member State—that is, the withholding tax on the dividend (in the country of the subsidiary paying the dividend) and the taxation of that dividend in the hands of the recipient company.

- A directive to facilitate cross-border mergers or divisions of companies by deferring any tax that would otherwise arise as a result of the transaction, such as tax depreciation recaptures, capital gains, and so on. This will facilitate a variety of corporate reorganizations, in-

cluding spin-offs, asset contributions, and stock swaps.

- A convention that creates an arbitration procedure for transfer pricing disputes between the revenue authorities in different Member States.

At the end of 1990, the Commission proposed two further measures to

- Eliminate the withholding tax that is currently imposed on interest and royalties paid by a subsidiary in one Member State to a parent company in another Member State

- Provide a measure of cross-border loss relief for losses incurred by a subsidiary (or branch) in one Member State against the profits of the parent company (or head office) in another Member State

A committee has been set up to look into the question of whether further harmonization of direct tax systems, rates, and bases is required to complete the Single Market. It is expected to report by the beginning of 1992.

FUNDING AND FINANCING SOURCES WITHIN THE EC

The EC has created a series of Structural Funds. These funds are under the management of the Commission. The collective goal of these funds is to help ensure that, as the Single Market develops, the EC itself will develop as a single integrated economic and social unit. To do this, the EC specifically is attempting to reduce the gap between its richer and poorer regions and communities, as well as between the privileged and the underprivileged in society.

As a group, the Structural Funds provide grants for investment in capital and human resources. The three Structural Funds are

- *The European Agricultural Guidance and Guarantee Fund—Guidance Section (EAGGF—Guidance Section)*. This fund, established to achieve the objectives of the Common Agricultural Policy (CAP), is operated to bring about "an increase in productivity through a rational development of agricultural production and an optimum use of [the] factors of production, in particular the work force."

- *The European Social Fund*. The European Social Fund (ESF) was established "to improve em-

ployment opportunities for workers in the Common Market and to contribute thereby to raising the standard of living."

- *The European Regional Development Fund*. The European Regional Development Fund (ERDF) aims to "redress the principal regional imbalances in the EC through participating in the development and structural adjustment of regions whose development is lagging behind and in the conversion of declining industrial regions."

In addition to the three Structural Funds, the EC has numerous other ways of providing loans and grants for "structural" purposes. These include

- *European Investment Bank*. The European Investment Bank (EIB) was set up to contribute to the balanced and steady development of the EC. It grants loans and provides guarantees for projects in less-developed regions of the EC, and for modernization and development activities.

- *Loans under the European Coal and Steel Community Treaty*. This treaty permits the Commission to make loans for industrial purposes, specifically to provide subsidized loans for redevelopment. The Commission also can provide resettlement and retraining grants for redundant coal and steel workers.

- *The Integrated Mediterranean Programs.* The Integrated Mediterranean Programs (IMPs) are designed to improve the socioeconomic structures of the EC's southern areas, particularly Greece. Running through 1992, the programs are supported by a combination of assistance from the Structural Funds, direct funding from the EC budget, and loans from the EIB.

- *Program to Modernize Portuguese Industry (PEDIP).* This program, aimed at assisting Portu-guese industry, provides grants over a period of five years. These grants supplement other assistance provided to Portugal by the Structural Funds.

Each Member State has its own investment and development incentive programs. However, operation of these programs may come under increasing review from the EC to make sure that they do not have anticompetitive effects. The long-term result of the EC's review will be that the investment and development incentives provided by the EC itself will become more important than those of the Member States as the Single Market Program progresses.

PROGRAMS OF ASSISTANCE FOR SMALL AND MEDIUM-SIZED ENTERPRISES (SMEs)

The EC believes small and medium-sized enterprises (SMEs) can make a vital contribution to solving its unemployment problems; therefore, it has made major efforts to assist these companies. A number of special EC initiatives and programs helping SMEs throughout the EC are projects of its SME Task Force; others are provided through the Commission's directorates-general and other Community institutions.

Euro Info Centres Provide Information

The EC has funded a series of centers, known as the Euro Info Centre NETwork (EICs) that provide information to businesses about European Commission policies and proposals, particularly those of interest to SMEs. In addition, the EICs are able to supply local businesses with information on national legislation and business practices in other Member States. All EICs have access to the EC's public databases (described in Parts III and IV).

Currently, 187 EICs are operating, and the number should exceed 200 in the near future. (See Appendix G for a listing of these centers.)

BC-Net Helps SMEs for Alliances

One EC program available to SMEs is the BC-Net, or Business Co-operation Network. This data-base helps SMEs form links with similar firms throughout the EC so they can establish business alliances.

BC-Net operates through a network of over 400 accredited business advisers based in organizations such as local chambers of commerce, scattered throughout the EC. Firms interested in BC-Net file an application form, which is entered into the BC-Net database. The identity of each applicant is kept confidential.

The goal of BC-Net is to match up the applicant firm with one or more of the 6000 other firms in BC-Net interested in one or more of 40 different types of business alliances, ranging from joint ventures to mergers. When a potential match is found, the business advisers assigned to the two SMEs are contacted and are free to explore the possibility of matching up their two SMEs. If the advisers conclude that the firms might be well matched, they can then contact their client firms. At this point, direct contact between the firms takes place.

Other Programs Assist SMEs

In addition to the Euro Info Centres and BC-Net, the EC has established many other programs of assistance for SMEs, among them:

- Business and Innovation Centres (BICs). These centers help set up SMEs having the potential for rapid growth, as well as those having an export orientation.

- Training programs in strategic management for SMEs.
- Eurotech Capital. This program encourages financial institutions to support high technology SME projects related to EC technology programs. These programs include Esprit (European Strategic Program for Research and Development in Information Technology) and Brite (Basic Research in Industrial Technologies in Europe).

- New Community Instrument (NCI). NCI, a financial program created in 1978, allows the Commission to borrow and relend to fund investment. Under it, the EIB borrows on behalf of the Commission. The EIB then loans the funds to financial institutions throughout the EC, and the institutions, in turn, relend to SMEs to promote industrial investment.

MAINTAINING A FAIR COMPETITIVE ENVIRONMENT

The EEC Treaty includes provisions designed to ensure that competition in the EC is not distorted. These rules operate in three main areas:

- *Regulation of Competition.* The Treaty of Rome itself includes a provision to prevent businesses from distorting trade rules or abusing their power in the marketplace by, for example, fixing prices among competitors, by agreeing on market shares, or by creating production quotas.
- *Regulation of Industrial Concentration.* A regulation adopted in September 1990 prevents excessive concentrations of economic power in the EC through company mergers and acquisitions. They permit the Commission to review and then to block or alter major business mergers that have a "Community dimension" and that would inhibit competition.
- *Regulation of State Aid.* The Treaty of Rome includes rules that enable the Commission to take action when a national, state, or local government grants aid, in whatever form, that favors particular businesses or products. These measures can involve, for example, cash grants, special subsidies, low-interest loans, or special tax advantages.

Regulating Competition

The core of the EC's competition policy is found in Articles 85 and 86 of the Treaty of Rome:

1. The following shall be prohibited as incompatible with the common market: all agreements between undertakings, decisions by associations of undertakings and concerted practices which may affect trade between Member States and which have as their object the prevention, restriction or distortion of competition within the Common Market, and in particular those which:

   a. directly or indirectly fix purchase or selling prices or any other trading conditions;

   b. limit or control production markets, technical development or investment;

   c. share markets or sources of supply;

   d. apply dissimilar conditions to equivalent transactions with other trading parties, thereby placing them at a competitive disadvantage;

   e. make the conclusion of contracts subject to acceptance by the other parties of supplementary obligations which, by their nature or according to commercial usage, have no connection with the subject of such contracts. (Treaty of Rome, Article 85)

Article 85 prohibits all agreements that may affect trade between Member States and that have as their object (or effect) the prevention, restriction, or distortion of competition. In practice, the Commission applies Article 85 only to "perceptible" restrictions. Thus, agreements between firms whose market share does not exceed 5 percent or whose combined annual gross income does not exceed 200 million ECUs are unlikely to be "perceptible."

Agreements can be exempted from the application of Article 85 in two ways:

- A specific application for exemption can be made to the Commission. Before approving the application, the Commission must be satisfied that the agreement involves either an economic or technical improvement, or that it provides a benefit to consumers. In addition, the Commission must find that the agreement is either "indispensable" or that its retention is an essential part of competition.

- The Commission adopts block exemptions in the form of regulations. These confer automatic exemptions on certain categories of agreements that fall within their terms.

Currently, there are block exemptions covering

- Franchise agreements
- Exclusive distribution agreements
- Patent licensing agreements
- Know-how licensing agreements
- Exclusive purchasing agreements
- Research and development agreements
- Selective distribution of motor vehicles

As the Single Market develops, other block exemptions, such as those for many insurance-related activities, will be developed and adopted.

Article 86 is aimed at abuses of competition by firms with "dominant positions" in the market. Having a dominant position in the market is not prohibited, but the article deals with practices that abuse such a position:

> Any abuse by one or more undertakings of a dominant position within the common market or in a substantial part of it shall be prohibited as incompatible with the common market in so far as it may affect trade between Member States.
>
> Such abuse may, in particular, consist in:
>
> a. directly or indirectly imposing unfair purchase or selling prices or other unfair trading conditions;
>
> b. limiting production, markets or technical development to the prejudice of consumers;
>
> c. applying dissimilar conditions to equivalent transactions with other trading parties, thereby placing them at a competitive disadvantage;
>
> d. making the conclusion of contracts subject to acceptance by the other parties of supplementary obligations which, by their nature or according to commercial usage, have no connection with the subject of such contracts. (Treaty of Rome, Article 86)

For Article 86 to apply, there must be an abuse of a dominant position; that is, a firm takes advantage of its position and causes injury to third parties, either consumers or competitors. Examples of practices subject to Article 86 are

- Imposing unfair prices or conditions
- A refusal to deal
- Unequal treatment of trading partners
- The use of tie-in sales

Regulating Mergers

Article 86 and, to a limited degree, Article 85 were also used by the Commission to control business concentrations. The former article requires a dominant position, and the latter article operates on a case-by-case basis only. This incomplete coverage has been corrected by the adoption of a new merger regulation that came into effect in September 1990.

That regulation lays down rules governing mergers that may "significantly impede effective competition in the [EC] or a substantial part of it." It gives the Commission the power to decide if mergers with a "Community dimension" are compatible with Community Law.

Controlling State Aid

Another aspect of the EC's competition policy is control of state aid. Under the EEC Treaty, this control is exercised by the Commission:

> [A]ny aid granted by a Member State or through State resources in any form whatsoever which distorts or threatens to distort competition by favoring certain undertakings or the production of certain goods shall, in so far as it affects trade between Member States, be incompatible with the common market. . . . (Treaty of Rome, Article 92)

The EC's position is that competition can be distorted when national, state, or local governments favor certain businesses by granting them aid, such as cash grants. The concept of "state aid" in the EC's competition laws covers any type of assistance given, directly or indirectly, by a Member State to businesses. The only exception to this definition is a measure aimed at the general promotion of the national economy. The position of tax incentives is complex and controversial.

As a general rule, state aid is deemed to be incompatible with the Single Market if it favors certain types of businesses or products and affects trade between Member States. However, certain types of state aid are regarded as compatible, provided the aid has a social character or is in response to damages caused by natural disasters. Other categories of aid may be acceptable—for example, aid to promote the economic development of areas with a very low standard of living and aid to promote a project of "common interest," such as Airbus Industrie.

The Commission is charged with reviewing existing state aid and with determining whether plans to grant or alter aid are compatible with the Single Market. Member States, therefore, are required to notify the Commission before implementing any plans to introduce new programs or change existing programs. This notification enables the Commission to determine whether the programs fall into one of the exempted categories and can be implemented. A Member State may not implement any aid plan until the Commission has made a final decision on its exemption.

Therefore, efforts by Member States to add investment incentives to those described in Part II are subject to prior review by the Commission.

Sanctioning Violators

If a company is found to have violated the competition laws, the Commission has several sanctions available:

- The prohibited agreement or practice is automatically void.
- The Commission can impose substantial fines, up to 1 million ECUs, or 10 percent of the businesses' gross revenues in the previous year, whichever is higher.
- The Commission can issue injunctions to enforce compliance.

In addition, third parties adversely affected by a company's actions may file claims for damages with national tribunals (to the extent that national law allows for this action).

If the Commission determines that state aid has been given illegally, it may order repayment of that aid.

IMPROVED ACCESSIBILITY OF DATA IN THE EC

The Official European System of Statistics: Eurostat

One consequence of the Single Market Program is a growing demand from the Commission and other EC institutions for current, accurate, and compatible statistics. The EC institutions need data in planning, administering, and reviewing Single Market programs. This need is met by Eurostat.

Eurostat, the common name for the Statistical Office of the European Communities, is a directorate-general of the Commission. (The Commission's directorate-generals are listed in Table 5.1.) Although the Commission is Eurostat's main customer for data, much of Eurostat's work in data collection, harmonization, and dissemination is of value to the business community and is available to the public.

To enable Eurostat to respond to the demand for reliable data, the EC adopted a formal statistical program covering the period from 1989 through 1992. This program defines and coordinates the Commission's requirements for statistics and the ability of the national statistical offices to meet the requirements.

The specific aim of the EC is to construct a European system of statistics. Eurostat's overall goal is to set statistical standards for the Community, chiefly by harmonizing the methodology, nomenclatures, and concepts of the 12 national systems to avoid discrepancies and ultimately to render them compatible. To do this, Eurostat not only works with the Member States on a regular basis, it also takes into account recommendations from international bodies. The process is designed to ensure that Eurostat's statistical output fits world statistical norms.

Increasing Availability of Information on EC Companies

The ability to obtain relatively current information on EC companies varies among the Member States. However, as the Single Market Program progresses, this information should become easier to obtain.

The amount of information on EC-based companies now available and easily accessible varies widely. Three basic questions illustrate this gap:

- Is basic registration and company information filed in a single central registry that is available for public inspection?

- Are current (at least annual) profit and loss statements required to be filed and made available for inspection?

- Are current (at least annual) balance sheets required to be filed and made available for inspection?

Even when national law requires companies to file certain documents, the actual information available on EC companies differs throughout the EC:

- Although current company records may have been provided to a country's central registry, the registry files themselves are not always kept up to date.

- Individual countries cannot or will not enforce their requirement for annual filings of financial information.

- There are often significant differences in the accounting principles used in different Member States.

In any case, the result is the same: records required to be available to the public do not necessarily provide directly comparable current financial information about the target companies.

Current practices should gradually become more uniform and efficient. To that end, an EC directive requires each state to provide all of the following:

- A registry of company documents. This is not necessarily a "central" registry; each Member State has established one or more registries to fit in with its existing system of commercial law administration.

- The initial filing of basic information on all companies.

- Annual filings of balance sheets and profit and loss statements.

Implementation of this directive has not led to uniformity. In particular:

- Partnerships are exempt from most filing requirements in many countries.

- Many countries have more than one "central" registry.

Variability of Information Among Member States

The availability of commercial and financial information on markets in general varies widely among Member States. A report released by the United Kingdom's Department of Trade and Industry has said:

> The UK has an unusually extensive range of financial and commercial information available at modest cost. . . .
>
> Similar information is available in some, but by no means all, other EC countries. In general, we would comment that the availability of such information is good in France, Germany and the Netherlands, but markedly inferior in extent, reliability or timeliness in Italy and, more so, in Spain. Among the smaller economies, lack of market information is also a significant problem . . . in Portugal and Greece. (Barriers to Takeovers in the European Community, 1989)

As with many other aspects of doing business in the EC, this is changing, but it may be some years before greater consistency is achieved.

The efforts of Eurostat, together with the regular reports and publications of the Organization for Economic Cooperation and Development (OECD), the General Agreement on Tariffs and Trade (GATT), the U.N., and the United Nations Economic Commission for Europe, provide a massive source of data on markets and industries. A large number of these reports and data series are updated regularly, providing a constantly renewing body of information. These sources are identified in Parts III and IV.

The EC is developing and refining its position on how its agencies and those of the Member States manage private data provided to public authorities. Efforts are being made to permit the legitimate exploitation of this data by businesses.

At the same time, the EC is seeking to protect the privacy of individuals who provide that data to a public authority, to supplement the existing international convention on this subject. Such protec- tion may include a right-to-know provision, as well as giving private persons limited control over the way data on them is released.

3

The Impact of the Single Market Program on Doing Business: Key Strategic Issues

Companies doing business anywhere in the EC today or planning to do business in the EC after the end of 1992 must be familiar with the Single Market Program's impact on an array of key strategic business issues.

This chapter identifies a number of the most important strategic issues that will be impacted by the Single Market Program and offers possible ways business may respond to the coming changes.

OVERVIEW

The whole Single Market Program is geared toward the removal of existing competitive restrictions. This objective will be achieved when the following are attained:

- *Freedom of establishment.* This will increase opportunities for corporate expansion into new domestic and pan-European markets and allow companies to achieve increased economies of scale and scope.

- *Freedom of movement of goods at lower cost.* This will open up domestic markets to transborder competition by removing the additional costs that currently arise because of physical and technical barriers and other hindrances to trade.

- *Harmonization of standards.* This will mean increased economies of scale in production, R&D, and so on.

- *Wider recognition of qualifications.* This will mean access to a broader range and depth of human resources.

- Free movement of capital will lead to a lower cost of capital, particularly in less developed capital markets.

- Broader public procurement will lead to increased opportunities by opening up previously restricted markets. It should also lead to economies of scale and other savings in industries such as telecommunications.

- Harmonization of labor force rights will remove unfair competitive advantages and ensure that the benefits of a single European market are shared throughout the EC.

- Alignment of indirect taxation will create new opportunities in certain countries.

Companies need to understand how these legislative changes will affect their businesses. The measures contained in the White Paper and developed since 1985 build on existing Community legislation. In many cases this legislation has and will have a very significant bearing on the development and operations of companies.

SECTIONS IN THIS CHAPTER

Impact on Competition Within the European Community

Impact on Customers and Buying Behavior

Impact on Distribution Systems

Impact on Pricing Strategy

Impact on Supplier Relations and Sourcing

Impact on Processing Technology and Production Strategy

Impact on Product Range and New Product Development

Impact on Cost Control

Impact on Organizational Structure and Human Resource Management

Impact on Resource Allocation and Financial Planning

Impact on Information Technology

IMPACT ON COMPETITION WITHIN THE EUROPEAN COMMUNITY

Changing Environmental Factors

The factors contributing to the creation of a wider market include public procurement liberalization, freedom of establishment, freedom to provide cross-frontier services, harmonization of technical standards, and closer alignment of indirect taxes.

The completion of the internal market will also be accompanied by modifications to Community competition policy. These will include

- Greater control over the provision of state aid by individual Member States to ensure that competition is not disturbed. The EC itself will continue to provide financial assistance, particularly to economically less developed Member States.

- Changes to controls over mergers and acquisitions within the Community. Mergers may be authorized even where they lead to or strengthen a dominant position, provided that the economic benefits outweigh their anticompetitive effects.

- Encouragement of cross-frontier cooperation of all forms, including joint ventures.

- Harmonization and liberalization of air and maritime transport in the Community.

- Harmonization of national laws relating to intellectual property, including those of relevance to the biotechnology industry and information technology-related industries.

Analysis of Competitive Environment

Competitive environment analysis will become much more complex. Companies will be faced with a larger market area, and an increased number of competitors will lead to greater complexity. Also, potential new entrants to their domestic markets will come from a larger geographical area: surprise is likely to become a more powerful strategic device for entering new markets. It is clear, then, that effective analysis combined with the ability to react quickly will give a decisive advantage to businesses that have good information systems.

"National champions" and other domestic market leaders will have to compare their competitive strengths against European industry as a whole, and market share calculations will also be made by taking the single market into account. Nevertheless, in certain industries, cultural differences will continue to be a major factor in penetrating the market.

Identification of Opportunities and Threats

The purpose of removing trade barriers within the Community is to offer businesses opportunities to sell their products and services in other markets to which, to date, access has been restricted. An increase in competitive pressure will be marked in areas previously protected. Public markets, so far protected by restrictive procurement practices, and high-technology markets segmented by differences in standards specifications, for example, will become tremendously attractive to new competitors. A number of specific proposals will contribute to creating a much more competitive environment:

- Freedom of establishment for services (including freedom to provide direct cross-frontier financial services) will change the approach that has to be used by players in services markets. In the banking sector, for example, freedom of establishment will allow firms operating in competitive environments to break into less efficient markets, thus taking advantage of their lower costs and larger product range to gain a share of those markets.

- Opportunities will also arise from intrasector transfers, particularly through increasing links between allied sectors. For example, subject to satisfying appropriate requirements, banks will be able to move more into the insurance business and benefit from their access to wide customer lists to achieve considerable economies of scale and scope. In West Germany, insurance firms will now be allowed to operate simultaneously in the life, credit and suretyship, legal, and general sectors, which so far have been fragmented by strict regulations.

- Harmonization of national laws relating to patent rights in the biotechnology industry will enable this sector to be more competitive against, in particular, the United States and Japan, where legislation provides significantly more protection than currently exists in the EC.

- Air carriers will be granted more freedom in planning routes and setting fares.

- Harmonization and mutual recognition of technical standards will open doors to new products in markets where they simply did not exist. Most importantly, this will enable firms to make economies of scale in producing larger quantities of similar goods for the whole European market. As a consequence, companies will see an increase in minimum efficient plant size in a number of sectors.

New Sources of Competitive Advantage

Artificial competitive advantages from which businesses in protected areas have benefited will disappear with the trade barriers. Following are a few examples:

- State aid to national champion companies in the car manufacturing sector will be reduced or eliminated.

- German beer producers will no longer be able to rely on technical standards of "product purity" to keep foreign competitors out of their domestic market.

- Telecommunications firms will no longer be able to count on public procurement national preferences to sell their products, all the more so as standards harmonization will destroy the monopoly power derived from being the only firms able to meet national norms and specifications.

Firms will, therefore, need to increase their real competitive advantage, for example, by selecting a number of key business areas on which to focus their efforts:

- Cost structures will become more critical as increased competitive pressures on prices squeeze profit margins. The degree to which higher margin levels can be recovered by companies will depend on their ability to bring their costs down.

- Company size will become more of an issue in a much wider market area, and economies of scale will be encouraged by the removal of technical barriers.

- Mergers and acquisitions will increase, because they are a means of achieving size and strengthening competitive position. EC legislation will encourage cross-border mergers and acquisitions by relaxing the relevant procedures within the Community. Consequently, consolidation will be apparent in most sectors: fewer, but larger, firms will share the market.

- Distribution will be a key factor of competitive advantage for European firms. Choosing the right channels and setting up efficient networks to reach new customers will often be decisive.

- Marketing and advertising will also play a major role in the new competitive environment. The creation of a Community trademark and the development of new technologies, such as direct satellite broadcasting, will enable firms to achieve economies of scale in spreading their marketing costs over a larger audience and will support global competition strategies.

Smaller players will be faced with three strategic options:

- They can rationalize their activities and concentrate on market niches where size is less important than specialist expertise.

- They can seek cross-frontier joint ventures. This should promote innovation, facilitate new technology transfers, and open new market opportunities.

- If the chances of surviving at their current size and organization structure appear to be low, small firms will look for acquisitions or purchasers.

Finally, in reviewing their strategies for 1992, firms will be concerned with the need for competitive advantage objectives to be set not only to meet European but also worldwide competitiveness standards. Through European integration, Community business will have a chance to increase its competitiveness against its U.S. and Japanese rivals. This issue is made particularly important by the emerging challenge posed to European companies by potential competitors from abroad and the enlarged single market. The invasion of Japanese and American companies with certain advantages, particularly pronounced in advanced technology, will be countered through the restructuring of European industries and the overall boost this will give to their competitiveness.

IMPACT ON CUSTOMERS AND BUYING BEHAVIOR

The term *customer* applies equally to corporate and government bodies and private individuals. Businesses should be aware of

- Who their customers are
- What they are looking for
- When and where they purchase
- How they pay
- Why they buy a particular product

Cultural differences in customer spending are unlikely to disappear overnight as a result of 1992. However, it is likely that many legislative differences will disappear.

Changing Environmental Factors

Customer buyer power may increase because of two major factors:

- Increased product and service availability due to new cross-border entrants within any given market; public procurement agencies will also be able to choose from among nonnational suppliers

- Pressure for prices to converge to a Community level

Potential decreases in buyer power derive from the following two causes:

- Increased internationalization and consolidation of companies, leading to the diminished relative importance of any individual customer.

- Increased numbers of customers due to new markets opening up. More companies will be able to adopt a global marketing approach, thus gaining economies of scale in marketing, production, and distribution.

The homogenization of markets that is already evident on a global scale will increase within the EC, especially in service areas (banking and insurance, for example) where the large and efficient national suppliers will expand their cross-border operations. The different standards are also significant in many manufacturing sectors. Ford has estimated that the cost of divergent specifications for volume passenger car models was no less than ECU 286 million. Higher technical standards will increase some manufacturers' costs where, currently, national standards are below any EC standards that may be developed.

Affluence in general is expected to increase once the Single Market is complete (as outlined in the Cecchini Report, volumes of which are cited by topic and industry in Parts III and IV of this book) and regional variations in wealth should decrease due to growing EC aid to depressed regions.

Possible Business Responses

Companies will need to know something of the markets they are contemplating entering before rushing blindly in. In conducting essential preliminary market research, companies will need to bear in mind the composition and structure of consumer groups, by social and/or economic group, by nationality, by region, and so on. They must have an idea as to consumer preferences, desires, and tastes, and their willingness to pay; why they buy certain products; and what their perceived value is. As a consequence of this research, a number of market segments will be identified. They need to think how the increasing

sophistication of consumers (due to wider product ranges, more and easier travel, and so on) will place new demands on them.

Companies should examine the major components of their business—that is, their value-chain activities. For production, companies will need to consider whether they can attain minimum efficient plant size to satisfy a greater number of consumers and where they should locate, perhaps nearer final consumers in new markets or nearer suppliers. For distribution they will have to think about the structure that will best fit in with their manufacturing strategy. Distribution will be made easier in some respects. Businesses will be able to distribute goods further afield. Again, this will involve issues of location, of setting up new systems, of vertical integration, and so on. Marketing may undergo major change as Communitywide channels become available and both physical delivery and advertising reach become more extensive. The availability of marketing information across Europe will encourage database marketing. Direct marketing, global advertising, and promotions across Europe may all be possible.

IMPACT ON DISTRIBUTION SYSTEMS

Distribution is the delivery of goods via a system or network, possibly containing several intermediate tiers between source and final destination. The critical decision in distribution is achieving the optimal balance between cost and level of service, the latter measured by speed, geographical area covered, security, reliability, and care. With the creation of pan-European entities there will be increased pressure to minimize the costs of distribution. For example, within the UK the cost of distribution as a percentage of sales has fallen over the last 10 years from an average of 15 percent to 5 percent of sales. There will be strong pressure to keep costs down to this level.

Changing Environmental Factors

Distribution will become more streamlined and competitive for a number of reasons:

- Removal of border and administrative controls will make access to new markets easier (as well as reducing costs).

- Abolition of border controls and reduction in paperwork will speed up distribution. The Cecchini Report gives an example: at present, a 1200-kilometer trip takes about 36 hours within the UK (that is, without any border crossings) and the same length of journey requires 58 hours, excluding Channel crossing, to Milan.

- Deregulation will lead to increased lorry load utilization. Cabotage limits should disappear.

- Increased competition between companies offering freight services will provide choices of suppliers and services and reduced prices.

- Harmonization of technical standards should make distribution simpler. It should also improve cross-border information flow.

Possible Business Responses

The responses required to capitalize on a borderless market will vary. Large multinational firms already transfer goods between European sites in an efficient and timely manner. However, smaller operations have been unable to do this and therefore should benefit.

The opening up of Europe will change market dynamics and will require a location analysis of present production, distribution, and warehouse facilities. Centralizing manufacturing facilities to take advantage of economies of scale must be balanced against additional distribution costs and the ability to meet customer needs, especially given the growing importance of "just-in-time" (JIT) delivery.

The reductions in travel time due to minimization of paperwork will allow a faster service to be offered and/or greater geographical reach. This will affect how firms organize their mix of transport modes (for example, rail/road, air/road), especially for the distribution of perishables.

As the size of operations increases there will be greater need for more sophisticated planning and forecasting systems.

The following are some examples of more specific actions and issues:

- Where necessary, companies will seek local distribution; local expertise will undoubtedly remain an important factor, so an increase in merger and acquisition activity will be seen.

- Mixing distribution systems: using third parties to reach new markets to complement existing integrated distribution.

- Alternative distribution methods may be adopted to improve services.

- Exclusive distributor relationships will be used to act as barriers to entry to the extent permitted under EC competition law.

- Where there is increased complexity due to growth, companies will need to upgrade their IT systems. (See Impact on Information Technology later in this chapter.)

- Traditional sources of competitive advantage may disappear. For example, freight forwarders have traded on their ability to efficiently process paperwork. With the removal of border controls and other obstacles to imported goods and services, such companies must seek new sources of competitive advantage.

- Because of increased competition among suppliers and price convergence, the selection of the most efficient distribution service will be more critical as profit margins become slimmer.

- Integration of the distribution system: Are there potential synergies in the system? Should you integrate upstream with, for example, component manufacturers or work-in-process distributors? Should you integrate forward into finished-goods distribution, buying independent distributors? Will you need extra tiers, such as new warehouses in new markets?

- Improved distribution will make decentralized production facilities more feasible, incorporating centrally produced common assemblies into different products to suit specific markets. JIT manufacturing strategies will be reconcilable to a greater extent with decentralization.

IMPACT ON PRICING STRATEGY

Pricing strategy should fulfill three main requirements: It should be a successful weapon against competition; it should meet profit-margin and market-share requirements; and it should reflect customers' expectations and perceived value of the goods and services. But price does not have the same strategic importance in all markets. The number and size of competitors in a given market will obviously be important, but so are the degree of product differentiation, nonprice competition, and price elasticity, which will vary from market to market. A firm's first objective, therefore, will be to determine the extent to which pricing can be used effectively as a weapon against competitors.

To be effective, a pricing strategy must take into account a number of factors, including the following:

- Overall market positioning strategy
- Cost structure
- Barriers to entry
- Price elasticity of demand
- Customers' perceptions of product value

Changing Environmental Factors

Pricing strategies will be dramatically affected by the following developments:

- Removing barriers that have protected some industries and opening up public procurement will allow price competition to develop in a market that previously was protected.

- The increased market size, combined with the removal of physical and technical barriers, will have an immediate effect on administrative and manufacturing costs. Larger markets encourage economies of scale in production and distribution/logistics. Such cost reductions will affect pricing strategies.

Possible Business Responses

There are several approaches that companies can select to implement a new pricing strategy. Companies can implement cost-reduction programs through trying to gain economies of scale—in some cases through mergers or acquisitions, or through the adoption of a cost-leadership strategy.

Alternatively, they can pursue a product-differentiation strategy or build a niche market.

It would be logical to consider moving into new markets, especially if they offer higher margins than the current one(s). Clearly, firms that are now active in open, competitive markets and that are used to operating on low margins should seek to extend their activities to new areas with higher margins. Conversely, the incumbents (those firms that have operated in protected markets) will need to reduce their margins to keep out these competitors. Companies need to define their information requirements in order to develop the best pricing strategy. They will need to determine the following:

- What the price range is for their products, across the Community, and where they stand in it

- What strategic decisions should be made to exploit the new opportunities and protect the company from threats identified through this analysis

IMPACT ON SUPPLIER RELATIONS AND SOURCING

Suppliers are the providers of goods and services. Selection of suitable suppliers that are timely and deliver a product of the right quality is a critical part of a business's strategy. Traditional supplier relationships are changing, particularly in view of JIT practices; such relationships are becoming closer and more exclusive.

Sourcing strategy is highly dependent on the type of business a company is in. For example, for some manufacturers, JIT techniques may call for a close or exclusive relationship with suppliers to ensure quality levels and timeliness. For others, the desire to play off several suppliers against each other entails a totally different kind of relationship.

As a result of 1992, sourcing strategy for manufacturing companies will very much depend on their overall manufacturing strategy, because of plant location, facilities, and so on. The nature of the product a company is sourcing will also have a bearing on strategy. A building contractor sourcing bricks will need to think differently from a computer manufacturer importing circuit boards.

Intermediate firms on the value chain will not be insulated from pressures affecting primary and finished-goods suppliers.

Changing Environmental Factors

The changes brought about by 1992 will affect companies' strategies with regard to suppliers in some of the following ways:

- Technical barriers that previously denied businesses alternative nondomestic supply sources will be removed. This is mainly due 'to the harmonization and mutual recognition of national standards and regulations. Its impact is likely to be felt most in the information technology and electronic goods sectors.

- Greater ease in locating abroad and freedom to provide cross-frontier services should broaden the range of suppliers available, especially in the insurance and banking sectors.

- Modifications to the rules governing cross-border mergers, acquisitions, and joint ventures within the Community could alter supplier relationships.

- The ability to integrate vertically will be eased by proposals relating to cross-border merger activity, acquisitions, and joint ventures. This ability could provide alternative means of reducing costs where horizontal integration is not achievable.

- Product substitution will be increasingly available.

Possible Business Responses

In the longer term, restructuring will take place as suppliers try to scale up production to take advantage of a larger market place. Economies of scale will be achieved, resulting in lower costs of supplies. There will be fewer but larger suppliers. Price disparity across the EC will decrease. Prices will probably move downward as a result of increased competitive pressure on suppliers, which will lead in some cases to cost-reduction programs.

There will be a number of changes to the relationship between suppliers and purchaser, including a potential decrease in supplier power because of increased variety of sources and product standardization.

The changes will vary according to type of product, the requirements of the buyer (JIT, pan-European manufacturing strategy, quality, and price). Purchasers for public procurement, which to date have operated within tight nationalist constraints, will see significant opportunities for reduced costs. For example, the Cecchini Report identified the following "effects" (benefits to purchasers) and the estimated savings:

- The *static trade effect*, whereby public authorities will be able to buy from the cheapest (that is, including foreign) suppliers (ECU 3 to 8 billion).

- The *competition effect*, which will lead to downward pressure on prices charged by domestic firms in previously closed sectors, as they strive to compete with foreign companies entering the market (ECU 1 to 3 billion).

- The *restructuring effect*, which is due to the longer-run effect of economies of scale, will occur as industry reorganizes under the pressure of new competitive conditions (ECU 4 to 8 billion). This saving is concentrated in high-tech sectors such as computers, telecommunications, and aerospace.

Any trend toward single sourcing will require strong coordination of purchasing needs and may lead companies to develop multisite, multicountry sources. The implications for IT resourcing are major.

Companies will need to consider upgrading their purchasing function. For example, they may need to recruit specialists who can negotiate in several languages or who have a good knowledge of sourcing potential. When the purchasing function grows in importance, companies will need to respond by considering its centralization or decentralization. Enhanced purchasing systems will require increased electronic data interchange (EDI) but will benefit from greater standardization in the IT field.

Various scenarios could occur as a result of changing buyer/supplier relationships. Such scenarios could well coexist, albeit in different industries, depending on whether such industries tend to favor vertical or horizontal mergers. For example,

- Ultimately, fewer and larger suppliers for any given clients. This will reduce the buyers' negotiating power, because their proportion of a supplier's sales will decrease.

- Same suppliers versus larger, pan-European clients. The reverse will happen to relative bargaining strength.

IMPACT ON PROCESSING TECHNOLOGY AND PRODUCTION STRATEGY

The methods and procedures that are used to produce goods and services can have an important impact on the profitability of a company. The criteria used to select the optimum method of processing in either manufacturing or service firms will not change as a consequence of 1992. What may change for any company are those factors that made previous processing decisions appropriate. In many instances, previously uneconomic alternatives may become the most cost-effective and appropriate means of production in the light of new market conditions. Many companies will need to completely reassess their production strategies in the pan-European market. The following issues should be addressed:

- Economics of the make-or-buy decision

- Facility-location strategy to balance production costs, including any new economies of scale, against distribution costs

- Adoption of advanced practices such as JIT or computer-integrated manufacturing (CIM)

- Impact of any changes to technical standards on manufacturing processes.

Changing Environmental Factors

Freedom of establishment and freedom of movement of goods will have significant logistical and distributional implications. The removal of competitive restrictions will inevitably lead to rationalization of industry on a pan-European basis as companies seek and are given the opportunity to pursue economies of scale in production, distribution, research and development, and other areas.

Possible Business Responses

The degree to which companies should integrate their operations along vertical lines will be influenced by the 1992 market environment. Some companies to date have been purchasing parts and components because it has been more cost-effective to buy them from external suppliers. With production levels increasing as firms start manufacturing for the whole European market, higher volumes of parts and components will be needed. Vertical integration may become attractive.

Improved opportunities for businesses to set up plants in countries where parts and components can be produced at lower cost will influence make-or-buy decisions. Freer movement of goods with-

in the Community, and reduced customs formalities and transport costs, will give companies more flexibility in organizing their manufacturing operations. Therefore, a trend toward multisite processing is likely to develop, with firms setting up specialized manufacturing units in carefully selected locations, where the best combination of economy and quality can be achieved.

Businesses will have a greater choice of possible locations after completion of the European market. Freedom of establishment will encourage geographical expansion, as will standardization of environmental controls. Companies will wish to select the most suitable locations for their facilities, on the basis of a number of criteria, including the following:

- Labor cost, availability, and skills

- Geographical considerations (proximity of supply sources, raw materials)

- Cost of land, construction, equipment, and so on

- Environmental controls

- Logistics (transportation costs, infrastructure, and so on)

- Availability of state aids, within EC law constraints

- Economies of scale

The competitive pressure on margins, which is expected to result from the opening up of the single market, will force businesses to reduce their costs or lose profitability. The adoption of advanced manufacturing practices and management of supply channels appear to be the areas with the most improvement potential. The removal of technical barriers will allow companies to manufacture the same products for the whole European market. Processing techniques will, therefore, become more standardized.

JIT methods and CIM are expected to become widespread across Europe. Due to a general increase in industrial competitiveness, firms will be looking for new ways of differentiating themselves, including enhancing their overall productivity. Investments in CIM may be extremely costly, but some businesses will see in them an opportunity to reach worldwide competitiveness standards.

IMPACT ON PRODUCT RANGE AND NEW PRODUCT DEVELOPMENT

Decisions about product range are central to business strategies, because they determine how companies position themselves on the market and choose to address specific customer needs. The opening up of the pan-European market will have considerable implications for an organization's product range strategy: the possibilities include rationalization, increased product range, and increased use of product platforms.

Changing Environmental Factors

A number of aspects of the 1992 program will influence the development of product range strategies. For example, there should be general recognition that goods produced or marketed in one Member State will have a right of access to all other Member States, once harmonization of differing Member State regulations and essential (safety) requirements has occurred. This includes the creation of European standards, to be set by the European Committee for Standardization (CEN), the European Committee for Electronic Standardization (CENELEC), and the European Telecommunications Standards Institute (ETSI). This development will eliminate duplication of certification and testing costs.

The following list illustrates the extent to which technical regulations and standards are considered to affect various manufacturing sectors (based on a survey of 11,000 businessmen across Europe, with industries listed in descending order of the amount of technical trade barriers imposed):

1. Motor vehicles
2. Electrical engineering
3. Mechanical engineering
4. Pharmaceuticals
5. Nonmetallic mineral products
6. Other transport equipment
7. Food and tobacco
8. Leather
9. Precision and medical equipment
10. Metal articles [a]

The circumstances under which Member States have a duty to notify the Commission of new

[a] Source: Cecchini Report.

regulations and standards in advance of their enactment will be extended. The Commission will decide whether such legislation is liable to trigger new technical barriers to intra-Community trade. Restrictive practices based on compliance with discriminatory standards will be banned.

Cost structures will also be an important factor in planning product range strategies. Sustaining different product lines is expensive, particularly if the costs involved cannot be spread over large markets. Decisions about the best way to increase both the profitability and competitiveness of a business can only be made by weighing the costs against the advantages of wide horizontal market coverage.

An example of how such changes will affect product range is the enhanced interoperability of telecommunications equipment. The Green Paper on the "Development of the Common Market for Telecommunications Services and Equipment" proposed a liberalization of public procurement, together with the creation of a European Standards Institute to accelerate common standards and technical specifications. Steps to achieve these objectives have already begun.

Another major factor is freedom of establishment and freedom to provide cross-frontier services, especially for banking and insurance. As a result, intersectoral transfers between these two industries are made easier, and restrictions on the range of different products that each of these sectors can provide are considerably reduced.

Possible Business Responses

Many large companies are expected to try to widen their product range to better serve customer needs. Different national consumer expectations of what should be included in a product range will be a factor. Medium-sized companies will need to either rationalize their product lines and concentrate on the ones in which, despite their size, they have a suitable competitive advantage or seek to create link-ups with national and foreign companies to increase their market coverage and reinforce their competitive position. Economies of scale will arise in some cases.

Smaller firms will be faced with two options: to focus on a niche market that they have the expertise to serve in a unique way or to diversify into similar niche markets abroad, possibly via intra-Community link-ups to share R&D efforts.

Firms will no longer need to devote a considerable share of their R&D budgets to the adjustment of technology to different national markets. The industries most likely to be affected by this situation are telecommunications equipment, automobiles, food stuffs, pharmaceuticals, and the building sector. Subject to marketing considerations (principally cultural differences), businesses in these sectors will be able to pursue global strategies that, although they were clearly suited to their sectoral characteristics, could not be implemented before.

Businesses should consider collaborative agreements to spread the cost of R&D. Companies will (1) find it easier to merge, and (2) find themselves competing Europe-wide with companies with large R&D resources that previously did not find it economically feasible to enter national markets (such as telecommunications firms). The reduction in the relative unit cost of bringing new products to market is expected to result in a greater number of new and innovative products.

On the one hand, 1992 will increase product standardization. This will benefit the automobile sector, which is currently incurring large product development costs due to differing requirements for engineering, production, product planning, type approval, certification, and other processes. The EC market integration will result in fewer car floorplan designs being needed for different car models. Thirty platforms are now used for passenger cars produced by six major car manufacturers (VW, Fiat, Renault, Ford, GM, and Volvo). This number could be reduced to 21 in a fully integrated market, resulting in considerable savings.

On the other hand, 1992 will lead to a more extensive product range. The West German insurance market—strictly divided at present by national legislation into life and nonlife sectors and within the nonlife sector among legal, credit suretyship, and other classes of insurance—will be partially liberalized. Insurers will be allowed to supply whatever classes of insurance they want, and the freedom to select the components of product range will be considerably increased.

IMPACT ON COST CONTROL

In competitive markets where selling prices are subject to great pressure, cost control is a key factor in business success. The pan-European market created in 1992 will result in immediate reductions in variable costs (customs, certification, and so forth). On a relative basis, fixed costs will also be reduced as volume increases.

Changing Environmental Factors

The impact of 1992 on cost issues will be twofold. Companies will see an immediate and direct effect on their costs as a result of certain measures to remove barriers to trade within the Community. But the opening up of the EC market will also give rise to indirect cost-reduction opportunities. The measures that should have an early effect on costs include

- The removal of technical barriers will reduce the inefficiencies caused by divergent product standards and, together with freedom of goods movement within the Community, will provide opportunities for greater economies of scale.

- The opening up of public procurement will give many manufacturers larger markets, which they have so far been denied. This will clearly increase their potential for unit cost savings.

- The removal of nontariff barriers will result in a reduction of primary costs, which will be reflected in lower intermediate consumption costs.

- A more significant impact on costs is expected from the indirect and dynamic effects of 1992 on industry efficiency. Moreover, with the harmonization of legislation for cross-border mergers and acquisitions, industry restructuring will be eased and will move toward rationalizing operations. Achieving more efficient size will be encouraged.

Lower costs of distribution, imported materials, transport, insurance, and banking services resulting from the opening up of the EC market have been identified as sources of large potential savings for companies in other sectors. In Greece, for example, industrialists consider lower banking costs to be the main reason for their own expected cost reduction. In Spain and Portugal, the lower cost of imported materials is regarded as the most important cost-reducing factor, but banking costs also rank high on the list.

As a result of these price pressures, an overall growth of demand is expected to arise that will affect the volume of goods produced and production-unit size.

Possible Business Response

As a result of the potentially larger markets, businesses will want to exploit economies of scale in certain sectors. Companies will need to determine what a technically efficient volume is for their sector and how unit costs increase below that volume. An assessment of the companies' business situations, in conjunction with their findings, will enable the firms to identify possible economies of scale (though economies of scale are not achievable in all sectors).

The development of cross-border mergers and acquisitions, which should be facilitated by changes to company and tax law, will increase the scope for economies of scale in manufacturing. Industry restructuring moves have already taken place in a number of sectors.

The abolition of technical barriers and the harmonization of national standards, including patents and trademarks, will give businesses new opportunities for economies in research and development, because the cost of product design and market research for new products, for example, will be spread over a larger volume of sales.

Businesses will also have to address the problems of maintaining margins. There is potential for lower input costs, but at the same time end-users will expect lower prices, given a greater level of

general competitiveness. Moreover, margins vary from country to country (for example, margins in the construction industry are high in the UK relative to France) and high-margin companies will need to know how to protect their positions or compete on lower margins.

Some businesses will have to look for alternative cost-rationalization strategies, in particular in those sectors where the potential for economies of scale is limited.

Certain sectors are now characterized by unused production capacity; inefficient allocation of human, physical, or financial resources; underemployment of certain factors; duplications; and redundancies. Often, these problems have developed as a result of insufficient competitive pressures.

As a result of increased competitive pressure, the reduction of excessive overhead costs will be a priority. In some instances, internal reorganization has been seen to reduce overhead costs by between 10 percent and 25 percent.

To take full advantage of cost-reduction opportunities, businesses should review all new alternative supply sources for goods and services that will emerge from increased competition. The success of cost-reduction strategies will depend, to a great extent, on businesses' ability to identify and fully exploit the cost-saving potential that will characterize the 1992 environment.

Most importantly, companies should remember that size will not always be a condition for cost efficiency in the 1992 context. Smaller niche players with light and flexible structures will see great opportunities for cost reductions through the learning effect (which brings down unit costs as a business acquires more experience). Increased specialization and rationalization of activities are key areas for the cost-reduction strategies of small businesses to exploit.

▼

Impact on Organizational Structure and Human Resource Management

The selection and recruitment of the best-suited human resources are essential to business success. Those companies that broaden the scope of their

activities, in particular by crossing borders into new markets, will put people who can operate in an international context—professionally, in a managerial capacity, and culturally—at a premium. The organization of such companies will need to change as they address different markets. Companies that become involved in merger or acquisition activity will be faced with a whole barrage of structural and cultural issues, national, regional, and corporate. Typical issues to be addressed are

- The organization structure to be used in a multibusiness, multicountry company

- Centralized or decentralized control and degrees of accountability

- Cultural issues when firms change structures or enter into mergers or joint ventures

- Mobility and flexibility of personnel

- The need for, and creation of, new skills to operate on a European basis or to deal with new businesses created by the European market

- Sourcing of people skills

- Industrial relations issues emerging across Europe

Changing Environmental Factors

The legal and statutory corporate requirements for companies that compete in the new Europe will change. This may entail changes in structure. There may be advantages to setting up an EEIG or one or more new companies to carry out Europe-wide functions and fully benefit from greater convergence in corporate and other relevant laws. An expert review of a company's current and planned trading environment, and an understanding of the implications of legislative changes in each country, will determine the feasibility of using new pan-European companies.

Many companies are currently organized on a geographical basis and compete in relatively few countries or in a very decentralized and autonomous fashion. Pressure will develop to trade across borders, in the whole market. This will raise the question of organizing functions on a European basis (such as marketing, production, corporate finance, and personnel), and product or segment marketing on a European basis. The latter move alone raises particular challenges for information systems and for management capability. It is, however, already a trend in industries such as banking, consumer products, and automotive, and the trend is likely to spread to food, pharmaceuticals, textiles, and others.

The economics and manageability of such structures will need to be questioned thoroughly. With advances in IT, assisted by common standards and specifications, the possibility of distributing data processing to employees (individuals or groups) will increase.

Companies will need to deal with pan-European functions and markets arranged on a different basis. They will be faced with language and cultural problems. The need for new managers with the ability to cope with these problems and the need for appropriate training will become more pressing. Particular new skills in areas such as telecommunications, logistics, and multinational marketing will become scarcer and, therefore, in greater demand. It will be important for companies to assess their managerial needs and look for new sources.

There will be increased visibility of and attention to labor force rights. Representation by unions, both on the shop floor and on company boards, will become an issue in certain countries. Central EC decisions will become increasingly important, especially in the long term, in their effect on the labor market.

Possible Business Response

Organizational structure has tended to be based on national boundaries in many industries. Competing in a European market may require pan-European management teams, European head offices, and a degree of central monitoring and control in order to plan the best use of resources. Companies in such industries will need to make decisions about achieving central control and maintaining local motivation and accountability.

Companies within some industries have already established European head offices and given them substantial autonomy. Such industries include computers, pharmaceuticals, consumer products, and—to some extent—financial services. Other companies considering setting up European head offices need to look at reporting arrangements; performance measurement systems; and proper accountability, locations, and communications.

Trading across borders and an increase in mergers and acquisitions will require companies to consider whether their current organizational structures and styles are appropriate for different national cultures. Carrying out an acquisition of a company in a different country, with the objective of merging functions and products into a single entity, will generate change-management issues.

The opportunities for movement of people and the standardizing of professional skill requirements should, in theory, make more companies look at how they can make the most economic use of personnel. Possible developments include

- Economies of scale through the setting up of centers of specialization to which people from different countries could be seconded or recruited. For example, a European design center in the automotive industry would be feasible.

- Larger companies investing in Europe-wide training facilities and training programs to gain economies of scale and meet the new skill requirements.

- The sharing of skills around European locations, depending on the demand. Engineers, computer experts, product designers, trainers, and others could be used as required as contractors for short-term projects, but organized on a central basis. There remain linguistic and cultural barriers to achieving these opportunities but they are worth investigating.

- Changes in the ways companies think about loyalty and retention. It is possible that with more movement and mobility, professionals and highly skilled workers will look at opportunities across the market.

IMPACT ON RESOURCE ALLOCATION AND FINANCIAL PLANNING

A correct assessment of current and future financial requirements is vital to effective corporate strategy. It is essential to plan the amount and sources of finance required to achieve your business objectives.

For example, expansion requires substantial resources and needs a sound financial base. As competitive pressure drives companies to develop aggressive expansion strategies, both in their domestic markets and abroad, it becomes increasingly important that financial resources be able to meet and support growth objectives. Having planned short- and long-term financial requirements, businesses will need to look for the most appropriate ways of raising the requisite resources either internally or externally, or both.

Changing Environmental Factors

The overall intensification of competitive activity stemming from market integration will have a considerable impact on firms' financial requirements. Some businesses, especially those with some protection at present, will want to reduce administrative and overhead costs, and to reorganize their business activities to be more productive and efficient. Normally, such a reduction will not happen without heavy investment, which will place great demands on their financial resources.

Apart from reinforcing their competitive positions in their domestic markets, businesses will also be looking for opportunities abroad. Expansion plans may require considerable investments in R&D, market research, marketing and advertising activities, new distribution networks, and human resources.

The liberalization of capital movements, together with a more progressive attitude toward profit repatriation, should give firms more flexibility in financial resources. They will be able to source funds from a greater number and variety of financial institutions. The liberalization of the European banking market will make cross-border financial operations easier and less expensive. Businesses will be able to choose from a wider range of competitive services, at lower cost. They will also benefit from the emergence of new products, because of increased innovation, that are better suited to their specific needs and requirements. Companies will be able to differentiate between countries and types of services to suit their financing needs.

Retail financial costs, currently less exposed to international competition, will be more affected than wholesale costs, which are already under competitive pressure.

Possible Business Responses

Businesses often seek external financing to fund ambitious expansion programs. This financing may include credit from financial organizations or capital injections from shareholders or business partners. Practices in fundraising (for example, German firms tend to go to banks where UK firms go to the stock market) should be reviewed as the cost of loans relative to equity alters. Companies should think more in terms of raising money from a broader European base. Mergers, acquisitions, and joint ventures will become more frequent as companies try to expand their financial bases. Companies will broaden their thinking and contemplate all these activities on a cross-border basis. Lower-cost finance will make more projects feasible by reducing the degree of risk.

Financial management on a European scale will increase. In addition, the treasury management function should spread, provided that companies are capable of handling multicurrency management.

Taxation changes will also become an issue.

▼

IMPACT ON INFORMATION TECHNOLOGY

Information technology (IT) can change the way companies compete, opening up new opportunities for business strategies. However, IT can also consume large amounts of company resources and management effort. Firms must be concerned with their ability to plan their IT strategy and to ensure that this strategy is made to happen.

Among many IT concerns are these:

- IT use has to be directly related to the changing business objectives of an organization.

- Top management will need increased access to information to plan, monitor, and control any new organization in Europe.

- Choice of IT strategies is governed by the way technology is organized and information delivered. Some of the issues here have a significant impact on control, cost, and flexibility.

Changing Environmental Factors

The creation of a pan-European market is the result of the removal of a number of barriers. Ways in which this removal will particularly affect IT strategy include the following:

- Pan-European professional recognition will open up opportunities for sharing and moving skills that may be a key part of an IT strategy.

- Moves toward common standards for communications technology will improve the viability of rapid clearing of and access to information across Europe.

- Companies will compete in a wider market arena in Europe. This will lead to marketing, manufacturing, supply of services, and distribution on a Europe-wide basis and to consequent increased demand for data communication.

Mergers and acquisitions will increase. This will affect IT considerations in different ways. For example, alliances will require that companies consider how common standards such as OSI will enable cost-effective communications. Acquisitions will create the need for flexible systems to allow a diversity of transaction and data types, and added volume.

Possible Business Response

Companies are increasingly turning to IT in the search for sustainable competitive advantage: changing an industry's structure to create barriers to entry or to tie in customers and suppliers; introducing new products and services; cost reduction (in processing and distribution); product differentiation; and niche businesses. All these general strategies create IT opportunities that will be enhanced by the 1992 measures.

A significant increase in the demand for distribution is expected. IT solutions to logistics and distribution problems will help existing distribution companies to compete better. They will also help clients not currently distributing on a European scale to develop major new distribution systems.

Drives toward economies of scale in production, leading to both larger and more flexible factories to supply a total European market, will cause an increase in the demand for CIM and other factory automation. Also, specialist manufacturing plants may be developed in particular countries as part of a Europe-wide production and manufacturing strategy. This might imply production planning, forecasting, and supply management on a European scale, with implications for the types of information systems needed. In consumer products and pharmaceutical companies, this particular trend is already emerging.

New services and businesses for the global market will emerge based on IT. These could include network and communication services, credit-card and financial services, and database marketing opportunities.

The availability of marketing information across Europe will encourage database marketing and the use of IT to find new ways of marketing across Europe. Direct marketing, global advertising, and coordination of promotions across Europe may all be possible. These techniques obviously need to address local marketing differences, but with the movement toward common products and product standards, opportunities will start opening up. IT may play a major part in changing the way sales and distribution happen across Europe. There may be a threat to the wholesalers and intermediaries in the distribution chain, who simply provide access to customers.

Financial management, on a European scale, may well be encouraged if IT can create real advantages here. Treasury management is likely to spread as a function, with the ability of new systems to handle multicurrency management, into companies in industrial sectors that historically are not used to investing in this area. Similarly, there may be advantages to looking at credit control and major processing functions on a European basis.

Other trends may occur:

- In purchasing and the supply of products, a trend toward single sourcing across Europe will require strong coordination of purchasing requirements and, again, moves companies toward multisite, multicountry management resources. IT implications here are of greater complexity with greater benefits.

- Personnel management systems on a European scale may also emerge, particularly where key skills, key resources, and key management capability should be monitored and moved across Europe. Remote or distributed data processing

may become more feasible, subject to concerns regarding privacy of personal data.

- There may be a streamlining of relationships resulting in smaller numbers of pan-European suppliers. This streamlining will push companies toward more use of electronic data interchange (EDI).

In many of these opportunity areas, there is potential movement toward functions being run on a European scale. Currently, organizations are very often set up within national boundaries but, as the opportunities for cross-boundary functions and coordination increase, there is a need emerging for collecting information across functions.

For the new senior management appearing as functional heads across Europe, and for the new managing directors who look for information across boundaries, there is a need for better, more flexible, and more complex management databases and executive information systems (EIS). The trend toward EIS is accelerating in general, and companies that compete in many European countries will reap considerable advantage if top management can be given rapid, economic access to critical planning and performance information. This implies the development of management databases supra Europe and significant investment in the same. There is a need to take into account multilinguistic capability in the reporting of information. Again, the implications for design may be considerable.

Beyond business requirements and associated information needs there are a number of implications for what IT will actually be needed by companies competing in global markets and across Europe, especially with hardware, software, IT organization, and other factors. The following possibilities and developments should be explored:

- Data centers operating on a European basis become more feasible and more economic. Some of the major multinationals are moving in this direction. They are encouraged by the use of common hardware, common communications standards, and the ability to move professional skills. This trend raises organizational and management issues.

- Significant changes are likely in the availability of public telecommunications services and tariffs, opening up opportunities for economies of scale and reorganization of telecommunications' infrastructures.

- In the opposite direction, availability of networks at more economic rates may lead to companies selectively using more decentralized procurement techniques. Mixed economies may develop. A balance of business risk, practicality, and economics will need to be weighed for each user of IT.

- Hardware suppliers are likely to restructure in order to look for new markets, seek strategic alliances, and find new marketing arrangements. Users of IT will, therefore, seek ways of exploiting the changes for better deals.

- The development of European communications and network strategies becomes a key part of the IT solution of a company competing Europe-wide. This development implies more experts and more attention to an area that has perhaps not been fully explored. The economics of communications become a key part of the strategy.

- Moves to standardization encourage common hardware and common application software. Traditional arguments about the differences between businesses in each country will gradually disappear. At the same time, companies should be seeking real benefits in systems development economics and in implementation timetables by sharing solutions. This implies significant changes to the way IT is organized and delivered and an ability to deal with organizational and political boundaries.

- When language difficulties remain a factor, there may be common application software providing translation facilities automatically.

- Centers of excellence may be developed for particular aspects of IT, capitalizing on particular strengths, that share their results around Europe. There may also be cases for multiple sites of excellence in particular applications.

- Companies in the business of supplying software services may seek new ways of gaining competitive advantage by setting up centers for development and production.

- Justification of the IT strategy in terms of costs and benefits must be done on a Europe-wide basis. Traditional measures of financial success by country, product group, or function may have to be discarded.

- Europe-wide service and support organizations will emerge as software and IT services companies identify economies of scale and recognize that resources can be moved and that clients or customers do not have easy and quick access to Europe-wide support.

- The information function will have to be organized and coordinated on a European basis.

- Economies of scale in systems development, resourcing, and implementation will encourage sharing of solutions and people. In implementation, economies of scale in areas such as education, training, and technology absorption programs could arise.

4

Understanding the Evolving European Monetary System

One of the most significant developments in the last year is the movement to create economic and monetary union throughout the EC. One aspect is the debate over the development and use of the European Currency Unit (ECU). Already, that "currency" is used among governments in the EC and in a limited number of commercial transactions.

Any business dealing with an EC-based firm or bank should understand what the ECU is and where it is going. Not only will its role in world commerce increase, but the ECU may well become the most important currency of the 1990s.

OVERVIEW

Originally used only to handle accounts of the Community agencies, over time the European Currency Unit has matured. Today, it is a standard way of handling transactions between governments; its use by companies has been slower to develop but is increasing. Within the next decade, it may evolve into the *only* currency in the EC.

The ECU is currently made up of a slice of each of the currencies of all 12 Member States.

The ECU is also the cornerstone of the European Monetary System (EMS), which has brought a significant degree of stability to the monetary systems of its members. Within the next decade, the EC expects to put into place its own separate central banking system, marking yet another major step toward the complete economic integration of Europe.

ASSISTANCE

Refer to Chapter 5 for background on the history and organizational design of the EC's institutions.

For additional help in using this sourcebook, refer to the Introduction to Part I.

THE ECU: CENTERPIECE OF THE EUROPEAN MONETARY SYSTEM

The ECU is a basket-type currency of the EC. That means it is composed of specific amounts of each Member State's currency. Precise rules have been laid down for the regular reexamination and modification of the composition of the basket.

Every business day, the Commission calculates the current exchange rate for the ECU, based on the Member States' currencies, using the exchange rates recorded at 2:30 P.M. in Brussels. This calculation produces official daily rates for the ECU, such as those in Table 4.1, which the Commission then publishes in the next day's edition of the *Official Journal of the European Communities ('C' Series)*, available by subscription from the Office for Official Publications for the EC in Luxembourg (see Chapter 19 for more information on the *Official Journal*).

PUBLIC AND PRIVATE SECTOR USES OF THE ECU

Public Sector Uses

First and foremost, the ECU is the unit of account used by all EC institutions for drawing up their budgets. In addition, the ECU is widely used for both Community and Member States' transactions:

- The ECU is used for fixing and collecting external customs duties, levies, refunds, and other intra-Community payments. Even the tax-free allowances for Community residents traveling between Member States or arriving from a nonmember state are set in ECUs.

- The Statistical Office of the European Communities uses the ECU to ensure direct comparability in EC data series.

- EC grants and loans to enterprises, as well as fines, such as those levied for infringing the Community's competition rules, are stated and paid in ECUs.

- The system of uniform agricultural prices established by the Common Agricultural Policy relies on the ECU.

- The European Development Fund uses the ECU to calculate its revenues and expenditures. It also uses the ECU to establish the Member States' contributions and payments to projects.

- The European Investment Bank issues public loans in ECUs. It was the first institution to do so.

- ECUs are used by the central banks of the countries participating in the European Monetary System (EMS) (which is discussed later in the chapter). These banks use the currency unit to settle a portion of the debts arising from compulsory interventions, under the exchange-rate mechanism, in support of their respective currencies.

- The ECU plays a role in Community credit facilities, which may be drawn on by Member States finding themselves in temporary balance-of-payments difficulties.

- The ECU is a reserve currency. Participants in the EMS have deposited 20 percent of their gold

Table 4.1
Value of the ECU—January 2, 1991

Country	Value of 1 ECU
Belgium	BEF 42.1944
Canada	$ 1.58721
Denmark	DKr 7.87374
France	FF 6.95237
Germany	Dm 2.04372
Greece	Dr 214.771
Ireland	Ir£ 0.768315
Italy	L 1539.95
Japan	Yen 183.931
Luxembourg	LUF 42.1944
The Netherlands	Dfl. 2.30567
Portugal	Esc 182.054
Spain	Pta 130.389
Sweden	Kr 7.67782
Switzerland	Fr 1.72997
UK	£ 0.706217
United States	$ 1.37006

Source: *Official Journal of the European Communities ('C' series).*

reserves and 20 percent of their U.S. dollar reserves with the European Monetary Co-operation Fund. In exchange, the fund has credited them with ECUs.

- National governments, including Spain, France, the UK, and Italy, are raising debt in ECUs.

Private Sector Uses

The ECU, intended for use by institutions of the Community and its Member States, is now also being used by the private sector. Any individual or company can use the currency in conducting its own financial or business transactions. This in-creasingly widespread use in the private sector can be seen from the following examples:

- The ECU is listed on stock exchanges in Europe, as well as on some markets outside the EC.
- It is possible for any business to borrow in ECUs. It also is possible to hold deposits in ECUs.
- Private loans and securities issues can be denominated in ECUs. On the ECU bond market, a company listed on a stock exchange can issue bonds denominated in ECUs. In addition, banks can join together and issue an ECU bond loan.
- The ECU is used in interbank transactions in the deposit and loan markets.
- EC-based corporations are structuring joint ventures with non-EC-based enterprises based on the ECU. For example, Fiat and the Soviet Union's Automobile Ministry have entered into a joint venture to produce cars in the U.S.S.R. That agreement provides that the new firm will operate within a "currency enclave" where all transactions will be denominated in ECUs.
- EC-based businesses are considering switching to ECU billing for intra-Community trade.
- It is possible to obtain EC-denominated travelers' checks.

The main factor behind the increasing use of the ECU by the private sector is the relative stability it provides in exchange and interest rates. This stability arises because the ECU is tied to the currencies of all of the 12 Member States.

The continued development of the ECU's use by the private sector is also due to all of these factors:

- The desire of some economists and those in some financial markets to draw back from the dollar and its relative volatility
- A desire by investors and enterprises for increased protection against the risk of exchange losses
- Strong encouragement by the EC's institutions

THE ECU'S ROLE IN THE EXCHANGE-RATE MECHANISM

The ECU is the principal pillar of the entire EMS. As such, it has been assigned four key functions. It is to function in all of the following roles:

- The key element of the exchange-rate mechanism. This determines the central rate of exchange of the Member States' currencies.

- The basis for the "divergence indicator." In that role, it measures the performance of each currency. This, in turn, can lead to intervention by the Member States' central banks on the foreign-exchange markets.

- The "numeraire," or currency for monetary intervention and for credit mechanisms between Member States.

- A reserve instrument and means of settlement between monetary authorities in the Community itself.

Fixing the Value of Participating Currencies

Participating in the EMS exchange-rate mechanism means that a central exchange rate, expressed in ECUs, is fixed for each participating currency. These ECU-related central rates then are used to establish a series of bilateral exchange rates.

Presently, 10 of the 12 EC currencies participate in the exchange-rate mechanism. The most recent addition was the British pound, which was added in October 1990. Only the Portuguese escudo and the Greek drachma do not yet participate.

Fluctuation margins of 2.25 percent are allowed on either side of the bilateral exchange rates. At present, the Spanish peseta and the British pound are allowed a wider range of fluctuations—a range of 6 percent. However, the pound is expected to move into the narrower range as soon as its domestic inflation permits.

Through the use of the ECU, any adjustment to the central rate of a particular currency becomes a matter of common interest to all participating Member States. The adjustment cannot be decided by any single government.

However, when central rates are adjusted, Member States' requests for revaluation or devaluation are negotiated on the basis of bilateral exchange rates. The new ECU-related central rates, thus, are to be calculated only as a second step.

Changing the ECU's Composition

Basically, the composition of the ECU can be changed on three different occasions:

- During a regular review of the ECU, held every five years. The first reexamination took place in 1984, the second took place in 1989, and the third is scheduled for 1994.

- On request of a member of the EC. This would happen if the weight of any of the currencies making up the ECU (detailed later in the chapter) changed by 25 percent or more.

- Following the addition of the currency of a new Member State to the ECU's basket. This was done when the drachma, the peseta, and the escudo were added.

The weight of each currency in the basket is fixed by a formula that applies predetermined economic criteria. These criteria are designed to reflect the relative strength of the national economies of the Members of the Community. The goal is to have the ECU reflect the overall economy of the EC.

The elements making up the weighting formula are as follows:

- The share of each Member State in the gross domestic product (GDP) of the EC

- The share of each Member State in the external trade—exports and imports of goods and services—of the EC, Europe, and the world

- The contribution of each Member State's central bank to the EMS's short-term monetary support mechanism

Table 4.2 lists a sample breakdown of the ECU by percentage for all the Member States.

The Future: Moves Toward Economic and Monetary Union

The EC still has a long way to go before it achieves complete economic and monetary union. However, the widening acceptance of the ECU and the relative success of the EMS provide support for future discussions on the development of that union.

Table 4.2
Composition of the ECU as of January 1991

Currency Unit	Composition of the ECU
Belgian Franc	7.60%
Danish Krone	2.45%
French Franc	19.00%
German Mark	30.10%
Greek Drachma	0.80%
Irish Pound	1.10%
Italian Lira	10.15%
Luxembourg Franc	0.30%
The Netherlands Guilder	9.40%
Portuguese Escudo	0.80%
Spanish Peseta	5.30%
UK Pound	13.00%

Continued progress toward using the ECU as a true European monetary unit will not come solely from official initiatives. In using the ECU, the private sector already has demonstrated that it needs, and is willing to use, a currency unit accepted across national boundaries.

The Member States have agreed in principle to move toward economic and monetary union (EMU) in three stages. The first stage, which has already started, will involve greater coordination of economic policy by national authorities and central banks. All currencies join the EMS in the 2.25 percent band.

In the second stage, a European System of Central Banks (ESCB), which some refer to as "Eurofed," will be achieved. A draft constitution for ESCB has already been prepared. ESCB would provide a means of achieving greater coordination and co-operation, but would not have power over individual countries' central banks. The permitted range of fluctuation within the EMS would be reduced to 1 percent.

In the third stage, exchange rates would be fixed and community institutions would be given full monetary competence. In effect, the ESCB would take over the responsibilities presently held by the central banks in each Member State. At this stage, it would be possible to adopt a common currency for use throughout the Community, possibly (as suggested by the UK) as a thirteenth currency. Much detail remains to be decided by the inter-governmental conference that started in Rome in December 1990. Current expectations are that stage 2 will begin in 1994 and stage 3 a few years later.

5

The History and Structure of the European Community

▼

Understanding the complicated way the EC works—specifically, its procedures for making decisions about the Single Market Program—requires a knowledge of the EC's history and of the legislative, executive, judicial, and advisory organizations that make up the EC.

This chapter provides an introduction to the EC's history as well as to the four principal institutions and three auxiliary bodies responsible for making the decisions that determine how the EC functions today and how it will operate in the future.

OVERVIEW

The European Community (EC) is the only international organization founded on a limited but real (and growing) transfer of sovereignty from its Member States to a supranational institution.

In the EC, authority is shared between Member States and Community institutions. Member States, however, have already relinquished the power to make unilateral rules governing agricultural and trade policy with non-EC countries. The EC's Commission, for instance, now speaks on behalf of all Member States at the international GATT (General Agreement on Tariffs and Trade) negotiations. It also protects EC interests against alleged unfair trade practices by non-EC countries.

In the future, it is expected that the EC institutions will acquire even greater political authority. This authority will result, in part, from an intergovernmental conference that was launched at a December 1990 "summit" meeting. At that meeting, the Member States agreed to review the roles and responsibilities of the EC institutions, and to consider the feasibility of achieving greater political union, paralleling the increasing unification of the Member States' economies.

SECTIONS IN THIS CHAPTER

History of the Single Market Program

Principal EC Institutions: Structure and Responsibilities

Auxiliary Bodies of the European Community

ASSISTANCE

Refer to Chapter 20 for descriptions of the annual reports that the EC's institutions release. Chapter 6 explains the role of the EC's institutions in making and interpreting EC legislation.

For additional help in using this sourcebook, refer to the Introduction to Part I.

HISTORY OF THE SINGLE MARKET PROGRAM

Figure 5.1 gives a chronology of milestone dates in the history of the European Community.

The European Coal and Steel Community

The foundation of the EC was laid in 1950. Robert Schuman, then the French foreign minister, put forward a plan for France and Germany to pool their coal and steel production. This plan became a reality with the signing in Paris of the treaty establishing the European Coal and Steel Community (ECSC) on April 18, 1951.

The European Economic Community and the European Atomic Energy Community

The next important step toward the development of the EC came on March 25, 1957, with the signing of the Treaty of Rome. Two additional "communities" were created: the European Economic Community (EEC) and the European Atomic Energy Community (EAEC), more usually known as Euratom.

Member States

Resulting from this series of treaties were three separate but parallel communities involved with the economic development of Europe: the ECSC, the EC, and the AEC. In 1958, when the Treaty of Rome came into effect, the three communities had the same six members:

• Belgium
• Federal Republic of Germany
• France
• Italy
• Luxembourg

• The Netherlands

Between 1958 and 1986, the number of Member States increased to 12, with the following new members:

• Denmark, Ireland, and the United Kingdom, on January 1, 1973
• Greece, on January 1, 1981
• Portugal and Spain, on January 1, 1986

Three Communities

Since 1957, these three separate communities have coexisted. Each operated in areas and in manners required by its own treaty, and each had its own institutions. Initially, some of these institutions were completely separate from similar institutions in the other communities. Now, however, the same institutions serve all three communities.

The European Community

In both the media and the commercial world, the three communities became regarded as a single entity—the European Community, or the EC. This perception was formalized by a resolution of the European Parliament on February 16, 1976, which proposed that the three communities be collectively designated as "the European Community."

Thus, for all practical purposes, the three original communities can now be regarded as one—the EC.

The 1985 White Paper

Two individuals are given most of the credit for the current movement toward the Single Market: Jacques Delors, president of the EC Commission, and Lord Cockfield, previously the EC commissioner responsible for the Single Market. They conceived the three concepts vital to that move-ment:

- Creating a package of specific changes (including both old and new proposals) needed to achieve that goal
- Setting a deadline to achieve enactment of these proposals
- Ensuring their ultimate implementation was guaranteed at the highest political levels

The catalyst for accomplishing this unity was the release of a "White Paper." In 1985, the Commission of the European Communities published a report by Lord Cockfield on the Single Market. This report, entitled *White Paper for the Completion of the Internal Market*, is commonly known as *The 1985 White Paper*. Its stated objective was to make the EC into a single market without internal frontiers.

The 1985 White Paper became the Commission's blueprint for achieving the Single Market. It detailed the necessary program to create the Single Market and tied it to a clear timetable for action. The 1985 White Paper sought to create, step by step, an integrated and coherent framework. It did this by attempting to identify all the existing physical, technical, and fiscal barriers to trade. These, it concluded, prevented the free functioning of the internal European market.

The White Paper for the first time provides a detailed and comprehensive plan to complete the internal market. The particular role that each citizen, each business and each government must play in this process has also become clearer. It is now a matter of working to make the plan a reality.

Date	Milestone
1950	Robert Schuman proposes that France and Germany pool coal and steel production.
1951	European Coal and Steel Community (ECSC) formed on April 18.
1957	Treaty of Rome signed, creating the European Economic Community (EEC) and European Atomic Energy Community (EAEC).
1958	Original Member States consist of Belgium, France, Germany, Italy, Luxembourg, and The Netherlands. Court of Justice and European Investment Bank are created as result of Treaty of Rome.
1967	Merger Treaty establishes a single Council and single Commission of the European Communities.
1973	Denmark, Ireland, and the UK become Member States on January 1.
1976	European Parliament proposes on February 16 that the ECSC, EEC, and EAEC be designated the European Community.
1977	Court of Auditors established in July.
1979	European Court of Justice settles the Cassis de Dijon case, establishing free circulation for products meeting essential safety criteria and mutual recognition of standards for product differences.
1981	Greece becomes a Member State on January 1.
1985	*White Paper for the Completion of the Internal Market* published by the Commission of the European Communities.
1986	Portugal and Spain become Member States on January 1. Single European Act (SEA) signed in February. The act took full effect July 1, 1987.
1988	Cecchini Report of 16 volumes published showing the results of the research on the "cost of non-Europe," which was performed by a number of independent consultants.
1990	Two intergovernment conferences started: one on economic and monetary union; the other on political union.

Figure 5.1 Chronology of EC Evolution

The great market will provide Europe's citizens with enormous new opportunities. It offers not only opportunities for big companies or State corporations, but for small and medium-sized companies and individuals. It will mean that there will be new opportunities for employment; that law-abiding travellers will be able to move freely to other parts of the Community with no fuss at borders; that there will be a wide range of the best products of each Member State for sale throughout the Community; that television and radio broadcasts will be available freely across frontiers; that goods will be transported across frontiers with minimum delay and costs; that students will be able to study in different countries and professionals will be able to practise freely in all countries. The list is endless. (*Europe Without Frontiers—Completing the Internal Market*, 3rd Edition, 1989.)

The 1985 White Paper contained nearly 300 specific proposals for the removal of these barriers. They have since been reshaped into a working, evolving list of approximately 279 proposals that address many diverse topics, including the following:

- Setting EC-wide technical standards for goods
- Adopting uniform laws governing the movement of agricultural products
- Creating an opportunity to compete for public procurement contracts offered by the EC as well as by its Member States
- Deregulating industries ranging from financial services to transportation
- Permitting the free movement of capital across the EC
- Providing for an EC-wide company (corporate) law

RELATED AREAS

The 1985 White Paper emphasized that the creation of the Single Market would necessarily affect different policies in many other areas. The policy areas most likely to be indirectly affected by the Single Market Program included employment, transportation, the environment, regional development, social affairs, competition, and external relations with other nations and groups of nations. As a result of preparing detailed measures to implement the 1985 White Paper proposals, there

are now over 500 measures that can properly be regarded as part of the Single Market Program.

STATUS OF THE SINGLE MARKET PROGRAM

The Commission has drafted detailed proposed directives and regulations for all the proposals in the 1985 White Paper. By the end of 1990, the Council had adopted (that is, approved) over 60 percent of the measures. However, these numbers do not completely reflect the status of the 1985 White Paper's proposals, for two reasons:

- Some of the most difficult issues, including many of the company law and tax measures, have yet to be approved (unanimity required).
- Many of the measures already adopted are directives—that is, they have to be converted into domestic legislation in each of the Member States. Some of the Member States lag behind others in doing this. In addition, the lead time to accomplish this for each proposal in each Member State may be substantial.

The Single European Act

The aim of the 1985 White Paper was both advanced and endorsed by the signing of the Single European Act in February 1986. This act, which was ratified by each Member State, actually supplemented and amended the treaties creating the three European Communities. It took full effect on July 1, 1987.

The Single European Act involved three key elements that have played important roles in accelerating the movement toward the Single Market:

- It changed the approval process governing EC legislation.
- It extended the scope of all of the treaties.
- It memorialized the Member States' political commitment to the 1992 deadline.

APPROVAL OF EC LEGISLATION

Before the Single European Act, virtually every decision of the Council of Ministers required unanimity. Now, as a result of this act, most measures require only a "qualified majority," which is 54 of 76 votes. Taxation and certain other measures still require unanimity.

The act also introduced a "cooperation procedure" into the process for adopting legislation. This process gives the European Parliament greater input into the EC legislative process than it had previously.

Amendments to Treaties

The act involved a number of amendments to the original treaties creating the ECSC, the EEC, and the EAEC. These expanded the scope of EC law. Now, EC legislation can encompass such varied subjects as economic and social cohesion, the environment, cooperation between the institutions of the EC, and political cooperation between and among the Member States.

Political Commitment

The Single European Act provided the necessary impetus to guarantee, at the highest political level, the completion of the Single Market Program. It did this by setting a firm and fixed deadline, which was accepted by each Member State when it approved the Single European Act.

It is important to note that the deadline of December 31, 1992, is not a final date. It is a *target* date for "the establishment of the internal market." Some of the necessary changes have already been made, others are in process, and a number are delayed. It is unlikely all of the measures mentioned in the 1985 White Paper will have been implemented by every Member State by the end of 1992. Indeed, some may not ever have been adopted by the Council of Ministers by that date.

The Cecchini Report

In 1988, the Commission released a 16-volume series of studies, entitled *Research on the Cost of Non-Europe*. These studies were directed by Paolo Cecchini (a Commission official) and are often referred to collectively as the *Cost of Non-Europe*, or the *Cecchini Report*.

Based on this series of reports, a number of macro- and microeconomic conclusions on both the benefits of a Single Market and the costs of failing to achieve that goal were developed, including

- The potential gain to the EC as a whole from completing the Single Market Program would add about 5 percent to the EC's gross domestic product (GDP).

- The impact of integration of the EC market would, in the medium term, deflate consumer prices by an average of 6 percent, while boosting output, employment, and living standards.

- Integration of the EC market would produce economies in public sector costs of about 2.2 percent of GDP, as well as boost the EC's trade with other countries by about 1 percent of GDP.

- The direct costs of frontier formalities were estimated to be about 1.8 percent of the value of all goods traded within the EC. The costs of other barriers to an internal market, such as differing national technical regulations on the making and selling of products, were estimated to be almost 2 percent of the companies' total costs.

- Aggregate cost savings from improved economies of scale in the EC would amount to about 2 percent of GDP.

Principal EC Institutions: Structure and Responsibilities

Responsibility for achieving the collective aims of the three communities, operating as the EC, now rests with four principal institutions:

- The Council of Ministers
- The Commission of the European Communities
- The European Parliament
- The Court of Justice

and with three auxiliary bodies:

- The Economic and Social Committee
- The European Investment Bank
- The European Court of Auditors

Until July 1967, the three communities had separate councils and executive commissions. In contrast, the European Parliament and the Court of Justice have been common institutions of the three communities since 1958.

In 1967, a "Merger Treaty" established a "single Council and a single Commission of the European Communities." The single Council and single Commission now exercise all the functions of their respective predecessors. Since the 1967 Merger Treaty, all three communities have had the same institutional structure.

Council of Ministers

The Council of Ministers (the Council) consists of representatives of all of the governments of the 12 Member States. Each government usually designates its foreign minister to serve as its member. The presidency of the Council, which is limited to a term of six months, rotates regularly among the Member States. The role of the Council is to balance and reconcile the individual interests of the Member States and the EC as a whole.

MEMBERSHIP

The membership of the Council varies with the subject under discussion. The foreign minister is regarded as a Member State's main representative on the Council. However, ministers for agriculture, transportation, social affairs, the environment, and so on, also may meet for specialized Council meetings.

FUNCTIONS

The Council serves the EC in both an executive and a legislative capacity. As an executive body, the Council is responsible for the coordination of the general economic policies of the Member States. As a legislative body, it makes the major legislative decisions of the EC.

VOTING

Although the Council has twelve members, one for each Member State, voting is done on a weighted basis. The votes are weighted as follows:

Germany, France, Italy, UK:	10 votes each
Spain:	8 votes
Belgium, Greece, The Netherlands, Portugal:	5 votes each
Denmark, Ireland:	3 votes each
Luxembourg:	2 votes

Until 1987, in practice all actions by the Council required unanimity among the Member States. Any individual Member State could effectively veto the adoption of EC legislation by asserting that its "vital interests" were adversely impacted. However, the Single European Act (explained later in this chapter) changed that process. Today, many decisions affecting the Single Market Program can be taken with a "qualified majority" and do not require unanimity.

A "qualified majority" means the proposal must receive at least 54 favorable votes (of the 76 possible). For very important matters, such as those dealing with taxation, unanimity is still required.

COREPER

In its daily operations, the Council is assisted by the Committee of Permanent Representatives, or COREPER. This committee is made up of the permanent representatives—the ambassadors—of the Member States.

The merger of the three communities in 1967 institutionalized COREPER and established its role, which now is primarily to prepare the ground for Council meetings.

COREPER does not have the power to issue formal decisions. Those decisions must be made by the Council of Ministers itself. However, the Council does not have to be consulted on certain categories of less important matters. Known as List "A" matters, these items are forwarded by COREPER to the Council for adoption without discussion. Others, known as List "B" matters, require action at the Council level.

EUROPEAN COUNCIL

The Council of Ministers should not be confused with the European Council. The European Council consists of the heads of state (or of government) of the 12 Member States, their foreign affairs ministers, the president of the Commission, and one vice president of the Commission. The European Council meets in "summit" conferences. That is, the meetings are held without civil servants or experts present.

The European Council provides a political impetus to the EC and determines long-term policy guidelines.

Over time, the importance of the European Council in the operation of the EC has increased. Beginning in 1986, however, its meetings were limited to two a year, except for special circumstances. This reduction of meetings helped limit the intervention of the European Council in the general management of the EC, retaining it as a forum for settling the most difficult and controversial policy disputes.

The Commission

The Commission of the European Communities (the CEC or the Commission) consists of 17 members. Five Member States designate two members each:

- France
- Germany
- Italy
- Spain
- UK

Each of the other seven Member States designates one member. The CEC members and its president are appointed by "common accord" of the Member States' governments for a renewable term of four years.

Historically, about 50 percent of the Commission serves a second term. A new Commission took office on January 1, 1989.

During their term, the members of the Commission must remain independent of both their own governments and of the Council of Ministers. This does not mean that they are not accountable to any other institution after they have been appointed. Although the Council of Ministers cannot remove any member of the Commission from office, the European Parliament can pass a motion of censure, which requires the Commission to resign as a body. If that should happen, the Commission would continue to handle routine business until a replacement was appointed.

The treaties assign the Commission a wide range of tasks and responsibilities:

- The Commission is the motive power and the initiating institution of EC policy. Every EC action begins there. The Commission initiates the proposals and drafts for EC rules that then go to the Council of Ministers.
- The Commission is the "guardian" of the treaties creating and defining the EC. It must ensure that the provisions of the treaties and of EC legislation are properly implemented and respected. When these provisions are infringed the Commission intervenes, either on its own initiative or on the basis of complaints from governments, firms, or private individuals.
- The Commission is an executive body. Its executive powers are concerned mainly with common EC policies (competition, agriculture, fisheries, and commercial policy) and with harmo-

nizing actions necessary for the completion of the Single Market. Each commissioner is responsible for one or more areas of EC policy, such as economic affairs, agriculture, environment, or energy. As a result, one or more directors-general report to each commissioner. However, because the Commission must act collectively, it cannot delegate the kinds of significant powers to an individual in his or her area that would give that commissioner independence equivalent to that of a cabinet secretary or national minister.

- The Commission is responsible for administering appropriations for the EC's public expenditures and four major EC funds:
  - European Social Fund (which deals with employment-related issues within the EC)
  - European Agricultural Guidance and Guarantee Fund (which supports the Common Agricultural Policy)
  - European Regional Development Fund (which aids the development of poorer and declining regions within the EC)
  - European Development Fund (which grants financial assistance to developing countries)

Administratively, the Commission is divided into 23 directorates-general, similar to cabinet departments. These are shown in Table 5.1. The Commission also supervises other offices and units, as follows:

- Consumer Policy Service
- Euratom Supply Agency
- European Centre for the Development of Vocational Training (CEDEFOP)
- European Foundation for the Improvement of Living and Working Conditions
- Forward Studies Unit
- Joint Interpreting and Conference Service
- Joint Research Centres
- Legal Service
- Office for Official Publications of the European Communities
- Secretariat-General
- Security Office
- Spokesman's Service
- Statistical Office

• Task Force for Human Resources, Education, Training, and Youth

• Translation Service

The Commission is unique within the EC, because its power is not limited by the treaties. Unlike the treaty provisions covering the other institutions of the EC, which limit their powers, the Commission is given its "own power of decision."

European Parliament

The European Parliament consists of 518 members (MEP) who are elected every five years by the citizens of the EC by direct universal suffrage. Each Member State uses its own national electoral system. The members are divided into political groups rather than national groups.

Parliament is directed by a president, assisted by 14 vice presidents. It meets in plenary session for one week each month (except August). Between the plenary sessions, two weeks are set aside for meetings of Parliament's committees (see the following list). One week is set aside for meetings of political groups within Parliament.

The standing committees of the European Parliament are as follows:

• Political Affairs Committee

• Committee on Agriculture, Fisheries, and Rural Development

• Committee on Budgets

• Committee on Economic and Monetary Affairs and Industrial Policy

• Committee on Energy, Research, and Technology

• Committee on External Economic Relations

• Committee on Legal Affairs and Citizens' Rights

• Committee on Social Affairs, Employment, and the Working Environment

• Committee on Regional Policy and Regional Planning

• Committee on Transport and Tourism

• Committee on the Environment, Public Health, and Consumer Protection

• Committee on Youth, Culture, Education, the Media, and Sport

• Committee on Development and Cooperation

• Committee on Budgetary Control

• Committee on Institutional Affairs

• Committee on the Rules of Procedure, the Verification of Credentials, and Immunities

• Committee on Women's Rights

• Committee on Petitions

Table 5.1
CEC Directorates-General

Directorate-General Number	Name
I	External Relations
II	Economic and Financial Affairs
III	Internal Market and Industrial Affairs
IV	Competition
V	Employment, Industrial Relations, and Social Affairs
VI	Agriculture
VII	Transport
VIII	Development
IX	Personnel and Administration
X	Information, Communication, and Culture
XI	Environment, Nuclear Safety, and Civil Protection
XII	Science, Research and Development
XIII	Telecommunications, Information Industries, and Innovation
XIV	Fisheries
XV	Financial Institutions and Company Law (includes direct taxation)
XVI	Regional Policy
XVII	Energy
XVIII	Credit and Investments
XIX	Budgets
XX	Financial Control
XXI	Customs Union and Indirect Taxation
XXII	Coordination of Structural Policies
XXIII	Enterprise Policy, Distributive Trades, Tourism, and Cooperatives

The European Parliament's formal powers are mainly advisory, supervisory, and budgetary. Compared with a national parliament, the European Parliament does not have significant legislative powers, as the following indicate:

- Parliament must assent to accession matters, that is, to the admission of new members into the EC. It also must assent to other agreements, such as the EC's association and cooperation agreements with the Mediterranean countries.

- Parliament participates with the Council of Ministers and the Commission in the decision-making process in matters such as the Single Market, social policy, economic and social cohesion, and research.

- Parliament has the last word on all "noncompulsory" EC expenditures—those that are not the inevitable consequence of EC legislation. These expenditures make up approximately 25 percent of the EC budget and include administrative costs and operational expenditures, covering items such as the Social Fund, the Regional Fund, and research and energy spending.

- Parliament can propose modifications to the "compulsory" expenditures of the EC. These are largely price supports under the Common Agricultural Policy. If the modifications do not increase the total expenditures, they are deemed accepted unless the Council rejects them by a qualified majority. Parliament also has the right to reject a budget in its entirety.

- Parliament has the power to require members of other EC agencies to publicize their stands on various issues.

- Parliament can dissolve the Commission by passing a censure motion.

In practice, much of the work of Parliament is handled by its committees.

Parliament's committees meet regularly with representatives of the Commission, monitoring the Commission's actions and proposals. The committees are responsible for preparing Parliament's opinions on Commission proposals, as well as motions to be brought before the full body. As a result, the committees receive a great deal of information. They also meet regularly with groups interested in Commission proposals. These groups range from independent experts to representatives of the organizations potentially affected by the proposals.

Court of Justice

The Court of Justice is made up of 13 judges, appointed by "common accord" of the governments of the Member States for a term of six years. It is assisted by six advocates-general.

The Court is responsible for ensuring that, "in the interpretation and application of the treaty, the law is observed." In practice, it determines the validity and correct interpretation of EC law.

It also ensures that neither EC institutions nor Member States overstep their powers. Historically, it has tended to interpret the Commission's authority and responsibility very broadly.

The Court can handle cases involving Member States, EC institutions, and individuals. Although it does not directly participate in the legislative process, its decisions have been a key force in European integration and the movement toward the Single Market. For example, the Court has forced Member States to eliminate specific barriers to freer trade within the EC.

The Court's rulings cannot be appealed.

In addition to handling actual cases, the Court can be called on to give preliminary rulings on questions referred to it by national courts of the Member States. The law, made up of the treaties and EC legislation based on the treaties, is increasingly becoming a part of the national law of the individual Member States. The Court's preliminary rulings permit EC law to be more uniformly enforced in all Member States and help build a consistent body of "European" case law.

In October 1988, a new "Court of First Instance" was established. This court has jurisdiction to hear certain classes of action brought by officials of the EC, competition cases, and actions for damages. Its decisions are subject to appeal to the Court of Justice on points of law. It is likely that the responsibilities of the Court of First Instance will expand and develop over the next few years.

Auxiliary Bodies of the European Community

Economic and Social Committee

The Economic and Social Committee (ESC) assists the Council and the Commission in EEC and Euratom matters but not in ECSC matters. It is a purely advisory body, composed of 189 representatives. Its members are selected to represent a wide range of specified socioeconomic categories and groups. The ESC must be consulted by other EC institutions before decisions are taken on a wide range of matters. It is also allowed to submit opinions on its own initiative.

European Investment Bank

The European Investment Bank (EIB) is a financing agency for the EC. Its primary aim is to achieve a "balanced and smooth development" of the EC. To accomplish this goal, the EIB provides loans and guarantees:

- To promote the development of less-developed regions
- To modernize or convert businesses
- To create new jobs
- To otherwise assist projects of common interest to Member States

Court of Auditors

The European Court of Auditors has 12 members who are appointed by unanimous decision of the Council, after consultation with Parliament. The purpose of the Court of Auditors is to audit the accounts of EC institutions, examining whether revenues and expenditures have been properly and lawfully handled. The Court helps to ensure that financial management has been sound and that proper accounting procedures have been followed. The Court then reports its findings to the EC institutions.

The Court of Auditors is permitted to extend its investigations beyond EC institutions. It can, for instance, investigate operations carried out in and by the Member States on behalf of the EC, such as spending on agriculture, as well as operations carried out in nonmember states that receive EC aid.

The investigatory powers, opinions, and annual report of the Court of Auditors are used by the Parliament as a part of its involvement in the EC budget process.

6

Community Legislation: Balancing the Needs of the EC and Its 12 Member States

The EC's directives and regulations are developed, adopted, and put into force through specific procedures. This chapter describes those procedures and explains how directives and other measures relate to the laws of each Member State. In doing so, the chapter should help you understand how the Single Market Program functions.

This chapter also details the special roles each EC institution has in developing and adopting new laws. Understanding these roles is vital for companies that want to have an impact on the outcome of proposals yet to become law.

OVERVIEW

The EC is authorized to adopt measures that can require the Member States to change their existing laws. The effectiveness and ultimate success of the Single Market Program rest on a balance between the interests of the Member States as sovereign nations and their commitment to a structure and process that operate in the interests of all residents of the EC.

SECTIONS IN THIS CHAPTER

ASSISTANCE

Refer to Chapter 5 for descriptions of EC institutions. Chapter 2 outlines the Single Market Program. Appendix D categorizes by topic and industry the directives and other measures making up the Single Market Program.

For additional help in using this sourcebook, refer to the Introduction to Part I.

TYPES OF EC LEGISLATION: RECOMMENDATIONS, OPINIONS, DECISIONS, DIRECTIVES, AND REGULATIONS

The way the Council and the Commission operate legislatively depends, in part, on which original treaty is being implemented. The specific treaty is important because differences in terminology under these separate instruments can cause problems. In most cases, the procedures used for legislation affecting the Single Market Program derive from the EEC Treaty.

Regardless of the treaty being implemented, the Court of Justice may be involved in all cases. The Court provides the Member States and individuals the assurance of compliance with the treaties and legislation. It also ensures uniform interpretation and enforcement of EC legislation, on its own and through national courts.

Operating Under the EEC and Euratom Treaties

When acting under the treaties that created the EEC and Euratom, the EC (operating through both the Council and the Commission) can take one of five types of action. It can adopt regulations or directives, make decisions, and issue recommendations and opinions as follows:

- *Regulations*, acts of general application, are binding in their entirety and apply to all Member States. They take effect directly as Community law in all Member States and do not require transformation into national law or even publi-

cation in national official journals. They are binding not only on Member States but on citizens of the Member States as well.

- *Directives* are binding on the Member States to which they are addressed and with respect to the results to be achieved. Each directive states an objective and specific provisions the Member States must enact within a specified period. However, the directives leave the form and method of achieving the results to the discretion of national authorities. Each Member State is required to "transform national legislation," making changes in national legislation needed to satisfy a specified provision of the treaties. This process may require a Member State to amend or repeal existing laws or pass new legislation.

- *Decisions* may be addressed to a government, an enterprise, or an individual. They are binding in their entirety only on those to whom they are addressed.

- *Recommendations* and *opinions* have no binding effect.

In EEC and Euratom affairs, the Council may act on its own, particularly when rendering a decision, making recommendations, or issuing opinions. More often (as described later in this chapter), the Commission acts in conjunction with the Council and the Parliament to adopt EC legislation. That legislation can take the form of either regulations or directives.

Operating Under the ECSC Treaty

When the Commission is acting under the treaty that created the European Coal and Steel Community (ECSC), it can make decisions or recommendations, or issue opinions:

- *Decisions* are binding in their entirety. They are usually addressed to individual persons, firms, or governments. However, they also may establish general rules, applicable throughout the EC, because the Commission has the power to make general rules under the ECSC Treaty.

- *Recommendations* are actually binding as to the ends to be achieved. They are not binding as to the means necessary to achieve them.

- *Opinions* are not binding.

In ECSC affairs, the Council acts mainly at the request of the Commission. It either states its opinion on a particular issue or it gives its assent, without which, in certain matters, the Commission cannot proceed.

Differences in Terminology

Because the actions taken by the EC have their roots in different treaties, the differences in terminology between the two systems can be confusing. The critical differences are the following:

- An EEC/Euratom *directive* is binding. It is equivalent to an ECSC *recommendation*.

- An EEC/Euratom *recommendation* is nonbinding, as is an EEC/Euratom *opinion*. They are both equivalent to an ECSC *opinion*.

The Legislative Process: How the Complex System Works

The legislative operation of the EC is complex and reflects a balance between the collective needs of the EC and the sovereignty of the 12 individual EC Member States.

Pre-Single European Act

Before the Single European Act took effect in mid-1987, the legislative process was slow, in large part because the Council had to approve most proposed legislation unanimously. Then, as now, the process involved the Commission, the Council, and Parliament.

Post-Single European Act

Changes made by the Single European Act have made the legislative process more complicated than it was previously. But they also have resulted in quicker passage of EC proposals. This acceleration was accomplished primarily by the elimination of the effective veto power formerly vested in the Council, and the use of a "qualified majority" to approve most measures.

Key Procedural Concepts

The process involved in the passage of any EC legislation includes three key concepts:

- Only the Commission has the power to propose legislation.

- Parliament can only influence the content and viability of any proposal. It cannot veto it.

- Ultimately, the Council must approve the final form of any legislative proposal, including all changes that have been made to it. At that point, a legislative proposal has been passed and becomes either an EC regulation or directive.

The main elements of the process are described here.

BEGINNING THE PROCESS

The legislative process begins with the Commission preparing and presenting a formal legislative proposal. That proposal is sent to the Council and to Parliament.

The Council begins deliberating on the Commission's proposal.

Parliament, operating through its committees, examines the proposal. Following that, Parliament gives an "opinion" on the proposal. This opinion is a nonbinding position, reflecting the judgment of elected representatives. It guides the agencies of the Community in their consideration of the proposal.

The Commission receives Parliament's opinion. The Commission then "takes a view" on the opinion by deciding whether to accept the opinion and to make changes in its own proposal based on the opinion.

From there, the process shifts to the Council. The Council, as a part of the review process, may make changes in the proposal. Whether or not it makes any changes in the Commission's proposal, the Council then must adopt a "common position." This common position is equivalent to a vote approving the proposal, with amendments added by the Council, if necessary. The common position is adopted by a qualified majority, except for those few cases requiring unanimity. In those cases, all members of the Council must vote in favor of the proposal.

COMMON POSITION

Once the Council has adopted a common position on the proposal, most proposals go back to Parliament, which has three months to act. Parliament may do any of the following:

- Approve the Council's common position.
- Take no position.
- Amend the Council's common position. This requires an absolute majority of the Members of Parliament.
- Reject the Council's common position.

If Parliament either approves the Council's common position or takes no position, the Council can then adopt the proposal. The proposal becomes EC law, ending the process.

If Parliament rejects the Council's common position by an absolute majority, the Council still may adopt the proposal. However, it must do so unanimously for the proposal to become law. If it fails to do that, the proposal dies.

If Parliament amends the Council's common position by an absolute majority of its members, the proposal returns to the Commission. The Commission then has one month to act on the amendments. The Commission reviews Parliament's amendments and can revise its own proposal to accept these amendments. If the Commission does so, the proposal becomes, in effect, the Commission's own proposal again. The Commission is not required to accept Parliament's amendments. After the Commission completes this stage, the proposal then goes to the Council.

At this point, the Council must act within three months (four if Parliament agrees to an extension). If the Council does not act, the Commission's proposal lapses and is deemed not to have been adopted.

The Council's actions at this point in the process can be any of the following options:

- The Council may adopt the Commission's proposal before it by a qualified majority. If so, the proposal takes effect and becomes EC law.
- The Council may adopt parliamentary amendments that were not approved by the Commission. If it does this unanimously, the proposal, as amended, becomes law.
- The Council may amend the Commission's proposal. If this is done unanimously, the proposal becomes law.

ENDORSING A PROPOSAL

At any stage where the Council must act unanimously on a Commission proposal, the Commission may accept the amendments under consideration. It does this by "endorsing" the text of the amended proposal. If the Commission endorses the new text of the proposal as its own, the document is treated as if it were a proposal of the Commission, and only a qualified majority of the Council is needed for its approval.

EVOLVING PRACTICES

In practice, the Council does not always wait for a Commission proposal and the Opinion of the Parliament before it becomes involved in the legislative process. Since the passage of the Single European Act, the Council has increasingly become involved earlier in the process. Now, the Council participates in the legislative process from the very beginning. Representatives of the Council may be included in discussions on possible legislative proposals from the drafting stage on.

This means there may be at least two versions of every proposal:

- The "official" version, which is the Commission's written proposal. Parliament can formally express an opinion only on this version or can try to amend only this version.

- An "unofficial" version, which is the Council's current compromise working text. Parliament

cannot express an opinion on this draft. But its contents, which indicate what the Council may accept, will influence what Parliament can and will do with the "official" version.

COMMUNITY LAW AND MEMBER STATE NATIONAL LAW: SEPARATE BUT INTERTWINED

The relationship between EC legislation and national laws is essentially one of primacy. The EC can adopt legislation that supersedes national law, because the EC legislation is founded on treaties previously approved by Member States.

Regulations

Some EC legislation—specifically regulations—takes effect across the EC as soon as it has been adopted (or on an implementation date specified in the regulation). The adopted regulation confers enforceable rights and imposes legal obligations directly on Community institutions, Member States, and legal persons (including individuals) in each Member State.

Directives

Much EC legislation—its directives—must be translated into national law before it can be put into effect. This translation can be slow. Normally each Member State must amend or repeal existing law, or must pass new legislation before the directive can take effect across the EC. However, under certain circumstances, once the stated implementation date has passed, certain directives can have direct effect even if not transposed into domestic legislation.

In either case, questions about the exact relationship between EC law and national law will continue to arise. The general rule is that when a conflict between Community law and national law exists, Community law must prevail over national law. In spite of this primacy, the two legal systems should actually complement each other. Over time, EC law and national law are becoming increasingly intertwined and interdependent.

Preliminary Rulings

The system of preliminary rulings provided by the Court of Justice is an example of the close relationship between the two legal systems. When a national court is in doubt about the correct interpretation of one of the treaties or about the measures taken by Community institutions, it can apply to the Court of Justice for a preliminary ruling. In fact, in some cases, a national court *must* make such an application. This preliminary ruling by the Court of Justice is sought to clarify the meaning of Community law.

This system is designed to help avoid the creation of conflicting interpretations of the treaties or of the EC's laws. The result is that Community law becomes an integral part of national law and takes precedence within the national legal system of each Member State.

ENSURING MEMBER STATES' CONFORMITY WITH COMMUNITY LAW

Complaints may arise that a Member State is not conforming to Community law. This most often occurs with respect to regulations and directives that are directly a part of the Single Market Program. The EC has developed a formal and an informal procedure for handling such complaints.

Formal Procedure

The formal procedure is as follows:

1. The Commission is informed of a possible infraction by a complaint. Complaints may come from persons or businesses that feel disadvan-

taged by a Member State's nonapplication of Community law. They may also result from questions raised in the European Parliament or from petitions filed with the EC.

2. The Commission examines the complaint, and informs the Member State involved of the complaint. It also asks other Member States to comment on the complaint.

3. If the complaint appears to be valid, the Commission then sends a "reasoned opinion" to the Member State. This threatens legal action against the Member State if it does not conform to the Commission's opinion.

4 If the problem is not then resolved by the Member State's voluntarily taking corrective action,

the case goes before the Court of Justice. If the Court rules in favor of the Commission, the Member State must conform to its decision.

Informal Procedure

In addition to its formal procedure, the Commission also has an informal procedure for dealing with noncompliance by Member States. This procedure is used before formal complaints are filed or as a part of the process of settling a complaint before it goes to the Court of Justice. The Commission encourages members of the European Parliament to use their positions to influence their national legislatures to accelerate compliance with EC legislation.

PART
II

Profiles of the European Community Member States

This part profiles the 12 Member States of the European Community, offering detailed information essential to making sound decisions about doing business in one or more of these countries.

Each of the 12 chapters in this part provides general information about that particular country's background and population, as well as key data directly affecting companies and their business operations.

STRUCTURE OF EACH CHAPTER

- *Background.* Includes general information on the country, its history, national language, and form of government.

- *Population.* Provides current estimates of the population of the country and its largest city. (Until the EC's statistical program is fully in place, some figures will be less current than others.)

- *Currency and Exchange Controls.* Names the national unit of currency and provides its recent exchange rate against the U.S. dollar. Notes

what exchange control programs, if any, are currently in operation in that country.

- *Establishing a Business.* Covers key issues facing a nonnational business interested in setting up a business in the country:

  - **Authorization.** Notes whether a business must get prior permission before setting up a subsidiary or branch in the country.

  - **Types of Businesses.** Summarizes in tabular format the most commonly used national business designations and abbreviations. Describes, in general terms, the most commonly used forms of subsidiaries and compares their operations with those of a branch office.

  - **Local Participation Requirements.** Discusses any laws or regulations requiring a nonnational business to have "local participation," which means a portion of the business must be owned by a national or a branch must be managed by a national.

  - **Employee Representation.** Discusses laws requiring that employees of a business must be involved in the decision-making processes of the business.

· **Investment Incentives.** Summarizes national-level programs, both tax and non-tax, that encourage business investments in the local economy.

· **Labor Laws.** Notes special laws or regulations that apply to nonnationals entering a country to work there.

• *Business Taxation.* Summarizes the existing national laws on business taxation, including the following:

· Tax year definition

· Scope of the tax laws, including income and sources to which the taxes apply

· Tax rates for various types of income

· Key elements of taxable income, including handling capital gains, dividends, and valuation of inventories

· Losses deducted from income

· Depreciation rates

· Treatment of undistributed profits for tax purposes

· Treatment of foreign income of a national company

· Taxes for foreign executives living in the country

· Payments by companies of national social security taxes

· An overview of the value added tax (VAT) system in the country

· Other taxes applicable to businesses, such as stamp, registration, or revenue taxes

· Rules and rates applicable to withholding taxes

· A list of some nations with which the country has a current tax treaty

The Single Market Program will have a major impact on how each Member State handles taxes. The EC already is working to bring VAT rates of its members closer together. In addition, it is seeking ways in which cross-border transactions will be treated more uniformly throughout the Community.

HIGHLIGHTS

Tables II.1 through II.3 summarize information from the 12 chapters in this part and present the data in tabular form to facilitate comparisons.

ASSISTANCE

In General

For additional help on using the resources in this part of the sourcebook, refer to the Introduction to this book.

Background and Population

Chapter 20 and Appendix G give additional background, population, and demographic information on the EC Member States.

Currency and Exchange Controls

Chapter 4 describes the EC's programs dealing with currency and monetary reform. Chapter 1 explains how the Single Market Program intends to deal with fiscal barriers to a single internal market. Chapter 30 lists sources for information on the EC's programs that provide for the free movement of capital throughout the Community.

Establishing a Business

Chapter 2 covers the European Economic Interest Grouping (EEIG), a new type of business entity in the EC, as well as the development of the European Company Law. Chapter 23 and Appendix C list sources for additional information on EEIG and European Community Law. Appendix C lists EC business designations and abbreviations used throughout this part.

Investment Incentives

Chapter 2 lists sources for additional information on economic and business development issues in the EC. Chapter 21 describes the EC's programs for economic development. Chapter 23 explores the relationship between the EC's competition laws and state aid for investments.

Employment

Chapter 22 lists sources of information on employment and labor-related issues. Chapter 25 includes sources for information on the EC's policies with respect to social services and welfare that can affect the employment relationship.

Taxation

Chapters 1 and 2 explain the impact of the Single Market Program on taxation. Chapter 25 gives sources of information on business taxation.

Table II.1
Comparing EC Member States: Population, Capital, and Major Language

EC Member State	Population (Millions)	Capital	Major Languages
Belgium	9.06	Brussels	French, Dutch, German
Denmark	5.14	Copenhagen	Danish
France	58.40	Paris	French
Germany	79.10	Berlin	German, English (business)
Greece	10.00	Athens	Greek
Ireland	3.60	Dublin City	English
Italy	57.40	Rome	Italian
Luxembourg	0.37	Luxembourg	Luxemburgish, French (business)
The Netherlands	15.00	Amsterdam	Dutch, English (business)
Portugal	9.80	Lisbon	Portuguese
Spain	39.30	Madrid	Spanish
United Kingdom	56.90	London	English

Table II.2
Comparing EC Member States: Currency and Exchange Rates as of April 1991

EC Member State	Currency	Exchange Rate (U.S. $1 =)
Belgium	Franc (BEF)	34.75
Denmark	Kroner (DKr)	6.50
France	Franc (FF)	5.74
Germany	Deutsche Mark (Dm)	1.69
Greece	Drachma (Dr)	177.00
Ireland	Pound (Ir£)	0.5813
Italy	Lira (L)	1261.00
Luxembourg	Franc (LUF)	33.78
The Netherlands	Florin/Guilder (Dfl.)	1.91
Portugal	Escudo (Esc)	148.90
Spain	Peseta (Pta)	105.15
United Kingdom	Pound Sterling (£)	0.5719

Table II.3
Comparing EC Member States: Corporate Tax Information

EC Member State	Tax Rate (Highest Rate %)	Loss Carryforward (in Years)
Belgium	41–39	Unlimited
Denmark	38	5
France	42	5
Germany	59.7	5 [a]
Greece	46	5
Ireland	40	Unlimited
Italy	47.826	5 (IRPEG only)
Luxembourg	33 [b]	Unlimited [c]
The Netherlands	40 [d]	8 [e]
Portugal	36 [f]	5
Spain	35	5
United Kingdom	35 [g]	Unlimited

Notes:

[a] Unlimited for losses in tax years ending after December 31, 1984.

[b] Increased by a municipal business tax to a maximum of 39.39%.

[c] Unlimited for losses in tax years ending after December 31, 1990.

[d] 40% for profits up to Dfl. 250,000 and 35% for the excess profits over Dfl. 250,000.

[e] Unlimited for losses realized in the first six years after the incorporation of the company.

[f] Increased by a municipal surcharge in many locations to 39.6%.

[g] 34% for year to March 31, 1991, and 33% for year to March 31, 1992, et seq.

Brussels

7

Belgium

SECTIONS IN THIS CHAPTER

ASSISTANCE

Chapter 20 lists resources that can provide macroeconomic, population, and census-type data on the EC and on most of its member states. For additional help on using the resources in this chapter, refer to the Introduction to Part II.

BACKGROUND

Belgium has an area of 30,507 square kilometers.

Belgium became independent in 1830 and became a constitutional monarchy in 1831. There are nine provinces and three regions: Flanders, Wallonia, and the Brussels metropolitan area. The Senate and the Chamber of Deputies are elected every four years, directly by the population, except in times of political crisis. The Belgian government is determined from the parliamentary majority.

In the past the Belgian economy has depended on agriculture, but today the country is mostly industrialized. Its overall economy is somewhat more dominated by the services and governmental sectors than the EC average, which is probably due to its geographic location and the presence of the EC's headquarters and associated activities in Bruxelles (Brussels). This trend is expected to continue, as the Government continues its efforts to make Bruxelles a major financial center.

Belgium is associated with The Netherlands and Luxembourg in the Benelux Economic Union. The official languages are French, Dutch, and German.

POPULATION

The population of Belgium is about 9.06 million. The population of the Flemish region is about 5.5 million, of the French region 2.8 million, and of the Brussels region is slightly less than 700 thousand.

CURRENCY AND EXCHANGE CONTROLS

Currency

The unit of currency is the Belgian franc (BEF). In April 1991, BEF 34.75 was equivalent to U.S. $1.

Exchange Controls

As of March 1990, Belgium abolished exchange controls. However, Belgium residents still must make reports on certain transactions:

- On all transactions to or from a bank account they own outside of Belgium or Luxembourg; and

- On all international transactions to or from a bank account in Belgium or Luxembourg. This report can be an oral one if the transaction does not exceed BEF 1,000,000. It must be in writing if it is larger.

These reports are made to the Belgian-Luxembourg Exchange Control Institute, through Belgian commercial banks.

ESTABLISHING A BUSINESS

Authorization

No prior authorization is required to establish a business in Belgium with the exception of a few specific types of industries, such as banking, insurance, and transportation.

Foreign companies can operate in Belgium through a subsidiary, incorporated under Belgian law, or through a Belgian branch of a company.

Most nonnationals who do business in Belgium set up a local corporation (Societe Anonyme, SA, or Naamloze Vennootschap, NV). No special consents are needed, although certain documents, such as bylaws, must be deposited with local authorities. In addition, each year 5 percent of the business's profits must be put in a legal reserve, until the reserve equals 10 percent of the capital issued. This reserve may not be distributed. There is no other limitation on the repatriation of profits, so long as the business's net asset value is adequate.

A foreign company that sets up a branch must also file certain documents and appoint a local representative.

▼ ▼

Types of Businesses

The designations and abbreviations for Belgian businesses are listed in Table 7.1.

COMPANIES

The following types of subsidiary companies may be used in Belgium, although a corporation (SA/NV) is the form most often chosen:

- Corporation, known either as a Societe Anonyme or a Naamloze Vennootschap (SA or NV);
- Private limited company, known either as a Societe de personnes a responsibilite limitee or a Besloten Vennootschap met Beperkte Aansprakelijkheid (SPRL or BVBA);
- Special partnership (SNC or VOF);
- Limited partnership (SCS or CV);
- Partnership limited by shares (SCA or VGA);
- Cooperative society (SC or Coop V).

A subsidiary set up as a Belgian company is required to comply with Belgian company law, regardless of whether the shareholders are foreign nationals or companies.

An SA (or NV) must have a minimum initial capital of BEF 1,250,000, in contrast with the required capitalization of the SPRL/BVBA, which is BEF 750,000. The law also requires a minimum of two shareholders. Company directors may be foreign nationals. There is no legal requirement that a Belgian national must own part of the corporation.

Every corporation must file its articles of incorporation, the names of its directors and statutory auditors, and its annual financial statements at the appropriate Register of Commerce and at the office of the clerk of the Commercial Court.

BRANCHES

Foreign companies may set up branches in Belgium. Branches are governed by the same regulations governing Belgian companies with respect to management and operations in Belgium.

Any foreign company wishing its Belgian branch or office to be involved in trade or manufacturing must file a certified copy of the parent company's articles of incorporation, together with any amendments, with the Trade Register of Commerce and with the office of the clerk of the Commercial Court. A statement by the parent company's board authorizing the establishment of the branch and delegating powers to the branch management, as well as the name and address of its official representative in Belgium, should also be filed.

Table 7.1
Belgium Business Designations and Abbreviations

Abbreviation	Name	Description
BVBA	Besloten Vennootschap met Beperkte Aansprakelijkheid	Belgium private limited liability company
Coop V	Cooperatieve Vennootschap	Belgium cooperative society
CV	Cooperatieve Vennootschap Cooperatie; Samenwerkende Vennootschap	Belgium cooperative society
NV	Naamloze Vennootschap	Belgium limited company
SC	Societe cooperative	Belgium cooperative society
SA	Societe anonyme	Belgium limited company
SCA	Societe en commandite par actions	Belgium partnership limited by shares
SCS	Societe en commandite simple	Belgium limited partnership
SNC	Societe en nom collectif	Belgium special partnership
SPRL	Societe de personnes a responsibilite limitee	Belgium private limited liability company
VGA	Vennootschap bij wijze van geldschieting op sandelen	Belgium partnership limited by shares
VOF	Vennootschap onder Firms	Belgium partnership

The branch must also register with the Register of Commerce where it is located, obtain a registration number, keep appropriate legal and accounting records, and file annual accounts.

Local Participation Requirements

There are no local participation requirements in foreign investments.

Employee Representation

Companies with 100 or more employees must set up a work council, made up of equal numbers of employer and employee representatives. It reviews work rules, employment practices, and the activities of the company.

Investment Incentives

TAX INCENTIVES

In some cases, new assets subsidized by the government may be depreciated at double the straight-line rate for three consecutive years.

An investment deduction, computed as a percentage of the amounts invested in assets used for income-generating activities in Belgium, may be deducted from taxable income.

Companies with high-tech operation that are located in an Employment Area are also entitled to special tax benefits for a period of ten years.

Companies carrying out investments with government assistance may be exempted from real estate taxes on assets acquired with the assistance for a period up to five years.

Contributions in cash or kind to companies in specific areas may be exempted from the registration tax.

Small businesses incorporated as subsidiaries through 1993 that operate and commercialize an "innovative high-technological process" can receive special tax benefits. Their stockholders may also be entitled to special tax benefits.

NONTAX INCENTIVES

The government has created Reconversion Areas to stimulate research, development, manufacturing, and marketing of new products, processes, and technologies. The government has made special benefits available to companies that locate in specific areas (these areas could differ from the reconversion areas mentioned earlier). These benefits include both capital and interest subsidies.

Special loans, some of which may even be interest-free, may be available to fund high-technology research. Loan guarantees and interest subsidies are also available under certain limited circumstances. In addition, Belgium has a number of special programs to encourage cooperation between businesses engaged in research and development programs and university research centers.

Labor Laws

An EC national can live or work in Belgium without restrictions. Other foreign nationals must obtain a work permit and a residence visa. These are valid for one year and must be renewed annually, unless the non-Belgium national is employed by a recognized coordination center.

The employer must obtain work permits from the *Ministere de l'Emploi et du Travail* before hiring the non-Belgium national employee. Non-Belgium nationals who intend to undertake independent business activities in Belgium must obtain a "professional card" from the same office.

BUSINESS TAXATION

Tax Year

The tax year in Belgium is the calendar year. A company's taxable period is the accounting year. If this ends on December 31, the relevant tax year is the following calendar year; otherwise, the relevant tax year is the calendar year in which the accounting year ends.

Scope

Corporate taxes apply on the worldwide profits (income and capital gains) of all resident companies as well as to the Belgian source profits of nonresidents of Belgium. A company is "resident" in Belgium if it is either domiciled or managed and controlled in Belgium. Profits reported in the annual accounts are adjusted for tax purposes.

Tax Rates

The basic rate of income tax on resident corporations is 41 percent for the 1991 tax year, and 39 percent for the 1992 tax year. This rate applies:

- Where corporate income exceeds BEF 14,800,000 for 1991 and BEF 13,000,000 for 1992;
- To all income of a company that has distributed more than 13 percent of its share capital;
- To all income of any company that is 50 percent or more owned by other legal entities; and
- To all income of any company that receives dividends exempted at 85 percent (holding companies).

The tax rate is increased to 43 percent for nonresident branches, subject to reductions required under tax treaties. Otherwise, a lower series of progressive rates apply.

Profits of permanent establishments of Belgian resident companies are taxed at 25 percent of the corporate tax rate, unless exempted by treaty.

Key Elements of Taxable Income

Capital gains on property held for five years or less are taxed at the normal corporate tax rate. If the property has been held for more than five years, the capital gains may receive more favorable treatment:

- *For assets other than shares or financial assets.* If the sales proceeds are reinvested within three years in qualifying assets, the taxation of gains can be deferred. That deferral runs for the period over which the replacement asset is depreciated.
- *For shares and financial assets.* The gains are taxable at 50 percent of the normal corporate tax rate, unless the sales proceeds are reinvested. That reinvestment must be made within three years in qualifying assets, and that asset must be held for three years. In that case, the gains are exempted from tax.

Qualifying dividends paid by a company subject to taxation that are similar to Belgium's corporate taxation are substantially exempted from taxes. They are exempt up to 85 percent or 90 percent of the dividend received.

Inventories are valued at the lower of cost or of market value. Direct cost and LIFO (for specific goods) costing methods may be used.

Losses

Losses are carried forward indefinitely. Losses cannot be carried back.

Depreciation

The average annual straight-line rates are as follows:

- Industrial buildings, 5 percent;
- Machinery, up to 20 percent;
- Purchased goodwill, 20 to 33 percent.

Accelerated depreciation also applies on a declining balance method at maximum rates of twice the straight-line rates.

An investment deduction on new assets used in Belgium is available. The applicable rate is determined annually, based on the index of prices. However, this percentage cannot be less than 3.5 percent nor more than 10.5 percent, adjusted for inflation for investments made after 1990. This deduction does not affect the cost basis of the asset.

Undistributed Profits

There is no difference in the taxation of distributed versus undistributed profits, other than the application of a withholding tax on dividends paid.

Foreign Income of Belgian Resident Companies

Worldwide profits of Belgian resident companies are taxable, but they may be able to obtain tax relief under Belgium's double tax treaties. Profits of permanent establishments of Belgian resident companies are taxed at 25 percent of normal rates, again subject to treaty relief.

Dividends received from foreign companies subject to taxation that is more favorable than Belgian taxation are fully taxed. However, certain foreign credits are also granted. In other cases, foreign dividends on shares held for the entire tax year are exempt up to 90 percent of the net amount received. "Nonpermanent" dividends are taxed after certain credit reliefs.

Social Security Taxes

Both the employer and employee pay social security taxes. Social security contributions paid by employees may be deducted in determining taxable income.

Foreign employees working in Belgium are normally liable for social security contributions, subject to relief under EC regulations or totalization agreements.

Taxation of Foreign Executives Living in Belgium

Foreign executives living and working temporarily in Belgium are granted a special tax status as nonresident, if they have been transferred to Belgium on a temporary basis by a multinational group. Belgian taxes apply on worldwide earned income, but a percentage of the income attributed to work performed outside Belgium is excluded from taxation (the travel exclusion).

Subject to a review of the nature and amounts by the Belgian tax authorities, additional expenses incurred by the employee as a result of the foreign assignment and reimbursed by the employer are (within certain limitations for a number of these allowances) excluded from taxable income. These include the following:

- Cost-of-living, housing, and tax equalization allowances; and
- Home leave, education, and relocation expenses.

Tax treaty provisions do not apply where the individual elects for the special tax status.

Value Added Tax (VAT)

The standard rates of value added tax vary with the commodity:

- Goods classified as necessities are charged at 6 percent;
- Standard goods at 19 percent; and
- Luxury goods are charged at 25 percent.

An additional 8 percent luxury tax (applied in addition to the 25 percent VAT) applies to goods such as jewelry, expensive cars, stereo equipment, and television sets.

Stamp Duty

Stamp duties are payable, for example, on documents providing a title to real estate, bills of exchange, and certain documents issued by the courts. Insurance contracts are also subject to an annual stamp duty of up to 9.25 percent.

Transactions in stocks, shares, or securities on the stock exchange are subject to duty at rates varying from 0.07 percent to 0.35 percent. There is an annual tax based on the total trading value of shares quoted of 0.4 percent per BEF 1000.

Other Taxes

Registration taxes apply as follows:

- 12.5 percent on transfers of real property;
- 0.2 percent on leases of real property; and
- 0.5 percent on capital contributions (except for mergers and splitting of companies).

Withholding Taxes

Withholdings arise on employee pay (for tax and social security) and on dividends, royalties, and interest payments. The rate relating to dividend payments is 25 percent. The rate relating to royalty and interest payments is either 10 percent or 25 percent, depending on the effective date of the underlying source of income. If a contract was concluded or a bond issued before March 1, 1990, the higher rate applies. However, tax treaties may provide for reductions or exemptions of withholding taxes in many cases. The rates of withholding taxes for key countries are listed in Table 7.2.

Tax Treaties

Belgium has tax treaties with the following:

- The countries of the EC;
- All other states of West Europe (except Iceland, Liechtenstein, San Marino, Monaco, Andorra, the Channel Islands, the Isle of Man, and Gibraltar);
- Several East Europe countries, including Czechoslovakia, Hungary, Poland, and Yugoslavia; and
- Australia, Brazil, Canada, Israel, India, Indonesia, Ivory Coast, Japan, Korea, Malaysia, Morocco, New Zealand, Pakistan, Philippines, Singapore, Sri Lanka, Thailand, Tunisia, and United States.

Table 7.2
Effective Rates for Withholding Taxes for Key Countries

Payee Resident in	Dividends (%)	Interest (%)
Belgium	25	10 [e]
Denmark	15	15
France	15 [b]	15
Germany	15	0 [c, i]
Greece	15	10
Ireland	15	15
Italy	15	15
Japan	15	15
Luxembourg [j]	15 [a]	0 [c, i]
The Netherlands	15 [d]	0 [a, i]
Portugal	15	15
Spain	15	15
United Kingdom	5 [f]	15 [h]
United States	5 [g]	15 [h]

Notes:

[a] 10% if the payee owns 25% or more of the payer, directly or indirectly.

[b] 10% if the payee owns 10% or more of the payer.

[c] 15% if the payee owns 25% or more of the payer, directly or indirectly.

[d] 5% if the payee owns directly 25% or more of the payer.

[e] 25% on interest received on contracts concluded and on bonds issued before March 1, 1990.

[f] 10% if the payee does not control, directly or indirectly, at least 25% or more of the voting power of the payer.

[g] 15% if the payee does not own, directly or indirectly, at least 10% of the payer.

[h] For interest payable by a Belgian company on loans concluded as of March 1, 1990, or later, the applicable withholding rate will be determined as follows: the lower of the Belgian tax rate (10%) or other tax treaty rate.

[i] Between enterprises.

[j] Tax treaty does not apply when the beneficiary is a Luxembourg company, subject to a preferential tax regime.

Copenhagen

8

Denmark

SECTIONS IN THIS CHAPTER

ASSISTANCE

Chapter 20 lists resources that can provide macroeconomic, population, and census-type data on the EC and on most of its member states. For additional help on using the resources in this chapter, refer to the Introduction to Part II.

BACKGROUND

Denmark is composed of the peninsula of Jylland (Jutland) in the North Sea, which borders on the south with Germany, and of numerous islands, the two largest being Sjaelland (Zealand) and Fyn (Funen). The country has an area of 43,069 square kilometers.

Denmark is a constitutional monarchy, with Queen Margrethe as the head of state. The Queen appoints the cabinet on the recommendation of the Parliament (Folketinget). In addition to Denmark itself, the Kingdom of Denmark also includes the overseas territories of Greenland and the Faroe Islands.

Danish is the official language. English is the foreign language spoken by most Danes, followed by German and French.

Until the 1950s, Denmark's economy was mainly based on agriculture. Within the last 40 years, the country has become heavily industrialized. When Denmark joined the EEC in 1973, this added further to the development of its industrial sector. In spite of this, Denmark's manufacturing sector is smaller than the EC average, primarily due to a smaller capital goods manufacturing sector.

POPULATION

Denmark's population is approximately 5.1 million. Copenhagen, the capital, has a population of approximately 1.5 million people.

The labor force is approximately 2.9 million.

CURRENCY AND EXCHANGE CONTROLS

Currency

The unit of currency is Danish kroner (DKr). As of April 1991, DKr 6.5 was equivalent to U.S. $1.

Exchange Controls

As of October 1, 1988, virtually all currency regulations were abolished as a part of Denmark's preparations for the Single Internal Market. However, the transfer of large amounts of funds must still take place through a bank or other authorized currency broker.

These transfers must also be reported to the Danish Central Bank (Danmarks Nationalbank). This reporting requirement has been maintained principally for statistical purposes.

ESTABLISHING A BUSINESS

Authorization

Foreign investments are encouraged. Accordingly, few restrictions are imposed on foreign investors setting up in Denmark. For example, the acquisition or establishment of a Danish company or branch by a company already domiciled in the EC can be made without permission from the Danish authorities.

Companies that are not domiciled in the EC, however, must obtain permission from the Ministry of Industry to set up a branch in Denmark. Such permission will normally be granted if a Danish company could receive permission to set up a branch in the corresponding foreign country.

In general, nonresidents of Denmark are free to make direct investments in Denmark up to a maximum amount of DKr 10 million per year. Investments exceeding this amount require the permission of the Ministry of Industry. This permission will normally be granted.

Types of Businesses

A foreign investor may establish either a subsidiary corporation or a branch in Denmark. Both subsidiaries and branches must register with the Companies' Registry. The designations and abbreviations for Danish businesses are listed in Table 8.1.

A subsidiary must file its financial statements with the Registry, whereas a branch must file audited financial statements of the head office, together with a branch manager's report. Material filed with the Registry is available to the general public.

A subsidiary may be established either as a private limited company (Anpartsselskab or ApS) or as a public limited company (Aktieselskab or A/S). From a legal and a tax point of view, the two types of companies are similar.

Private Limited Company
The principal purpose of a private limited company is to facilitate the establishment of small companies with limited liability, for instance, for smaller undertakings or closely held family businesses. A private limited company must have a paid-in capital of at least DKr 80,000. If the paid-in capital is less than DKr 300,000, a board of directors need not be elected. However, at least one general manager must be appointed.

Public Limited Company
A public limited company must have a share capital of at least DKr 300,000. The company must have a board of directors, with a minimum of three members and at least one general manager.

A registration fee of DKr 1700 plus 0.4 percent of the share capital is payable to the Companies' Registry on registration of either type of company. In addition, a capital duty of 1 percent of the registered capital must be paid. Future increases in the share capital are subject to the same duties.

Branches
A foreign company can register a branch in Denmark, provided that the company is registered in its home country. One or more branch manager(s) must be appointed.

A registration fee of DKr 1700, plus 0.4 percent of the foreign company's share capital, to a maximum of DKr 100,000, is payable on registration.

Partnership
Business may also be conducted through a partnership. A partnership can either be organized as a general partnership (Interessentskab or I/S) or a limited partnership (Kommanditselskab or K/S). In either case, the income is taxed in the hands of the individual partners.

Local Participation Requirements

Danish ownership participation is not mandatory when foreign companies wish to invest in Denmark.

If a subsidiary is established, at least half the members of the board of directors and all members of the management must be either Danish residents or EC nationals. However, the Ministry of Industry may grant an exemption from this requirement.

If a company sets up a branch, the branch manager must be a Danish resident or an EC national. However, the Ministry of Industry may grant an exemption from this requirement.

Employee Representation

If a company employs more than an average of 35 employees over a period of three years, the employees may demand representation on the company's board.

Investment Incentives

Tax Incentives
There are no specific tax incentives for investment in Denmark.

Other Incentives
Certain government-supported loans and grants are available to promote research and development projects in Denmark. These programs offer grants or loans for product development of up to 75 percent of the total cost of approved projects.

Also, certain joint export efforts may receive support, through refunds of up to 40 percent of direct costs on export activities such as marketing analysis, participation in exhibitions, export manuals, leaflets, advertisements, and travel.

Table 8.1
Danish Business Designations and Abbreviations

Abbreviation	Name	Description
A/S	Aktieselskab	Danish public limited company
ApS	Anpartsselskab	Danish private limited company
I/S	Interessentskab	Danish general partnership
K/S	Kommanditselskab	Danish limited partnership

The Export Credit Council can issue guarantees for loans granted by Danish banks for the purpose of financing export. The Council can also issue guarantees to cover losses on claims on foreign trade debts resulting from commercial and political risk.

A number of areas in Denmark have been designated as development areas, and special incentives are available to businesses that locate there.

Labor Laws

Citizens of other Scandinavian countries (that is, Norway and Sweden) do not need work permits to work in Denmark. EC nationals may work in Denmark for up to three months before seeking a residence permit. A work permit is not required.

In all other cases, a foreign individual who intends to work in Denmark must apply to a Danish embassy or consulate for a work and a residence permit. At that time, the individual must provide the name of his Danish employer. The Danish Aliens Authority will then confirm the employment with the Danish employer. After that, the permit can be obtained from the embassy or consulate. Permits are granted for an initial period of six months and thereafter annually.

On arrival in Denmark, the foreign individual must register with both the National Register and the local police authorities, presenting his or her passport and permits.

BUSINESS TAXATION

Tax Year

A company is free to choose its financial year. Corporation tax is paid in November for the financial year ending on or before March 31.

Scope

Corporations resident in Denmark are subject to Danish taxation on their worldwide income. A company is deemed to be resident in Denmark when it is incorporated in accordance with Danish company law, regardless of where its management is situated and its trading activities take place.

Corporations not resident in Denmark are subject to tax on certain types of income from sources in Denmark, including profits from permanent establishments, income from land, royalties, and dividends.

Rates

The rate of income tax on resident as well as nonresident corporations (that is, branches) is 38 percent. A 30 percent withholding tax applies to distributions from a Danish company, subject to tax treaty provisions.

Key Elements of Taxable Income

Taxable income is determined from the income shown in statutory financial statements, adjusted to comply with applicable tax provisions.

Capital gains are normally taxed as income. Gains on certain bonds and debentures bought at a discount, on shares held for at least three years, and on buildings owned for more than seven years are exempt, unless sold as part of normal business activities. Capital gains realized from the sale of goodwill are also exempt.

Dividends received from domestic companies, in which at least 25 percent of the share capital has been held for the whole accounting year, are tax-free. For other domestic dividends, companies fully liable to taxation in Denmark must declare 66 percent of the dividends received. The effective tax rate is reduced to 25 percent.

An allowance of up to 30 percent of the net book value of inventories may be taken for tax purposes, regardless of any other tax-deductible provisions for obsolete and slow-moving items. This allowance must be added to income in the following accounting year, at which time another allowance may be taken based on that year's ending inventory value.

Losses

Losses may be carried forward for five years and may be offset against taxable income in that period. Losses cannot be carried back.

Depreciation

Using the declining balance method, machinery and equipment, cars, and ships may all be depreciated by a maximum of 30 percent per year.

Buildings used for commercial purposes, except office buildings, may be depreciated using the straight-line method. An office building attached to a depreciable building may, in certain instances, be depreciated.

Buildings for agricultural, industrial, and retail use may be depreciated by 6 percent of cost per year until 60 percent has been depreciated and thereafter by 2 percent per year until fully depreciated.

Buildings for entertainment and hotel purposes may be depreciated by a maximum of 4 percent per year until 40 percent has been depreciated and thereafter by 1 percent per year until fully depreciated.

Undistributed Profits

There are no provisions relating to undistributed profits.

Foreign Income of Danish Resident Companies

A Danish company may elect to be jointly taxed with its wholly owned foreign and domestic subsidiaries. In this case, it is taxed on income of the subsidiary as earned.

A Danish company with branches or jointly taxed foreign subsidiaries may obtain relief amounting to 50 percent of the Danish corporation tax levied on the net taxable income of the foreign entities. The effect of this relief is that, under certain circumstances, the effective Danish tax rate can be reduced for a company with branches or jointly taxed foreign subsidiaries.

Dividends from foreign companies that are not jointly taxed are taxable as received. If at least 25 percent of the share capital has been held for the whole accounting year the dividend is tax-free, provided the paying company is subject to a corporate tax that is not significantly different from Danish taxation.

Social Security Taxes

Contributions to social security are paid as part of the national income tax. However, monthly contributions to a supplementary pension fund are made at the rate of DKr 64.80 for employees and DKr 129.60 for employers.

Taxation of Foreign Executives Living in Denmark

Foreign executives who are living temporarily in Denmark are subject to taxation in Denmark on their worldwide income and net wealth, following the normal Danish tax rules applicable to individuals.

However, expatriates who:
- Are assigned to Denmark for a period not exceeding three years;
- Continue to be employed and paid directly by the foreign employer during the assignment to Denmark; and
- Have been employed by the foreign employer for a certain period of time before the transfer to Denmark

may be granted an annual allowance for 24 months to cover the extra cost of living. The allowance is the lower of DKr 8000 plus 5 percent of gross earned income or 25 percent of gross earned income. The allowance is granted as a deduction in taxable income.

Value Added Tax (VAT)

The basic value added tax (VAT) rate in Denmark is set at 22 percent. This rate is charged on the net invoice price for both goods and services.

Most services and all goods sold in Denmark are subject to the VAT. Certain types of activities are exempted from VAT:
- Hospital, medical, and dental care;
- Education;
- Certain cultural and sports activities;
- Taxi, bus, and train fares; and
- The sale of real estate, stock, and bonds.

Although no VAT is charged on export sales, imported goods are subject to VAT.

Stamp Duty

A stamp duty is imposed on the value represented or transferred by certain documents, including mortgages (1.5 percent to 4 percent), deeds of properties (1.2 percent), leases (1 percent to 4 percent), and loan agreements (0.3 percent).

Withholding Taxes

Withholding tax applies to employee pay, dividends, and royalties. The withholding tax rate applicable to royalties is 30 percent, but most tax treaties reduce the rate to 0. Payments of interest to persons previously resident in Denmark may in certain circumstances be subject to a 30 percent withholding tax. The rates of withholding taxes for key countries are listed in Table 8.2.

Tax Treaties

Denmark has tax treaties with the following:

- The countries of the EC, except for Greece;

- The Nordic countries (Norway, Sweden, Finland, and Iceland), Faroe Islands, and Greenland;

- Numerous Western and Eastern European countries, including Austria, Bulgaria, Cyprus, Czechoslovakia, Hungary, Malta, Poland, Rumania, Switzerland, Turkey, U.S.S.R., and Yugoslavia; and

- Australia, Brazil, Canada, China, India, Indonesia, Israel, Jamaica, Japan, Kenya, Malaysia, New Zealand, Pakistan, The Philippines, Singapore, South Korea, Sri Lanka, Tanzania, Thailand, Trinidad and Tobago, Tunisia, United States, and Zambia.

Table 8.2
Effective Rates for Withholding Taxes for Key Countries

Payee Resident in	Dividends (%)	Interest [c] (%)
Belgium	15	15
Denmark	30	0
France	0	0
Germany	10 [a]	0
Ireland	0	0
Italy	15	15
Japan	10 [a]	10
Luxembourg	5 [a]	0
The Netherlands	0 [a]	0
Portugal	10 [a]	15
Spain	10 [b]	10
United Kingdom	0 [a]	0
United States	5 [a]	0

Notes:

[a] 15% if payee owns less than 25% of the payer.

[b] 15% if payee owns less than 50% of payer.

[c] Payment of interest to individuals who previously have been resident in Denmark may in certain circumstances be subject to a 30% withholding tax, which, however, may be reduced due to tax treaty provisions. For companies and other individuals, no withholding tax is levied on interest payments from Denmark.

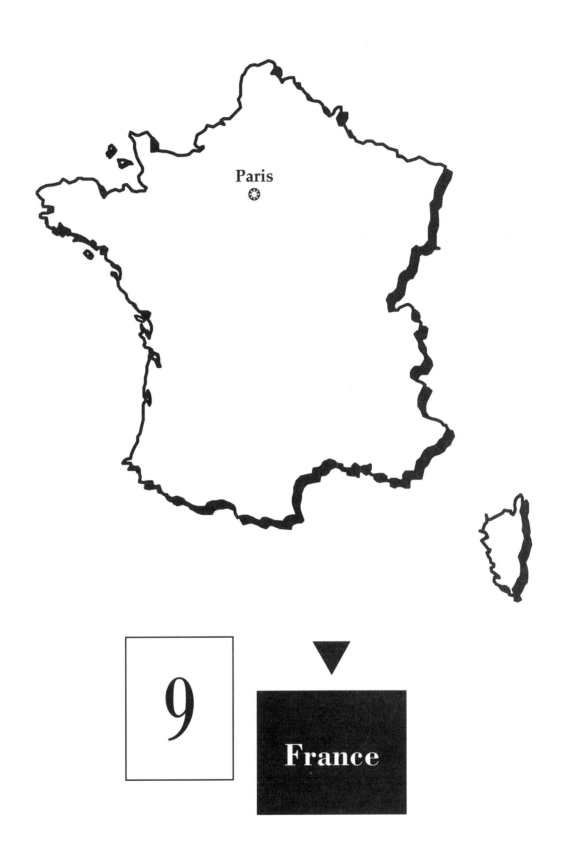

Paris

9

France

ASSISTANCE

Chapter 20 lists resources that can provide macroeconomic, population, and census-type data on the EC and on most of its member states. For additional help on using the resources in this chapter, refer to the Introduction to Part II.

BACKGROUND

The French Republic covers an area of approximately 551,800 square kilometers. Continental France, together with the island of Corsica, constitutes metropolitan France. Four overseas departments and various overseas territories also form an integral part of the republic.

France was a monarchy for many years, becoming a republic after the French Revolution in 1792. Under the current constitution, France is a democratic republic with a president serving as head of state. The president is elected for a seven-year period and appoints the prime minister. The French Parliament consists of two bodies: the National Assembly and the Senate.

France was one of the founding members of the EC.

The official language is French; there are also several regional dialects.

Paris, the capital, is also the largest city in France.

France is now a largely industrial nation, with an important agricultural sector. Currently, manufacturing industry accounts for over 80 percent of all French exports, whereas agricultural exports amount to about 18 percent of the total. The industrial sector employs 22 percent of the work force to produce 27 percent of GDP, whereas 7 percent of the work force employed in agriculture produces only 4 percent of GDP. The outlook for expansion of France's agricultural sector is limited because of food surpluses due to world overproduction.

POPULATION

The estimated population of France is 58.4 million.

The capital, Paris, has a population of approximately 10.3 million (Ile de France).

CURRENCY
AND EXCHANGE CONTROLS

Currency

The unit of currency is the French franc (FF). As of April 1991, FF 5.74 was equivalent to U.S. $1.

Exchange Controls

French exchange control has been diminishing in recent years. Direct foreign investment in France is free. Restrictions apply in principle to non-EC investments.

ESTABLISHING A BUSINESS

Authorization

No exchange control regulations apply to the establishment of a new business in France, by either EC or non-EC residents. However, all investments have to be reported.

Types of Businesses

Table 9.1 summarizes the types of businesses the French use. Most foreigners doing business in France set up a local company, either a Societe anonyme (SA) or a Societe a responsibilite limitee (SARL). Cash contributions to these companies involve a registration tax of 1 percent, up to a maximum of FF 430 and contributions in kind between 1 percent and 11.4 percent. All such enterprises must be registered at the Register of Commerce and Corporations.

An SA needs at least seven shareholders and a minimum capital of FF 250,000, which must be deposited in a French bank. Cash contributions to these companies involve a registration tax of 1 percent, up to a maximum of FF 430, and contributions in kind between 1 percent and 11.4 percent.

An SARL must have at least 2 shareholders but not more than 50. The minimum capital for an SARL, FF 50,000, must be paid up in full before a business may start. This kind of company cannot undertake certain activities, such as banking and insurance.

Any foreign company that sets up a branch must deposit certain documents (translated into French) and register certain information with the authorities.

Local Participation Requirements

There are no local participation requirements for foreign investments in France.

Employee Representation

French labor law provides that employee representatives should be elected when companies have more than 10 employees. Moreover, a company committee (with employee representatives and a chairman) should be set up and union representatives may be appointed when companies have at least 50 employees.

Investment Incentives

Three free zones have been created in the areas of Dunkerque, Aubagne-La Ciotat, and Toulon-La Seyne. Corporations established within five years from the creation of such free zones—that is, through October 1, 1991—may receive an exemption from some corporation taxes and from the minimum tax on corporations until 1996.

Labor Laws

Residence permits are required, if a non-French individual wishes to stay in France for a continuous period of more than three months. A special residence permit is issued to residents of EC countries.

Foreign individuals, other than EC citizens, must have work permits if they are employed by a resident person or business. Additional permits are also required for certain senior foreign executives who are not EC residents.

BUSINESS TAXATION

Tax Year

The tax year is usually the calendar year ending on December 31.

Scope

The French corporate tax applies to profits arising in France of both resident and nonresident companies. (A company is resident if it is incorporated in France or if it has its effective seat of management in France.)

Profits of nonresident companies are deemed to be distributed and face an immediate withholding tax of 25 percent (that rate may be reduced by a tax treaty), unless the company proves that such profits are distributed to French residents, or that the total dividends distributed by the nonresident company to its shareholders are less than the branch's after-tax profits.

Taxable profits are based on the difference between net assets at the beginning and end of the year as shown by the company's accounts, or on the profits disclosed in those accounts. Expenditures incurred for business purposes are generally deductible unless they are of capital nature.

New corporations may be fully exempt from taxes during the first two years of activity, and partly during the third, fourth, and fifth years of activity, provided that certain conditions are met.

Rates

As of January 1, 1991, the French corporation tax is levied at a normal rate of 34 percent per annum. However, a higher rate of 42 percent is applied on profits distributed by the corporation.

Table 9.1
French Business Designations and Abbreviations

Abbreviation	Name	Description
G.I.E.	Groupement d'interet economique	Intercompany partnership
SA	Societe anonyme	French limited company
SARL	Societe a responsibilite limitee	French private limited liability company
SCA	Societe en commandite par actions	French partnership limited by shares

Key Elements of Taxable Income

The following are viewed as short-term capital gains:

- The profit on a sale of assets owned for less than two years; and

- Recaptured depreciation on assets owned for longer than two years.

Short-term capital gains have to be included in the taxable basis of the year when they are realized and are taxed as operating profits. Long-term gains—that is, the profit on assets held for longer than two years—are taxed at 19 percent, plus a complementary tax of 23 percent if distributed.

Short-term losses can be used to reduce ordinary income. Long-term losses may be carried forward for ten years to be set off against long-term gains.

Dividends received by a company are, in principle, included in the parent's taxable income, with the benefit of a tax credit. The credit is against the "avoir fiscal" for domestic dividends or withholding tax for foreign dividends. However, a company owning more than 10 percent of its "subsidiary" (whether French or foreign) can exclude distributions received (minus a 5 percent service charge) from its taxable income.

Stock valuation is set by generally accepted accounting principles. The valuation is the lower of cost or net realizable value.

Interest on shareholders' loans and advances is only deductible when all shares are fully paid and then at the prescribed interest rate (average rate of French private bonds). Interest relief is restricted on loans from a foreign parent company that exceed 150 percent of the subsidiary's capital.

Losses

Tax losses can be carried forward for five years. However, the carryforward of losses attributable to depreciation has no time limit.

Losses can be carried back for three years, if certain conditions are met.

The tax credit, based on the excess tax paid in prior years after the carryback, can be carried forward for five years. The tax credit may be refunded if it is not used during the five-year carryforward period.

Losses may be offset against profits arising in a group of related companies, those that are at least 95 percent owned, in the same period, under certain conditions.

Depreciation

The average rates for straight-line depreciation are 2 percent to 5 percent for buildings, 10 percent to 15 percent for machinery, 10 percent to 20 percent for equipment, and 20 percent to 25 percent for vehicles. Accelerated depreciation is available under certain conditions.

Undistributed Profits

The undistributed profits of a company are taxed at an effective rate of 34 percent in 1991; they are taxed at an effective rate of 42 percent if distributed. Although the profits of a branch are normally taxed at the same rate, it is possible to benefit from the 34 percent rate, if it is shown that such profits are not remitted to a foreign parent.

Foreign Income of Resident Companies

In general, the profits and losses from foreign permanent establishments are not taken into account in calculations of the taxable income of French resident companies. A distribution tax is due on the distribution of such profits.

Foreign dividends, other than from a 10 percent held subsidiary, are taxed in full.

Value Added Tax (VAT)

The value added tax (VAT or TVA) is levied at 18.6 percent on most products and services produced in France. It also applies to all imports at the time of entry into French customs territory on a c.i.f. basis. A higher tax of 22 percent applies to luxury products (such as photographic equipment and materials, record players, and radios). A reduced rate of 5.5 percent applies to food and some services.

Other Taxes

Other business taxes include a registration tax, a local business license tax, and a payroll tax for companies not subject to VAT.

Withholding Taxes

Withholding tax applies to dividends, royalty payments, and payments for certain services rendered in France. Since June 1987 there has been no withholding tax on interest paid to nonresidents under certain conditions. The rates of withholding taxes for key countries are listed in Table 9.2.

Tax Treaties

France has tax treaties with the following:

- All of the countries of the EC;

- Numerous Western and Eastern European countries, including Austria, Bulgaria, Cyprus, Czechoslovakia, Finland, Hungary, Malta, Monaco, Norway, Poland, Rumania, Sweden, Switzerland, U.S.S.R., and Yugoslavia; and

- Algeria, Argentina, Australia, Bangladesh, Benin, Brazil, Canada, China, Egypt, India, Indonesia, Iran, Israel, Ivory Coast, Japan, Jordan, Korea (South), Kuwait, Lebanon, Madagascar, Malaysia, Mali, Morocco, New Caledonia, New Zealand, Niger, Pakistan, Philippines, Saudi Arabia, Senegal, Singapore, Sri Lanka, Thailand, Togo, Trinidad and Tobago, Tunisia, United States, and Zambia/Malawi.

Table 9.2
Effective Rates for Withholding Taxes for Key Countries

Payee Resident in	Dividends (%)
Belgium	15 [a]
Denmark	
Germany	[h]
Greece	25
Ireland	15 [c]
Italy	15
Japan	[b, g]
Luxembourg	15 [d]
The Netherlands	15 [d]
Portugal	15
Spain	15 [f]
United Kingdom	15 [e]
United States	15 [e]

Notes:

[a] 10% if payee owns more than 10%.

[b] 15% where "avoir fiscal" (imputed credit) is granted.

[c] 10% if payee owns more than 50%.

[d] 5% if payee owns more than 25%.

[e] 5% if payee owns more than 10%.

[f] 10% if payee owns more than 25%.

[g] 10% if payee owns more than 15%.

[h] Special provisions apply.

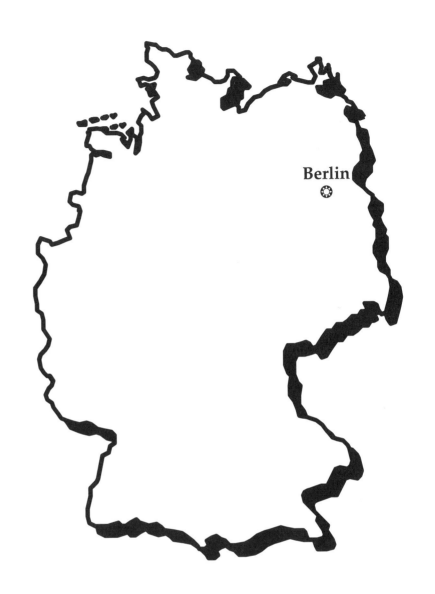

Berlin

10

Germany

SECTIONS IN THIS CHAPTER

ASSISTANCE

Chapter 20 lists resources that can provide macroeconomic, population, and census-type data on the EC and on most of its member states. For additional help on using the resources in this chapter, refer to the Introduction to Part II.

BACKGROUND

Germany covers an area of over 357,000 square kilometers. In 1949, four years after the end of World War II, the Federal Republic of Germany was founded on the territory of the three Western zones of occupation. In 1990, the former German Democratic Republic became a part of the Federal Republic and ceased to exist.

Germany has a bicameral parliamentary system, and each of the federal states also has its own legislature and government.

The capital of the Federal Republic of Germany is Berlin. The seat of government is Bonn.

The national language is German, but in business life most people also speak English.

The Federal Republic of Germany ranks among the top three trading nations in the world. The most important growth industries are the production of cars and trucks, machinery, electrical engineering, and the chemical industry.

Declining industries include mining and ship-building. Moreover, much of the industrial plant that had been state-supported by the former German Democratic Republic is aging and unproductive. In addition, Germany is expected to need to make substantial investments in the infrastructure of areas encompassing the former German Democratic Republic, including telecommunications, highways, and airports.

POPULATION

The estimated population of Germany in 1990 was 79.1 million.

CURRENCY AND EXCHANGE CONTROLS

Currency

The unit of currency is the Deutsche Mark (DM). As of April 1991, DM 1.69 was equivalent to U.S. $1.

Exchange Controls

There are no exchange controls in Germany, with the exception of certain reporting provisions contained in its foreign trade laws. These require a report to the Federal Bank (Bundesbank) if more than 20 percent of an existing company's capital is acquired or if a company or branch is created, acquired, sold, or liquidated, and the investment exceeds DM 50,000.

ESTABLISHING A BUSINESS

Authorization

Except in a limited number of trades, permission is not required to set up a corporation or a branch in Germany. It is, however, necessary to register the business and to file the appropriate legal documents. Local resident shareholders and directors are generally not required.

Types of Businesses

Table 10.1 summarizes the types of businesses Germans use. Most nonnationals who do business in Germany set up a limited liability company (Gesellschaft mit beschrankter Haftung, or GmbH) rather than a stock corporation (Aktiengesellschaft or AG).

A GmbH needs a minimum nominal share capital of DM 50,000 of which at least 25 percent (or a minimum amount of DM 25,000, whichever is greater) must be paid up. The minimum share capital of an AG is DM 100,000. Until January 1, 1992, a capital transfer tax (1 percent) is due on the paid-up capital. That tax will be abolished as of that date.

A branch can also be set up following the registration of certain documents.

Local Participation Requirements

In general, there are no local ownership participation requirements in Germany.

Employee Representation

Germany's codetermination law requires the participation of employee representatives on the board, if the company has 500 or more employees (Plant Council Law, Betriebsverfassungsgesetz).

Investment Incentives

Special depreciation rates of up to 75 percent in the first year are possible for investments in undeveloped areas. Higher depreciation rates are also available for investments in research and development (40 percent), shipbuilding (40 percent), and mining (up to 50 percent).

In addition, in West Berlin, there is a reduction in the tax rate to 22.5 percent for corporations. For the territories that formerly made up the German Democratic Republic, special promotional incentives, covering up to 33 percent of the amount invested, have been established.

Other Incentives

Germany's Ministry of Science and Technology supervises the federal research and development programs. Under these programs, grants may be available for up to 50 percent of the costs of a project. In addition, each of the German states offers its own programs, which may include credit guarantees, grants, loans, and technical assistance.

BUSINESS TAXATION

Tax Year

The normal tax year is the calendar year. Other fiscal years are permitted for newly set-up companies. For existing companies, a change from the calendar year to an irregular tax year needs official approval. A tax year and a stub period tax year must not exceed 12 months.

Scope

A corporation is either resident or nonresident in Germany. A corporation that is incorporated or that has its central management and control in Germany is a German resident.

A resident corporation is taxable on its worldwide income. A nonresident corporation is taxable only on income derived from sources within Germany.

Rates

Resident companies (whether GmbH or AG) pay corporate income tax at a 50 percent rate on undistributed profits and at 36 percent on distributed profits. In addition, all business activities are subject to a municipal trade tax, which averages 17 percent of the income. The municipal trade tax is deductible for corporate income tax purposes.

The total effective tax rate on distributed profits is therefore 47 percent (including the average municipal trade tax but not counting dividend withholding tax). Special lower tax rates apply for West Berlin, where corporate income tax is reduced by 22.5 percent and municipal trade tax on income is roughly half the normal rates.

Table 10.1
German Business Designations and Abbreviations

Abbreviation	Name	Description
AG	Aktiengesellschaft	German public stock corporation
GmbH & Co KG	Gesellschaft mit beschrankter Haftung Kommanditgesellschaft	German private limited company—partnership composed of partners with limited liability and a general partner in the legal form of a GmbH
GmbH	Gesellschaft mit beschrankter Haftung	German private limited liability company
KGaA	Kommanditgesellschaft auf Aktien	German partnership limited by shares
OHG	Offene Handelsgesellschaft	German general partnership

Key Elements of Taxable Income

Capital gains are taxed at the normal rate. Gains on the sale of certain assets used to acquire similar assets may be deferred.

Dividends received from resident companies are effectively tax exempt. Dividends from a foreign corporation in a treaty country are generally excluded from income tax.

Inventories are valued according to German generally accepted accounting principles (GAAP), at the lower of cost or net realizable value. For price increases of raw materials and supplies, a tax deductible reserve may be created if the market price has increased by more than 10 percent over the last year. The reserve must be dissolved after six years at the latest. Furthermore, for some imported supplies, a special deduction is allowed against inventories.

Shareholder loans and corresponding interest are only accepted for taxable purposes if the corporation is not thinly capitalized. Generally, thin capitalization is presumed if the corporation's equity is not more than 10 percent of its assets. However, new legislation on this subject is expected to modify these rules.

Losses

Losses of up to DM 10,000,000 must be carried back to the two prior years. Any remaining losses generated in tax years ending after December 31, 1984, can be carried forward indefinitely.

Depreciation

The acceptable methods of depreciation are the straight-line and the declining balance methods.

Straight-line depreciation on buildings built after January 1, 1925, is normally 2 percent per year, or 2.5 percent per year on buildings built before January 1, 1925, but a declining balance method may be used. For commercial buildings for which building permits were granted after March 31, 1985, which are owned and used for business purposes (except for personal residences), the regular straight-line depreciation rate is 4 percent per year. The declining balance method is also applicable.

Movable assets may be depreciated under the declining balance method at three times the straight-line rates, with a maximum rate of 30 percent. Average straight-line rates are 10 percent for machinery and 20 percent to 25 percent for cars. More favorable rates apply for research and development, and ecological and development areas.

Undistributed Profits

As mentioned earlier, undistributed profits are taxed at a higher rate of 50 percent compared with 36 percent on distributed profits.

Foreign Income of Resident Companies

The foreign income of a resident corporation is subject to German tax, unless the applicable tax treaty provides for tax exemption. A credit is possible for foreign taxes on taxable foreign income. As an alternative, foreign taxes can be deducted from the taxable income.

Other Taxes

NET ASSET TAX

Net assets of companies are subject to wealth tax at 0.6 percent. Because only 75 percent of the business-related net assets are actually subject to tax, the effective rate is 0.45 percent. The net asset tax is not deductible as an expenditure for corporate income tax purposes.

MUNICIPAL TRADE TAX

The regional communities impose a municipal trade tax on income and on capital from business activities. The tax is deductible from corporate income tax. Long-term debts and corresponding interest expenses are not fully deductible. The tax rates vary from community to community.

VALUE ADDED TAX (VAT)

Sales of goods and services, including imported goods, are subject to the value added tax (VAT), which is generally 14 percent of the net sales price, less VAT. A reduced rate of 7 percent applies generally to food, printed matter, certain health and public services, prosthetic devices, and works of art.

Certain specified transactions are exempt from VAT. VAT is also waived on exports, if the necessary documents (proof of export) are prepared and provided to the authorities.

Transfer Tax

The transfer of real property is subject to real estate transfer tax at 2 percent. Furthermore, a transfer of real property is deemed to exist by the transfer of shares of a company that owns real property if by this transaction all shares are united directly or indirectly or if all shares of the company are sold.

Withholding Taxes

Tax withholding is required from employee pay (for tax and social security), on dividends, and on certain royalty payments to nonresidents. The rates of withholding taxes for key countries are listed in Table 10.2.

Tax Treaties

Germany has tax treaties with the following:

- All of the countries of the EC;

- Numerous Western and Eastern European countries, including Austria, Bulgaria, Czechoslovakia, Finland, Hungary, Iceland, Malta, Norway, Poland, Rumania, Sweden, Switzerland, U.S.S.R., and Yugoslavia; and

- Argentina, Australia, Brazil, Canada, China, Cyprus, Ecuador, Egypt, India, Indonesia, Iran, Israel, Ivory Coast, Jamaica, Japan, Kenya, Kuwait, Liberia, Malaysia, Mauritius, Morocco, New Zealand, Pakistan, Philippines, Singapore, South Africa, South Korea, Sri Lanka, Thailand, Trinidad and Tobago, Tunisia, United States, and Zambia.

Data and the Unification of Germany

The unification of Germany in October 1990 is causing some problems for businesspeople seeking data about the unified Germany.

Historical Data

It is very misleading simply to combine data reported from the Federal Republic of Germany (FRG) with that collected by the former German Democratic Republic (GDR) to determine totals for the unified Germany. Primarily, this is because

Table 10.2
Effective Rates for Withholding Taxes for Key Countries

Payee Resident in	Dividends (%)	Interest (%)
Belgium	15	15 [b]
Denmark	15/10	0
France	15	0
Germany	25	0 [b]
Ireland	15	0
Italy	25	25
Japan	15	10 [b]
Luxembourg	15/10	0
The Netherlands	15	0
Portugal	15	15 [b]
Spain	15	10 [b]
United Kingdom	15	0
United States	10 [a]	0

Notes:

[a] The rate will be reduced to 5% in 1992.

[b] There are certain exceptions.

some of the data collection and analysis processes used by the GDR in the past are regarded as lacking in objectivity. In addition, the GDR did not always collect data that is compatible with that collected by the FRG.

The result is that only population data statistics produced by the FRG and GDR before unification are fully comparable. All other data has problems of accuracy, compatibility, and even of availability.

To overcome this problem, before the unification the FRG and GDR established a working group of statisticians to review historical data (particularly that of the most recent vintage). The aim of this group is to supply reliable data of the types needed to facilitate the unification process and the management of the newly created economy.

Current Data

Germany is currently harmonizing the statistical procedures formerly used by the GDR with those of the FRG. The result is that the collection of current data on employment, external trade, and output will produce numbers that can be used with some confidence in their accuracy.

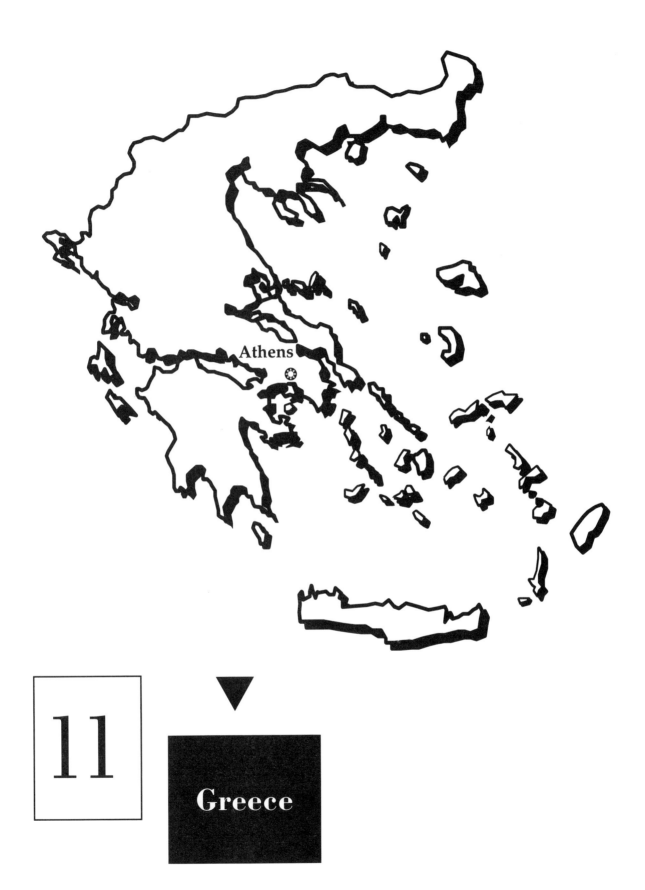

Athens

11

Greece

SECTIONS IN THIS CHAPTER

ASSISTANCE

Chapter 20 lists resources that can provide macroeconomic, population, and census-type data on the EC and on most of its member states. For additional help on using the resources in this chapter, refer to the Introduction to Part II.

BACKGROUND

The Republic of Greece covers a total area of 132,000 square kilometers. To the south, east, and west of the mainland lie numerous Greek islands, which represent about 19 percent of its area. The largest of these is Crete.

Greece became an independent country in 1829, following nearly four centuries of Turkish rule. The country is now a Presidential Republic. The Greek Constitution provides for the separation of powers among the legislative, executive, and judicial branches of the state.

The executive branch consists of the prime minister and his or her cabinet. Usually the prime minister is the leader of the majority party in parliament.

The native language is Greek.

Greece has traditionally been an agricultural nation. It still has rather a large agricultural sector, the main crops of which are cereals and fresh and dried fruit.

Whereas approximately 29 percent of the working population is engaged in agriculture, the industrial sector is rapidly growing in importance, with manufactured exports now representing 56 percent of total exports. In addition, mineral deposits have been intensively exploited, and tourism and shipping also play a major role in the Greek economy. However, long-term industrial development may be adversely affected by Greece's relatively low levels of investment in its infrastructure over the past 10 years.

POPULATION

The population of Greece is estimated to be about 10 million, of which the work force totals 3.8 million.

Approximately 3 million people live in Athinai (Athens), the capital of Greece. About half the population live in cities that have over 10,000 inhabitants.

CURRENCY AND EXCHANGE CONTROLS

Currency

The unit of currency is the drachma (Dr). As of April 1991, Drs 177.00 were equivalent to U.S. $1.

Exchange Controls

Exchange controls had been in force in Greece for many years. However, in 1986 to harmonize exchange control regulations with those of the EC, Greece removed restrictions on most capital movements to Greece from within the EC, as well as from non-EC countries.

The capital movements now permitted include foreign capital used for direct investment in Greece. This includes capital to be used to establish branches and subsidiaries as well as to participate in Greek companies. Capital is also allowed to enter Greece for the acquisition of real estate and of stocks listed on the Athens Stock Exchange.

ESTABLISHING A BUSINESS

Authorization

The establishment of a business presence in Greece requires no prior permission from the Greek authorities, unless it is done through the creation of a subsidiary corporation or a branch. Because there are special governmental incentives provided for businesses that invest in manufacturing and advanced technology, the approval of the Ministry of National Economy is required before a non-Greek company can obtain governmental investment grants.

Types of Businesses

Table 11.1 summarizes the types of businesses the Greeks use. A foreign enterprise may be established in Greece either as a subsidiary or as a branch. Approval for the establishment and registration of both subsidiaries and branches must be obtained from the competent Prefecture of the district in which the business will be located. If a subsidiary is used it is usually a corporation, an Anonymos Eteria (AE), rather than a private company with limited liabilities, an Eteria Periorismenis Efthinis (EPE).

An AE requires at least two shareholders (who may be foreigners) and a minimum capital of 5 million drachmas. The business's annual financial statements must be filed and, in the case of a subsidiary, published. For the formation of an EPE, the minimum capital required is 200,000 drachmas.

If a foreign company sets up a branch rather than a subsidiary, the parent foreign company must meet a minimum capitalization test. It must have a capital of 5 million drachmas if it is a corporation (AE) or a capital of 200,000 drachmas if it is a limited liability company (EPE). These minimum capital requirements are expected to be increased from Drs 200,000 to Drs 5 million for an EPE and from Drs 5 million to Drs 30 million for an AE.

Local Participation Requirements

In general, there are no local participation requirements in Greece. Specifically, all shareholdings in an AE may be foreign.

Table 11.1
Greek Business Designations and Abbreviations

Abbreviation	Name	Description
AE	Anonymos Eteria	Greek corporation
EE	Eterorrythmos Eteria	Greek limited partnership
EPE	Eteria Periorismenis Efthinis	Greek private company with limited liabilities

However, EC nationals (natural persons or legal entities) cannot acquire real estate in "border areas" (as defined by Greek law) without the prior authorization of a special governmental committee. In addition, the prior approval of the Minister of National Defense is required in cases involving non-EC nationals.

Employee Participation

Greece has no provisions for employee participation in company management.

Investment Incentives

Foreign enterprises are granted special benefits if they establish offices in Greece that are engaged in activities conducted outside Greece. However, ministerial approval is required to establish such offices. These special benefits include, among others, a tax exemption on income earned abroad and an import tax exemption on equipment imported.

Government assistance is provided for "productive investments" in less-developed areas as well as for investments in high technology. This assistance includes investment grants and bank interest subsidies. Approval of the Ministry of National Economy is required for these incentives.

An enterprise making "productive investments" in less-developed areas in Greece is also entitled to increased depreciation at rates between 20 and 150 percent, depending on the amount of use and location of the assets.

Undistributed profits of corporations receiving government assistance in the form of investment grants and bank interest subsidies are taxed at 40 percent. This rate drops to 35 percent for manufacturing, handicraft, and mining enterprises.

Labor Laws

Foreign individuals working in Greece must have both residence and work permits. These permits are issued by the Ministries of Public Order and of Employment. At present there is special treatment for EC nationals who are employed on a salaried basis in Greece. They are entitled to a five-year residence permit without the need for a prior work permit.

BUSINESS TAXATION

Tax Year

The tax year is normally the calendar year ending on December 31, although the tax years of AEs and EPEs may end on June 30. In addition, the tax year of branches of foreign companies may end on the same day that the tax year of the foreign company ends. This also applies to Greek companies in which a foreign company owns 51 percent or more of the stock.

Scope

The corporate tax applies to the worldwide profits of Greek resident companies and also to the Greek source profits of nonresidents. A company is resident if it is incorporated in Greece or has a "permanent establishment" in Greece. The meaning of "permanent establishment" is set by Greek law and includes offices, agencies, shops, annexes, warehouses, factories, and laboratories.

Taxable income is based on the profits disclosed in the annual accounts, after the deduction of authorized expenses.

An EPE is not taxed separately. The company's profits are divided among the partners, who then include their shares of profits on their own tax returns.

Rates

The undistributed profits of an AE are taxed at a rate of 46 percent. Greek companies employed in certain industries, such as manufacturing and mining, are taxed at 40 percent, unless they are registered on the Athens Stock Exchange, in which case the rate is 35 percent.

Branches of foreign entities that operate in Greece are taxed at the same general rate as AEs—46 percent. No additional tax is charged on remittances from the branch to the parent.

Key Elements of Taxable Income

Dividends received are taxable. The tax withheld depends on the status of the stock from which the dividend is derived. For example, registered shares listed on the Athens Stock Exchange have a 42 percent rate, whereas in contrast, bearer shares that are unlisted face a 50 percent rate.

Gains arising from the sale or from the revaluation of fixed assets are taxed as income. However, gains that arise from the sale of immovable property and ships are exempt. Gains on sales of intangible assets are taxed at the rates described earlier—46 percent, 40 percent, or 35 percent, depending on the kind of shares and/or the objects of the corporation.

Losses

Losses may be carried forward for five years but may not be carried back.

Depreciation

Depreciation is usually calculated on a straight-line basis, using the following rates:

- 8 percent for industrial buildings;
- Between 4 percent and 20 percent for machinery and equipment; and
- 20 percent for commercial vehicles (trucks) and computers.

Rates for productive assets may be increased by up to 150 percent, depending on their location and use.

Undistributed Profits

Under Greek law, the corporation must credit at least 5 percent of the net profits each year to a legal reserve. After crediting this amount, at least 35 percent of the net profits must be distributed as a dividend to shareholders. This dividend must also equal at least 6 percent of value of the paid-in capital stock. The 35 percent requirement may be waived by a total 95 percent vote of the shareholders at a general meeting.

Foreign Income of Resident Companies

Greek companies are taxed on foreign income. Within certain limits, overseas taxes paid can be credited against Greek corporate taxes.

Taxation of Foreign Executives Living in Greece

Residents of countries with which Greece has a tax treaty are exempt from Greek income tax in respect of income from personal services rendered in Greece, provided

- They are present in Greece for not more than 183 days in the tax year;
- The services are performed for, and on behalf of, a resident of the treaty country; and
- The remuneration is not ultimately borne by a permanent establishment in Greece.

In the case of U.S. residents, the second requirement is deemed to be met if the remuneration received does not exceed $10,000 and the final requirement is waived altogether.

As of October 1, 1990, all foreigners working in Greece are subject to social security taxes, starting from the first day they are employed in Greece.

Value Added Tax (VAT)

The normal VAT rate applied to the transfer of goods and rendering of services is 18 percent. This rate is reduced to 8 percent for free professional services, transportation, certain food products, and other basic necessities. It is increased to 36 percent for luxury categories of goods and services. Certain categories of goods or services, such as exports, sales to ships, and duty-free sales are exempt from VAT.

Other Taxes

Transfers of real estate are subject to two types of taxes:

- Those paid by the purchaser. They amount to 12 to 14 percent of the value of the real estate transferred. That value is determined by the Ministry of Finance, according to tables it has generated.
- Those paid by the seller. This is a capital gains tax, based on the difference between the purchase price and selling price, with an adjustment based on the cost of living while the property was held by the seller. The tax is computed at rates ranging from 10 percent to 25 percent.

A stamp duty applies to a wide range of legal documents. The current rates range from 0.6 to 3.6 percent.

Withholding Taxes

Withholdings arise on employee pay (for tax and social security) and on dividends, interest, and royalty payments. Special rates of withholding taxes are provided if the beneficiaries of the income are residents of a country with which Greece has a tax treaty. For example, the rates of withholding taxes on transfers to residents of representative countries are listed in Table 11.2.

Tax Treaties

Greece has tax treaties with the following:

- Within the EC: Belgium, France, Germany, Italy, The Netherlands, and the United Kingdom; and
- Austria, Cyprus, Czechoslovakia, Finland, Hungary, India, Sweden, Switzerland, and United States.

Table 11.2
Effective Rates for Withholding Taxes for Key Countries

Payee Resident in	Dividends (%)	Interest (%)
Belgium	25	15
France	[a]	10
Germany	25	10
Italy	25	10
The Netherlands	35	10 [b]
United Kingdom	[a]	
United States	[a]	[c]

Notes:

[a] Registered shares: unlisted 47%
                listed 42%

     Bearer shares: unlisted 50%
                listed 45%

[b] 8% if payee is a bank, and so forth.

[c] Special provisions apply.

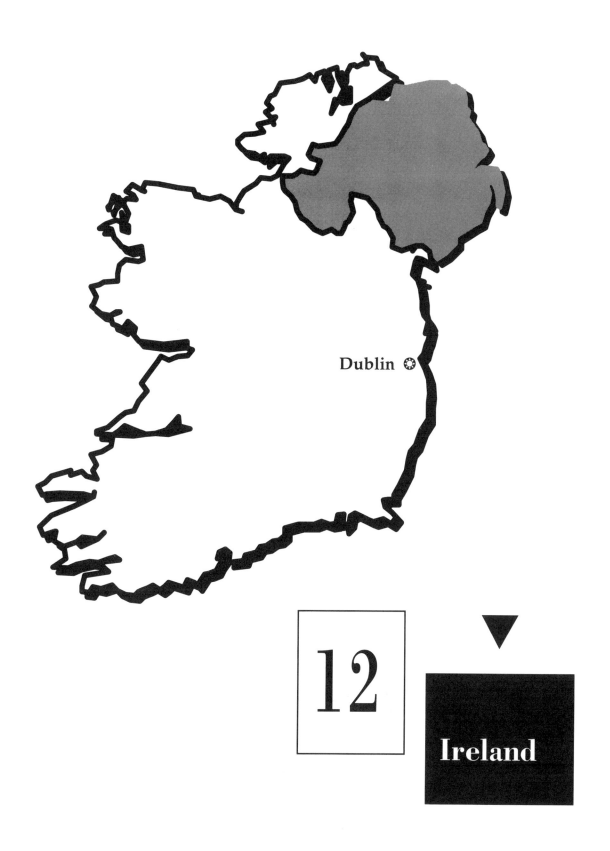

Dublin ⊙

12

▼

Ireland

▼ ▼

Sections in This Chapter

Background

Population

Currency and Exchange Controls

Establishing a Business

Business Taxation

Assistance

Chapter 20 lists resources that can provide macroeconomic, population, and census-type data on the EC and on most of its member states. For additional help on using the resources in this chapter, refer to the Introduction to Part II.

Background

The island of Ireland lies 60 miles to the west of Great Britain. Today, that island includes two separate political entities: the independent Republic of Ireland and Northern Ireland, which is a part of the United Kingdom.

The Republic of Ireland is a parliamentary democracy with a written constitution containing provisions creating and protecting fundamental rights of the person, the family, education, private property, and religion.

The head of state in the Republic of Ireland is the president, who is elected for a period of seven years. The legislative power of Ireland is vested in the national parliament, which consists of two houses, the Dail and the Seanad. The Dail has 166 members and the Seanad has 60.

The Dail, which is presided over by the speaker, is a representative assembly elected by the population.

The Seanad, which is presided over by the chairman, contains both appointed and specially elected members.

Proposed legislation is introduced in the Dail or Seanad. If it passes both the Dail and the Seanad and is signed by the president, it then becomes law.

English is the main language.

Traditionally, Ireland's economy was based on agriculture. The country's most significant natural resource is its grassland, on which its beef and dairy agribusinesses are based. Agricultural exports still form a substantial proportion of its total exports.

However, there has been rapid and significant industrial expansion over the last 25 years. As a result, the percentage of the work force employed in industry and in services has increased steadily. Ireland's most rapid areas of expansion to date have been in the areas of electrical, electronics, engineering, food, pharmaceutical, health care, and consumer products.

Ireland has also become established as an important source of base metals, exploiting its deposits of lead, zinc, and copper. In addition, a commercial gas field has been developed off its south coast and oil is known to exist in Irish waters.

Population

The estimated population of Ireland is about 3.6 million. The majority of the population of Ireland is centered in five counties: Cork, Limerick, Waterford, Galway, and Dublin.

The capital of Ireland, Dublin City, has a population of over 500,000. Dublin County, of which Dublin City is a part, has a total population of approximately 1 million people.

The labor force is estimated to be about 1.3 million.

Currency and Exchange Controls

Currency

The unit of currency is the Irish pound (IR£). As of April 1991, IR£ 0.5813 was equivalent to U.S. $1.

Exchange Controls

Inward direct investment involving total financing in excess of IR£ 1 million is subject to general reporting requirements, which are not usually restrictive or limiting. A decision from the Central Bank of Ireland with respect to such applications is usually given within 2 or 3 weeks. At that time, outline permission for the payment of dividends and repatriation of funds is normally granted.

Exchange controls have been significantly alleviated in recent years. They are due to be removed for all capital movements between Ireland and the EC before the end of 1992.

ESTABLISHING A BUSINESS

Authorization

It is not generally necessary to obtain approval from the Irish government before setting up a business in Ireland, except with respect to certain industries or sectors, such as banking and insurance.

Types of Businesses

Table 12.1 summarizes the types of businesses the Irish use. The types of business entities used in Ireland are quite similar to those used in the United Kingdom, due to the close historical links between the two countries.

A foreign company may operate in Ireland either by establishing an Irish subsidiary, usually a private company (carrying the designation Ltd. or Teo), or by establishing a branch.

Most Irish companies are private companies—that is, they have less than 50 members and are subject to certain restrictions dealing with the transfer of their shares. There is no minimum share capital.

Every Irish company and any overseas company establishing a place of business in Ireland must submit its memorandum of association (charter) and articles of association (bylaws), translated into English where necessary, together with certain other particulars to the Registrar of Companies.

Business may also be conducted in Ireland through a partnership. In such cases, the income of the partnership is taxed in the hands of the individual partners.

Table 12.1
Irish Business Designations and Abbreviations

Abbreviation	Name	Description
Ltd	Limited Company	Irish private limited company
PLC	Public Limited Company	Irish public company
Teo	Teoranta	Irish private limited company

Although less common, it is also possible for a trust to trade in Ireland. However, trading trusts are subject to income tax at the rate of 29 percent and may also be liable for a 20 percent surcharge on the trust's undistributed income.

Local Participation Requirements

There are no local participation requirements.

Employee Participation

Ireland has no requirements that employees participate in the management of a company.

Investment Incentives

TAX INCENTIVES

Companies that manufacture in Ireland are taxed on their manufacturing profits at 10 percent. *Manufacturing* is broadly defined, and can include a wide range of service activities, such as software development, data processing, shipping activities, and aircraft maintenance.

Companies that locate in the Shannon area may also qualify for this 10 percent rate on their non-manufacturing activities, provided that they contribute to the use of Shannon Airport and are export-oriented.

Certain activities at the Customs House Docks Area of Dublin can qualify for the 10 percent special tax rate. These services must, among other stipulations, contribute to the development of that area as an "International Financial Services Centre" and generally consist of transactions with, or services to, nonresidents in non-Irish currencies. A wide range of services may qualify for this rate, including the following:

- Fund management;
- Financial advice;
- Brokerage operations;
- Insurance;
- "Back office" operations;
- Leasing and factoring; and
- Credit card operations.

Special incentives apply to certain unit trusts and "undertakings for collective investment in transferable securities" (UCITS), located in either the Shannon region or in the International Financial Services Centre in Dublin. The unit trusts/UCITS funds are free from Irish tax on both income and gains.

The 10 percent rate is to apply until the year 2005 for qualifying Shannon and financial service activities, and until the year 2010 for manufacturing activities.

Income from patents is tax free, provided that the work on the development of the patent was carried out in Ireland. If this type of income is received by a company, the tax-free status flows through on dividends to shareholders.

OTHER INCENTIVES

The Irish government provides assistance for industrial investment through a variety of schemes, which vary according to the location and type of project. They are normally given selectively after negotiation with the Irish Development Authority (IDA).

In addition, the Irish Science and Technology Agency makes cash grants available for up to 50 percent of the costs of certain research and development expenditures (with a project ceiling of IR£ 250,000).

Cash grants are given toward capital expenditures on new buildings and machinery or plant that are used wholly or mainly for qualifying manufacturing and certain other activities. The maximum grant is two-thirds for investment in designated areas (mainly the West and North-West of Ireland).

Other incentives include training grants, loan guarantees and interest subsidies, ready-to-occupy factories, rent subsidies, and advisory services.

If a company is receiving government grants, the government body will require that shareholders' equity, in the form of either share capital or subordinated loan, should exceed a minimum level, normally set at the amount of grants received.

Labor Laws

Non-United Kingdom nationals staying more than three months in the Republic of Ireland must register with the police. Work permits must be obtained by the employer from the Department of Labour for non-EC nationals and, until 1992, for nationals of Spain and Portugal.

BUSINESS TAXATION

The Tax Year

The corporate tax year is the calendar year ending December 31. It is not necessary for the company's year end to be coterminous with the tax year.

Scope

A resident company pays corporation tax on its profits, wherever they arise. A company is *resident* if it is centrally managed and controlled in Ireland. *Profits* are defined as income plus chargeable gains, but generally excluding distributions received from other resident companies.

A nonresident company with an Irish branch or agency pays corporation tax on the profits connected with that branch or agency. A nonresident company with no Irish branch or agency is liable to income tax on its Irish source income as well as to a capital gains tax on certain Irish assets.

Resident companies must account for an advance corporation tax (ACT) on all distributions. ACT may be set off, within certain limits, against tax on income, but not against chargeable gains. It can be carried forward indefinitely or back (within limits). ACT is not payable on dividends paid by an Irish-resident company to a foreign 75 percent parent company resident in a country with which Ireland has a tax treaty.

Rates

The standard rate of corporation tax is 40 percent. The standard income tax rate is 29 percent. The corporation tax rate is reduced to 10 percent for a wide range of manufacturing activities and for certain financial, shipping, and services activities. See the discussion on Tax Incentives.

The rate of ACT depends on the rate of tax paid on profits with which the distributions are identified. The standard ACT rate is 25/75. The ACT on dividends from 10 percent taxed profits is 1/18.

Capital gains are taxed at effective rates of between 30 percent and 50 percent, depending on how long the asset sold was held.

Key Elements of Taxable Income

The tax basis of capital assets will be adjusted for inflation when the holding period exceeds 1 year.

Capital gains on the disposal of certain assets used in a trade may be deferred, if the proceeds are reinvested in assets similarly used within 12 months before, or 3 years after, the disposal. Capital losses may be carried forward indefinitely for offset against future capital gains.

Dividends received from resident companies are generally exempt from taxation.

Inventories (stocks) are valued at the lower of cost or net realizable value. LIFO and base stock methods are not acceptable. There are specific rules on transfer pricing in certain situations.

Losses

Trading losses may be offset against total profits (not including "development land gains") in the same accounting period. Any remaining balance may be offset against profits from the immediately preceding accounting period. Unused trading losses are carried forward indefinitely against income from the same trade.

Losses may be offset against profits arising within an Irish group of companies (at least 75 percent owned) in the same period. There are some restrictions on the use of losses from 10 percent taxed activities and from leasing.

Depreciation

Plant and machinery are depreciated on a declining balance method, at rates that depend on the type and condition of the equipment involved. For new equipment, the rates are 10 percent, 12.5 percent, or 20 percent. New industrial buildings and hotels are depreciated on a straight-line basis, at 4 percent and 10 percent, respectively.

In general, government grants are deducted from the cost of the plant and buildings in computing the allowance.

Accelerated depreciation of between 25 percent and 100 percent may be available in respect of expenditures incurred before March 31, 1992, and expenditures for projects approved for Government grants before December 31, 1990. Accelerated depreciation of 100 percent continues for operations at the International Financial Services Centre and at Shannon.

Depreciation is not available on most intangible assets or on commercial buildings, except those in government-designated areas. These commercial buildings are eligible for allowances ranging from 50 percent to 100 percent.

Undistributed Profits

Closely held companies must distribute investment and estate income, including exempt distributions from resident companies, within a period of 18 months from the end of the accounting period in which the relevant income was derived. Failure to distribute that income will result in an additional 20 percent corporation tax charged on the relevant income. This additional tax is nonrecoverable and is not creditable to the shareholder on any subsequent distribution of the relevant income.

Closely held professional service companies must operate a full distribution policy to avoid a similar additional tax charge.

Foreign Income of Resident Companies

The foreign income of a resident corporation is subject to tax in Ireland. In the absence of a double tax treaty providing otherwise, a deduction for foreign taxes incurred is allowed against the gross income derived from the foreign source, and no credit is given for foreign tax incurred.

Dividends from foreign subsidiaries can be exempted from tax. This is possible if the dividends are used for the purpose of an approved investment plan directed toward the creation or maintenance of employment in the state.

Other Taxes

VALUE ADDED TAX (VAT)
VAT applies at the standard rate of 21 percent. A lower rate of 12.5 percent applies to certain goods and services, such as personal clothing, footwear, theater, and certain other services. A 10 percent rate applies to building, newspapers, and certain tourist related services. Most food, books, and oral medicines, among other items, are zero-rated.

CAPITAL DUTIES
A capital duty of 1 percent is payable on the issue of share capital by a limited company.

STAMP DUTIES
Stamp duties of up to 6 percent apply to certain legal documents.

Withholding Taxes

Withholdings arise on employee pay (for income tax and social security) and on certain interest and royalty payments at a 29 percent rate. There is no withholding tax on dividends, although ACT is payable, except on dividends paid to foreign parents under certain conditions. The rates of withholding taxes for key countries are listed in Table 12.2.

Tax Treaties

The Republic of Ireland has tax treaties with the following:

- All of the countries of the EC except Greece, Portugal, and Spain;

- Numerous Western European countries, including Austria, Cyprus, Finland, Norway, Sweden, and Switzerland; and

- Australia, Canada, Japan, New Zealand, Pakistan, United States, and Zambia.

There are also shipping and air transport treaties with Spain and South Africa.

Table 12.2
Effective Rates for Withholding Taxes for Key Countries

Payee Resident in	Dividends (%)	Interest (%)
Belgium		15
Denmark		
France		
Germany		
Ireland		29
Italy		10
Japan		10
Luxembourg		
The Netherlands		
United Kingdom	[a]	
United States		29 [b]

Notes:

[a] Individuals and companies owning less than 10% can reclaim part of the ACT.

[b] 0% if the payee controls or owns less than 50% of voting power.

Rome

13

Italy

SECTIONS IN THIS CHAPTER

ASSISTANCE

Chapter 20 lists resources that can provide macroeconomic, population, and census-type data on the EC and on most of its member states. For additional help on using the resources in this chapter, refer to the Introduction to Part II.

BACKGROUND

Italy is a peninsula of 301,250 square kilometers. Italy is a founding member of the EC.

Italy became politically united in 1861 and has been a republic since the end of World War II. The Italian system of government is a democracy, founded on a bicameral system of government in which both legislative bodies have equal powers. The President of the Republic is elected by the Parliament. Many parties, even very small ones, are represented in the Parliament, so that governments in recent years have always been coalition governments. By law, elections must be held every five years.

The capital city, Roma (Rome), is also the largest city in the nation. Its population is approximately 2.8 million. From an economic point of view, other cities, such as Milan (with a population of approximately 1.5 million), are at least as important. Other economically important Italian cities include Torino (Turin), Venezia (Venice), Napoli (Naples), and Palermo.

The main language is Italian.

Italy has a shortage of natural resources and therefore has developed a significant manufacturing economy. The leading industrial activities are those associated with mechanical products, textile products, and food. State-owned industrial firms represent a substantial element in Italian economic activity. However, the number of people employed in agricultural activities is still relatively high, particularly in Southern Italy ("Mezzogiorno"), which also faces a higher unemployment rate than do the Northern and Central sections.

Import and export trade plays a substantial role in the Italian economy.

POPULATION

The estimated population of Italy in 1990 was 57.4 million.

CURRENCY AND EXCHANGE CONTROLS

Currency

The unit of currency is the Italian lira (L). In April 1991, L 1261.00 was equivalent to U.S. $1.

Exchange Controls

Since the beginning of 1989, all economic and financial transactions with Italy have been substantially liberalized. Now, nonresidents can freely reexport previously imported foreign currency or lire, and can also export available funds deposited in banks appointed as agents of the Bank of Italy.

No direct exchange control restrictions are provided for residents. They are free to carry out any kind of transaction in foreign currency. However, some indirect controls have been introduced, primarily for tax purposes. They are designed to monitor transactions carried out by residents.

ESTABLISHING A BUSINESS

Authorization

In general, there are no broad-scale government restrictions on foreign investment in Italy, other than the limited exchange controls noted earlier. However, certain controls and restrictions do apply to industries designated as affecting the national security or the economy. These include banking, insurance, and communications.

Types of Businesses

Table 13.1 summarizes the types of businesses Italians use. A foreign corporation may establish a subsidiary, a branch, or a representative office to do business in Italy.

A subsidiary, which is a resident enterprise, can be either of the following:

- Societa per Azioni (SpA), a limited company; or
- Societa a responsibilita limitata (Srl), a private limited liability company.

An SpA has a minimum share capital of L 200 million, whereas an Srl has a minimum of L 20 million.

Both types of companies are taxed in the same manner. Also, with both type of companies, a registration tax is collected, which is based on initial net worth of the company. The tax rate varies from 1 percent to 15 percent, according to the kind of goods contributed to the company's capital.

Both the SpA and the Srl have to be registered with the district court and the local Chamber of Commerce. Also, their incorporation documents are published, and annual financial statements have to be filed with the district court.

Setting up a branch office is subject to many of the same formalities that apply to establishing a corporate subsidiary. Also, branch taxation and accounting requirements do not substantially differ from those applicable to subsidiaries.

Business may also be conducted through a partnership (unlimited liability). Partnerships are subject to the local income tax (ILOR), whereas their earned income (even if not distributed) is attributed to the individual partners, which affects the partnerships' personal tax liabilities.

Local Participation Requirements

There are no general limitations as to the nationality of directors or shareholders.

Table 13.1
Italian Business Designations and Abbreviations

Abbreviation	Name	Description
SAp A	Societa in Accomandita per Azioni	Italian partnership limited by shares
SpA	Societa per Azioni	Italian limited company
Srl	Societa a responsibilita limitata	Italian private limited liability company

Employee Participation

There are no requirements for employee participation in the management of a company.

Investment Incentives

A wide range of tax incentives are provided for investments in Southern Italy. The National Income Tax (IRPEG) is reduced to zero for companies established in Italy (even outside the Mezzogiorno) that have as their purpose setting up new productive ventures within the Mezzogiorno.

This tax abatement lasts 10 years from the time the company is established. It is also granted a 10-year tax abatement for the local income tax (ILOR) purposes to the extent that taxable income is derived from enterprises located in the Mezzogiorno.

Profits of an Italian company not located in the Mezzogiorno are also exempt from ILOR if directly reinvested in the construction or expansion of industrial plants in the Mezzogiorno.

In addition, Italy has two funds that offer cash grants and subsidized loans, respectively, for approved projects: the Research and Development Fund and the Technological Innovation Revolving Fund. The funds can be used for the project itself or to defray the costs of related technology transfer, technical assistance, and consulting studies.

Labor Laws

All foreigners must get a temporary residence permit from the Police Department. A work permit, followed by a "working residence" permit, must then be obtained from the Ministry of Labor and the Ministry of the Interior, respectively. However, EC residents do not need to get a working residence permit.

BUSINESS TAXATION

Tax Year

A corporation's tax year is identical to the accounting year that is, in general, the calendar year.

Scope

A corporation is resident in Italy in the following cases:

- A corporation incorporated in Italy is always resident.
- A corporation incorporated outside Italy can be nonetheless considered resident if it is actually managed in Italy or its principal activity is performed in Italy.

Both resident and nonresident corporations are subject to IRPEG and to ILOR. Resident corporations are subject to national income tax on their worldwide income; nonresident corporations are taxed only on income derived from Italy. Local income tax is, on the contrary, always levied only on Italian sources of income.

Rates

The IRPEG's rate is 36 percent. The ILOR's rate is 16.2 percent. Because 75 percent of the ILOR is deducted when computing IRPEG, the total tax rate is 47.826.

Taxable income is computed from profits as determined from the corporation's profit and loss account, adjusted for tax purposes. There is no distinction between distributed and undistributed profits, with one exception: exempt profits are subject to a compensatory tax of 36 percent only when distributed.

Key Elements of Taxable Income

Capital gains are included in operating income and are usually taxable in the period in which they are realized. However, at the taxpayer's option, they may be taxed in equal annual installments over a period not to exceed five years.

Inventory is generally valued at the lower of cost or normal value during the last three months of the tax year. Cost is calculated on the LIFO basis. Alternative methods to LIFO are allowable, provided the cost value exceeds LIFO.

Dividends are exempt for ILOR purposes. However, for IRPEG purposes, a full-imputation system applies when both the distributing and the receiving companies are residents of Italy. That results in the receiving company receiving a tax credit equal to 9/16 of the dividends received.

Losses

For IRPEG purposes, operating losses may be carried forward for a maximum of five years.

However, no carryback is allowed. No loss deduction applies for ILOR purposes.

Depreciation

Both tangible and intangible assets can be depreciated. Depreciation is claimed on a straight-line basis, with rates dependent on the nature of the assets as well as the industry in which the assets are used. For the first three years of use, accelerated depreciation of up to two times the basic rates may be applicable.

Undistributed Profits

There are no provisions relating to undistributed profits. However, exempt profits are subject to a compensatory tax of 36 percent when they are distributed.

Foreign Income of Resident Companies

Foreign income is subject to the IRPEG but is exempt from the ILOR. Relief from potential double taxation is available either under the provisions of an applicable tax treaty or by way of a foreign tax credit, up to the Italian tax, on the relevant income.

When an Italian company owns at least 10 percent of a foreign company, only 40 percent of the dividends received from that company are taxable.

Taxation of Foreign Executives Living in Italy

A resident of a treaty country is normally exempt from Italian taxes on remuneration from an employer in the treaty country, provided that he or she spends less than 183 days in Italy (90 days in the case of residents of The Netherlands).

If there is no specific treaty provision dealing with temporary visitors, their earnings are normally taxed in the country in which the services are performed.

Other Taxes

VALUE ADDED TAX (VAT)

A tax on added value (IVA) is imposed at a standard rate of 19 percent. Some household items are taxed at the lower rates of 4 percent and 9 percent. In addition, luxury products such as jewelry and cars with engines of over 2000 cc are taxable at 38 percent.

STAMP DUTY

A nominal stamp duty is imposed on certain documents, such as receipts, statements of account, checks, and notes receivable.

REGISTRATION TAX

A registration tax is imposed on certain transactions not subject to IVA. The most important of these are sales of real property (10 percent) and leases of real property (2 percent).

Withholding Taxes

Withholding taxes apply to employee pay (for IRPEG and social security) as well as to dividends, royalties, and interest. The rates of withholding taxes for key countries are listed in Table 13.2.

Tax Treaties

Italy has tax treaties with the following:

* All of the countries of the EC;

* Numerous Western and Eastern European countries, including Austria, Cyprus, Czechoslovakia, Finland, Hungary, Malta, Norway, Rumania, Sweden, Switzerland, and Yugoslavia; and

* Argentina, Australia, Brazil, Canada, China, Egypt, India, Israel, Ivory Coast, Japan, Kenya, Malaysia, New Zealand, Morocco, Singapore, Tanzania, Thailand, Trinidad and Tobago, Tunisia, United States, and Zambia.

Table 13.2
Effective Rates for Withholding Taxes for Key Countries

Payee Resident in	Dividends (%)	Interest (%)
Belgium	15	15
Denmark	15	15
France	15	15
Germany	32.4	0 [d]
Greece	25 [g]	10
Ireland	15	10
Italy	10	[f]
Japan	15 [b]	10
Luxembourg	15 [d]	10 [d]
The Netherlands	32.4 [a]	[h]
Portugal	15	15
Spain	15	12
United Kingdom	15 [c]	[d]
United States	15 [e]	15

Notes:

[a] 0%, if the recipient owns 75% of the payer.

[b] 10%, if the recipient owns 25% of the payer.

[c] 5%, if the recipient owns 51% of the payer.

[d] Special provisions apply.

[e] 5%, if the recipient owns 51% of the payer for 12 months; 10%, if the recipient owns 10% of the payer for 12 months.

[f] 30%, 15%, or 12.5%. Special provisions apply.

[g] When the Italy-Greece tax treaty comes into force, it will provide for a withholding tax on dividends equal to 15%.

[h] Domestic legislation applies.

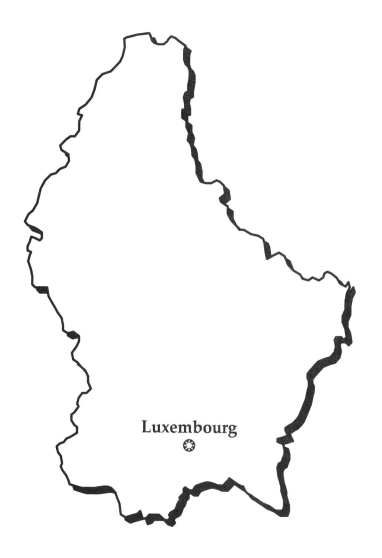

Luxembourg

14

Luxembourg

SECTIONS IN THIS CHAPTER

Background

Population

Currency and Exchange Controls

Establishing a Business

Business Taxation

ASSISTANCE

Chapter 20 lists resources that can provide macroeconomic, population, and census-type data on the EC and on most of its member states. For additional help on using the resources in this chapter, refer to the Introduction to Part II.

BACKGROUND

The Grand Duchy of Luxembourg, encompassing 2600 square kilometers, is an independent state, in which the Grand Duke Jean serves as head of state. The Grand Duke succeeded to the throne in 1964 and is married to the Princess Josephine-Charlotte of Belgium.

Executive power in Luxembourg is in the hands of the Grand Duke and a cabinet of 12 ministers. The legislative power is exercised by a 60-member Parliament (Chamber of Deputies), which is elected by all citizens over the age of 18.

Prior to their enactment, all bills are submitted for advice to the 21-member Council of State, appointed by the sovereign.

Luxembourg is associated with Belgium and The Netherlands in the Benelux Economic Union. In addition, special economic and financial ties link Luxembourg with Belgium.

Luxemburgish is the national language and is used by the majority of the population. The main languages used for administrative purposes are French and German. However, English is also widely spoken, especially in business circles.

The iron and steel industry was the basis of the Luxembourg economy until the early 1970s. It still represents an important element of the national economy. In addition, about 5 percent of the population is employed in the agricultural sector, including the wine production and dairy industries.

Since 1975, the financial and governmental service sectors have grown rapidly. Today, Luxembourg is home to a number of major EC organizations, to almost 200 international banking institutions, and to hundreds of investment funds. Also, the government is seeking to stimulate activity with respect to the telecommunications and broadcasting industries.

POPULATION

The population of Luxembourg is approximately 372,000, of which about 30 percent are foreigners. Luxembourg has a labor force of about 170,000.

CURRENCY AND EXCHANGE CONTROLS

Currency

The unit of currency is the Luxembourg franc (LUF), which is at par with the Belgian franc. As of April 1991, LUF 33.78 was equivalent to U.S. $1.

Exchange Controls

There is virtually no exchange control in Luxembourg. The Belgium/Luxembourg Exchange Control Institute, which previously controlled some transactions, now exists for statistical purposes only.

ESTABLISHING A BUSINESS

Authorization

There are no particular limitations on establishing a business, except for specific industries and activities, such as banking and financial services. There are also no restrictions on foreign investors and no limits regarding their investments.

A company seeking to do business in Luxembourg may have to obtain a business license, depending on the type of business. The license is issued based on the professional skills and qualifications needed for the particular line of business.

If a branch is set up in Luxembourg, this must also be licensed and registered.

Types of Businesses

Table 14.1 summarizes the types of businesses Luxembourgers use.

The most common forms for business operations are S.a.r.l.s, S.A.s, and branch operations. Branches enjoy the same legal rights and obligations as corporations.

For most types of companies, the articles of incorporation have to be executed by a notary.

After the incorporation, the articles and the names of the directors as well as the statutory auditors must be filed with the district court and published in the official journal (Memorial). The same filing and publication requirements apply to all subsequent changes.

A capital contribution duty of 1 percent of the subscribed capital is due on incorporation and on all subsequent increases in capital.

Local Participation Requirements

There are no local participation requirements in Luxembourg.

Employee Participation

Companies with more than 15 employees must have employee delegates. These delegates must meet regularly with the company's management.

Investment Incentives

The grant of many tax and other incentives is often a matter of negotiation between the government and the company. In granting these benefits, the government requires that the business project meet the following standards:

- Sound management;
- Viability of project economics;

- Contribution to the growth or to the structural improvement of the economy; and
- Provision for better geographical distribution of economic activity.

TAX INCENTIVES

Twenty-five percent of a corporation's taxable income can be exempted from tax for the first eight years of operations.

An investment tax credit of 12 percent may be granted for additional investments in depreciable assets other than land and buildings. A further credit of 2 percent to 6 percent is allowed in respect of certain new investment in tangible assets, other than buildings and motor vehicles. These credits are deductible from corporate income tax. Unused credits may be carried forward to the following four years.

OTHER INCENTIVES

A National Investment Credit Bank has been established by the government to operate as a public banking institution. It provides public funds for economic development. Medium- and long-term loans can be obtained for investment programs. The National Investment Credit Bank may, under certain conditions, contribute part of the capital on the creation of a company or participate in a capital increase.

With specific arrangement with the government, other investment incentives may be also obtained, covering part of the costs incurred in connection with training of an employer's work force. Export credits are also available for the export of equipment and goods produced in Luxembourg. Also, eligible research and development projects can qualify for grants of up to 50 percent of the project's costs.

Financial incentives are available for land acquisition for industrial sites. Specifically, the government may acquire, develop, and make available

Table 14.1
Luxembourg Business Designations and Abbreviations

Abbreviation	Name	Description
S.A.	Societe anonyme	Luxembourg joint stock company
S.a.r.l.	Societe a responsabilite limitee	Luxembourg limited liability company
SC	Societe cooperative	Luxembourg cooperative society
S.E.C.A.	Societe en commandite par actions	Luxembourg partnership limited by shares
SECS	Societe en commandite simple	Luxembourg limited partnership
S.E.N.C.	Societe en nom collectif	Luxembourg general partnership

industrial land to manufacturing companies. The location and amount of the land is determined by mutual agreement between the government and the company. The government can also undertake the construction of industrial buildings, which it can sell or lease. The government can also contribute to the financing of the building of industrial or business premises.

Labor Laws

EC nationals working in Luxembourg are automatically entitled to a residence permit. They do not need a work permit.

Non-EC residents must obtain a work permit before applying for a residence permit.

BUSINESS TAXATION

Tax Year

The tax year is usually the same as the calendar year. However, a business can seek approval from the Revenue to use a different tax year.

Scope

A company is considered to be a resident of Luxembourg if any of the following is in Luxembourg:

- Its statutory domicile;
- Its principal establishment; and
- Its management.

The corporate income tax applies to the worldwide income of resident companies and to the Luxembourg source income of nonresident companies.

Taxable profits are based on the profits disclosed in the annual accounts approved by the shareholders, adjusted for tax purposes.

In addition, a municipal business tax is levied by the Revenue Service on behalf of Luxembourg's communes. This is partially based on trade income and partially based on trade capital. This business tax is imposed on all businesses situated in Luxembourg, regardless of their legal form of ownership.

Rates

The corporate income tax rate on both resident and nonresident corporations is 33 percent, plus a 1 percent surcharge for unemployment compensation. In addition, all business activities are subject to the municipal business tax that is set at 9.09 percent. Allowing for the deductibility of the municipal business tax, this creates a total effective rate of 39.39 percent.

Key Elements of Taxable Income

Capital gains are taxed as ordinary income. However, the tax on gains from certain fixed assets, such as real estate and securities, that have been held for at least five years, may be deferred. This is accomplished by a reinvestment in business assets within the following years.

Capital gains arising from the disposal of a participation are tax exempt if:

- The parent company is a corporation resident in Luxembourg and is subject to corporate income taxes.
- The subsidiary is a resident, fully taxable corporation, or a nonresident corporation subject to an income tax comparable to the Luxembourg corporate income tax (that is, subject to corporate income tax of at least 15 percent).
- The parent company holds at least 25 percent of the capital of the subsidiary or the cost of the participation must be at least LUF 250 million.
- The investment is held for a period of at least 12 months as of the beginning of the year it is sold.

Dividends received from a Luxembourg corporation are exempt if the shareholder is a corporation and has at least 10 percent of the company (or LUF 50 million in value) and the stock has been owned for 12 months before the dividend is received.

Inventories are valued at the lower of cost or market value. FIFO and LIFO methods may be used if appropriate.

Losses

Losses may be carried forward for an unlimited period but may not be carried back.

Depreciation

The use of the straight-line method of depreciation is customary. The following are typical rates:

- 2 to 4 percent for buildings;
- 10 percent for office equipment; and
- 20 percent for machinery.

The declining-balance method, up to 30 percent, is available except for buildings and intangible assets.

Undistributed Profits

There are no requirements relating to undistributed profits.

Foreign Income of Resident Companies

Unless exempted by treaty, foreign income is fully taxable to domestic corporations. However, a credit may be claimed for foreign taxes paid, but that credit is limited to the amount of Luxembourg tax on the foreign income. Excess foreign tax that does not qualify for tax credit can be deducted from the corporation's taxable income.

Other Taxes

VALUE ADDED TAX (VAT)
VAT is levied on most transactions with respect to both goods and services. The basic rates range from 6 percent to 12 percent, which are among the lowest in the EC.

NET WORTH TAX
Luxembourg imposes an annual tax on net worth. This is imposed on corporations, individuals, nonresidents, and branches of businesses. For nonresidents and branches of businesses, the tax is based only on the assets owned in Luxembourg.

SUBSCRIPTION TAX
Luxembourg holding companies and investment funds are subject to an annual subscription tax on paid-up share capital. The rates applicable to this are 0.2 percent for holding companies and 0.06 percent for investment funds.

Withholding Taxes

Withholdings apply to dividends and certain interest and royalty payments, but not to holding company dividends. Dividends paid from a Luxembourg corporation to another Luxembourg corporation are exempt from withholding tax if:

- The parent company is a resident, fully taxable corporation.

- The subsidiary is a resident, fully taxable corporation or a nonresident corporation subject in its home country to an income tax similar to the Luxembourg corporate income tax.

- The parent company holds at least 10 percent of the capital of the subsidiary or the cost of the investment is at least LUF 50 million.

- The investment is held without interruption for a period of at least 12 months before the year-end closing.

The rates of withholding taxes for key countries are listed in Table 14.2.

Tax Treaties

Luxembourg has tax treaties with the following:

- All of the countries of the EC, except Greece and Portugal;

- Western European countries, including Austria, Finland, Norway, and Sweden; and

- Brazil, Canada, Hungary, Morocco, South Korea, and the United States.

Table 14.2
Effective Rates for Withholding Taxes for Key Countries

Payee Resident in	Dividends (%)	Interest (%)
Austria	15 [a]	0
Belgium	15 [c,g]	0
Denmark	15 [a,g]	0
France	15 [a,g]	0
Germany	15 [c,g]	0
Ireland	15 [a,g]	0
Italy	15 [e,g]	0
Luxembourg	15 [f]	0
The Netherlands	15 [d,g]	0
Spain	15 [a,g]	0
United Kingdom	15 [a,g]	0
United States	7.5 [b]	0

Notes:

[a] 5% if payee owns 25% or more of payer.

[b] Special provisions apply, reducing the rate to 5%.

[c] 10% if payee owns 25% or more of payer.

[d] 2.5% if payee owns 25% or more of payer.

[e] No reduced rate.

[f] 0% if payee owns 10% or more of payer.

[g] Dividend payments to a parent company in another EC country will be exempt from Luxembourg withholding tax if the parent holds at least 25 percent of the Luxembourg subsidiary and the relevant holding was held without interruption for at least two years at the date the dividend is paid.

Amsterdam

15

The Netherlands

SECTIONS IN THIS CHAPTER

ASSISTANCE

Chapter 20 lists resources that can provide macroeconomic, population, and census-type data on the EC and on most of its member states. For additional help on using the resources in this chapter, refer to the Introduction to Part II.

BACKGROUND

The Netherlands has a land area of 41,800 square kilometers. About 40 percent of the country is below sea level and is protected by dikes.

The Netherlands is a constitutional monarchy, whose reigning sovereign is Queen Beatrix. The basis of the government is a democratic parliamentary system based on a written constitution that provides safeguards for individual liberties.

Legislative power is exercised by the Parliament and the Cabinet. The First Chamber of the Parliament consists of 75 members, elected for six-year terms by the 12 provincial legislatures.

The Second Chamber consists of 150 members, who are elected for four-year terms by all citizens 18 years of age or older. Votes are generally cast for parties, not individual candidates.

Legislation can be introduced or amended only in the Second Chamber; the First Chamber has the right to approve or reject proposed bills.

Executive power is exercised by the prime minister and a cabinet, consisting of the heads of the ministries. Cabinet members are appointed by the queen, based on their political support. The ministers are responsible to Parliament and may speak in both its chambers. Ministers may not be members of either chamber.

Amsterdam is the capital and principal financial, commercial, and cultural center. Rotterdam, with a slightly smaller population, is the world's lead-ing port and an important trading center, particularly for commodities. The city of Gravenhagen (The Hague) is the seat of government. The business community is widespread across the country.

Dutch is the official language. English is widely spoken and most business houses correspond in English.

The Netherlands has traditionally earned a living from international trading and shipping. Agricultural exports still remain important. However, in the last 35 years, industrialization has been rapid and widespread. As a result, earnings from overseas trading and shipping have been overtaken by exports of industrial goods and natural gas, and by trade in petrochemicals. Also, the government has been involved in a program to increase efficiency in the economy, including the sale of publicly held stock in many large industrial and financial corporations.

The Netherlands has a highly developed economy, notable for its interdependence with those of other countries as well as its degree of foreign participation through investment.

POPULATION

The Netherlands is one of the most densely populated countries in the world. The population in 1990 was estimated to be 15 million, a density of nearly 359 per square kilometer. Amsterdam has a population of about 700,000 people, and Rotterdam is slightly smaller.

CURRENCY AND EXCHANGE CONTROLS

Currency

The unit of currency is the Dutch florin (also known as the Dutch guilder), Dfl. As of April 1991, Dfl. 1.91 was equivalent to U.S. $1.

Exchange Controls

The Netherlands has moderate exchange control regulations. Approval is necessary only for a limited number of financial transactions between residents and nonresidents. For international payments or receipts in excess of Dfl. 25,000 (or the equivalent in foreign currency), special foreign exchange forms must be completed. These are provided by De Nederlandse Bank (The Central Bank of the Netherlands), and are required for statistical purposes.

Establishing a Business

Authorization

Every business enterprise has to be registered with the trade register of the Chamber of Commerce within one week after its incorporation. Registration with the tax and social security authorities is also necessary.

If an NV or BV is used, a request for incorporation must be filed with the Ministry of Justice, giving specified information, such as the names of the directors and shareholders.

Types of Businesses

Table 15.1 summarizes the types of busines the Dutch use. Various forms of business enterprises are allowed under Dutch law.

The legal and administrative requirements for the incorporation and control of an NV or BV are very similar. However, the BV does not have to disclose as much financial information as does the NV; also, the transferability of its shares is restricted.

The minimum share capital for an NV is Dfl. 100,000 and for a BV, Dfl. 40,000. The minimum type of representation is a branch office (permanent establishment).

Local Participation Requirements

There are no local participation requirements in The Netherlands.

Table 15.1
Dutch Business Designations and Abbreviations

Abbreviation	Name	Description
BV	Besloten Vennootschap	Netherlands private limited company
CV	Commanditaire Vennootschap	Netherlands partnership
NV	Naamloze Vennootschap	Netherlands limited company
VOF	Vennootschap onder Firma	Netherlands partnership

Employee Participation

A company with 35 or more employees must establish a works council. Depending on the type of company action, the council may have a right to receive information from the company, to review the action, or even to approve it.

Investment Incentives

As of January 1, 1990, the Netherlands created an investment grant for small-scale investment in fixed assets. This is granted as a deduction from taxable income on a sliding scale. Qualifying investments include those in buildings and equipment.

A variety of other allowances and grants are available for the training of employees, transport of employees, research and development activities, and investments made in antipollution and energy-saving areas. The allowances and grants include the following: Innovation Stimulation Scheme (INSTIR) that provides subsidies for research and development-related wages to small and medium-sized information technology businesses, and the Technical Development Loans (TOK), which are available to smaller companies for their development costs of new products, processes, or services.

These are all provided through the Ministry of Economic Affairs. They are paid out and are not adjustments to tax liability. In fact, they are either taxable or lower the depreciation basis of the company.

Labor Laws

A foreigner must register with the police and with the municipality in which he or she is residing. Foreigners should also apply for a residence permit if they intend to stay more than three months.

EC residents do not have to apply for work permits. However, an employer must apply for work permits for any non-EC employee. Permits for skilled workers are freely granted.

Business Taxation

Tax Year

In general, the tax year is the calendar year. However, in its articles of incorporation, a company may elect a book year differing from the calendar year.

Scope

Those companies that are either incorporated in The Netherlands or have their central management in The Netherlands are considered to be resident companies. Resident companies are taxed on their worldwide taxable income, which is defined as the book profits as disclosed in the annual accounts, adjusted for tax purposes.

Nonresident companies are, in general, taxed only on any Dutch source income earned through a Dutch permanent establishment.

Rates

The present corporate income tax rate has two steps:

- The first Dfl. 250,000 of net profits are taxed at 40 percent.
- The balance of corporate income will be taxed at 35 percent.

Key Elements of Taxable Income

Capital gains are generally taxed as ordinary income, with the exception of capital gains on the sale of shares in subsidiaries and those on certain portfolio investments (see Participation Exemption).

Gains on certain assets can be deferred if the proceeds are reinvested in similar assets and certain other conditions are met. First, the gain is credited to a replacement reserve. When the new asset is purchased within five years after setting up the reserve, the gain is deducted from the acquisition price of the new asset, which results in a lower annual depreciation.

Dividend income is subject to Dutch corporate income taxation unless the Participation Exemption (noted later in the chapter) is applicable. However, the Dutch dividend withholding tax may be credited by a Dutch company against its overall Dutch corporate income tax liability in cases where the dividend income is subject to Dutch tax.

Participation Exemption

Dividend income and capital gains from an investment in a domestic or foreign subsidiary can be transferred free of Dutch corporate income tax by a Dutch (holding) company if the Dutch company is eligible for the Participation Exemption.

The Participation Exemption applies if the Dutch company owns at least 5 percent of the shares of the subsidiary.

If the investment is in a foreign subsidiary, in addition the foreign subsidiary should be subject to an income tax similar to Dutch corporate income tax. Also, the investment may not be a portfolio investment or be held as inventory. The former means that the foreign subsidiary should be involved in an active trade or business, and the latter refers to dormant companies used for sales.

If the Participation Exemption applies, losses on investments in subsidiaries are not tax deductible, except for liquidation losses. However, liquidation losses are only deductible if no tax relief is granted with respect to the liquidation.

Foreign withholding taxes on dividends from the foreign investment cannot be credited against Dutch corporate income tax if the Participation Exemption applies. Also, no Dutch withholding tax is levied on dividend distributions by a domestic investment to its Dutch parent company if the exemption applies.

Losses

Losses can be carried back to offset taxable income of the previous three years and carried forward for eight years. Losses incurred in the first six years of a company's operations can be carried forward for an indefinite period of time.

Depreciation

Assets with limited useful lives, whether tangible or intangible, may be depreciated. Several methods, including straight-line and declining-balance depreciation, may be used.

The average depreciation rates on a straight-line basis are as follows:

- Buildings   2.5%– 4%   (25–40 yrs)
- Machinery and
  equipment   10%–20%   (5–10 yrs)
- Office furniture   20%–33.33%   (3–5 yrs)
- Goodwill   20%   (5 yrs)

No depreciation is available on land.

Undistributed Profits

For operating companies, there are no provisions related to undistributed profits in The Netherlands. However, individual Dutch shareholders of a foreign investment company may be taxed on the deemed investment income from the company.

Foreign Income of Resident Companies

Resident companies are taxed on their worldwide income, although dividend income is free of Dutch corporate tax if the Participation Exemption applies.

For Dutch resident companies, double taxation is usually avoided by the application of a double tax treaty between The Netherlands and the foreign taxing country. In the absence of a double tax treaty, the Dutch unilateral rules for the avoidance of double taxation may apply.

In either case, a credit for foreign taxes on income is given in the proportion that the foreign income bears to total income, except for foreign withholding taxes. These can be offset as a credit against the Dutch tax liability on the worldwide income if certain conditions are met.

Other Taxes

Value Added Tax (VAT)

Value added tax is imposed on the delivery or importation of goods and on the performance of services within The Netherlands. Tax is due on the total amount charged, excluding the tax itself. A general rate of 18.5 percent is imposed on most transactions, with a lower rate, 6 percent, charged on goods classified as basic necessities. A special zero rate applies to exports and related transactions.

Registration Duty

A registration duty of 6 percent of the sales price is payable on the transfer of real property, unless the transaction is subject to VAT.

A tax of 1 percent is due on the contribution of capital (or paid-in surplus) to Dutch companies. There is an exemption for certain reorganizations and mergers.

Withholding Taxes

Withholdings arise on dividends, but in The Netherlands there is no interest (except on profit-shar-

ing bonds) or royalty withholding tax. The rates of withholding taxes for key countries are listed in Table 15.2.

Tax Treaties

The Netherlands has tax treaties with the following:

- All of the countries of the EC, except Portugal;

- Western and Eastern European countries, including Austria, Czechoslovakia, Finland, Hungary, Malta, Norway, Poland, Rumania, Sweden, Switzerland, U.S.S.R., Yugoslavia; and

- Australia, Canada, China, India, Indonesia, Israel, Japan, South Korea, Malaysia, Malawi, Morocco, Netherlands Antilles, New Zealand, Pakistan, Philippines, Singapore, South Africa, Sri Lanka, Suriname, Thailand, Turkey, United States, Zambia, and Zimbabwe.

Table 15.2
Effective Rates for Withholding Taxes for Key Countries

Payee Resident in	Dividends (%)	Interest on Profit-Sharing Bonds (%)
Belgium	15 [c,d]	10
Denmark	15 [a]	
France	15 [d]	10
Germany	15 [c,e]	15 [c]
Ireland	15 [a]	
Italy	Nil [h]	
Japan	15 [d]	15 [d]
Luxembourg	15 [f]	15 [f]
The Netherlands	25 [g]	25 [g]
Spain	15 [b,c]	15 [b,c]
United Kingdom	15 [c,d]	15 [c,d]
United States	15 [c,d]	15 [c,d]

Notes:

[a] Nil where payee owns 25% or more of payer.

[b] 5% where payee owns 50% or more of payer.

[c] Special conditions apply.

[d] 5% where payee owns 25% or more of payer.

[e] 10% where payee owns 25% or more of payer.

[f] 2.5% where payee owns 25% or more of payer (excluding qualifying holding companies).

[g] 0% where payee owns 5% or more of payer.

[h] A new tax treaty may enter into force in 1991, resulting in: 5% where the payee owns 50% or more of the payer; 10% if the payee owns 10% or more of the payer; and 15% in all other cases.

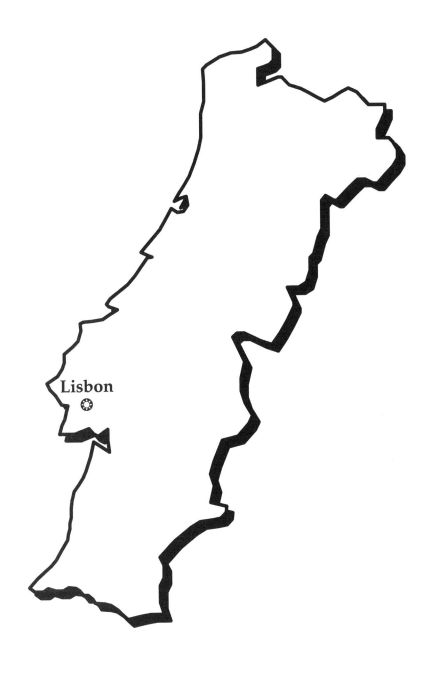

Lisbon

16

Portugal

SECTIONS
IN THIS CHAPTER

Background

Population

Currency and Exchange Controls

Establishing a Business

Business Taxation

ASSISTANCE

Chapter 20 lists resources that can provide macroeconomic, population, and census-type data on the EC and on most of its member states. For additional help on using the resources in this chapter, refer to the Introduction to Part II.

BACKGROUND

Portugal comprises 88,500 square kilometers on the mainland of Europe, plus the islands of Madeira (797 square kilometers) and the Azores (2344 square kilometers) in the Atlantic Ocean. The country is a republic, with a president as head of state and a prime minister as head of government.

The main language is Portuguese.

Portugal is an industrialized country, with its service sector the major contributor to GDP, followed by industry. The public sector has also played a substantial role in the Portuguese economy due to the nationalization of important branches of the economy in the past. However, since 1989, a process of reprivatization has been in effect, gradually reversing this trend.

Portugal's principal trading partners are the other countries of the EC, Spain in particular, as well as the United States. Trade with former colonies in Africa is also considerable.

Its major exports are textiles, footwear, clothing, primary products (canned fish, tomatoes, wine, wood, and cork), machinery, and chemicals. Portugal's major imports are grain and other food products, machinery and transportation equipment, oil, chemicals, and metal products.

POPULATION

The population is about 9.795 million. The largest cities in Portugal are Lisboa (Lisbon), the capital of the country, with a population of about 1,350,000 people, and Porto (Oporto), with about 347,000.

CURRENCY
AND EXCHANGE CONTROLS

Currency

The unit of currency is the escudo (Esc). As of April 1991, Esc 148.90 was equivalent to U.S. $1.

Exchange Controls

Portuguese exchange controls are being liberalized during the transitional period of the full entry of Portugal to the EC. That period ends on January 1, 1993. In spite of that, cross-border borrowing and investments may continue to be controlled for a further three years.

Now, all direct investments in Portugal by residents of Member States of EC are unrestricted. The acquisition of fixed assets in Portugal and the repatriation of the proceeds of sale of investments in fixed assets in Portugal was entirely liberalized on January 1, 1991. Already, foreign investment is now allowed in all economic sectors open to private enterprise.

However, foreign investment in Portugal is still subject to a system of prior declaration. In addition, large-scale investments may be subject to a separate contract with the Portuguese state.

Capital imports and exports require authorization by the Bank of Portugal, unless their value does not exceed certain limits or they involve the import of certain articles. In the latter case, a credit institution with the competence to deal with foreign exchange transactions may carry out the transfers under authority delegated to it by the Bank of Portugal.

Technical assistance contracts or other agreements that may give rise to "current invisible" transfers are subject to registration at the Bank of Portugal.

With respect to foreign trade, there are almost no restrictions. Registration of foreign trade operations is required only for statistical purposes. Only in a few specific sectors, such as the textile and the automobile industries, do some protective measures remain.

Portugal guarantees the transfer abroad of dividends and profits, after deduction of depreciation and taxes due, and after taking into account the participation of nonresidents in the company's capital. Foreign investors may also transfer abroad, after the payment of the taxes due, the proceeds of their investments.

All operations in foreign currencies must be made through a competent credit institution.

ESTABLISHING A BUSINESS

Authorization

Individuals seeking to do business in Portugal must register with the tax and social security authorities, the Commercial Registry, and the Commerce Department. They must also obtain a "certificado de comerciante."

Types of Businesses

Table 16.1 summarizes the types of businesses the Portuguese use. Business can be conducted in Portugal in any of the following ways:

- By individuals;
- By special partnerships (Sociedade em nome colectivo) or limited partnerships (Sociedade em comandita simples or Sociedade em comandita por accoes);
- By limited liability companies (Sociedades por Quotas or Lda); or
- By corporations (Sociedades Anonima or SA).

The latter two, the Lda and SA, are the most common forms used by foreign companies operating in Portugal. Although it is possible to establish a branch of a foreign company in Portugal, this form of business organization is generally regarded less favorably by the regulatory authorities.

The Lda, a limited liability company, is a convenient form of organization for small and medium-sized enterprises having few stockholders or owners, and not in need of capital from the public. The minimum capital is Esc 400,000 and the minimum number of shareholders is two. Annual accounts must be audited when, for two successive years, two of the following three limits are exceeded:

- The company's assets total or exceed Esc 180 million.
- The turnover equals or exceeds Esc 370 million.
- The average number of employees is 50 or more.

The SA, or corporation, is generally used for larger, widely held entities. The corporation must have at least five shareholders and can have an administrative structure consisting of either a board of directors and an audit board or management, general board, and statutory auditor.

The minimum capital for a corporation is Esc 5 million. The accounts of an SA must be audited each year. Annual accounts must be published in the Official Gazette and in one daily newspaper.

Local Participation Requirements

There are no local participation requirements in foreign investments.

Employee Participation

There are no requirements dealing with employee participation in company management.

Investment Incentives

TAX INCENTIVES

In 1989, Portugal adopted a wide range of tax incentives for investment. Among those of greatest interest to foreign companies is that any gain realized by a foreign company (without a presence

Table 16.1
Portuguese Business Designations and Abbreviations

Abbreviation	Name	Description
EP	Empresa Publica	State-owned Portuguese company
Lda	Sociedades por Quotas	Portuguese private limited liability company
SA	Sociedades Anonima	Portuguese limited company
CIA	Sociedade em nome colectivo	Portuguese special partnership in collective name
	Sociedade em comandita simples	Portuguese limited partnership
	Sociedade em comandita por accoes	Portuguese partnership limited by shares

in Portugal) on the sale of shares in Portuguese companies is exempt from tax.

OTHER INCENTIVES

Portugal has in place a system of regional-based aids and incentives designed to stimulate the creation of new jobs in industry and tourism, with particular emphasis on the less-developed parts of the country. These incentives are referred to in abbreviated terms in Portuguese as follows:

- PEDIP—Specific Programme for the Development of Portuguese Industry. This extensive EC-funded program is designed to assist industrial modernization in the period up to 1992.

- SIBR—System of Regional-Based Financial Incentives. This consists of cash grants up to 75 percent of the qualifying expenditure, limited to Esc 250 million per project. The incentive depends on the geographical location of the project and the number of jobs created.

- SIFIT—System of Incentives for Investment in Tourism. This is the equivalent of SIBR in the tourism sector. Cash grants up to a maximum of the lesser of Esc 220 million or 60 percent of the qualifying expenditure are available. The amount of the grant is determined by the geographical location of each project and the number of jobs created.

- SIPE—System of Incentives for the Development of Local Potential. This is aimed at stimulating local potential by investments in small and medium sized enterprises.

Other incentives are also available. They include an exemption from social security (related to the creation of new jobs for young workers), technical and financial assistance for employee training, and financial and other incentives in agriculture, craft-work, and energy sectors.

Labor Laws

Non-EC foreigners who work in Portugal for more than six months are required to obtain both a work permit and a residence permit. For shorter periods, only a work permit and special visa renewable every 60 days are required. Foreign workers' labor contracts have to be in writing and registered with the Labor Ministry.

Foreign workers from EC countries may enter Portugal on the presentation of their identity cards or their passports. They need a residence card if they plan to stay and work in Portugal for more than three months. If their stay lasts less than a year, they are required to have a temporary residence card. If they remain for a longer period or plan to establish a business in Portugal, they are obliged to obtain a residence card for EC nationals or a normal residence card, as appropriate.

BUSINESS TAXATION

Tax Year

The tax year is the calendar year ending on December 31, although branches and subsidiaries of foreign companies may request authorization to use a different tax year.

Scope

A legal entity is considered a resident of Portugal if it has its registered office or place of effective management in Portugal.

Generally, the Portuguese corporate income tax and a municipal surcharge apply to the following:

- Worldwide profits of resident companies;

- Incomes of nonresidents (such as branches of foreign companies) from Portuguese permanent establishments; and

- Specific earnings from Portuguese sources by a nonresident without a permanent establishment in Portugal.

Profit is defined in balance sheet terms, prepared according to the Official Plan of Accounts, being the difference between net equity at the beginning and end of the accounting period, adjusted in accordance with the corporate income tax code. Reasonable expenses incurred in generating profit are deductible. If the company's records are not regarded as acceptable, tax liabilities are estimated.

Rates

The current rate of corporate tax is 36 percent. The rate of tax applicable to a nonresident without a permanent establishment is, in general, 25 percent. However, for some categories of income, special reduced rates apply. The tax applicable to nonresidents is deducted at source for dividends, interest, royalties, rentals, and technical assistance fees.

The municipal surcharge is established by the municipalities, and may not exceed 10 percent of the corporate income tax.

Key Elements of Taxable Income

Ninety-five percent of the dividends distributed by resident businesses are excluded from the taxable income of the recipient where

- The recipient is a resident company that has held the investment for two years or since incorporation of the distributing entity.
- The recipient holds at least 25 percent of the capital of the distributing entity.

Taxpayers that do not meet these requirements are taxed on the full dividend received, with a credit for 20 percent of the underlying corporate tax as well as for the withholding tax on the dividend. The 1991 State budget proposed increasing this to 35 percent.

Inventories (stocks) must be valued consistently in accordance with recognized criteria. Changing the applicable criteria is allowed only with the authorization of the tax authorities. The devaluation of inventory stock is allowed when the inventories' market price on the last day of the tax year is lower than the acquisition or production cost.

Provisions for doubtful debts may be made according to the time the debt is overdue. If a debtor is declared bankrupt, a 100 percent provision is allowed.

Work in progress must be valued under the percentage of completion method, in the case of contract construction works lasting more than a year. Other long-term production processes may use other valuation criteria.

Capital gains are taxed as income, but rollover relief is available for reinvestment of sales proceeds.

Losses

Losses may be carried forward for five years, but may not be carried back.

Depreciation

Depreciation is normally allowed on a straight-line basis. The normal rates are as follows:

- Industrial buildings, 5 percent;
- Commercial buildings, 2 percent;
- Plant and machinery, 5 to 25 percent;
- Cars, 25 percent;
- Commercial vehicles, 16.66-20 percent; and
- Startup expenses, 33.3 percent.

The taxpayer may use lower rates, but if these are less than one-half the maximum rates, the difference may not be carried forward.

Foreign Income of Resident Companies

Portuguese resident companies are taxed on their worldwide revenues, including branch income and foreign dividends. Under Portuguese tax treaties, a credit for foreign taxes is generally granted up to the amount of Portuguese tax payable on the foreign income.

Other Taxes

VALUE ADDED TAX (VAT)

Portugal introduced VAT in 1986. The tax applies to a wide range of goods and services supplied in the course of business and also to the importation of goods.

The standard rate is 17 percent. There is a reduced rate of 8 percent for certain items, such as textiles and some food products, and a luxury rate of 30 percent, covering items such as liquor, perfume, furs, motorcycles, and firearms. Items exempted from VAT include basic foodstuffs, newspapers, printed matter, pharmaceutical products, and orthopedic appliances.

STAMP DUTY

Certain documents and transactions, including negotiable securities, bills of exchange, and deeds, are subject to a stamp duty.

CONVEYANCING TAX

Transfers of real estate and of shareholdings of 75 percent or more in limited liability companies holding properties attract conveyance tax (SISA) at rates of 8 percent or 10 percent.

Withholding Taxes

Withholdings apply to employee remuneration (for tax and social security) and to dividends, interest, royalties, technical assistance fees, and rental income. The rates of withholding taxes for key countries are listed in Table 16.2.

Tax Treaties

Portugal has tax treaties with the following:

- Within the EC: Belgium, Denmark, France, Ger-many, Italy, Spain, and the United Kingdom; and

- Austria, Brazil, Finland, Norway, and Switzer-land.

Table 16.2
Effective Rates for Withholding Taxes for Key Countries

Payee Resident in	Dividends (%)	Interest (%)
Belgium	15	15
Denmark	15 [a]	15
France	15	12
Germany	15	15 [b]
Italy	15	15
Portugal	25 [c]	20 [d]
Spain	15 [e]	15
United Kingdom	15 [f]	10

Notes:

[a] 10% where payee owns 25% or more of payer.

[b] 10% on interest on bank loans.

[c] When the company is an SA, there is an additional 5% Gift and Inheritance Tax withholding, which may not be reduced under any of the treaties.

[d] 25% on corporate bond interest.

[e] 10% where payee owns 50% or more of payer in the prior year.

[f] 10% where payee owns 25% or more of the voting capital of the payer. The difference in the withholding rates may be obtained only through a refund. This may take a number of years.

Madrid

17

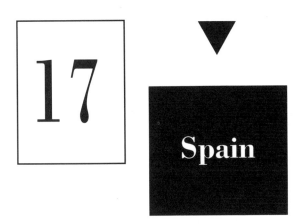

Spain

SECTIONS IN THIS CHAPTER

Background

Population

Currency and Exchange Controls

Establishing a Business

Business Taxation

ASSISTANCE

Chapter 20 lists resources that can provide macroeconomic, population, and census-type data on the EC and on most of its member states. For additional help on using the resources in this chapter, refer to the Introduction to Part II.

BACKGROUND

The kingdom of Spain occupies an area of slightly more than 500,000 square kilometers. Spanish territory also includes the Balearic Islands (in the Mediterranean), the Canary Islands (in the Atlantic off North Africa), and the provinces of Ceuta and Melilla on the Mediterranean north coast of Africa.

Spain is a parliamentary monarchy, with the King as head of state. The 1978 Constitution provides for a bicameral Parliament (Congress and Senate), which are elected for a four-year term.

Administratively, Spain is divided into 17 financially autonomous communities. These can share in the proceeds of national taxes or surcharges, or the communities can levy their own taxes.

The basic language is Castilian Spanish. Castilian Spanish is used jointly with other official languages (that is, Catalan, Basque, and Galician) in certain of the autonomous communities.

The capital and largest city of Spain is Madrid. The second largest city is Barcelona.

In recent years, there have been important changes in Spain's general economic framework. The impact of these changes has been to begin to move Spain to a place among the industrialized countries. For example, although agriculture is a very important economic sector for Spain, the relative weight of agriculture in the economy has declined, so that the leading economic sector is now servic-

es. In addition, Spain has attained an appreciable degree of industrial and commercial development. All of this has resulted in strong economic growth, averaging over 5 percent per year for the past several years.

The consequences of Spain's accession to the EC have been significant. One of the most important events is that import tariffs on goods from other EC countries are being reduced and will be finally abolished by January 1, 1993.

Spain's internal market is supplemented by the vast numbers of foreign tourists who visit Spain each year.

POPULATION

The population of Spain is approximately 39.3 million. Madrid has a population of approximately 3.1 million people. Approximately 25 percent of the Spanish population lives in cities of over 500,000 inhabitants, and slightly more than half of all Spaniards live in cities of over 50,000 inhabitants.

CURRENCY AND EXCHANGE CONTROLS

Currency

The unit of currency is the peseta (Pta.). As of April 1991, Ptas. 105.15 were equivalent to U.S. $1.

Exchange Controls

Businesses with registered offices in Spain and Spanish branches of foreign companies, regardless of their ownership, are considered as residents of Spain for exchange control purposes.

Exchange controls apply to most transactions between Spanish residents and nonresidents that involve payments abroad or receipts from abroad. However, payments abroad with respect to most types of transactions are not hampered by exchange controls. These include remittance of branch profits and the payment of dividends.

Foreign investments must be registered with the Spanish Foreign Investment Register. This also safeguards the repatriation of funds invested in Spain.

ESTABLISHING A BUSINESS

Authorization

Investments by private nonresident investors generally do not require prior governmental authorization. However, prior clearance of the projected investment by the Department of Foreign Transactions (DGTE) is required as a control measure for the following types of foreign investment, among others:

- The acquisition of more than 50 percent of the capital of Spanish companies, and the formation of branches or establishments. However, if these types of foreign investments are under Ptas. 25 million, they are normally exempted from the clearance procedures.

- The acquisition of real property by a legal entity (such as a corporation), and, in certain cases, the acquisition of real property by foreign individuals who are not resident in Spain.

- The acquisition of unlisted private-sector, fixed-interest securities (or of listed securities as described but not acquired through the stock market).

Some sectors of the economy, such as air transport, telecommunications, and defense, are subject to special rules.

Investments made by foreign governments or by official foreign sovereignty entities require special authorization by the Council of Ministers. However, the Spanish authorities have recently deregulated investments made by governments of EC countries now subject to the general regime.

Types of Businesses

Table 17.1 summarizes the types of businesses Spaniards use. A foreign investor may operate in Spain in many ways. The most common is through a subsidiary corporation, a branch, or a joint venture.

Table 17.1
Spanish Business Designations and Abbreviations

Abbreviation	Name	Description
SA	Sociedad Anonima	Corporation
SL	Sociedad de Responsabilidad Limitada	Limited liability company

---

A minimum of three shareholders (acting on their own behalf or on behalf of other persons or companies) are required for the formation of a corporation (Sociedad Anonima or SA). Spain requires a minimum capital stock of Ptas. 10 million in order to form an SA. There is no required debt-to-equity ratio.

A branch must have an assigned capital, but there is no stipulated minimum amount. The branch must have a legal representative who is empowered by the home office to administer the affairs of the branch. Other than these, the requirements for forming and operating through a Spanish branch are very similar to those for incorporating a subsidiary.

Local Participation Requirements

In general, there are no local participation requirements in Spain. However, special rules apply to foreign investments in some economic sectors that may restrict the permitted levels of foreign participation. Restrictions normally do not apply to EC countries.

Employee Participation

In general, there are no requirements dealing with employee participation in company management.

Investment Incentives

There are many legal measures in Spain to encourage investment and job creation, which generally apply equally to Spanish and to foreign-owned companies.

TAX INCENTIVES

Spain provides an exemption from tax on the proceeds of the disposal of tangible fixed assets, if such proceeds are reinvested and certain requirements are complied with.

A tax credit of 5 percent of the investment is available when a company invests in new fixed assets that are kept for at least five years.

A tax credit of 15 percent of the investment is available for certain investments, including:

- Acquisition of holdings in foreign companies and the formation of branches and subsidiaries abroad for export purposes; and

- Publicity and advertising expenditures for the development of new products or markets abroad.

Tax credits are also available for investment in research and development programs for new products or new industrial processes. The current rates are 15 percent on intangible expenses and 30 percent on assets.

All of the tax credits just described are subject to a ceiling of 25 percent of the taxes payable.

Job creation efforts qualify for a tax credit of Ptas. 500,000 for each worker-year of increase in the average labor force. The credit is increased in cases dealing with handicapped persons.

Certain tax benefits are also available for temporary joint ventures and combinations of companies, and on mergers and spin-offs.

OTHER INCENTIVES

Other incentives include subsidies for generating jobs or innovative investments, as well as reduced social security costs and hiring subsidies. There are also special incentives for investment in certain industries or certain regions of Spain. These include nonrepayable subsidies, preferential access to official credit, and relief from certain taxes.

Labor Laws

There are no restrictions on the employment of foreign nationals in Spain. However, residence and work permits must first be obtained for them. (These permits will not be necessary for EC country workers after January 1, 1993.) Foreign individuals working in Spain are subject to full social security contributions, except when exempted by a social security treaty or by EC regulations.

BUSINESS TAXATION

Tax Year

A company's taxable period is its business year, which normally—although not necessarily—coincides with the calendar year.

Scope

A corporation is either resident or nonresident in Spain. A corporation is resident if

- It is incorporated under Spanish law.
- It has its registered offices or effective management headquarters in Spanish territory.

Resident corporations are subject to tax on their worldwide income. Taxable income includes all profits from operations, income from investments not relating to the company's regular business purpose, and capital gains.

Nonresident companies are taxable on their Spanish-source gross income, as defined by Spanish law. The key factor in determining the taxability of nonresident businesses is whether they have a permanent establishment in Spain. If they have a permanent establishment in Spain, they will be taxed on the full amount of the income attributable to that establishment.

If they do not have a permanent establishment or do not use one in Spain, they are taxed on the following items of gross income:

- Income arising from services, technical assistance, loans, work, or capital provided or used in Spain;
- Income from marketable securities issued by companies resident in Spain, or by foreign companies with a permanent establishment in Spain;
- Income from property located in Spain; and
- Capital gains on the disposal of assets located in Spain.

However, the following items of income are deemed not to be obtained in Spain, and therefore they are not taxable in Spain (provided that they were not obtained through a permanent establishment):

- Interest and capital gains on movable assets obtained by individuals or companies resident in any EC member state. Exceptions are capital gains arising in connection with companies whose assets consist, either directly or indirectly, mainly of real estate located in Spain, and capital gains arising as a consequence of a transfer in which the transferor has had a holding of at least 25 percent in the capital stock or net worth of the company during the 12 months preceding the transfer.
- Interest and capital gains on government debt securities.

These exemptions (for interest and capital gains) will not be applicable if the income was obtained through a country defined as a tax haven.

Rates

The rate of income tax on resident companies is 35 percent. This rate is also applicable to the profits of branches of nonresident corporations.

Income earned in Spain by nonresident companies without a permanent Spanish establishment is taxed at the following principal rates:

- General income (dividends, interest, and so forth)—25 percent;
- Fees for management support services—14 percent; and
- Capital gains—35 percent.

An EC directive, due to be implemented by January 1, 1992, would eliminate the taxation on dividends paid by a Spanish corporation to its parent company, if the parent is resident in an EC country.

Distributions of profits by a Spanish branch to its home office are not subject to taxation in Spain. However, draft legislation is currently being debated under which a 25 percent withholding tax could be made on such distributions.

The provisions of tax treaties may reduce or even eliminate these charges.

Key Elements of Taxable Income

Capital gains are taxable as ordinary income at the standard rate of 35 percent. However, there is a tax exemption for capital gains arising on the sale of business fixed assets, if the proceeds of the sale are reinvested in other fixed assets for use in the business.

Dividends received from resident companies are taxed but receive a credit relief of 50 percent of that tax. If the payee company owns more than 25 percent of the payer company and has been such an owner during the year in which the dividend was distributed and during the preceding year, the payee may receive 100 percent tax relief.

The main tax credits available, apart from the dividend tax credit, are the investment tax credit and the job creation tax credit.

Losses

Losses can be carried forward for offset against the taxable income of the following five years. However, they cannot be carried back.

Depreciation

Depreciation is permitted on virtually all assets except land and certain types of intangible assets (such as goodwill). Depreciation qualifies as a deductible expense only if it is "effective" and is recorded in the accounts. There are official guidelines that, if complied with, relieve the company of the need to prove effectiveness.

The declining balance method of depreciation can be used for certain new assets. Companies can seek prior approval from the Spanish tax administration for higher annual rates of depreciation. Unrestricted depreciation for certain categories of companies and certain industries will apply according to their specific legislation.

Undistributed Profits

There are no minimum distribution requirements for companies or any special rates for undistributed profits.

However, the profits of "transparent" companies are imputed to the shareholders and taxed accordingly, whether the profits are distributed or not. Transparent companies are essentially closely held investment companies whose main corporate purpose is the ownership of assets.

The tax treatment of nonresident shareholders of Spanish transparent companies has been a controversial issue for many years. However, an internal regulation has clarified the tax treatment. Thus, in general, if a tax treaty applies the income imputed to the nonresident shareholder will not be taxed in Spain until a distribution takes place. The distribution of the dividend will subject it to withholding tax at the rate stated in the corresponding tax treaty. If a tax treaty is not applicable, a withholding of 25 percent will be levied on the income imputed. Subsequent distributions will not bear any taxation.

Further changes are expected in connection with tax transparency in 1992.

Foreign Income of Resident Companies

Spanish tax-resident companies are subject to taxation on their worldwide income. Subject to specific treaty provisions, the following general rules apply to prevent double taxation of foreign-source income:

- Spanish tax calculated on gross worldwide income may be reduced by the lower of the tax paid abroad or the Spanish tax that would be payable if the income had arisen in Spain.

- An amendment to the Spanish international double-taxation tax credit is under consideration. If adopted, it will change the rules after January 1, 1992.

Other Taxes

VALUE ADDED TAX (VAT)
Value added tax is the basic indirect tax levied on the sale of goods and the provision of services in Spain, including imports. The standard rate of VAT is 12 percent, which is applied to most goods and services. A reduced rate of 6 percent is applied to basic necessities such as foodstuffs, medicines, books, and printed matter. An increased rate, 33 percent, is applicable to certain luxury goods and services, such as cars and recreational vehicles, jewelry and luxury furs. Exemptions include health care, education, financial investments and insurance, exports, and new artwork transactions.

TRANSFER TAX
A transfer tax is levied on a limited number of transactions, including:

- 1 percent on corporate transactions, such as incorporation and capital increases or reductions;
- 6 percent on transfers of real estate;
- 4 percent on transfers of movable assets;
- 1 percent on certain rights in real estate; and
- 0.5 percent on certain mercantile public deeds.

If the seller is a company or an individual developer, the transfer of buildable land or the first delivery of a building will be subject to VAT.

Transfers of shares of Spanish companies are generally not subject to any indirect taxation, except when more than 50 percent of the assets of the company consist of real estate located in Spain. In that case, the transaction is considered to be a transfer of real estate, subject to a transfer tax of 6 percent.

Transfer taxes are paid by the buyer.

Withholding Taxes

Withholding taxes are applied to resident employees' pay, at rates ranging from 0 percent to 42 percent. Payments to commission agents, independent agents, and professional practitioners will be subject to a withholding tax of 15 percent, and directors' fees at 30 percent. They are also applied to dividends, interest, royalties, and rents of movable goods from Spanish sources at a 25 percent rate. These rates apply to resident individuals or corporations.

Nonresident individuals and nonresident businesses operating without a permanent establishment in Spain are subject to taxation in Spain. That tax is applied to their Spanish source gross income at a flat rate of 25 percent (35 percent on capital gain), unless a tax treaty is applicable. The rates of withholding taxes for key countries are listed in Table 17.2.

Tax Treaties

Spain has tax treaties with the following:

- Within the EC: all members except Ireland and Greece; and
- Austria, Brazil, Canada, Czechoslovakia, Finland, Hungary, Japan, Morocco, Norway, Poland, Rumania, Sweden, Switzerland, Tunisia, United States, and U.S.S.R.

Table 17.2
Effective Rates for Withholding Taxes for Key Countries

Payee resident in	Dividends [a] (%)	Interest [b] (%)
Austria	15 (10)	5
Belgium	15	15
Denmark	15 (10)	10
France	15 (10)	10
Germany	15 (10)	10
Italy	15	12
Japan	15 (10)	10
Luxembourg	15 (10)	10
The Netherlands	15 (10)	10
Portugal	15 (10)	15
United Kingdom	15 (10)	12
United States	15 (10)	10

Notes:

[a] The lower rates shown in parentheses generally apply to recipients that are corporations with substantial shareholdings in the Spanish payer company.

[b] Special provisions apply to interest on certain types of loans.

The United Kingdom

18 ▶

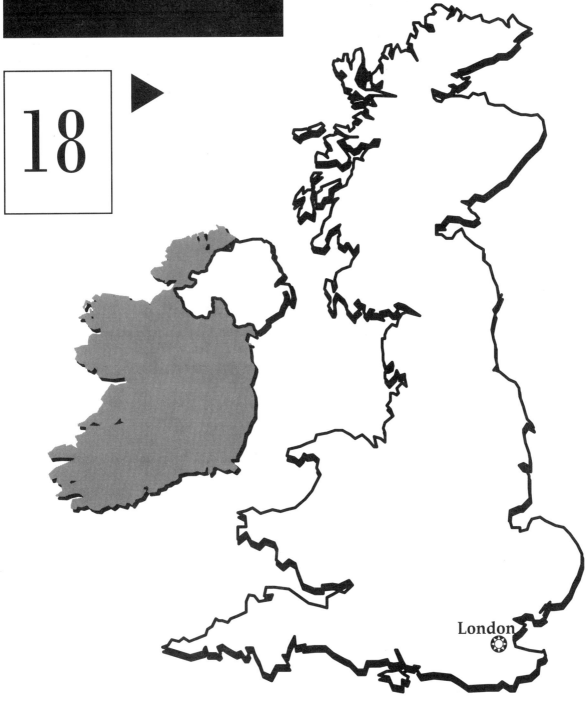

London

Sections in This Chapter

Assistance

Chapter 20 lists resources that can provide macroeconomic, population, and census-type data on the EC and on most of its member states. For additional help on using the resources in this chapter, refer to the Introduction to Part II.

Background

The United Kingdom consists of Great Britain (England, Scotland, and Wales), together with adjacent smaller islands, as well as the six counties of Northern Ireland.

The head of state is the Queen. The legislative body is Parliament, which contains two Chambers.

The House of Commons is a representative assembly consisting of 650 Members of Parliament. The members of the House of Commons are elected by universal adult suffrage. Elections for the House of Commons are due every five years, although the government may call an election before the term officially ends.

The House of Lords is the second legislative chamber. Its members are not elected, but consist of senior members of the Church of England together with hereditary and life peers.

Proposed legislation must generally be approved by both Chambers before it can become law. However, the House of Lords has limited powers, as, in the event of conflict with the House of Commons, its members can only delay legislation.

Although many links remain between the United Kingdom and the other members of the British Commonwealth, most of the preferential trading arrangements with the Commonwealth countries ceased following the United Kingdom's membership in the EC.

The United Kingdom is one of the world's leading industrial nations, with a diversified economic base. It has an important oil and gas industry, based mainly around the North Sea. The City of London, the capital, is one of the leading financial markets in the world.

Population

The population of the United Kingdom is approximately 56.9 million. London, its capital, has a population of approximately 6.7 million people. Other major centers of population are Birmingham, Glasgow, Leeds, and Manchester.

Currency and Exchange Controls

Currency

The unit of currency is the pound sterling (£). As of April 1991, £0.5719 was equivalent to U.S. $1.

Exchange Controls

The United Kingdom has no exchange controls.

Establishing a Business

Authorization

No permission is usually required to establish a business presence in the United Kingdom. However, there are specific rules for specialized industries, such as finance and defense.

Types of Businesses

Table 18.1 summarizes the two types of companies used in the U.K. A foreign corporation may establish either a subsidiary or a branch in the United Kingdom. Most foreign corporations set up a local private company (Ltd) rather than a public limited company (PLC).

In either case, no government consents are needed. In addition, no local shareholders or directors are required, nor are there minimum capital rules applicable to private companies. (However, a minimum of two shareholders is required.) Certain documents, such as the articles of incorporation, do have to be filed with local authorities.

A foreign corporation that sets up a U.K. branch must, within 30 days, register certain documents (with an English translation, if needed) and appoint a local representative.

Local Participation Requirements

There are no local participation requirements in the United Kingdom.

Employee Participation

There are no requirements dealing with employee participation in company management.

Investment Incentives

TAX INCENTIVES

Accelerated depreciation, equal to 100 percent, is available for certain types of expenditures in government-designated "enterprise zones."

OTHER INCENTIVES

Various regional incentives are available for establishing businesses in "development areas." In addition there are certain employment incentives, assistance for major projects in the national interest, and assistance for new technology.

The Department of Trade and Industry (DTI) offers most of these programs, including the following:

- Small Firms Merit Award for Research and Technology (SMART). These awards are open to small firms in the U.K. and are designed to encourage potential commercial projects that lack funding.

- The LINK Initiative. This is aimed at improving cooperation between industry and universities in the U.K. LINK can offer support, up to 50 percent of project costs, for approved high-technology projects.

- The Advanced Technology Programmes. This program offers financial support up to 50 percent of project costs in designated areas of electronics and electronics-related technology. All projects must involve at least three independent partners.

Labor Laws

EC nationals may freely enter the United Kingdom. If they produce an employer's certificate within six months of arrival, they will be granted a residence permit, valid for five years, which is renewable.

Special rules apply for certain Commonwealth citizens in respect of immigration and employment control.

Non-EC nationals who are visiting the United Kingdom for business or vacation purposes may stay six months in the United Kingdom. After that period, an extension must be obtained from the Home Office.

Where employment is to be undertaken in the United Kingdom, the U.K. employer must obtain a work permit before the prospective employee arrives. This is obtained from the Department of Employment. It is valid for the period required and is renewable, up to a maximum of four years.

Non-EC nationals wishing to undertake business on their own account must obtain permission from the British Consulate in their home country.

BUSINESS TAXATION

Tax Year

The tax year is the fiscal year ended March 31. It is not necessary for a company's year end to be coterminous with the fiscal year end.

Scope

A corporation is resident in the United Kingdom if it was incorporated in the U.K. on or after March 15, 1988, or if its central management and control is exercised from the U.K.

Resident corporations are subject to taxation on their worldwide profits, both income and capital gains. Nonresident corporations are taxed only on U.K. source profits.

Business may also be conducted through a partnership, in which case the income is taxed in the hands of the individual partners.

Table 18.1
United Kingdom Business Designations and Abbreviations

Abbreviation	Name	Description
Ltd	Limited Company	British private limited company
PLC	Public Limited Company	British public company

Rates

The rate of taxation on resident corporations and nonresident corporations, operating through a branch in the United Kingdom, is the same:

- 33 percent —Financial year commencing April 1, 1991
- 34 percent—Financial year commencing April 1, 1990
- 35 percent—Earlier years

A lower rate of 25 percent is charged if profits do not exceed £200,000. This amount is reduced proportionately by the number of associated companies.

Close investment companies (CICs), however, are not entitled to this reduced rate. A CIC is a *close company*, that is, a company that is controlled by five or fewer individuals or its directors, which exists wholly or mainly for the purpose of investment (other than in land). Holding companies of subsidiaries that are trading or land investment companies are excluded.

A company must account for an advance corporation tax (ACT) of one-third of all dividends it pays. The company can set off, subject to certain limits, the ACT paid against its corporation tax liability.

Key Elements of Taxable Income

Taxable profits are based on the profits disclosed in the statutory accounts, adjusted for tax purposes.

Costs are deductible if they were incurred wholly and exclusively for trade purposes and are not of a capital nature. Entertainment costs are nondeductible.

Capital gains, after reduction for indexation relief, are taxed in the same ways as income. Certain gains may be deferred if the proceeds are reinvested in certain assets 12 months before or 3 years after the disposal.

Capital losses can be carried forward against capital gains without time limit.

Dividends received from resident companies are exempt.

Losses

Trading losses may be carried forward without time limit against income from the same trade or may be offset against any profits of the same or previous period. (Losses incurred after April 1, 1991, may be carried back 3 years.) Losses may be offset against profits arising in group companies (at least 75 percent owned) in the same period.

Depreciation

Depreciation for tax purposes is given according to statutory rules by reference to asset classes. For machinery a 25 percent allowance, on a reducing balance basis, is applicable. New industrial buildings, on the other hand, use a 4 percent annual allowance on a straight-line basis. Scientific research can use a 100 percent allowance.

No depreciation is allowed for goodwill and commercial buildings, except those in government-designated "enterprise zones." These buildings can be 100 percent depreciated in the first year.

Undistributed Profits

There are no specific provisions relating to undistributed profits.

Foreign Income of Resident Companies

Dividends from foreign sources are taxable. However, there is a credit allowed for withholding taxes and, in many cases, the appropriate proportion of underlying overseas tax paid may be credited as well. Certain income of a tax haven subsidiary of a U.K. company can be deemed distributed to the U.K. company.

Other Taxes

VALUE ADDED TAX (VAT)

The standard rate of value added tax (VAT) is 17.5 percent (15 percent until March 1991), applied to all goods and services produced in the United Kingdom with certain exceptions. Specifically, insurance, education, finance, and items such as food, books, and transport are not normally taxed. VAT is not charged on the export of goods and services; goods and certain services imported to the U.K. also carry VAT at a 17.5 percent rate.

STAMP DUTY

A stamp duty is imposed on documents connected with the transfer of shares and securities, land, and certain other assets. The duty is normally 0.5 percent for shares and securities, and 1 percent for other assets. The duty on shares is due to be abolished by March 1992.

Withholding Taxes

Withholdings arise on employee pay (for tax and social security) and on certain interest and royalty payments. The rates of withholding taxes for key countries are listed in Table 18.2.

Tax Treaties

The United Kingdom has a comprehensive series of tax treaties with most of the major countries of the world, including the following:

- All of the members of the EC;

- Most of Western and Eastern Europe, including Austria, Cyprus, Finland, Guernsey, Hungary, Isle of Man, Jersey, Malta, Norway, Poland, Rumania, Sweden, Switzerland, U.S.S.R., and Yugoslavia; and

- Australia, Bangladesh, Barbados, Belize, Botswana, Brunei, Burma, Canada, China, Egypt, Fiji, Gambia, Ghana, Grenada, India, Indonesia, Israel, Ivory Coast, Jamaica, Japan, Kenya, Korea, Lesotho, Malawi, Malaysia, Mauritius, Morocco, Namibia, New Zealand, Pakistan, Philippines, St. Christopher (St Kitts) and Nevis, Sierra Leone, Singapore, Solomon Islands, South Africa, Sri Lanka, Sudan, Swaziland, Thailand, Trinidad and Tobago, Tunisia, Turkey, Uganda, United States, Zambia, and Zimbabwe.

Table 18.2
Effective Rates for Withholding Taxes for Key Countries

Payee resident in	Dividends (%)	Interest (%)
Belgium	b,c	15
Denmark	a,c	0
France	a	0
Germany	0	0
Ireland	a	0
Italy	a,c	10 [d]
Japan	a	10
Luxembourg	a,c	0
The Netherlands	a,c	0
Portugal		10
Spain	a	12
United Kingdom		25
United States	a,c	

Notes:

[a] If payee is a company owning under 10% of payer, or is an individual, dividend is increased by the ACT less 15% on revised gross income.

[b] If the payee owns under 10% of the voting power of the payer or is an individual, the dividend is increased by ACT, less 20% on the revised gross income.

[c] If corporate payee owns 10% or more of payer, dividend is increased by half of ACT less 5% on revised gross income.

[d] 0% rate applies if the interest is paid in connection with the sale on credit of industrial, commercial, or scientific equipment or in connection with the sale on credit of goods delivered by one enterprise to another enterprise. Additionally, no withholding is due if the payer of the interest is the government or a local authority or if the interest is paid on a loan made, guaranteed, or insured by the Export Credits Insurance Company (Italy) or by the United Kingdom Export Credits Guarantee Department.

PART III

Sources on EC

1992 by Topic

INTRODUCTION

This part of the sourcebook provides sources of information on the Single Market Program, arranged by broad business topic. The part comprises seven chapters, each covering a broad range of related topics. The topics, in chapter (alphabetical) order are

- Tracking the Progress of the Single Market
- EC-Wide Macroeconomic, Population, and Census-Type Data

- Economic and Business Development and Assistance
- Employment and Labor
- Regulation of Businesses and Competition
- Science and Technology
- Social and Economic Policy

STRUCTURE OF EACH CHAPTER

Each chapter begins with a section noting the Single Market Program's impact to date on the topics covered in the chapter followed by a short list of key issues about the topics still facing the Single Market Program.

These two sections are not intended to be complete summaries of how the Single Market Program will affect these broad topics. Rather, they give a perspective of the relationship between the Single Market Program and these topics.

Under the Assistance heading, the chapter lists other places in the book you can scan for further information or help to use these materials.

For each set of topics, the Sourcebook provides:

- *A list and table of EC contacts.* Includes Committees of the European Parliament and offices within the Commission of the European Communities. This list offers the most specific EC offices possible as a starting contact point and includes the name of the contact office, its address, and its telephone, telex, and fax numbers. For subdirectorate contacts, refer to the table that summarizes all the sources at the EC headquarters for that topic.

- *A list of associations and organizations in the EC most directly concerned with the specific topics.* Provides the name and official acronym of the association, its address, telephone, and, when available, telex and fax numbers.

- *A list of data sources and publications that deal with the topics.* Each entry includes information on the publication's publisher as well as on its contents.

- *A list of related topics.* Refers to other chapters in Part III.

WHEN TO USE THIS PART

- To develop information on specific Single Market Program issues, such as safety in the workplace or environmental protection, that affect how you do business in the EC

- To find sources through which you can track broad issues involving the Single Market Program, such as the development and application of its competition rules and exemptions

- To locate demographic, macroeconomic, and other aggregated data needed to help evaluate potential markets for products and services

HOW TO USE THIS PART

1. *Review Chapter Opening.* Review the opening of the chapter to make sure it deals with the topics that interest you.

2. *Turn to Appendix D.* You can also make sure the chapter deals with topics that interest you by turning to Appendix D (which has divided EC measures paralleling this part) and finding the measures corresponding to the chapter you are reviewing. If the subjects covered there seem familiar, this is probably the best place for you to start.

3. *Scan EC Contact Names.* After you have determined this is the correct chapter, scan the names of the EC contacts listed in the section you are reading. Doing so will help you immediately understand what the EC sees as the current policy issues, because the listing shows which EC offices can provide information about the Single Market Program with respect to this topic.

4. *Review Association Listing.* Review the list of associations to get an overview of the specific industries and other interest groups in the EC that deal with the topic in question.

5. *Scan Resources and Publications Listing.* Scan the data resources and publications list, which shows the wide variety of resources available and the scope of each resource.

Which Sources Should Be Used?

Once you have a sense of the contents of the chapter and section, consider which sources can be most helpful. The following should give you an idea of what to use:

- *EC Contacts.* Profiles useful contacts for up-to-date information on the progress of the Single Market Program as it relates to the narrow areas for which each office is responsible.

- *Associations.* Provides contacts for developing information on the status of past and current Single Market Program initiatives affecting areas in which the associations are primarily interested.

▼ ▼

• *Data Sources and Publications.* Lists data resources and publications that are most useful in providing a sense of perspective on the Single Market Program in this particular area. The data resources may also provide specific information on the sectors being affected by the Single Market Program.

How to Use the Sources

EC CONTACTS

For several reasons, it is best to communicate with EC contacts in writing rather than by telephone :

• Making a request in writing helps minimize communications problems caused by language difficulties.

• Referring a written request to another office is substantially easier than referring a telephone request.

• Following up on a written request is easier than following up on a telephone call.

You can make a request by letter, fax, or telex. In all cases, you should observe several basic rules.

Specify the office to which you are writing. Many EC offices share common addresses, telex numbers, and even fax numbers. In corresponding with CEC offices, prominently note the directorate-general (DG), as well as the directorate and the subdirectorate with which you are corresponding. This can be done in either of two ways:

• Use all of the numbers and letters that refer to that office, starting with the directorate-general, then the directorate, and finally the subdirectorate, such as DG XIX/A/3.

• Use the key words from the title of that office, such as Budgets/Expenditure/Structural Funds.

Identify yourself and your affiliation. Provide your full name and title, if any. Also provide your *full* return address, as well as telephone numbers, fax numbers, and telex numbers.

State why you are writing and what kind of information or help you are seeking. Be as specific as possible. If you have been referred to this office by another office, state that. If you already have obtained copies of reports, studies, or other materials that deal with the topic on which you are writing, explain what you already have. This way, you will avoid receiving duplicates.

If you are operating under a deadline, indicate what it is. Be reasonable in what you expect to receive and when you expect to receive it.

If you have questions about a specific adopted or proposed measure, first identify that measure as well as you can. Describe what it is about and where you heard about it. If you have materials carrying some reference numbers, provide them. Then, ask your questions as precisely as possible.

Allow enough time for a reply. The CEC and the European Parliament's committees are very busy offices. Their primary mission is to advance the Single Market Program, and although assisting in your inquiry may be a part of that mission, they face other assignments as well.

If time is a constraint or your inquiry is *very precise and limited,* consider making a direct call. In that case, follow these guidelines in *preparing* to make your call. They will help you develop a full command of what you want, what you need, and when you need it. The hints in Appendix F's Etiquette in Government Calls may also be useful. Even when time is a problem, consider using a fax rather than a call.

ASSOCIATIONS

When you contact an association or organization listed in this book, remember the association exists *primarily* to further the interests of its own member organizations in terms of the EC. However, as a part of their operations, many associations have assembled substantial amounts of information on their own industry and on their own members. Some associations even provide statistical information and research services to nonmembers (often for a fee) as well as to their members.

As long as an association or organization perceives that fulfilling a request for information is in the best interests of its members, it usually will try to respond to requests for information. It may provide the information directly or identify other sources of data. These sources can be specialized research groups with which the association or organization may be affiliated, national-level associations or organizations, or even its own members.

In general, when you communicate with an association or organization, follow the same guidelines that apply to dealings with EC offices. In addition:

- Indicate if you are a member of an association in your home country that parallels the association you are contacting.

- Offer to pay for documents and services but set an initial price limit. Or you can ask the association to advise you of any costs involved before it proceeds.

DATA SOURCES AND PUBLICATIONS

When you order any data source or publication, find out the following before you complete the order:

- Whether the material is available locally, through a library, national commercial development office, graduate school of business or economics, or other information center, such as Euro Info Centres.

- If the document is other than a one-time publication, what year (or edition) is being shipped. Confirm that this edition is the latest published. Not all distributors receive current editions of all publications.

- Details about the materials, such as length and language of publication. Ask whether the supplier (listed in Appendix E) can send you more information about the materials, such as a brochure.

- The total cost, including delivery charges.

- When the materials will be shipped and when you can expect to receive them. If that delivery is too slow, find out about express or rush charges.

- Data resources now available on either a microcomputer diskette or online databases are marked with the following symbols: ☥ for resources available through a database; ■ for ones available on a microcomputer diskette.

ADDRESSES IN TABLES OF EC CONTACTS

In tables throughout this part, key contacts in the EC's directorates and subdirectorates often are presented in a tabular format.

The name of the directorate-general has been removed, leaving only the DG number. The names of all of the DGs are provided in Table 5.1 in Chapter 5.

Because many of these offices are in the same office complexes in Belgium and often use a common number, information is given in an abbreviated form. In each table of EC contacts, "CEC, HQ, Belgium" means:

▲ Commission of the European Communities

Address: rue de la Loi
            B-1049 Bruxelles
            Belgium
Telephone: 2/235 11 11
Telex: 21877 COMEU B

Any variation from the common telephone, fax line, or telex number is set out separately in the table.

CITY AND COUNTRY TELEPHONE CODES

Throughout the sourcebook telephone and fax numbers are preceded by corresponding city codes (or in the United States, area codes). Luxembourg is the one exception, because it has no city code, only a country code.

The city codes used for London (71 and 81) throughout the Sourcebook assume telephone calls will originate from outside Great Britain. When you are making intracountry calls, however, a zero should precede the designated city codes (071 and 081).

Although International Country Codes are necessary to place intercountry calls, these codes have not been included with the telephone and fax numbers listed in the sourcebook. Selected country codes, together with the time difference from Greenwich Mean Time (GMT) are shown in Table III.1.

ASSISTANCE

For additional help on understanding and using the resources in this part, refer to Appendixes A through H, as well as to the Introduction to this book.

Table III.1
EC Member States' Country Telephone Codes

Country	Code	Difference from GMT
Belgium	32	+1
Canada (Ottawa)	1	–5
Denmark	45	+1
France	33	+1
Germany, Federal Republic of	49/37 *	+1
Greece	30	+2
Ireland, Northern	44	0
Ireland, Republic of	353	0
Italy	39	+1
Japan	81	+9
Luxembourg	352	+1
The Netherlands	31	+1
Portugal	351	0
Spain	34	+1
Switzerland	41	+1
United Kingdom	44	0
USA (New York)	1	–5

* Use 37 when you dial the former German Democratic Republic.

19

Tracking the Progress of the Single Market Program

TRACKING THE PROGRESS OF THE SINGLE MARKET PROGRAM: HIGHLIGHTS

As described in Chapter 1, the Single Market Program has three broad objectives:

- The removal of physical barriers
- The removal of technical barriers
- The removal of fiscal barriers

The 1985 White Paper's proposals are aimed at accomplishing all of these goals by the end of 1992. The Commission has drafted all the measures referred to in the 1985 White Paper, other than those that are now not considered necessary to complete the Single Market. The Council of Ministers, in turn, has adopted over 60 percent of them. However, implementation at the national level has been somewhat slower, so that not all of the proposals that have been acted on by the EC are fully a part of the national law of all of the Member States.

KEY ISSUES FACING THE SINGLE MARKET PROGRAM

- Completing action on all remaining White Paper proposals
- Accelerating implementation of the Single Market Program at the national level
- Establishing a new relationship with the European Free Trade Association (EFTA)
- Defining the EC's relationship with Central and Eastern Europe
- Moves toward Political Union (PU)

▼ ━━━━━━━━━━━━━━━━━━━━━━━━━━━━ ▼

• Moves toward Economic and Monetary Union (EMU)

Sections in This Chapter

EC Contacts

Data Resources and Publications

━━━━ ▼ ━━━━

EC Contacts

Table 19.1 lists official European Community directorates and subdirectorates that provide information about the progress of the Single Market Program. For the complete address of the Commission of the European Communities headquarters (CEC HQ in the table) refer to the Introduction to Part III.

Commission of the European Communities
▲ Directorate-General I—External Relations

Address: rue de la Loi 200
        B-1049 Bruxelles
        Belgium
Telephone: 235 11 11
Telex: 21877 COMEU B

Commission of the European Communities
▲ Directorate-General XXII—Coordination of Structural Policies

Address: rue de la Loi 200
        B-1049 Bruxelles
        Belgium
Telephone: 235 11 11
Telex: 21877 COMEU B

Commission of the European Communities
▲ Office for Official Publications of the European Communities

Address: 2, rue Mercier
        L-2985 Luxembourg
Telephone: 499 28-1
Telex: 1324 PUBOF LU; 1322 PUBOF LU (sales department only)

Assistance

Chapter 6 describes how the EC transforms proposals into legislation, as well as how that legislation relates to national law.

Appendix D contains a list of the Single Market measures dealing with the progress of the Single Market Program of 1992. For additional help on using the resources in this chapter, refer to the Introduction to Part III.

Commission of the European Communities
▲ Spokesman's Service

Address: rue de la Loi 200
        B-1049 Bruxelles
        Belgium
Telephone: 2/235 81 18
Telex: 21877 COMEU B

Commission of the European Communities
▲ Statistical Office

Directorate A/2—Dissemination and Computer Processing/Public Relations, Dissemination and Statistical Digests

Address: Batiment Jean Monnet
        rue Alcide de Gasperi
        L-2920 Luxembourg
Telephone: 430 11
Telex: 3423/3446/3476 COMEUR LU

European Parliament
▲ Secretariat General

Directorate-General III—Information and Public Relations

Address: Centre Europeen
        Plateau du Kirchberg
        L-2929 Luxembourg
Telephone: 430 01
Telex: 3493 EUPARL LU; 2894 EUPARL LU

DATA RESOURCES AND PUBLICATIONS

1992 and Beyond

Publisher: Office for Official Publications of the European Communities
Frequency of Publication: One time
Scope: Summary of the Single Market Program and its future

1992: The European Social Dimension

Publisher: Office for Official Publications of the European Communities
Frequency of Publication: One time
Scope: Discussion of the "social dimension" of the Single Market Program

Annual Report—CEDEFOP

Publisher: Office for Official Publications of the European Communities
Frequency of Publication: Annual
Scope: Official summary of actions of CEDE-FOP, the European Centre for the Development of Vocational Training

Annual Report of the Economic and Social Committee

Publisher: Office for Official Publications of the European Communities
Frequency of Publication: Annual
Scope: Summary of activities and positions taken by ESC, including opinions issued, studies initiated, and information reports released

Bulletin of the Economic and Social Committee

Publisher: Office for Official Publications of the European Communities
Frequency of Publication: Monthly
Scope: Report on all plenary (working) sessions of the ESC, together with reports of other actions taken by the ESC

Table 19.1
CEC Subdirectorates—Tracking the Progress of the Single Market Program

Directorate and Subdirectorate Name	Directorate/ Subdirectorate Number	Directorate-General	Address
Economic Evaluation of Community Policies	B	II	CEC HQ, Belgium
Industrial Economy, Service Industries, Non-member Countries, Raw Materials	A	III	CEC HQ, Belgium
Internal Market and Industrial Affairs I	B	III	CEC HQ, Belgium
Internal Market and Industrial Affairs II	C	III	CEC HQ, Belgium
Approximation of Laws, Freedom of Establishment and Freedom to Provide Services	D	III	CEC HQ, Belgium
Public Procurement	F	III	CEC HQ, Belgium
Agro-Economic Legislation	B-I	VI	CEC HQ, Belgium Telex: 22037 AGREC B
Priority Programmes and Decentralized Information	A	X	CEC HQ, Belgium Telephone: 2/235 81 18
Communication	B	X	CEC HQ, Belgium Telephone: 2/235 81 18

Bulletin of the European Communities

Publisher: Office for Official Publications of the European Communities

Frequency of Publication: 11 times a year

Scope: Coverage of main EC events: policy development, external relations, financing, and news in brief; prepared by the Secretariat-General of the Commission

Collected Agreements Concluded Within the Framework of European Cooperation in the Field of Scientific and Technical Research

Publisher: Office for Official Publications of the European Communities

Frequency of Publication: Annual

Scope: Official texts of all agreements adopted or amended during the year; prepared by the Council of the European Communities

COM Documents

Publisher: Office for Official Publications of the European Communities

Frequency of Publication: Approximately daily

Scope: Official documents before the CEC, including proposals for new EC legislation, new policy initiatives, and progress and action reports; selective subscriptions available

Committee Reports of the European Parliament

Publisher: Office for Official Publications of the European Communities

Frequency of Publication: Periodically

Scope: Official reports made by EP committees and related activities

The Community Budget: The Facts in Figures

Publisher: Office for Official Publications of the European Communities

Frequency of Publication: One time

Scope: Overview of the EC budget

Community Public Finance—The European Budget After the Reform

Publisher: Office for Official Publications of the European Communities

Frequency of Publication: One time

Scope: Description of how the EC budget is created and managed

Completing the Internal Market: Current Status Report

Publisher: Office for Official Publications of the European Communities

Frequency of Publication: One time

Scope: Coverage of all policy directives adopted by the European Parliament through December 1989, and the current status of measures to achieve each one; five volumes

Court of Auditors: Annual Report

Publisher: Office for Official Publications of the European Communities

Frequency of Publication: Annual

Scope: Review of the financial year by the Court of Auditors, including replies from the EC institutions audited

Court of Auditors of the European Communities

Publisher: Office for Official Publications of the European Communities

Frequency of Publication: One time

Scope: Details of work and responsibilities of the Court of Auditors

Debates of the European Parliament

Publisher: Office for Official Publications of the European Communities

Frequency of Publication: Periodically

Scope: Reports of the proceedings of the EP; published as an annex to the *Official Journal of the EC*

Digest of Case-Law Relating to the European Communities: A Series

Publisher: Office for Official Publications of the European Communities

Frequency of Publication: Periodically

Scope: Judgments of the Court of Justice of the EC, relating to the EEC, ECSC, and EAEC treaties and secondary law.

Directory of Community Legislation in Force and Other Acts of the Community Institutions

Publisher: Office for Official Publications of the European Communities

Frequency of Publication: Annual

Scope: Two volumes covering all official legislation of the EC; updated and recompiled each year; with chronological and alphabetical indexes

Directory of Public Databases

Publisher: Office for Official Publications of the European Communities
Frequency of Publication: Approximately annual
Scope: Description of official databases available to the public, lists of hosts and distributors providing access to them, prepared by the Commission of the European Communities

Documents

Publisher: Office for Official Publications of the European Communities
Frequency of Publication: Monthly
Scope: Bibliographic notices of documents released by CEC, EP, and ESC

ECLAS

Database Producer: Central Library of the European Commission
Distributors/Hosts: Eurobases
Frequency of Update: As needed
Scope: European Commission's Library Automated System, a bibliographic database including EC official publications and publications of other international organizations, commercial publishers, and national governments

ECU-EMS Information

Publisher: Office for Official Publications of the European Communities
Frequency of Publication: Monthly
Scope: EMS and private uses of the ECU, including a series of ECU indicators that deal with the official and private use of the ECU; prepared by the Statistical Office of the EC

EEC Competition Policy in the Single Market

Publisher: Office for Official Publications of the European Communities
Frequency of Publication: Periodically
Scope: Guide to EC competition rules applicable to companies of all sizes

EIB-Information

Publisher: European Investment Bank
Frequency of Publication: Monthly
Scope: Newsletter on activities of the European Investment Bank

EP News

Publisher: European Parliament Information Office
Frequency of Publication: Monthly
Scope: Recent news of the European Parliament's activities

Euratom Supply Agency—Annual Report

Publisher: Office for Official Publications of the European Communities
Frequency of Publication: Annual
Scope: Reviews activities of Euratom (EAEC)

Eurecom

Publisher: Commission of the European Community, New York office
Frequency of Publication: Monthly
Scope: Current news on EC economic and financial affairs

Europe—Magazine of the European Communities

Publisher: EC Information Office in Washington, D.C.
Frequency of Publication: Monthly
Scope: Current events in the EC for a U.S. audience

Europe Without Frontiers—Completing the Internal Market

Publisher: Office for Official Publications of the European Communities
Frequency of Publication: One time
Scope: Summary of the Single Market Program's background and goals

The European Commission and the Administration of the Community

Publisher: Office for Official Publications of the European Communities
Frequency of Publication: One time
Scope: Description of the European Civil Service in operation; prepared by the CEC

European Development Fund—Annual Report

Publisher: Office for Official Publications of the European Communities
Frequency of Publication: Annual
Scope: Description of activities of the EDF; prepared by the CEC

European Economy

Publisher: Office for Official Publications of the European Communities

Frequency of Publication: 4 times a year

Scope: Annual economic reports, communications from the Commission to the Council and to the Parliament on important economic developments; also presents reports and studies on problems concerning economic policy; prepared by DG II

European File

Publisher: Office for Official Publications of the European Communities

Frequency of Publications: 24 times a year

Scope: Newsletter on current EC activities; prepared by DG X

The European Financial Common Market

Publisher: Office for Official Publications of the European Communities

Frequency of Publication: One time

Scope: Summary of progress toward a financial common market as of June 1989

European Investment Bank—Annual Report

Publisher: Office for Official Publications of the European Communities

Frequency of Publication: Annual

Scope: Review of the year's activities, with emphasis on loans granted within the EC

Eurostat News

Publisher: Office for Official Publications of the European Communities

Frequency of Publication: 4 times a year

Scope: Report on the current activities of the Statistical Office of the EC

Facts Sheets on the European Parliament and the Activities of the European Community

Publisher: Office for Official Publications of the European Communities

Frequency of Publication: One time

Scope: Brief summaries of structure and role of the European Parliament within the EC and the Single Market Program

Financial Report

Publisher: Office for Official Publications of the European Communities

Frequency of Publication: Annual

Scope: Reviews financial and other activities of the European Coal and Steel Community

Forging Ahead: European Parliament 1952-1988

Publisher: Office for Official Publications of the European Communities

Frequency of Publication: One time

Scope: Historical activities of the European Parliament

A Frontier-Free Europe

Publisher: Office for Official Publications of the European Communities

Frequency of Publication: One time

Scope: Brief overviews of the goals of the Single Market Program

General Report on the Activities of the European Communities

Publisher: Office for Official Publications of the European Communities

Frequency of Publication: Annual

Scope: Summary of the activity of the previous year, prepared by the Commission of the European Communities

Guide to the Council of the European Communities

Publisher: Office for Official Publications of the European Communities

Frequency of Publication: Annual

Scope: Coverage of the Council of the European Communities, including lists of representatives of each Member State

A Guide to the European Community

Publisher: Office for Official Publications of the European Communities

Frequency of Publication: Annual

Scope: Highlights of the EC and its activities, prepared by the Commission of the European Communities

Guide to the Reform of the Community's Structural Funds

Publisher: Office for Official Publications of the European Communities
Frequency of Publication: One time
Scope: Details about EC's structural funds, their operations and goals

Integration Processes in Europe and North America

Publisher: United Nations Economic Commission for Europe
Frequency of Publication: One time
Scope: Comprehensive look at the economic integration processes now under way in Europe and North America and their possible effects

Minutes of Sittings of the European Parliament

Publisher: Office for Official Publications of the European Communities
Frequency of Publication: Periodically
Scope: Summaries of official actions of the EP

Official Journal of the European Communities

Publisher: Office for Official Publications of the European Communities
Frequency of Publication: Daily
Scope: Activities of all EC institutions

Official Journal of the European Communities, Series C: Information and Notices

Publisher: Office for Official Publications of the European Communities
Frequency of Publication: Daily
Scope: Coverage of proposals for legislation, reports from the Court of Justice, resolutions of the European Parliament, exchange rates for the ECU, notices of job vacancies, and certain invitations for tenders

Official Journal of the European Communities, Series L: Legislation

Publisher: Office for Official Publications of the European Communities
Frequency of Publication: Daily
Scope: Text and descriptions of all the legislative acts whose publication is required by the treaties establishing the EC, as well as many acts that are not required to be published

Opinions and Reports of the Economic and Social Committee

Publisher: Office for Official Publications of the European Communities
Frequency of Publication: Periodically
Scope: Official reports of the ongoing actions of the ESC

Panorama of EC Industry

Publisher: Office for Official Publications of the European Communities
Frequency of Publication: Annual
Scope: Description of 165 manufacturing and service industries, plus evaluations of the impact of the Single Market Program

Progress in Structural Reform

Publisher: OECD
Frequency of Publication: Periodically
Scope: Reviews of economic activities of all OECD members, as well as EC specifically, in areas including financial markets, investment, taxation, competition policy, trade, agriculture, industrial policy, and labor markets; a supplement to selected issues of OECD's *Economic Outlook*

Publications of the European Communities

Publisher: Office for Official Publications of the European Communities
Frequency of Publication: 4 times a year
Scope: Bibliographic notices of monographs, series and periodicals published by EC institutions

RAPID

Database Producer: *European Commission's Spokesman's Service*

Distributors/Hosts: Eurobases
Frequency of Update: As needed
Scope: Full text of press release materials filed by the European Commission's Spokesman's Service in Brussels

Report on Competition Policy

Publisher: Office for Official Publications of the European Communities

Frequency of Publication: Annual

Scope: Survey of the competition policy during the prior year, its application to companies, state aid, and adjustments of national monopolies

Report on Economic and Monetary Union in the European Community

Publisher: Office for Official Publications of the European Communities

Frequency of Publication: One time

Scope: Collection of papers submitted to the Committee for the Study of Economic and Monetary Union

Reports of Cases Before the Court

Publisher: Office for Official Publications of the European Communities

Frequency of Publication: Periodically

Scope: Official reports of cases before the Court of Justice of the EC

Research on the "Cost of Non-Europe"—Studies on the Economics of Integration

Publisher: Office for Official Publications of the European Communities

Frequency of Publication: One time

Scope: Explanation of basis for determining the costs of nonintegration of the European marketplace, including results of surveys of 11,000 EC companies conducted for the study; Volume 2 of the Cecchini study on the "cost of non-Europe"

Research on the "Cost of Non-Europe"— Summaries of the Reports

Publisher: Office for Official Publications of the European Communities

Frequency of Publication: One time

Scope: Summary of 15 volumes of studies on the costs of nonintegration for all major market sectors, and shows the potential gains from market integration; Volume 1 of the Cecchini study on the "cost of non-Europe"

Research on the "Cost of Non-Europe"—The Completion of the Internal Market: A Survey of European Industry's Perception of the Likely Effects

Publisher: Office for Official Publications of the European Communities

Frequency of Publication: One time

Scope: Survey of 11,000 EC businesses showing expected increases in sales and investments, as well as other responses that EC businesses would make to a Single Market; Volume 3 of the Cecchini study on the "cost of non-Europe"

Results of the Business Survey Carried Out Among Managements in the Community

Publisher: Office for Official Publications of the European Communities

Frequency of Publication: Monthly

Scope: Results of regular surveys on various issues dealing with the Single Market Program; prepared by DG II

Review of the Council's Work

Publisher: Office for Official Publications of the European Communities

Frequency of Publication: Annual

Scope: Summary of the actions taken by the Council of the European Community on the EC legislation and other matters brought before it

SCAD Bulletin

Publisher: Office for Official Publications of the European Communities

Frequency of Publication: Weekly

Scope: Analytical bibliography of main EC acts, publications of the EC institutions, and current articles; also includes cumulative volumes at irregular intervals

Social Europe—Review

Publisher: Office for Official Publications of the European Communities

Frequency of Publication: 3 times a year

Scope: Critical review of the social aspects of the Single Market Program and the Common Agricultural Policy; prepared by DG V

Social Europe—Supplement: The Social Aspects of the Internal Market

Publisher: Office for Official Publications of the European Communities

Frequency of Publication: One time

Scope: Summarizes the results of six seminars; prepared by DG V

Social Europe: The Impact of the Internal Market by Industry Sector: The Challenge for the Member States

Publisher: Office for Official Publications of the European Communities

Frequency of Publication: One time

Scope: Follow-up to the "Cost of Non-Europe" research, focusing on 40 industry sectors, showing the current and projected impacts of the Single Market Program on each

Statement of the Broad Lines of Commission Policy

Publisher: Office for Official Publications of the European Communities

Frequency of Publication: One time

Scope: Position of the CEC on major policy issues, in the form of a reply to a Parliamentary debate

Synopsis of the Work of the Court of Justice of the European Communities and Record of Formal Sittings

Publisher: Office for Official Publications of the European Communities

Frequency of Publication: Every 2 years

Scope: Synopses for judges, lawyers, and practitioners of EC law

Target 92

Publisher: Office for Official Publications of the European Communities

Frequency of Publication: Monthly

Scope: Newsletter on the Single Internal Market, prepared by DG X

Texts Adopted by the European Parliament

Publisher: Office for Official Publications of the European Communities

Frequency of Publication: Periodically

Scope: Official texts of amendments to draft legislation, resolutions, reports, and other actions taken by the European Parliament

The Week

Publisher: Commission of the European Communities, DG X

Frequency of Publication: Weekly during EP sessions

Scope: Brief summary of the European Parliament's current session

Women of Europe/Information Bulletin

Publisher: Office for Official Publications of the European Communities

Frequency of Publication: 2 times a month

Scope: Newsletter prepared by DG X

Working Together: The Institutions of the European Community

Publisher: Office for Official Publications of the European Communities

Frequency of Publication: One time

Scope: Monograph prepared by Emile Noel, providing a brief overview of the organizations making up the EC

EC-Wide Macroeconomic, Population, and Census-Type Data

20

THE IMPACT OF THE SINGLE MARKET PROGRAM ON MACROECONOMIC, POPULATION, AND CENSUS-TYPE DATA: HIGHLIGHTS

One consequence of the Single Market Program is a growing demand from the Commission and other EC institutions for current, accurate, and compatible statistics. The EC institutions need such statistics to plan, administer, and review Single Market Programs. That demand is now being met by Eurostat, the Statistical Office of the European Communities.

To enable Eurostat to respond to this demand for reliable data, the EC adopted a formal statistical program covering the period from 1989 through 1992. It defines and coordinates the Commission's requirements for statistics and deals with the ability of the national statistical offices to meet these needs.

Eurostat's ultimate goal is to set statistical standards for the Community. The standards harmonize the methodology, nomenclatures, and concepts of the 12 national statistical systems, preventing discrepancies and ultimately rendering them comparable.

KEY ISSUES FACING THE SINGLE MARKET PROGRAM

- Continuing the development of an EC-wide system of statistical standards

- Developing a system to collect trade statistics after the abolition of all remaining internal frontiers

- Dealing with the problems posed by the merger of the German Democratic Republic (GDR) into the Federal Republic of Germany (FRG)

Sections in This Chapter

Macroeconomic Data

Population and Census-Type Data

Statistical Offices of Member Countries (by Country)

Assistance

Chapter 10 describes the statistical problems caused by the merger of the German Democratic Republic (GDR) into the Federal Republic of Germany (FRG). Appendix D contains a list of the Single Market measures dealing with macroeconomic, population, and census-type data. For additional help on using the resources in this chapter, refer to the Introduction to Part III.

Macroeconomic Data

EC Contacts

Table 20.1 lists official European Community directorates and subdirectorates that provide information about macroeconomic data. For the complete address of the Commission of the European Communities headquarters (CEC HQ in the table), refer to the Introduction to Part III.

Commission of the European Communities
▲ Statistical Office

Directorate B—Economic Statistics and National Accounts, Prices and Coordination Relating to the Single Market

Address: Batiment Jean Monnet
rue Alcide de Gasperi
L-2920 Luxembourg
Telephone: 430 11
Telex: 3423/3446/3476 COMEUR LU

Commission of the European Communities
▲ Statistical Office

Directorate E/4—Social and Regional Statistics/ Regional Statistics and Accounts

Address: Batiment Jean Monnet
rue Alcide de Gasperi
L-2920 Luxembourg
Telephone: 430 11
Telex: 3423/3446/3476 COMEUR LU

Data Resources and Publications

Annual Bulletin of General Energy Statistics for Europe

Publisher: United Nations and the United Nations Economic Commission for Europe
Frequency of Publication: Annual
Scope: Basic data on the energy situation as a whole, including the production of energy by form, overall energy balance sheets, and deliveries of petroleum products for internal consumption

Annual National Accounts: Main Aggregates

Publisher: OECD
Frequency of Publication: Annual
Scope: Series of national accounts of OECD members that is available on microcomputer diskette and in hardcopy ■

Basic Statistics of the Community

Publisher: Office for Official Publications of the European Communities
Frequency of Publication: Annual
Scope: Selected data, including comparisons with the United States, Japan, and the U.S.S.R.

Table 20.1
CEC Subdirectorates—Macroeconomic Data

Directorate and Subdirectorate Name	Directorate/ Subdirectorate Number	Directorate-General	Address
National Economies	A	I	CEC HQ, Belgium
Macroeconomic Analyses and Policies	C	II	CEC HQ, Belgium

CEFIC Energy Statistics (Consumption)

Publisher: Chemicals Industries Association, Ltd

Frequency of Publication: Annual

Scope: Report made of the EC Association CEFIC; published by a private press

Consumer Price Index

Publisher: Office for Official Publications of the European Communities

Frequency of Publication: Monthly

Scope: Detailed price indexes, as well as inflation rates and consumer prices of EC member states; also available online via the Cronos database; prepared by the Statistical Office of the EC ⊛

Cronos

Database Producer: Eurostat

Distributors/Hosts: Eurostat, WEFA, Datacentralen, GSI-ECO, DSI

Frequency of Update: Regular, depending on data series involved

Scope: Macroeconomic time series covering every part of the economy, broken down into 23 different parts ⊛

Demographic Yearbook

Publisher: United Nations

Frequency of Publication: Annual

Scope: Demographic statistics, including data on population, natality, infant mortality, marriage, and divorce

EC Agricultural Price Indices: Monthly Results/ Half Yearly Statistics

Publisher: Office for Official Publications of the European Communities

Frequency of Publication: 2 times a year

Scope: Trends of monthly indexes of producer prices, agricultural inputs, and production; also available online via the Cronos database; prepared by the Statistical Office of the EC ⊛

Economic Bulletin for Europe

Publisher: United Nations Economic Commission for Europe

Frequency of Publication: Annual

Scope: World trade and the economies of Europe, including output and trade, economic development, trade, and financing

Economic Survey of Europe

Publisher: United Nations

Frequency of Publication: Annual

Scope: World trade and the economies of Europe, including output and trade, economic development, trade, and financing

Economies in Transition

Publisher: OECD

Frequency of Publication: One time

Scope: Reviews structural adjustment of economies of OECD countries in the recent past

European Economy

Publisher: Office for Official Publications of the European Communities

Frequency of Publication: 4 times a year

Scope: Annual economic reports, communications from the Commission to the Council and to the Parliament on important economic developments, as well as reports and studies on problems concerning economic policy; prepared by DG II

European Economy—Supplement—Series A: Recent Economic Trends

Publisher: Office for Official Publications of the European Communities

Frequency of Publication: 11 times a year

Scope: Recent economic conditions in the EC, together with macroeconomic forecasts, prepared by DG II

European Economy—Supplement—Series B: Business and Consumer Survey Results

Publisher: Office for Official Publications of the European Communities

Frequency of Publication: 11 times a year

Scope: Results of surveys on prospective economic trends, prepared by DG II

Europe in Figures

Publisher: Office for Official Publications of the European Communities

Frequency of Publication: Annual

Scope: Overview of the EC and its member states, including population, education, labor, employment, as well as agricultural and industrial production

Eurostat Review

Publisher: Office for Official Publications of the European Communities

Frequency of Publication: Annual

Scope: Most important EC statistics over a 10-year period

Eurostatistics—Data for Short-Term Economic Analysis

Publisher: Office for Official Publications of the European Communities

Frequency of Publication: Monthly

Scope: Recent economic data on the EC together with comparative statistics from the United States and Japan, such as exchange rates, interest rates, money supply, industrial and agricultural indexes, and foreign trade; also available online via the Cronos database; prepared by the Statistical Office of the EC

External Debt Statistics

Publisher: OECD

Frequency of Publication: Annual

Scope: Total external debt and other liabilities for members of the OECD and other nations; available on microcomputer diskette and in hardcopy   ■

Financial Statistics—Part I: Monthly Statistics

Publisher: OECD

Frequency of Publication: 24 times a year

Scope: Statistics on international and domestic financial markets during the previous 30 days

Financial Statistics—Part II: Financial Accounts

Publisher: OECD

Frequency of Publication: Annual

Scope: Booklets on each of the 20 OECD members, including flow-of-funds accounts and the balance sheets for each country

Financial Statistics—Part III: Non-Financial Enterprises Financial Statements

Publisher: OECD

Frequency of Publication: Annual

Scope: Balance sheets and statements of income, as well as details on the sources and uses of funds, for a sample of enterprises for 16 countries

General Government Accounts and Statistics: 1970-1986

Publisher: Office for Official Publications of the European Communities

Frequency of Publication: One time

Scope: Historical summary of governmental accounts; prepared by Statistical Office of the EC

Government Financing of Research and Development

Publisher: Office for Official Publications of the European Communities

Frequency of Publication: Annual

Scope: Summarizes spending on research and development and related areas; prepared by the Statistical Office of the EC

Handbook of International Trade and Development Statistics

Publisher: United Nations

Frequency of Publication: Annual

Scope: Basic statistical data dealing with world trade and development

Industrial Production—Quarterly Statistics

Publisher: Office for Official Publications of the European Communities

Frequency of Publication: 4 times a year

Scope: Production of industrial products; also available online via the Cronos database; prepared by the Statistical Office of the EC

Industrial Statistics Yearbook

Publisher: United Nations
Frequency of Publication: Annual
Scope: Statistics of industrial establishments, employers/employees, wages, output in various sectors, investments, and commodity production data of individual products, among others

Industrial Structure Statistics

Publisher: OECD
Frequency of Publication: Annual
Scope: Statistics of production, value added, number of establishments, employment, wages and salaries, exports, imports, and investment

Industrial Trends—Monthly Statistics

Publisher: Office for Official Publications of the European Communities
Frequency of Publication: Monthly
Scope: Industrial activity, such as data for each industrial branch and for the industry as a whole, including indexes for the value of imports and exports in these branches; also available online via the Cronos database; prepared by the Statistical Office of the EC

International Comparison of Gross Domestic Product in Europe

Publisher: United Nations
Frequency of Publication: One time
Scope: Conversion and comparison of the 20 European nations' GDPs with a common basis

International Rates on International and Domestic Markets

Publisher: OECD
Frequency of Publication: Monthly
Scope: Microdiskette summary of selected interest rates that appear in the OECD publication *Financial Statistics Monthly—Section 2—Domestic Markets—Interest Rates* ■

International Sectoral Databank

Publisher: OECD
Frequency of Publication: Annual
Scope: Standardized data for 14 of the OECD countries on subjects including gross domestic product, total employment, compensation of employees, and capital stock; also available on microdiskette ■

International Trade

Publisher: GATT
Frequency of Publication: Annual
Scope: Review of trade performance of all GATT members, and developments by economic sector; also includes over 150 separate statistical tables on trade-related issues

Leading Indicators and Business Surveys

Publisher: OECD
Frequency of Publication: Monthly
Scope: Leading economic indicators of industrial production; available on microcomputer diskettes ■

Main Economic Indicators

Publisher: OECD
Frequency of Publication: Monthly
Scope: Summary of most recent changes in the economy of OECD countries, as well as statistics on national accounts, industrial production, deliveries, construction, internal trade, labor, prices, and interest rates; also the name of a set of microcomputer diskettes, containing most (but not all) of the data from the hardcopy publication ■

Money and Finances

Publisher: Office for Official Publications of the European Communities
Frequency of Publication: 4 times a year
Scope: Structural financial indicators plus quarterly and monthly time-series data; also available online via the Cronos database; prepared by the Statistical Office of the EC

Monthly Bulletin of Statistics

Publisher: United Nations
Frequency of Publication: Monthly
Scope: Data on 74 social and economic subjects from over 200 countries; includes quarterly data for regional groups including the EC

National Accounts ESA—Aggregates 1970-1979

Publisher: Office for Official Publications of the European Communities
Frequency of Publication: One time
Scope: Historical summary of national accounts of EC members; prepared by Statistical Office of the EC

National Accounts Statistics

Publisher: United Nations
Frequency of Publication: Annual
Scope: International statistical data on national accounts, specifically gross domestic product, national income and capital transactions, government and consumer expenditures, social security, and household funds

OECD Economic Outlook

Publisher: OECD
Frequency of Publication: 2 times a year
Scope: Survey of latest economic development in the OECD area, together with analysis and projections of economic activity

OECD Economic Studies

Publisher: OECD
Frequency of Publication: 2 times a year
Scope: Applied economic and statistical analysis within OECD and on an international basis

OECD Economic Surveys

Publisher: OECD
Frequency of Publication: Periodically
Scope: Series of country-level surveys on members of OECD

Overall Economic Perspective to the Year 2000

Publisher: United Nations Economic Commission for Europe
Frequency of Publication: One time
Scope: Exploration of long-term economic problems, their evolution, and present recommendations for solving them

Panorama of EC Industry

Publisher: Office for Official Publications of the European Communities
Frequency of Publication: Annual
Scope: Description of 165 manufacturing and service industries, including the macroeconomic outlook, plus evaluations of the impact of the Single Market Program

Quarterly National Accounts

Publisher: OECD
Frequency of Publication: 4 times a year
Scope: More than 1000 quarterly series of main national accounts aggregates; also available on microcomputer diskettes ■

Quarterly National Accounts—ESA

Publisher: Office for Official Publications of the European Communities
Frequency of Publication: 4 times a year
Scope: Annual and quarterly trends in the main aggregates of national accounts, in both volume and price; also available online via the Cronos database; prepared by the Statistical Office of the EC

Regio

Database Producer: Eurostat
Distributors/Hosts: Eurostat
Frequency of Update: Annual or more frequently
Scope: Macroeconomic statistics on various regions of the EC, including demography, economic accounts, unemployment, labor force sample survey, industry, agriculture, the EC's financial participation in investments, and transport

Statistical Yearbook

Publisher: United Nations
Frequency of Publication: Annual
Scope: Reports on population, agriculture, manufacturing, construction, transport, commodity import/export trade, balance of payments, national income, education, and culture, for more than 270 countries; presented on an internationally comparable basis, using overall world summary tables and data by country

Statistics on External Indebtedness

Publisher: OECD
Frequency of Publication: Annual
Scope: Bank and trade-related nonbank external claims on individual borrowing countries, provided on microcomputer diskette, issued jointly by the OECD and the Bank for International Settlements ■

Structure and Activity of Industry—Annual Inquiry

Publisher: Office for Official Publications of the European Communities
Frequency of Publication: Annual
Scope: Industrial census of the EC; regional data volumes also available; prepared by the Statistical Office of the EC

TES

Database Producer: Eurostat
Distributors/Hosts: Eurostat
Frequency of Update: Every 5 years
Scope: Input-output tables of the national accounts of EC members, covering 5-year periods   ⊛

POPULATION AND CENSUS-TYPE DATA

EC Contacts

Commission of the European Communities
▲ Statistical Office

Directorate E/2—Social and Regional Statistics/ Living and Working Conditions

Address: Batiment Jean Monnet
            rue Alcide de Gasperi
            L-2920 Luxembourg
Telephone: 430 11
Telex: 3423/3446/3476 COMEUR LU

Commission of the European Communities
▲ Statistical Office

Directorate E/3—Social and Regional Statistics/ Social Digests

Address: Batiment Jean Monnet
            rue Alcide de Gasperi
            L-2920 Luxembourg
Telephone: 430 11
Telex: 3423/3446/3476 COMEUR LU

Commission of the European Communities
▲ Statistical Office

Directorate E/4—Social and Regional Statistics/ Regional Statistics and Accounts

Address: Batiment Jean Monnet
            rue Alcide de Gasperi
            L-2920 Luxembourg
Telephone: 430 11
Telex: 3423/3446/3476 COMEUR LU

Data Resources and Publications

Advanced Population Aging in Europe and North America—Demographic and Economic Aspects

Publisher: United Nations Economic Commission for Europe
Frequency of Publication: One time
Scope: Demographics of population aging, including effects of changing vital rates on aging, as well as the impact of aging on the economy, public expenditures, and the labor market

▼ ▼

Annual Bulletin of Housing and Building Statistics for Europe

Publisher: United Nations and the United Nations Economic Commission for Europe

Frequency of Publication: Annual

Scope: Statistics on dwelling construction, materials used, and employment in the construction industry, plus wholesale price indexes of building materials '

Basic Statistics of the Community

Publisher: Office for Official Publications of the European Communities

Frequency of Publication: Annual

Scope: Basic econometric and statistical data, including comparisons with the United States, Japan, and the U.S.S.R.

Compendium of OECD Environmental Data

Publisher: OECD

Frequency of Publication: Every 2 years

Scope: Data on the environment and environmental protection in OECD member countries

Demographic Statistics

Publisher: Office for Official Publications of the European Communities

Frequency of Publication: Annual

Scope: Summary of country-level demographic data; prepared by the Statistical Office of the EC

Demographic Yearbook

Publisher: United Nations

Frequency of Publication: Annual

Scope: Data on population, natality, infant mortality, marriage, and divorce

Employment in Europe—1989

Publisher: Office for Official Publications of the European Communities

Frequency of Publication: One time

Scope: Employment statistics

Europe in Figures

Publisher: Office for Official Publications of the European Communities

Frequency of Publication: Annual

Scope: Overview of the EC and its member states, including population, education, labor, employment, and agricultural and industrial production

Eurostat Review

Publisher: Office for Official Publications of the European Communities

Frequency of Publication: Annual

Scope: Most important EC statistics over a 10-year period

FSSRS

Database Producer: Eurostat

Distributors/Hosts: Eurostat

Frequency of Update: Every 2 to 3 years

Scope: Results of EC surveys on the structure of farm holdings, including the size, physical and economic form of the holdings, management of the holdings, crops and livestock, and workers ✆

Handbook of International Trade and Development Statistics

Publisher: United Nations

Frequency of Publication: Annual

Scope: Summary of basic statistical data dealing with world trade and development

Industrial Structure Statistics

Publisher: OECD

Frequency of Publication: Annual

Scope: Statistics of production, value added, number of establishments, employment, wages and salaries, exports, imports, and investment

Industry—Statistical Yearbook

Publisher: Office for Official Publications of the European Communities

Frequency of Publication: Annual

Scope: Statistical overview of industry and commerce; prepared by the Statistical Office of the EC

International Sectoral Databank

Publisher: OECD
Frequency of Publication: Annual
Scope: Standardized data for 14 of the OECD countries on subjects including gross domestic product, total employment, compensation of employees, and capital stock; also available on microdiskette ■

Living Conditions in the OECD Countries

Publisher: OECD
Frequency of Publication: One time
Scope: Evaluation of living conditions in OECD countries using a common set of social indicators

Main Economic Indicators

Publisher: OECD
Frequency of Publication: Monthly
Scope: Most recent changes in the economies of OECD countries, as well as international statistics on economic developments affecting the OECD area, including national accounts, industrial production, deliveries, construction, internal trade, labor, prices, and interest rates; also the name of a set of microcomputer diskettes, containing most (but not all) data from the hardcopy ■

Population and Vital Statistics Report

Publisher: United Nations
Frequency of Publication: 4 times a year
Scope: Latest census data, plus worldwide demographic statistics

Population Bulletin of the United Nations

Publisher: United Nations
Frequency of Publication: Annual
Scope: Articles on population and population research

Programme for Research and Actions on the Development of the Labor Market

Publisher: Office for Official Publications of the European Communities
Frequency of Publication: One time
Scope: Overview of trends and distribution of incomes; prepared by the European Federation for Economic Research

Regio

Database Producer: Eurostat
Distributors/Hosts: Eurostat
Frequency of Update: Periodically
Scope: Summary of demography, economic accounts, unemployment, labor force sample survey, industry, agriculture, the EC's financial participation in investments, and transport ⊛

Statistical Yearbook

Publisher: United Nations
Frequency of Publication: Annual
Scope: Population, agriculture, manufacturing, construction, transport, commodity import/export trade, balance of payments, national income, education, and culture, for more than 270 countries, presented on an internationally comparable basis, using overall world summary tables and data by country

Structure and Activity of Industry—Annual Inquiry

Publisher: Office for Official Publications of the European Communities
Frequency of Publication: Annual
Scope: Industrial census of the EC; regional data volumes also available; prepared by the Statistical Office of the EC

Transport and Communications—Statistical Yearbook

Publisher: Office for Official Publications of the European Communities
Frequency of Publication: Annual
Scope: Country and EC-level data on all aspects of transportation and communications; prepared by the Statistical Office of the EC

Trends in Enterprises
Publisher: OECD
Frequency of Publication: One time
Scope: Study of business trends in OECD
member countries

World Statistics in Brief
Publisher: United Nations
Frequency of Publication: Periodically
Scope: Broad range of data, on worldwide,
regional, and national bases

STATISTICAL OFFICES OF MEMBER COUNTRIES (BY COUNTRY)

▲ L'Institut National de Statistique

Address: rue de Louvain 44
B-1000 Bruxelles
Belgium
Telephone: 2/513 96 50

▲ Danmark Statistik

Address: Sejrogade 11
DK-2100 Copenhagen O
Denmark
Telephone: 3/1298 222

▲ INSEE (Institute National de la Statistique et des Etudes Economiques)

Address: 18, bd. Adolphe Pinard
Paris Cedex 14
France
Telephone: 1/45 40 01 12

▲ Statistisches Bundesamt

Address: Gustav-Stresemann-Ring 11
D-6200 Wiesbaden
Germany
Telephone: 611/751

▲ Central Statistical Office—Information Services Division

Address: Government Offices
Great George Street
GB-London SW1P 3AQ
Great Britain
Telephone: 71/233 6315

▲ National Statistical Service of Greece

Address: 14-16 Lycourgou St.
GR-10166 Athens
Greece
Telephone: 1/324 4746

▲ Central Statistics Office

Address: St. Stephen's Green House
Earlsfort Terrace
Dublin 2
Ireland
Telephone: 12/767531

▲ ISTAT (Istituto Central de Statistica)

Address: via Cesare Balbo 16
I-00100 Roma
Italy
Telephone: 6/4673

▲ STATEC (Service Central de la Statistique et des Etudes Economiques)

Address: 19-21, bd. Royale
L-2013 Luxembourg
Telephone: 47941

▲ Centraal Bureau voor de Statistiek

Address: Prinses Beatrixlaan 428
P.O. Box 959
NL-2270 AZ Voorburg
Netherlands
Telephone: 70/694 341

▲ Instituto Nacional de Estatistica

Address: Avenida Antonio Jose de Almeida
P-1078 Lisbon
Portugal
Telephone: 1/802 080

▲ Institute Nacional de Estadistica

Address: Paseo de la Castellana
E-28046 Madrid
Spain
Telephone: 1/279 9300

21

Economic and Business Development and Assistance

THE IMPACT OF THE SINGLE MARKET PROGRAM ON ECONOMIC AND BUSINESS DEVELOPMENT AND ASSISTANCE: HIGHLIGHTS

Economic and Regional Development

The EC is directly involved in many efforts designed to strengthen the economic and social cohesion of the Community. Among the most important are the activities of the EC's Structural Funds. These are operated to achieve several goals:

- Assisting in the development of the EC's agricultural sector

- Improving employment opportunities for workers throughout the Community

- Helping the development of regions of the EC that are "lagging behind" in economic terms

In addition to the activities of the Structural Funds, the EC operates numerous special programs that address particular problems in economic and regional development. One of the more recently initiated programs is Pedip, a program to help modernize Portuguese industry, focusing on the fishing industry.

SMEs

The future of small and medium-sized enterprises (SMEs) is an important concern of the EC, because the SMEs are seen as a major source of future economic growth. The Single Market Program plans additional efforts to strengthen the existing links among these businesses and with the EC, such as the Business Cooperation Network (BC-Net) program.

KEY ISSUES FACING THE SINGLE MARKET PROGRAM

- Supervising changes in the industrial development programs of Member States to ensure that they do not violate the EC's competition laws

- Continuing the expansion of the EuroInfo Centre program

- Assisting SMEs through special financing programs

- Preparing additional rural assistance programs to deal with the consequences of potential reductions in agricultural subsidies

SECTIONS IN THIS CHAPTER

Economic Development
Regional and Rural Development
Small and Medium-Sized Businesses

ASSISTANCE

Chapter 2 describes the EC's Structural Funds and their role in economic and business development as well as some of the assistance programs for small and medium-sized enterprises already in place in the EC. Chapter 3 analyzes the EC's competition rules and how they may limit the aid that the Member States can provide to businesses.

Appendix D contains a list of the Single Market measures dealing with economic and business development. For additional help on using the resources in this chapter, refer to the Introduction to Part III.

ECONOMIC DEVELOPMENT

EC Contacts

Table 21.1 lists official European Community directorates and subdirectorates that provide information about economic development. For the complete address of the Commission of the European Communities headquarters (CEC HQ in the table), refer to the Introduction to Part III.

European Parliament
▲ Committee on Development and Cooperation

Address: 97-113, rue Belliard
B-1040 Bruxelles
Belgium
Telephone: 2/284 21 21; 2/284 27 53
Fax: 2/230 68 56; 2/231 12 57

Address: Palais de l'Europe
F-67006 Strasbourg Cedex
France
Telephone: 88/374 001; 88/374 917
Fax: 88/369 214; 88/256 516

Address: Centre Europeen
Plateau du Kirchberg
L-2929 Luxembourg
Telephone: 430 01
Telex: 3493 EUPARL LU; 2894 EUPARL LU
Fax: 436 972; 435 359

European Parliament
▲ Committee on Economic and Monetary Affairs and Industrial Policy

Address: 97-113, rue Belliard
B-1040 Bruxelles
Belgium
Telephone: 2/284 21 21; 2/284 35 40
Fax: 2/230 68 56; 2/231 12 57

Address: Palais de l'Europe
F-67006 Strasbourg Cedex
France
Telephone: 88/374 001; 88/375 484
Fax: 88/369 214; 88/256 516

Address: Centre Europeen
Plateau du Kirchberg
L-2929 Luxembourg
Telephone: 430 01
Telex: 3493 EUPARL LU; 2894 EUPARL LU
Fax: 436 972; 435 359

Data Sources and Publications

Agricultural Policies, Markets, and Trade

Publisher: OECD
Frequency of Publication: Annual
Scope: Policies for agriculture, markets, and trade in OECD member countries

Annual Report of the EIB

Publisher: European Investment Bank
Frequency of Publication: Annual
Scope: Details of EIB financing and loans inside and outside of the EC

Bulletin of Statistics on World Trade in Engineering Products

Publisher: United Nations and the United Nations Economic Commission for Europe
Frequency of Publication: Annual
Scope: Statistics on the flow of machinery, transport, scientific, medical, optical, and measuring equipment; watches; and clocks

Business Creation by Women: Motivations, Situations, and Perspectives

Publisher: Office for Official Publications of the European Communities
Frequency of Publication: One time
Scope: Final report of a study for the Commission of the European Communities

Commodity Trade Statistics

Publisher: United Nations
Frequency of Publication: Every other week
Scope: Analysis of more than 150 groups of commodities exported or imported by the world's principal trading nations

Table 21.1
CEC Subdirectorates—Economic Development

Directorate and Subdirectorate Name	Directorate/ Subdirectorate Number	Directorate-General	Address
National Economies	A	II	CEC HQ, Belgium
Industrial Economy, Service Industries, Non-member Countries, Raw Materials			
Industrial Economy	A/3	III	CEC HQ, Belgium Telephone: 2/236 30 12
General Competition Policy and Coordination			
Economic Questions and Studies	A/3	IV	CEC HQ, Belgium
State Aids			
General Aid Schemes	E/1	IV	CEC HQ, Belgium
Industry Aids I	E/4	IV	CEC HQ, Belgium
Industry Aids II	E/5	IV	CEC HQ, Belgium
Development Activities and Trade Policy	A	VIII	CEC HQ, Belgium Telephone: 2/236 30 12
Operations in Regions Whose Development is Lagging Behind—Objective 1: Greece, Ireland, Northern Ireland, and Portugal	B	XVI	CEC HQ, Belgium
Operations in Regions Whose Development is Lagging Behind—Objective 1: Spain, France, and Italy	B	XVI	CEC HQ, Belgium

Directory of Non-Governmental Development Organisations in OECD Member Countries

Publisher: OECD

Frequency of Publication: Periodically

Scope: Descriptions of the aims, development educational work, and development activities of over 2,000 nongovernment organizations in OECD countries

Economic Bulletin for Europe

Publisher: United Nations Economic Commission for Europe

Frequency of Publication: Annual

Scope: World trade and the economies of Europe, including output and trade, economic developments, trade, and financing

Economic Outlook

Publisher: OECD

Frequency of Publication: 2 times a year

Scope: A series of forecasts for all OECD member countries that also includes historical data; available on microcomputer diskette and in hard copy ∎

Economic Survey of Europe

Publisher: United Nations

Frequency of Publication: Annual

Scope: World trade and the economies of Europe, including output and trade, economic developments, trade, and financing

Education and the Economy in a Changing Society

Publisher: OECD

Frequency of Publication: One time

Scope: Studies on the role of education and its impact on economic growth and development

EIB-Information

Publisher: European Investment Bank

Frequency of Publication: Monthly

Scope: Newsletter reporting EIB information

Elise

Database Producer: European Community, DG V

Distributors/Hosts: ECHO

Frequency of Update: 4 times per year

Scope: The European network for information exchange on local employment schemes

⊛

Entrepreneurship and Economic Development

Publisher: United Nations

Frequency of Publication: One time

Scope: Analysis of the role of entrepreneurship in economic growth and development in industrial and nonindustrial countries

European Development Fund—Annual Report

Publisher: Office for Official Publications of the European Communities

Frequency of Publication: Annual

Scope: Description of activities of the EDF; prepared by the CEC

European Investment Bank—Annual Report

Publisher: Office for Official Publications of the European Communities

Frequency of Publication: Annual

Scope: Review of the year's activities, with emphasis on loans granted within the EC

The Export Credit Financing Systems in OECD Member Countries

Publisher: OECD

Frequency of Publication: Every 3 years

Scope: Describes export credit insurance and guarantee programs, as well as export financing support in OECD countries, including overseas development assistance programs that bear on export credit activities

Foreign Direct Investment and Transnational Corporations in Services

Publisher: United Nations

Frequency of Publication: One time

Scope: Review of established policy patterns of multinational businesses in direct investment in service industries

Guide to the Reform of the Community's Structural Funds

Publisher: Office for Official Publications of the European Communities
Frequency of Publication: One time
Scope: Details of EC's structural funds, their operations and goals

Handbook of International Trade and Development Statistics

Publisher: United Nations
Frequency of Publication: Annual
Scope: Summary of basic statistical data dealing with world trade and development

Indicators of Industrial Activity

Publisher: OECD
Frequency of Publication: 4 times a year
Scope: Overview of short-term economic developments in different industries for all OECD members

Industrial Policy Development in OECD Countries

Publisher: OECD
Frequency of Publication: Annual
Scope: Recently adopted or soon to be applied industrial policy measures in OECD member countries

Industrial Policy in OECD Countries

Publisher: OECD
Frequency of Publication: Annual
Scope: Exploration of industrial developments in member countries

Industrial Structure Statistics

Publisher: OECD
Frequency of Publication: Annual
Scope: Statistics on production, value added, number of establishments, employment, wages and salaries, exports, imports, and investment

The Informal Sector Revisited

Publisher: OECD
Frequency of Publication: One time
Scope: Survey of existing knowledge and discussion of agenda for research addressing the further development of policies and programs for the informal sector, a leading provider of first-time jobs

International Direct Investment and the New Economic Environment

Publisher: OECD
Frequency of Publication: One time
Scope: Review of roles of direct investment in assisting economic development

International Trade Statistics Yearbook

Publisher: United Nations
Frequency of Publication: Annual
Scope: Summary of foreign trade statistics, showing overall trade by regions and countries and showing world exports by origin, area of destination, and product

Investment Incentives and Disincentives: Effects on International Direct Investment

Publisher: OECD
Frequency of Publication: One time
Scope: Summary of effects of investment incentives and disincentives on private direct investment

Leading Indicators and Business Surveys

Publisher: OECD
Frequency of Publication: Monthly
Scope: Set of microcomputer diskettes showing leading indicators of industrial production

Main Economic Indicators

Publisher: OECD
Frequency of Publication: Monthly
Scope: Summary of the most recent changes in the economy of OECD countries and a set of international statistics on economic developments affecting the OECD area, including national accounts, industrial production, deliveries, construction, internal trade, labor, prices, and interest rates; also the name of a set of microcomputer diskettes, containing most (but not all) of the data from the hardcopy publication of the same name

Main Science and Technology Indicators

Publisher: OECD
Frequency of Publication: 2 times a year
Scope: Research and development spending as compared with gross domestic product; available in hardcopy or on microcomputer diskette

OECD Economic Outlook

Publisher: OECD
Frequency of Publication: 2 times a year
Scope: Survey of latest economic development in the OECD area, together with analysis and projections of economic activity

The OECD Observer

Publisher: OECD
Frequency of Publication: 6 times a year
Scope: Important issues handled by the OECD, including economic growth, employment and unemployment, social problems, agriculture, energy, financial markets, fiscal policy, multinational enterprises, the environment, and science and technology

Operations of the European Community Concerning Small and Medium-Sized Enterprises

Publisher: Office for Official Publications of the European Communities
Frequency of Publication: One time
Scope: Guide to operation of SMEs in EC, including information on business cooperation, grants, and loans

Pabil

Database Producer: European Community, DG VII
Distributors/Hosts: ECHO
Frequency of Update: 6 times a year
Scope: Monitor of the progress of the EC's development programs

Panorama of EC Industry

Publisher: Office for Official Publications of the European Communities
Frequency of Publication: Annual
Scope: Description of 165 manufacturing and service industries, including internal investment, plus evaluations of the impact of the Single Market Program

Progress in Structural Reform

Publisher: OECD
Frequency of Publication: Periodically
Scope: Review of economic activities of all OECD members, as well as EC specifically, in areas including financial markets, investment, taxation, competition policy, trade, agriculture, industrial policy, and labor markets; a supplement to selected issues of OECD's *Economic Outlook*

Statistical Yearbook

Publisher: United Nations
Frequency of Publication: Annual
Scope: Summary of statistical data for more than 270 countries on population, agriculture, manufacturing, construction, transport, commodity import/export trade, balance of payments, national income, education, and culture; presented on an internationally comparable basis, using overall world summary tables and data by country

Statistics of World Trade in Steel

Publisher: United Nations and the United Nations Economic Commission for Europe
Frequency of Publication: Annual
Scope: Exports of semifinished and finished steel products

Survey on State Aids in the European Community

Publisher: Office for Official Publications of the European Communities
Frequency of Publication: One time
Scope: Analysis of direct and indirect assistance provided to businesses by EC member countries

Transnational Corporations in World Development, Trends, and Prospects

Publisher: United Nations
Frequency of Publication: One time
Scope: Major emerging transnationalization trends and strategic responses of major multinational businesses, particularly those dealing with economic development; executive summary also available

Western Europe . . . A Tax Tour

Publisher: Arthur Andersen & Co.
Frequency of Publication: As needed
Scope: Background information on each
country, highlights of the main features
of each country's business and personal
tax systems, plus factors that could
influence a decision regarding investment within the country

Related Topics and Industries

Regulation of Businesses and Competition; Social Services and Welfare. See also *Part IV—Sources on EC 1992 by Industry*

REGIONAL AND RURAL DEVELOPMENT

EC Contacts

Table 21.2 lists official European Community directorates and subdirectorates that provide information about regional and rural development. For the complete address of the Commission of the European Communities headquarters (CEC HQ in the table), refer to the Introduction to Part III.

Commission of the European Communities
▲ Statistical Office

Directorate E/4 (Social and Regional Statistics/ Regional Statistics and Accounts)

Address: Batiment Jean Monnet
rue Alcide de Gasperi
L-2920 Luxembourg
Telephone: 430 11
Telex: 3423/3446/3476 COMEUR LU

Table 21.2
CEC Subdirectorates—Regional and Rural Development

Directorate and Subdirectorate Name	Directorate/ Subdirectorate Number	Directorate- General	Address
State Aids			
Regional Aids	E/3	IV	CEC HQ, Belgium
European Social Fund	C	V	CEC HQ, Belgium
Rural Development I	F-I	VI	CEC HQ, Belgium Telex: 22037 AGREC B
Rural Development II	F-II	VI	CEC HQ, Belgium Telex: 22037 AGREC B
European Agricultural Guidance and Guarantee Fund	G	VI	CEC HQ, Belgium Telex: 22037 AGREC B
Formulation and Launching of Regional Policies	A	XVI	CEC HQ, Belgium
Operations in Regions Affected by Industrial Decline—Objective 2—and in Rural Areas—Objective 5b; and ECSC Conversion Methods		XVI	CEC HQ, Belgium

European Parliament

▲ Committee on Agriculture, Fisheries, and Rural Development

Address: 97-113, rue Belliard
            B-1040 Bruxelles
            Belgium
Telephone: 2/284 21 21; 2/284 28 08
Fax: 2/230 68 56; 2/231 12 57

Address: Palais de l'Europe
            F-67006 Strasbourg Cedex
            France
Telephone: 88/374 001; 88/374 589; 88/374 554
Fax: 88/369 214; 88/256 516

Address: Centre Europeen
            Plateau du Kirchberg
            L-2929 Luxembourg
Telephone: 430 01
Telex: 3493 EUPARL LU; 2894 EUPARL LU
Fax: 436 972; 435 359

European Parliament

▲ Committee on Regional Policy and Regional Planning

Address: Palais de l'Europe
            F-67006 Strasbourg Cedex
            France
Telephone: 88/374 001; 88/374 618
Fax: 88/369 214; 88/256 516

Address: Centre Europeen
            Plateau du Kirchberg
            L-2929 Luxembourg
Telephone: 430 01
Telex: 3493 EUPARL LU; 2894 EUPARL LU
Fax: 436 972; 435 359

Data Resources and Publications

Directory of Bodies Concerned with Urban and Regional Research

Publisher: United Nations Economic Commission for Europe
Frequency of Publication: One time
Scope: Organization of urban and regional research in EC countries with addresses of government ministries, departments, institutes, specialized agencies, and universities dealing with research in this field

E.C. International Investment Partners

Publisher: Office for Official Publications of the European Communities
Frequency of Publication: One time
Scope: Description of the EC "financial facility" established to promote joint ventures in Asia, Latin America, and the Mediterranean region

European Development Fund—Annual Report

Publisher: Office for Official Publications of the European Communities
Frequency of Publication: Annual
Scope: Description of activities of the EDF; prepared by the CEC

FSSRS

Database Producer: Eurostat
Distributors/Hosts: Eurostat
Frequency of Update: Every 2 to 3 years
Scope: Results of EC surveys on the structure of farm holdings, including the size, physical and economic form of the holdings, the management of the holdings, the crops and livestock, and workers

The Future of Rural Society

Publisher: Office for Official Publications of the European Communities
Frequency of Publication: One time
Scope: Analysis of the long-term prospects for the EC's rural areas

Guide to the Reform of the Community's Structural Funds

Publisher: Office for Official Publications of the European Communities
Frequency of Publication: One time
Scope: Details about EC's structural funds, their operations and goals

Initial and Continuing Vocational Training and Work Migration in Europe

Publisher: Office for Official Publications of the European Communities
Frequency of Publication: One time
Scope: Study of vocational education and employment and their impact on employment mobility in the EC

New Rules in Rural Policymaking

Publisher: OECD
Frequency of Publication: One time
Scope: Review of current policies of OECD members toward rural development

Pabil

Database Producer: European Community, DG VIII
Distributors/Hosts: ECHO
Frequency of Update: 6 times a year
Scope: Monitor of the progress of the EC's development programs ⊛

Partnerships for Rural Development

Publisher: OECD
Frequency of Publication: One time
Scope: Review of organizational and policy aspects that underpin effective partnerships, and assessment of prospects for successful use of institutional partnerships to carry out rural development

Regio

Database Producer: Eurostat
Distributors/Hosts: Eurostat
Frequency of Update: Periodically
Scope: Macroeconomic statistics on various regions of the EC; covers demography, economic accounts, unemployment, labor force sample survey, industry, agriculture, the EC's financial participation in investments, and transport ⊛

Regions

Publisher: Office for Official Publications of the European Communities
Frequency of Publication: Annual
Scope: Main aspects of the economic and social life of the EC's many regions; also available online via the database Regio; prepared by the Statistics Office of the EC ⊛

STAR

Publisher: Office for Official Publications of the European Communities
Frequency of Publication: One time
Scope: Brief summary of the operations of STAR, an EC program designed to give improved access to advanced telecommunications systems in "less-favored" regions of the EC

Strategic Partnering and Local Employment Initiatives

Publisher: Office for Official Publications of the European Communities
Frequency of Publication: One time
Scope: Summary in 2 volumes of case studies throughout the EC

Structure and Activity of Industry—Annual Inquiry

Publisher: Office for Official Publications of the European Communities
Frequency of Publication: Annual
Scope: Industrial census of the EC; regional data volumes also available; prepared by the Statistical Office of the EC

Survey on State Aids in the European Community

Publisher: Office for Official Publications of the European Communities
Frequency of Publication: One time
Scope: Analysis of direct and indirect assistance provided to businesses by EC member countries

Western Europe . . . A Tax Tour

Publisher: Arthur Andersen & Co.
Frequency of Publication: As needed
Scope: Background information on each country, highlights of the main features of each country's business and personal tax systems, as well as factors that could influence a decision regarding investment within the country

Related Topics and Industries

Employment and Labor; Regulation of Businesses and Competition; Social Services and Welfare. See also *Part IV—Sources on EC 1992 by Industry*

SMALL AND MEDIUM-SIZED BUSINESSES

EC Contacts

Commission of the European Communities

▲ Directorate-General XXIII (Enterprise Policy, Distributive Trades, Tourism, and Cooperatives)

Directorate (Enterprise Policy and Small and Medium-Sized Enterprises [SME])

Address: rue de la Loi 200
B-1049 Bruxelles
Belgium
Telephone: 2/235 81 18
Telex: 21877 COMEU B

European Parliament

▲ Committee on Economic and Monetary Affairs and Industrial Policy

Address: 97-113, rue Belliard
B-1040 Bruxelles
Belgium
Telephone: 2/284 21 21; 2/284 35 40
Fax: 2/230 68 56; 2/231 12 57

Address: Palais de l'Europe
F-67006 Strasbourg Cedex
France
Telephone: 88/374 001; 88/375 484
Fax: 88/369 214; 88/256 516

Address: Centre Europeen
Plateau du Kirchberg
L-2929 Luxembourg
Telephone: 430 01
Telex: 3493 EUPARL LU; 2894 EUPARL LU
Fax: 436 972; 435 359

Associations

▲ CEDI (European Confederation of Independent European Businesses)

Address: Oberbexbacherstrasse 7
D-6652 Bexbach
Germany
Telephone: 6826/1470 - 2188
Fax: 6826/50904

▲ Centre for European Business Information—Small Firms Service

Address: Ebury Bridge House
2-18 Ebury Bridge Road
GB-London SW1W 8QD
Great Britain
Telephone: 71/730 8815

▲ CLD (Liaison Committee of Associations of European Franchisers)

Address: av. A Lacomble 17
B-1040 Bruxelles
Belgium
Telephone: 2/736 05 31
Telex: 64192 GEDIS B
Fax: 2/736 05 42

▲ EMSU (European Medium and Small Business Union)

Address: Deutscher Bundestag
Hochhaus Tulpenfeld HT 304/305
Postfach 120443
D-5300 Bonn 1
Germany
Telephone: 228/16 76 54
Telex: 8869350 BTHT D
Fax: 228/16 32 73 (HT 305)

▲ EUROPMI (European Committee for Small and Medium-Sized Independent Companies)

Address: rue de Stalle 90
B-1180 Bruxelles
Belgium
Telephone: 2/376 85 57
Fax: 2/376 01 71

▲ UEAPME (European Association of Craft, Small and Medium-Sized Enterprises)

Address: rue de Spa 8
B-1040 Bruxelles
Belgium
Telephone: 2/238 06 71/72
Fax: 2/230 93 54

Data Sources and Publications

Continuing Training in Enterprises for Techno-logical Change

Publisher: Office for Official Publications of the European Communities
Frequency of Publication: One time
Scope: Strategy for the future for entrepreneurs

Data Banks of Interest to SMEs

Publisher: Office for Official Publications of the European Communities
Frequency of Publication: One time
Scope: Directory of public databases of interest to small and medium-sized businesses in the EC; prepared by the SME Task Force of the EC

Evaluation of Policy Measures for the Creation and Development of Small and Medium-Sized Enterprises

Publisher: Office for Official Publications of the European Communities
Frequency of Publication: One time
Scope: Status report as of October 1988

Implementing Change: Entrepreneurship and Local Initiative

Publisher: OECD
Frequency of Publication: One time
Scope: Description of new trends in entrepreneurship and financial mechanisms that create employment and foster entrepreneurship

Industrial Relations in Small and Medium-Sized Enterprises

Publisher: Office for Official Publications of the European Communities
Frequency of Publication: One time
Scope: Study of management-labor relations problems in small and medium-sized businesses

Management Education for Small and Medium-Sized Enterprises in the European Communities

Publisher: Office for Official Publications of the European Communities
Frequency of Publication: One time
Scope: Summary of management education activities for SMEs; prepared by CEDEFOP

Methods of Promoting the Supply of Risk Capital

Publisher: Office for Official Publications of the European Communities
Frequency of Publication: One time
Scope: Study on using banking to improve the equity capital resources of SMEs

Operations of the European Community Concerning Small and Medium-Sized Enterprises

Publisher: Office for Official Publications of the European Communities
Frequency of Publication: One time
Scope: Guide to operation of SMEs in the EC, including information on business cooperation, grants, and loans

Terms of Payment for Small and Medium-Sized Enterprises and a Challenge in the Internal Market

Publisher: Office for Official Publications of the European Communities
Frequency of Publication: One time
Scope: Prepared by DG XXIII

Training in Innovative Management

Publisher: Office for Official Publications of the European Communities
Frequency of Publication: One time
Scope: Prepared by DG XIII

Trends in Enterprises

Publisher: OECD
Frequency of Publication: One time
Scope: Study of business trends in OECD member countries

Related Topics and Industries

Employment and Labor; Regulation of Businesses and Competition; Social Services and Welfare. See also *Part IV—Sources on EC 1992 by Industry*

22 Employment and Labor

▼

THE IMPACT OF THE SINGLE MARKET PROGRAM ON EMPLOYMENT AND LABOR: HIGHLIGHTS

Free Movement of Labor

One of the key goals of the Single Market Program is the "free movement of persons" throughout the Community. This could eventually eliminate national requirements for residence and work permits, once the visa policies of all Member States are coordinated. The free movement of labor forces among EC nations is intimately related to achieving the EC goal of free movement for all persons.

Employee-Employer Relations

Among the important impacts of the Single Market on employment throughout the Community will be the eventual adoption of pending proposals dealing with many aspects of the employment relationship, including employment contracts, providing for increased employee participation and consultation, and incentives for greater employment of the handicapped.

Protecting and Benefiting Employees

In addition, Single Market Program measures are being adopted that may have a significant impact on employees and employers alike. They deal with a wide variety of topics, including the following:

- Health and safety in the work place
- Occupational diseases
- Allowing leaves for employees to receive vocational education
- Financial protection, including social security and job protection during maternity leave

KEY ISSUES FACING THE SINGLE MARKET PROGRAM

- Continuing the development and improvement of vocational education programs, such as CEDEFOP, the European Centre for the Development of Vocational Training
- Adopting additional Directives dealing with health and safety in the work place
- Deciding whether any European Company law will require businesses to provide for employee participation or consultation in management and business decision making

SECTIONS IN THIS CHAPTER

Training

Unemployment

Wages, Benefits, and Working Conditions

Other Topics in Employment and Labor

ASSISTANCE

Appendix D contains a list of the Single Market measures dealing with employment and labor. For additional help on using the resources in this chapter, refer to the Introduction to Part III.

TRAINING

EC Contacts

Commission of the European Communities

▲ European Centre for the Development of Vocational Training (CEDEFOP)

Address: Bundesallee 22
              D-1000 Berlin
              Germany
Telephone: 30/88 41 20
Telex: 184163 EUCEN D

Commission of the European Communities

▲ Task Force for Human Resources, Education, Training, and Youth

Address: rue de la Loi 200
              B-1049 Bruxelles
              Belgium
Telephone: 2/235 11 11
Telex: 21877 COMEU B

European Parliament

▲ Committee on Legal Affairs and Citizens' Rights

Address: 97-113, rue Belliard
              B-1040 Bruxelles
              Belgium
Telephone: 2/284 21 21; 2/284 33 45
Fax: 2/230 68 56; 2/231 12 57

Address: Palais de l'Europe
              F-67006 Strasbourg Cedex
              France
Telephone: 88/374 001; 88/374 164
Fax: 88/369 214; 88/256 516

Address: Centre Europeen
              Plateau du Kirchberg
              L-2929 Luxembourg
Telephone: 430 01
Telex: 3493 EUPARL LU; 2894 EUPARL LU
Fax: 436 972; 435 359

European Parliament

▲ Committee on Social Affairs, Employment, and the Working Environment

Address: 97-113, rue Belliard
              B-1040 Bruxelles
              Belgium
Telephone: 2/284 21 21; 2/284 35 04
Fax: 2/230 68 56; 2/231 12 57

Address: Palais de l'Europe
              F-67006 Strasbourg Cedex
              France
Telephone: 88/374 001; 88/374 037; 88/374 548
Fax: 88/369 214; 88/256 516

Address: Centre Europeen
              Plateau du Kirchberg
              L-2929 Luxembourg
Telephone: 430 01
Telex: 3493 EUPARL LU; 2894 EUPARL LU
Fax: 436 972; 435 359

European Parliament

▲ Committee on Youth, Culture, Education, the Media and Sport

Address: 97-113, rue Belliard
              B-1040 Bruxelles
              Belgium
Telephone: 2/284 21 21; 2/284 25 11
Fax: 2/230 68 56; 2/231 12 57

Address: Palais de l'Europe
              F-67006 Strasbourg Cedex
              France
Telephone: 88/374 001; 88/374 522
Fax: 88/369 214; 88/256 516

Address: Centre Europeen
Plateau du Kirchberg
L-2929 Luxembourg
Telephone: 430 01
Telex: 3493 EUPARL LU; 2894 EUPARL LU
Fax: 436 972; 435 359

Data Resources and Publications

Annual Report—CEDEFOP

Publisher: Office for Official Publications of the European Communities
Frequency of Publication: Annual
Scope: Official summary of actions of CEDE-FOP, the European Centre for the Development of Vocational Training

CEDEFOP News

Publisher: Office for Official Publications of the European Communities
Frequency of Publication: Occasional
Scope: Information on vocational training; prepared by CEDEFOP

Continuing Training in Enterprises for Technological Change

Publisher: Office for Official Publications of the European Communities
Frequency of Publication: One time
Scope: Study of on-site vocational training to deal with changing technologies; prepared by CEDEFOP

Evaluation of the Comett Programme

Publisher: Office for Official Publications of the European Communities
Frequency of Publication: One time
Scope: Review of Comett, EC's Community Program in Education and Training for Technology

First Invitation Conference on Databases for Education and Training

Publisher: Office for Official Publications of the European Communities
Frequency of Publication: One time
Scope: Proceedings of meeting on the use of computers in education and training in the EC; organized by CEDEFOP

Higher Education in the European Community

Publisher: Office for Official Publications of the European Communities
Frequency of Publication: Every 2 years
Scope: Directory of courses and institutions in the EC, including vocational and technical education

Industrial Training

Publisher: United Nations
Frequency of Publication: Regularly updated
Scope: Directory of basic industrial information sources

Initial and Continuing Vocational Training and Work Migration in Europe

Publisher: Office for Official Publications of the European Communities
Frequency of Publication: One time
Scope: Vocational education and employment

Management Education for Small and Medium-Sized Enterprises in the European Communities

Publisher: Office for Official Publications of the European Communities
Frequency of Publication: One time
Scope: Summary of management education activities for SMEs; prepared by CEDEFOP

Occupational Hygiene Education in the EEC: A Survey of Existing Programs

Publisher: Office for Official Publications of the European Communities
Frequency of Publication: One time
Scope: Survey of national education programs on occupational hygiene; prepared by DG V

Promotion of Cooperation Among Research and Development Organizations in the Field of Vocational Training

Publisher: Office for Official Publications of the European Communities
Frequency of Publication: Annual
Scope: Working meeting papers of CEDEFOP-sponsored meetings on vocational training in R&D enterprises

The Role of the Two Sides of Industry in Initial and Continuing Training

Publisher: Office for Official Publications of the European Communities

Frequency of Publication: One time

Scope: Documentation from a CEDEFOP-sponsored conference on the roles of labor and management in training

The Social Dialogue in the Member States of the European Community in the Field of Vocational Training and Continuing Training

Publisher: Office for Official Publications of the European Communities

Frequency of Publication: One time

Scope: Report on the "social dimension" of the Single Market Program and its impact on training; prepared by CEDEFOP

Social Work Training in the European Community

Publisher: Office for Official Publications of the European Communities

Frequency of Publication: One time

Scope: Brief discussion of social work training

Tecnet

Database Producer: European Centre for Work and Society, Maastricht, The Netherlands

Distributors/Hosts: ECHO

Frequency of Update: As needed

Scope: Demonstration projects of the Eurotecnet network; these projects represent a cross section of training approaches in the field of new information technologies and vocational training ✇

Training in Innovation Management

Publisher: Office for Official Publications of the European Communities

Frequency of Publication: One time

Scope: Reports on training in industries facing product and technological innovation; prepared by DG XIII

Vocational Training—Information Bulletin

Publisher: Office for Official Publications of the European Communities

Frequency of Publication: 3 times a year

Scope: Information about vocational program reports and studies carried out by CEDEFOP, the European Centre for the Development of Vocational Training

Related Topics and Industries

Economic and Business Development; Science and Technology; Social and Economic Policy. See also Part IV—Sources on EC 1992 by Industry

▼

UNEMPLOYMENT

EC Contacts

Commission of the European Communities

▲ Statistical Office

Directorate E/1 (Social and Regional Statistics/Employment and Unemployment)

Address: Batiment Jean Monnet
rue Alcide de Gasperi
L-2920 Luxembourg

Telephone: 430 11

Telex: 3423/3446/3476 COMEUR LU

European Parliament

▲ Committee on Social Affairs, Employment, and the Working Environment

Address: 97-113, rue Belliard
B-1040 Bruxelles
Belgium

Telephone: 2/284 21 21; 2/284 35 04

Fax: 2/230 68 56; 2/231 12 57

Address: Palais de l'Europe
F-67006 Strasbourg Cedex
France
Telephone: 88/374 001; 88/374 037; 88/374 548
Fax: 88/369 214; 88/256 516

Address: Centre Europeen
Plateau du Kirchberg
L-2929 Luxembourg
Telephone: 430 01
Telex: 3493 EUPARL LU; 2894 EUPARL LU
Fax: 436 972; 435 359

Data Resources and Publications

Employment and Unemployment

Publisher: Office for Official Publications of the
European Communities
Frequency of Publication: Annual
Scope: Reports on employment statistics from
EC member states; prepared by the
Statistical Office of the EC

Employment in Europe—1989

Publisher: Office for Official Publications of the
European Communities
Frequency of Publication: One time
Scope: Employment statistics

Measures to Assist the Long-Term Unemployed: Recent Experiences in Some OECD Countries

Publisher: OECD
Frequency of Publication: One time
Scope: Summary of policies and results experi-
enced by major OECD members in
dealing with long-term unemployment
and the unemployed

Quarterly Labour Force Statistics

Publisher: OECD
Frequency of Publication: 4 times a year
Scope: Annual and quarterly data on the total
labor force and its components, such as
types of activity and unemployment,
covering 15 countries; available in
hardcopy and on microcomputer
diskette ▪

Regio

Database Producer: Eurostat
Distributors/Hosts: Eurostat
Frequency of Update: Periodically
Scope: Macroeconomic statistics on various
regions of the EC; covers demography,
economic accounts, unemployment,
labor force sample survey, industry,
agriculture, the EC's financial participation in investments, and transport ⊛

Social Europe—Supplement: Policy Measures for Combating Long-Term Unemployment in the European Community Since the 1984 Council Resolution

Publisher: Office for Official Publications of the
European Communities
Frequency of Publication: One time
Scope: Analysis of actions taken by EC member
countries from 1984 through 1988;
prepared by DG V

Social Europe—Supplement: Youth and Unemployment

Publisher: Office for Official Publications of the
European Communities
Frequency of Publication: One time
Scope: Report of conference on unemployment
problem of young adults and teenagers;
prepared by DG V

Strategic Partnering and Local Employment Initiatives

Publisher: Office for Official Publications of the
European Communities
Frequency of Publication: One time
Scope: Case studies of employment initiatives
in 2 volumes

Taking Action About Long-Term Unemployment in Europe

Publisher: Office for Official Publications of the
European Communities
Frequency of Publication: One time
Scope: Summary of 20 local projects through
the EC dealing with long-term and
structural unemployment in the EC

Unemployment

Publisher: Office for Official Publications of the European Communities

Frequency of Publication: Monthly

Scope: Absolute and relative figures for unemployed persons; also available online via the Cronos database; prepared by the Statistical Office of the EC

Related Topics and Industries

Economic and Business Development; Science and Technology; Social and Economic Policy. See also *Part IV—Sources on EC 1992 by Industry*

WAGES, BENEFITS, AND WORKING CONDITIONS

EC Contacts

Table 22.1 lists official European Community directorates and subdirectorates that provide information about wages, benefits, and working conditions. For the complete address of the Commission of the European Communities headquarters (CEC HQ in the table), refer to the Introduction to Part III.

Commission of the European Communities
▲ Consumer Policy Service

Unit 2 (Health, Safety, and Quality)

Address: rue de la Loi 200
B-1049 Bruxelles
Belgium
Telephone: 2/235 11 11
Telex: 21877 COMEU B

Commission of the European Communities
▲ Statistical Office

Directorate E/2 (Social and Regional Statistics/Living and Working Conditions)

Address: Batiment Jean Monnet
rue Alcide de Gasperi
L-2920 Luxembourg
Telephone: 430 11
Telex: 3423/3446/3476 COMEUR LU

Commission of the European Communities
▲ European Foundation for the Improvement of Living and Working Conditions

Address: Loughlinstown House
Shankill
IRL-CO. Dublin
Ireland
Telephone: 12/826888
Telex: 30726 EURF

European Parliament
▲ Committee on Social Affairs, Employment, and the Working Environment

Address: 97–113, rue Belliard
B-1040 Bruxelles
Belgium
Telephone: 2/284 21 21; 2/284 35 04
Fax: 2/230 68 56; 2/231 12 57

Address: Palais de l'Europe
F-67006 Strasbourg Cedex
France
Telephone: 88/374 001; 88/374 037; 88/374 548
Fax: 88/369 214; 88/256 516

Table 22.1
CEC Subdirectorates—Wages, Benefits, and Working Conditions

Directorate and Subdirectorate Name	Directorate/ Subdirectorate Number	Directorate- General	Address
Living and Working Conditions and Welfare	B	V	CEC HQ, Belgium
Health and Safety	D	V	CEC HQ, Belgium

▼ ──────────────────────────────────── ▼

Address: Centre Europeen
Plateau du Kirchberg
L-2929 Luxembourg
Telephone: 430 01
Telex: 3493 EUPARL LU; 2894 EUPARL LU
Fax: 436 972; 435 359

European Parliament
▲ Committee on the Environment, Public
Health, and Consumer Protection

Address: 97–113, rue Belliard
B-1040 Bruxelles
Belgium
Telephone: 2/284 21 21; 2/284 28 48
Fax: 2/230 68 56; 2/231 12 57

Address: Palais de l'Europe
F-67006 Strasbourg Cedex
France
Telephone: 88/374 001; 88/374 418
Fax: 88/369 214; 88/256 516

Address: Centre Europeen
Plateau du Kirchberg
L-2929 Luxembourg
Telephone: 430 01
Telex: 3493 EUPARL LU; 2894 EUPARL LU
Fax: 436 972; 435 359

Data Resources and Publications

Adapting Shiftwork Arrangements
Publisher: Office for Official Publications of the
European Communities
Frequency of Publication: One time
Scope: Study of ways to improve employee
productivity

Earnings: Industry and Services
Publisher: Office for Official Publications of the
European Communities
Frequency of Publication: 2 times a year
Scope: Detailed results of statistics on earnings
of manual and nonmanual workers in
industry and certain groups of activities
in the service sector; also available
online via the Cronos database; prepared by the Statistical Office of the EC

⊛

EF News
Publisher: Office for Official Publications of the
European Communities
Frequency of Publication: 5 times a year
Scope: Newsletter of the European Foundation
for the Improvement of Living and
Working Conditions

Related Topics and Industries

*Economic and Business Development; Regulation of
Businesses and Competition; Social and Economic
Policy.* See also *Part IV—Sources on EC 1992 by
Industry*

─── ▼ ───

OTHER TOPICS IN EMPLOYMENT AND LABOR

EC Contacts

Table 22.2 lists official European Community directorates and subdirectorates that provide information about other topics in employment and
labor. For the complete address of the Commission of the European Communities headquarters
(CEC HQ in the table), refer to the Introduction to
Part III.

Commission of the European Communities
▲ Statistical Office

Directorate E/1 (Social and Regional Statistics/
Employment and Unemployment)

Address: Batiment Jean Monnet
rue Alcide de Gasperi
L-2920 Luxembourg
Telephone: 430 11
Telex: 3423/3446/3476 COMEUR LU

European Parliament

▲ Committee on Legal Affairs and Citizens' Rights

Address: 97–113, rue Belliard
            B-1040 Bruxelles
            Belgium
Telephone: 2/284 21 21; 2/284 33 45
Fax: 2/230 68 56; 2/231 12 57

Address: Palais de l'Europe
            F-67006 Strasbourg Cedex
            France
Telephone: 88/374 001; 88/374 164
Fax: 88/369 214; 88/256 516

Address: Centre Europeen
            Plateau du Kirchberg
            L-2929 Luxembourg
Telephone: 430 01
Telex: 3493 EUPARL LU; 2894 EUPARL LU
Fax: 436 972; 435 359

Associations

▲ EFCGU (European Federation of Chemical and General Workers' Unions)

Address: av. Emile de Beco 109
            B-1050 Bruxelles
            Belgium
Telephone: 2/648 24 97
Fax: 2/648 43 16

Table 22.2
CEC Subdirectorates—Other Topics in Employment and Labor

Directorate and Subdirectorate Name	Directorate/ Subdirectorate Number	Directorate-General	Address
Approximation of Laws, Freedom of Establishment, and Freedom to Provide Services			
Free Movement of Self-employed Persons and Recognition of Diplomas	D/2	III	CEC HQ, Belgium Telephone: 2/236 30 12
Employment			
Employment and Labour Market Policy	A/1	V	CEC HQ, Belgium
Action on Employment and Equality for Women	A/4	V	CEC HQ, Belgium
Nuclear Safety, Impact of Industry on the Environment, and Waste Management			
Economic Aspects, Employment, and Statistics	A/4	XI	CEC HQ, Belgium
Company Law, Company and Capital Movements Taxation			
Company Law, Industrial Democracy, and Accounting Standards	B/2	XV	CEC HQ, Belgium Telephone: 2/235 53 47

▲ ETUC (European Trade Union Confederation)

Address: rue Montagne aux
                   Herbes Potageres 37
                   B-1000 Bruxelles
                   Belgium
Telephone: 2/218 31 00
Telex: 62241 DK
Fax: 2/218 35 66

▲ ETUI (European Trade Union Institute)

Address: bd. de l'Imperatrice 66 (Bte 4)
                   B-1000 Bruxelles
                   Belgium
Telephone: 2/512 30 70
Fax: 2/514 17 31

▲ Union of Industrial and Employers' Confederations of Europe

Address: rue Joseph 11 40 (Bte 4)
                   B-1040 Bruxelles
                   Belgium
Telephone: 2/237 65 11
Telex: 26013 B
Fax: 2/231 14 45

Data Sources and Publications

Advanced Population Aging in Europe and North America—Demographic and Economic Aspects

Publisher: United Nations Economic Commission for Europe
Frequency of Publication: One time
Scope: Demographic aspects of population aging, including effects of changing vital rates on aging, as well as the impact of aging on the economy, public expenditures, and the labor market

Annual Review of Engineering Industries and Automation

Publisher: United Nations Economic Commission for Europe
Frequency of Publication: Annual
Scope: Analyses of data on production, investments, staffing, and price indexes

The Changing Face of Work: Researching and Debating the Issues

Publisher: Office for Official Publications of the European Communities
Frequency of Publication: One time
Scope: Analyses of changes in employee roles and the work place

Elise

Database Producer: European Community, DG V
Distributors/Hosts: ECHO
Frequency of Update: 4 times a year
Scope: European network for information exchange on local employment schemes

                                                                                ⊛

Employment Outlook

Publisher: OECD
Frequency of Publication: Annual
Scope: Trends in the labor markets of OECD members, including total hours worked, patterns in regional labor markets, and data on people who lose jobs; also includes a statistical annex

Erasmus Newsletter

Publisher: Office for Official Publications of the European Communities
Frequency of Publication: 3 times a year
Scope: Developments in the Erasmus program —the European Community Action Scheme for the Mobility of University Students; prepared by DG V

The European Commission and the Administration of the Community

Publisher: Office for Official Publications of the European Communities
Frequency of Publication: One time
Scope: Description of the European Civil Service

European Information Bulletin

Publisher: Office for Official Publications of the European Communities
Frequency of Publication: 4 times a year
Scope: Newsletter for trade unionists

Freedom of Movement in the Community— Entry and Residence

Publisher: Office for Official Publications of the European Communities

Frequency of Publication: One time

Scope: Information on travel and residence requirements throughout the EC

FSSRS

Database Producer: Eurostat

Distributors/Hosts: Eurostat

Frequency of Update: Every 2 to 3 years

Scope: Results of EC surveys on the structure of farm holdings, including the size and physical and economic form of the holdings, the management of the holdings, the crops and livestock, and workers   ⊛

A Guide to Working in a Europe Without Frontiers

Publisher: Office for Official Publications of the European Communities

Frequency of Publication: One time

Scope: Handbook for employees on the impact of the Single Market Program on labor mobility

Industrial Relations in Small and Medium-Sized Enterprises

Publisher: Office for Official Publications of the European Communities

Frequency of Publication: One time

Scope: Management-labor relations in small and medium-sized businesses

Industrial Structure Statistics

Publisher: OECD

Frequency of Publication: Annual

Scope: Statistics for such topics as production, value added (to products and services), number of establishments, employment, wages and salaries, exports, imports, and investment

The Informal Sector Revisited

Publisher: OECD

Frequency of Publication: One time

Scope: Surveys of existing knowledge and discusses an agenda for research addressing the further development of policies and programs for the "informal sector," a leading provider of first-time jobs

Innovation and Employment

Publisher: OECD

Frequency of Publication: 4 times a year

Scope: Reviews of developments in innovation policy as they affect employment; prepared jointly with the Commission of the European Communities

International Sectoral Databank

Publisher: OECD

Frequency of Publication: Monthly

Scope: Standardized data for 14 of the OECD countries on subjects including Gross Domestic Product, Total Employment, Compensation of Employees, and Capital Stock; available on microdiskette   ∎

Iron and Steel—Monthly Statistics

Publisher: Office for Official Publications of the European Communities

Frequency of Publication: Monthly

Scope: Data on employment; consumption of raw materials; and production of iron ore, pig iron, crude steel, finished steel products, and end products; also available online via the Cronos database; prepared by the Statistical Office of the EC   ⊛

Labor Market Policies for the 1990s

Publisher: OECD

Frequency of Publication: One time

Scope: Outlines the thrust and emphasis of future labor market policies in OECD countries

Main Economic Indicators

Publisher: OECD

Frequency of Publication: Monthly

Scope: Description of the most recent changes in the economy of OECD countries, as well as statistics on labor, prices, and interest rates; also the name of a set of microcomputer diskettes, containing most (but not all) of the data from the hardcopy publication of the same name ■

Misep

Database Producer: ECWS (European Centre for Work and Society, Maastricht, The Netherlands)

Distributors/Hosts: ECHO

Frequency of Update: 2 times a year

Scope: Biographical references to documents published within the context of the Misrep (Mutual Information System on Employment Policies in Europe) program ⊛

New Forms of Work

Publisher: Office for Official Publications of the European Communities

Frequency of Publication: One time

Scope: Labor law and social security in the EC; prepared by the European Foundation for the Improvement of Living and Working Conditions

New Information Technology and Participation in Europe: The Potential for Social Dialogue

Publisher: Office for Official Publications of the European Communities

Frequency of Publication: One time

Scope: Analysis of the impact of information technology on worker and consumer participation in business decision making; prepared by the European Foundation for the Improvement of Living and Working Conditions

New Semi-Sheltered Forms of Employment for Disabled Persons

Publisher: Office for Official Publications of the European Communities

Frequency of Publication: One time

Scope: Analysis of "landmark" measures in the EC member states; prepared by CEDEFOP

The OECD Observer

Publisher: OECD

Frequency of Publication: 6 times a year

Scope: Key problems dealt with by the OECD, including economic growth, employment, social problems, energy, financial markets, the environment, and science and technology

Participation Review

Publisher: Office for Official Publications of the European Communities

Frequency of Publication: One time

Scope: Reviews studies on employee participation in management decision making made by the European Foundation for the Improvement of Living and Working Conditions

Preparation for Retirement in the Member States of the European Community

Publisher: Office for Official Publications of the European Communities

Frequency of Publication: One time

Scope: Reports on 1988 seminar on retirement-related issues

Programme for Research and Actions on the Development of the Labor Market

Publisher: Office for Official Publications of the European Communities

Frequency of Publication: One time

Scope: Overview of trends and distribution of incomes; prepared by the European Federation for Economic Research

Progress in Structural Reform

Publisher: OECD

Frequency of Publication: Periodically

Scope: Reviews economic activities of OECD members, including specific coverage of the EC, in areas including agriculture, industrial policy, and labor markets; a supplement to selected issues of OECD's *Economic Outlook*

Quarterly Labour Force Statistics

Publisher: OECD

Frequency of Publication: 4 times a year

Scope: Coverage of 15 countries on the total labor force and its components, such as types of activity and unemployment; available in hardcopy and on microcomputer diskette ∎

Reforming Public Pensions

Publisher: OECD

Frequency of Publication: One time

Scope: Analysis of the funding and future burdens of public pensions in OECD countries, with suggestions for long-term reform

Research Manpower

Publisher: OECD

Frequency of Publication: One time

Scope: Suggestions for managing the supply of and demand for skilled researchers

Social Europe—Review

Publisher: Office for Official Publications of the European Communities

Frequency of Publication: 3 times a year

Scope: Critical review of the social aspects of the Single Market Program, including information on employment; prepared by DG V

Social Europe—Supplement: The Leading Edge

Publisher: Office for Official Publications of the European Communities

Frequency of Publication: One time

Scope: Reviews of the growth of school/industry partnerships in the EC; prepared by DG V

Related Topics and Industries

Economic and Business Development; Regulation of Businesses and Competition; Social and Economic Policy. See also *Part IV—Sources on EC 1992 by Industry*

23

Regulation of Businesses and Competition

THE IMPACT OF THE SINGLE MARKET PROGRAM ON THE REGULATION OF BUSINESSES AND COMPETITION:
HIGHLIGHTS

Although the goal of the Single Market Program is to remove barriers to internal trade within the EC, the EC continues to deal with a wide variety of collateral regulatory issues in moving toward that goal:

European Company Law. One of the most important subjects still under consideration by the EC as Europe moves toward the Single Market is the creation of a Community-wide company statute.

Competition Policy. Controlling competition and regulating mergers and acquisitions continues to be a topic of importance to the EC. The EC has created a mechanism for reviewing major mergers on a Community-wide basis.

Protecting Consumers. Improvements in consumer protection, including the regulation of the safety of goods and products, will continue to occupy an important place as the EC moves toward a Single Market. This area already encompasses measures covering topics such as safety standards for specific products, banning particular substances, and requiring increased uniformity in food labeling.

Environmental Protection. Efforts to protect the environment will become more significant as the Single Market Program progresses. Environmental protection measures include controlling or eliminating nitrates in the water, phosphates in detergents, and burning by-products of toxic waste.

KEY ISSUES FACING THE SINGLE MARKET PROGRAM

- Adopting an EC company statute
- Developing an EC-wide intellectual and property protection program
- Clarifying the liability of companies for harm caused by waste and defective products

SECTIONS IN THIS CHAPTER

Advertising and Consumer Protection

Competition and Trade Regulation

Environmental Protection

Organizing a Business

Patents, Trademarks, and Other Copyright Protection

Product Standards, Safety, and Certifications

Other Topics in the Regulation of Business and Competition

ASSISTANCE

Appendix D contains a list of the Single Market measures dealing with the regulation of businesses and competition. For additional help on using the resources in this chapter, refer to the Introduction to Part III.

▬▬▬ ▼ ▬▬▬

ADVERTISING AND CONSUMER PROTECTION

EC Contacts

Table 23.1 lists the units of the European Community Consumer Policy Service that provide information about consumerism efforts of the EC. Contact any of these units using the general address for the CEC headquarters.

Commission of the European Communities
▲ Directorate-General III (Internal Market and Industrial Affairs)

Directorate D/4 (Approximation of Laws, Freedom of Establishment, and Freedom to Provide Services/Copyright, Unfair Competition, and International Aspects of Intellectual Property)

Address: rue de la Loi 200
B-1049 Bruxelles
Belgium
Telephone: 2/236 30 12
Telex: 21877 COMEU B

European Parliament
▲ Committee on Legal Affairs and Citizens' Rights

Address: 97–113, rue Belliard
B-1040 Bruxelles
Belgium
Telephone: 2/284 21 21; 2/284 33 45
Fax: 2/230 68 56; 2/231 12 57

Address: Palais de l'Europe
F-67006 Strasbourg Cedex
France
Telephone: 88/374 001; 88/374 164
Fax: 88/369 214; 88/256 516

Address: Centre Europeen
Plateau du Kirchberg
L-2929 Luxembourg
Telephone: 430 01
Telex: 3493 EUPARL LU; 2894 EUPARL LU
Fax: 436 972; 435 359

Table 23.1
Consumer Policy Service Units of the CEC and Areas of Consumer Concerns

Unit	Title
1	General Matters; Relations with the Community Institutions and Consumer Organizations
2	Health, Safety, and Quality
3	Transactions Involving Consumers
4	Consumer Information and Training

European Parliament

▲ Committee on the Environment, Public Health, and Consumer Protection

Address: 97–113, rue Belliard
B-1040 Bruxelles
Belgium
Telephone: 2/284 21 21; 2/284 28 48
Fax: 2/230 68 56; 2/231 12 57

Address: Palais de l'Europe
F-67006 Strasbourg Cedex
France
Telephone: 88/374 001; 88/374 418
Fax: 88/369 214; 88/256 516

Address: Centre Europeen
Plateau du Kirchberg
L-2929 Luxembourg
Telephone: 430 01
Telex: 3493 EUPARL LU; 2894 EUPARL LU
Fax: 436 972; 435 359

European Parliament

▲ Committee on Youth, Culture, Education, the Media and Sport

Address: 97–113, rue Belliard
B-1040 Bruxelles
Belgium
Telephone: 2/284 21 21; 2/284 25 11
Fax: 2/230 68 56; 2/231 12 57

Address: Palais de l'Europe
F-67006 Strasbourg Cedex
France
Telephone: 88/374 001; 88/374 522
Fax: 88/369 214; 88/256 516

Address: Centre Europeen
Plateau du Kirchberg
L-2929 Luxembourg
Telephone: 430 01
Telex: 3493 EUPARL LU; 2894 EUPARL LU
Fax: 436 972; 435 359

Associations

▲ BEUC (Bureau Europeen des Unions des Consommateurs [Consumers' Associations])

Address: rue Royale 29 (Bte 3)
B-1000 Bruxelles
Belgium
Telephone: 2/218 30 93
Telex: 63772 B
Fax: 2/218 70 55

▲ Common Market Group of the World Federation of Advertisers

Address: rue des Colonies 54 (Bte 13)
B-1000 Bruxelles
Belgium
Telephone: 2/219 06 98
Fax: 2/219 54 64

▲ EAAA (European Association of Advertising Agencies)

Address: av. du Barbeau 28
B-1160 Bruxelles
Belgium
Telephone: 2/672 43 36
Telex: 62864 EAAA B
Fax: 2/672 00 14

▲ EAT (European Advertising Tripartite)

Address: av. du Barbeau 28
B-1160 Bruxelles
Belgium
Telephone: 2/672 43 36
Fax: 2/672 00 14

▲ EGTA (European Group of Television Advertising)

Address: Knighton House
56 Mortimer Street
GB-London W1N 8AN
Great Britain
Telephone: 71/636 6866
Telex: 262988 G
Fax: 71/580 7892

▲ EURO COOP (European Community of Consumer Cooperatives)

Address: rue Archimede 17A
B-1040 Bruxelles
Belgium
Telephone: 2/230 14 11
Fax: 2/231 07 57

Data Resources and Publications

Consumer Policies in OECD Countries

Publisher: OECD
Frequency of Publication: Every 2 years
Scope: Main developments in consumer protection policies in OECD countries

Individual Choice and Higher Growth—The Task of European Consumer Policy

Publisher: Office for Official Publications of the European Communities
Frequency of Publication: One time
Scope: Description of consumer's role in a frontier-free Europe

Related Topics and Industries

See *Part IV—Sources on EC 1992 by Industry*

▼

COMPETITION AND TRADE REGULATION

EC Contacts

Table 23.2 lists official European Community directorates and subdirectorates that provide information about competition and trade regulation. For the complete address of the Commission of the European Communities headquarters (CEC HQ in the table), refer to the Introduction to Part III.

European Parliament

▲ Committee on Economic and Monetary Affairs and Industrial Policy

Address: 97–113, rue Belliard
B-1040 Bruxelles
Belgium
Telephone: 2/284 21 21; 2/284 35 40
Fax: 2/230 68 56; 2/231 12 57

Address: Palais de l'Europe
F-67006 Strasbourg Cedex
France
Telephone: 88/374 001; 88/375 484
Fax: 88/369 214; 88/256 516

Address: Centre Europeen
Plateau du Kirchberg
L-2929 Luxembourg
Telephone: 430 01
Telex: 3493 EUPARL LU; 2894 EUPARL LU
Fax: 436 972; 435 359

Data Resources and Publications

Barriers to Entry and Intensity of Competition in European Markets

Publisher: Office for Official Publications of the European Communities
Frequency of Publication: One time
Scope: Study of competition and the impact of entry barriers throughout the EC

Competition in Banking

Publisher: OECD
Frequency of Publication: One time
Scope: Review of policies of OECD member countries toward permitting competition in banking and with banks

Competition Policy and Intellectual Property Rights

Publisher: OECD
Frequency of Publication: One time
Scope: Patent and know-how licensing from the point of view of EC competition policy, among others

Competition Policy in OECD Countries

Publisher: OECD
Frequency of Publication: Annual
Scope: Current developments in competition policy, including antitrust and merger policies

Table 23.2
CEC Subdirectorates—Competition and Trade Regulation

Directorate and Subdirectorate Name	Directorate/ Subdirectorate Number	Directorate- General	Address
Approximation of Laws, Freedom of Establishment, and Freedom to Provide Services			
Copyright, Unfair Competition, and International Aspects of Intellectual Property	D/4	III	CEC HQ, Belgium Telephone: 2/236 30 12
General Competition Policy and Coordination			
General Policy and International Aspects; Relations with the European Parliament and the Economic and Social Commitee	A/1	IV	CEC HQ, Belgium
Coordination of Competition Decisions	A/4	IV	CEC HQ, Belgium
Public Enterprises and State Monopolies and Implementation of Articles 101 and 102	A/5	IV	CEC HQ, Belgium
Restrictive Practices, Abuse of Dominant Positions, and Other Distortions of Competition I	B	IV	CEC HQ, Belgium
Restrictive Practices, Abuse of Dominant Positions, and Other Distortions of Competition II	C	IV	CEC HQ, Belgium
Restrictive Practices, Abuse of Dominant Positions, and Other Distortions of Competition III	D	IV	CEC HQ, Belgium
Agroeconomic Legislation			
Competition	B-I/2	VI	CEC HQ, Belgium Telex: 22037 AGREC B
Telecommunications Policy, Technology Transfer, and Innovation			
Regulatory Aspects, Analyses, and Studies by Sector	D/2	XIII	CEC HQ, Belgium Telephone: 2/235 24 48

EEC Competition Policy in the Single Market

Publisher: Office for Official Publications of the European Communities
Frequency of Publication: Periodically
Scope: Guide to EC competition rules applicable to companies of all sizes

Innovation in the EC Automotive Industry

Publisher: Office for Official Publications of the European Communities
Frequency of Publication: One time
Scope: Analysis of state aid policy and the automotive industry

International Mergers and Competition Policy

Publisher: OECD
Frequency of Publication: One time
Scope: Summary of policies of major OECD members toward mergers and acquisitions

Predatory Pricing

Publisher: OECD
Frequency of Publication: One time
Scope: Review of competition rules in OECD members, including the EC, covering legality of low pricing

Progress in Structural Reform

Publisher: OECD
Frequency of Publication: Periodically
Scope: Reviews of the economic activities of all OECD members, as well as EC specifically, in areas including financial markets, investment, taxation, competition policy, trade, agriculture, industrial policy, and labor markets; a supplement to selected issues of OECD's *Economic Outlook*

Report on Competition Policy

Publisher: Office for Official Publications of the European Communities
Frequency of Publication: Annual
Scope: Survey of the competition policy during the prior year, its application to companies, state aid, and adjustments of national monopolies

Survey on State Aids in the European Community

Publisher: Office for Official Publications of the European Communities
Frequency of Publication: One time
Scope: Analysis of direct and indirect assistance provided to businesses by EC member countries

Related Topics and Industries

Economic and Business Development; Social and Economic Policy. See also *Part IV—Sources on EC 1992 by Industry*

ENVIRONMENTAL PROTECTION

EC Contacts

Table 23.3 lists official European Community directorates and subdirectorates that provide information about environmental protection. For the complete address of the Commission of the European Communities headquarters (CEC HQ in the table), refer to the Introduction to Part III.

Commission of the European Communities

▲ Directorate-General XII (Science, Research and Development)

Joint Research Centre
Institute for the Environment

Address: I-21020 Ispra (VA)
Italy
Telephone: 332/78 91 11
Telex: 380042/380058/324878/324880 EUR I
Fax: 332/78 90 45

Data Resources and Publications

Agricultural and Environmental Policies

Publisher: OECD
Frequency of Publication: One time
Scope: Summary of OECD member country policies dealing with the impact on the environment of agriculture

Bioconversion of Agricultural Wastes

Publisher: United Nations
Frequency of Publication: Periodically
Scope: Directory of basic industrial information sources

Table 23.3
CEC Subdirectorates—Environmental Protection

Directorate and Subdirectorate Name	Directorate/ Subdirectorate Number	Directorate-General	Address
Air Transport; Transport Infrastructure; Social and Ecological Aspects of Transport			
Social and Ecological Aspects of Transport	C/3	VII	CEC HQ, Belgium Telephone: 2/236 27 42
Nuclear Safety, Impact of Industry on the Environment, and Waste Management			
Monitoring of Chemical Substances, Industrial Hazards, and Biotechnology	A/2	XI	CEC HQ, Belgium
Waste Management, Clean Technologies, Soil Protection, and Prevention of Noise Pollution	A/3	XI	CEC HQ, Belgium
Protection of Water and the Air, and Conservation; Civil Protection			
Protection and Management of Water	B/1	XI	CEC HQ, Belgium
Monitoring of Atmospheric Pollution	B/2	XI	CEC HQ, Belgium
Agriculture, Nature Conservation, and Relations with Other Policies	B/4	XI	CEC HQ, Belgium
Environment and Nonnuclear Energy Sources			
Environment and Waste Recycling	E/1	XII	CEC HQ, Belgium
Climatology and Natural Hazards	E/2	XII	CEC HQ, Belgium

Compendium of OECD Environmental Data

Publisher: OECD

Frequency of Publication: Every 2 years

Scope: Data on the environment and environmental protection in OECD member countries

EABS

Database Producer: European Commission, DG XIII

Distributors/Hosts: ECHO

Frequency of Update: Monthly

Scope: References to the published results of scientific and technical research programs, sponsored in whole or in part by the EC; covers a wide range of topics including nuclear research, new sources, or energy and environmental research ⊛

Ecdin

Database Producer: EC Joint Research Center for Information Technology and Electronics, Ispra (CITE)

Distributors/Hosts: CITE

Frequency of Update: Periodically

Scope: Data on chemical products that actually or potentially affect the environment or human health, by their manufacture, use, transport, or disposal ⊛

Economic Instruments for Environmental Protection

Publisher: OECD

Frequency of Publication: One time

Scope: Provides alternative approaches to using market forces to provide for environmental protection

Environmental Data

Publisher: OECD

Frequency of Publication: Annual

Scope: Environmental data for most OECD countries

The European Community and the Problems of Its Waters

Publisher: Office for Official Publications of the European Communities

Frequency of Publication: One time

Scope: Brief summary of the water supply problems facing the EC; prepared by DG XI

Ground Water in Eastern and Northern Europe

Publisher: United Nations

Frequency of Publication: One time

Scope: Survey of ground water resources and demands in portions of Europe

National Strategies for Protection of Flora, Fauna, and Their Habitats

Publisher: United Nations Economic Commission for Europe

Frequency of Publication: One time

Scope: Review of general problems in protecting the major ecosystems; analysis of the legislative basis, administration, and policy instruments applied in member countries

The OECD Observer

Publisher: OECD

Frequency of Publication: 6 times a year

Scope: Key problems dealt with by the OECD, including economic growth, employment, social problems, energy, financial markets, the environment, and science and technology

Panorama of EC Industry

Publisher: Office for Official Publications of the European Communities

Frequency of Publication: Annual

Scope: Description of 165 manufacturing and service industries, including external industrial trade, plus evaluations of the impact of the Single Market Program

Pesticides Industry

Publisher: United Nations

Frequency of Publication: Periodically

Scope: Directory of basic industrial information sources

Regional Strategy for Environmental Protection and Rational Use of Natural Resources

Publisher: United Nations Economic Commission for Europe

Frequency of Publication: One time

Scope: Collective experiences and insights of UNECE member countries on critical environmental problems and possible solutions

REM

Database Producer: EC Joint Research Center for Information Technology and Electronics, Ispra (CITE)
Distributors/Hosts: CITE
Frequency of Update: 4 times a year
Scope: Radioactivity data from the national network of Member Countries of the EC

Tourism Policy and International Tourism in OECD Member Countries

Publisher: OECD
Frequency of Publication: One time
Scope: Reviews the impact of tourist growth and transport deregulation, government policies toward tourism, and tourism on the environment

Transport Policy and the Environment: ECMT Ministerial Session

Publisher: OECD
Frequency of Publication: One time
Scope: Analysis of challenges of coordinating transport policies with environmental protection and examines how some Ministers of Transport are addressing them

Related Topics and Industries

Economic and Business Development; Science and Technology. See also *Part IV—Sources on EC 1992 by Industry*

ORGANIZING A BUSINESS

EC Contacts

Table 23.4 lists official European Community directorates and subdirectorates that provide information about organizing a business. For the complete address of the Commission of the European Communities headquarters (CEC HQ in the table), refer to the Introduction to Part III.

Commission of the European Communities
▲ Directorate-General XXIII (Enterprise Policy, Distributive Trades, Tourism, and Cooperatives)

Directorate (Enterprise Policy and Small and Medium-Sized Enterprises [SMEs])

Address: rue de la Loi 200
B-1049 Bruxelles
Belgium
Telephone: 2/235 11 11
Telex: 21877 COMEU B

European Parliament
▲ Committee on Economic and Monetary Affairs and Industrial Policy

Address: 97–113, rue Belliard
B-1040 Bruxelles
Belgium
Telephone: 2/284 21 21; 2/284 35 40
Fax: 2/230 68 56; 2/231 12 57

Address: Palais de l'Europe
F-67006 Strasbourg Cedex
France
Telephone: 88/374 001; 88/375 484
Fax: 88/369 214; 88/256 516

Address: Centre Europeen
Plateau du Kirchberg
L-2929 Luxembourg
Telephone: 430 01
Telex: 3493 EUPARL LU; 2894 EUPARL LU
Fax: 436 972; 435 359

European Parliament
▲ Committee on Legal Affairs and Citizens' Rights

Address: 97–113, rue Belliard
B-1040 Bruxelles
Belgium
Telephone: 2/284 21 21; 2/284 33 45
Fax: 2/230 68 56; 2/231 12 57

Address: Palais de l'Europe
F-67006 Strasbourg Cedex
France
Telephone: 88/374 001; 88/374 164
Fax: 88/369 214; 88/256 516

▼ ▼

Address: Centre Europeen
Plateau du Kirchberg
L-2929 Luxembourg
Telephone: 430 01
Telex: 3493 EUPARL LU; 2894 EUPARL LU
Fax: 436 972; 435 359

Data Resources and Publications

Business Creation by Women: Motivations, Situations, and Perspectives

Publisher: Office for Official Publications of the European Communities
Frequency of Publication: One time
Scope: Final report of a study for the Commission of the European Communities

Disclosure Requirements for Branches—Single-Member Private Limited Companies

Publisher: Office for Official Publications of the European Communities
Frequency of Publication: One time
Scope: Summarizes information disclosure requirements established by the EC

Evaluation of Policy Measures for the Creation and Development of Small and Medium-Sized Enterprises

Publisher: Office for Official Publications of the European Communities
Frequency of Publication: One time
Scope: Status report as of October 1988

Table 23.4
CEC Subdirectorates—Organizing a Business

Directorate and Subdirectorate Name	Directorate/ Subdirectorate Number	Directorate- General	Address
General Questions and Instruments of External Economic Policy			
Questions of Community Law in the Field of Member States Trade and Cooperation Agreements; Infringements; Law of the Sea; and General Questions	C/3	I	CEC HQ, Belgium
Approximation of Laws, Freedom of Establishment, and Freedom to Provide Services			
Civil and Economic Law, Criminal Law, and Law of Procedure; Citizens' Rights	D/1	III	CEC HQ, Belgium
General Competition Policy and Coordination	A	IV	CEC HQ, Belgium
Company Law, Company and Capital Movements Taxation			
Company Law, Industrial Democracy, and Accounting Standards	B/2	XV	CEC HQ, Belgium
Multinationals, Groups of Companies, and the European Company	B/3	XV	CEC HQ, Belgium

Western Europe . . . A Tax Tour

Publisher: Arthur Andersen & Co.
Frequency of Publication: As needed
Scope: Background information on each
country, highlights of the main features
of each country's business and personal
tax systems, and factors that could
influence a decision regarding investment within the country

Related Topics and Industries

Economic and Business Development; Employment and Labor. See also Part IV—Sources on EC 1992 by Industry.

PATENTS, TRADEMARKS, AND OTHER COPYRIGHT PROTECTION

EC Contacts

Commission of the European Communities

▲ Directorate-General III (Internal Market and
Industrial Affairs), Directorate D/4 (Approxi-
mation of Laws, Freedom of Establishment,
and Freedom to Provide Services/Copyright,
Unfair Competition, and International
Aspects of Intellectual Property)

Address: rue de la Loi 200
B-1049 Bruxelles
Belgium
Telephone: 2/236 30 12
Telex: 21877 COMEU B

European Parliament

▲ Committee on Economic and Monetary
Affairs and Industrial Policy

Address: 97–113, rue Belliard
B-1040 Bruxelles
Belgium
Telephone: 2/284 21 21; 2/284 35 40
Fax: 2/230 68 56; 2/231 12 57

Address: Palais de l'Europe
F-67006 Strasbourg Cedex
France
Telephone: 88/374 001; 88/375 484
Fax: 88/369 214; 88/256 516

Address: Centre Europeen
Plateau du Kirchberg
L-2929 Luxembourg
Telephone: 430 01
Telex: 3493 EUPARL LU; 2894 EUPARL LU
Fax: 436 972; 435 359

European Parliament

▲ Committee on Energy, Research and
Technology

Address: Palais de l'Europe
F-67006 Strasbourg Cedex
France
Telephone: 88/374 001; 88/375 485
Fax: 88/369 214; 88/256 516

Address: Centre Europeen
Plateau du Kirchberg
L-2929 Luxembourg
Telephone: 430 01
Telex: 3493 EUPARL LU; 2894 EUPARL LU
Fax: 436 972; 435 359

European Parliament

▲ Committee on Legal Affairs and Citizens'
Rights

Address: 97–113, rue Belliard
B-1040 Bruxelles
Belgium
Telephone: 2/284 21 21; 2/284 33 45
Fax: 2/230 68 56; 2/231 12 57

Address: Palais de l'Europe
F-67006 Strasbourg Cedex
France
Telephone: 88/374 001; 88/374 164
Fax: 88/369 214; 88/256 516

Address: Centre Europeen
Plateau du Kirchberg
L-2929 Luxembourg
Telephone: 430 01
Telex: 3493 EUPARL LU; 2894 EUPARL LU
Fax: 436 972; 435 359

European Parliament

▲ Committee on Youth, Culture, Education, the Media and Sport

Address: 97–113, rue Belliard
            B-1040 Bruxelles
            Belgium
Telephone: 2/284 21 21; 2/284 25 11
Fax: 2/230 68 56; 2/231 12 57

Address: Palais de l'Europe
            F-67006 Strasbourg Cedex
            France
Telephone: 88/374 001; 88/374 522
Fax: 88/369 214; 88/256 516

Address: Centre Europeen
            Plateau du Kirchberg
            L-2929 Luxembourg
Telephone: 430 01
Telex: 3493 EUPARL LU; 2894 EUPARL LU
Fax: 436 972; 435 359

Associations

▲ AIM (European Association of Industries of Branded Products)

Address: rue de l'Orme 19
            B-1040 Bruxelles
            Belgium
Telephone: 2/733 12 64
Telex: 61473 ECCO B
Fax: 2/734 67 02

▲ TII (European Association for the Transfer of Technologies, Innovation, and Industrial Information)

Address: 3, rue des Capucins
            L-1313 Luxembourg
Telephone: 46 30 35
Telex: 610511 GMA LU
Fax: 46 21 85

Data Resources and Publications

Competition Policy and Intellectual Property Rights
Publisher: OECD
Frequency of Publication: One time
Scope: Patent and know-how licensing from the point of view of EC competition policy, among others

Euro Abstracts—Scientific and Technical Publications and Patents/Section I: Euratom and EEC R & D and Demonstration Projects
Publisher: Office for Official Publications of the European Communities
Frequency of Publication: Monthly
Scope: Abstracts of research contracts, publications, and the resulting patents; prepared by DG XIII

Euro Abstracts—Scientific and Technical Publications and Patents/Section II: Coal, Steel, and Related Social Research
Publisher: Office for Official Publications of the European Communities
Frequency of Publication: Monthly
Scope: Abstracts of research contracts, publications, and the resulting patents; prepared by DG XIII

Related Topics and Industries

Economic and Business Development; Social and Economic Policy. See also *Part IV—Sources on EC 1992 by Industry*

PRODUCT STANDARDS, SAFETY, AND CERTIFICATIONS

EC Contacts

Commission of the European Communities

▲ Directorate-General III (Internal Market and Industrial Affairs)

Directorate B/4 (Internal Market and Industrial Affairs I/Standardization and Certification; Relations with Standardization Bodies; Notification Procedures)

Address: rue de la Loi 200
        B-1049 Bruxelles
        Belgium
Telephone: 236 30 12
Telex: 21877 COMEU B

European Parliament

▲ Committee on Energy, Research and Technology

Address: Palais de l'Europe
        F-67006 Strasbourg Cedex
        France
Telephone: 88/374 001; 88/375 485
Fax: 88/369 214; 88/256 516

Address: Centre Europeen
        Plateau du Kirchberg
        L-2929 Luxembourg
Telephone: 430 01
Telex: 3493 EUPARL LU; 2894 EUPARL LU
Fax: 436 972; 435 359

European Parliament

▲ Committee on Legal Affairs and Citizens' Rights

Address: 97–113, rue Belliard
        B-1040 Bruxelles
        Belgium
Telephone: 2/284 21 21; 2/284 33 45
Fax: 2/230 68 56; 2/231 12 57

Address: Palais de l'Europe
        F-67006 Strasbourg Cedex
        France
Telephone: 88/374 001; 88/374 164
Fax: 88/369 214; 88/256 516

Address: Centre Europeen
        Plateau du Kirchberg
        L-2929 Luxembourg
Telephone: 430 01
Telex: 3493 EUPARL LU; 2894 EUPARL LU
Fax: 436 972; 435 359

European Parliament

▲ Committee on Social Affairs, Employment and the Working Environment

Address: 97–113, rue Belliard
        B-1040 Bruxelles
        Belgium
Telephone: 2/284 21 21; 2/284 35 04
Fax: 2/230 68 56; 2/231 12 57

Address: Palais de l'Europe
        F-67006 Strasbourg Cedex
        France
Telephone: 88/374 001; 88/374 037; 88/374 548
Fax: 88/369 214; 88/256 516

Address: Centre Europeen
        Plateau du Kirchberg
        L-2929 Luxembourg
Telephone: 430 01
Telex: 3493 EUPARL LU; 2894 EUPARL LU
Fax: 436 972; 435 359

Associations

▲ CEN (European Committee for Standardization)

Address: rue Brederode 2
        B-1000 Bruxelles
        Belgium
Telephone: 2/519 68 11
Fax: 2/519 68 19

▲ CENELEC (European Committee for Electro-technical Standardization)

Address: rue Brederode 2
        B-1000 Bruxelles
        Belgium
Telephone: 2/519 68 11
Fax: 2/519 68 19

▲ CEOC (Confederation of European Technical Organizations)

Address: 191, rue de Vaugirard
       F-75015 Paris
       France
Telephone: 1/45 66 99 44
Fax: 1/45 67 90 47

▲ ECPSA (European Consumer Product Safety Association)

Address: P.O. Box 5169
       NL-1007 AD Amsterdam
       Netherlands
Telephone: 20/573 03 70
Telex: 10486 SCV NL
Fax: 20/662 80 50

▲ European Committee for Standardization

Address: rue Brederode 2 (Bte 5)
       B-1000 Bruxelles
       Belgium
Telephone: 2/519 68 11
Telex: 26257 CENLEC B
Fax: 2/519 68 19

Data Resources and Publications

Common Standards for Enterprises

Publisher: Office for Official Publications of the European Communities
Frequency of Publication: One time
Scope: Explanation of the EC standardization system and how it interfaces with national systems

ERSA (European Safety and Reliability Association) Newsletter

Publisher: Office for Official Publications of the European Communities
Frequency of Publication: 3 times a year
Scope: Newsletter on product safety; prepared by the EC Joint Research Centre

Europe in the Pharmaceutical Industry

Publisher: Office for Official Publications of the European Communities
Frequency of Publication: One time
Scope: Review of current pharmaceutical markets and industries, and analysis of the impact of Single Market Program on pricing, production, and product testing; Volume 15 of the Cecchini study on the "cost of non-Europe"

Green Paper on the Development of European Standardization: Action for Faster Technological Integration in Europe

Publisher: Office for Official Publications of the European Communities
Frequency of Publication: One time
Scope: Outline of the significance of the EC standardization program in the context of the Single Market Program

Monthly Review of Ongoing Activities in European Standards

Publisher: CEN/CENELEC
Frequency of Publication: Monthly
Scope: Listings of documents from CEN/CENELEC made available from new EC drafts sent for a formal vote, new EC drafts sent for public comments, and new proposals for EC standards projects

Research on the "Cost of Non-Europe"—Technical Trade Barriers in the EC: An Illustration in Six Industries—Some Case Studies on Technical Barriers

Publisher: Office for Official Publications of the European Communities
Frequency of Publication: One time
Scope: Identification of technical trade barriers, including standards, legal requirements, testing and certification procedures, and evaluation of their impact in the foodstuffs, pharmaceuticals, automobile, building materials, telecommunications, and electrical products and machinery industries; Volume 6 of the Cecchini study on the "cost of non-Europe"

Research on the "Cost of Non-Europe"—The Benefits of Completing the Internal Market for Telecommunications Equipment and Services in the Community

Publisher: Office for Official Publications of the European Communities

Frequency of Publication: One time

Scope: Review of standards for telecommunications equipment and services in the EC and estimates the benefits of eliminating technical barriers throughout the EC; Volume 10 of the Cecchini study on the "cost of non-Europe"

Related Topics and Industries

Economic and Business Development; Social and Economic Policy. See also Part IV—Sources on EC 1992 by Industry

---

OTHER TOPICS IN THE REGULATION OF BUSINESS AND COMPETITION

EC Contacts

Table 23.5 lists official European Community directorates and subdirectorates that provide information about other topics in the regulation of businesses and competition. For the complete address of the Commission of the European Communities headquarters (CEC HQ in the table), refer to the Introduction to Part III.

Commission of the European Communities

▲ Directorate-General XXIII (Enterprise Policy, Distributive Trades, Tourism, and Cooperatives)

Directorate (Enterprise Policy and Small and Medium-sized Enterprises [SME])

Address: rue de la Loi 200
B-1049 Bruxelles
Belgium
Telephone: 2/235 81 18
Telex: 21877 COMEU B

Associations

▲ AEVPC (European Mail Order Traders Association)

Address: av. E. Lancomble 17
B-1040 Bruxelles
Belgium
Telephone: 2/736 03 48
Telex: 64192 FIGEMA B
Fax: 2/736 05 42

▲ FEWITA (Federation of European Wholesale and International Trade Associations)

Address: av. d'Auderghem 33–35
B-1040 Bruxelles
Belgium
Telephone: 2/231 08 31
Telex: 26946 TRACED B
Fax: 2/230 00 78

Data Resources and Publications

Accounting Standards Harmonization: Operating Results of Insurance Companies

Publisher: OECD

Frequency of Publication: One time

Scope: Summary of current practices pertaining to insurance companies in OECD countries

Conclusions on Accounting and Reporting by Transnational Corporations

Publisher: United Nations

Frequency of Publication: One time

Scope: Guide for preparers and users of financial statements of multinational businesses

CTC Reporter

Publisher: United Nations
Frequency of Publication: 2 times a year
Scope: Coverage of matters concerning multinational corporations, in governmental and nongovernmental organizations; prepared by Center on Transnational Corporations

Deregulation and Airline Competition

Publisher: OECD
Frequency of Publication: One time
Scope: Summary of current policies in OECD member countries toward regulation and deregulation of competition in the airline industry

Entrepreneurship and Economic Development

Publisher: United Nations
Frequency of Publication: One time
Scope: Analysis of the role of entrepreneurship in economic growth and development in industrial and nonindustrial countries

Reports of Cases Before the Court

Publisher: Office for Official Publications of the European Communities
Frequency of Publication: Periodically
Scope: Official reports of cases before the Court of Justice of the EC

Table 23.5
CEC Subdirectorates—Other Topics in the Regulation of Businesses and Competition

Directorate and Subdirectorate Name	Directorate/ Subdirectorate Number	Directorate- General	Address
Approximation of Laws, Freedom of Establishment, and Freedom to Provide Services			
Civil and Economic Law, Criminal Law, and Law of Procedure; Citizen's Rights	D/1	III	CEC HQ, Belgium Telephone: 2/236 30 12
Industrial Policy and Broadcasting Policy	D/3	III	CEC HQ, Belgium Telephone: 2/236 30 12
Organization of Markets in Crop Products	C	VI	CEC HQ, Belgium Telex: 22037 AGREC B
Organization of Markets in Livestock Products	D	VI	CEC HQ, Belgium Telex: 22037 AGREC B
Organization of Markets in Specialized Products	E	VI	CEC HQ, Belgium Telex: 22037 AGREC B
Telecommunications Policy, Technology Transfer, and Innovation			
Regulatory Aspects, Analyses and Studies by Sector	D/2	XIII	CEC HQ, Belgium Telephone: 2/235 24 48

Research on the "Cost of Non-Europe"—The Cost of Non-Europe: Obstacles to Transborder Business Activity

Publisher: Office for Official Publications of the European Communities

Frequency of Publication: One time

Scope: Analysis of impact of industrial policies, corporate laws, fiscal regulations, border controls, financing, and social measures on intra-EC business operations; Volume 7 of the Cecchini study on the "cost of non-Europe"

Role and Extent of Competition in Improving the Performance of Public Enterprises

Publisher: United Nations

Frequency of Publication: One time

Scope: Studies of the importance of competition in changing the way in which the public sector operates

Related Topics and Industries

Social and Economic Policy. See also *Part IV— Sources on EC 1992 by Industry*

24 Science and Technology

THE IMPACT OF THE SINGLE MARKET PROGRAM ON SCIENCE AND TECHNOLOGY: HIGHLIGHTS

Research and Technology Strategy

The EC is already making significant efforts to develop an overall research and technology strategy, and to improve coordination among the Member States in this area. These efforts will supplement the extensive activities that the EC is already undertaking in science and technology. These efforts include

- Its own direct research
- Support for concerted Community-wide action
- Funding for cost-sharing programs in industrial sectors, ranging from transportation (Drive) to health and medicine (AIM), and from telecommunications (RACE) to biotechnology (Bridge)

Patents

One other result of the Single Market Program will be the creation of an EC-wide European Patent Office, providing for central registration of all patents.

KEY ISSUES FACING THE SINGLE MARKET PROGRAM

- Establishing legal protection for semiconductor designs, computer programs, and the products of biotechnology
- Managing and expanding existing programs supporting research and development, as well as technology transfer
- Assuring an adequate supply of technically educated personnel for EC-based industries

Sections in This Chapter

Research and Innovation

Technology Transfer and Productivity

Other Topics in Science and Technology

Assistance

Appendix D contains a list of the Single Market measures dealing with science and technology. For additional help on using the resources in this chapter, refer to the Introduction to Part III.

Research and Innovation
EC Contacts

Table 24.1 lists official European Community directorates and subdirectorates that provide information about research and innovation. For the complete address of the Commission of the European Communities headquarters (CEC HQ in the table), refer to the Introduction to Part III.

Commission of the European Communities
▲ Directorate-General XII (Science, Research, and Development)

Fusion programme

Address: rue de la Loi 200
B-1049 Bruxelles
Belgium
Telephone: 2/235 11 11
Telex: 21877 COMEU B

Commission of the European Communities
▲ Directorate-General XII (Science, Research, and Development)

Joint Research Centre
Central Bureau for Nuclear Measurements

Address: Steenweg op Retie
B-2440 Geel
Belgium
Telephone: 14/57 12 11
Telex: 33589 EURAT B
Fax: 14/58 42 73

Commission of the European Communities
▲ Directorate-General XII (Science, Research, and Development)

Joint Research Centre
Centre for Information Technologies and Electronics

Address: I-21020 Ispra (VA)
Italy
Telephone: 332/78 91 11
Telex: 380042/380058/324878/324880 EUR I
Fax: 332/78 90 45

Commission of the European Communities
▲ Directorate-General XII (Science, Research, and Development)

Joint Research Centre
Institute for Advanced Materials

Address: I-21020 Ispra (VA)
Italy
Telephone: 332/78 91 11
Telex: 380042/380058/324878/324880 EUR I
Fax: 332/78 90 45

and

Address: Westerduinweg 3
Postbus Nr. 2
NL-1755 ZG Petten (N.-H.)
Netherlands
Telephone: 22/46 5656
Telex: 57211 REACP
Fax: 22/46 10 02

Table 24.1
CEC Subdirectorates—Research and Innovation

Directorate and Subdirectorate Name	Directorate/ Subdirectorate Number	Directorate-General	Address
State Aids			
Aids to Research and Development	E/2	IV	CEC HQ, Belgium
Employment			
Social Aspects of Industrial Policies, New Technologies, and Industrial Relations	A/2	V	CEC HQ, Belgium
Inland Transport; Market Analysis; Transport Safety; Research and Technology			
Transport Safety, Research, and Technology	B/3	VII	CEC HQ, Belgium Telephone: 2/236 27 42
Nuclear Safety, Impact of Industry on the Environment, and Waste Management			
Waste Management, Clean Technologies, Soil Protection, and Prevention of Noise Pollution	A/3	XI	CEC HQ, Belgium
Means of Action			
R&TD Contract Policy and Management	B/2	XII	CEC HQ, Belgium
Scientific and Technological Policy			
Researchers' Europe, and Integration with Other Community Policies	A/3	XII	CEC HQ, Belgium
Technological Research			
Materials Research	C/3	XII	CEC HQ, Belgium
Environment and Nonnuclear Energy Sources			
Rational Energy Use and Energy Systems Analysis	E/5	XII	CEC HQ, Belgium
Advanced Fuel Technology	E/6	XII	CEC HQ, Belgium
Biology			
CUBE (Concertation Unit for Biotechnology in Europe)	F/1	XII	CEC HQ, Belgium
Agro-Industrial Research	F/3	XII	CEC HQ, Belgium
Medical Research	F/6	XII	CEC HQ, Belgium

Table 24.1
CEC Subdirectorates—Research and Innovation *(continued)*

Directorate and Subdirectorate Name	Directorate/ Subdirectorate Number	Directorate- General	Address
Science and Technology Policy Support			
Evaluation of R&D Programmes (Spear)	H/4	XII	CEC HQ, Belgium
Espace: Strategy and Coordination	H/5	XII	CEC HQ, Belgium
Information Technology and Esprit			
Basic Research and Scientific Liaison on IT [Information Technology]	A/7	XIII	CEC HQ, Belgium Telephone: 2/235 24 48
Exploitation of Research and Technological Development, Technology Transfer, and Innovation			
Policy on Innovation and Protection of Research and Technological Development Results	C/1	XIII	CEC HQ, Belgium Telephone: 2/235 24 48
Promotion of the Exploitation of Community Research and Technological Development	C/2	XIII	CEC HQ, Belgium Telephone: 2/235 24 48

Commission of the European Communities
▲ Directorate-General XII (Science, Research, and Development)

Joint Research Centre
Institute for Prospective Technological Studies
Address: I-21020 Ispra (VA)
          Italy
Telephone: 332/78 91 11
Telex: 380042/380058/324878/324880 EUR I
Fax: 332/78 90 45

Commission of the European Communities
▲ Directorate-General XII (Science, Research, and Development)

Joint Research Centre
Institute for Remote Sensing Applications
Address: I-21020 Ispra (VA)
          Italy
Telephone: 332/78 91 11
Telex: 380042/380058/324878/324880 EUR I
Fax: 332/78 90 45

Commission of the European Communities

▲ Directorate-General XII (Science, Research, and Development)

Joint Research Centre
Institute for Safety Technology

Address: I-21020 Ispra (VA)
Italy
Telephone: 332/78 91 11
Telex: 380042/380058/324878/324880 EUR I
Fax: 332/78 90 45

Commission of the European Communities

▲ Directorate-General XII (Science, Research, and Development)

Joint Research Centre
Institute for Systems Engineering

Address: I-21020 Ispra (VA)
Italy
Telephone: 332/78 91 11
Telex: 380042/380058/324878/324880 EUR I
Fax: 332/78 90 45

Commission of the European Communities

▲ Directorate-General XII (Science, Research, and Development)

Joint Research Centre
Institute for the Environment

Address: I-21020 Ispra (VA)
Italy
Telephone: 332/78 91 11
Telex: 380042/380058/324878/324880 EUR I
Fax: 332/78 90 45

Commission of the European Communities

▲ Directorate-General XII (Science, Research, and Development)

Joint Research Centre
Institute for Transuranium Elements

Address: Linkenheim
Postfach 2350
D-7500 Karlsruhe
Germany
Telephone: 72/47 841
Telex: 7825483 EU D
Fax: 72/40 46

European Parliament

▲ Committee on Energy, Research and Technology

Address: Palais de l'Europe
F-67006 Strasbourg Cedex
France
Telephone: 88/374 001; 88/375 485
Fax: 88/369 214; 88/256 516

Address: Centre Europeen
Plateau du Kirchberg
L-2929 Luxembourg
Telephone: 430 01
Telex: 3493 EUPARL LU; 2894 EUPARL LU
Fax: 436 972; 435 359

Data Sources and Publications

Advanced Materials

Publisher: OECD
Frequency of Publication: One time
Scope: Discussion of development of advanced materials, in particular government policies and their impact on technological change

Agree

Database Producer: European Community, DG VI
Distributors/Hosts: Datacentralen, Dimdi
Frequency of Update: Annual
Scope: Listings of titles of agricultural research projects dealing with agriculture, silviculture, pisciculture, and food processing that are current at the time of collection; includes the names and addresses of the organizations where the work is being done ⓐ

The Community's Research and Development Programme on Radioactive Waste Management and Storage—Shared Cost Action

Publisher: Office for Official Publications of the European Communities
Frequency of Publication: Annual
Scope: Progress report on EC radioactive waste management programs; prepared by DG XII

Contract Research Organizations in the EEC

Publisher: Office for Official Publications of the European Communities

Frequency of Publication: One time

Scope: Directory of research organizations throughout the EC; prepared by DG XIII

ECSC Coal Research—Annual Report

Publisher: Office for Official Publications of the European Communities

Frequency of Publication: Annual

Scope: Summary of work of the technical coal research programs sponsored by ECSC; prepared by DG XVII

Energy in Europe

Publisher: Office for Official Publications of the European Communities

Frequency of Publication: 3 times a year

Scope: Short-term energy outlook for the EC, plus ongoing information on energy policy developments, research programs, conferences, and publications; prepared by DG XVII

ESPRIT—Annual Report

Publisher: Office for Official Publications of the European Communities

Frequency of Publication: Annual

Scope: Reviews of activities of Esprit (European Strategic Program for Research and Development in Information Technology); prepared by DG XII

Euro Abstracts—Scientific and Technical Publications and Patents/Section I: Euratom and EEC R&D and Demonstration Projects

Publisher: Office for Official Publications of the European Communities

Frequency of Publication: Monthly

Scope: Abstracts of research contracts, publications, and the resulting patents; prepared by DG XIII

Euro Abstracts—Scientific and Technical Publications, and Patents/Section II: Coal, Steel, and Related Social Research

Publisher: Office for Official Publications of the European Communities

Frequency of Publication: Monthly

Scope: Abstracts of research contracts, publications, and the resulting patents; prepared by DG XIII

Government Financing of Research and Development

Publisher: Office for Official Publications of the European Communities

Frequency of Publication: Annual

Scope: Summary of spending on research and development and related areas; prepared by the Statistical Office of the EC

Government Policies and the Diffusion of Microelectronics

Publisher: OECD

Frequency of Publication: One time

Scope: Summary of policies of OECD members toward research and development activities in the microelectronics industry

HTM-DB

Database Producer: EC Joint Research Center for Information Technology and Electronics, Ispra (CITE)

Distributors/Hosts: CITE

Frequency of Update: Periodically

Scope: High-temperature materials databank; combines a computerized databank and evaluation system for mechanical properties of technically relevant engineering materials

IES-DC1

Database Producer: European Commission, DG XIII

Distributors/Hosts: ECHO

Frequency of Update: Periodically

Scope: Basic information on publicly funded research and development programs and projects in the EC in telecommunications, the information industries, and innovation, including Esprit, RACE, Eureka, Alvey, COST, and Docdel; includes detailed project information, project partners, and project description ⊛

Information, Computer and Communications Policy: Major R&D Programmes for Information Technology

Publisher: OECD

Frequency of Publication: One time

Scope: Summary of major research and development programs and policies of selected OECD countries in information, computer, and communications industries

Innovation and Employment

Publisher: OECD

Frequency of Publication: 4 times a year

Scope: Reviews developments in innovation policy as they affect employment; prepared jointly with the Commission of the European Communities

Innovation in the EC Automotive Industry

Publisher: Office for Official Publications of the European Communities

Frequency of Publication: One time

Scope: Analysis of state aid policy and the automotive industry

Innovations from Community Research— Selection 1987

Publisher: Office for Official Publications of the European Communities

Frequency of Publication: One time

Scope: Illustrations of commercial results of EC-sponsored R&D; prepared by DG XIII

Introducing Innovation into Europe's Traditional Industries

Publisher: Office for Official Publications of the European Communities

Frequency of Publication: One time

Scope: Description of the Sprint (Strategic Program for Innovation and Technology Transfer) network of industrial research associations

Needs for Strategic R&D in Support of Improved Energy Efficiency in the Processing Industries

Publisher: Office for Official Publications of the European Communities

Frequency of Publication: One time

Scope: Summary of views of energy research experts

Promotion of Cooperation Among Research and Development Organizations in the Field of Vocational Training

Publisher: Office for Official Publications of the European Communities

Frequency of Publication: Annual

Scope: Working meeting papers of CEDEFOP-sponsored meetings

Research Manpower

Publisher: OECD

Frequency of Publication: One time

Scope: Suggestions for managing the supply and demand for skilled researchers

Sesame

Database Producer: European Commission, DG XVII and DG XII

Distributors/Hosts: ECHO, Datacentralen

Frequency of Update: Weekly

Scope: EC energy research and development and technology projects, including R&D demonstration projects, as well as hydrocarbon projects and national projects ⊛

Training in Innovative Management

Publisher: Office for Official Publications of the European Communities

Frequency of Publication: One time

Scope: Report on innovative management training techniques; prepared by DG XIII

Transnational Corporations in Biotechnology

Publisher: United Nations

Frequency of Publication: One time

Scope: Exploration of roles of major multinational businesses in the biotechnology industry, including investment and research and development

The Utilization of Solid Fuels—Catalogue of R&D Contracts 1988

Publisher: Office for Official Publications of the European Communities

Frequency of Publication: One time

Scope: Catalogue of EC research and development contracts on the use of solid fuels; prepared by DG XVII

Utilization of the Results of Public Research and Development

Publisher: Office for Official Publications of the European Communities

Frequency of Publication: One time

Scope: Coverage of public activities in R&D for individual EC Member States in separate volumes; most EC Member States included; prepared by DG XIII

Related Topics and Industries

Economic and Business Development; Social and Economic Policy. See also Part IV—Sources on EC 1992 by Industry

TECHNOLOGY TRANSFER AND PRODUCTIVITY

EC Contacts

Commission of the European Communities

▲ Directorate-General XII (Science, Research, and Development)

Directorate C/1 (Technological Research/Development and Application of Advanced Technology)

Address: rue de la Loi 200
B-1049 Bruxelles
Belgium
Telephone: 2/235 11 11
Telex: 21877 COMEU B

European Parliament

▲ Committee on Energy, Research, and Technology

Address: Palais de l'Europe
F-67006 Strasbourg Cedex
France
Telephone: 88/374 001; 88/375 485
Fax: 88/369 214; 88/256 516

Address: Centre Europeen
Plateau du Kirchberg
L-2929 Luxembourg
Telephone: 430 01
Telex: 3493 EUPARL LU; 2894 EUPARL LU
Fax: 436 972; 435 359

European Parliament

▲ Committee on Social Affairs, Employment, and the Working Environment

Address: 97–113, rue Belliard
B-1040 Bruxelles
Belgium
Telephone: 2/284 21 21; 2/284 35 04
Fax: 2/230 68 56; 2/231 12 57

Address: Palais de l'Europe
F-67006 Strasbourg Cedex
France
Telephone: 88/374 001; 88/374 037; 88/374 548
Fax: 88/369 214; 88/256 516

Address: Centre Europeen
Plateau du Kirchberg
L-2929 Luxembourg
Telephone: 430 01
Telex: 3493 EUPARL LU; 2894 EUPARL LU
Fax: 436 972; 435 359

Associations

▲ AECNP (European Association of National Productivity Centres)

Address: rue de la Concorde 60
B-1050 Bruxelles
Belgium
Telephone: 2/511 71 00
Fax: 2/511 71 00

▲ TII (European Association for the Transfer of Technologies, Innovation, and Industrial Information)

Address: 3, rue des Capucins
L-1313 Luxembourg
Telephone: 46 30 35
Telex: 6105111 GMA LU
Fax: 46 21 85

Data Resources and Publications

Eurotec

Publisher: Office for Official Publications of the European Communities
Frequency of Publication: Periodically
Scope: Newsletter on technology in Europe

Industrial Processes

Publisher: Office for Official Publications of the European Communities
Frequency of Publication: One time
Scope: Proceedings of a meeting of contractors; prepared by DG XII

Industrial Quality Control

Publisher: United Nations
Frequency of Publication: Periodically
Scope: Directory of basic industrial information sources

Introducing Innovation into Europe's Traditional Industries

Publisher: Office for Official Publications of the European Communities
Frequency of Publication: One time
Scope: Description of the Sprint (Strategic Program for Innovation and Technology Transfer) network of industrial research associations

New Technology in the 1990s: A Socio-Economic Strategy

Publisher: OECD
Frequency of Publication: One time
Scope: Suggestions of governmental strategies for dealing with new technology, based on experiences of OECD members

The Role of Technology in Iron and Steel Developments

Publisher: OECD
Frequency of Publication: One time
Scope: Study on impact of technology on the iron and steel industries of OECD member countries

Sesame

Database Producer: European Commission, DG XVII and DG XII
Distributors/Hosts: ECHO, Datacentralen
Frequency of Update: Weekly
Scope: EC energy research and development and energy technology projects, including R&D demonstration projects, as well as hydrocarbon projects and national projects

Social Europe—Supplement: New Technologies in Printing and Publishing

Publisher: Office for Official Publications of the European Communities
Frequency of Publication: One time
Scope: Summary of technological developments impacting printing and publishing industries, including impacts on employment; prepared by DG V

Related Topics and Industries

Economic and Business Development; Social and Economic Policy. See also *Part IV—Sources on EC 1992 by Industry*

Other Topics in Science and Technology

EC Contacts

Table 24.2 lists official European Community directorates and subdirectorates that provide information about other topics in science and technology. For the complete address of the Commission of the European Communities headquarters (CEC HQ in the table), refer to the Introduction to Part III.

Euronet Diane

▲ European Network for Scientific and Technical Information

Address: bd. Mahon
177 Route d'Esch
L-1471 Luxembourg

Data Resources and Publications

Biorep

Database Producer: The Library of the Royal Netherlands Academy of Arts and Sciences
Distributors/Hosts: ECHO
Frequency of Update: Annual
Scope: Biotechnical projects carried out in the Member States of the EC

Biotechnology and the Changing Role of Government

Publisher: OECD
Frequency of Publication: One time
Scope: Studies on the role of OECD governments in the emerging biotechnology industries

The Changing Role of Government Research Laboratories

Publisher: OECD
Frequency of Publication: One time
Scope: Study of OECD member countries experience with government-funded research laboratories

Collected Agreements Concluded Within the Framework of European Cooperation in the Field of Scientific and Technical Research

Publisher: Office for Official Publications of the European Communities
Frequency of Publication: Annual
Scope: Official texts of all agreements adopted or amended during the year; prepared by the Council of the European Communities

Comparison of Scientific and Technological Policies of the Community Member States

Publisher: Office for Official Publications of the European Communities
Frequency of Publication: One time
Scope: Study of the EC's scientific and technological efforts, including resources for increasing the Community's competitiveness

Domis

Database Producer: ECHO
Distributors/Hosts: ECHO
Frequency of Update: Periodically
Scope: Directory of materials, information sources, and services currently available in Europe; intended for those involved in industry, research, and administration; provides details on currently available information sources, such as databanks and databases, technical centers, scientific and technical laboratories, and experts; areas covered include metals, alloys and steel; ceramics and glass; composite materials; coatings and joints; and plastics and rubber; updated using information from questionnaires

Table 24.2
CEC Subdirectorates—Other Topics in Science and Technology

Directorate and Subdirectorate Name	Directorate/ Subdirectorate Number	Directorate-General	Address
Scientific and Technological Policy			
Framework Programme; Overall Formulation of Scientific and Technological Policy	A/1	XII	CEC HQ, Belgium
Coordination of Scientific and Technological Policies of Member States and Crest	A/2	XII	CEC HQ, Belgium
Technological Research			
Production and Materials Technology	C/2	XII	CEC HQ, Belgium
Technical Research—Steel	C/4	XII	CEC HQ, Belgium
Mineral Raw Materials	C/5	XII	CEC HQ, Belgium
Community Bureau of Reference [BCR—Metrology and Reference Materials]	C/6	XII	CEC HQ, Belgium
Biology			
Biomass	F/4	XII	CEC HQ, Belgium
Scientific and Technical Cooperation with Nonmember Countries			
Scientific and Technical Cooperation with the EFTA countries and COST	G/1	XII	CEC HQ, Belgium
Science and Technology Policy Support			
Strategic Analysis of Science and Technology [SAST]	H/2	XII	CEC HQ, Belgium
Science and Technology Forecasting [FAST])	H/3	XII	CEC HQ, Belgium
RACE Programme and Development of Advanced Telematics Services			
Telecommunications Technologies	F/2	XIII	CEC HQ, Belgium Telephone: 2/235 24 48
Information and Telecommunications Technologies Applied to Road Transport—Drive Programme	F/5	XIII	CEC HQ, Belgium Telephone: 2/235 24 48
Information and Telecommunications Technologies Applied to Health—AIM Programme	F/6	XIII	CEC HQ, Belgium Telephone: 2/235 24 48
Energy Technology	D	XVII	CEC HQ, Belgium Telephone: 2/236 27 99

▼ ▼

EABS

Database Producer: European Commission, DG XIII

Distributors/Hosts: ECHO

Frequency of Update: Monthly

Scope: References to the published results of scientific and technical research programs, sponsored in whole or in part by the EC, covering a wide range of topics including nuclear research, new sources of energy, and environmental research ⊛

Eurodicautom

Database Producer: European Commission, DG IX

Distributors/Hosts: ECHO

Frequency of Update: Periodically

Scope: Automated directory, containing technical and scientific terms, contextual phrases, and abbreviations ⊛

Evaluation of the Comett Programme

Publisher: Office for Official Publications of the European Communities

Frequency of Publication: One time

Scope: Review of Comett, EC's Community Program in Education and Training for Technology

I'M: Information Market

Publisher: Office for Official Publications of the European Communities

Frequency of Publication: Periodically

Scope: Articles in various languages on the IMPACT program and the language industry; prepared by DG XIII

Joint Research by Trade Unions and Universities into the Technological Society of Tomorrow

Publisher: Office for Official Publications of the European Communities

Frequency of Publication: One time

Scope: Conference proceedings

New Technologies in Commerce: The Potential and the Cost

Publisher: Office for Official Publications of the European Communities

Frequency of Publication: One time

Scope: Report on changes in commerce and distribution; prepared by DG III

Newsletter: Innovation and Technology Transfer

Publisher: Office for Official Publications of the European Communities

Frequency of Publication: 5 to 6 times a year

Scope: Updates of developments in technology transfer; prepared by DG XIII

The OECD Observer

Publisher: OECD

Frequency of Publication: 6 times a year

Scope: Key problems dealt with by the OECD, including economic growth, employment, social problems, energy, financial markets, the environment, and science and technology

A Review of COST Cooperation Since Its Beginnings

Publisher: Office for Official Publications of the European Communities

Frequency of Publication: One time

Scope: Summary of actions under the COST program (European Co-operation on Scientific and Technical Research); prepared by DG XII

STI—Science, Technology, Industry Review

Publisher: OECD

Frequency of Publication: 2 times a year

Scope: Reports and articles on science, technology, and industry policy issues of current interest to member countries of the OECD

Value (1989-1992): Dissemination and Utilization of Results from Scientific and Technological Research

Publisher: Office for Official Publications of the European Communities

Frequency of Publication: One time

Scope: Description of VALUE, the EC program for the dissemination and use of research results; prepared by DG XIII

Related Topics and Industries

Economic and Business Development; Social and Economic Policy. See also Part IV—Sources on EC 1992 by Industry

25

Social and Economic Policy

THE IMPACT OF THE SINGLE MARKET PROGRAM ON SOCIAL AND ECONOMIC POLICY: HIGHLIGHTS

Efforts to increase the coordination of the social and economic policies of the Member States of the EC, particularly on matters of trade, public procurement, taxation, and education, continue as 1992 draws near:

Trade. One of the keys to the creation of the Single Market is assurance of the free movement of goods throughout the EC. As impediments to the movement of goods within the EC continue to fall, it is anticipated that the volume of intra-EC trade will continue to grow.

Government Contracts. Efforts to open EC public procurement are continuing. One impact of these efforts would be to enable companies anywhere in the EC to bid for and be awarded most major public sector projects initiated by national and local governments as well as those initiated by the Commission, the EIB, and other agencies of the EC.

Taxation. One of the stated goals of the Single Market Program is to achieve greater convergence on value added tax (VAT) and excise duties across the community.

KEY ISSUES FACING THE SINGLE MARKET PROGRAM

- Greater convergence of rates of value added tax (VAT) systems among the Member States
- Continuing the process of opening public procurement contracts to competitive bidding from companies throughout the EC
- Changing the EC's Common Agricultural Policy

Sections in This Chapter

Business Taxation

Government Contracts

Social Services and Welfare

Trade

Assistance

Appendix D contains a list of the Single Market measures dealing with social and economic policy. For additional help on using the resources in this chapter, refer to the Introduction to Part III.

Business Taxation

EC Contacts

Table 25.1 lists official European Community directorates and subdirectorates that provide information about business taxation. For the complete address of the Commission of the European Communities headquarters (CEC HQ in the table), refer to the Introduction to Part III.

European Parliament

▲ Committee on Economic and Monetary Affairs and Industrial Policy

Address: 97–113, rue Belliard
B-1040 Bruxelles
Belgium
Telephone: 2/284 21 21; 2/284 35 40
Fax: 2/230 68 56; 2/231 12 57

Address: Palais de l'Europe
F-67006 Strasbourg Cedex
France
Telephone: 88/374 001; 88/375 484
Fax: 88/369 214; 88/256 516

Address: Centre Europeen
Plateau du Kirchberg
L-2929 Luxembourg
Telephone: 430 01
Telex: 3493 EUPARL LU; 2894 EUPARL LU
Fax: 436 972; 435 359

European Parliament

▲ Committee on Legal Affairs and Citizens' Rights

Address: 97–113, rue Belliard
B-1040 Bruxelles
Belgium
Telephone: 2/284 21 21; 2/284 33 45
Fax: 2/230 68 56; 2/231 12 57

Address: Palais de l'Europe
F-67006 Strasbourg Cedex
France
Telephone: 88/374 001; 88/374 164
Fax: 88/369 214; 88/256 516

Address: Centre Europeen
Plateau du Kirchberg
L-2929 Luxembourg
Telephone: 430 01
Telex: 3493 EUPARL LU; 2894 EUPARL LU
Fax: 436 972; 435 359

Data Sources and Publications

CTC Reporter

Publisher: United Nations
Frequency of Publication: 2 times a year
Scope: Coverage of matters concerning transnational corporations, in governmental and multigovernmental organizations; prepared by Center on Transnational Corporations

Energy Prices and Taxes

Publisher: OECD
Frequency of Publication: 4 times a year
Scope: International compilation of available energy prices at all market levels; available in hardcopy or on microcomputer diskette; prepared by the IEA ■

Eurecom

Publisher: Commission of the European Community, New York office
Frequency of Publication: Monthly
Scope: Current news on EC economic and financial affairs

Industrial Structure Statistics

Publisher: OECD
Frequency of Publication: Annual
Scope: Statistics on production, value added, number of establishments, employment, wages and salaries, exports, imports, and investment

International Tax Agreements

Publisher: United Nations
Frequency of Publication: Periodically
Scope: Updates on the status of international taxation agreements on income and assets; movable capital; commercial, industrial, and agricultural enterprises; and maritime and air transport enterprises

The Personal Income Tax Base: A Comparative Survey

Publisher: OECD
Frequency of Publication: One time
Scope: Sources of income that are taxed, plus data on the personal income tax base for 17 OECD countries based on a common methodology

Revenue Statistics of OECD Member Countries

Publisher: OECD
Frequency of Publication: Annual
Scope: Information on tax levels and structures in OECD member countries

Table 25.1
CEC Subdirectorates—Business Taxation

Directorate and Subdirectorate Name	Directorate/ Subdirectorate Number	Directorate- General	Address
Financial Institutions			
General Matters; Supervision of the Application of Community Provisions	A/4	XV	CEC HQ, Belgium Telephone: 2/235 53 47
Company Law, Company and Capital Movements Taxation			
Company Taxation and Other Direct Taxation; Capital Duty; Taxes on Transactions in Securities	B/1	XV	CEC HQ, Belgium Telephone: 2/235 53 47
Company Law, Industrial Democracy, and Accounting Standards	B/2	XV	CEC HQ, Belgium Telephone: 2/235 53 47
Multinationals, Groups of Companies, and the European Company	B/3	XV	CEC HQ, Belgium Telephone: 2/235 53 47
Indirect Taxation Including Elimination of Tax Frontiers			
VAT and Other Turnover Taxes	C/1	XXI	CEC HQ, Belgium
Indirect Taxation Other Than Turnover Taxes	C/2	XXI	CEC HQ, Belgium
Elimination of Tax Frontiers and the VAT Clearing System	C/3	XXI	CEC HQ, Belgium

Progress in Structural Reform
Publisher: OECD
Frequency of Publication: Periodically
Scope: Reviews of economic activities of all OECD members, as well as EC specifically, in areas including financial markets, investment, taxation, competition policy, trade, agriculture, industrial policy, and labor markets; a supplement to selected issues of OECD's *Economic Outlook*

Tax Law and Cross Border Cooperation Between Companies
Publisher: Office for Official Publications of the European Communities
Frequency of Publication: One time
Scope: Review of recent trends and developments in tax law and cross border cooperation between companies

The Taxation of Fringe Benefits
Publisher: OECD
Frequency of Publication: One time
Scope: Report on policies of OECD members dealing with taxability of fringe benefits

Taxing Consumption
Publisher: OECD
Frequency of Publication: One time
Scope: Study of proposals for taxes on consumption and experiences of OECD member countries

Taxpayers' Rights and Obligations: A Survey of the Legal Situation in OECD
Publisher: OECD
Frequency of Publication: One time
Scope: Provision of details and analysis of legal provisions relating to taxpayers' rights in 22 OECD countries

Western Europe . . . A Tax Tour
Publisher: Arthur Andersen & Co.
Frequency of Publication: As needed
Scope: Background information on each country, highlights of the main features of each country's business and personal tax systems, as well as factors that could influence a decision regarding investment within the country

Related Topics and Industries

Economic and Business Development; Regulation of Businesses and Competition. See also *Part IV— Sources on EC 1992 by Industry*

GOVERNMENT CONTRACTS

EC Contacts
Commission of the European Communities
▲ Directorate-General III (Internal Market and Industrial Affairs)

Directorate F (Public Procurement)
Address: rue de la Loi 200
B-1049 Bruxelles
Belgium
Telephone: 2/236 30 12
Telex: 21877 COMEU B

European Parliament
▲ Committee on Institutional Affairs

Address: 97–113, rue Belliard
B-1040 Bruxelles
Belgium

Telephone: 2/284 21 21; 2/284 35 10
Fax: 2/230 68 56; 2/231 12 57

Address: Palais de l'Europe
F-67006 Strasbourg Cedex
France
Telephone: 88/374 001; 88/377 013
Fax: 88/369 214; 88/256 516

Address: Centre Europeen
Plateau du Kirchberg
L-2929 Luxembourg
Telephone: 430 01
Telex: 3493 EUPARL LU; 2894 EUPARL LU
Fax: 436 972; 435 359

European Parliament

▲ Committee on Legal Affairs and Citizens' Rights

Address: 97–113, rue Belliard
B-1040 Bruxelles
Belgium
Telephone: 2/284 21 21; 2/284 33 45
Fax: 2/230 68 56; 2/231 12 57

Address: Palais de l'Europe
F-67006 Strasbourg Cedex
France
Telephone: 88/374 001; 88/374 164
Fax: 88/369 214; 88/256 516

Address: Centre Europeen
Plateau du Kirchberg
L-2929 Luxembourg
Telephone: 430 01
Telex: 3493 EUPARL LU; 2894 EUPARL LU
Fax: 436 972; 435 359

Data Sources and Publications

Notices of Public Contracts
Supplement to the Official Journal of the
European Communities, Series S

Publisher: Office for Official Publications of the
European Communities
Frequency of Publication: 4 days a week
Scope: Notices of public works, contracts, and
public supply contracts and invitations
to tender of the European Development
Fund, and public works and supply
contracts of the EC

Public Procurement and Construction—To-
wards an Integrated Market

Publisher: Office for Official Publications of the
European Communities
Frequency of Publication: Annual
Scope: Report on developments in public
procurement

Public Procurement in the Excluded Sectors

Publisher: Office for Official Publications of the
European Communities
Frequency of Publication: One time
Scope: Official CEC communication, accompanied by proposals for directives relating
to water, energy, transport, and telecommunications procurement

Research on the "Cost of Non-Europe"—The
Cost of Non-Europe in Public Procurement
Sector

Publisher: Office for Official Publications of the
European Communities
Frequency of Publication: One time
Scope: Analysis of the benefits of improved
access to public contracts in the EC, as
well as information on national purchasing practices throughout the EC; Volume 5 of the Cecchini study on the "cost
of non-Europe"

Role and Extent of Competition in Improving
the Performance of Public Enterprises

Publisher: United Nations
Frequency of Publication: One time
Scope: Studies of the importance of competition in changing the way in which the
public sector operates

TED

Database Producer: Office for Official Publica-
tions of the EC
Distributors/Hosts: ECHO, Centre francais du
commerce exterieur,
Cerved, ICEX, Infotap,
Ministerie van Ekonomische
Zaken, Profile Information,
Saarbrucker Zeitung,
ODAV, Stjernquist
Frequency of Update: Daily
Scope: Description of tenders for public works,
supply, and service contracts; corre-
sponds to the *Official Journal of the*
European Communities—Series S   ⬬

TED Fax

Publisher: ECHO
Frequency of Publication: Daily
Scope: Selected tenders for public works,
supply, and service contracts provided
by fax; taken from the *Official Journal of*
the European Communities—Series S

Related Topics and Industries

Economic and Business Development; Science and
Technology. See also Part IV—Sources on EC 1992 by
Industry

SOCIAL SERVICES AND WELFARE

EC Contacts

Table 25.2 lists official European Community directorates and subdirectorates that provide information about social services and welfare. For the complete address of the Commission of the European Communities headquarters (CEC HQ in the table), refer to the Introduction to Part III.

Commission of the European Communities
▲ Statistical Office

Directorate E/3 (Social and Regional Statistics/ Social Digests)

Address: Batiment Jean Monnet
rue Alcide de Gasperi
L-2920 Luxembourg
Telephone: 430 11
Telex: 3423/3446/3476 COMEUR LU

Commission of the European Communities
▲ Task Force for Human Resources, Education, Training and Youth

Address: rue de la Loi 200
B-1049 Bruxelles
Belgium
Telephone: 2/235 11 11
Telex: 21877 COMEU B

European Parliament
▲ Committee on Social Affairs, Employment, and the Working Environment

Address: 97–113, rue Belliard
B-1040 Bruxelles
Belgium
Telephone: 2/284 21 21; 2/284 35 04
Fax: 2/230 68 56; 2/231 12 57

Address: Palais de l'Europe
F-67006 Strasbourg Cedex
France
Telephone: 88/374 001; 88/374 037; 88/374 548
Fax: 88/369 214; 88/256 516

Address: Centre Europeen
Plateau du Kirchberg
L-2929 Luxembourg
Telephone: 430 01
Telex: 3493 EUPARL LU; 2894 EUPARL LU
Fax: 436 972; 435 359

European Parliament
▲ Committee on Youth, Culture, Education, the Media, and Sport

Address: 97–113, rue Belliard
B-1040 Bruxelles
Belgium
Telephone: 2/284 21 21; 2/284 25 11
Fax: 2/230 68 56; 2/231 12 57

Address: Palais de l'Europe
F-67006 Strasbourg Cedex
France
Telephone: 88/374 001; 88/374 522
Fax: 88/369 214; 88/256 516

Address: Centre Europeen
Plateau du Kirchberg
L-2929 Luxembourg
Telephone: 430 01
Telex: 3493 EUPARL LU; 2894 EUPARL LU
Fax: 436 972; 435 359

Associations

▲ COFACE (Confederation of Family Organizations in the European Community)

Address: rue de Londres 17
B-1050 Bruxelles
Belgium
Telephone: 2/511 41 79

Data Resources and Publications

1992: The European Social Dimension

Publisher: Office for Official Publications of the European Communities
Frequency of Publication: One time
Scope: Discussion of the "social dimension" of the Single Market Program

Aging Populations

Publisher: OECD
Frequency of Publication: One time
Scope: Studies of the social policy implications of the increasing numbers of the aged in OECD countries

Bulletin of the Economic and Social Committee

Publisher: Office for Official Publications of the European Communities
Frequency of Publication: Monthly
Scope: Report on all plenary sessions of the Economic and Social Committee

Curriculum Reform

Publisher: OECD
Frequency of Publication: One time
Scope: Reviews of policies in OECD countries toward reform in educational curricula

Directory of Bodies Concerned with Urban and Regional Research

Publisher: United Nations Economic Commission for Europe
Frequency of Publication: One time
Scope: Organization of urban and regional research in EC countries with addresses of government ministries, departments, institutes, specialized agencies, and universities dealing with research in this field

Disabled Youth

Publisher: OECD
Frequency of Publication: One time
Scope: Reviews of government policies toward disabled youth, including their right to status as adults

Education and the Economy in a Changing Society

Publisher: OECD
Frequency of Publication: One time
Scope: Studies on the role of education and its impact on economic growth and development

Education in OECD Countries

Publisher: OECD
Frequency of Publication: Annual
Scope: Comparative statistics on all the education systems in OECD countries

Erasmus—The Joint Study Programme Newsletter of the Commission

Publisher: Office for Official Publications of the European Communities
Frequency of Publication: 2 times a year
Scope: Newsletter about current activities of Erasmus (European Community Action Scheme for the Mobility of University Students)

Table 25.2
CEC Subdirectorates—Social Services and Welfare

Directorate and Subdirectorate Name	Directorate/ Subdirectorate Number	Directorate- General	Address
Employment			
Social Aspects of Industrial Policies, New Technologies, and Industrial Relations	A/2	V	CEC HQ, Belgium
ECSC Readaptation and Social Aspects of Iron and Steel Policies	A/3	V	CEC HQ, Belgium
Action on Employment and Equality for Women	A/4	V	CEC HQ, Belgium
Living and Working Conditions and Welfare			
Social Security and Social Action Programmes	B/1	V	CEC HQ, Belgium
European Social Fund	C	V	CEC HQ, Belgium

▼ ▼

Europe Against Cancer

Publisher: Office for Official Publications of the European Communities

Frequency of Publication: One time

Scope: Discussion of topics for 1989, the European year of information on cancer, targeting a 15 percent reduction in cancer by the year 2000

European University News

Publisher: Office for Official Publications of the European Communities

Frequency of Publication: 6 times a year

Scope: Newsletter about higher education in the EC; prepared by DG X

Evaluation of the Comett Programme

Publisher: Office for Official Publications of the European Communities

Frequency of Publication: One time

Scope: Review of Comett, EC's Community Program in Education and Training for Technology

First Invitation Conference on Databases for Education and Training

Publisher: Office for Official Publications of the European Communities

Frequency of Publication: One time

Scope: Proceedings of meeting on the use of computers in education and training in the EC; organized by CEDEFOP

The Future of Social Protection

Publisher: OECD

Frequency of Publication: One time

Scope: Studies of options for providing a wide range of social programs

Higher Education Management

Publisher: OECD

Frequency of Publication: 3 times a year

Scope: Survey of institutional management, including current research reports and articles

Information Technologies in Education

Publisher: OECD

Frequency of Publication: One time

Scope: Review of the demands for software for use in education

Monthly Bulletin of Statistics

Publisher: United Nations

Frequency of Publication: Monthly

Scope: Data on 74 social and economic subjects from over 200 countries; includes quarterly data for regional groups such as the EC

New Forms of Work

Publisher: Office for Official Publications of the European Communities

Frequency of Publication: One time

Scope: Coverage of labor law and social security in the EC; prepared by the European Foundation for the Improvement of Living and Working Conditions

New Semi-Sheltered Forms of Employment for Disabled Persons

Publisher: Office for Official Publications of the European Communities

Frequency of Publication: One time

Scope: Analysis of measures in the EC Member States; prepared by CEDEFOP

The OECD Observer

Publisher: OECD

Frequency of Publication: 6 times a year

Scope: Key problems dealt with by the OECD, including economic growth, employment, social problems, energy, financial markets, the environment, and science and technology

Preparation for Retirement in the Member States of the European Community

Publisher: Office for Official Publications of the European Communities

Frequency of Publication: One time

Scope: Reports from a seminar on retirement-related issues

Reforming Public Pensions

Publisher: OECD

Frequency of Publication: One time

Scope: Analysis of the funding and future burdens of public pensions in OECD countries, with suggestions for long-term reform

Rent Policy in the EC Countries

Publisher: United Nations Economic Commission for Europe
Frequency of Publication: One time
Scope: Rent policy in relation to housing production, subsidy systems, housing quality, rent legislation, and developments in 20 Eastern and Western European countries

Role and Extent of Competition in Improving the Performance of Public Enterprises

Publisher: United Nations
Frequency of Publication: One time
Scope: Studies importance of competition in changing the way in which the public sector operates

The Social and Economic Situation of Older Women in Europe

Publisher: Office for Official Publications of the European Communities
Frequency of Publication: One time
Scope: Short analysis of the economic position of older women in the EC

Social Europe—Review

Publisher: Office for Official Publications of the European Communities
Frequency of Publication: 3 times a year
Scope: Critical review of the social aspects of the Single Market Program, including information on employment; prepared by DG V

Social Europe—Supplement: The Fight Against Poverty

Publisher: Office for Official Publications of the European Communities
Frequency of Publication: One time
Scope: Report on EC action program to combat poverty; prepared by DG V

Social Europe—Supplement: The Leading Edge

Publisher: Office for Official Publications of the European Communities
Frequency of Publication: One time
Scope: Reviews of the growth of school/industry partnerships in the EC; prepared by DG V

Social Europe—Supplement: The Social Aspects of the Internal Market

Publisher: Office for Official Publications of the European Communities
Frequency of Publication: One time
Scope: Summary of the results of six seminars concerning social aspects of the intra-EC market; prepared by DG V

Social Europe—Supplement: Youth and Unemployment

Publisher: Office for Official Publications of the European Communities
Frequency of Publication: One time
Scope: Report of 1987 conference on unemployment problems of young adults and teenagers; prepared by DG V

Social Expenditure 1960–1990

Publisher: OECD
Frequency of Publication: One time
Scope: Study of the problems of growth in social expenditures and proposals for controlling that growth

Social Work Training in the European Community

Publisher: Office for Official Publications of the European Communities
Frequency of Publication: One time
Scope: Brief discussion of social work training

Trends in Research on Human Settlements in EC Countries

Publisher: United Nations Economic Commission for Europe
Frequency of Publication: One time
Scope: Trends in research and related policies, as well as current and future research requirements for settlement development

Who Cares for Europe's Children?

Publisher: Office for Official Publications of the European Communities
Frequency of Publication: One time
Scope: Report of the European Childcare Network

Related Topics and Industries

Economic and Business Development; Employment and Labor. See also *Part IV—Sources on EC 1992 by Industry*

TRADE

EC Contacts

Table 25.3 lists official European Community directorates and subdirectorates that provide information about trade. For the complete address of the Commission of the European Communities headquarters (CEC HQ in the table), refer to the Introduction to Part III.

Commission of the European Communities
▲ Statistical Office

Directorate C (International Trade Statistics and Relations with ACP and Other Countries)

Address: Batiment Jean Monnet
              rue Alcide de Gasperi
              L-2920 Luxembourg
Telephone: 430 11
Telex: 3423/3446/3476 COMEUR LU

European Parliament
▲ Committee on Agriculture, Fisheries, and Rural Development

Address: Centre Europeen
              Plateau du Kirchberg
              L-2929 Luxembourg
Telephone: 430 01
Telex: 3493 EUPARL LU; 2894 EUPARL LU

European Parliament
▲ Committee on Development and Cooperation

Address: Centre Europeen
              Plateau du Kirchberg
              L-2929 Luxembourg
Telephone: 430 01
Telex: 3493 EUPARL LU; 2894 EUPARL LU

European Parliament
▲ Committee on External Economic Relations

Address: Centre Europeen
              Plateau du Kirchberg
              L-2929 Luxembourg
Telephone: 430 01
Telex: 3493 EUPARL LU; 2894 EUPARL LU

Associations

▲ FEWITA (Federation of European Wholesale and International Trade Associations)

Address: av. d'Auderghem 33–35
          B-1040 Bruxelles
          Belgium
Telephone: 2/231 08 31
Telex: 26946 TRACED B
Fax: 2/230 00 78

▲ IUCAB (International Union of Commercial Agents and Brokers)

Address: Herengracht 376
              NL-1016 CH Amsterdam
              Netherlands
Telephone: 20/22 19 44
Telex: 18313 GEBO NL
Fax: 20/26 0557

Data Sources and Publications

Commodity Trade Statistics

Publisher: United Nations
Frequency of Publication: Every 2 weeks
Scope: Analysis of more than 150 groups of commodities exported or imported by the world's principal trading nations

Comtext

Database Producer: Eurostat
Distributors/Hosts: Eurostat, WEFA, Business and Trade Statistics
Frequency of Update: Monthly
Scope: Statistics on trade between the Member States of the EC and on their trade with non-Member Countries   ☿

The Cost of Restricting Imports

Publisher: OECD
Frequency of Publication: One time
Scope: Analysis of the impact of import restrictions on the automobile industry

Table 25.3
CEC Subdirectorates—Trade

Directorate and Subdirectorate Name	Directorate/ Subdirectorate Number	Directorate- General	Address
General Questions and Instruments of External Economic Policy			
Antidumping Strategy: Policy (Dumping), Investigations and Measures; New Trade Policy Instrument; and Export Arrangements	C/1	I	CEC HQ, Belgium
Antidumping Strategy: Policy (Injury), Investigations and Measures; Antisubsidy Strategy; Import Arrangements; and Article 115	C/2	I	CEC HQ, Belgium
Internal Market and Industrial Affairs I			
Safeguard Measures and Removal of Nontariff Barriers	B/1	III	CEC HQ, Belgium Telephone: 2/236 30 12
General Competition Policy and Coordination			
Legal and Procedural Problems, Regulation, Infringement Procedures, and Intra-Community Dumping	A/2	IV	CEC HQ, Belgium
External Tariff Questions			
Combined Nomenclature	A/1	XXI	CEC HQ, Belgium
Economic Tariff Questions	A/2	XXI	CEC HQ, Belgium
Customs Valuation	A/3	XXI	CEC HQ, Belgium
Integrated Tariff	A/4	XXI	CEC HQ, Belgium
Customs Union Legislation			
Movement of Goods, Procedures, and Coordination of Agricultural Questions	B/1	XXI	CEC HQ Belgium
Origin of Goods	B/2	XXI	CEC HQ, Belgium
General Customs Legislation	B/3	XXI	CEC HQ, Belgium
Customs Procedures with Economic Impact and General Matters	B/4	XXI	CEC HQ, Belgium

Table 25.3
CEC Subdirectorates—Trade (continued)

Directorate and Subdirectorate Name	Directorate/ Subdirectorate Number	Directorate-General	Address
Indirect Taxation Including Elimination of Tax Frontiers			
VAT and Other Turnover Taxes	C/1	XXI	CEC HQ, Belgium
Indirect Taxation Other Than Turnover Taxes	C/2	XXI	CEC HQ, Belgium
Elimination of Tax Frontiers and the VAT Clearing System	C/3	XXI	CEC HQ, Belgium

Economic Bulletin for Europe

Publisher: United Nations Economic Commission for Europe

Frequency of Publication: Annual

Scope: World trade and the economies of Europe, including output and trade, economic developments, and financing

Economic Survey of Europe

Publisher: United Nations

Frequency of Publication: Annual

Scope: World trade and the economies of Europe, including output and trade, economic developments, and financing

The Export Credit Financing Systems in OECD Member Countries

Publisher: OECD

Frequency of Publication: Every 3 years

Scope: Description of export credit insurance and guarantee programs, as well as export financing support in OECD countries, including overseas development assistance programs that bear on export credit activities

External Trade—Monthly Statistics

Publisher: Office for Official Publications of the European Communities

Frequency of Publication: Monthly

Scope: Trade statistical data by country and commodity; prepared by the Statistical Office of the EC

Foreign Trade Statistics—Series A

Publisher: OECD

Frequency of Publication: Monthly

Scope: Over 12,000 time series, including total trade, trade of OECD groupings by main region, trade of OECD countries with OECD grouping, volume and average value indexes, trade by SITC sections; available on microcomputer diskette and in hardcopy; OECD also makes available a service to extract specific data

GATT Activities

Publisher: GATT

Frequency of Publication: Annual

Scope: Report on the current state of trade negotiations, including a background on current trade disputes

GATT Focus

Publisher: GATT

Frequency of Publication: 10 times a year

Scope: Newsletter on trade negotiations, including features on economic developments and major trade policy issues

GATT, What It Is, What It Does

Publisher: GATT

Frequency of Publication: Periodically

Scope: Origins and activities of GATT

Handbook of International Trade and Development Statistics

Publisher: United Nations
Frequency of Publication: Annual
Scope: Basic statistical data dealing with world trade and development

Industrial Structure Statistics

Publisher: OECD
Frequency of Publication: Annual
Scope: Statistics on production, value added, number of establishments, employment, wages and salaries, exports, imports, and investment

Industrial Trends—Monthly Statistics

Publisher: Office for Official Publications of the European Communities
Frequency of Publication: Monthly
Scope: Statistical data on trends in industrial activity, such as data for each industrial branch and for the industry as a whole, including indexes for the value of imports and exports in these branches; available online via the Cronos database; prepared by the Statistical Office of the EC

International Trade

Publisher: GATT
Frequency of Publication: Annual
Scope: Review of trade performance of all GATT members, and developments by economic sector; also includes over 150 separate statistical tables on trade-related issues

International Trade Statistics Yearbook

Publisher: United Nations
Frequency of Publication: Annual
Scope: Summary of foreign trade statistics, showing overall trade by product and by regions and countries, world exports by origin, and area of destination

News of the Uruguay Round

Publisher: GATT
Frequency of Publication: Periodically
Scope: Press bulletins on discussions in various trade negotiating bodies

Panorama of EC Industry

Publisher: Office for Official Publications of the European Communities
Frequency of Publication: Annual
Scope: Description of 165 manufacturing and service industries, including external industrial trade and evaluations of the impact of the Single Market Program

Progress in Structural Reform

Publisher: OECD
Frequency of Publication: Periodically
Scope: Reviews of economic activities of all OECD members, as well as EC specifically, in areas including financial markets, investment, taxation, competition policy, trade, agriculture, industrial policy, and labor markets; a supplement to selected issues of OECD's *Economic Outlook*

Research on the "Cost of Non-Europe"—The Cost of Non-Europe: Border Related Controls and Administrative Formalities—An Illustration of the Road Haulage Sector

Publisher: Office for Official Publications of the European Communities
Frequency of Publication: One time
Scope: Results of a survey on the costs of customs controls and formalities to businesses, including estimates of trade lost due to current customs barriers; Volume 4 of the Cecchini study on the "cost of non-Europe"

Statistical Yearbook

Publisher: United Nations
Frequency of Publication: Annual
Scope: Summary of statistical data for more than 270 countries on population, agriculture, manufacturing, construction, transport, commodity import/export trade, balance of payments, national income, education, and culture; presented on an internationally comparable basis, using overall world summary tables and data by country

Statistics of Foreign Trade. Series A: Monthly Statistics of Foreign Trade

Publisher: OECD
Frequency of Publication: Monthly
Scope: Trade data for individual OECD members with most of their partner countries

Statistics of Foreign Trade. Series C: Foreign Trade by Commodities

Publisher: OECD
Frequency of Publication: Annual (in five separate volumes during the year)
Scope: Detailed data on trade of individual OECD members by commodity

Related Topics and Industries

Economic and Business Development. See also *Part IV—Sources on EC 1992 by Industry*

PART

IV

Sources on
EC 1992 by
Industry

INTRODUCTION

In this part of the sourcebook you'll find sources of information on the Single Market Program as it impacts specific businesses and industries. The part is divided into 12 chapters, each covering a broad range of related industries, including these:

- Agriculture and Food Stuffs
- Communications and Information
- Consumer Products and Services
- Energy
- Financial Services and Insurance
- Health Care and Medicine
- Housing and Infrastructure
- Industrial Products
- Manufacturing
- Natural Resources
- Professions and Service Industries
- Transportation

STRUCTURE OF EACH CHAPTER

Each chapter begins by noting other places in the sourcebook you can look for assistance.

Each major section of every chapter covers a broad range of industries. For each grouping of industries, the sourcebook provides

- *A list and table of EC contacts.* Includes committees of the European Parliament and offices within the Commission of the European Communities. This list provides the most specific EC offices possible as a starting contact point and includes the name of the contact office; its address; and its telephone, telex, and fax numbers. For subdirectorate contacts, refer to the table that summarizes all the sources at the EC headquarters for that industry.

- *A list of associations and organizations in the EC most directly concerned with the specific businesses and industries.* Provides the name and official acronym of the association, as well as its address, telephone, and, when available, telex and fax numbers.

- *A list of data sources and publications that deal with the businesses and industries.* Each entry includes information on the publication's publisher as well as on its contents.

- *A list of related industries.* Refers to other chapters in Part IV.

WHEN TO USE THIS PART

- To identify and monitor specific Single Market Program issues that impact your industry and related industries.

- To track current activity and key participants in markets of particular interest.

- To provide access to EC-based competitors, suppliers, and customers.

HOW TO USE THIS PART

1. *Review Chapter Opening.* Review the opening of the chapter to make sure it deals with the topics that interest you.

2. *Turn to Appendix D.* You can also make sure the chapter deals with topics that interest you by turning to Appendix D (which has divided EC Single Market measures paralleling this part)

and finding the measures corresponding to the chapter you are reviewing. If the subjects covered there seem familiar, this is probably the best place for you to start.

3. *Scan EC Contact Names.* After you have determined this is the correct chapter, scan the names of the EC contacts listed in the section you are reading. Doing so will help you immediately understand what the EC sees as the most important current policy issues. The listing shows which EC offices can provide information about the Single Market Program with respect to this industry.

4. *Review Association Listing.* Review the list of associations to get an overview of the specific industries and other interest groups in the EC that deal with the Single Market Program.

5. *Scan Resources and Publications Listing.* Scan the data resources and publications list, which shows the wide variety of resources available and the scope of each resource.

Which Sources Should Be Used?

Once you have a sense of the contents of the chapter and section, consider which sources can be most helpful. The following should give you an idea of what to use:

- *EC Contacts.* Profiles useful contacts for up-to-date information on the progress of the Single Market Program as it relates to the narrow areas for which each office is responsible.

- *Associations.* Provides contacts for developing information on the status of past and current Single Market Program initiatives affecting areas in which the associations are primarily interested.

- *Data Sources and Publications.* Lists data resources and publications that are most useful in providing a sense of perspective on the Single Market Program in this particular area. The data resources may also provide specific information on the sectors being affected by the Single Market Program.

How to Use the Sources

EC CONTACTS

For several reasons, it is best to communicate with EC contacts in writing rather than by telephone:

- Making a request in writing helps minimize communications problems caused by language difficulties.

- Referring a written request to another office is substantially easier than referring a telephone request.
- Following up on a written request is easier than following up on a telephone call.

You can make a request by letter, fax, or telex. In all cases, you should observe several basic rules.

Specify the office to which you are writing. Many EC offices share common addresses, telex numbers, and even fax numbers. In corresponding with CEC offices, prominently note the directorate-general (DG), as well as directorate and subdirectorate with which you are corresponding. This can be done in either of two ways:

- Use all of the numbers and letters that refer to that office, starting with the directorate-general, then the directorate, and finally the subdirectorate, such as DG XIX/A/3; or
- Use the key words from the title of that office, such as Budgets/Expenditure/Structural Funds.

Identify yourself and your affiliation. Provide your full name and title (if any). Also provide your *full* return address, as well as telephone numbers, fax numbers, and telex numbers.

State why you are writing and what kind of information or help you are seeking. Be as specific as possible. If you have been referred to this office by another office, state that. If you already have obtained copies of reports, studies, or other materials that deal with the industry about which you are writing, explain what you already have. This way, you will avoid receiving duplicates.

If you are operating under a deadline, indicate what it is. Be reasonable in what you expect to receive and when you expect to receive it.

If you have questions about specific adopted or proposed measures, first identify that measure as well as you can. Describe what it is about and where you heard about it. If you have materials carrying some reference numbers, provide them. Then, ask your questions as precisely as possible.

Allow enough time for a reply. The CEC and the European Parliament's committees are very busy offices. Their primary mission is to advance the Single Market Program, and although assisting in your inquiry may be a part of that mission, they face other assignments as well.

If time is a constraint or your inquiry is *very precise and limited,* you may wish to consider a direct call. In that case, follow these guidelines in *preparing* to make the call. They will help you develop a full command of what you want, what you need, and when you need it. The hints in Appendix F's Etiquette in Government Calls may also be useful. Even when time is a problem, consider using a fax rather than a call.

ASSOCIATIONS

When you contact an association or organization listed in this book, remember the association exists *primarily* to further the interests of its own member organizations in terms of the EC. However, as a part of their operations, many associations have assembled substantial amounts of information on their own industry and on their own members. Some associations even provide statistical information and research services to nonmembers (often for a fee) as well as to their members.

As long as an association or organization perceives that fulfilling a request for information is in the best interests of its members, it usually will try to respond to requests for information. It may provide the information directly or identify other sources of data. These sources can be specialized research groups with which the association or organization may be affiliated, national-level associations or organizations, or even its own members.

In general, when you communicate with an association or organization, follow the same guidelines that apply to dealings with EC offices. In addition:

- Indicate if you are a member of an association in your home country that parallels the association you are contacting.
- Offer to pay for documents and services but set an initial price limit. Or you can ask the association to advise you of any costs involved before it proceeds.

DATA SOURCES AND PUBLICATIONS

When you order any data source or publication, find out the following before you complete the order:

- Whether the material is locally available through a library, national commercial development office, graduate school of business or economics, or other information center, such as Euro Info Centres.

• If the document is other than a one-time publication, what year (or edition) is being shipped. Confirm that this edition is the latest published. Not all distributors receive current editions of all publications.

• Details about the materials, such as length and language of publication. Ask whether the supplier (listed in Appendix E) can send you more information about the materials, such as a brochure.

• The total cost, including delivery charges.

• When the materials will be shipped and when you can expect to receive them. If that delivery is too slow, find out about express or rush charges.

• Data resources now available on either a microcomputer diskette or online databases are marked with the following symbols: ☯ for available through a database; ■ for available on a microcomputer diskette.

ADDRESSES IN TABLES OF EC CONTACTS

In tables throughout this part, key contacts in the EC's directorates and subdirectorates often are presented in a tabular format.

The name of the directorate-general has been removed, leaving only the DG number. The names of all of the DGs are provided in Table 5.1 in Chapter 5.

Because many of these offices are in the same office complexes in Belgium and often use a common number, information is given in an abbreviated form. In each table of EC contacts, "CEC HQ, Belgium" means:

▲ Commission of the European Communities

Address: rue de la Loi
            B-1049 Bruxelles
            Belgium
Telephone: 2/235 11 11
Telex: 21877 COMEU B

Any variation from the common telephone, fax line, or telex number is set out separately in the table.

CITY AND COUNTRY TELEPHONE CODES

Throughout the sourcebook telephone and fax numbers are preceded by corresponding city codes (or in the United States, area codes). Luxembourg is the one exception, because it has no city code, only a country code.

The city codes used for London (71 and 81) throughout the Sourcebook assume telephone calls will originate from outside Great Britain. When you are making intracountry calls, however, a zero should precede the designated city codes (071 and 081).

Although International Country Codes are necessary to place intercountry calls, these codes have not been included with the telephone and fax numbers listed in the sourcebook. Selected country codes, together with the time difference from Greenwich Mean Time (GMT) are shown in Table IV.1.

ASSISTANCE

For additional help on understanding and using the resources in this part, refer to Appendixes A through H, as well as to the Introduction to this book.

Table IV.1
EC Member States' Country Telephone Codes

Country	Code	Difference from GMT
Belgium	32	+1
Canada (Ottawa)	1	−5
Denmark	45	+1
France	33	+1
Germany, Federal Republic of	49/37 *	+1
Greece	30	+2
Ireland, Northern	44	0
Ireland, Republic of	353	0
Italy	39	+1
Japan	81	+9
Luxembourg	352	+1
The Netherlands	31	+1
Portugal	351	0
Spain	34	+1
Switzerland	41	+1
United Kingdom	44	0
USA (New York)	1	−5

* Use 37 when you dial the former German Democratic Republic.

26

Agriculture

and

Food Stuffs

SECTIONS IN THIS CHAPTER

Agricultural Support Policies

Fish and Fisheries

Food, Dairy, and Livestock

Other Agricultural and Food Stuffs Industries

ASSISTANCE

Appendix D contains a list of the Single Market measures dealing with agriculture and food stuffs. For additional help on using the resources in this chapter, refer to the Introduction to Part IV.

AGRICULTURAL SUPPORT POLICIES

EC Contacts

Table 26.1 lists official European Community directorates and subdirectorates that provide information about agricultural support policies. For the complete address of the Commission of the European Communities headquarters (CEC HQ in the table), refer to the Introduction to Part IV.

European Parliament

▲ Committee on Agriculture, Fisheries, and Rural Development

Address: 97–113, rue Belliard
B-1040 Bruxelles
Belgium
Telephone: 2/284 21 21; 2/284 28 08
Fax: 2/230 68 56; 2/231 12 57

Address: Palais de l'Europe
F-67006 Strasbourg Cedex
France
Telephone: 88/374 001; 88/374 589; 88/374 554
Fax: 88/369 214; 88/256 516

Address: Centre Europeen
Plateau du Kirchberg
L-2929 Luxembourg
Telephone: 430 01
Telex: 3493 EUPARL LU; 2894 EUPARL LU
Fax: 436 972; 435 359

European Parliament

▲ Committee on Budgets

Address: 97–113, rue Belliard
B-1040 Bruxelles
Belgium
Telephone: 2/284 21 21; 2/284 27 94
Fax: 2/230 68 56; 2/231 12 57

Address: Palais de l'Europe
F-67006 Strasbourg Cedex
France
Telephone: 88/374 001; 88/377 069
Fax: 88/369 214; 88/256 516

Address: Centre Europeen
Plateau du Kirchberg
L-2929 Luxembourg
Telephone: 430 01
Telex: 3493 EUPARL LU; 2894 EUPARL LU
Fax: 436 972; 435 359

European Parliament

▲ Committee on External Economic Relations

Address: 97–113, rue Belliard
B-1040 Bruxelles
Belgium
Telephone: 2/284 21 21; 2/284 27 49
Fax: 2/230 68 56; 2/231 12 57

Address: Palais de l'Europe
F-67006 Strasbourg Cedex
France
Telephone: 88/374 001; 88/374 021
Fax: 88/369 214; 88/256 516

Address: Centre Europeen
Plateau du Kirchberg
L-2929 Luxembourg
Telephone: 430 01
Telex: 3493 EUPARL LU; 2894 EUPARL LU
Fax: 436 972; 435 359

Data Resources and Publications

Agricultural and Environmental Policies

Publisher: OECD
Frequency of Publication: One time
Scope: Summary of OECD member country policies dealing with the impact on the environment of agriculture

Agricultural Markets: Prices

Publisher: Office for Official Publications of the European Communities
Frequency of Publication: 4 times a year
Scope: Official support prices and derived prices used to operate the Common Agricultural Policy (CAP); a publication of DG VI

Agricultural Policies for the 1990s

Publisher: OECD
Frequency of Publication: One time
Scope: Discussion of the problems and prospects for international agricultural development and trade

Table 26.1
CEC Subdirectorates—Agricultural Support Policies

Directorate and Subdirectorate Name	Directorate/ Subdirectorate Number	Directorate-General	Address
Organization of Markets in Crop Products	C	VI	CEC HQ, Belgium Telex: 220376 AGREC B
Organization of Markets in Livestock Products	D	VI	CEC HQ, Belgium Telex: 220376 AGREC B
Organization of Markets in Specialized Products	E	VI	CEC HQ, Belgium Telex: 220376 AGREC B
Rural Development I	F-I	VI	CEC HQ, Belgium Telex: 220376 AGREC B
Rural Development II	F-II	VI	CEC HQ, Belgium Telex: 220376 AGREC B
European Agricultural Guidance and Guarantee Fund	G	VI	CEC HQ, Belgium Telex: 220376 AGREC B

Agricultural Policies, Markets, and Trade

Publisher: OECD
Frequency of Publication: Annual
Scope: Description of agricultural policies, markets, and trade in OECD member countries

The Agricultural Situation in the Community

Publisher: Office for Official Publications of the European Communities
Frequency of Publication: Annual
Scope: Description of the structure of agricultural markets, status of the Common Agricultural Policy (CAP), and market outlook for agricultural products

A Common Agricultural Policy for the 1990s

Publisher: Office for Official Publications of the European Communities
Frequency of Publication: One time
Scope: Details about the Common Agricultural Policy (CAP) of the EC and its status

Guide to the Reform of the Community's Structural Funds

Publisher: Office for Official Publications of the European Communities
Frequency of Publication: One time
Scope: Details EC's structural funds, their operations, and goals

Social Europe—Supplement: Seminar on the Social Aspects of the Common Agricultural Policy

Publisher: Office for Official Publications of the European Communities
Frequency of Publication: One time
Scope: Proceedings of a seminar about the social factors in the EC agricultural policy; prepared by DG V

Related Topics and Industries

Natural Resources. See also *Part III—Sources on EC 1992 by Topic*

Fish and Fisheries

EC Contacts

Table 26.2 lists official European Community directorates and subdirectorates that provide information about fish and fisheries. For the complete address of the Commission of the European Communities headquarters (CEC HQ in the table), refer to the Introduction to Part IV.

European Parliament

▲ Committee on Agriculture, Fisheries, and Rural Development

Address: 97–113, rue Belliard
           B-1040 Bruxelles
           Belgium
Telephone: 2/284 21 21; 2/284 28 08
Fax: 2/230 68 56; 2/231 12 57

Address: Palais de l'Europe
           F-67006 Strasbourg Cedex
           France
Telephone: 88/374 001; 88/374 589; 88/374 554
Fax: 88/369 214; 88/256 516

Address: Centre Europeen
           Plateau du Kirchberg
           L-2929 Luxembourg
Telephone: 430 01
Telex: 3493 EUPARL LU; 2894 EUPARL LU
Fax: 436 972; 435 359

Associations

▲ AIPCEE (Association des Industries du Poisson de la Communaute Economique Europeen {Fish})

Address: 1 Green Street
           Grosvenor Square
           GB-London W1Y 3RG
           England
Telephone: 71/629 0655
Fax: 71/499 9095

▲ CEP (Federation of National Organizations of Fish Wholesalers)

Address: c/o Danmarks Fiskeindustri og
           Eksportforening
           Kronprinsessegade 32
           DK-1306 Kobenhavn
           Denmark

▲ EUROPECHE (Association of National Organisations of Fishing Enterprises in the EEC)

Address: rue de la Science 23–25 (Bte 15)
           B-1040 Bruxelles
           Belgium
Telephone: 2/230 48 40
Telex: 25816 B
Fax: 2/230 26 80

Table 26.2
CEC Subdirectorates—Fish and Fisheries

Directorate and Subdirectorate Name	Directorate/ Subdirectorate Number	Directorate- General	Address
Internal Market and Industrial Affairs II			
Shipbuilding, Wood, Leather, Paper and Miscellaneous Industries	C/4	III	CEC HQ, Belgium Telephone: 2/236 30 12
Markets and External Resources	A	XIV	CEC HQ, Belgium
Internal Resources and Monitoring	B	XIV	CEC HQ, Belgium

▲ Union of Associations of Fish Meal Manufacturers in the European Economic Community

Address: Wachmannstrasse 95
D-2800 Bremen 1
Germany
Telephone: 421/34 47 53
Telex: 238633 FISRE D
Fax: 421/349 90 31

Data Resources and Publications

Agrep

Database Producer: European Community, DG VI
Distributors/Hosts: Datacentralen, Dimdi
Frequency of Update: Annual
Scope: Titles of agricultural research projects dealing with agriculture, silviculture, pisciculture, and food processing that are current at the time of collection; includes the names and addresses of the organizations where the work is being done ☸

Aquaculture

Publisher: OECD
Frequency of Publication: One time
Scope: Reviews of recent experience in the aquaculture industry, and discusses its development as a new industry

Review of Fisheries in OECD Countries

Publisher: OECD
Frequency of Publication: Annual
Scope: Major developments affecting commercial fisheries of OECD countries

Related Topics and Industries

Consumer Products and Services; Natural Resources; Transportation. See also Part III—Sources on EC 1992 by Topic

─── ▼ ───

FOOD, DAIRY, AND LIVESTOCK

EC Contacts

Table 26.3 lists official European Community directorates and subdirectorates that provide information about food, dairy, and livestock. For the complete address of the Commission of the European Communities headquarters (CEC HQ in the table), refer to the Introduction to Part IV.

Table 26.3
CEC Subdirectorates—Food, Dairy, and Livestock

Directorate and Subdirectorate Name	Directorate/ Subdirectorate Number	Directorate-General	Address
Internal Market and Industrial Affairs I			
Food Stuffs	B/2	III	CEC HQ, Belgium Telephone: 2/236 30 12
Restrictive Practices, Abuse of Dominant Positions, and Other Distortions of Competition II			
Processed Chemical Products, Agricultural Products and Food Stuffs	C/3	IV	CEC HQ, Belgium Telephone: 2/235 22 24

▼ ▼

European Parliament

▲ Committee on Agriculture, Fisheries, and Rural Development

Address: 97–113, rue Belliard
    B-1040 Bruxelles
    Belgium
Telephone: 2/284 21 21; 2/284 28 08
Fax: 2/230 68 56; 2/231 12 57

Address: Palais de l'Europe
    F-67006 Strasbourg Cedex
    France
Telephone: 88/374 001; 88/374 589; 88/374 554
Fax: 88/369 214; 88/256 516

Address: Centre Europeen
    Plateau du Kirchberg
    L-2929 Luxembourg
Telephone: 430 01
Telex: 3493 EUPARL LU; 2894 EUPARL LU
Fax: 436 972; 435 359

European Parliament

▲ Committee on the Environment, Public Health, and Consumer Protection

Address: 97–113, rue Belliard
    B-1040 Bruxelles
    Belgium
Telephone: 2/284 21 21; 2/284 28 48
Fax: 2/230 68 56; 2/231 12 57

Address: Palais de l'Europe
    F-67006 Strasbourg Cedex
    France
Telephone: 88/374 001; 88/374 418
Fax: 88/369 214; 88/256 516

Address: Centre Europeen
    Plateau du Kirchberg
    L-2929 Luxembourg
Telephone: 430 01
Telex: 3493 EUPARL LU; 2894 EUPARL LU
Fax: 436 972; 435 359

Associations

▲ AEMB (European Association of Livestock Markets)

Address: rue de la Loi 81 A (Bte 9)
    B-1040 Bruxelles
    Belgium
Telephone: 2/230 86 86
Telex: 64685 UECBV B
Fax: 2/230 94 00

▲ AIFLD (European Organization of the Dehydrated Fruit and Vegetable Industries)

Address: av. de Cortenbergh 172 (Bte 6)
    B-1040 Bruxelles
    Belgium
Telephone: 2/735 81 70
Telex: 26246 SIA B
Fax: 2/736 81 75

▲ AIFLV (Association of the Industry of Fruit and Vegetables in Vinegar, Brine, Oil, and Similar Products of the EC)

Address: av. de Cortenbergh 182 (Bte 6)
    B-1040 Bruxelles
    Belgium
Telephone: 2/735 81 70
Telex: 26246 B
Fax: 2/736 81 75

▲ AMFEP (Association of Microbial Food Enzyme Producers in Western Europe)

Address: av. de Cortenbergh 172 (Bte 6)
    B-1040 Bruxelles
    Belgium
Telephone: 2/735 81 70
Telex: 26246 FIA B
Fax: 2/736 81 75

▲ ASFALEC (Association of Preserved Milk Manufacturers of the EEC)

Address: 140, bd. Haussmann
    F-75008 Paris
    France
Telephone: 1/45 62 12 51
Telex: 643488 F
Fax: 1/42 25 44 39

▲ ASSIFONTE (Association de l'Industrie de la Fonte de Fromage de la CEE {Cheeses})

Address: Schedestrasse 11
D-5300 Bonn
Germany
Telephone: 228/21 70 05
Telex: 2283839 D
Fax: 228/26 16 94

▲ ASSILEC (EC Dairy Trade Association)

Address: 140, bd. Haussmann
F-75008 Paris
France
Telephone: 1/45 62 12 51
Telex: 643488 F
Fax: 1/42 25 44 39

▲ AVEC (Association of Poultry Processors and Poultry Import and Export Trade in the EC Communities)

Address: Vester Farimagsgade 1 (Suite 3410)
DK-1606 Kobenhavn
Denmark
Telex: 27101 ROSET DK

▲ CEES (European Committee for the Study of Salt)

Address: 11, bis. av. Victor Hugo
F-75116 Paris
France
Telephone: 1/45 01 72 62
Telex: 630731 COMESEL F
Fax: 1/45 00 64 78

▲ CEFS (Comite Europeen des Fabricants de Sucre {Sugar Makers})

Address: av. de Tervueren 182
B-1150 Bruxelles
Belgium
Telephone: 2/762 07 60
Telex: 63788 B
Fax: 2/771 00 26

▲ CIAA (Confederation des Industries Agro-Alimentaires de la CEE {Food Products})

Address: rue Joseph 11 40 (Bte 16)
B-1040 Bruxelles
Belgium
Telephone: 2/237 66 60
Telex: 20682 CIAA B
Fax: 2/231 14 81

▲ CIDE (European Dehydrators Association)

Address: 5, quai Voltaire
F-75007 Paris
France
Telephone: 1/42 61 72 94
Fax: 1/49 27 02 73

▲ CLITRAVI (Liaison Center for the European Meat Processing Industry)

Address: av. de Cortenbergh 172
B-1040 Bruxelles
Belgium
Telephone   2/735 81 70
Telex: 26246 SIA B
Fax: 2/736 81 75

▲ COBCCEE (Butchers and Meatcutters)

Address: av. de Cortenbergh 116
B-1040 Bruxelles
Belgium
Telephone: 2/735 24 70
Fax: 2/736 64 93

▲ COCERAL (Commerce Committee for Agricultural Supply Trade)

Address: rue Belliard 197 (Bte 6)
B-1040 Bruxelles
Belgium
Telephone: 2/230 61 70
Telex: 26047 B
Fax: 2/230 30 63

▲ COFALEC (Committee of Bakers' Yeast Producers in the European Economic Community)

Address: 15, rue du Louvre
F-75001, Paris
France
Telephone: 1/45 08 54 82
Fax: 1/42 21 02 14

▲ CPIV (Permanent International Vinegar Committee—Common Market)

Address: Reuterstrasse 151
D-5300 Bonn 1
Germany
Telephone: 228/21 20 17
Telex: 8869489 D
Fax: 228/22 94 60

▲ EFEMA (European Food Emulsifier Manufacturers' Association)

Address: av. Louise 250 (Bte 64)
B-1050 Bruxelles
Belgium
Telephone: 2/640 20 95
Telex: 62498 B
Fax: 2/647 87 06

▲ EFPA (European Food Service and Packaging Association)

Address: Waldeggstrasse 22B
CH-3800 Interlaken
Switzerland
Telephone: 36/22 22 26
Telex: 923152 OVI CH
Fax: 36/22 40 41

▲ EUCOLAIT (European Union of Producers of Dairy Products)

Address: av. Livingstone 26
B-1040 Bruxelles
Belgium
Telephone: 2/230 44 48
Telex: 22688 EUCO B
Fax: 2/230 40 44

▲ EURA (European Renderers Association)

Address: Heer Bokelweg 157B
NL-3032 AD Rotterdam
The Netherlands
Telephone: 10/467 31 88
Telex: 26560 CVG NL
Fax: 10/467 87 61

EUROGLACES (Association of the Ice Cream Industries of the EEC)

Address: 51–53, rue Fondary
F-75015 Paris
France
Telephone: 1/45 79 80 75
Telex: 205705 F
Fax: 1/45 79 61 29

▲ European Industrial Food Additives and Food Enzymes Liaison Committee

Address: Veraartlaan 8
NL-2288 GM Rijswijk
The Netherlands
Telephone: 70/90 34 64
Telex: 31172 NL
Fax: 70/98 98 93

▲ EUTECA (European Technical Caramel Association)

Address: rue de l'Orme 19
B-1040 Bruxelles
Belgium
Telephone: 2/733 12 40
Telex: 61473 ECCO B
Fax: 2/734 67 02

▲ EUVEPRO (European Vegetable Protein Federation)

Address: Leuvensestraat 29
B-1800 Vilvoorde
Belgium
Telephone: 2/252 10 52
Telex: 21260 FOODIN B
Fax: 2/252 41 99

▲ EUWEP (European Union of Wholesale with Eggs, Egg Products, Poultry, and Game)

Address: Buschstrasse 2
D-5300 Bonn 1
Germany
Telephone: 228/21 20 37
Telex: 886429 D
Fax: 228/22 09 62

▲ Federation des Associations de Fabricants de Produits Alimentaires Surgeles de la CEE {Raw Food Products}

Address: av. de Cortenbergh 172 (Bte 6)
B-1040 Bruxelles
Belgium
Telephone: 2/735 81 70
Telex: 26246 SIA B
Fax: 2/736 81 75

▲ FEDESA (European Federation of Animal Health)

Address: rue Defacqz 1 (Bte 8)
B-1050 Bruxelles
Belgium
Telephone: 2/537 21 25
Fax: 2/537 00 49

▲ FEDIOL (EEC Seed Crushers' and Oil Processors' Federation)

Address: rue de la Loi 74 (Bte 4)
B-1040 Bruxelles
Belgium
Telephone: 2/230 31 25
Telex: 23628 OLMA B
Fax: 2/230 22 74

▲ FEDOLIVE (Federation de l'Industrie de l'Huile d'Olive de la Communaute Economique Europeo {Olive Oil})

Address: Via del Governo Vecchio 3
I-00186 Roma
Italy
Telephone: 6/687 90 63
Telex: 630288 I
Fax: 6/689 61 76

▲ FRUCOM (European Federation of the Trade in Dried Fruit, Edible Nuts, Preserved Food, Spices, Honey, and Similar Foodstuffs)

Address: Plan 5
D-2000 Hamburg 1
Germany
Telephone: 40/32 64 14
Telex: 2162680 D
Fax: 40/32 26 39

▲ IMAGE (Association of the Margarine Industries of the EEC Countries)

Address: rue de la Loi 74
B-1040 Bruxelles
Belgium
Telephone: 2/230 48 10
Telex: 23628 OLMA B
Fax: 2/230 22 74

▲ NATCOL (Natural Food Colours Association)

Address: P.O. Box 3225
CH-4002
Switzerland
Telephone: 61/688 30 27
Telex: 962292 HLV CH
Fax: 61/691 93 91

▲ OECIT (Association of European Tomato Processing Industries)

Address: av. de Cortenbergh 172 (Bte 6)
B-1040 Bruxelles
Belgium
Telephone: 2/735 81 70
Telex: 26246 SIA B
Fax: 2/736 81 75

▲ OEITFL (Association of European Fruit and Vegetable Processing Industries)

Address: av. de Cortenbergh 172 (Bte 6)
B-1040 Bruxelles
Belgium
Telephone: 2/735 81 70
Telex: 26246 SIA B
Fax: 2/736 81 75

▲ PAO (Federation of Associations of Oat and Barley Millers in the EC)

Address: Postfach 190165
D-5300 Bonn 1
Germany
Telephone: 228/21 93 50
Telex: 886654 STVBN D
Fax: 228/22 28 12

▲ UECBV (European Livestock and Meat Trading Union)

Address: rue de la Loi 81A (Bte 9)
             B-1040 Bruxelles
             Belgium
Telephone: 2/230 46 03
Telex: 64685 UECBV B
Fax: 2/230 94 00

▲ UEEA (European Abattoirs Union)

Address: rue Belliard 197 (Bte 6)
             B-1040 Bruxelles
             Belgium
Telephone: 2/230 61 70
Telex: 26047 COCEAL B
Fax: 2/230 30 63

▲ UEITP (Union Europeen des Industries de Transformation de la Pomme de Terre {Potato Products})

Address: Van Stolkweg 31
             NL-2585 JN's Gravenhage
             The Netherlands
Telephone: 70/51 24 61
Telex: 31423 NL

▲ UNAFPA (Union of Organizations of Manufacturers of Pasta Products in the EEC)

Address: 6, Catherine Street
             London WC2B 5JJ
             Great Britain
Telephone: 71/836 2460
Telex: 299388 FDF G
Fax: 71/836 0580

▲ UNECOLAIT (European Federation of Dairy Retailers)

Address: 19, Cornwall Terrace
             GB-London NW1 4QP
             Great Britain
Telephone: 71/486 7244
Telex: 262027 DAIRY F G
Fax: 71/487 4734

▲ UNEGA (Union Europeen des Fondeurs et Fabricants de Corps Gras Animaux {Animal Products and By-Products})

Address: 10A, rue de la Paix
             F-75002 Paris
             France
Telephone: 1/42 61 66 81
Telex: 230905 STABILI F
Fax: 1/47 03 98 78

▲ Union des Associations des Semouliers des Communautes Europeen {Flour Milling}

Address: Via dei Crociferi 44
             I-00187 Roma
             Italy
Telephone: 6/678 54 09
Fax: 6/678 30 54

Data Resources and Publications

Agrep

Database Producer: European Community, DG VI
Distributors/Hosts: Datacentralen, Dimdi
Frequency of Update: Annual
Scope: Titles of agricultural research projects dealing with agriculture, silviculture, pisciculture, and food processing that are current at the time of collection; includes the names and addresses of the organizations where the work is being done ☿

Agricultural Markets: Prices

Publisher: Office for Official Publications of the European Communities
Frequency of Publication: 4 times a year
Scope: Official support prices and derived prices used to operate the Common Agricultural Policy; a publication of DG VI

Agricultural Review of Europe: An Annual Survey

Vol. I: General Review—A Review of the Current Agricultural Situation and of Agricultural Policy Developments

Vol. II: Agricultural Trade—Recent Developments in Agricultural Trade in Europe, Including the Quality of Agricultural and Food Products and Trade Flows

Vol. III: The Grain Market—Review of the Grain Situation and Outlook for Supply and Demand

Vol. IV: The Livestock and Meat Market—The European Market for Live Cattle, Live Pigs, Live Sheep, Poultry, and Game

Vol. V: The Milk and Dairy Products Market—Information on Production, Consumption, and Prices for Milk, Butter, Cheese, Whole Milk, Skim Milk, and Whey Powders, Condensed Milk, and Casein

Vol. VI: The Egg Market—Information on Production, Consumption, Prices, and Trade

Publisher: United Nations Economic Commission for Europe and the United Nations

Frequency of Publication: Annual

Scope: Six-volume survey of all aspects of agriculture in Europe

The Agricultural Situation in the Community

Publisher: Office for Official Publications of the European Communities

Frequency of Publication: Annual

Scope: Structure of agricultural markets, status of the Common Agricultural Policy, and market outlook for agricultural products

Agricultural Prices

Publisher: Office for Official Publications of the European Communities

Frequency of Publication: 4 times a year

Scope: Agricultural price series; available online via the Cronos database; a publication of the Statistical Office of the EC ⊛

Animal Production

Publisher: Office for Official Publications of the European Communities

Frequency of Publication: 4 times a year

Scope: Animal production, including meat, milk, poultry, and egg products; available online via the Cronos database; a publication of the Statistical Office of the EC ⊛

Canning Industry

Publisher: United Nations

Frequency of Publication: Periodically

Scope: Directory of basic industrial information sources

Commodity Trade Statistics

Publisher: United Nations

Frequency of Publication: Every other week

Scope: Analysis of more than 150 groups of commodities exported or imported by the world's principal trading nations

The Dairy Products Manufacturing Industry

Publisher: United Nations

Frequency of Publication: Periodically

Scope: Directory of basic industrial information sources about dairy products

EC Agricultural Price Indices: Monthly Results/ Half Yearly Statistics

Publisher: Office for Official Publications of the European Communities

Frequency of Publication: 2 times a year

Scope: Statements about trends of monthly indexes of producer prices, agricultural inputs, and production; available online via the Cronos database; prepared by the Statistical Office of the EC ⊛

The International Market for Meat

Publisher: GATT

Frequency of Publication: Annual

Scope: Highlights about the main trends in the international trade of bovine meat

Meat Balances in OECD Countries

Publisher: OECD

Frequency of Publication: Annual

Scope: International comparisons of production, trade, and consumption for each category of meat for a period of five years

Meat Processing Industry

Publisher: United Nations

Frequency of Publication: Periodically

Scope: Directory of basic industrial information sources for meat processors

Milk and Milk Product Balances in OECD Countries

Publisher: OECD

Frequency of Publication: Every other year

Scope: International comparison of production, trade, and consumption for each category of milk and milk products for a period of seven years

Presentation of an Application for Assessment of a Food Additive Prior to Its Authorization

Publisher: Office for Official Publications of the European Communities

Frequency of Publication: One time

Scope: Procedures for gaining approval of food additives

Prices of Agricultural Products and Selected Inputs in Europe and North America

Publisher: United Nations Economic Commission for Europe

Frequency of Publication: Annual

Scope: General price changes in agricultural price policies and in prices received by farmers, prices of individual products, and prices of selected inputs

Research on the "Cost of Non-Europe"— Technical Trade Barriers in the EC: An Illustration in Six Industries—Some Case Studies on Technical Barriers

Publisher: Office for Official Publications of the European Communities

Frequency of Publication: One time

Scope: Identifies technical trade barriers— including standards, legal requirements, testing and certification procedures— and evaluates their impact on the food stuffs, pharmaceuticals, automobile, building materials, telecommunications, and electrical products and machinery industries; Volume 6 of the Cecchini study on the "cost of non-Europe"

Research on the "Cost of Non-Europe"—The Cost of Non-Europe in the Foodstuffs Industry

Publisher: Office for Official Publications of the European Communities

Frequency of Publication: One time

Scope: Identifies nontariff trade barriers in major food stuff sectors, plus comparisons of the operations of US- and EC-based food companies in Europe; Volume 12 of the Cecchini study on the "cost of non-Europe"

Trends in Distributive Trades/Retail Sales— Registration of Cars

Publisher: Office for Official Publications of the European Community

Frequency of Publication: Annually

Scope: Volume of retail sales in three groups of products—food, clothing, and household equipment—as well as car registrations; available online via the Cronos database; prepared by the Statistical Office of the EC

The World Market for Dairy Products

Publisher: GATT

Frequency of Publication: Annually

Scope: Key trends in trade, production, consumption, and prices of fresh milk, milk powders, butter, and cheeses; compiled by the GATT Secretariat for members of the International Dairy Arrangement

Related Topics and Industries

Consumer Products and Services; Natural Resources. See also *Part III—Sources on EC 1992 by Topic*

OTHER AGRICULTURAL AND FOOD STUFFS INDUSTRIES

EC Contacts

Table 26.4 lists official European Community directorates and subdirectorates that provide information about other agricultural and food stuffs industries. For the complete address of the Commission of the European Communities headquarters (CEC HQ in the table), refer to the Introduction to Part IV.

Associations

▲ CECD (European Confederation of Retailers)

Address: av. d'Auderghem 33–35
B-1040 Bruxelles
Belgium

Telephone: 2/231 07 99

Telex: 26946 TRACED B

Fax: 2/230 00 78

▲ CEMA (European Committee of Agricultural Machine Builders)

Address: 19, rue Jacques Bingen
F-75017 Paris
France
Telephone: 1/47 66 02 20
Telex: 640362 F
Fax: 1/40 54 95 60

▲ CEOAH (European Committee for Agricultural and Horticultural Tools and Implements)

Address: 16, av. Hoche
F-75008 Paris
France
Telephone: 1/45 63 93 23
Telex: 280900 FEDEMEC F
Fax: 1/45 63 59 86

▲ COGECA (General Committee of Agricultural Cooperation in the EEC)

Address: rue de la Science 23–25
B-1040 Bruxelles
Belgium
Telephone: 2/230 39 45
Telex: 25816 B
Fax: 2/230 40 46

▲ COPA (Committee of Agricultural Organizations in the EEC)

Address: rue de la Science 23–25
B-1040 Bruxelles
Belgium
Telephone: 2/230 39 45
Telex: 25816 B
Fax: 2/230 40 46

Table 26.4
CEC Subdirectorates—Other Agricultural and Food Stuffs Industries

Directorate and Subdirectorate Name	Directorate/ Subdirectorate Number	Directorate-General	Address
General Matters, and Relations with the European Parliament, and the Economic and Social Committee			
Statistical Information, Quantity Studies, and Forecasts	A/2	VI	CEC HQ, Belgium Telex: 22037 AGREC B
Reports, Publications, Studies and Documentation	A/5	VI	CEC HQ, Belgium Telex: 22037 AGREC B
Agroeconomic Legislation	B-I	VI	CEC HQ, Belgium Telex: 22037 AGREC B
Quality and Health	B-II	VI	CEC HQ, Belgium Telex: 22037 AGREC B
Priority Programmes and Decentralized Information			
Agricultural Information	A/2	X	CEC HQ, Belgium
Protection of Water and the Air, and Conservation; Civil Protection			
Agriculture, Nature Conservation, and Relations with Other Policies	B/4	XI	CEC HQ, Belgium
Biology			
Agroindustrial Research	F/3	XII	CEC HQ, Belgium

▲ EFA (European Federation of Agricultural Workers' Unions)

Address: rue Fosse-aux-Loups 38 (Bte 8)
            B-1000 Bruxelles
            Belgium
Telephone: 2/218 53 08
Telex: 62241 ETUC B
Fax: 2/217 59 63

▲ EFMA (European Fertilizer Manufacturers Association)

Address: av. Louise 250 (Bte 54)
            B-1050 Bruxelles
            Belgium
Telephone: 2/640 54 02
Telex: 62444 B
Fax: 2/641 93 17

▲ EUREAU (Union of the Water Supply Associations from Countries of the European Communities)

Address: ch. de Waterloo 255 (Bte 6)
            B-1060 Bruxelles
            Belgium
Telephone: 2/537 43 02

▲ FEFAC (European Federation of the Compound Feed Manufacturers)

Address: rue de la Loi 223 (Bte 3)
            B-1040 Bruxelles
            Belgium
Telephone: 2/230 87 15
Telex: 23993 B
Fax: 2/230 57 22

▲ FEFANA (European Federation of Feed Additive Manufacturers)

Address: Roonstrasse 5
            D-5300 Bonn 2
            Germany
Telephone: 228/35 24 00
Telex: 886391 AWT D
Fax: 228/36 13 97

▲ FEWITA (Federation of European Wholesale and International Trade Associations)

Address: av. d'Auderghem 33–35
            B-1040 Bruxelles
            Belgium
Telephone: 2/231 08 31
Telex: 26946 TRACED B
Fax: 2/230 00 78

▲ International Liaison Committee for the Manufacturers and Restorers of Agricultural Machinery

Address: Wilhelminalaan 1
            NL-3732 GJ De Bilt
            The Netherlands
Telephone: 30/20 48 11
Telex: 76231 MU NL
Fax: 30/20 48 99

▲ Technical Centre for Agricultural and Technical Cooperation

Address: De Rietkampen Galvinstraat 19
            Ede
            The Netherlands

Data Resources and Publications
Agrep

Database Producer: European Community, DG VI
Distributors/Hosts: Datacentralen, Dimdi
Frequency of Update: Annual
Scope: Titles of agricultural research projects dealing with agriculture, silviculture, pisciculture, and food processing, that are current at the time of collection; includes the names and addresses of the organizations where the work is being done   ⊛

Agricultural Implements and Machinery Industry

Publisher: United Nations
Frequency of Publication: Periodically
Scope: Directory of basic industrial information sources

Agricultural Policies, Markets and Trade

Publisher: OECD
Frequency of Publication: Annual
Scope: Agricultural policies, markets, and trade in OECD member countries

Agricultural Review for Europe—Volume II: Agricultural Trade

Publisher: United Nations and the United Nations Economic Commission for Europe
Frequency of Publication: Annual
Scope: Recent developments in agricultural trade in Europe, including the quality of agricultural and food products and trade flows

The Agricultural Situation in the Community

Publisher: Office for Official Publications of the European Communities
Frequency of Publication: Annual
Scope: Structure of agricultural markets, status of the Common Agricultural Policy, and market outlook for agricultural products

Analysis of Agricultural Trade—EC-Developing Countries—1970–1986

Publisher: Office for Official Publications of the European Communities
Frequency of Publication: One time
Scope: Draft report on value and trends of EC agricultural trade with developing countries

Coffee, Cocoa, Tea, and Spices Industry

Publisher: United Nations
Frequency of Publication: Periodically
Scope: Directory of basic industrial information sources on basic agricultural industries

Economic Accounts for Agriculture and Forestry—1982–1987

Publisher: Office for Official Publications of the European Communities
Frequency of Publication: One time
Scope: Aggregated data on agriculture and forestry industries

Eurostatistics—Data for Short-term Economic Analysis

Publisher: Office for Official Publications of the European Communities
Frequency of Publication: Monthly
Scope: Recent economic data on the EC together with comparative statistics from the United States and Japan, such as exchange rates, interest rates, money supply, industrial and agricultural indexes, and foreign trade; available online via the Cronos database; prepared by the Statistical Office of the EC

Fertilizer Industry

Publisher: United Nations
Frequency of Publication: Periodically
Scope: Directory of basic industrial information sources

Flour Milling and the Bakery Products Industries

Publisher: United Nations
Frequency of Publication: Periodically
Scope: Directory of basic industrial information sources

FSSRS

Database Producer: Eurostat
Distributors/Hosts: Eurostat
Frequency of Update: Every 2 to 3 years
Scope: Results of EC surveys on the structure of farm holdings, including the size, physical and economic form of the holdings, the management of the holdings, the crops and livestock, and workers

Grain Processing and Storage

Publisher: United Nations
Frequency of Publication: Periodically
Scope: Directory of basic industrial information sources

Green Europe

Publisher: Office for Official Publications of the European Communities
Frequency of Publication: Monthly
Scope: Newsletter of agricultural developments; also available online via the Cronos database; prepared by DG VI ✆

The Impact of Biotechnology on Agriculture in the European Community to the Year 2005

Publisher: Office for Official Publications of the European Communities
Frequency of Publication: One time
Scope: Study on intensive farming and the impact on the environment and rural economy

Leather and Leather Products

Publisher: United Nations
Frequency of Publication: Periodically
Scope: Directory of basic industrial information sources

Panorama of EC Industry

Publisher: Office for Official Publications of the European Communities
Frequency of Publication: Annual
Scope: Description of 165 manufacturing and service industries, including the animal feed and agrochemical industries, plus evaluations of the impact of the Single Market Program

Progress in Structural Reform

Publisher: OECD
Frequency of Publication: Periodically
Scope: Reviews economic activities of all OECD members, as well as EC specifically, in areas including financial markets, investment, taxation, competition policy, trade, agriculture, industrial policy, and labor markets; a supplement to selected issues of OECD's *Economic Outlook*

Regio

Database Producer: Eurostat
Distributors/Hosts: Eurostat
Frequency of Update: Regularly
Scope: Macroeconomic statistics on various regions of the EC; covers demography, economic accounts, unemployment, labor force sample survey, industry, agriculture, the EC's financial participation in investments, and transport ✆

The Rules Governing Medicinal Products in the European Community

Publisher: Office for Official Publications of the European Communities
Frequency of Publication: One time
Scope: Five volumes of rules dealing with manufacturing, testing, and marketing authorization for medicinal products (human and veterinary) in the member states of the EC

Utilization of Agricultural Residues for the Production of Panels, Pulp, and Paper

Publisher: United Nations
Frequency of Publication: Periodically
Scope: Directory of basic industrial information sources

Related Topics and Industries

Consumer Products and Services; Industrial Products; Natural Resources. See also *Part III—Sources on EC 1992 by Topic*

27

Communications
and Information

ASSISTANCE

Appendix D contains a list of the Single Market measures dealing with communications and information. For additional help on using the resources in this chapter, refer to the Introduction to Part IV.

INFORMATION TECHNOLOGY

EC Contacts

Table 27.1 lists official European Community directorates and subdirectorates that provide information about information technology. For the complete address of the Commission of the European Communities headquarters (CEC HQ in the table), refer to the Introduction to Part IV.

Commission of the European Communities

▲ Directorate-General XII (Science, Research, and Development)

Joint Research Centre

Centre for Information Technologies and Electronics

Address: I-21020 Ispra (VA)
Italy
Telephone: 332/78 91 11
Telex: 380042/380058/324878/324880 EUR I
Fax: 332/78 90 45

European Parliament

▲ Committee on Energy, Research, and Technology

Address: Palais de l'Europe
F-67006 Strasbourg Cedex
France
Telephone: 88/374 001; 88/375 485
Fax: 88/369 214; 88/256 516

Address: Centre Europeen
Plateau du Kirchberg
L-2929 Luxembourg
Telephone: 430 01
Telex: 3493 EUPARL LU; 2894 EUPARL LU
Fax: 436 972; 435 359

Table 27.1
CEC Subdirectorates—Information Technology

Directorate and Subdirectorate Name	Directorate/ Subdirectorate Number	Directorate-General	Address
Restrictive Practices, Abuse of Dominant Positions, and Other Distortions of Competition I			
Electrical and Electronic Manufactured Products, Information Industries, and Telecommunications	B/1	IV	CEC HQ, Belgium
Information Technology and Esprit			
Strategy and Evaluation	A/1	XIII	CEC HQ, Belgium Telephone: 2/235 24 48
Microelectronics	A/3	XIII	CEC HQ, Belgium Telephone: 2/235 24 48
Software and Advanced Information Processing	A/4	XIII	CEC HQ, Belgium Telephone: 2/235 24 48
Office Systems	A/5	XIII	CEC HQ, Belgium Telephone: 2/235 24 48
Computer Integrated Manufacturing	A/6	XIII	CEC HQ, Belgium Telephone: 2/235 24 48

Basic Research and Scientific Liaison on IT [Information Technology]	A/7	XIII	CEC HQ, Belgium Telephone: 2/235 24 48
Information Industry and Market			
Information Services Policy	B/1	XIII	CEC HQ, Belgium Telephone: 2/235 24 48
Computerized Language Processing	B/3	XIII	CEC HQ, Belgium Telephone: 2/235 24 48
Exploitation of Research and Technological Development, Technology Transfer, and Innovation			
Scientific and Technical Communication	C/3	XIII	CEC HQ, Belgium Telephone: 2/235 24 48
Telecommunications Policy, Technology Transfer, and Innovation			
Regulatory Aspects, Analyses and Studies by Sector	D/2	XIII	CEC HQ, Belgium Telephone: 2/235 24 48
General Affairs			
Economic and International Aspects	E/3	XIII	CEC HQ, Belgium Telephone: 2/235 24 48
Information, Documentation, Public Relations	E/5	XIII	CEC HQ, Belgium Telephone: 2/235 24 48
RACE Programme and Development of Advanced Telematics Services			
Information and Telecommunications Technologies Applied to Education—Delta Programme	F/4	XIII	CEC HQ, Belgium Telephone: 2/235 24 48
Information and Telecommunications Technologies Applied to Road Transport— Drive Programme	F/5	XIII	CEC HQ, Belgium Telephone: 2/235 24 48
Information and Telecommunications Technologies Applied to Health—AIM Programme	F/6	XIII	CEC HQ, Belgium Telephone: 2/235 24 48

European Parliament

▲ Committee on Youth, Culture, Education, the Media, and Sport

Address: 97–113, rue Belliard
B-1040 Bruxelles
Belgium
Telephone: 2/284 21 21; 2/284 25 11
Fax: 2/230 68 56; 2/231 12 57

Address: Palais de l'Europe
F-67006 Strasbourg Cedex
France
Telephone: 88/374 001; 88/374 522
Fax: 88/369 214; 88/256 516

Address: Centre Europeen
Plateau du Kirchberg
L-2929 Luxembourg
Telephone: 430 01
Telex: 3493 EUPARL LU; 2894 EUPARL LU
Fax: 436 972; 435 359

Associations

▲ ECMA (European Computer Manufacturers Association)

Address: rue du Rhone 114
CH-1204 Geneve
Switzerland
Telephone: 22/35 36 34
Telex: 413237
Fax: 22/786 52 31

Data Resources and Publications

CCL-Train

Database Producer: European Community, DG XII
Distributors/Hosts: ECHO
Frequency of Update: Not updated
Scope: A training file for the common command language (CCL), containing abstracts of scientific and technical publications from the EC ⊛

ESPRIT—*Annual Report*

Publisher: Office for Official Publications of the European Communities
Frequency of Publication: Annual
Scope: Reviews of activities of Esprit (European Strategic Program for Research and Development in Information Technology); prepared by DG XII

IES-DC1

Database Producer: European Community, DG XIII
Distributors/Hosts: ECHO
Frequency of Update: Periodically
Scope: Basic information on publicly funded research and development programs and projects in the EC in telecommunications, the information industries, and innovation, such as Esprit, RACE, Eureka, Alvey, COST, and Docdel; includes detailed project information, project partners, and project description ⊛

I'M: *Information Market*

Publisher: Commission of the European Communities, DG XIII
Frequency of Publication: 6 times a year
Scope: Information industry and EC developments; also available online through ECHO ⊛

Information, Computer, and Communications Policy: Information Technology and New Growth Opportunities

Publisher: OECD
Frequency of Publication: One time
Scope: Reviews new growth opportunities in OECD countries due to information technology changes

Information, Computer, and Communications Policy: Major R&D Programs for Information Technology

Publisher: OECD
Frequency of Publication: One time
Scope: Summary of major research and development programs and policies of selected OECD countries in information, computer, and communications industries

Information Technologies in Education

Publisher: OECD
Frequency of Publication: One time
Scope: Review of the demands for software for use in education

New Information Technology and Participation in Europe: The Potential for Social Dialogue

Publisher: Office for Official Publications of the European Communities
Frequency of Publication: One time
Scope: Analysis of the impact of information technology on worker and consumer participation in business decision making; prepared by the European Foundation for the Improvement of Living and Working Conditions on employee participation

Panorama of EC Industry

Publisher: Office for Official Publications of the European Communities
Frequency of Publication: Annual
Scope: Description of 165 manufacturing and service industries, including information, software and computing services, plus evaluations of the impact of the Single Market Program

Public Procurement in the Excluded Sectors

Publisher: Office for Official Publications of the European Communities
Frequency of Publication: One time
Scope: Study accompanied by proposals for directives relating to water, energy, transport, and telecommunications procurement; official CEC communication

Tecnet

Database Producer: European Centre for Work and Society, Maastricht, The Netherlands
Distributors/Hosts: ECHO
Frequency of Update: As needed
Scope: Demonstration projects of the Eurotecnet network, representing a cross-section of training approaches in the field of new information technologies and vocational training

Telecommunications in Europe: Free Choice for the Use in Europe's 1992 Market

Publisher: Office for Official Publications of the European Communities
Frequency of Publication: One time
Scope: Analysis of the main elements of the telecommunications industry, including the characteristics of the European markets

Towards a Free Sky for Border-Free Europe

Publisher: Office for Official Publications of the European Communities
Frequency of Publication: One time
Scope: A "Green Paper" on a common approach in satellite communications in the EC

Related Topics and Industries

Manufacturing. See also *Part III—Sources on EC 1992 by Topic*

MASS MEDIA AND TELECOMMUNICATIONS

EC Contacts

Table 27.2 lists official European Community directorates and subdirectorates that provide information about the mass media and telecommunications. For the complete address of the Commission of the European Communities headquarters (CEC HQ in the table), refer to the Introduction to Part IV.

Table 27.2
CEC Subdirectorates—Mass Media and Telecommunications

Directorate and Subdirectorate Name	Directorate/ Subdirectorate Number	Directorate- General	Address
Approximation of Laws, Freedom of Establishment, and Freedom to Provide Services			
Industrial Policy and Broadcasting Policy	D/3	III	CEC HQ, Belgium Telephone: 2/236 30 12
Restrictive Practices, Abuse of Dominant Positions, and Other Distortions of Competition I			
Electrical and Electronic Manufactured Products, Information Industries, and Telecommunications	B/1	IV	CEC HQ, Belgium
Information Technology and Esprit			
Strategy and Evaluation	A/1	XIII	CEC HQ, Belgium Telephone: 2/235 24 48
Exploitation of Research and Technological Development, Technology Transfer, and Innovation			
Scientific and Technical Communication	C/3	XIII	CEC HQ, Belgium Telephone: 2/235 24 48
Telecommunications Policy, Technology Transfer, and Innovation			
Telecommunications Market and Network Equipment	D/1	XIII	CEC HQ, Belgium Telephone: 2/235 24 48
Regulatory Aspects, Analyses and Studies by Sector	D/2	XIII	CEC HQ, Belgium Telephone: 2/235 24 48
Space and Rural Telecommunications and Posts	D/3	XIII	CEC HQ, Belgium Telephone: 2/235 24 48
Relationship between Telecommunications and Broadcasting	D/4	XIII	CEC HQ, Belgium Telephone: 2/235 24 48
Electronic Data Interchange	D/5	XIII	CEC HQ, Belgium Telephone: 2/235 24 48

General Affairs

Economic and International Aspects	E/3	XIII	CEC HQ, Belgium Telephone: 2/235 24 48
Information, Documentation, Public Relations	E/5	XIII	CEC HQ, Belgium Telephone: 2/235 24 48

RACE Programme and Development
of Advanced Telematics Services

Development and Implementation Strategies for Integrated Broadband Communications	F/1	XIII	CEC HQ, Belgium Telephone: 2/235 24 48
Telecommunications Technologies	F/2	XIII	CEC HQ, Belgium Telephone: 2/235 24 48
Integration of Services and Telecommunications Systems Engineering	F/3	XIII	CEC HQ, Belgium Telephone: 2/235 24 48
Information and Telecommunications Technologies Applied to Education—Delta Programme	F/4	XIII	CEC HQ, Belgium Telephone: 2/235 24 48
Information and Telecommunications Technologies Applied to Road Transport—Drive Programme	F/5	XIII	CEC HQ, Belgium Telephone: 2/235 24 48
Information and Telecommunications Technologies Applied to Health—AIM Programme	F/6	XIII	CEC HQ, Belgium Telephone: 2/235 24 48

Commission of the European Communities
▲ Directorate-General XII (Science, Research and Development)

Joint Research Centre
Centre for Information Technologies and Electronics
Address: I-21020 Ispra (VA)
                Italy
Telephone: 332/78 91 11
Telex: 380042/380058/324878/324880 EUR I
Fax: 332/78 90 45

European Parliament
▲ Committee on Energy, Research, and Technology

Address: Palais de l'Europe
                F-67006 Strasbourg Cedex
                France
Telephone: 88/374 001; 88/375 485
Fax: 88/369 214; 88/256 516

Address: Centre Europeen
                Plateau du Kirchberg
                L-2929 Luxembourg
Telephone: 430 01
Telex: 3493 EUPARL LU; 2894 EUPARL LU
Fax: 436 972; 435 359

European Parliament

▲ Committee on Youth, Culture, Education, the Media, and Sport

Address: 97–113, rue Belliard
              B-1040 Bruxelles
              Belgium
Telephone: 2/284 21 21; 2/284 25 11
Fax: 2/230 68 56; 2/231 12 57

Address: Palais de l'Europe
              F-67006 Strasbourg Cedex
              France
Telephone: 88/374 001; 88/374 522
Fax: 88/369 214; 88/256 516

Address: Centre Europeen
              Plateau du Kirchberg
              L-2929 Luxembourg
Telephone: 430 01
Telex: 3493 EUPARL LU; 2894 EUPARL LU
Fax: 436 972; 435 359

Associations

▲ CEPT (The European Conference of Posts and Telecommunications)

Address: Liaison Office
              Seilerstr. 22
              Case Postale 1283
              CH-3001 Berne
              Switzerland

▲ ECTEL (European Telecommunications and Professional Electronics Industry)

Address: c/o ZVEI, Stresemannallee 19
              Postfach 70 09 69
              D-6000 Frankfurt/Main 70
              Germany

▲ EUROTELCAB (European Conference of Associations of Telecommunication Cables Industries)

Address: Postfach 100645
              Pipinstrasse 16
              D-5000 Koln 1
              Germany
Telephone: 221/204 62 10
Telex: 8881342 D
Fax: 221/204 62 48

▲ EUTELSAT (European Telecommunications Satellite Organisation)

Address: Andrea Caruso
              Tour Marie Montparnasse
              33, av. du Maine
              F-75755 Paris Cedex 15
              France

▲ GEJ-FIJ (European Group of Journalists— International Federation of Journalists)

Address: bd. Charlemagne 1 (Bte 5)
              B-1041 Bruxelles
              Belgium
Telephone: 2/238 09 51
Telex: 61275 IPC B
Fax: 2/230 36 33

▲ IPTT (European Committee of the Postal, Telegraph, and Telephone International)

Address: 38, av. du Lignon
              CH-1219 Le Lignon/Geneve
              Switzerland
Telephone: 22/796 83 11
Telex: 418735 IPTT CH
Fax: 22/796 39 75

Data Resources and Publications

Engineering Industries and Automation

Publisher: United Nations Economic Commission for Europe
Frequency of Publication: Annual
Scope: General developments of engineering industries, including computer, telecommunications, machine tool, industrial robot, and automotive industries; includes data on trade in engineering products

Green Paper on the Development of the Common Market for Telecommunications Services and Equipment

Publisher: Office for Official Publications of the European Communities
Frequency of Publication: One time
Scope: Analysis of policy options for the telecommunications services and equipment industries

IES-DC1

Database Producer: European Community, DG XIII
Distributors/Hosts: ECHO
Frequency of Update: Periodically
Scope: Basic information on publicly funded research and development programs and projects in the EC in telecommunications, the information industries, and innovation, including Esprit, RACE, Eureka, Alvey, COST, and Docdel; includes detailed project information, project partners, and project description

I'M: Information Market

Publisher: Office for Official Publications of the European Communities
Frequency of Publication: Monthly
Scope: Articles on the IMPACT programme and the language industry; prepared by DG XIII

Information, Computer, and Communications Policy: New Telecommunications Services, Videotex Development Strategies

Publisher: OECD
Frequency of Publication: One time
Scope: Summary of government policy options and strategies for dealing with new telecommunications services

Information, Computer, and Communications Policy: Telecommunication Network-Based Services

Publisher: OECD
Frequency of Publication: One time
Scope: Review of policy options and implications of network-based services

Information, Computer, and Communications Policy: The Telecommunications Industry

Publisher: OECD
Frequency of Publication: One time
Scope: Review of implications of continuing structural changes in the telecommunications industry

Panorama of EC Industry

Publisher: Office for Official Publications of the European Communities
Frequency of Publication: Annual
Scope: Description of 165 manufacturing and service industries, including the telecommunications equipment industry, plus evaluations of the impact of the Single Market Program

Printing and Graphic Industry

Publisher: United Nations
Frequency of Publication: Periodically
Scope: Directory of basic industrial information sources

Public Procurement in the Excluded Sectors

Publisher: Office for Official Publications of the European Communities
Frequency of Publication: One time
Scope: Study accompanied by proposals for Directives relating to water, energy, transport, and telecommunications procurement; official CEC communication

Research on the "Cost of Non-Europe"—Technical Trade Barriers in the EC: An Illustration in Six Industries—Some Case Studies on Technical Barriers

Publisher: Office for Official Publications of the European Communities
Frequency of Publication: One time
Scope: Identifies technical trade barriers, including standards, legal requirements, testing and certification procedures, and evaluates their impact in the foodstuffs, pharmaceuticals, automobile, building materials, telecommunications, and electrical products and machinery industries; Volume 6 of the Cecchini study on the "cost of non-Europe"

▼ ▼

Research on the "Cost of Non-Europe"—The Benefits of Completing the Internal Market for Telecommunications Equipment and Services in the Community

Publisher: Office for Official Publications of the European Communities
Frequency of Publication: One time
Scope: Review of standards for telecommunications equipment and services in the EC and estimates the benefits of eliminating technical barriers throughout the EC; Volume 10 of the Cecchini study on the "cost of non-Europe"

STAR

Publisher: Office for Official Publications of the European Communities
Frequency of Publication: One time
Scope: Brief summary of the operations of STAR, an EC program designed to give improved access to advanced telecommunications systems in "less-favored" regions of the EC

Telecommunications in Europe

Publisher: Office for Official Publications of the European Communities
Frequency of Publication: One time
Scope: Review of policies of EC with respect to telecommunications and their impact on consumers; prepared by DG XIII

Related Topics and Industries

Manufacturing; Professions and Service Industries. See also Part III—Sources on EC 1992 by Topic

─── ▼ ───

OTHER COMMUNICATIONS AND INFORMATION INDUSTRIES

EC Contacts

Commission of the European Communities
▲ Directorate-General XIII (Telecommunications, Information Industries and Innovation)

Directorate B/2 (Information Industry and Market/New Information Services)

Address: rue de la Loi 200
B-1049 Bruxelles
Belgium
Telephone: 2/235 24 48
Telex: 21877 COMEU B

Associations

▲ CEPT (The European Conference of Posts and Telecommunications)

Address: Liaison Office
Seilerstr. 22
Case Postale 1283
3001 Berne
Switzerland

▲ GALC (Group of Booksellers Associations in the EEC)

Address: Ter Borchtlaan
B-2520 Edegem
Belgium

▲ IPTT (European Committee of the Postal, Telegraph and Telephone International)

Address: 38, av. du Lignon
CH-1219 Le Lignon/Geneve
Switzerland
Telephone: 22/796 83 11
Telex: 418735 IPTT CH
Fax: 22/796 39 75

Data Resources and Publications

Brokersguide

Database Producer: ECHO
Distributors/Hosts: ECHO
Frequency of Update: Monthly
Scope: Directory of information brokers, currently active in the EC, who offer fee-based information search services; provides information on areas of specialization, activities, and services, and lists the names of the different databases and host services used ⊛

Engineering Industries: Dynamics of the Eighties

Publisher: United Nations Economic Commission for Europe
Frequency of Publication: One time
Scope: Study and assessment of the role and place of engineering industries in national and world economics over the period 1979–1986; reviews current trends and foreseeable developments in engineering industries

Guidelines for Improving the Synergy Between the Public and Private Sectors in the Information Market

Publisher: Office for Official Publications of the European Communities
Frequency of Publication: One time
Scope: EC guidelines to coordinate products and the public services that interface with them; prepared by DG XIII

IES-DC1

Database Producer: European Community, DG XIII
Distributors/Hosts: ECHO
Frequency of Update: Periodically
Scope: Basic information on publicly funded research and development programs and projects in the EC in telecommunications, the information industries, and innovation, including Esprit, RACE, Eureka, Alvey, COST, and Docdel; includes detailed project information, project partners, and project description ⊛

Information, Computer, and Communications Policy: Satellites and Fibre Optics

Publisher: OECD
Frequency of Publication: One time
Scope: Analysis of competitive relationships between two new modes of communications: satellites and fiber optics

Research on the "Cost of Non-Europe"—The Cost of Non-Europe in Business Services

Publisher: Office for Official Publications of the European Communities
Frequency of Publication: One time
Scope: Identifies barriers to providing engineering, architectural, management, legal, computing, marketing, public relations, research and development, accounting, and financial services throughout the EC; Volume 8 of the Cecchini study on the "cost of non-Europe"

Related Topics and Industries

Manufacturing. See also Part III—Sources on EC 1992 by Topic

28

Consumer Products and Services

ASSISTANCE

Appendix D contains a list of the Single Market measures that deal with consumer products and services. For additional help on using the resources in this chapter, refer to the Introduction to Part IV.

APPLIANCES AND LIGHTING

Associations

▲ CECED (European Committee of Manufacturers of Electrical Domestic Equipment)

Address: Leicester House
8 Leicester Street
GB-London WC2H 7BN
Great Britain
Telephone: 71/437 0678
Telex: 253536 G
Fax: 71/494 1094

▲ ELC (European Lighting Council)

Address: rue Montoyer 31 (Bte 1)
B-1040 Bruxelles
Belgium
Telephone: 2/513 60 85
Fax: 2/514 33 86

▲ ELMO (European Laundry and Dry Cleaning Machinery Manufacturers Organization)

Address: Lyoner Strasse 18
D-6000 Frankfurt/Main
Germany
Telephone: 69/66 03 271
Telex: 411321 D
Fax: 69/66 03 511

Data Resources and Publications

Panorama of EC Industry

Publisher: Office for Official Publications of the European Communities
Frequency of Publication: Annual
Scope: Description of 165 manufacturing and service industries, including the consumer electronics industry, plus evaluations of the impact of the Single Market Program

Trends in Distributive Trades / Retail Sales— Registration of Cars

Publisher: Office for Official Publications of the European Community; prepared by the Statistical Office of the EC
Frequency of Publication: Annual
Scope: Data on the volume of retail sales in three groups of products—food, clothing, and household equipment—as well as car registrations. Also available online via the Cronos-Eurostatistics database.

Related Topics and Industries

Manufacturing. See also *Part III—Sources on EC 1992 by Topic*

CLOTHING AND FOOTWEAR

EC Contacts

Table 28.1 lists official European Community directorates and subdirectorates that provide information about clothing and footwear. For the complete address of the Commission of the European Communities headquarters (CEC HQ in the table), refer to the Introduction to Part IV.

Associations

▲ AEDT (European Association of National Organizations of Textile Retailers)

Address: rue de Spa 8
B-1040 Bruxelles
Belgium
Telephone: 2/238 06 51
Fax: 2/230 93 54

▲ AEIH (European Association of Clothing Industries)

Address: rue Montoyer 24
B-1040 Bruxelles
Belgium
Telephone: 2/511 87 31
Fax: 2/514 17 81

▲ CEC (European Confederation of the Footwear Industry)

Address: rue F. Bossaerts 53
B-1030 Bruxelles
Belgium
Telephone: 2/736 58 10
Telex: 65625 RSCEC B
Fax: 2/736 12 76

▼ ▼

▲ CELIBRIDE (International Liaison Committee for Embroideries, Curtains and Laces)

Address: 7, rue Louis le Grand
F-75002 Paris
France
Telephone: 1/42 61 56 29
Telex: 64969 F
Fax: 1/42 86 81 77

▲ EBIF (European Button Industries Federation)

Address: 63, Stanley Hill Avenue
Amersham
GB-Bucks HP7 9BA
Great Britain

▲ European Trade Union Committee: Textiles, Clothing and Leather

Address: rue Joseph Stevens 8
B-1000 Bruxelles
Belgium
Telephone: 2/511 54 77
Fax: 2/511 09 04

▲ FEGAP (European Federation of Leather Glovemakers)

Address: 38, bd. de l'Ayrolle
F-12100 Millau
France

▲ OECT (European Organization of Textile Wholesalers)

Address: Adriaan Goekooplaan 5
NL-2517 JX Den Haag
The Netherlands
Telephone: 70/54 68 11
Fax: 70/55 13 00

Data Resources and Publications

Leather and Leather Products

Publisher: United Nations
Frequency of Publication: Periodically
Scope: Directory of basic industrial information sources

Panorama of EC Industry

Publisher: Office for Official Publications of the European Communities
Frequency of Publication: Annual
Scope: Description of 165 manufacturing and service industries, including the clothing and footwear industries, plus evaluations of the impact of the Single Market Program

Table 28.1
CEC Subdirectorates—Clothing and Footwear

Directorate and Subdirectorate Name	Directorate/ Subdirectorate Number	Directorate-General	Address
Internal Market and Industrial Affairs II			
Textiles and Clothing	C/3	III	CEC HQ, Belgium Telephone: 2/236 30 12
Restrictive Practices, Abuse of Dominant Positions and Other Distortions of Competition I			
Mechanical Manufactured Products and the Textile, Clothing, Leather, and Other Manufacturing Industries	B/2	IV	CEC HQ, Belgium

Research on the "Cost of Non-Europe"—The Cost of Non-Europe in the Textile and Clothing Industry

Publisher: Office for Official Publications of the European Communities
Frequency of Publication: One time
Scope: Review of intra-EC trade, prices and consumption patterns, as well as barriers facing these industries and probable benefits of their elimination; Volume 14 of the Cecchini study on the "cost of non-Europe"

Trends in Distributive Trades: Retail Sales—Registration of Cars

Publisher: Office for Official Publications of the European Communities
Frequency of Publication: Annual
Scope: Volume of retail sales in three groups of products—food, clothing and household equipment, as well as car registrations; also available online via the Cronos database; prepared by the Statistical Office of the EC

Related Topics and Industries

Manufacturing. See also *Part III—Sources on EC 1992 by Topic*

FOOD AND BEVERAGES

Associations

▲ AECGV (European Association of Fresh Meat Sellers)

Address: 29, rue Fortuny
F-75017 Paris
France
Telephone: 1/46 22 93 80
Fax: 1/44 40 48 62

▲ AICV (Association of the Cider and Fruit Wine Industry of the EEC)

Address: av. de Cortenbergh 172 (Bte 6)
B-1040 Bruxelles
Belgium
Telephone: 2/735 81 70
Telex: 26246 SIA B
Fax: 2/736 81 75

▲ Association of National Organizations in the Bakery and Confectionery in the EEC

Address: bd. L. Mettewie 83 (Bte 42)
B-1080 Bruxelles
Belgium
Telephone: 2/465 20 00
Fax: 2/465 06 40

▲ CAEC (Committee of Associations of European Coffee Importers)

Address: Artillery House
Artillery Row, Westminster
GB-London SW1P 1RY
Great Britain
Telephone: 71/222 0940
Telex: 8812923 COMMET G
Fax: 71/799 1852

▲ CAOBISCO (Association of the Chocolate, Biscuit, and Confectionery Industries of the EEC)

Address: 1 rue Defacqz (Bte 7)
B-1050 Bruxelles
Belgium
Telephone: 2/539 18 00
Telex: 24000 B
Fax: 2/539 15 75

▲ CEDT (European Tea Committee)

Address: Tourniairestraat 3
NL-1006 KK Amsterdam
The Netherlands
Telephone: 20/17 03 14
Telex: 18765 VRIES NL

▲ CIMSCEE (Comite des Industries des Mayonnaises et Sauces Condimentairs de la Communaute Economique Europeen {Mayonnaise and Sauces})

Address: av. de Cortenbergh 172 (Bte 6)
B-1040 Bruxelles
Belgium
Telephone: 2/735 81 70
Telex: 26246 B
Fax: 2/736 81 75

▲ Committee of the European Economic Community for the Wine and Spirits Industry

Address: Rond-Point Schuman 9 (Bte 4)
B-1040 Bruxelles
Belgium
Telephone: 2/230 99 70
Telex: 61177 B
Fax: 2/230 43 23

▲ ECF-IUF (European Committee of Food, Catering, and Allied Workers Unions Within the IUF)

Address: rue Fosse-aux-Loups 38 (Bte 3)
B-1000 Bruxelles
Belgium
Telephone: 2/218 77 30
Fax: 2/217 59 63

▲ ECSA (European Chips and Snacks Association)

Address: Swiss Centre
10, Wardour Street
GB-London W1V 3HG
Great Britain
Telephone: 71/439 2567
Telex: 297939 G
Fax: 71/439 2673

▲ EDMMA (European Dessert Mixes Manufacturers' Association)

Address: 6, Catherine Street
GB-London WC2B 5JJ
Great Britain
Telephone: 71/836 2460
Telex: 299388 FDF G
Fax: 71/836 0580

▲ EEC Wine and Spirit Importers Group

Address: Van Eeghenlaan 27
NL-1071 EN Amsterdam
The Netherlands
Telephone: 20/73 03 31
Fax: 20/664 54 66

▲ EFPA (European Food Service and Packaging Association)

Address: Waldeggstrasse 22B
CH-3800 Interlaken
Switzerland
Telephone: 36/22 22 26
Telex: 923152 OVI CH
Fax: 36/22 40 41

▲ EHIA (European Herbal Infusions Association)

Address: Gotenstrasse 21
D-2000 Hamburg 1
Germany
Telephone: 40/236 01 60
Telex: 2/162388 WGA D
Fax: 40/236 01 610

▲ EHPM (European Federation of Associations of Health Product Manufacturers)

Address: Hindenburgring 18
D-6380 Bad Homburg
Germany

▲ EUCA (Federation of European Coffee Roasters' Associations)

Address: Tourniairestraat 3
NL-1065 KK Amsterdam
The Netherlands
Telephone: 20/17 08 14
Telex: 18765 VRIES NL
Fax: 20/15 75 09

▲ EUROMALT (Working Committee of the EC Malting Industry)

Address: rue de l'Orme 19
B-1040 Bruxelles
Belgium
Telephone: 2/733 12 64
Telex: 61473 ECCO B
Fax: 2/734 67 02

▲ FIVS (International Federation of Wines & Spirits)

Address: 116, bd. Haussmann
F-75008 Paris
France
Telephone: 1/42 94 18 27
Telex: 280054 CNVS F
Fax: 1/42 94 14 46

▲ GEAMR (European Associations of Health Food Stores)

Address: Waldstrasse 6
D-6370 Oberursel 4
Germany
Telephone: 6172/32002
Fax: 6172/303967

▲ IDACE (Association of the Dietetic Foods Industries of the EEC)

Address: 194, rue de Rivoli
75001 Paris
France
Telephone: 1/42 97 53 80
Telex: 680553 UNICHOCO F
Fax: 1/42 61 95 34

▲ IFIWA (International Federation of Importers' and Wholesale Grocers' Associations)

Address: Parkstraat 99
NL-2414 JH's Gravenhage
Netherlands
Telephone: 70/65 08 71
Fax: 70/64 33 43

▲ UEAES (Union Europeen des Alcools, Eaux-de-vie et Spiritueux {Alcoholic Beverages})

Address: av. de Tervueren 192 (Bte 6)
B-1150 Bruxelles
Belgium
Telephone: 2/771 77 35
Telex: 63954 UNALCO B
Fax: 2/772 01 09

▲ UIDA (International Federation of Grocers' Associations)

Address: Falkenplatz 1
Postfach 2740
CH-3001 Bern
Switzerland
Telephone: 31/23 76 46
Fax: 31/23 76 46

▲ UIPCG (International Union of Confectioners, Pastrycooks, and Ice-Cream Makers)

Address: 41, rue Glesener
L-1631 Luxembourg
Telephone: 40 00 22-1
Telex: 2215 CHMET LU
Fax: 49 23 80

Data Resources and Publications

Beer and Wine Industry

Publisher: United Nations
Frequency of Publication: Periodically
Scope: Directory of basic industrial information sources

Canning Industry

Publisher: United Nations
Frequency of Publication: Periodically
Scope: Directory of basic industrial information sources

Coffee, Cocoa, Tea, and Spices Industry

Publisher: United Nations
Frequency of Publication: Periodically
Scope: Directory of basic industrial information sources

The Dairy Products Manufacturing Industry

Publisher: United Nations
Frequency of Publication: Periodically
Scope: Directory of basic industrial information sources

Flour Milling and the Bakery Products Industries

Publisher: United Nations
Frequency of Publication: Periodically
Scope: Directory of basic industrial information sources

▼

▼

Non-Alcoholic Beverages Industry

Publisher: United Nations
Frequency of Publication: Periodically
Scope: Directory of basic industrial information sources

Panorama of EC Industry

Publisher: Office for Official Publications of the European Communities
Frequency of Publication: Annual
Scope: Description of 165 manufacturing and service industries, including the food and beverage industries, plus evaluations of the impact of the Single Market Program

Research on the "Cost of Non-Europe"—The Cost of Non-Europe in the Foodstuffs Industry

Publisher: Office for Official Publications of the European Communities
Frequency of Publication: One time
Scope: Identifies nontariff trade barriers in major food stuff sectors, plus comparisons of the operations of U.S.- and EC-based food companies in Europe; Volume 12 of the Cecchini study on the "cost of non-Europe"

Related Topics and Industries

Agriculture and Food Stuffs; Manufacturing. See also *Part III—Sources on EC 1992 by Topic*

▼

OTHER CONSUMER PRODUCTS AND SERVICES

EC Contacts

European Parliament

▲ Committee on the Environment, Public Health, and Consumer Protection

Address: 97–113, rue Belliard
B-1040 Bruxelles
Belgium
Telephone: 2/284 21 21; 2/284 28 48
Fax: 2/230 68 56; 2/231 12 57

Address: Palais de l'Europe
F-67006 Strasbourg Cedex
France
Telephone: 88/374 001; 88/374 418
Fax: 88/369 214; 88/256 516

Address: Centre Europeen
Plateau du Kirchberg
L-2929 Luxembourg
Telephone: 430 01
Telex: 3493 EUPARL LU; 2894 EUPARL LU
Fax: 436 972; 435 359

European Parliament

▲ Committee on Transport and Tourism

Address: 97–113, rue Belliard
B-1040 Bruxelles
Belgium
Telephone: 2/284 21 21; 2/284 35 02
Fax: 2/230 68 56; 2/231 12 57

Address: Palais de l'Europe
F-67006 Strasbourg Cedex
France
Telephone: 88/374 001; 88/374 035
Fax: 88/369 214; 88/256 516

Address: Centre Europeen
Plateau du Kirchberg
L-2929 Luxembourg
Telephone: 430 01
Telex: 3493 EUPARL LU; 2894 EUPARL LU
Fax: 436 972; 435 359

European Parliament

▲ Committee on Youth, Culture, Education, the Media, and Sport

Address: 97–113, rue Belliard
B-1040 Bruxelles
Belgium
Telephone: 2/284 21 21; 2/284 25 11
Fax: 2/230 68 56; 2/231 12 57
Address: Palais de l'Europe
F-67006 Strasbourg Cedex
France
Telephone: 88/374 001; 88/374 522
Fax: 88/369 214; 88/256 516

Address: Centre Europeen
Plateau du Kirchberg
L-2929 Luxembourg
Telephone: 430 01
Telex: 3493 EUPARL LU; 2894 EUPARL LU
Fax: 436 972; 435 359

Associations

▲ AIS (International Association of the Soap and Detergent Industry)

Address: sq. Marie-Louise 49
B-1040 Bruxelles
Belgium
Telephone: 2/230 83 71
Telex: 23167 FECHIM B
Fax: 2/230 82 88

▲ CECD (European Confederation of Retailers)

Address: av. d'Auderghem 33–35
B-1040 Bruxelles
Belgium
Telephone: 2/231 07 99
Telex: 26946 TRACED B
Fax: 2/230 00 78

▲ CEDIM (European Committee of National Federations of Morocco-leather Manufacturers, Travel Articles, and Associated Industries)

Address: 59, bd. Magenta
F-75005 Paris
France
Telephone: 1/42 41 44 55
Fax: 1/42 41 31 70

▲ CERAME-UNIE (Liaison Office of Ceramic Industries of the Common Market)

Address: rue des Colonies 18–24 (Bte 17)
B-1000 Bruxelles
Belgium
Telephone: 2/511 30 12
Telex: 21598 B
Fax: 2/511 51 74

▲ COLIPA (Liaison Committee for European Associations of Perfume, Cosmetic, and Toilet Article Manufacturers)

Address: rue de la Loi 223 (Bte 2)
B-1040 Bruxelles
Belgium
Telephone: 2/230 91 79
Telex: 21908 B
Fax: 2/231 15 87

▲ CPIV (Standing Committee of the EC Glass Industries)

Address: av. Louise 89
B-1050 Bruxelles
Belgium
Telephone: 2/538 44 46
Telex: 25694 CPIV B
Fax: 2/537 84 69

▲ EFF (European Franchise Federation)

Address: av. de Broqueville 5
B-1150 Bruxelles
Belgium
Telephone: 2/736 64 64
Fax: 2/736 72 26

▲ EFVA (European Federation of Vending Associations)

Address: rue Marianne 34
B-1180 Bruxelles
Belgium

▲ ETV (European Wholesale Tobacco)

Address: Stadtwaldgurtel 44
D-5000 Koln 41
Germany
Telephone: 221/40 50 25
Fax: 221/40 75 91

▲ EUREMAIL (Association of the European Manufacturers of Vitreous Enamelled Hollow Ware)

Address: Neuenhofer Strasse 24
D-5650 Solingen
Germany
Telephone: 212/88 01 40
Telex: 8514772 D
Fax: 212/88 01 35

▲ EURO-FIET (European Regional Organisation of the International Federation of Commercial, Clerical, Professional, and Technical Employees)

Address: 15, av. de Balexert
CH-1219 Chatelaine/Geneve
Switzerland
Telephone: 22/796 27 33
Telex: 418736 FIET CH
Fax: 22/796 53 21

▲ EUROMAT (Federation of European Coin Machine Associations)

Address: place princesse Elisabeth 44 (Bte 3)
B-1030 Bruxelles
Belgium
Telephone: 2/242 71 74/77
Fax: 2/242 24 19

▲ European Association of Candlemakers

Address: 10A, rue de la Paix
F-75002 Paris
France
Telephone: 1/42 61 61 54
Telex: 230905 STABILI F
Fax: 1/47 03 98 78

▲ European Association of Toy Retailers

Address: Sigmundstrasse 220
D-8500 Nurnberg 80
Germany
Telephone: 911/6556-213
Telex: 623154 D
Fax: 911/6556 251

▲ European Toy Federation

Address: 47, rue Berthier
F-75017 Paris
France
Telephone: 1/43 80 60 75
Telex: 643919 F
Fax: 1/42 27 82 72

▲ FEA (Federation of European Aerosol Associations)

Address: sq. Marie-Louise 49
B-1040 Bruxelles
Belgium
Telephone: 2/230 40 90
Telex: 23167 FECHIM B
Fax: 2/230 82 88

▲ FEC (Federation of the European Cutlery and Flatware Industries)

Address: 58, rue du Louvre
F-75002 Paris
France
Telephone: 1/42 33 61 33
Telex: 680377 BOCI F
Fax: 1/40 26 29 51

▲ FEDIAF (European Pet Food Industry Federation)

Address: sq. Marie-Louise 89
B-1050 Bruxelles
Belgium
Telephone: 2/537 41 75
Telex: 25695 CPIV B
Fax: 2/537 84 69

▲ FEIBP (Federation of European Industries of Hardware and Houseware Manufacturers)

Address: rue Royale 109–111
B-1000 Bruxelles
Belgium
Telephone: 2/217 63 65
Telex: 64143 FEHOUT B
Fax: 2/217 59 04

▲ FEP (European Federation of Associations of Floor Covering Manufacturers)

Address: Fullenbachstr. 6
D-4000 Dusseldorf 30
Germany
Telephone: 211/43 49 04; 211/45 41 374

▲ FEPD (European Federation of Perfume Retailers)

Address: 21, rue du Chateau d'Eau
F-75010 Paris
France

▲ FEPF/MC (Common Market Committee of the European Federation of Porcelain and Earthenware Tableware and Ornamental Ware Industries)

Address: rue des Colonies 18–24 (Bte 17)
B-1000 Bruxelles
Belgium
Telephone: 2/511 30 12
Telex: 21598 B
Fax: 2/511 51 74

▲ FEUPF (European Federation of Professional Florists)

Address: c/o Federfiori
Via Massena 20
I-10128 Torino
Italy
Telephone: 11/54 70 51
Fax: 11/53 38 69

▲ FEVSD (European Direct Selling Federation)

Address: av. de Tervueren 14 (Bte 1)
B-1040 Bruxelles
Belgium
Telephone: 2/736 10 14
Fax: 2/736 34 97

▲ FEWITA (Federation of European Wholesale and International Trade Associations)

Address: av. d'Auderghem 33–35
B-1040 Bruxelles
Belgium
Telephone: 2/231 08 31
Telex: 26946 TRACED B
Fax: 2/230 00 78

▲ FIGED (International Federation of Retail Distributors)

Address: av. Edouard Lacomble 17
B-1040 Bruxelles
Belgium
Telephone: 2/736 04 04
Fax: 2/736 05 42

▲ FIHBJO (International Federation of Retailers in Horology, Jewelry, Gold- and Silverware of the EEC)

Address: 65, rue des Grandes Arcades
F-67000 Strasbourg
France

▲ GEDIS (European Multiple Retailers Association)

Address: av. Edouard Lacomble 17
B-1040 Bruxelles
Belgium
Telephone: 2/736 02 51
Telex: 64192 GEDIS B
Fax: 2/736 05 42

▲ IEACS (European Institute of the Gun Trade)

Address: rue Charles Morren 3
B-4000 Liege
Belgium
Telephone: 41/53 39 86 - 71 37 78
Fax: 41/53 39 89

▲ International Commission of Hairdressers of the Common Market

Address: Centre International Rogier
Residence Iris (Bte 10)
B-1210 Bruxelles
Belgium
Telephone: 2/217 85 09

▲ UEA (European Furniture Manufacturers Federation)

Address: rue de l'Association 15
B-1000 Bruxelles
Belgium
Telephone: 2/218 18 89
Telex: 61933 MEUBEL UEA B
Fax: 2/219 27 01

▲ UENCPB (European Union of Leatherware Buyers)

Address: Bourse de commerce
2, rue de Viarmes
F-75040 Paris Cedex 01
France
Telephone: 1/45 08 08 54

▲ UNEBIF (Union of European Imitation Jewelry Manufacturers)

Address: 40, Greenacres
Hendon Lane
GB-London N3 3SF
Great Britain
Telephone: 81/346 0742
Fax: 81/405 1462

▲ UNIC (International Union of Cinemas)

Address: 10, rue de Marignan
F-75008 Paris
France
Telephone: 1/43 59 16 76
Fax: 1/40 74 08 64

Data Resources and Publications

Furniture and Joinery Industry

Publisher: United Nations
Frequency of Publication: Periodically
Scope: Directory of basic industrial information sources

Individual Choice and Higher Growth—The Task of European Consumer Policy

Publisher: Office for Official Publications of the European Communities
Frequency of Publication: One time
Scope: Discussion of the consumer's role in a frontier-free Europe

Panorama of EC Industry

Publisher: Office for Official Publications of the European Communities
Frequency of Publication: Annual
Scope: Description of 165 manufacturing and service industries, including the consumer product manufacturing, distribution, tourism, furniture, tobacco, soap, and detergent industries, plus evaluations of the impact of the Single Market Program

Soap and Detergent Industry

Publisher: United Nations
Frequency of Publication: Periodically
Scope: Directory of basic industrial information sources

Telecommunications in Europe

Publisher: Office for Official Publications of the European Communities
Frequency of Publication: One time
Scope: Review of policies of EC with respect to telecommunications and their impact on consumers; prepared by DG XIII

Tourism Policy and International Tourism in OECD Member Countries

Publisher: OECD
Frequency of Publication: One time
Scope: Review of impacts of tourist growth and transport deregulation and the impact of government policies toward tourism, as well as the impact of tourism on the environment

Related Topics and Industries

Health Care and Medicine; Housing and Infrastructure; Manufacturing; Professions and Service Industries. See also *Part III—Sources on EC 1992 by Topic*

29

Energy

ASSISTANCE

Appendix D contains a list of the Single Market measures dealing with energy. For additional help on using the resources in this chapter, refer to the Introduction to Part IV.

ELECTRIC POWER

EC Contacts

Commission of the European Communities
▲ Directorate-General XVII (Energy)

Directorate C/1 (Industries and markets II: Non-fossil energy/Electricity)

Address: rue de la Loi 200
                 B-1049 Bruxelles
                 Belgium
Telephone: 2/236 27 99
Telex: 21877 COMEU B

European Parliament
▲ Committee on Energy, Research, and Technology

Address: Palais de l'Europe
                 F-67006 Strasbourg Cedex
                 France
Telephone: 88/374 001; 88/375 485
Fax: 88/369 214; 88/256 516

Address: Centre Europeen
                 Plateau du Kirchberg
                 L-2929 Luxembourg
Telephone: 430 01
Telex: 3493 EUPARL LU; 2894 EUPARL LU
Fax: 436 972; 435 359

Associations

▲ EUROPOWERCAB (European Conference of Associations of Power Cable Industries)

Address: 56, Palace Road
                 East Molesey
                 GB-Surrey KT8 9DW
                 Great Britain
Telephone: 1/941 4079
Telex: 24893 ELECAB G
Fax: 1/783 0104

Data Resources and Publications

Annual Bulletin of Electric Energy Statistics for Europe and North America
Publisher: United Nations Economic Commission for Europe and the United Nations
Frequency of Publication: Annual
Scope: Basic data on the energy situation and details of the production of energy by form, overall energy balance sheets, deliveries of petroleum products for internal consumption, liquid fuels, and nuclear, hydrothermal, and geothermal energy

Bulletin of Energy Prices
Publisher: Office for Official Publications of the European Communities
Frequency of Publication: 2 times a year
Scope: Description of import and consumer prices for oil, coal, gas, and electricity in the EC, prepared by DG XVII

COST 302—Prospects for Electrical Vehicles in Europe
Publisher: Office for Official Publications of the European Communities
Frequency of Publication: One time
Scope: Proceedings of a seminar held under the auspices of the COST program (European Cooperation on Scientific and Technical Research); prepared by DG VII and XII

Energy Balances and Electricity Profiles
Publisher: United Nations
Frequency of Publication: Every two years
Scope: National-level data on energy resources and utilization

Energy Policies and Programmes of IEA Countries—Review
Publisher: OECD
Frequency of Publication: Annual
Scope: Analysis of energy policies, together with country-level data; prepared by the IEA

Nuclear Energy Data

Publisher: OECD
Frequency of Publication Annual
Scope: Statistics on electricity generation and nuclear power in the OECD; prepared by the OECD Nuclear Energy Agency

Panorama of EC Industry

Publisher: Office for Official Publications of the European Communities
Frequency of Publication: Annual
Scope: Description of 165 manufacturing and service industries, including energy, plus evaluations of the impact of the Single Market Program

Projected Costs of Generating Electricity from Power Stations for Commissioning in the Period 1995–2000

Publisher: OECD
Frequency of Publication: One time
Scope: Study estimating costs of electric power in OECD countries for the end of the decade

Related Topics and Industries

Natural Resources. See also *Part III—Sources on EC 1992 by Topic*

NUCLEAR ENERGY

EC Contacts

Table 29.1 lists official European Community directorates and subdirectorates that provide information about nuclear energy. For the complete address of the Commission of the European Communities headquarters (CEC HQ in the table), refer to the Introduction to Part IV.

Commission of the European Communities
▲ Directorate-General XII (Science, Research, and Development)

Fusion Programme

Address: rue de la Loi 200
B-1049 Bruxelles
Belgium
Telephone: 235 11 11
Telex: 21877 COMEU B

Commission of the European Communities
▲ Directorate-General XII (Science, Research, and Development)

Joint Research Centre

Central Bureau for Nuclear Measurements

Address: Steenweg op Retie
B-2440 Geel
Belgium
Telephone: 14/57 12 11
Telex: 33589 EURAT B
Fax: 14/58 42 73

Commission of the European Communities
▲ Directorate-General XII (Science, Research, and Development)

Joint Research Centre

Institute for Transuranium Elements

Address: Linkenheim
Postfach 2350
D-7500 Karlsruhe
Germany
Telephone: 72/47 841
Telex: 7825483 EU D
Fax: 72/40 46

European Parliament
▲ Committee on Energy, Research, and Technology

Address: Palais de l'Europe
F-67006 Strasbourg Cedex
France
Telephone: 88/374 001; 88/375 485
Fax: 88/369 214; 88/256 516

Address: Centre Europeen
Plateau du Kirchberg
L-2929 Luxembourg
Telephone: 430 01
Telex: 3493 EUPARL LU; 2894 EUPARL LU
Fax: 436 972; 435 359

Associations

▲ FORATOM (Association of European Atomic Forums)

Address: 22, Buckingham Gate
GB-London SW1E 6LB
Great Britain
Telephone: 71/828 0116
Telex: 264476 G
Fax: 71/828 0110

Data Resources and Publications

The Community's Research and Development Program on Decommissioning of Nuclear Installations

Publisher: Office for Official Publications of the European Communities
Frequency of Publication: Annual
Scope: Progress report of DG XII's activities in the decommissioning of nuclear reactors in the EC

The Community's Research and Development Programme on Radioactive Waste Management and Storage—Shared Cost Action

Publisher: Office for Official Publications of the European Communities
Frequency of Publication: Annual
Scope: Progress report on the EC's radioactive waste management program, in two volumes; prepared by DG XII

EABS

Database Producer: European Commission, DG XIII
Distributors/Hosts: ECHO
Frequency of Update: Monthly
Scope: References to the published results of scientific and technical research programs, sponsored in whole or in part by the EC, covering a wide range of topics, including nuclear research, new sources of energy, and environmental research ⊛

Table 29.1
CEC Subdirectorates—Nuclear Energy

Directorate and Subdirectorate Name	Directorate/ Subdirectorate Number	Directorate- General	Address
Nuclear Safety, Impact of Industry on the Environment, and Waste Management			
Radiation Protection	A/1	XI	Batiment Jean Monnet Rue Alcide de Gasperi L-2920 Luxembourg Telephone: 430 11 Telex: 3423/3466/3476 COMEUR LU
Economic Aspects, Employment, and Statistics	A/4	XI	CEC HQ, Belgium
Nuclear Safety Research	D	XII	CEC HQ, Belgium
Industries and Markets II: Non-fossil Energy			
Nuclear Energy	C/3	XVII	CEC HQ, Belgium Telephone: 2/236 27 99
Nuclear Conventions	C/4	XVII	CEC HQ, Belgium Telephone: 2/236 27 99
Euratom Safeguards	E	XVII	Batiment Jean Monnet Rue Alcide de Gasperi L-2920 Luxembourg Telephone: 430 11 Telex: 3423/3466/3476 COMEUR LU

▼ ▼

Euratom Supply Agency—Annual Report

Publisher: Office for Official Publications of the European Communities
Frequency of Publication: Annual
Scope: Review of activities of EAEC, the EC's nuclear power agency

Nuclear Energy Data

Publisher: OECD
Frequency of Publication: Annual
Scope: Summary of basic statistics on electricity generation and nuclear power in the OECD; prepared by the OECD Nuclear Energy Agency

Nuclear Energy in Perspective

Publisher: OECD
Frequency of Publication: One time
Scope: Insights on five major issues associated with nuclear power generation

OECD Nuclear Energy Agency Activities

Publisher: OECD
Frequency of Publication: Annual
Scope: Brief review of the activities of the NEA during the previous year

OECD Nuclear Energy Data

Publisher: OECD
Frequency of Publication: Annual
Scope: Brief summary of key nuclear energy data of OECD members; also annual report of the NEA

Operation of Nuclear Power Stations

Publisher: Office for Official Publications of the European Communities
Frequency of Publication: Annual
Scope: Regular report on nuclear power plants in the EC; prepared by DG XVII

Panorama of EC Industry

Publisher: Office for Official Publications of the European Communities
Frequency of Publication: Annual
Scope: Description of 165 manufacturing and service industries, including nuclear fuels, plus evaluations of the impact of the Single Market Program

Uranium—Resources, Production, and Demand

Publisher: OECD
Frequency of Publication: Periodically
Scope: Uranium resources and production data, plus projections of the nuclear industry's future uranium requirements; joint report of the OECD Nuclear Energy Agency and International Atomic Energy Agency

Related Topics and Industries

Natural Resources. See also *Part III—Sources on EC 1992 by Topic*

▼

ENERGY POLICY AND PLANNING

EC Contacts

Table 29.2 lists official European Community directorates and subdirectorates that provide information about energy policy and planning. For the complete address of the Commission of the European Communities headquarters (CEC HQ in the table), refer to the Introduction to Part IV.

Commission of the European Communities

▲ Statistical Office of the Commission of the European Communities

Directorate D/1 (Business Statistics/Energy)

Address: Batiment Jean Monnet
rue Alcide de Gasperi
L-2920 Luxembourg
Telephone: 430 11
Telex: 3423/3446/3476 COMEUR LU

European Parliament

▲ Committee on Energy, Research, and Technology

Address: Palais de l'Europe
F-67006 Strasbourg Cedex
France
Telephone: 88/374 001; 88/375 485
Fax: 88/369 214; 88/256 516

Address: Centre Europeen
Plateau du Kirchberg
L-2929 Luxembourg
Telephone: 430 01
Telex: 3493 EUPARL LU; 2894 EUPARL LU
Fax: 436 972; 435 359

Associations

▲ UNIPEDE (International Union of Producers and Distributors of Electrical Energy)

Address: 39, av. de Friedland
F-75008 Paris
France
Telephone: 1/40 42 37 08
Telex: 644471 F
Fax: 1/40 42 60 52

Data Resources and Publications

Annual Bulletin of General Energy Statistics for Europe and North America
Publisher: United Nations and the United Nations Economic Commission for Europe
Frequency of Publication: Annual
Scope: Basic data on the energy situation as a whole, including the production of energy by form, overall energy balance sheets, and deliveries of petroleum products for internal consumption

Bulletin of Energy Prices
Publisher: Office for Official Publications of the European Communities
Frequency of Publication: 2 times a year
Scope: Import and consumer prices for oil, coal, gas, and electricity in the EC, prepared by DG XVII

Collection of Legislation and Acts Relating to Energy
Publisher: Office for Official Publications of the European Communities
Frequency of Publication: Periodically
Scope: Official EC legislation and other acts dealing with energy

Table 29.2
CEC Subdirectorates—Policy and Planning

Directorate and Subdirectorate Name	Directorate/ Subdirectorate Number	Directorate- General	Address
Nuclear Safety, Impact of Industry on the Environment, and Waste Management			
Economic Aspects, Employment, and Statistics	A/4	XI	CEC HQ, Belgium
Energy Policy			
Policymaking	A/1	XVII	CEC HQ, Belgium Telephone: 2/236 27 99
Analyses and Forecasts	A/2	XVII	CEC HQ, Belgium Telephone: 2/236 27 99
Energy Planning	A/3	XVII	CEC HQ, Belgium Telephone: 2/236 27 99

Energy Balances for Europe and North America 1970–2000

Publisher: United Nations Economic Commission for Europe

Frequency of Publication: One time

Scope: Official government energy balances and projections to the year 2000 for all members of the UNECE

Energy Balances of OECD Countries

Publisher: OECD

Frequency of Publication: Annual

Scope: Companion to *Energy Statistics of OECD Countries*, providing comparisons on a common basis, millions of tons of oil equivalent; available in hardcopy or on microcomputer diskette; prepared by the IEA

Energy Efficiency in European Industry

Publisher: United Nations Economic Commission for Europe

Frequency of Publication: One time

Scope: Energy supply and demand projections to the year 2000, including the impact of conservation measures on energy imports and exports of North America, Western Europe, Eastern Europe, and the U.S.S.R.

Energy Efficiency in Land Transport

Publisher: Office for Official Publications of the European Communities

Frequency of Publication: One time

Scope: Seminar proceedings on developments in improving energy efficiency of cars, trucks, and trams; prepared by DG XVII

Energy in Europe

Publisher: Office for Official Publications of the European Communities

Frequency of Publication: 3 times a year

Scope: Short-term energy outlook for the EC, plus ongoing information on energy policy developments, research programs, conferences, and publications; prepared by DG XVII

Energy in Europe: Major Themes in Energy

Publisher: Office for Official Publications of the European Communities

Frequency of Publication: One time

Scope: Brief overview of major policy issues; prepared by DG XVII

Energy in Europe: The Internal Energy Market

Publisher: Office for Official Publications of the European Communities

Frequency of Publication: One time

Scope: Brief overview of major policy issues; prepared by DG XVII

Energy—Monthly Statistics

Publisher: Office for Official Publications of the European Communities,

Frequency of Publication: Monthly

Scope: Update service covering principal statistical series tracking short-term trends in the energy economy, including coal, oil, gas, and electrical energy; also available online via the Cronos database; prepared by the Statistical Office of the EC

Energy Policies and Programmes of IEA Countries—Review

Publisher: OECD

Frequency of Publication: Annual

Scope: Analysis of energy policies, together with country-level data; prepared by the IEA

Energy Prices and Taxes

Publisher: OECD

Frequency of Publication: 4 times a year

Scope: International compilation of available energy prices at all market levels; available in hardcopy or on microcomputer diskette; prepared by the IEA

Energy Statistics of OECD Countries

Publisher: OECD

Frequency of Publication: Annual

Scope: Overview of supply and use of fuels in OECD countries, including detailed data on production, trade, stock, and consumption by sector; available in hardcopy or on microcomputer diskette; prepared by the IEA

Energy Statistics Yearbook

Publisher: United Nations

Frequency of Publication: Annual

Scope: Global framework for comparable data on trends and developments in the supply of all forms of energy, providing data for all forms of energy, for each type of fuel, and aggregate data for the total mix of commercial fuels

The OECD Observer

Publisher: OECD

Frequency of Publication: Bimonthly

Scope: Key problems dealt with by the OECD, including economic growth, employment, social problems, energy, financial markets, the environment, and science and technology

Public Procurement in the Excluded Sectors

Publisher: Office for Official Publications of the European Communities

Frequency of Publication: One time

Scope: Official CEC communication, accompanied by proposals for directives relating to water, energy, transport, and telecommunications procurement

Sesame

Database Producer: European Commission, DG XVII and DG XII

Distributors/Hosts: ECHO, Datacentralen

Frequency of Update: Weekly

Scope: Updates on EC energy research and development and technology projects, including R&D demonstration projects, as well as hydrocarbon projects and national projects

Related Topics and Industries

Natural Resources. See also Part III—Sources on EC 1992 by Topic

OTHER ENERGY SOURCES

EC Contacts

Table 29.3 lists official European Community directorates and subdirectorates that provide information about other energy sources. For the complete address of the Commission of the European Communities headquarters (CEC HQ in the table), refer to the Introduction to Part IV.

Data Resources and Publications

EABS

Database Producer: European Commission, DG XIII

Distributors/Hosts: ECHO

Frequency of Update: Monthly

Scope: References to the published results of scientific and technical research programs, sponsored in whole or in part by the EC, covering a wide range of topics including nuclear research, new sources of energy, and environmental research

▼ ▼

Energy Balances and Electricity Profiles

Publisher: United Nations
Frequency of Publication: Every two years
Scope: Energy data and overall energy balances

Energy Policies and Programmes of IEA Countries—Review

Publisher: OECD
Frequency of Publication: Annual
Scope: Analysis of energy policies, together with country-level data; prepared by the IEA

Energy—Statistical Yearbook

Publisher: Office for Official Publications of the European Communities
Frequency of Publication: Annual
Scope: Summary of annual energy data for the EC and its member states; prepared by the Statistical Office of the EC

Energy Statistics of OECD Countries

Publisher: OECD
Frequency of Publication: Annual
Scope: Overview of supply and use of fuels in OECD countries, including detailed data on production, trade, stock, and consumption by sector; available in hardcopy or on microcomputer diskette; prepared by the IEA ■

Monthly Oil and Gas Trade Data

Publisher: OECD
Frequency of Publication: Monthly
Scope: Trade flows by country or origin and country of destination, including the OECD countries; complements the basic service provided in *Monthly Oil and Gas Statistics*; also on microcomputer diskette; prepared by the IEA ■

Table 29.3
CEC Subdirectorates—Other Energy Sources

Directorate and Subdirectorate Name	Directorate/ Subdirectorate Number	Directorate-General	Address
Restrictive Practices, Abuse of Dominant Positions, and Other Distortions of Competition II			
Energy {Other Than Coal}, Basic Products of the Chemical Industry	C/2	IV	CEC HQ, Belgium
Environment and Non-nuclear Energy Sources			
Renewable Energy Sources	E/3	XII	CEC HQ, Belgium
Geothermal Energy	E/4	XII	CEC HQ, Belgium
Rational Energy Use and Energy Systems Analysis	E/5	XII	CEC HQ, Belgium
Advanced Fuel Technology	E/6	XII	CEC HQ, Belgium
Industries and Markets II: Nonfossil Energy			
New and Renewable Sources of Energy [NRSE] and Rational Use of Energy [RUE]	C/2	XVII	CEC HQ, Belgium Telephone: 2/236 27 99
Energy Technology	D	XVII	CEC HQ, Belgium Telephone: 2/236 27 99

Oil and Gas Information

Publisher: OECD
Frequency of Publication: Annual
Scope: Current world oil and gas market trends and prospects, including data on supply and trade, consumption and prices; available in hardcopy or on microcomputer diskette; prepared by the IEA ■

Panorama of EC Industry

Publisher: Office for Official Publications of the European Communities
Frequency of Publication: Annual
Scope: Description of 165 manufacturing and service industries, including energy, plus evaluations of the impact of the Single Market Program

Sesame

Database Producer: European Commission, DG XVII and DG XII
Distributors/Hosts: ECHO, Datacentralen
Frequency of Update: Weekly
Scope: EC energy research and development and technology projects, including R&D demonstration projects, as well as hydrocarbon projects and national projects   ⊛

Related Topics and Industries

Natural Resources. See also *Part III—Sources on EC 1992 by Topic*

30

Financial Services and Insurance

ASSISTANCE

Appendix D contains a list of the Single Market measures dealing with financial services and insurance. For additional help on using the resources in this chapter, refer to the Introduction to Part IV.

BANKING, INVESTMENT BANKING, AND VENTURE CAPITAL

EC Contacts

Table 30.1 lists official European Community directorates and subdirectorates that provide information about banking, investment banking, and venture capital. For the complete address of the Commission of the European Communities headquarters (CEC HQ in the table), refer to the Introduction to Part IV..

European Parliament
▲ Committee on Economic and Monetary Affairs and Industrial Policy

Address: 97–113, rue Belliard
        B-1040 Bruxelles
        Belgium
Telephone: 2/284 21 21; 2/284 35 40
Fax: 2/230 68 56; 2/231 12 57

Address: Palais de l'Europe
        F-67006 Strasbourg Cedex
        France
Telephone: 88/374 001; 88/375 484
Fax: 88/369 214; 88/256 516

Address: Centre Europeen
        Plateau du Kirchberg
        L-2929 Luxembourg
Telephone: 430 01
Telex: 3493 EUPARL LU; 2894 EUPARL LU
Fax: 436 972; 435 359

Associations

▲ Association of Cooperative Banks of the EC

Address: rue de la Science 23–25 (Bte 9)
        B-1040 Bruxelles
        Belgium
Telephone: 2/230 11 24
Fax: 2/230 06 49

▲ CICP (International Confederation for Cooperative Banks)

Address: Le Ponant de Paris
        5, rue Leblanc
        F-75511 Paris Cedex 15
        France
Telephone: 1/40 39 66 19
Telex: 270483 F
Fax: 1/40 39 60 60

▲ EUROFINAS (European Federation of Finance Houses)

Address: av. de Tervueren 267 (Bte 10)
        B-1150 Bruxelles
        Belgium
Telephone: 2/771 21 07

Table 30.1
CEC Subdirectorates—Banking, Investment Banking, and Venture Capital

Directorate and Subdirectorate Name	Directorate/ Subdirectorate Number	Directorate- General	Address
Restrictive Practices, Abuse of Dominant Positions, and Other Distortions of Competition I			
Banking and Insurance and Other Service Industries	B/3	IV	CEC HQ, Belgium
Financial Institutions			
Banks and Financial Establishments	A/1	XV	CEC HQ, Belgium

▲ European Banks Advisory Committee

Address: c/o European Banks International Co.
av. Louise 61
B-1050 Bruxelles
Belgium
Telephone: 2/538 62 40

▲ European Federation of Building Societies

Address: 3 Savile Row
GB-London W1X 1AF
Great Britain
Telephone: 71/437 9655

▲ EVCA (European Venture Capital Association)

Address: Minervastraat (bte 6)
B-1970 Zaventem
Belgium
Telephone: 2/720 60 10
Fax: 2/725 30 36

▲ Federation Bancaire de la Communaute Europeenne

Address: av. de Tervueren 168
B-1150 Bruxelles
Belgium
Telephone: 2/771 00 94

▲ Federation of Bankers of the European Community

Address: rue Montoyer 10
B-1040 Bruxelles
Belgium
Telephone: 2/511 78 00
Fax: 2/511 23 28

▲ GCECEE (Savings Banks Group of the European Economic Community)

Address: av. de la Renaissance 12
B-1040 Bruxelles
Belgium
Telephone: 2/739 16 11
Fax: 2/736 09 55

▲ Groupment des Caisses d'Epargne de la CEE {Savings Banks}

Address: Square E Plasky 92-94
B-1040 Bruxelles
Belgium
Telephone: 2/736 80 47

▲ Groupment des Cooperatives d'Epargne et de Credit de la CEE {Savings Societies}

Address: rue de la Science 23–25 (Bte 9)
B-1040 Bruxelles
Belgium
Telephone: 2/230 11 24

▲ International Union of Building Societies and Savings Associations

Address: 20 North Wacker Drive, Suite 2267
Chicago, IL 60606
USA
Telephone: 312/726-6676
Telex: 9102213834

Data Resources and Publications

Competition in Banking

Publisher: OECD
Frequency of Publication: One time
Scope: Review of policies of OECD member countries toward permitting competition in banking and with banks

Human Resources and Corporate Strategy

Publisher: OECD
Frequency of Publication: One time
Scope: Study of technological change in banks and insurance companies in France, Germany, Japan, Sweden, and the United States

Methods of Promoting the Supply of Risk Capital

Publisher: Office for Official Publications of the European Communities
Frequency of Publication: One time
Scope: Study on using banking to improve the equity capital resources of SMEs

Panorama of EC Industry

Publisher: Office for Official Publications of the European Communities
Frequency of Publication: Annual
Scope: Description of 165 manufacturing and service industries, including the banking industry, plus evaluations of the impact of the Single Market Program

Research on the "Cost of Non-Europe"—The Cost of Non-Europe in Financial Services

Publisher: Office for Official Publications of the European Communities
Frequency of Publication: One time
Scope: Analysis of structure, operations, and profitability of banking, insurance, and securities industries, including macro-economic data for EC member states; discusses the link between freedom of capital markets and trade in financial products; Volume 9 of the Cecchini study on the "cost of non-Europe"

Related Topics and Industries

Professions and Service Industries. See also *Part III—Sources on EC 1992 by Topic*

▼

INSURANCE

EC Contacts

Table 30.2 lists official European Community directorates and subdirectorates that provide information about insurance. For the complete address of the Commission of the European Communities headquarters (CEC HQ in the table), refer to the Introduction to Part IV.

European Parliament

▲ Committee on Economic and Monetary Affairs and Industrial Policy

Address: 97–113, rue Belliard
B-1040 Bruxelles
Belgium
Telephone: 2/284 21 21; 2/284 35 40
Fax: 2/230 68 56; 2/231 12 57

Address: Palais de l'Europe
F-67006 Strasbourg Cedex
France
Telephone: 88/374 001; 88/375 484
Fax: 88/369 214; 88/256 516

Address: Centre Europeen
Plateau du Kirchberg
L-2929 Luxembourg
Telephone: 430 01
Telex: 3493 EUPARL LU; 2894 EUPARL LU
Fax: 436 972; 435 359

Table 30.2
CEC Subdirectorates—Insurance

Directorate and Subdirectorate Name	Directorate/ Subdirectorate Number	Directorate-General	Address
Restrictive Practices, Abuse of Dominant Positions, and Other Distortions of Competition I			
Banking and Insurance and Other Service Industries	B/3	IV	CEC HQ, Belgium
Financial Institutions			
Insurance	A/2	XV	CEC HQ, Belgium

Associations

▲ AEAI (Association Europeenne des Assures de l'Industrie {Industrial Insurance})

Address: rue Montoyer 51
B-1040 Bruxelles
Belgium
Telephone: 2/516 77 02
Telex: 21541 B
Fax: 2/513 63 31

▲ CEA (European Committee of Insurers)

Address: 3 bis, rue de la Chaussee d'Antin
F-75009 Paris
France
Telephone: 1/48 24 66 00
Telex: 281829 CEA F
Fax: 1/47 70 03 75

▲ Standing Committee of the Economic Community—International Bureau of Insurers and Reinsurers

Address: av. Albert-Elisabeth 40
B-1200 Bruxelles
Belgium
Telephone: 2/735 60 48

Data Resources and Publications

Accounting Standards Harmonization: Operating Results of Insurance Companies

Publisher: OECD
Frequency of Publication: One time
Scope: Summary of current practices pertaining to insurance companies in OECD countries

Automobile Insurance and Road Accident Prevention

Publisher: OECD
Frequency of Publication: One time
Scope: Review of the existing and potential roles of automobile insurers in road accident prevention

The Creation of the Internal Market in Insurance

Publisher: Office for Official Publications of the European Communities
Frequency of Publication: One time
Scope: Trace of the regulatory framework governing insurance in the EC

Human Resources and Corporate Strategy

Publisher: OECD
Frequency of Publication: One time
Scope: Study of technological change in banks and insurance companies in France, Germany, Japan, Sweden, and the United States

Panorama of EC Industry

Publisher: Office for Official Publications of the European Communities
Frequency of Publication: Annual
Scope: Description of 165 manufacturing and service industries, including the insurance industry, plus evaluations of the impact of the Single Market Program

Research on the "Cost of Non-Europe"—The Cost of Non-Europe in Financial Services

Publisher: Office for Official Publications of the European Communities
Frequency of Publication: One time
Scope: Analysis of structure, operations, and profitability of banking, insurance, and securities industries, including macroeconomic data for EC member states; discusses the link between freedom of capital markets and trade in financial products; Volume 9 of the Cecchini study on the "cost of non-Europe"

Related Topics and Industries

Professions and Service Industries. See also *Part III—Sources on EC 1992 by Topic*

SECURITIES AND CAPITAL MARKETS

EC Contacts

Table 30.3 lists official European Community directorates and subdirectorates that provide information about securities and capital markets. For the complete address of the Commission of the European Communities headquarters (CEC HQ in the table), refer to the Introduction to Part IV.

European Parliament

▲ Committee on Economic and Monetary Affairs and Industrial Policy

Address: 97–113, rue Belliard
B-1040 Bruxelles
Belgium
Telephone: 2/284 21 21; 2/284 35 40
Fax: 2/230 68 56; 2/231 12 57

Address: Palais de l'Europe
F-67006 Strasbourg Cedex
France
Telephone: 88/374 001; 88/375 484
Fax: 88/369 214; 88/256 516

Address: Centre Europeen
Plateau du Kirchberg
L-2929 Luxembourg
Telephone: 430 01
Telex: 3493 EUPARL LU; 2894 EUPARL LU
Fax: 436 972; 435 359

Associations

▲ Federation of Stock Exchanges in the European Community

Address: rue du Midi 2 (5e etage)
B-1000 Bruxelles
Belgium
Telephone: 2/513 05 18; 2/511 85 35
Fax: 2/512 49 05

Data Resources and Publications

Panorama of EC Industry

Publisher: Office for Official Publications of the European Communities
Frequency of Publication: Annual
Scope: Description of 165 manufacturing and service industries, including the securities industry, plus evaluations of the impact of the Single Market Program

Research on the "Cost of Non-Europe"—The Cost of Non-Europe in Financial Services

Publisher: Office for Official Publications of the European Communities
Frequency of Publication: One time
Scope: Analysis of structure, operations, and profitability of banking, insurance, and securities industries, including macroeconomic data for EC member states; discusses the link between freedom of capital markets and trade in financial products; Volume 9 of the Cecchini study on the "cost of non-Europe"

Securities Markets—Community Measures Adopted or Proposed

Publisher: Office for Official Publications of the European Communities
Frequency of Publication: One time
Scope: Status report, as of June 1989, on the EC's progress toward a unified market for securities

Related Topics and Industries

See *Part III—Sources on EC 1992 by Topic*

Table 30.3
CEC Subdirectorates—Securities and Capital Markets

Directorate and Subdirectorate Name	Directorate/ Subdirectorate Number	Directorate-General	Address
Financial Institutions			
Stock Exchanges and Securities	A/3	XV	CEC HQ, Belgium
Company Law, Company and Capital Movements Taxation			
Company Taxation and Other Direct Taxation; Capital Duty; Taxes on Transaction in Securities	B/1	XV	CEC HQ, Belgium

Transfers of Capital

EC Contacts

Table 30.4 lists official European Community directorates and subdirectorates that provide information about transfers of capital. For the complete address of the Commission of the European Communities headquarters (CEC HQ in the table), refer to the Introduction to Part IV.

European Parliament

▲ Committee on Economic and Monetary Affairs and Industrial Policy

Address: 97–113, rue Belliard
B-1040 Bruxelles
Belgium
Telephone: 2/284 21 21; 2/284 35 40
Fax: 2/230 68 56; 2/231 12 57

Address: Palais de l'Europe
F-67006 Strasbourg Cedex
France
Telephone: 88/374 001; 88/375 484
Fax: 88/369 214; 88/256 516

Table 30.4
CEC Subdirectorates—Transfers of Capital

Directorate and Subdirectorate Name	Directorate/ Subdirectorate Number	Directorate- General	Address
Financial Institutions			
General Matters; Supervision of the Application of Community Provisions	A/4	XV	CEC HQ, Belgium Telephone: 2/235 53 47
Company Law, Company and Capital Movements Taxation			
Company Taxation and Other Direct Taxation; Capital Duty; Taxes on Transactions in Securities	B/1	XV	CEC HQ, Belgium Telephone: 2/235 53 47
Company Law, Industrial Democracy and Accounting Standards	B/2	XV	CEC HQ, Belgium Telephone: 2/235 53 47
Multinationals, Groups of Companies and the European Company	B/3	XV	CEC HQ, Belgium Telephone: 2/235 53 47
Indirect Taxation, Including Elimination of Tax Frontiers			
VAT and Other Turnover Taxes	C/1	XXI	CEC HQ, Belgium
Indirect Taxation Other Than Turnover Taxes	C/2	XXI	CEC HQ, Belgium
Elimination of Tax Frontiers and the VAT Clearing System	C/3	XXI	CEC HQ, Belgium

Address: Centre Europeen
Plateau du Kirchberg
L-2929 Luxembourg
Telephone: 430 01
Telex: 3493 EUPARL LU; 2894 EUPARL LU
Fax: 436 972; 435 359

European Parliament
▲ Committee on External Economic Relations

Address: 97–113, rue Belliard
B-1040 Bruxelles
Belgium
Telephone: 2/284 21 21; 2/284 27 49
Fax: 2/230 68 56; 2/231 12 57

Address: Palais de l'Europe
F-67006 Strasbourg Cedex
France
Telephone: 88/374 001; 88/374 021
Fax: 88/369 214; 88/256 516

Address: Centre Europeen
Plateau du Kirchberg
L-2929 Luxembourg
Telephone: 430 01
Telex: 3493 EUPARL LU; 2894 EUPARL LU
Fax: 436 972; 435 359

Data Sources and Publications

Economic Bulletin for Europe
Publisher: United Nations Economic Commission for Europe
Frequency of Publication: Annual
Scope: Review of the previous year's developments in world trade and the economies of Europe, including output and trade, economic developments, trade and financing

Economic Survey of Europe
Publisher: United Nations
Frequency of Publication: Annual
Scope: Review of the previous year's developments in world trade and the economies of Europe, including output and trade, economic developments, trade, and financing

Foreign Direct Investment and Transnational Corporations in Services
Publisher: United Nations
Frequency of Publication: One time
Scope: Review of established policy patterns of multinational businesses in direct investment in service industries

General Arrangements Applicable to Capital Movements
Publisher: Office for Official Publications of the European Communities
Frequency of Publication: One time
Scope: Summary of EC rules governing the free movement of capital; prepared by DG II

Industrial Structure Statistics
Publisher: OECD
Frequency of Publication: Annual
Scope: Statistics that summarize production, value added, number of establishments, employment, wages and salaries, exports, imports, and investment

Research on the "Cost of Non-Europe"—The Cost of Non-Europe in Financial Services
Publisher: Office for Official Publications of the European Communities
Frequency of Publication: One time
Scope: Analysis of structure, operations, and profitability of banking, insurance, and securities industries, including macro-economic data for EC member states; discusses the link between freedom of capital markets and trade in financial products; Volume 9 of the Cecchini study on the "cost of non-Europe"

Related Topics and Industries

See *Part III—Sources on EC 1992 by Topic*

OTHER FINANCIAL SERVICES AND INSURANCE INDUSTRIES

EC Contacts

Table 30.5 lists official European Community directorates and subdirectorates that provide information about other financial services and insurance industries. For the complete address of the Commission of the European Communities headquarters (CEC HQ in the table), refer to the Introduction to Part IV.

Commission of the European Communities
▲ Directorate-General XVIII (Credit and Investments)

Address: Batiment Jean Monnet
rue Alcide de Gasperi
L-2920 Luxembourg
Telephone: 430 11
Telex: 3423/3466/3476 COMEUR LU; 2331
EUCRED LU; 3366 EURFIN LU

Associations

▲ CICA (International Confederation of Agricultural Credit Corporations)

Address: Birmensdorferstrasse 67
CH-8004 Zurich
Switzerland
Telephone: 1/291 05 75
Telex: 817675 CICA CH
Fax: 1/291 07 66

▲ EUROFINAS (European Federation of Finance House Associations)

Address: av. de Tervueren 267 (Bte 10)
B-1150 Bruxelles
Belgium
Telephone: 2/771 21 08
Fax: 2/770 75 96

▲ FHCEE (European Community Mortgage Federation)

Address: av. de la Joyeuse Entree 14 (Bte 2)
B-1040 Bruxelles
Belgium
Telephone: 2/230 25 51
Fax: 2/230 64 11

▲ LEASEUROPE (European Federation of Equipment Leasing Company Associations)

Address: av. de Tervueren 267 (Bte 9)
B-1150 Bruxelles
Belgium
Telephone: 2/771 21 08
Fax: 2/770 75 96

Data Resources and Publications

E.C. International Investment Partners

Publisher: Office for Official Publications of the European Communities
Frequency of Publication: One time
Scope: Description of the EC "financial facility" established to promote joint ventures in Asia, Latin America, and the Mediterranean region

Table 30.5
CEC Subdirectorates—Other Financial Services and Insurance Industries

Directorate and Subdirectorate Name	Directorate/ Subdirectorate Number	Directorate-General	Address
Financial Engineering and Capital Movements	E	II	CEC HQ, Belgium
Financial Institutions			
General Matters; Supervision of the Application of Community Provisions	A/4	XV	CEC HQ, Belgium Telephone: 2/235 53 47

Electronic Funds Transfer: Plastic Cards and the Consumer

Publisher: OECD
Frequency of Publication: One time
Scope: Review of policies toward electronic funds transfer (EFT) in OECD countries, as well as consumer attitudes toward EFT

Eurecom

Publisher: Commission of the European Community, New York office
Frequency of Publication: Monthly
Scope: Current news on EC economic and financial affairs

The European Financial Common Market

Publisher: Office for Official Publications of the European Communities
Frequency of Publication: One time
Scope: Summary, as of June 1989, of the EC's progress toward a unified financial marketplace

European Investment Bank—Annual Report

Publisher: Office for Official Publications of the European Communities
Frequency of Publication: Annual
Scope: Review of the year's activities, with emphasis on loans granted within the EC

The Export Credit Financing Systems in OECD Member Countries

Publisher: OECD
Frequency of Publication: Every 3 years
Scope: Description of export credit insurance and guarantee programs, as well as export financing support in OECD countries, including overseas development assistance programs that bear on export credit activities

Financial Market Trends

Publisher: OECD
Frequency of Publication: 3 times a year
Scope: Assessment of trends and prospects in the international and major domestic financial markets of the OECD area

Financial Statistics—Part I: Monthly Statistics

Publisher: OECD
Frequency of Publication: 24 times a year
Scope: Activities of both international and domestic financial markets during the previous 30 days

International Rates on International and Domestic Markets

Publisher: OECD
Frequency of Publication: Monthly
Scope: This is microdiskette summary of selected interest rates that appear in the OECD publication *Financial Statistics Monthly—Section 2—Domestic Markets— Interest Rates.* ∎

The OECD Observer

Publisher: OECD
Frequency of Publication: 6 times a year
Scope: Key problems dealt with by the OECD, including economic growth, employment, social problems, energy, financial markets, the environment, and science and technology

Panorama of EC Industry

Publisher: Office for Official Publications of the European Communities
Frequency of Publication: Annual
Scope: Description of 165 manufacturing and service industries, including the financial sector, plus evaluations of the impact of the Single Market Program

Progress in Structural Reform

Publisher: OECD
Frequency of Publication: Periodically
Scope: Review of economic activities of all OECD members, as well as EC specifically, in areas including financial markets, investment, taxation, competition policy, trade, agriculture, industrial policy, and labor markets; a supplement to selected issues of OECD's *Economic Outlook*

Report on Economic and Monetary Union in the European Community

Publisher: Office for Official Publications of the European Communities
Frequency of Publication: One time
Scope: Collection of papers submitted to the Committee for the Study of Economic and Monetary Union

Urban Housing Finance

Publisher: OECD
Frequency of Publication: One time
Scope: Report on OECD member countries relating to policies of funding urban housing and housing programs

Related Topics and Industries

See *Part III—Sources on EC 1992 by Topic*

31

Health Care and Medicine

ASSISTANCE

Appendix D contains a list of the Single Market measures dealing with health care and medicine. For additional help on using the resources in this chapter, refer to the Introduction to Part IV.

HEALTH CARE PROFESSIONALS AND HOSPITALS

EC Contacts

Table 31.1 lists official European Community directorates and subdirectorates that provide information about health care professionals and hospitals. For the complete address of the Commission of the European Communities headquarters (CEC HQ in the table), refer to the Introduction to Part IV.

Commission of the European Communities

▲ Directorate-General V—Employment, Industrial Relations, and Social Affairs

Coordination of the Programme of Action Against Cancer, and of Health Aspects of a People's Europe

Address: rue de la Loi 200
B-1049 Bruxelles
Belgium
Telephone: 2/235 11 11
Telex: 21877 COMEU B

European Parliament

▲ Committee on the Environment, Public Health, and Consumer Protection

Address: 97–113, rue Belliard
B-1040 Bruxelles
Belgium
Telephone: 2/284 21 21; 2/284 28 48
Fax: 2/230 68 56; 2/231 12 57

Address: Palais de l'Europe
F-67006 Strasbourg Cedex
France
Telephone: 88/374 001; 88/374 418
Fax: 88/369 214; 88/256 516

Address: Centre Europeen
Plateau du Kirchberg
L-2929 Luxembourg
Telephone: 430 01
Telex: 3493 EUPARL LU; 2894 EUPARL LU
Fax: 436 972; 435 359

European Parliament

▲ Committee on Youth, Culture, Education, the Media, and Sport

Address: 97–113, rue Belliard
B-1040 Bruxelles
Belgium
Telephone: 2/284 21 21; 2/284 25 11
Fax: 2/230 68 56; 2/231 12 57

Address: Palais de l'Europe
F-67006 Strasbourg Cedex
France
Telephone: 88/374 001; 88/374 522
Fax: 88/369 214; 88/256 516

Address: Centre Europeen
Plateau du Kirchberg
L-2929 Luxembourg
Telephone: 430 01
Telex: 3493 EUPARL LU; 2894 EUPARL LU
Fax: 436 972; 435 359

Associations

▲ AESCO (European Association of Schools and Colleges of Optometry)

Address: 134, rue de Chartres
F-91440 Bures/Yvette
France
Telephone: 1/69 07 67 37
Fax: 1/69 28 78 06

▲ CEHP (Comite Europeen de l'Hospitalisation Privee {Private Hospitals})

Address: av. F. Roosevelt 81
B-1050 Bruxelles
Belgium
Telephone: 2/640 93 95

▲ CLEO (Liaison Committee of European Osteopaths)

Address: 1, rue Hoche
F-93500 Pantin
France
Telephone: 1/845 91 36

▲ EEC Midwives Liaison Committee

Address: 15, Mansfield Street
        GB-London W1M 0BE
        Great Britain
Telephone: 71/580 6523
Fax: 71/436 3951

▲ EFOMP (European Federation of Organisations for Medical Physics)

Address: Josef Schneider Strasse 11
        D-8700 Wurzburg
        Germany
Telephone: 931/2230-2240

▲ GOMAC (Opticians Group of the Common Market)

Address: 45, rue de Lancry
        F-75010 Paris
        France
Telephone: 1/42 06 07 31
Fax: 1/42 45 77 40

▲ GPCE (Pharmaceutical Group of the European Community)

Address: sq. Ambiorix 13
        B-1040 Bruxelles
        Belgium
Telephone: 2/736 72 81
Fax: 2/736 02 06

▲ GPPIP-CEE (Industrial Pharmacists Group of the European Economic Community)

Address: rue de Moerkerke 10
        B-1210 Bruxelles
        Belgium
Telephone: 2/216 63 46

▲ Hospital Committee of the European Community

Address: Kapucijnenvoer 35
        B-3000 Leuven
        Belgium
Telephone: 16/21 69 02/01

▲ INTERBOR (International Union of Orthopedics)

Address: rue Prince Baudouin 108
        B-1000 Bruxelles
        Belgium
Telephone: 2/426 99 66
Fax: 2/424 07 82

▲ Liaison Committee for Dentistry in the EEC

Address: 64, Wimpole Street
        GB-London W1M 8AL
        Great Britain
Telephone: 71/935 0875
Fax: 71/487 5232

Table 31.1
CEC Subdirectorates—Health Care Professionals and Hospitals

Directorate and Subdirectorate Name	Directorate/ Subdirectorate Number	Directorate- General	Address
Approximation of Laws, Freedom of Establishment, and Freedom to Provide Services			
Free Movement of Self-employed Persons and Recognition of Diplomas	D/2	III	CEC HQ, Belgium Telephone: 2/236 30 12
RACE Programme and Development of Advanced Telematics Services			
Information and Telecommunications Technologies Applied to Health—AIM Programme	F/6	XIII	CEC HQ, Belgium Telephone: 2/235 24 48

▲ Standing Committee of Doctors of the EEC

Address: Villanueva 11
E-28001 Madrid
Spain
Telephone: 1/431 77 80
Fax: 1/275 95 48

▲ Standing Committee of Nurses of the EC

Address: 11, Fitzwilliam Place
IRL-Dublin 2
Ireland
Telephone: 1/76 01 37/38

▲ UEMS (European Union of Medical Specialists)

Address: av. de la Couronne 20
B-1050 Bruxelles
Belgium
Telephone: 2/649 51 64
Fax: 2/649 26 90

Related Topics and Industries

Professions and Service Industries. See also *Part III—Sources on EC 1992 by Topic*

▼

MEDICAL EQUIPMENT

EC Contacts

Table 31.2 lists official European Community directorates and subdirectorates that provide information about medical equipment. For the complete address of the Commission of the European Communities headquarters (CEC HQ in the table), refer to the Introduction to Part IV.

European Parliament
▲ Committee on Energy, Research, and Technology

Address: Palais de l'Europe
F-67006 Strasbourg Cedex
France
Telephone: 88/374 001; 88/375 485
Fax: 88/369 214; 88/256 516

Address: Centre Europeen
Plateau du Kirchberg
L-2929 Luxembourg
Telephone: 430 01
Telex: 3493 EUPARL LU; 2894 EUPARL LU
Fax: 436 972; 435 359

European Parliament
▲ Committee on the Environment, Public Health, and Consumer Protection

Address: 97–113, rue Belliard
B-1040 Bruxelles
Belgium
Telephone: 2/284 21 21; 2/284 28 48
Fax: 2/230 68 56; 2/231 12 57

Table 31.2
CEC Subdirectorates—Medical Equipment

Directorate and Subdirectorate Name	Directorate/ Subdirectorate Number	Directorate-General	Address
Biology			
Medical Research	F/6	XII	CEC HQ, Belgium
RACE Programme and Development of Advanced Telematics Services			
Information and Telecommunications Technologies Applied to Health—AIM Programme	F/6	XIII	CEC HQ, Belgium Telephone: 2/235 24 48

Address: Palais de l'Europe
F-67006 Strasbourg Cedex
France
Telephone: 88/374 001; 88/374 418
Fax: 88/369 214; 88/256 516

Address: Centre Europeen
Plateau du Kirchberg
L-2929 Luxembourg
Telephone: 430 01
Telex: 3493 EUPARL LU; 2894 EUPARL LU
Fax: 436 972; 435 359

Associations

▲ AEA (European Association of Hearing Aid Dispensers)

Address: Postbus 1
NL-6955 ZG Ellecom
The Netherlands
Telephone: 8330/22688

▲ COCIR (Coordination Committee of the Radiological and Electromedical Industries)

Address: Via Algardi 2
I-20148 Milano
Italy
Telephone: 2/326 42 27
Telex: 321616 I
Fax: 2/326 42 12

▲ EUCOMED (European Confederation of Medical Suppliers Associations)

Address: 551 Finchley Road
GB-Hampstead NW3 7BJ
Great Britain
Telephone: 71/431 2187
Telex: 923753 MONREF G
Fax: 71/794 5271

Data Sources and Publications

Bulletin of Statistics on World Trade in Engineering Products

Publisher: United Nations and the United Nations Economic Commission for Europe
Frequency of Publication: Annual
Scope: Flow of machinery, transport, scientific, medical, optical and measuring equipment, watches, and clocks

Health Care and Nursing Education in the 21st Century

Publisher: Office for Official Publications of the European Communities
Frequency of Publication: One time
Scope: Symposium proceedings on the future of health care and related issues in the EC

Health Care Systems in Transition: The Search for Efficiency

Publisher: OECD
Frequency of Publication: One time
Scope: Review of managerial tools and the philosophies underpinning the evolution of expenditures on health care in OECD member countries

Related Topics and Industries

See *Part III—Sources on EC 1992 by Topic*

MEDICINE AND DRUGS

EC Contacts

Table 31.3 lists official European Community directorates and subdirectorates that provide information about medicine and drugs. For the complete address of the Commission of the European Communities headquarters (CEC HQ in the table), refer to the Introduction to Part IV.

European Parliament

▲ Committee on Energy, Research, and Technology

Address: Palais de l'Europe
F-67006 Strasbourg Cedex
France
Telephone: 88/374 001; 88/375 485
Fax: 88/369 214; 88/256 516

Address: Centre Europeen
Plateau du Kirchberg
L-2929 Luxembourg
Telephone: 430 01
Telex: 3493 EUPARL LU; 2894 EUPARL LU
Fax: 436 972; 435 359

European Parliament

▲ Committee on the Environment, Public Health, and Consumer Protection

Address: 97–113, rue Belliard
B-1040 Bruxelles
Belgium
Telephone: 2/284 21 21; 2/284 28 48
Fax: 2/230 68 56; 2/231 12 57

Address: Palais de l'Europe
F-67006 Strasbourg Cedex
France
Telephone: 88/374 001; 88/374 418
Fax: 88/369 214; 88/256 516

Address: Centre Europeen
Plateau du Kirchberg
L-2929 Luxembourg
Telephone: 430 01
Telex: 3493 EUPARL LU; 2894 EUPARL LU
Fax: 436 972; 435 359

Associations

▲ AESGP (The European Proprietary Medicines Manufacturers Association)

Address: av. de Tervueren 7
B-1040 Bruxelles
Belgium

▲ EFPIA (European Federation of Pharmaceutical Industries Associations)

Address: av. Louise 250 (Bte 91)
B-1050 Bruxelles
Belgium
Telephone: 2/640 68 15
Telex: 64405 EFPIA B
Fax: 2/647 60 49

▲ EUCOMED (European Confederation of Medical Suppliers Associations)

Address: 551 Finchley Road
GB-Hampstead NW3 7BJ
Great Britain
Telephone: 71/431 2187
Telex: 923753 MONREF G
Fax: 71/794 5271

▲ GIRP (International Association of Pharmaceutical Distributors of the European Community)

Address: Savignystrasse 42
D-6000 Frankfurt/Main
Germany
Telephone: 69/74 04 77
Telex: 413494 BPG D
Fax: 69/74 04 70

Table 31.3
CEC Subdirectorates—Medicine and Drugs

Directorate and Subdirectorate Name	Directorate/ Subdirectorate Number	Directorate-General	Address
Internal Market and Industrial Affairs I			
Pharmaceuticals and Veterinary Medicines	B/6	III	CEC HQ, Belgium Telephone: 2/236 30 12
Biology			
Medical Research	F/6	XII	CEC HQ, Belgium

▲ GPCE (Pharmaceutical Group of the European Community)

Address: sq. Ambiorix 13
B-1040 Bruxelles
Belgium
Telephone: 2/736 72 81
Fax: 2/736 02 06

▲ GPPIP-CEE (Industrial Pharmacists Group of the European Economic Community)

Address: Delegation aux Affaires Exterieures
rue de Moerkerke 10
B-1210 Bruxelles
Belgium
Telephone: 2/216 63 46

▲ UEPS (European Union of the Social Pharmacies)

Address: ch. de Mons 602
B-1070 Bruxelles
Belgium
Telephone: 2/522 56 90
Fax: 2/522 93 00

Data Resources and Publications

Future System for Free Movement of Medicinal Products in the European Communities

Publisher: Office for Official Publications of the European Communities
Frequency of Publication: One time
Scope: Summary of the Commission's proposal on the free movement of human and veterinary medical products throughout the EC

Panorama of EC Industry

Publisher: Office for Official Publications of the European Communities
Frequency of Publication: Annual
Scope: Description of 165 manufacturing and service industries, including the pharmaceutical and nonpharmaceutical industries, plus evaluations of the impact of the Single Market Program

Pharmaceutical Industry

Publisher: United Nations
Frequency of Publication: Regularly updated
Scope: Directory of basic industrial information sources

Research on the "Cost of Non-Europe"—Technical Trade Barriers in the EC: An Illustration in Six Industries—Some Case Studies on Technical Barriers

Publisher: Office for Official Publications of the European Communities
Frequency of Publication: One time
Scope: Identifies technical trade barriers, including standards, legal requirements, testing, and certification procedures, and evaluates their impact in the food stuffs, pharmaceuticals, automobile, building materials, telecommunications, and electrical products and machinery industries; Volume 6 of the Cecchini study on the "cost of non-Europe"

Research on the "Cost of Non-Europe"—The Cost of Non-Europe in the Pharmaceutical Industry

Publisher: Office for Official Publications of the European Communities
Frequency of Publication: One time
Scope: Review of current pharmaceutical markets and industries, and analysis of the impact of the Single Market Program on pricing, production, and product testing; Volume 15 of the Cecchini study on the "cost of non-Europe"

The Rules Governing Medicinal Products in the European Community

Publisher: Office for Official Publications of the European Communities
Frequency of Publication: One time
Scope: Five volumes of rules dealing with manufacturing, testing, and marketing authorization for medicinal products (human and veterinary) in the Member States of the EC

Related Topics and Industries

See *Part III—Sources on EC 1992 by Topic*

OTHER HEALTH CARE AND MEDICAL INDUSTRIES

EC Contacts

Table 31.4 lists official European Community directorates and subdirectorates that provide information about other health care and medical industries. For the complete address of the Commission of the European Communities headquarters (CEC HQ in the table), refer to the Introduction to Part IV.

Commission of the European Communities

▲ Directorate-General V—Employment, Industrial Relations, and Social Affairs

Coordination of the Programme of Action Against Cancer, and of Health Aspects of a People's Europe

Address: rue de la Loi 200
B-1049 Bruxelles
Belgium
Telephone: 2/235 11 11
Telex: 21877 COMEU B

Associations

▲ AESCO (European Association of Schools and Colleges of Optometry)

Address: 134, rue de Chartres
F-91440 Bures/Yvette
France
Telephone: 1/69 07 67 37
Fax: 1/69 28 78 06

▲ EURO-FIET (European Regional Organisation of the International Federation of Commercial, Clerical, Professional, and Technical Employees)

Address: 15 av. de Balexert
CH-1219 Chatelaine/Geneve
Switzerland
Telephone: 22/796 27 33
Telex: 418736 FIET CH
Fax: 22/796 53 21

Data Resources and Publications

Europe Against Cancer

Publisher: Office for Official Publications of the European Communities
Frequency of Publication: One time
Scope: Discusses 1989, the European year of information on cancer, which targeted a 15 percent reduction in cancer by the year 2000

Financing and Delivering Health Care

Publisher: OECD
Frequency of Publication: One time
Scope: A comparative analysis of the policies and practices in OECD countries of health care financing and delivery systems

Related Topics and Industries

See *Part III—Sources on EC 1992 by Topic*

Table 31.4
CEC Subdirectorates—Other Health Care and Medical Industries

Directorate and Subdirectorate Name	Directorate/ Subdirectorate Number	Directorate- General	Address
Health and Safety	D	V	CEC HQ, Belgium
Biology			
Medical Research	F/6	XII	CEC HQ, Belgium
RACE Programme and Development of Advanced Telematics Services			
Information and Telecommunications Technologies Applied to Health—AIM Programme	F/6	XII	CEC HQ, Belgium Telephone: 2/235 24 48

32

Housing and Infrastructure

ASSISTANCE

Appendix D contains a list of the Single Market measures dealing with housing and infrastructure. For additional help on using the resources in this chapter, refer to the Introduction to Part IV.

CONSTRUCTION

EC Contacts

Table 32.1 lists official European Community directorates and subdirectorates that provide information about construction. For the complete address of the Commission of the European Communities headquarters (CEC HQ in the table), refer to the Introduction to Part IV.

European Parliament

▲ Committee on Regional Policy and Regional Planning

Address: Palais de l'Europe
F-67006 Strasbourg Cedex
France
Telephone: 88/374 001; 88/374 618
Fax: 88/369 214; 88/256 516

Address: Centre Europeen
Plateau du Kirchberg
L-2929 Luxembourg
Telephone: 430 01
Telex: 3493 EUPARL LU; 2894 EUPARL LU
Fax: 436 972; 435 359

Associations

▲ AIE (International Association of Electrical Contractors)

Address: 5, rue de Hamelin
F-75116 Paris
France
Telephone: 1/47 27 97 49
Telex: 620993 FELEC F
Fax: 1/47 55 00 47

▲ CECE (Committee for European Construction Equipment)

Address: Carolyn House
22–26 Dingwall Road
GB-Croydon
Surrey CRO 9XF
Great Britain
Telephone: 81/688 2727
Telex: 9419625 G
Fax: 81/681 2134

▲ CEEC (European Committee of Construction Economists)

Address: 12 Great George Street
GB-London SW1P 3AD
Great Britain
Telephone: 71/222 7000
Telex: 9155443 RICS G
Fax: 71/222 9430

▲ CEETB (European Committee for Building Equipment)

Address: 5, rue de Hamelin
F-75116 Paris
France
Telephone: 1/47 27 97 49
Telex: 620993 F
Fax: 1/47 55 00 47

▲ CLAEU (Liaison Committee of the Architects of United Europe)

Address: rue de Livourne 158 (Bte 5)
B-1050 Bruxelles
Belgium
Telephone: 2/647 06 69

▲ EDA (European Demolition Association)

Address: Wassenaarseweg 80
NL-2596 CZ's Gravenhage
The Netherlands
Telephone: 70/326 42 51
Telex: 32576 ECON NL
Fax: 70/324 51 18

▲ EUROBUILD (European Organisation for the Promotion of New Techniques and Methods in Building)

Address: 142, rue de Rivoli
F-75001 Paris
France
Telephone: 1/40 13 00 64
Telex: 217004 F
Fax: 1/47 20 76 50

▲ EUROPLANT {Construction of Industrial Plants}

Address: rue des Drapiers 21
B-1050 Bruxelles
Belgium
Telephone: 2/510 25 31
Telex: 21078 FABRIM B
Fax: 2/510 23 01

▲ FESI (European Federation of Associations of Insulation Contractors)

Address: 10, rue du Debarcadere
F-75852 Paris Cedex 17
France
Telephone: 1/40 55 13 70
Telex: 644044 FPB F
Fax: 1/45 74 12 47

▲ FIEC (European Construction Industry Federation)

Address: 128, rue de la Boetie
F-75008 Paris
France
Telephone: 1/49 53 50 50
Telex: 290918 F
Fax: 1/45 63 52 84

▲ UECL (European Union of Independent Home-Builders)

Address: rue du Lombard 36
B-1000 Bruxelles
Belgium
Telephone: 2/510 46 51
Telex: 64956 COBO B
Fax: 2/513 30 04

▲ UICP (International Union of Plumbers)

Address: 9, rue La Perouse
F-75784 Paris Cedex 16
France
Telephone: 1/47 20 10 20
Telex: 611975 FEDEBAT F
Fax: 1/47 23 02 84

Data Resources and Publications

Construction Statistics Yearbook

Publisher: United Nations
Frequency of Publication: Annually
Scope: Dwelling construction for each country over a 10-year period

Table 32.1
CEC Subdirectorates—Construction

Directorate and Subdirectorate Name	Directorate/ Subdirectorate Number	Directorate-General	Address
Internal Market and Industrial Affairs I			
Construction	B/5	III	CEC HQ, Belgium Telephone: 2/236 30 12
Restrictive Practices, Abuse of Dominant Positions, and Other Distortions of Competition II			
Non-ferrous Metals, Non-metallic Mineral Products, Construction, Timber, Paper, Glass, and Other Distortions of Competition	C/1	IV	CEC HQ, Belgium

Panorama of EC Industry

Publisher: Office for Official Publications of the European Communities

Frequency of Publication: Annual

Scope: Description of 165 manufacturing and service industries, including the building and construction industries, plus evaluations of the impact of the Single Market Program

Public Procurement and Construction—Towards an Integrated Market

Publisher: Office for Official Publications of the European Communities

Frequency of Publication: Annual

Scope: Report on developments in public procurement

Transnational Corporations in the Construction and Design Industry

Publisher: United Nations

Frequency of Publication: One time

Scope: Role of major multinational businesses in the construction and design industries, including investment and research and development

Urban Housing Finance

Publisher: OECD

Frequency of Publication: One time

Scope: Report on OECD member countries' policies of funding urban housing and housing programs

Related Topics and Industries

See *Part III—Sources on EC 1992 by Topic*

CONSTRUCTION MATERIALS

Associations

▲ BIBM (International Bureau for Precast Concrete)

Address: bd. A. Reyers 207–209
B-1040 Bruxelles
Belgium
Telephone: 2/735 60 69
Fax: 2/734 77 95

▲ CECM (European Convention for Constructional Steelwork)

Address: av. des Ombrages 32–36 (Bte 20)
B-1200 Bruxelles
Belgium
Telephone: 2/762 09 35
Fax: 2/762 09 35

▲ CLC (Liaison Committee of the Cement Industries in the EEC)

Address: rue d'Arlon 55
B-1040 Bruxelles
Belgium
Telephone: 2/234 10 11
Telex: 27203 CEMBUR B
Fax: 2/230 47 20

▲ European Confederation for Trade in Paint Wall- and Floor-Coverings

Address: 42, av. Marceau
F-75008 Paris
France
Telephone: 1/47 23 64 48
Fax: 1/47 20 90 30

▲ FECS (European Federation of Sanitary Ceramic Fabricators)

Address: Piazza Liberty 8
I-20121 Milano
Italy
Telephone: 2/79 07 25
Telex: 383825 FEDECE I
Fax: 2/76 00 93 80

▲ FEIC (European Federation of Laminated Wood Industries)

Address: 30, av. Marceau
F-75008 Paris
France
Telephone: 1/47 20 17 31
Telex: 611968 FILBOIS F
Fax: 1/47 20 76 31

▲FEP (European Federation of Associations of Floor Covering Manufacturers)

Address: Fullenbachstr. 6
D-4000 Dusseldorf 30
Germany
Telephone: 211/43 49 04; 211/45 41 374

▲ FEPF (European Federation of Producers of Fibre-Cement)

Address: bd. E. Jacqmain 162 (Bte 37)
B-1210 Bruxelles
Belgium
Telephone: 2/211 04 11
Telex: 21696 B
Fax: 2/219 69 08

▲ FESYP (European Federation of Associations of Particleboard Manufacturers)

Address: Wilhelmstrasse 25
D-6300 Giessen
Germany
Telephone: 641/78091
Telex: 482877 VHI D
Fax: 641/72145

▲ TBE (European Federation of Brick and Tile Manufacturers)

Address: rue des Poissonniers 13 (Bte 22)
B-1000 Bruxelles
Belgium
Telephone: 2/511 25 81
Fax: 2/513 26 40

Data Resources and Publications

Cement and Concrete Industry

Publisher: United Nations
Frequency of Publication: Periodically
Scope: Directory of basic industrial information sources

Paint and Varnish Industry

Publisher: United Nations
Frequency of Publication: Periodically
Scope: Directory of basic industrial information sources

Panorama of EC Industry

Publisher: Office for Official Publications of the European Communities
Frequency of Publication: Annual
Scope: Description of 165 manufacturing and service industries, including the construction materials industry, plus evaluations of the impact of the Single Market Program

Research on the "Cost of Non-Europe"—Technical Trade Barriers in the EC: An Illustration in Six Industries—Some Case Studies on Technical Barriers

Publisher: Office for Official Publications of the European Communities
Frequency of Publication: One time
Scope: Identification of technical trade barriers, including standards, legal requirements, testing, and certification procedures, and evaluation of their impact in the food stuffs, pharmaceuticals, automobile, building materials, telecommunications, and electrical products and machinery industries; Volume 6 of the Cecchini study on the "cost of non-Europe"

Research on the "Cost of Non-Europe"—The Cost of Non-Europe in Construction Products

Publisher: Office for Official Publications of the European Communities
Frequency of Publication: One time
Scope: Analysis of the cost of differences in technical standards among EC member states and benefits of completing the Single Market; Volume 13 of the Cecchini study on the "cost of non-Europe"

Woodworking Industry Machinery

Publisher: United Nations
Frequency of Publication: Periodically
Scope: Directory of basic industrial information sources

Related Topics and Industries

See *Part III—Sources on EC 1992 by Topic*

OTHER HOUSING AND INFRASTRUCTURE INDUSTRIES

Associations

▲ AFECI (Association of European Manufacturers of Instantaneous Gas Water Heaters and Wall-Hung Boilers)

Address: rue des Drapiers 21
B-1050 Bruxelles
Belgium
Telephone: 2/510 23 11
Telex: 21078 FABRIM B
Fax: 2/510 23 01

▲ AIPC (International Association for Bridge and Structural Engineering IVBH)

Address: ETH-Honggerberg
CH-8093 Zurich
Switzerland
Telephone: 1/377 26 47
Telex: 822186 IABS CH

▲ AQUA EUROPA (European Water Conditioning Association)

Address: rue des Drapiers 21
B-1050 Bruxelles
Belgium
Telephone: 2/510 23 11
Telex: 21078 FABRIM B
Fax: 2/510 23 01

▲ ARGE (The European Federation of Associations of Lock and Builders Hardware Manufacters)

Address: Offerstrasse 12
D-5620 Velbert 1
Germany
Telephone: 2051/4367
Telex: 8597507 FVSB D
Fax: 2051/4360

▲ EFLA (European Foundation for Landscape Architecture)

Address: av. Brugmann 52
B-1060 Bruxelles
Belgium

▲ European Commission of the International Federation of Real Estate Valuers

Address: 23, av. Bosquet
F-75007 Paris
France
Telephone: 1/45 50 45 49
Telex: 201339 F
Fax: 1/45 50 42 00

▲ European Council of Town Planners

Address: 26, Portland Place
GB-London W1N 4BE
Great Britain
Telephone: 71/636 9107
Fax: 71/323 1582

▲ EUROVENT (European Committee of Air Handling and Air Conditioning Equipment)

Address: rue des Drapiers 21
B-1050 Bruxelles
Belgium
Telephone: 2/510 23 11
Telex: 21078 FABRIM B
Fax: 2/510 23 01

▲ FAECF (Federation of European Window Manufacturers Associations)

Address: Bockenheimer Anlage 13
D-6000 Frankfurt 1
Germany
Telephone: 69/55 00 68
Telex: 0416547 D
Fax: 69/59 73 644

▲ GCI (Climate Engineers International Union of Associations of Heating and Ventilating Contractors)

Address: 9, rue La Perouse
F-75784 Paris Cedex 16
France
Telephone: 1/47 20 10 20
Telex: 611975 F
Fax: 1/45 53 58 77

▲ UIPI (Union Internationale de la Propriete Immobiliere {Real Estate})

Address: rue Joseph II, 17
            B-1050 Bruxelles
            Belgium

Data Resources and Publications

Annual Bulletin of Housing and Building Statistics for Europe

Publisher: United Nations and the United Nations Economic Commission for Europe
Frequency of Publication: Annual
Scope: Review of previous year's activity in dwelling construction as well as the materials used and employment in the construction industry; also includes wholesale price indexes of building materials

Cities and Transport

Publisher: OECD
Frequency of Publication: One time
Scope: Study of policies toward metropolitan transit issues in OECD countries

Crop Production

Publisher: Office for Official Publications of the European Communities
Frequency of Publication: Quarterly
Scope: Most recent data on land use, arable crops, and fruit and vegetable production; also available online via the Cronos database; prepared by Statistical Office of the EC   ⊛

Green Paper on the Urban Environment

Publisher: Office for Official Publications of the European Communities
Frequency of Publication: One time
Scope: Reports on the 1989–1990 conferences about the problems facing EC cities, with suggested solutions

Public Procurement in the Excluded Sectors

Publisher: Office for Official Publications of the European Communities
Frequency of Publication: One time
Scope: Coverage of proposals for directives relating to water, energy, transport, and telecommunications procurement; official CEC communication

Rent Policy in the EC Countries

Publisher: United Nations Economic Commission for Europe
Frequency of Publication: One time
Scope: Rent policy in relation to housing production, subsidy systems, housing quality, rent legislation, and developments in 20 East and West European countries

Trends in Research on Human Settlements in EC Countries

Publisher: United Nations Economic Commission for Europe
Frequency of Publication: One time
Scope: Research on settlement patterns and related policies, as well as current and future research requirements

Related Topics and Industries

Transportation. See also Part III—Sources on EC 1992 by Topic

33 Industrial Products

SECTIONS IN THIS CHAPTER

ASSISTANCE

Appendix D contains a list of the Single Market measures dealing with industrial products. For additional help on using the resources in this chapter, refer to the Introduction to Part IV.

BIOTECHNOLOGY

EC Contacts

Table 33.1 lists official European Community directorates and subdirectorates that provide information about biotechnology. For the complete address of the Commission of the European Communities headquarters (CEC HQ in the table), refer to the Introduction to Part IV.

European Parliament

▲ Committee on Energy, Research, and Technology

Address: Palais de l'Europe
F-67006 Strasbourg Cedex
France
Telephone: 88/374 001; 88/375 485
Fax: 88/369 214; 88/256 516

Address: Centre Europeen
Plateau du Kirchberg
L-2929 Luxembourg
Telephone: 430 01
Telex: 3493 EUPARL LU; 2894 EUPARL LU
Fax: 436 972; 435 359

European Parliament

▲ Committee on the Environment, Public Health, and Consumer Protection

Address: 97–113, rue Belliard
B-1040 Bruxelles
Belgium
Telephone: 2/284 21 21; 2/284 28 48
Fax: 2/230 68 56; 2/231 12 57

Address: Palais de l'Europe
F-67006 Strasbourg Cedex
France
Telephone: 88/374 001; 88/374 418
Fax: 88/369 214; 88/256 516

Address: Centre Europeen
Plateau du Kirchberg
L-2929 Luxembourg
Telephone: 430 01
Telex: 3493 EUPARL LU; 2894 EUPARL LU
Fax: 436 972; 435 359

Data Resources and Publications

Biorep

Database Producer: The Library of the Royal Netherlands Academy of Arts and Sciences
Distributors/Hosts: ECHO
Frequency of Update: Annual
Scope: Listing of biotechnical projects carried out in the Member States of the EC each year

Biotechnology and the Changing Role of Government

Publisher: OECD
Frequency of Publication: One time
Scope: Studies on the role of OECD governments in the emerging biotechnology industries

Table 33.1
CEC Subdirectorates—Biotechnology

Directorate and Subdirectorate Name	Directorate/ Subdirectorate Number	Directorate-General	Address
Nuclear Safety, Impact of Industry on the Environment, and Waste Management			
Monitoring of Chemical Substances, Industrial Hazards, and Biotechnology	A/2	XI	CEC HQ, Belgium
Biology			
CUBE [Concertation Unit for Biotechnology in Europe]	F/1	XII	CEC HQ, Belgium
Biotechnology	F/2	XII	CEC HQ, Belgium

Biotechnology: Economic and Wider Impacts

Publisher: OECD
Frequency of Publication: One time
Scope: Analysis of economic and social impact of biotechnology in OECD member countries

The Impact of Biotechnology on Agriculture in the European Community to the Year 2005

Publisher: Office for Official Publications of the European Communities
Frequency of Publication: One time
Scope: Study on intensive farming and the impact on the environment and rural economy

Membrane Technology in the Chemical Industry

Publisher: United Nations Economic Commission for Europe
Frequency of Publication: One time
Scope: Listing of major European suppliers of membranes, membrane modules, and membrane process equipment

Transnational Corporations in Biotechnology

Publisher: United Nations
Frequency of Publication: One time
Scope: Role of major multinational businesses in the biotechnology industry, including investment, research, and development

Related Topics and Industries

Health Care and Medicine; Natural Resources. See also Part III—Sources on EC 1992 by Topic

CHEMICALS, PLASTICS, AND PETROLEUM-BASED PRODUCTS

EC Contacts

Table 33.2 lists official European Community directorates and subdirectorates that provide information about chemicals, plastics, and petroleum-based products. For the complete address of the Commission of the European Communities headquarters (CEC HQ in the table), refer to the Introduction to Part IV.

European Parliament
▲ Committee on Energy, Research, and Technology

Address: Palais de l'Europe
F-67006 Strasbourg Cedex
France
Telephone: 88/374 001; 88/375 485
Fax: 88/369 214; 88/256 516

Address: Centre Europeen
Plateau du Kirchberg
L-2929 Luxembourg
Telephone: 430 01
Telex: 3493 EUPARL LU; 2894 EUPARL LU
Fax: 436 972; 435 359

European Parliament
▲ Committee on the Environment, Public Health, and Consumer Protection

Address: 97–113, rue Belliard
B-1040 Bruxelles
Belgium
Telephone: 2/284 21 21; 2/284 28 48
Fax: 2/230 68 56; 2/231 12 57

Address: Palais de l'Europe
F-67006 Strasbourg Cedex
France
Telephone: 88/374 001; 88/374 418
Fax: 88/369 214; 88/256 516

Address: Centre Europeen
              Plateau du Kirchberg
              L-2929 Luxembourg
Telephone: 430 01
Telex: 3493 EUPARL LU; 2894 EUPARL LU
Fax: 436 972; 435 359

Associations

▲ AEC (European Association of Fabricators of Plastic Leaf, Membranes, and Surfacings)

Address: rue Capouillet 19
              B-1060 Bruxelles
              Belgium
Telephone: 2/536 86 54
Fax: 2/536 86 00

▲ AIS (International Association of the Soap and Detergent Industry)

Address: sq. Marie-Louise 49
              B-1040 Bruxelles
              Belgium
Telephone: 2/230 83 71
Telex: 23167 FECHIM B
Fax: 2/230 82 88

▲ BLA (Liaison Bureau of Syndicated European Producers of Essences/Aromatics)

Address: sq. Marie-Louise 49
              B-1040 Bruxelles
              Belgium
Telephone: 2/230 40 90
Telex: 23167 FECHIM B
Fax: 2/231 13 01

Table 33.2
CEC Subdirectorates—Chemicals, Plastics, and Petroleum-Based Products

Directorate and Subdirectorate Name	Directorate/ Subdirectorate Number	Directorate-General	Address
Internal Market and Industrial Affairs II			
Chemicals, Plastics, and Rubber	C/5	III	CEC HQ, Belgium Telephone: 2/236 30 12
Restrictive Practices, Abuse of Dominant Positions, and Other Distortions of Competition II			
Energy {other than Coal}, Basic Products of the Chemical Industry	C/2	IV	CEC HQ, Belgium
Processed Chemical Products, Agricultural Products, and Foodstuffs	C/3	IV	CEC HQ, Belgium
Nuclear Safety, Impact of Industry on the Environment, and Waste Management			
Monitoring of Chemical Substances, Industrial Hazards, and Biotechnology	A/2	XI	CEC HQ, Belgium

▲ CEFIC (European Council of Chemical Manufacturers Federations)

Address: av. Louise 250 (Bte 71)
B-1050 Bruxelles
Belgium
Telephone: 2/640 20 95
Telex: 62444 CEFIC B
Fax: 2/640 19 81

▲ ECCC (European Communities Chemistry Committee)

Address: Burlington House
Piccadilly
GB-London W1V OBN
Great Britain
Telephone: 71/437 8656
Telex: 268001 G
Fax: 71/437 8883

▲ EFCGU (European Federation of Chemical and General Workers' Unions)

Address: av. Emile de Beco 109
B-1050 Bruxelles
Belgium
Telephone: 2/648 24 97
Fax: 2/648 43 16

▲ EUROMAP (European Committee of Builders of Machinery for Plastics and India Rubber)

Address: 5, Belgrave Square
GB-London SW1X 8PD
Great Britain
Telephone: 71/235 9483
Telex: 8951528 PLAFED G
Fax: 71/235 8045

▲ FECC (European Federation of the Chemical Trade)

Address: sq. Marie-Louise 49
B-1040 Bruxelles
Belgium
Telephone: 2/230 40 90
Telex: 23167 FECHIM B
Fax: 2/230 82 88

▲ GIFAP (International Group of National Associations of Pesticide Manufacturers)

Address: av. A. Lancaster 79A
B-1180 Bruxelles
Belgium
Telephone: 2/375 68 60
Telex: 62120 B
Fax: 2/375 27 93

▲ GPRMC (European Organisation of Reinforced Plastics-Composite Materials)

Address: rue des Drapiers 21
B-1050 Bruxelles
Belgium
Telephone: 2/511 23 70
Telex: 21078 FABRIM B
Fax: 2/510 23 01

▲ International Association of Chemical Expertise

Address: 1, rue Gabriel-Vicare
F-75003 Paris
France
Telephone: 1/48 87 53 63

▲ PLASTEUROTEC (European Group of Fabricators of Technical Plastic Parts)

Address: Am Hauptbahnhof
D-6000 Frankfurt/Main 1
Germany
Telephone: 69/271 05 35
Telex: 411122 D
Fax: 69/23 27 99

▲ UEIL (European Union of Independent Lubricant Manufacturers)

Address: 15, rue de Bruxelles
F-75009 Paris
France
Telephone: 1/42 81 18 22
Fax: 1/42 80 45 60

Data Resources and Publications

Annual Bulletin of Trade in Chemical Products

Publisher: United Nations
Frequency of Publication: Annual
Scope: Summary of imports and exports of chemical products, covering over 60 commodities

Annual Review of the Chemical Industry

Publisher: United Nations and United Nations Economic Commission for Europe

Frequency of Publication: Annual

Scope: Facts about production, imports, and exports of chemical products, as well as employment in the industry

Ecdin

Database Producer: EC Joint Research Center for Information Technology and Electronics, Ispra (CITE)

Distributors/Hosts: CITE

Frequency of Update: Periodically

Scope: Data on chemical products that actually or potentially affect the environment or human health by their manufacture, use, transport, or disposal ⊛

Membrane Technology in the Chemical Industry

Publisher: United Nations Economic Commission for Europe

Frequency of Publication: One time

Scope: Listing of major European suppliers of membranes, membrane modules, and membrane process equipment

Natural and Synthetic Rubber

Publisher: United Nations

Frequency of Publication: Periodically

Scope: Directory of basic industrial information sources

Paint and Varnish Industry

Publisher: United Nations

Frequency of Publication: Periodically

Scope: Directory of basic industrial information sources

Panorama of EC Industry

Publisher: Office for Official Publications of the European Communities

Frequency of Publication: Annual

Scope: Description of 165 manufacturing and service industries, including the printing ink, chemicals, rubber, plastics processing, and agrochemicals industries, plus evaluations of the impact of the Single Market Program

Pesticides Industry

Publisher: United Nations

Frequency of Publication: Periodically

Scope: Directory of basic industrial information sources

Petrochemical Industry

Publisher: United Nations

Frequency of Publication: Periodically

Scope: Directory of basic industrial information sources

Soap and Detergent Industry

Publisher: United Nations

Frequency of Publication: Periodically

Scope: Directory of basic industrial information sources

Related Topics and Industries

Manufacturing; Energy; Natural Resources. See also *Part III—Sources on EC 1992 by Topic*

METALS OTHER THAN STEEL

Associations

▲ Bismuth Institute Information Centre

Address: 47, rue de Ligne
B-1000 Bruxelles
Belgium

Telephone: 2/218 60 40

Telex: 62162 BISMUT

▲ Cadmium Association

Address: 34 Berkeley Square
GB-London W1X 6AJ
Great Britain

Telephone: 71/499 8425

Telex: 261286

▲ CAEF (Committee of European Foundry Associations)

Address: 2, rue de Bassano
F-75783 Paris Cedex 16
France
Telephone: 1/47 23 55 50
Telex: 620617 SYGEFON F
Fax: 1/47 20 44 15

▲ CEMAFON (European Committee for Materials and Products for Foundries)

Address: Lyoner Strasse 18
D-6000 Frankfurt/Main 71
Germany
Telephone: 69/660 34 13
Telex: 411321 D
Fax: 69/660 35 11

▲ Chromium Association

Address: 30, bd. Haussmann
F-75008 Paris
France
Telephone: 1/43 87 53 65

▲ Cobalt Development Institute

Address: Ravenstein 3
B-1000 Bruxelles
Belgium

▲ Comite de Liaison du Negoce des Metaux Non-Ferreux de la CCE {Non-Ferrous Metals}

Address: place du Samedi 13
B-1000 Bruxelles
Belgium

▲ Contact Office—Inter Trade Union of Miners' and Metalworkers' Free Trade Unions in the European Communities

Address: rue de Moniteur 18
B-1000 Bruxelles
Belgium
Telephone: 2/218 37 93

▲ ELDEC (European Lead Development Committee)

Address: 42, Weymouth Street
GB-London W1N 3LQ
Great Britain
Telephone: 71/499 8422
Telex: 261286 G
Fax: 71/493 1555

▲ EMF (European Metalworkers' Federation in the Community)

Address: rue Fosse-aux-Loups 38 (Bte 4)
B-1000 Bruxelles
Belgium
Telephone: 2/217 27 47
Fax: 2/217 59 63

▲ EUROFORGE (Liaison Committee for the European Stamping and Forging Industries)

Address: Goldene Pforte 1
D-5800 Hagen
Germany
Telephone: 2331/510 41
Telex: 823806 D
Fax: 2331/510 46

▲ EUROMETAUX (European Association of Metals)

Address: rue Montoyer 47
B-1040 Bruxelles
Belgium
Telephone: 2/511 72 73
Telex: 22077 CNOFER B
Fax: 2/514 45 13

▲ European Aluminium Association

Address: Konigsallee 30
P.O. Box 1207
D-4000 Dusseldorf 1
Germany
Telephone: 211/808 71
Telex: 8587 407 D

▲ European Coil Coating Association

Address: rue Montoyer 47 (Bte 4)
B-1040 Bruxelles
Belgium
Telephone: 2/513 60 52
Telex: 20689 B

▲ European Zinc Institute

Address: P.O. Box 2126
            NL-5600 CC Eindhoven
            The Netherlands
Telephone: 40/122 497

▲ International Lead and Zinc Study Group

Address: Metro House
            58 St. James' Street
            GB-London SW1A 1LD
            Great Britain
Telephone: 71/499 9373
Telex: 299819

▲ International Primary Aluminium Institute

Address: New Zealand House
            Haymarket
            GB-London SW1Y 4TE
            Great Britain
Telephone: 71/930 0582-9
Telex: 917837

▲ Liaison Committee for Non-Ferrous Metal Trade Within the EEC

Address: place du Samedi 13 (Bte 5–6)
            B-1000 Bruxelles
            Belgium
Telephone: 2/217 99 93
Telex: 61965 BIR B
Fax: 2/219 00 22

▲ Manganese Centre

Address: 17, av. Hoche
            F-75008 Paris
            France
Telephone: 1/45 63 06 34

▲ Non-Ferrous Metals Information Centre

Address: 47, rue de Montoyer
            B-1040 Bruxelles
            Belgium
Telephone: 2/513 86 34
Telex: 22077
Fax: 2/511 75 53

▲ Organization of European Aluminium Smelters

Address: Grad-Adolf Str. 18
            P.O. Box 200 840
            D-4000 Dusseldorf
            Germany
Telephone: 211/320 672
Telex: 8582508

▲ Tantalum-Niobium International Study Center

Address: 40, rue Washington
            B-1050 Bruxelles
            Belgium
Telephone: 2/649 51 58
Telex: 65080 INAC B
Fax: 2/649 32 69

▲ World Bureau of Metal Statistics

Address: 41, Doughty Street
            GB-London WC1N 2LF
            Great Britain
Telephone: 71/405 2771
Telex: 298970

Data Resources and Publications

Panorama of EC Industry

Publisher: Office for Official Publications of the European Communities
Frequency of Publication: Annual
Scope: Description of 165 manufacturing and service industries, including nonferrous metals, plus evaluations of the impact of the Single Market Program

Related Topics and Industries

Manufacturing; Natural Resources. See also Part III—Sources on EC 1992 by Topic

▼ ——————————————————————————————————— ▼

Steel

EC Contacts

Table 33.3 lists official European Community directorates and subdirectorates that provide information about steel. For the complete address of the Commission of the European Communities headquarters (CEC HQ in the table), refer to the Introduction to Part IV.

European Parliament

▲ Committee on Economic and Monetary Affairs and Industrial Policy

Address: 97–113, rue Belliard
B-1040 Bruxelles
Belgium
Telephone: 2/284 21 21; 2/284 35 40
Fax: 2/230 68 56; 2/231 12 57

Address: Palais de l'Europe
F-67006 Strasbourg Cedex
France
Telephone: 88/374 001; 88/375 484
Fax: 88/369 214; 88/256 516

Address: Centre Europeen
Plateau du Kirchberg
L-2929 Luxembourg
Telephone: 430 01
Telex: 3493 EUPARL LU; 2894 EUPARL LU
Fax: 436 972; 435 359

Associations

▲ CAEF (Committee of European Foundry Associations)

Address: 2, rue de Bassano
F-75783 Paris Cedex 16
France
Telephone: 1/47 23 55 50
Telex: 620617 SYGEFON F
Fax: 1/47 20 44 15

Table 33.3
CEC Subdirectorates—Steel

Directorate and Subdirectorate Name	Directorate/ Subdirectorate Number	Directorate- General	Address
Steel			
General Objectives and Industrial Structures	E/2	III	CEC HQ, Belgium Telephone: 2/236 30 12
Analysis and Forecasts for the Internal Market in Steel	E/3	III	CEC HQ, Belgium Telephone: 2/236 30 12
Restrictive Practices, Abuse of Dominant Positions, and Other Distortions of Competition III			
Steel and Coal	D/1	IV	CEC HQ, Belgium
Employment			
ECSC Readaptation and Social Aspects of Iron and Steel Policies	A/3	V	CEC HQ, Belgium
Technological Research			
Technical Research— Steel	C/4	XII	CEC HQ, Belgium

▲ CECM (European Convention for Constructional Steelwork)

Address: av. des Ombrages 32–36 (Bte 20)
B-1200 Bruxelles
Belgium
Telephone: 2/762 09 35
Fax: 2/762 09 35

▲ CEMAFON (European Committee for Materials and Products for Foundries)

Address: Lyoner Strasse 18
D-6000 Frankfurt/Main 71
Germany
Telephone: 69/660 34 13
Telex: 411321 D
Fax: 69/660 35 11

▲ Club des Marchands de Fer de la CECA {Iron Merchants}

Address: rue de la Bonte 4 (Bte 1)
B-1050 Bruxelles
Belgium
Telephone: 2/537 43 43

▲ COFENAF (Committee of the National Ferrous Scrap Federations and Associations of the Common Market)

Address: place du Samedi 13 (Btes 5–6)
B-1000 Bruxelles
Belgium
Telephone: 2/217 99 93
Telex: 61965 BIR B
Fax: 2/219 00 22

▲ Contact Office-Inter Trade Union of Miners' and Metalworkers' Free Trade Unions in the European Communities

Address: rue de Moniteur 18
B-1000 Bruxelles
Belgium
Telephone: 2/218 37 93

▲ EMF (European Metalworkers' Federation in the Community)

Address: rue Fosse-aux-Loups 38 (Bte 4)
B-1000 Bruxelles
Belgium
Telephone: 2/217 27 47
Fax: 2/217 59 63

▲ EUROFER (European Confederation of Iron and Steel Industries)

Address: sq. de Meeus 5 (Bte 9)
B-1040 Bruxelles
Belgium
Telephone: 2/512 98 30
Telex: 62112 EURFER B
Fax: 2/512 01 46

▲ EUROFORGE (Liaison Committee for the European Stamping and Forging Industries)

Address: Goldene Pforte 1
D-5800 Hagen
Germany
Telephone: 2331/510 41
Telex: 823806 D
Fax: 2331/510 46

▲ EUROMETAUX (European Association of Metals)

Address: rue Montoyer 47
B-1040 Bruxelles
Belgium
Telephone: 2/511 72 73
Telex: 22077 CNOFER B
Fax: 2/514 45 13

▲ European Coil Coating Association

Address: 4th Floor, rue Montoyer 47
B-1040 Bruxelles
Belgium
Telephone: 2/513 60 52
Telex: 20689

▲ European Independent Steelworks Association

Address: 205, rue Belliard (Bte 18)
B-1040 Bruxelles
Belgium
Telephone: 2/230 79 62

▲ International Iron and Steel Institute

Address: rue Col Bourg 120
B-1140 Bruxelles
Belgium
Telephone: 2/735 90 75
Telex: 22639

▲ International Pig Iron Secretariat

Address: Breite Str. 69
Postfach 6709
D-4000 Dusseldorf
Germany
Telephone: 211/085 82 286

▲ Liaison Committee of the European Community Steel Tube Industry

Address: 25, rue d'Astorg
F-75008 Paris
France
Telephone: 1/42 66 93 70
Telex: 290319 TELPA F
Fax: 1/42 66 94 21

▲ Liaison Committee of the Ferro Alloy Manufacturers of the European Economic Community

Address: Calle Castello 117
Despacho 650
E-28006 Madrid
Spain
Telephone: 1/262 65 99
Telex: 43465 IMBAR E
Fax: 1/261 13 96

▲ World Bureau of Metal Statistics

Address: 41, Doughty Street
London WC1N 2LF
Great Britain
Telephone: 71/405 2771
Telex: 298970

Data Resources and Publications

Annual Bulletin of Steel Statistics for Europe

Publisher: United Nations Economic Commission for Europe and the United Nations
Frequency of Publication: Annual
Scope: Statistics about the development of steel production and trade, consumption and trade of raw materials, movements of scrap, consumption of energy in the steel industry, and steel deliveries to consuming industries

Financial Report

Publisher: Office for Official Publications of the European Communities
Frequency of Publication: Annual
Scope: Review of finances and other activities of the European Coal and Steel Community

The Importance of the Iron and Steel Industry for the Economic Activity of the EC Member Countries

Publisher: United Nations Economic Commission for Europe
Frequency of Publication: One time
Scope: Description of the importance of the steel industry in the economy; describes its structure

Investment in the Community Coalmining and Iron and Steel Industries

Publisher: Office for Official Publications of the European Communities
Frequency of Publication: Annual
Scope: Actual and forecast capital expenditures of the coal mining industry, coking plants, iron-ore mines, and the iron and steel industry; also available online via the Cronos database; prepared by DG XVIII ✆

Iron and Steel Industry

Publisher: United Nations
Frequency of Publication: Periodically
Scope: Directory of basic industrial information sources

The Iron and Steel Industry

Publisher: OECD
Frequency of Publication: Annual
Scope: Review of previous year's production and consumption of steel and iron

Iron and Steel—Monthly Statistics

Publisher: Office for Official Publications of the European Communities

Frequency of Publication: Monthly

Scope: Statistics by month for iron and steel industry employment; consumption of raw materials; and production of iron ore, pig iron, crude steel, finished steel products, and end products; also available online via the Cronos database; prepared by the Statistical Office of the European Community ⓐ

Iron and Steel—Statistical Yearbook

Publisher: Office for Official Publications of the European Communities

Frequency of Publication: Annual

Scope: Statistics on the structure and economic situations of the EC's iron and steel industry; prepared by the Statistical Office of the EC

Panorama of EC Industry

Publisher: Office for Official Publications of the European Communities

Frequency of Publication: Annual

Scope: Description of 165 manufacturing and service industries, including the iron and steel industries, plus evaluations of the impact of the Single Market Program

The Role of Technology in Iron and Steel Developments

Publisher: OECD

Frequency of Publication: One time

Scope: Study on impact of technology on the iron and steel industries of OECD member countries

Statistics of World Trade in Steel

Publisher: United Nations and the United Nations Economic Commission for Europe

Frequency of Publication: Annual

Scope: Statistics about exports of semifinished and finished steel products

The Steel Market

Publisher: United Nations and the United Nations Economic Commission for Europe

Frequency of Publication: Annual

Scope: Monitor of the steel market's international development, including statistical information submitted by governments, as well as reports on steel market trends and their outlook on a country-by-country basis

The Steel Market and Outlook

Publisher: OECD

Frequency of Publication: Annual

Scope: Brief review of steel industry in OECD countries, together with outlook for prospects for the following year

Related Topics and Industries

Housing and Infrastructure; Manufacturing; Natural Resources. See also Part III—Sources on EC 1992 by Topics

OTHER INDUSTRIAL PRODUCTS

EC Contacts

Table 33.4 lists official European Community directorates and subdirectorates that provide information about other industrial products. For the complete address of the Commission of the European Communities headquarters (CEC HQ in the table), refer to the Introduction to Part IV.

▲ Joint Research Centre

Institute for Advanced Materials

Address: I-21020 Ispra (VA)
Italy

Telephone: 39/332 78 91 11

Telex: 380042/380058/324878/324880 EUR I

Fax: 39/332 78 90 45

▲ Joint Research Centre

Institute for Advanced Materials

Address: Westerduinweg 3
Postbus Nr. 2
NL-1755 ZG Petten (N.H.)
The Netherlands
Telephone: 31/22 46-5656
Telex: 57211 REACP
Fax: 31/22 46 10 02

Commission of the European Communities
▲ Statistical Office

Directorate D/2—Business Statistics/Industry

Address: Batiment Jean Monnet
rue Alcide de Gasperi
L-2920 Luxembourg
Telephone: 430 11
Telex: 3423/3446/3476 COMEUR LU

Associations

▲ AECMA (Association of European Constructors of Aerospace Materials)

Address: 88, bd. Malesherbes
F-75008 Paris
France
Telephone: 1/45 63 82 85
Telex: 642701 AECMA F
Fax: 1/42 25 15 48

▲ AEEF (European Association of Refrigeration Enterprises—Common Market Committee)

Address: av. de Broqueville 272 (Bte 4)
B-1200 Bruxelles
Belgium
Telephone: 2/771 36 35
Telex: 26458 B
Fax: 2/762 94 25

▲ AIA/EAC (European Advisory Council of the Asbestos International Association)

Address: bd. E. Jacqmain 162 (Bte 32)
B-1210 Bruxelles
Belgium
Telephone: 2/218 63 29
Telex: 21696 B
Fax: 2/219 69 08

▲ BLIC (Liaison Office of the Rubber Industry in the European Economic Community)

Address: av. des Arts 2 (Bte 12)
B-1040 Bruxelles
Belgium
Telephone: 2/218 49 40
Telex: 62291 BLIC B
Fax: 2/281 61 62

Table 33.4
CEC Subdirectorates—Other Industrial Products

Directorate and Subdirectorate Name	Directorate/ Subdirectorate Number	Directorate- General	Address
Internal Market and Industrial Affairs II			
Shipbuilding, Wood, Leather, Paper, and Miscellaneous Industries	C/4	III	CEC HQ, Belgium Telephone: 2/236 30 12
Restrictive Practices, Abuse of Dominant Positions, and Other Distortions of Competition II			
Non-ferrous Metals, Non-metallic Mineral Products, Construction, Timber, Paper, Glass, and Rubber Industries	C/1	IV	CEC HQ, Belgium

▲ CECE (Committee for European Construction Equipment)

Address: Carolyn House
22–26, Dingwall Road
GB-Croydon, Surrey CRO 9XF
Great Britain
Telephone: 81/688 2727
Telex: 9419625 G
Fax: 81/681 2134

▲ CECIP (European Committee for the Constructors of Instruments for Weighing)

Address: 36, av. Hoche
F-75008 Paris
France
Telephone: 1/45 61 18 51
Telex: 280900 FEDEMEC F
Fax: 1/45 63 59 86

▲ CECOF (European Committee of Industrial Furnace and Heating Equipment Associations)

Address: Lyoner Strasse 18
D-6000 Frankfurt/Main 71
Germany
Telephone: 69/03 413
Telex: 411321 D
Fax: 69/03 511

▲ CECT (European Committee of Boiler, Vessel, and Pipework Manufacturers)

Address: Etelranta 10
SF-00130 Helsinki
Finland
Telephone: 0/19 231
Telex: 124997 FIMET SF
Fax: 0/82 25 46

▲ CEIR (European Committee for the Valves and Fittings Industry)

Address: Lyoner Strasse 18
D-6000 Frankfurt/Main 71
Germany
Telephone: 69/66 03 241
Telex: 411321 D
Fax: 69/66 03 634

▲ CEPE (European Committee of Paint, Printing Ink, and Artists Colours Manufacturers Associations)

Address: sq. Marie-Louise 49
B-1040 Bruxelles
Belgium
Telephone: 2/230 40 90 (ext. 179)
Telex: 23167 B
Fax: 2/230 14 09

▲ CERAME-UNIE (Liaison Office of Ceramic Industries of the Common Market)

Address: rue des Colonies 18–24 (Bte 17)
B-1000 Bruxelles
Belgium
Telephone: 2/511 30 12
Telex: 21598 B
Fax: 2/511 51 74

▲ COTREL (Committee of Associations of Transformer Manufacturers in the Common Market)

Address: Stresemanallee 19
D-6000 Frankfurt/Main 70
Germany
Telephone: 69/630 22 32/33
Telex: 69980010 D
Fax: 69/630 22 79

▲ EFPA (European Food Service and Packaging Association)

Address: Waldeggstrasse 22B
CH-3800 Interlaken
Switzerland
Telephone: 36/22 22 26
Telex: 923152 OVI CH
Fax: 36/22 40 41

▲ EIFI (European Industrial Fasteners Institute)

Address: Blundell House
Torrington Avenue
GB-Coventry CV4 9GV
Great Britain
Telephone: 203/466 496
Fax: 203/466 074

▲ EUROCORD (Liaison Committee of EEC Twine and Cordage Industries)

Address: 3, av. du President Wilson
              F-75116 Paris
              France
Telephone: 1/47 23 64 51
Telex: 611792 EURTEXT F
Fax: 1/40 70 92 39

▲ EUROM (European Federation of Optical and Precision Instruments Industry)

Address: Carolyn House
              22–26, Dingwall Road
              GB-Croydon CRO 9XF
              Great Britain
Telephone: 81/681 1680
Telex: 9419625 FMEC G
Fax: 81/681 2134

▲ EUROPLANT {Construction of Industrial Plants}

Address: rue des Drapiers 21
              B-1050 Bruxelles
              Belgium
Telephone: 2/510 25 31
Telex: 21078 FABRIM B
Fax: 2/510 23 01

▲ EUROPOWERCAB (European Conference of Associations of Power Cable Industries)

Address: 56, Palace Road
              East Molesey
              GB-Surrey KT8 9DW
              Great Britain
Telephone: 81/941 4079
Telex: 24893 ELECAB G
Fax: 81/783 0104

▲ EURORAD (European Association of Manufacturers of Radiators)

Address: Obstgartenstrasse 19
              Postfach 7190
              CH-8023 Zurich
              Switzerland
Telephone: 1/361 30 60
Telex: 817538 CH
Fax: 1/382 83 61

▲ EUROTELCAB (European Conference of Associations of Telecommunication Cables Industries)

Address: Postfach 100645
              Pipinstrasse 16
              D-5000 Koln 1
              Germany
Telephone: 221/204 62 10
Telex: 8881342 D
Fax: 221/204 62 48

▲ EUROVENT (European Committee of Air Handling and Air Conditioning Equipment)

Address: rue des Drapiers 21
              B-1050 Bruxelles
              Belgium
Telephone: 2/510 23 11
Telex: 21078 FABRIM B
Fax: 2/510 23 01

▲ EWRIS (European Wire Rope Information Service)

Address: Fountain Precinct
              1, Balm Green
              GB-Sheffield S1 3AF
              Great Britain
Telephone: 742/766 789
Telex: 54170 G
Fax: 742/766 213

▲ FEA (Federation of European Aerosol Associations)

Address: sq. Marie-Louise 49
              B-1040 Bruxelles
              Belgium
Telephone: 2/230 40 90
Telex: 23167 FECHIM B
Fax: 2/230 82 88

▲ FECS (European Federation of Sanitary Ceramic Fabricators)

Address: Piazza Liberty 8
              I-20121 Milano
              Italy
Telephone: 2/79 07 25
Telex: 383825 FEDECE I
Fax: 2/76 00 93 80

▲ FEICA (Association of European Adhesives Manufacturers)

Address: Ivo-Beucker-Strasse 43
       Postfach 230169
       D-4000 Dusseldorf 1
       Germany
Telephone: 211/67931-0
Telex: 8584860 VCID D
Fax: 211/67931-88

▲ FEPA (European Federation of Manufacturers of Abrasives)

Address: 20, av. Reille
       F-75014 Paris
       France
Telephone: 1/45 81 25 90
Telex: 203860 F
Fax: 1/45 89 69 53

▲ FIFE (International Federation of Associations of Maintenance Products Manufacturers)

Address: sq. Marie-Louise 49
       B-1040 Bruxelles
       Belgium
Telephone: 2/230 40 90
Telex: 23167 FECHIM B
Fax: 2/230 82 88

▲ GROUPISOL (Association of the EEC Manufacturers of Technical Ceramics for Electronic, Electrical, Mechanical, and Other Applications)

Address: rue des Colonies
       B-1000 Bruxelles
       Belgium
Telephone: 2/511 70 25
Telex: 21598 B
Fax: 2/511 51 74

▲ SEFEL (European Secretariat of Manufacturers of Light Metal Packaging)

Address: rue des Drapiers 21
       B-1050 Bruxelles
       Belgium
Telephone: 2/510 23 11
Telex: 21078 FABRIM B
Fax: 2/510 23 01

Data Resources and Publications

Advanced Materials

Publisher: OECD
Frequency of Publication: One time
Scope: Discussion of how advanced materials are developed, in particular government policies and their impact on technological change

Cement and Concrete Industry

Publisher: United Nations
Frequency of Publication: Periodically
Scope: Directory of basic industrial information sources

Ceramics Industry

Publisher: United Nations
Frequency of Publication: Periodically
Scope: Directory of basic industrial information sources

Domis

Database Producer: ECHO
Distributors/Hosts: ECHO
Frequency of Update: Periodically
Scope: Directory of information sources in the materials field. Covers metals, alloys, and steel; ceramics and glass; composite materials; coatings and joints; and plastics and rubber

Earnings: Industry and Services

Publisher: Office for Official Publications of the European Communities
Frequency of Publication: 2 times a year
Scope: Earnings of manual and nonmanual workers in industry and certain groups of activities in the service sector; also available online via the Cronos database; prepared by Statistical Office of the EC

Engineering Industries: Dynamics of the Eighties

Publisher: United Nations Economic Commission for Europe
Frequency of Publication: One time
Scope: Study and assessment of the role and place of engineering industries in national and world economics over the period 1979–1986; reviews current trends and foreseeable developments in engineering industries

Fertilizer Industry

Publisher: United Nations
Frequency of Publication: Periodically
Scope: Directory of basic industrial information sources

Foundry Industry

Publisher: United Nations
Frequency of Publication: Periodically
Scope: Directory of basic industrial information sources

Glass Industry

Publisher: United Nations
Frequency of Publication: Periodically
Scope: Directory of basic industrial information sources

HTM-DB

Database Producer: EC Joint Research Center for Information Technology and Electronics, Ispra (CITE)
Distributors/Hosts: CITE
Frequency of Update: Periodically
Scope: High-temperature materials databank, combining a computerized databank and evaluation system for mechanical properties of technically relevant engineering materials

Industrial Maintenance and Repair

Publisher: United Nations
Frequency of Publication: Periodically
Scope: Directory of basic industrial information sources

Industrial Processes

Publisher: Office for Official Publications of the European Communities
Frequency of Publication: One time
Scope: Proceedings of a meeting of contractors on research and development in industrial processes; prepared by DG XII

Industrial Production—Quarterly Statistics

Publisher: Office for Official Publications of the European Communities
Frequency of Publication: 4 times a year
Scope: Statistics about production of industrial products; also available online via the Cronos database; prepared by the Statistical Office of the EC

Industrial Quality Control

Publisher: United Nations
Frequency of Publication: Periodically
Scope: Directory of basic industrial information sources

Industrial Trends—Monthly Statistics

Publisher: Office for Official Publications of the European Communities
Frequency of Publication: Monthly
Scope: Industrial activity, such as data for each industrial branch and for the industry as a whole, including indexes for the value of imports and exports in these branches; also available online via the Cronos database; prepared by the Statistical Office of the EC

Needs for Strategic R&D in Support of Improved Energy Efficiency in the Processing Industries

Publisher: Office for Official Publications of the European Communities
Frequency of Publication: One time
Scope: Summary of views of research experts on energy efficiency in the processing industries

Panorama of EC Industry

Publisher: Office for Official Publications of the European Communities

Frequency of Publication: Annual

Scope: Description of 165 manufacturing and service industries, including the metal goods, glass and ceramic goods industries, plus evaluations of the impact of the Single Market Program

Progress in Structural Reform

Publisher: OECD

Frequency of Publication: Periodically

Scope: Review of economic activities of all OECD members, as well as EC specifically, in areas including financial markets, investment, taxation, competition policy, trade, agriculture, industrial policy, and labor markets; a supplement to selected issues of OECD's *Economic Outlook*

The Rules Governing Medicinal Products in the European Community

Publisher: Office for Official Publications of the European Communities

Frequency of Publication: One time

Scope: Five volumes of rules dealing with manufacturing, testing, and marketing authorization for medicinal products (human and veterinary) in the Member States of the EC

Structure and Activity of Industry—Annual Inquiry

Publisher: Office for Official Publications of the European Communities

Frequency of Publication: Annual

Scope: Industrial census of the EC; regional data volumes also available; prepared by the Statistical Office of the EC

Related Topics and Industries

Manufacturing; Natural Resources. See also *Part III—Sources on EC 1992 by Topic*

Manufacturing

Sections in This Chapter

Computers

Electrical and Electronics Equipment

Textiles

Tools and Machine Tools

Other Manufacturing Industries

Assistance

Appendix D contains a list of the Single Market measures dealing with manufacturing. For additional help on using the resources in this chapter, refer to the Introduction to Part IV.

COMPUTERS

EC Contacts

Table 34.1 lists official European Community directorates and subdirectorates that provide information about computers. For the complete address of the Commission of the European Communities headquarters (CEC HQ in the table), refer to the Introduction to Part IV.

European Parliament

▲ Committee on Energy, Research, and Technology

Address: Palais de l'Europe
F-67006 Strasbourg Cedex
France
Telephone: 88/374 001; 88/375 485
Fax: 88/369 214; 88/256 516

Address: Centre Europeen
Plateau du Kirchberg
L-2929 Luxembourg
Telephone: 430 01
Telex: 3493 EUPARL LU; 2894 EUPARL LU
Fax: 436 972; 435 359

Associations

▲ ECMA (European Computer Manufacturers Association)

Address: rue du Rhone 114
CH-1204 Geneve
Switzerland
Telephone: 22/35 36 34
Telex: 413237
Fax: 22/786 52 31

▲ EUROBIT (European Association of Manufacturers of Business Machines and Data Processing Equipment)

Address: P.O. Box 710109
Lyoner Str. 28
D-6000 Frankfurt am Main 71
Germany

Data Resources and Publications

Engineering Industries and Automation

Publisher: United Nations Economic Commission for Europe
Frequency of Publication: Annual
Scope: Report of general developments of engineering industries, including computer, telecommunications, machine tool, industrial robot, and automotive industries; includes data on trade in engineering products

Information, Computer, and Communications Policy: The Internationalization of Software and Computer Services

Publisher: OECD
Frequency of Publication: One time
Scope: Review of policy options for dealing with the use of similar computer services and software throughout the world

Table 34.1
CEC Subdirectorates—Computers

Directorate and Subdirectorate Name	Directorate/ Subdirectorate Number	Directorate-General	Address
Information Technology and Esprit			
Computer Integrated Manufacturing	A/6	XIII	CEC HQ, Belgium Telephone: 2/235 24 48

Panorama of EC Industry

Publisher: Office for Official Publications of the European Communities

Frequency: Annual

Scope: Description of 165 manufacturing and service industries, including the computer and office equipment industry, software and computing services, plus evaluations of the impact of the Single Market Program

Related Topics and Industries

Communications and Information; Industrial Products. See also *Part III—Sources on EC 1992 by Topics*

ELECTRICAL AND ELECTRONICS EQUIPMENT

EC Contacts

Table 34.2 lists official European Community directorates and subdirectorates that provide information about electrical and electronics equipment. For the complete address of the Commission of the European Communities headquarters (CEC HQ in the table), refer to the Introduction to Part IV.

▲ Joint Research Centre

Centre for Information Technologies and Electronics

DG XII: Science, Research and Development

Address: I-21020 Ispra (VA)
Italy

Telephone: 332/78 91 11

Telex: 380042/380058/324878/324880 EUR I

Fax: 332/78 90 45

Associations

▲ CAPIEL (Coordinating Committee for Common Market Associations of Manufacturers of Electrical Switchgear and Controlgear)

Address: 11, rue Hamelin
F-75783 Paris Cedex 16
France

Telephone: 1/45 05 70 70

Telex: 611045 SYCEL F

Fax: 1/47 04 68 57

Table 34.2
CEC Subdirectorates—Electrical and Electronics Equipment

Directorate and Subdirectorate Name	Directorate/ Subdirectorate Number	Directorate- General	Address
Restrictive Practices, Abuse of Dominant Positions, and Other Distortions of Competition I			
Electrical and Electronic Manufactured Products, Information Industries, and Telecommunications	B/1	IV	CEC HQ, Belgium
Information Technology and Esprit			
Microelectronics	A/3	XIII	CEC HQ, Belgium Telephone: 2/235 24 48

▲ CECED (European Committee of Manufacturers of Electrical Domestic Equipment)

Address: Leicester House
8 Leicester Street
GB-London WC2H 7BN
Great Britain
Telephone: 071/437 0678
Telex: 253536 g
Fax: 71/494 1094

▲ ECTEL (European Telecommunications and Professional Electronics Industry)

Address: Secretary General
c/o ZVEI
Stresemannallee 19
Postfach 70 09 69
D-6000 Frankfurt/Main 70
Germany

▲ EECA (European Electronic Component Manufacturers Association)

Address: av. Louis 430 (Bte 12)
B-1050 Bruxelles
Belgium
Telephone: 2/647 50 11

▲ EUROCAE (European Organisation for Civil Aviation Electronics)

Address: 11, rue Hamelin
F-75783 Paris Cedex 16
France
Telephone: 1/45 05 71 88
Telex: 611045 SYCELEC F
Fax: 1/45 53 03 93

Data Resources and Publications

Electronic Industry

Publisher: United Nations
Frequency of Publication: Periodically
Scope: Directory of basic industrial information sources

Government Policies and the Diffusion of Microelectronics

Publisher: OECD
Frequency of Publication: One time
Scope: Summary of policies of OECD members toward research and development activities in microelectronics industry

Green Paper on the Development of the Common Market for Telecommunications Services and Equipment

Publisher: Office for Official Publications of the European Communities
Frequency of Publication: One time
Scope: Analysis of policy options for the telecommunications services and equipment industries

Panorama of EC Industry

Publisher: Office for Official Publications of the European Communities
Frequency: Annual
Scope: Description of 165 manufacturing and service industries, including electrical and electronic engineering equipment industries, plus evaluations of the impact of the Single Market Program

Research on the "Cost of Non-Europe"—Technical Trade Barriers in the EC: An Illustration in Six Industries—Some Case Studies on Technical Barriers

Publisher: Office for Official Publications of the European Communities
Frequency of Publication: One time
Scope: Identification of technical trade barriers, including standards, legal requirements, testing, and certification procedures, and evaluation of their impact on the food stuffs, pharmaceuticals, automobile, building materials, telecommunications, and electrical products and machinery industries; Volume 6 of the Cecchini study on the "cost of non-Europe"

Related Topics and Industries

Communications and Information; Housing and Infrastructure; Industrial Products. See also *Part III—Sources on EC 1992 by Topic*

▼ ——————————————————————————————— ▼

TEXTILES

EC Contacts

Table 34.3 lists official European Community directorates and subdirectorates that provide information about textiles. For the complete address of the Commission of the European Communities headquarters (CEC HQ in the table), refer to the Introduction to Part IV.

European Parliament

▲ Committee on External Economic Relations

Address: 97–113, rue Belliard
B-1040 Bruxelles
Belgium
Telephone: 2/284 21 21; 2/284 27 49
Fax: 2/230 68 56; 2/231 12 57

Address: Palais de l'Europe
F-67006 Strasbourg Cedex
France
Telephone: 88/374 001; 88/374 021
Fax: 88/369 214; 88/256 516

Address: Centre Europeen
Plateau du Kirchberg
L-2929 Luxembourg
Telephone: 430 01
Telex: 3493 EUPARL LU; 2894 EUPARL LU
Fax: 436 972; 435 359

Associations

▲ AIUFFASS (International Association of Users of Yarn of Man-Made Fibres and of Natural Silk)

Address: Martelaarslaan 39
B-9000 Gent
Belgium
Telephone: 91/25 35 97
Fax: 91/23 66 42

▲ CEMATEX (European Committee of Textile Material Constructors)

Address: Kirchenweg 4
CH-8032 Zurich
Switzerland
Telephone: 1/384 48 44
Telex: 816519 VSM CH
Fax: 1/384 48 48

▲ CICL (International Linen and Hemp Confederation)

Address: 27, bd. Malesherbes
F-75008 Paris
France
Telephone: 1/42 65 88 52
Telex: 290772 PUBLIN F
Fax: 1/42 65 51 15

Table 34.3
CEC Subdirectorates—Textiles

Directorate and Subdirectorate Name	Directorate/ Subdirectorate Number	Directorate-General	Address
Internal Market and Industrial Affairs II			
Textiles and Clothing	C/3	III	CEC HQ, Belgium Telephone: 2/236 30 12
Restrictive Practices, Abuse of Dominant Positions and Other Distortions of Competition I			
Mechanical Manufactured Products and the Textile, Clothing, Leather, and Other Manufacturing Industries	B/2	IV	CEC HQ, Belgium

▲ CIRFS (International Rayon and Synthetic Fibres Committee)

Address: 25, rue de Maubeuge
             F-75009 Paris
             France
Telephone: 1/42 81 97 62
Telex: 282591 F
Fax: 1/42 81 97 63

▲ COMITEXTIL (Coordination Committee for the Textile Industries in the EEC)

Address: rue Montoyer 24
             B-1040 Bruxelles
             Belgium
Telephone: 2/230 95 80
Telex: 22380 EURTEX B
Fax: 2/230 60 54

▲ EATP (European Association for Textile Polyolefins)

Address: 29, rue de Courcelles
             F-75008 Paris
             France
Telephone: 1/42 56 27 76
Telex: 650931 CIRFS F
Fax: 1/42 89 23 12

▲ EUROCOTON (Committee of the Cotton and Allied Textile Industries of the EEC)

Address: rue Montoyer 24
             B-1040 Bruxelles
             Belgium
Telephone: 2/230 32 39
Telex: 22380 B
Fax: 2/230 36 22

▲ European Trade Union Committee: Textiles, Clothing and Leather

Address: rue Joseph Stevens 8
             B-1000 Bruxelles
             Belgium
Telephone: 2/511 54 77
Fax: 2/511 09 04

▲ INTERLAINE (Committee of the Wool Textile Industry in the EEC)

Address: rue de Luxembourg 19 (Bte 14)
             B-1040 Bruxelles
             Belgium
Telephone: 2/513 06 20
Telex: 26885 WOOL B
Fax: 2/514 06 65

▲ International Textile Manufacturers Federation

Address: Am Schanzengraben 29
             CH-8039 Zurich
             Switzerland
Telephone: 1/2017080 or 2017747
Telex: 56798
Fax: 1/2017134

▲ MAILLEUROP (Committee for the Knitting Industries in the EEC)

Address: rue Montoyer 24
             B-1040 Bruxelles
             Belgium
Telephone: 2/230 91 27
Telex: 22380 EURTEX B
Fax: 2/230 86 69

Data Resources and Publications

Panorama of EC Industry

Publisher: Office for Official Publications of the European Communities
Frequency of Publication: Annual
Scope: Description of 165 manufacturing and service industries, including the textile industry, plus evaluations of the impact of the Single Market Program

Research on the "Cost of Non-Europe"—The Cost of Non-Europe in the Textile and Clothing Industry

Publisher: Office for Official Publications of the European Communities
Frequency of Publication: One time
Scope: Review of intra-EC trade, prices and consumption patterns, as well as barriers facing these industries and probable benefits of their elimination; Volume 14 of the Cecchini study on the "cost of non-Europe"

▼ ▼

Related Topics and Industries

Consumer Products and Services; Industrial Products.
See also *Part III—Sources on EC 1992 by Topic*

▼

TOOLS AND MACHINE TOOLS

EC Contacts

Table 34.4 lists official European Community directorates and subdirectorates that provide information about tools and machine tools. For the complete address of the Commission of the European Communities headquarters (CEC HQ in the table), refer to the Introduction to Part IV.

Commission of the European Communities
▲ Business Statistics/Industry

Directorate D/2
Statistical Office

Address: Batiment Jean Monnet
               rue Alcide de Gasperi
               L-2920 Luxembourg
Telephone: 430 11
Telex: 3423/3446/3476 COMEUR LU

Associations

▲ CECIMO (European Committee for Cooperation of the Machine Tool Industries)

Address: rue des Drapiers 21
               B-1050 Bruxelles
               Belgium
Telephone: 2/510 23 50
Telex: 21078 B
Fax: 2/510 23 01

▲ CEI-BOIS (European Confederation of Woodworking Industries)

Address: rue Royale 109–111
               B-1000 Bruxelles
               Belgium
Telephone: 2/217 63 65
Telex: 64143 B
Fax: 2/217 59 04

Table 34.4
CEC Subdirectorates—Tools and Machine Tools

Directorate and Subdirectorate Name	Directorate/ Subdirectorate Number	Directorate- General	Address
Internal Market and Industrial Affairs II			
Shipbuilding, Wood, Leather, Paper, and Miscellaneous Industries	C/4	III	CEC HQ, Belgium Telephone: 2/236 30 12
Restrictive Practices, Abuse of Dominant Positions, and Other Distortions of Competition I			
Electrical and Electronic Manufactured Products, Information Industries, and Telecommunications	B/1	IV	CEC HQ, Belgium
Mechanical Manufactured Products and the Textile, Clothing, Leather, and Other Manufacturing Industries	B/2	IV	CEC HQ, Belgium

▲ CEMA (European Committee of Agricultural Machine Builders)

Address: 19, rue Jacques Bingen
             F-75017 Paris
             France
Telephone: 1/47 66 02 20
Telex: 640362 F
Fax: 1/40 54 95 60

▲ CEMAFON (European Committee for Materials and Products for Foundries)

Address: Lyoner Strasse 18
             D-6000 Frankfurt/Main 71
             Germany
Telephone: 69/660 34 13
Telex: 411321 D
Fax: 69/660 35 11

▲ CEMATEX (European Committee of Textile Material Constructors)

Address: Kirchenweg 4
             CH-8032 Zurich
             Switzerland
Telephone: 1/384 48 44
Telex: 816519 VSM CH
Fax: 1/384 48 48

▲ CEO (European Tool Committee)

Address: Elberfelder Strasse 77
             Postfach 100360
             D-5630 Remscheid
             Germany
Telephone: 2191/438 20
Telex: 8513802 INDU D
Fax: 2191/438 79

▲ CEOAH (European Committee for Agricultural and Horticultural Tools and Implements)

Address: 16, av. Hoche
             F-75008 Paris
             France
Telephone: 1/45 63 93 23
Telex: 280900 FEDEMEC F
Fax: 1/45 63 59 86

▲ CEPAC (European Confederation of Pulp, Paper and Board Industries)

Address: rue Defacqz 1
             B-1050 Bruxelles
             Belgium
Telephone: 2/534 10 10
Telex: 65080 INAC B
Fax: 2/534 14 24

▲ CITPA (International Committee of Paper and Board Converters in the Common Market)

Address: Arndstrasse 47
             D-6000 Frankfurt 1
             Germany
Telephone: 69/74 03 11
Telex: 411925 D
Fax: 69/74 77 14

▲ CLEDIPA (Liaison Committee for European Manufacturers of Automobile Equipment)

Address: bd. de la Woluwe 46 (Bte 9)
             B-1200 Bruxelles
             Belgium
Telephone: 2/771 00 80
Fax: 2/771 16 55

▲ COMEL (Coordinating Committee for Common Market Associations of Manufacturers of Rotating Electrical Machinery)

Address: Leicester House
             8 Leicester Street
             GB-London WC2H 7BN
             Great Britain
Telephone: 71/437 0678
Telex: 263536 G
Fax: 71/437 4901

▲ CPIV (Standing Committee of the EC Glass Industries)

Address: av. Louise 89
             B-1050 Bruxelles
             Belgium
Telephone: 2/538 44 46
Telex: 25694 CPIV B
Fax: 2/537 84 69

▲ ECTA (European Cutting Tools Association)

Address: Light Trades House
Melbourne Avenue
GB-Sheffield S10 2QJ
Great Britain
Telephone: 742/663 084
Telex: 547676 G
Fax: 742/670 910

▲ EFCEM (European Federation of Catering
Equipment Manufacturers)

Address: 10, av. Hoche
F-75008 Paris
France
Telephone: 1/45 63 02 00
Telex: 643996 F
Fax: 1/45 63 59 86

▲ ELMO (European Laundry and Dry Cleaning
Machinery Manufacturers Organization)

Address: Lyoner Strasse 18
D-6000 Frankfurt/Main
Germany
Telephone: 69/66 03 271
Telex: 411321 D
Fax: 69/66 03 511

▲ EPTA (European Power Tool Association)

Address: Leuschnerstrasse 41–47
Postfach 101444
D-7000 Stuttgart 1
Germany
Telephone: 711/66 65 0
Telex: 722057 D
Fax: 711/66 65 249

▲ EUMAPRINT (European Committee of
Printing and Paper Converting Machinery
Manufacturers)

Address: 1899 Preston White Drive
Reston VA 22091
USA
Telephone: 703/264-7200
Telex: 901753
Fax: 703/620-0994

▲ EUROCLAMP (European Clamping Tools
Association)

Address: Lyoner Strasse 18
D-6000 Frankfurt 71
Germany
Telephone: 69/60 03 251
Telex: 411321 VDMA D
Fax: 69/66 03 511

▲ EUROFORGE (Liaison Committee for the
European Stamping and Forging Industries)

Address: Goldene Pforte 1
D-5800 Hagen
Germany
Telephone: 2331/51041
Telex: 823806 d
Fax: 2331/51046

▲ EUROMAP (European Committee of Builders
of Machinery for Plastics and India Rubber)

Address: 5, Belgrave Square
GB-London SW1X 8PD
Great Britain
Telephone: 71/235 9483
Telex: 8951528 PLAFED G
Fax: 71/235 8045

▲ EWA (European Welding Association)

Address: Wassenaarseweg 80
NL-2596 CZ Den Haag
The Netherlands
Telephone: 70/36 23 41
Telex: 32576 ECON NL
Fax: 70/34 51 18

▲ International Tube Association

Address: P.O. Box 84
Leamington Spa
GB-Warwickshire CV32 5FX
Great Britain
Telephone: 926/34 137
Telex: 312548 INTRAS G
Fax: 926/314 755

▲ ISTA (International Special Tooling Association)

Address: Lyoner Strasse 18
             Postfach 710864
             D-6000 Frankfurt 71
             Germany
Telephone: 69/660 32 51
Telex: 411321 D
Fax: 69/660 35 11

▲ Liaison Committee of the European Community Steel Tube Industry

Address: 25, rue d'Astorg
             F-75008 Paris
             France
Telephone: 1/42 66 93 70
Telex: 290319 TELPA F
Fax: 1/42 66 94 21

▲ PNEUROP (European Committee of Manufacturers of Compressors, Vacuum Pumps, and Pneumatic Tools)

Address: Leicester House
             8, Leicester Street
             GB-London WC2H 7BN
             Great Britain
Telephone: 71/437 0678
Telex: 263536 G
Fax: 71/437 4901

Data Resources and Publications

Earnings: Industry and Services

Publisher: Office for Official Publications of the European Communities
Frequency: 2 times a year
Scope: Reports on earnings of manual and nonmanual workers in industry and certain groups of activities in the service sector; also available online via the Cronos database; prepared by the Statistical Office of the EC   ⊛

Engineering Industries and Automation

Publisher: United Nations Economic Commission for Europe
Frequency of Publication: Annual
Scope: General developments of engineering industries, including computer, telecommunications, machine tool, industrial robot, and automotive industries; includes data on trade in engineering products

Panorama of EC Industry

Publisher: Office for Official Publications of the European Communities
Frequency: Annual
Scope: Description of 165 manufacturing and service industries, including tool and machine tool industries, plus evaluations of the impact of the Single Market Program

The Pulp and Paper Industry in OECD Member Countries

Publisher: OECD
Frequency: Annual
Scope: Production and consumption of pulp and paper products, capacity and utilization, and foreign trade

Woodworking Industry Machinery

Publisher: United Nations
Frequency of Publication: Periodically
Scope: Directory of basic industrial information sources

Related Topics and Industries

Industrial Products; Manufacturing. See also Part III— Sources on EC 1992 by Topic

▼ ▼

OTHER MANUFACTURING INDUSTRIES

EC Contacts

Table 34.5 lists official European Community directorates and subdirectorates that provide information about other manufacturing industries. For the complete address of the Commission of the European Communities headquarters (CEC HQ in the table), refer to the Introduction to Part IV.

Commission of the European Communities
▲ Business Statistics/Industry

Directorate D/2
Statistical Office

Address: Batiment Jean Monnet
rue Alcide de Gasperi
L-2920 Luxembourg
Telephone: 430 11
Telex: 3423/3446/3476 COMEUR LU

Associations

▲ AEGRAFLEX (Association of Rubber Stamp Manufacturers)

Address: Postfach 1869
Biebricher Allee 79
D-6200 Wiesbaden 1
Germany
Telephone: 6121/80 31 15
Telex: 4186888 BVD D
Fax: 6121/80 31 13

▲ CECOF (European Committee of Industrial Furnace and Heating Equipment Associations)

Address: Lyoner Strasse 18
D-6000 Frankfurt/Main 71
Germany
Telephone: 69/66 03 413
Telex: 411321 D
Fax: 69/66 03 511

Table 34.5
CEC Subdirectorates—Other Manufacturing Industries

Directorate and Subdirectorate Name	Directorate/ Subdirectorate Number	Directorate- General	Address
Internal Market and Industrial Affairs I			
Pharmaceuticals and Veterinary Medicines	B/6	III	CEC HQ, Belgium Telephone: 2/236 30 12
Internal Market and Industrial Affairs II			
Shipbuilding, Wood, Leather, Paper, and Miscellaneous Industries	C/4	III	CEC HQ, Belgium Telephone: 2/236 30 12
Restrictive Practices, Abuse of Dominant Positions, and Other Distortions of Competition I			
Mechanical Manufactured Products and the Textile, Clothing, Leather, and Other Manufacturing Industries	B/2	IV	CEC HQ, Belgium

▲ CECOMAF (European Committee of Manufacturers of Refrigeration Equipment)

Address: rue des Drapiers 21
B-1050 Bruxelles
Belgium
Telephone: 2/510 23 11
Telex: 21078 B
Fax: 2/510 23 01

▲ CEMAFON (European Committee for
Materials and Products for Foundries)

Address: Lyoner Strasse 18
D-6000 Frankfurt/Main 71
Germany
Telephone: 69/660 34 13
Telex: 411321 D
Fax: 69/660 35 11

▲ EFCEM (European Federation of Catering
Equipment Manufacturers)

Address: 10, av. Hoche
F-75008 Paris
France
Telephone: 1/45 63 02 00
Telex: 643996 F
Fax: 1/45 63 59 86

▲ ELMO (European Laundry and Dry Cleaning
Machinery Manufacturers Organization)

Address: Lyoner Strasse 18
D-6000 Frankfurt/Main
Germany
Telephone: 69/66 03 271
Telex: 411321 D
Fax: 69/66 03 511

▲ EPDCC (European Pressure Die Casting
Committee)

Address: 42, Weymouth Street
GB-London W1N 3LQ
Great Britain
Telephone: 71/499 6636
Telex: 261286 G
Fax: 71/493 1555

▲ EUROPUMP (European Committee of Pump
Manufacturers)

Address: Artillery House
Artillery Row
GB-London SW1P 1RT
Great Britain
Telephone: 71/222 0830
Telex: 8812939 G
Fax: 71/799 1852

▲ EUROTRANS (European Committee of
Associations of Manufacturers of Gears and
Transmission Parts)

Address: 162, bd. Malesherbes
F-75017 Paris
France
Telephone: 1/43 80 04 09
Telex: 643788 F
Fax: 1/40 54 82 95

▲ EWA (European Welding Association)

Address: Wassenaarseweg 80
NL-2596 CZ Den Haag
The Netherlands
Telephone: 70/36 23 41
Telex: 32576 ECON NL
Fax: 70/34 51 18

▲ FEMB (European Federation of Office Furniture)

Address: 4, place Valois
F-75001 Paris
France
Telephone: 1/42 86 81 89
Fax: 1/42 86 82 65

▲ International Liaison Committee for the
Manufacturers and Restorers of Agricultural
Machinery

Address: Wilhelminalaan 1
NL-3732 GJ De Bilt
The Netherlands
Telephone: 30/20 48 11
Telex: 76231 MU NL
Fax: 30/20 48 99

▲ **International Tube Association**

Address: P.O. Box 84
Leamington Spa
GB-Warwickshire CV32 5FX
Great Britain
Telephone: 926/341 37
Telex: 312548 INTRAS G
Fax: 926/314 755

▲ **International Wrought Copper Council**

Address: 6 Bathurst Street
Sussex Square
GB-London W2 2SD
Great Britain
Telephone: 71/723 7465
Telex: 23556
Fax: 71/724 0308

▲ **PNEUROP (European Committee of Manufacturers of Compressors, Vacuum Pumps and Pneumatic Tools)**

Address: Leicester House
8, Leicester Street
GB-London WC2H 7BN
Great Britain
Telephone: 71/437 0678
Telex: 263536 G
Fax: 71/437 4901

Data Resources and Publications

Agricultural Implements and Machinery Industry

Publisher: United Nations
Frequency of Publication: Periodically
Scope: Directory of basic industrial information sources

Bulletin of Statistics on World Trade in Engineering Products

Publisher: United Nations and the United Nations Economic Commission for Europe
Frequency of Publication: Annual
Scope: Statistics about the flow of machinery, transport, scientific, medical, optical and measuring equipment, watches, and clocks

Earnings: Industry and Services

Publisher: Office for Official Publications of the European Communities
Frequency of Publication: 2 times a year
Scope: Reports on earnings of manual and nonmanual workers in industry and certain groups of activities in the service sector; also available online via the Cronos database; prepared by the Statistical Office of the EC

Engineering Industries: Dynamics of the Eighties

Publisher: United Nations Economic Commission for Europe
Frequency of Publication: One time
Scope: Study and assessment of the role and place of engineering industries in national and world economics over the period 1979–1986; review of current trends and foreseeable developments in engineering industries

Furniture and Joinery Industry

Publisher: United Nations
Frequency of Publication: Periodically
Scope: Directory of basic industrial information sources

Industrial Quality Control

Publisher: United Nations
Frequency of Publication: Periodically
Scope: Directory of basic industrial information sources

Packaging Industry

Publisher: United Nations
Frequency of Publication: Periodically
Scope: Directory of basic industrial information sources

Printing and Graphic Industry

Publisher: United Nations
Frequency of Publication: Periodically
Scope: Directory of basic industrial information sources

Utilization of Agricultural Residues for the Production of Panels, Pulp, and Paper

Publisher: United Nations
Frequency of Publication: Periodically
Scope: Directory of basic industrial information sources

Related Topics and Industries

Industrial Products; Natural Resources. See also *Part III—Sources on EC 1992 by Topic*

35 Natural Resources

ASSISTANCE

Appendix D contains a list of the Single Market measures dealing with natural resources. For additional help on using the resources in this chapter, refer to the Introduction to Part IV.

COMMODITIES AND RAW MATERIALS

EC Contacts

Table 35.1 lists official European Community directorates and subdirectorates that provide information about commodities and raw materials. For the complete address of the Commission of the European Communities headquarters (CEC HQ in the table), refer to the Introduction to Part IV.

Commission of the European Communities
▲ Statistical Office

Directorate D/3—Business Statistics/Iron and Steel

Address: Batiment Jean Monnet
rue Alcide de Gasperi
L-2920 Luxembourg
Telephone: 430 11
Telex: 3423/3446/3476 COMEUR LU

European Parliament
▲ Committee on Agriculture, Fisheries, and Rural Development

Address: 97–113, rue Belliard
B-1040 Bruxelles
Belgium
Telephone: 2/284 21 21; 2/284 28 08
Fax: 2/230 68 56; 2/231 12 57

Address: Palais de l'Europe
F-67006 Strasbourg Cedex
France
Telephone: 88/374 001; 88/374 589; 88/374 554
Fax: 88/369 214; 88/256 516

Address: Centre Europeen
Plateau du Kirchberg
L-2929 Luxembourg
Telephone: 430 01
Telex: 3493 EUPARL LU; 2894 EUPARL LU
Fax: 436 972; 435 359

Associations

▲ AFG (Association of the Glucose Producers in the EC)

Address: av. de la Joyeuse Entree 1 (Bte 10)
B-1040 Bruxelles
Belgium
Telephone: 2/230 20 31
Telex: 22283 AACCEE B
Fax: 2/230 02 45

▲ AIA/EAC (European Advisory Council of the Asbestos International Association)

Address: bd. E. Jacqmain 162 (Bte 32)
B-1210 Bruxelles
Belgium
Telephone: 2/218 63 29
Telex: 21696 B
Fax: 2/219 69 08

▲ ANGO (Association of Animal and Vegetable Fat and Oil Traders)

Address: rue Belliard 197 (Bte 6)
B-1040 Bruxelles
Belgium
Telephone: 2/230 61 70
Telex: 26047 B
Fax: 2/230 30 63

▲ API (Association of Producers of Isoglucose of the EC)

Address: av. de la Joyeuse Entree 1 (Bte 10)
B-1040 Bruxelles
Belgium
Telephone: 2/230 20 31
Telex: 22283 AACCEE B
Fax: 2/230 02 45

▲ ASSUC (Association of Organizations of Sugar Traders of the European Economic Community)

Address: av. de la Brabanconne 18 (Bte 8)
B-1040 Bruxelles
Belgium
Telephone: 2/736 15 84
Telex: 24395 SACAR B
Fax: 2/734 87 71

Table 35.1
CEC Subdirectorates—Commodities and Raw Materials

Directorate and Subdirectorate Name	Directorate/ Subdirectorate Number	Directorate-General	Address
Industrial Economy, Service Industries, Non-Member Countries, Raw Materials			
Raw Materials	A/5	III	CEC HQ, Belgium Telephone: 2/236 30 12
Internal Market and Industrial Affairs II			
Shipbuilding, Wood, Leather, Paper, and Miscellaneous Industries	C/4	III	CEC HQ, Belgium Telephone: 2/236 30 12
Chemicals, Plastics, and Rubber	C/5	III	CEC HQ, Belgium Telephone: 2/236 30 12
Restrictive Practices, Abuse of Dominant Positions, and Other Distortions of Competition I			
Mechanical Manufactured Products, and the Textile, Clothing, Leather, and Other Manufacturing Industries	B/2	IV	CEC HQ, Belgium
Restrictive Practices, Abuse of Dominant Positions, and Other Distortions of Competition II			
Non-ferrous Metals, Non-metallic Mineral Products, Construction, Timber, Paper, Glass, and Rubber Industries	C/1	IV	CEC HQ, Belgium
Restrictive Practices, Abuse of Dominant Positions, and Other Distortions of Competition III			
Steel and Coal	D/1	IV	CEC HQ, Belgium
Employment			
ECSC Readaptation and Social Aspects of Iron and Steel Policies	A/3	V	CEC HQ, Belgium
Health and Safety			
Mines and Other Extractive Industries	D/4	V	CEC HQ, Belgium
Technological Research			
Mineral Raw Materials	C/5	XII	CEC HQ, Belgium

Biology

Renewable Raw Materials [Timber]	F/5	XII	CEC HQ, Belgium
Markets and External Resources {Fisheries}	A	XIV	CEC HQ, Belgium
Internal Resources and Monitoring {Fisheries}	B	XIV	CEC HQ, Belgium

▲ CAEC (Committee of Associations of European Coffee Importers)

Address: Artillery House
Artillery Row
Westminster
GB-London SW1P 1RY
Great Britain
Telephone: 71/222 0940
Telex: 8812923 COMMET G
Fax: 71/799 1852

▲ CELCAA (European Liaison Committee of Agricultural Commodities)

Address: rond-point Schuman 9 (Bte 4)
B-1040 Bruxelles
Belgium
Telephone: 2/230 99 70
Telex: 61177 ASSCIM B
Fax: 2/230 43 23

▲ CEPAC (European Confederation of Pulp, Paper, and Board Industries)

Address: rue Defacqz 1
B-1050 Bruxelles
Belgium
Telephone: 2/534 10 10
Telex: 65080 INAC B
Fax: 2/534 14 24

▲ CIPF (EEC Standing Committee of the International Straw, Fodder, and Peat Trade Confederation)

Address: Bureau 286
Bourse de Commerce
2, rue de Viarmes
F-75040 Paris Cedex 01
France
Telephone: 1/42 36 84 35
Telex: 790484 F
Fax: 1/45 21 04 09

▲ Contact Office—Inter Trade Union of Miners' and Metalworkers' Free Trade Unions in the European Communities

Address: rue de Moniteur 18
B-1000 Bruxelles
Belgium
Telephone: 2/218 37 93

▲ COSEMCO (Seed Committee of the Common Market)

Address: av. de la Joyeuse Entree 1–5 (Bte 19)
B-1040 Bruxelles
Belgium
Telephone: 2/231 03 71
Telex: 64518 COSMEC B
Fax: 2/230 22 40

▲ ECCTO (The European Community Cocoa Trade Organisation)

Address: Commodity Quay
St. Katherine Docks
GB-London E1 9AX
Great Britain
Telephone: 71/481 2980
Telex: 884370 G

▲ EFAPIT (Euromarket Federation of Animal Protein Importers and Traders)

Address: Adolphsplatz 1
Borse-Kontor 24
D-2000 Hamburg 11
Germany
Telephone: 40/36 20 25
Telex: 17403968 D
Fax: 40/36 20 29

▼ ━━━ ▼

▲ ELDEC (European Lead Development Committee)

Address: 42, Weymouth Street
GB-London W1N 3LQ
Great Britain
Telephone: 71/499 8422
Telex: 261286 G
Fax: 71/493 1555

▲ EUCOFEL (European Commercial Union for Importing and Exporting Fruit and Beans)

Address: av. de la Brabanconne 18 (Bte 8)
B-1040 Bruxelles
Belgium
Telephone: 2/736 15 84
Telex: 24395 B
Fax: 2/734 87 71

▲ EUROGYPSUM (Working Community of the European Gypsum Industry)

Address: 3, rue Alfred Roll
F-75849 Paris Cedex 17
France
Telephone: 1/47 66 03 64
Telex: 641394 F
Fax: 1/40 54 03 28

▲ European Trade Union Committee: Textiles, Clothing, and Leather

Address: rue Joseph Stevens 8
B-1000 Bruxelles
Belgium
Telephone: 2/511 54 77
Fax: 2/511 09 04

▲ European Union of Hop Merchants

Address: Hauptplatz 14/1
D-8068 Pfaffenhofen/Ilm
Germany
Telephone: 8441/6035
Telex: 55562 RAKHKV D
Fax: 8441/3915

▲ FEB (European Timber Association)

Address: Rostocker Strasse 16
Postfach 1867
D-6200 Wiesbaden
Germany
Telephone: 6121/50 20 91
Telex: 4186515 D
Fax: 6121/50 96 12

▲ Federation of Commodity Associations

Address: 1, Commodity Quay
St. Katherine Docks
GB-London E1 9AX
Great Britain
Telephone: 71/481 2080
Telex: 884370 G
Fax: 71/702 9924

▲ FIPA (International Federation of Agricultural Producers)

Address: 1, rue d'Hauteville
F-75010 Paris
France
Telephone: 1/42 46 94 55
Telex: 287120 CHAMBAG F
Fax: 1/48 00 94 85

▲ UCBT (Union of Timber Importers)

Address: rue Royale 109
B-1000 Bruxelles
Belgium
Telephone: 2/219 43 73
Fax: 2/217 30 03

▲ UCEPCEE (Union of Fertilizer Traders)

Address: Luikersteenweg 37
B-3500 Hasselt
Belgium
Telephone: 11/22 30 98
Fax: 11/22 35 69

Data Resources and Publications

Agricultural Policies, Markets and Trade
Publisher: OECD
Frequency of Publication: Annual
Scope: Agricultural policies, markets, and trade in OECD member countries

Agricultural Review for Europe—Vol. II: Agricultural Trade
Publisher: United Nations and the United Nations Economic Commission for Europe
Frequency of Publication: Annual
Scope: Recent developments in agricultural trade in Europe, including the quality of agricultural and food products and trade flows

The Agricultural Situation in the Community

Publisher: Office for Official Publications of the European Communities

Frequency of Publication: Annual

Scope: Overview of the structure of agricultural markets, status of the Common Agricultural Policy, and market outlook for agricultural products

Animal Production

Publisher: Office for Official Publications of the European Communities

Frequency of Publication: 4 times a year

Scope: Statistics about animal production, including meat, milk, poultry, and egg products; also available online via the Cronos database; prepared by the Statistical Office of the EC ⊛

Coffee, Cocoa, Tea, and Spices Industry

Publisher: United Nations

Frequency of Publication: Regularly updated

Scope: Directory of basic industrial information sources

Crop Production

Publisher: Office for Official Publications of the European Communities

Frequency of Publication: 4 times a year

Scope: Updated data on land use, arable crops, and fruit and vegetable production; also available online via the Cronos database; prepared by the Statistical Office of the EC ⊛

EC Agricultural Price Indices: Monthly Results/ Half Yearly Statistics

Publisher: Office for Official Publications of the European Communities

Frequency of Publication: 2 times a year

Scope: Trend of monthly indexes of producer prices, agricultural inputs, and production; also available online via the Cronos database; prepared by the Statistical Office of the EC ⊛

Economic Accounts for Agriculture and Forestry—1982-1987

Publisher: Office for Official Publications of the European Communities

Frequency of Publication: One time

Scope: Aggregated data on agriculture and forestry industries

Natural and Synthetic Rubber

Publisher: United Nations

Frequency of Publication: Regularly updated

Scope: Directory of basic industrial information sources

Panorama of EC Industry

Publisher: Office for Official Publications of the European Communities

Frequency of Publication: Annual

Scope: Description of 165 manufacturing and service industries, including the wood processing, paper, and pulp industries, plus evaluations of the impact of the Single Market Program

The Pulp and Paper Industry in OECD Member Countries

Publisher: OECD

Frequency of Publication: Annual

Scope: Updates of production and consumption of pulp and paper products, production capacity and utilization, and foreign trade

Timber Bulletin

Publisher: United Nations Economic Commission for Europe

Frequency of Publication: 9 times a year

Scope: Coverage of all aspects of the timber and forest products market in Europe, including prices, statistics, trade data, and future prospects

Related Topics and Industries

Agriculture and Food Stuffs; Industrial Products; Manufacturing. See also Part III—Sources on EC 1992 by Topic

FUELS

EC Contacts

Table 35.2 lists official European Community directorates and subdirectorates that provide information about fuels. For the complete address of the Commission of the European Communities headquarters (CEC HQ in the table), refer to the Introduction to Part IV.

▲ Euratom Supply Agency

Address: rue de la Loi 200
B-1049 Bruxelles
Belgium
Telephone: 2/235 11 11
Telex: 21877 COMEU B

European Parliament
▲ Committee on Energy, Research, and Technology

Address: Palais de l'Europe
F-67006 Strasbourg Cedex
France
Telephone: 88/374 001; 88/375 485
Fax: 88/369 214; 88/256 516

Address: Centre Europeen
Plateau du Kirchberg
L-2929 Luxembourg
Telephone: 430 01
Telex: 3493 EUPARL LU; 2894 EUPARL LU
Fax: 436 972; 435 359

European Parliament
▲ Committee on the Environment, Public Health, and Consumer Protection

Address: 97–113, rue Belliard
B-1040 Bruxelles
Belgium
Telephone: 2/284 21 21; 2/284 28 48
Fax: 2/230 68 56; 2/231 12 57

Address: Palais de l'Europe
F-67006 Strasbourg Cedex
France
Telephone: 88/374 001; 88/374 418
Fax: 88/369 214; 88/256 516

Address: Centre Europeen
Plateau du Kirchberg
L-2929 Luxembourg
Telephone: 430 01
Telex: 3493 EUPARL LU; 2894 EUPARL LU
Fax: 436 972; 435 359

Associations

▲ AEGPL (European Association of the Liquified Petroleum Gas Industry)

Address: 16, av. Kleber
F-75116 Paris
France
Telephone: 1/45 01 23 95
Fax: 1/47 47 25 42

Table 35.2
CEC Subdirectorates—Fuels

Directorate and Subdirectorate Name	Directorate/ Subdirectorate Number	Directorate-General	Address
Restrictive Practices, Abuse of Dominant Positions, and Other Distortions of Competition III			
Steel and Coal	D/1	IV	CEC HQ, Belgium
Industries and Markets I (Fossil Fuels)			
Solid Fuels	B/1	XVII	CEC HQ, Belgium Telephone: 2/236 27 99
Hydrocarbons	B/2	XVII	CEC HQ, Belgium Telephone: 2/236 27 99

▲ CEPCEO (Association of the Coal Producers of the European Community)

Address: av. de Tervueren 168 (Bte 11)
B-1150 Bruxelles
Belgium
Telephone: 2/771 99 74
Telex: 24046 CEPCEO
Fax: 2/771 41 04

▲ COMETEC-GAZ (Economic Research Committee of the Gas Industry)

Address: av. Palmerston 4
B-1040 Bruxelles
Belgium
Telephone: 2/230 43 85
Fax: 2/230 44 80

▲ MARCOGAZ (Union of the Gas Industries of the Common Market)

Address: av. Palmerston 4
B-1040 Bruxelles
Belgium
Telephone: 2/230 43 85
Fax: 2/230 44 80

▲ UPEI (Union of European Oil Independents)

Address: 10, rue de Laborde
F-75008 Paris
France
Telephone: 1/43 87 00 01
Telex: 281997 F
Fax: 1/43 87 43 46

Data Resources and Publications

Annual Bulletin of Coal Statistics for Europe and North America

Publisher: United Nations Economic Commission for Europe and the United Nations
Frequency of Publication: Annual
Scope: Yearly developments in the field of solid fuels

Annual Bulletin of Gas Statistics for Europe and North America

Publisher: United Nations Economic Commission for Europe and the United Nations
Frequency of Publication: Annual
Scope: Yearly developments and trends in consumption and production of gas

Annual Oil Market Report

Publisher: OECD
Frequency of Publication: Annual
Scope: Examination of major developments in world oil markets and also presentation of key current statistics and selected historical data on consumption, supply, stock, and prices; prepared by the IEA

Bulletin of Energy Prices

Publisher: Office for Official Publications of the European Communities
Frequency of Publication: 2 times a year
Scope: Survey of import and consumer prices for oil, coal, gas, and electricity in the EC; prepared by DG XVII

Coal Information

Publisher: OECD
Frequency of Publication: Annual
Scope: Current world coal market trends and prospects, including data on coal supply and trade, consumption, and prices; prepared by the IEA, and available in hardcopy or on microcomputer diskette

ECSC Coal Research—Annual Report

Publisher: Office for Official Publications of the European Communities
Frequency of Publication: Annual
Scope: Summary of technical coal research programs conducted during the year and sponsored by ECSC; prepared by DG XVII

Energy Statistics of OECD Countries

Publisher: OECD

Frequency of Publication: Annual

Scope: Overview of supply and use of fuels in OECD countries, including detailed data on production, trade, stock, and consumption by sector; available in hardcopy or on microcomputer diskette; prepared by the IEA ■

Euratom Supply Agency—Annual Report

Publisher: Office for Official Publications of the European Communities

Frequency of Publication: Annual

Scope: Official review of activities of EAEC for each fiscal year

Investment in the Community Coalmining and Iron and Steel Industries—Survey

Publisher: Office for Official Publications of the European Communities

Frequency of Publication: Annual

Scope: Study results of yearly actual and forecast capital expenditures of the coalmining industry, coking plants, iron-ore mines, and the iron and steel industry; also available online via the Cronos database; prepared by DG XVIII

Monthly Oil and Gas Statistics

Publisher: OECD

Frequency of Publication: Monthly

Scope: Statistical supply data for past two years for the OECD countries; available on microcomputer diskette; prepared by the IEA ■

Monthly Oil and Gas Trade Data

Publisher: OECD

Frequency of Publication: Monthly

Scope: Trade flows each month by country of origin and country of destination; complements the *Monthly Oil and Gas Statistics*; on microcomputer diskette, prepared by the IEA ■

Oil and Gas Information

Publisher: OECD

Frequency of Publication: Annual

Scope: Current world oil and gas market trends and prospects, including data on supply and trade, consumption, and prices; available in hardcopy or on microcomputer diskette; prepared by the IEA ■

Panorama of EC Industry

Publisher: Office for Official Publications of the European Communities

Frequency of Publication: Annual

Scope: Description of 165 manufacturing and service industries, including nuclear fuels, plus evaluations of the impact of the Single Market Program

Quarterly Oil Statistics and Energy Balances

Publisher: OECD

Frequency of Publication: 4 times a year

Scope: Supply and demand data on oil and gas, covering all 24 OECD countries, plus regional breakdowns, including the EC

Substitute Fuels for Road Transport: A Technology Assessment

Publisher: OECD

Frequency of Publication: One time

Scope: Assessment of the prospects of fuel that might substitute for gasoline in cars and trucks

Uranium—Resources, Production, and Demand

Publisher: OECD

Frequency of Publication: Periodically

Scope: Data summaries for uranium resources and production, plus projections of the nuclear industry's future uranium requirements; joint report of the OECD Nuclear Energy Agency and International Atomic Energy Agency

The Utilization of Solid Fuels—Catalogue of R&D Contracts 1988

Publisher: Office for Official Publications of the European Communities

Frequency of Publication: One time

Scope: Catalog of research and development contacts prepared by DG XVII

Related Topics and Industries

Energy; Industrial Products; Manufacturing. See also *Part III—Sources on EC 1992 by Topic*

IRON

EC Contacts

Table 35.3 lists official European Community directorates and subdirectorates that provide information about iron. For the complete address of the Commission of the European Communities headquarters (CEC HQ in the table), refer to the Introduction to Part IV.

Associations

▲ Club des Marchands de Fer de la CECA {Iron Merchants}

Address: rue de la Bonte 4 (Bte 1)
B-1050 Bruxelles
Belgium
Telephone: 2/053 74343

▲ Contact Office—Inter Trade Union of Miners' and Metalworkers' Free Trade Unions in the European Communities

Address: rue de Moniteur 18
B-1000 Bruxelles
Belgium
Telephone: 2/218 37 93

▲ EUROFER (European Confederation of Iron and Steel Industries)

Address: sq. de Meeus 5 (Bte 9)
B-1040 Bruxelles
Belgium
Telephone: 2/512 98 30
Telex: 62112 EURFER B
Fax: 2/512 01 46

▲ EUROMETAUX (European Association of Metals)

Address: rue Montoyer 47
B-1040 Bruxelles
Belgium
Telephone: 2/511 72 73
Telex: 22077 CNOFER B
Fax: 2/514 45 13

▲ European Independent Steelworks Association

Address: 205, rue Belliard (Bte 18)
B-1040 Bruxelles
Belgium
Telephone: 2/230 7962

▲ International Iron and Steel Institute

Address: rue Colebourg 120
B-1140 Bruxelles
Belgium
Telephone: 2/735 9075
Telex: 22639

▲ International Pig Iron Secretariat

Address: Breite Str. 69
Postfach 6709
D-4000 Dusseldorf
Germany
Telephone: 211/08 58 2286

Data Resources and Publications

Financial Report

Publisher: Office for Official Publications of the European Communities
Frequency of Publication: Annual
Scope: Review of finances and other activities of the European Coal and Steel Community

The Importance of the Iron and Steel Industry for the Economic Activity of the EC Member Countries

Publisher: United Nations Economic Commission for Europe
Frequency of Publication: One time
Scope: Description of the importance of the steel industry in the economy and of the industry's structure

Investment in the Community Coal-Mining and Iron and Steel Industries

Publisher: Office for Official Publications of the European Communities
Frequency of Publication: Annual
Scope: Actual and forecast capital expenditures of the coal mining industry, coking plants, iron-ore mines, and the iron and steel industry; also available online via the Cronos database; prepared by DG XVIII

Iron and Steel Industry

Publisher: United Nations
Frequency of Publication: Periodically
Scope: Directory of basic industrial information sources

The Iron and Steel Industry

Publisher: OECD
Frequency of Publication: Annual
Scope: Production and consumption of steel and iron

Iron and Steel—Monthly Statistics

Publisher: Office for Official Publications of the European Communities
Frequency of Publication: Monthly
Scope: Employment, consumption of raw materials, production of iron ore, pig iron, crude steel, finished steel products, and end products; also available online via the Cronos database; prepared by Statistical Office of the EC

Iron and Steel—Statistical Yearbook

Publisher: Office for Official Publications of the European Communities
Frequency of Publication: Annual
Scope: Statistics on the structure and economic situations of the EC's iron and steel industry; prepared by the Statistical Office of the EC

Panorama of EC Industry

Publisher: Office for Official Publications of the European Communities
Frequency of Publication: Annual
Scope: Description of 165 manufacturing and service industries, including the iron and steel industry, plus evaluations of the impact of the Single Market Program

The Role of Technology in Iron and Steel Developments

Publisher: OECD
Frequency of Publication: One time
Scope: Study on the impact of technology on the iron and steel industries of OECD member countries

Related Topics and Industries

Industrial Products; Manufacturing. See also *Part III—Sources on EC 1992 by Topic*

Table 35.3
CEC Subdirectorates—Iron

Directorate and Subdirectorate Name	Directorate/ Subdirectorate Number	Directorate-General	Address
Employment			
ECSC Readaptation and Social Aspects of Iron and Steel Policies	A/3	V	CEC HQ, Belgium

MINERALS

Associations

▲ Bismuth Institute Information Centre

Address: 47 Rue de Ligne
B-1000 Bruxelles
Belgium
Telephone: 2/218 6040
Telex: 62162 BISMUT

▲ Cadmium Association

Address: 34 Berkeley Square
GB-London W1X 6AJ
Great Britain
Telephone: 71/499 8425
Telex: 261286

▲ Chromium Association

Address: 30, Bd. Haussmann
F-75008 Paris
France
Telephone: 1/438 75365

▲ Cobalt Development Institute

Address: Ravenstein 3
B-1000 Bruxelles
Belgium

▲ Comite de Liaison du Negoce des Metaux
Non-Ferreux de la CCE {Non-Ferrous Metals}

Address: place du Samedi 13
B-1000 Bruxelles
Belgium

▲ Contact Office-Inter Trade Union of Miners'
and Metalworkers' Free Trade Unions in the
European Communities

Address: rue de Moniteur 18
B-1000 Bruxelles
Belgium
Telephone: 2/218 37 93

▲ ELDEC (European Lead Development
Committee)

Address: 42, Weymouth Street
GB-London W1N 3LQ
Great Britain
Telephone: 71/499 8422
Telex: 261286 G
Fax: 71/493 1555

▲ EMF (European Metalworkers' Federation in
the Community)

Address: rue Fosse-aux-Loups 38 (Bte 4)
B-1000 Bruxelles
Belgium
Telephone: 2/217 27 47
Fax: 2/217 59 63

▲ EUROGYPSUM (Working Community of the
European Gypsum Industry)

Address: 3, rue Alfred Roll
F-75849 Paris Cedex 17
France
Telephone: 1/47 66 03 64
Telex: 641394 F
Fax: 1/40 54 03 28

▲ EUROMETAUX (European Association of
Metals)

Address: rue Montoyer 47
B-1040 Bruxelles
Belgium
Telephone: 2/511 72 73
Telex: 22077 CNOFER B
Fax: 2/514 45 13

▲ European Aluminium Association

Address: Konigsallee 30
P.O. Box 1207
D-4000 Dusseldorf 1
Germany
Telephone: 211/80 871
Telex: 8587 407

▲ European Zinc Institute

Address: P.O. Box 2126
NL-5600 CC Eindhoven
The Netherlands
Telephone: 40/122 497

▲ International Lead & Zinc Study Group

Address: Metro House
58 St. James' Street
GB-London SW1A 1LD
Great Britain
Telephone: 71/499 9373
Telex: 299819

▲ International Primary Aluminium Institute

Address: New Zealand House
Haymarket
GB-London SW1Y 4TE
Great Britain
Telephone: 71/930 0582-9
Telex: 917837

▲ Liaison Committee for Non-Ferrous Metal
Trade Within the EEC

Address: place du Samedi 13 (Bte 5–6)
B-1000 Bruxelles
Belgium
Telephone: 2/217 99 93
Telex: 61965 BIR B
Fax: 2/219 00 22

▲ Manganese Centre

Address: 17, av. Hoche
F-75008 Paris
France
Telephone: 1/45 63 06 34

▲ Non-Ferrous Metals Information Centre

Address: 47, rue de Montoyer
B-1040 Bruxelles
Belgium
Telephone: 2/513 86 34
Telex: 22077
Fax: 2/511 75 53

▲ Organization of European Aluminium
Smelters

Address: Grad-Adolf Str. 18
P.O. Box 200 840
D-4000 Dusseldorf
Germany
Telephone: 211/320 672
Telex: 8582508

▲ Tantalum-Niobium International Study
Center

Address: 40, rue Washington
B-1050 Bruxelles
Belgium
Telephone: 2/649 51 58
Telex: 65080 INAC B
Fax: 2/649 32 69

▲ World Bureau of Metal Statistics

Address: 41, Doughty Street
GB-London WC1N 2LF
Great Britain
Telephone: 71/405 2771
Telex: 298970

Data Resources and Publications

Panorama of EC Industry

Publisher: Office for Official Publications of the
European Communities
Frequency of Publication: Annual
Scope: Description of 165 manufacturing and
service industries, including the mining
industry, plus evaluations of the impact
of the Single Market Program

Related Topics and Industries

Industrial Products; Manufacturing. See also *Part III—
Sources on EC 1992 by Topic*

OTHER NATURAL RESOURCES

EC Contacts

Table 35.4 lists official European Community directorates and subdirectorates that provide information about other natural resources. For the complete address of the Commission of the European Communities headquarters (CEC HQ in the table), refer to the Introduction to Part IV.

Table 35.4
CEC Subdirectorates—Other Natural Resources

Directorate and Subdirectorate Name	Directorate/ Subdirectorate Number	Directorate-General	Address
Internal Market and Industrial Affairs I			
Pharmaceuticals and Veterinary Medicines	B/6	III	CEC HQ, Belgium Telephone: 2/236 30 12
General Matters, and Relations with the European Parliament and the Economic and Social Committee			
Statistical Information, Quantity Studies, and Forecasts	A/2	VI	CEC HQ, Belgium Telex: 22037 AGREC B
Reports, Publications, Studies, and Documentation	A/5	VI	CEC HQ, Belgium Telex: 22037 AGREC B
Agroeconomic Legislation	B-I	VI	CEC HQ, Belgium Telex: 22037 AGREC B
Quality and Health	B-II	VI	CEC HQ, Belgium Telex: 22037 AGREC B
Organization of Markets in Crop Products	C	VI	CEC HQ, Belgium Telex: 22037 AGREC B
Organization of Markets in Livestock Products	D	VI	CEC HQ, Belgium Telex: 22037 AGREC B
Organization of Markets in Specialized Products	E	VI	CEC HQ, Belgium Telex: 22037 AGREC B
Priority Programmes and Decentralized Information			
Agricultural Information	A/2	X	CEC HQ, Belgium
Biology			
Agroindustrial Research	F/3	XII	CEC HQ, Belgium
Protection of Water and the Air, and Conservation; Civil Protection			
Agriculture, Nature Conservation, and Relations with Other Policies	B/4	XI	CEC HQ, Belgium

Associations

▲ AQUA EUROPA (European Water Conditioning Association)

Address: rue des Drapiers 21
B-1050 Bruxelles
Belgium
Telephone: 2/510 23 11
Telex: 21078 FABRIM B
Fax: 2/510 23 01

▲ CEMA (European Committee of Agricultural Machine Builders)

Address: 19, rue Jacques Bingen
F-75017 Paris
France
Telephone: 1/47 66 02 20
Telex: 640362 F
Fax: 1/40 54 95 60

▲ CEOAH (European Committee for Agricultural and Horticultural Tools and Implements)

Address: 16, av. Hoche
F-75008 Paris
France
Telephone: 1/45 63 93 23
Telex: 280900 FEDEMEC F
Fax: 1/45 63 59 86

▲ COGECA (General Committee of Agricultural Cooperation in the EEC)

Address: rue de la Science 23–25
B-1040 Bruxelles
Belgium
Telephone: 2/230 39 45
Telex: 25816 B
Fax: 2/230 40 46

▲ COPA (Committee of Agricultural Organizations in the EEC)

Address: rue de la Science 23–25
B-1040 Bruxelles
Belgium
Telephone: 2/230 39 45
Telex: 25816 B
Fax: 2/230 40 46

▲ COTANCE (Confederation of National Associations of Tanners and Dressers of the European Community)

Address: 122, rue de Provence
F-75008 Paris
France
Telephone: 1/45 22 96 45
Telex: 290785 F
Fax: 1/42 93 37 44

▲ EFA (European Federation of Agricultural Workers' Unions)

Address: rue Fosse-aux-Loups 38 (Bte 8)
B-1000 Bruxelles
Belgium
Telephone: 2/218 53 08
Telex: 62241 ETUC B
Fax: 2/217 59 63

▲ EFMA (European Fertilizer Manufacturers Association)

Address: av. Louise 250 (Bte 54)
B-1050 Bruxelles
Belgium
Telephone: 2/640 54 02
Telex: 62444 B
Fax: 2/641 93 17

▲ EUREAU (Union of the Water Supply Associations from Countries of the European Communities)

Address: ch. de Waterloo 255 (Bte 6)
B-1060 Bruxelles
Belgium
Telephone: 2/537 43 02

▲ EUROPECHE (Association of National Organisations of Fishing Enterprises in the EEC)

Address: rue de la Science 23–25 (Bte 15)
B-1040 Bruxelles
Belgium
Telephone: 2/230 48 40
Telex: 25816 B
Fax: 2/230 26 80

▲ FEFAC (European Federation of the Compound Feed Manufacturers)

Address: rue de la Loi 223 (Bte 3)
B-1040 Bruxelles
Belgium
Telephone: 2/230 87 15
Telex: 23993 B
Fax: 2/230 57 22

▲ FEFANA (European Federation of Feed Additive Manufacturers)

Address: Roonstrasse 5
D-5300 Bonn 2
Germany
Telephone: 228/35 24 00
Telex: 886391 AWT D
Fax: 228/36 13 97

▲ International Liaison Committee for the Manufacturers and Restorers of Agricultural Machinery

Address: Wilhelminalaan 1
NL-3732 GJ De Bilt
The Netherlands
Telephone: 30/20 48 11
Telex: 76231 MU NL
Fax: 30/20 48 99

Data Resources and Publications

Agricultural Policies, Markets, and Trade

Publisher: OECD
Frequency of Publication: Annual
Scope: Agricultural policies, markets, and trade in OECD member countries

Bioconversion of Agricultural Wastes

Publisher: United Nations
Frequency of Publication: Periodically
Scope: Directory of basic industrial information sources

Essential Oils

Publisher: United Nations
Frequency of Publication: Periodically
Scope: Directory of basic industrial information sources

The European Community and the Problems of Its Waters

Publisher: Office for Official Publications of the European Communities
Frequency of Publication: One time
Scope: Brief summary of the water supply problems facing the EC; prepared by DG XI

Eurostatistics—Data for Short-Term Economic Analysis

Publisher: Office for Official Publications of the European Communities
Frequency of Publication: Monthly
Scope: Recent economic data on the EC together with comparative statistics from the United States and Japan, such as exchange rates, interest rates, money supply, industrial and agricultural indexes, and foreign trade; also available online via the Cronos database; prepared by the Statistical Office of the EC ⓐ

Green Europe

Publisher: Office for Official Publications of the European Communities
Frequency of Publication: Monthly
Scope: Newsletter of agricultural matters; also available online via the Cronos database; prepared monthly by DG VI ⓐ

Ground Water in Eastern and Northern Europe

Publisher: United Nations
Frequency of Publication: One time
Scope: Survey of ground water resources and demands in portions of Europe

National Strategies for Protection of Flora, Fauna, and Their Habitats

Publisher: United Nations Economic Commission for Europe
Frequency of Publication: One time
Scope: General problems of protecting the major ecosystems; analysis of the legislative basis, administration, and policy instruments applied in member countries

Needs for Strategic R&D in Support of Improved Energy Efficiency in the Processing Industries

Publisher: Office for Official Publications of the European Communities
Frequency of Publication: One time
Scope: Summary of views of research experts on energy efficiency research and development

Regional Strategy for Environmental Protection and Rational Use of Natural Resources

Publisher: United Nations Economic Commission for Europe
Frequency of Publication: One time
Scope: Collective experiences and insights of UNECE member countries on critical environmental problems and possible solutions

Renewable Natural Resources

Publisher: OECD
Frequency of Publication: One time
Scope: Report on economic incentives for improved management of renewable natural resources

Utilization of Agricultural Residues for the Production of Panels, Pulp and Paper

Publisher: United Nations
Frequency of Publication: Periodically
Scope: Directory of basic industrial information sources

Water Resource Management

Publisher: OECD
Frequency of Publication: One time
Scope: Study of integrated policies of selected OECD member countries

Related Topics and Industries

Industrial Products; Manufacturing. See also *Part III—Sources on EC 1992 by Topic*

36

Professions and Service Industries

ASSISTANCE

Appendix D contains a list of the Single Market measures dealing with professions and service industries. For additional help on using the resources in this chapter, refer to the Introduction to Part IV.

ADVERTISING, MARKETING, AND PUBLIC RELATIONS

EC Contacts

European Parliament

▲ Committee on Legal Affairs and Citizens' Rights

Address: 97–113, rue Belliard
        B-1040 Bruxelles
        Belgium
Telephone: 2/284 21 21; 2/284 33 45
Fax: 2/230 68 56; 2/231 12 57

Address: Palais de l'Europe
        F-67006 Strasbourg Cedex
        France
Telephone: 88/374 001; 88/374 164
Fax: 88/369 214; 88/256 516

Address: Centre Europeen
        Plateau du Kirchberg
        L-2929 Luxembourg
Telephone: 430 01
Telex: 3493 EUPARL LU; 2894 EUPARL LU
Fax: 436 972; 435 359

European Parliament

▲ Committee on Social Affairs, Employment, and the Working Environment

Address: 97–113, rue Belliard
        B-1040 Bruxelles
        Belgium
Telephone: 2/284 21 21; 2/284 35 04
Fax: 2/230 68 56; 2/231 12 57

Address: Palais de l'Europe
        F-67006 Strasbourg Cedex
        France
Telephone: 88/374 001; 88/374 037; 88/374 548
Fax: 88/369 214; 88/256 516

Address: Centre Europeen
        Plateau du Kirchberg
        L-2929 Luxembourg
Telephone: 430 01
Telex: 3493 EUPARL LU; 2894 EUPARL LU
Fax: 436 972; 435 359

European Parliament

▲ Committee on the Environment, Public Health, and Consumer Protection

Address: 97–113, rue Belliard
        B-1040 Bruxelles
        Belgium
Telephone: 2/284 21 21; 2/284 28 48
Fax: 2/230 68 56; 2/231 12 57

Address: Palais de l'Europe
        F-67006 Strasbourg Cedex
        France
Telephone: 88/374 001; 88/374 418
Fax: 88/369 214; 88/256 516

Address: Centre Europeen
        Plateau du Kirchberg
        L-2929 Luxembourg
Telephone: 430 01
Telex: 3493 EUPARL LU; 2894 EUPARL LU
Fax: 436 972; 435 359

Associations

▲ CERP (European Confederation of Public Relations)

Address: 35–41, rue de l'Oasis
        F-90600 Puteaux
        France
Telephone: 1/47 73 60 72
Telex: 612293 F
Fax: 1/45 06 53 43

▲ Common Market Group of the World Federation of Advertisers

Address: rue des Colonies 54 (Bte 13)
        B-1000 Bruxelles
        Belgium
Telephone: 2/219 06 98
Fax: 2/219 54 64

▲ EAAA (European Association of Advertising Agencies)

Address: av. du Barbeau 28
            B-1160 Bruxelles
            Belgium
Telephone: 2/672 43 36
Telex: 62864 EAAA B
Fax: 2/672 00 14

▲ EAT (European Advertising Tripartite)

Address: av. du Barbeau 28
            B-1160 Bruxelles
            Belgium
Telephone: 2/672 43 36
Fax: 2/672 00 14

▲ EGTA (European Group of Television Advertising)

Address: Knighton House
            56, Mortimer Street
            GB-London W1N 8AN
            Great Britain
Telephone: 71/636 6866
Telex: 262988 G
Fax: 71/580 7892

Data Resources and Publications

Panorama of EC Industry

Publisher: Office for Official Publications of the European Communities
Frequency of Publication: Annual
Scope: Description of 165 manufacturing and service industries, including marketing and advertising professions, plus evaluations of the impact of the Single Market Program

Research on the "Cost of Non-Europe"—The Cost of Non-Europe in Business Services

Publisher: Office for Official Publications of the European Communities
Frequency of Publication: One time
Scope: Identification of barriers to providing engineering, architectural, management, legal, computing, marketing, public relations, research and development, accounting, and financial services throughout the EC; Volume 8 of the Cecchini study on the "cost of non-Europe"

Related Topics and Industries

Consumer Products and Services. See also *Part III—Sources on EC 1992 by Topic*

ENGINEERING

EC Contacts

Table 36.1 lists official European Community directorates and subdirectorates that provide information about engineering and engineers. For the complete address of the Commission of the European Communities headquarters (CEC HQ in the table), refer to the Introduction to Part IV.

European Parliament
▲ Committee on Energy, Research, and Technology

Address: Palais de l'Europe
            F-67006 Strasbourg Cedex
            France
Telephone: 88/374 001; 88/375 485
Fax: 88/369 214; 88/256 516

Address: Centre Europeen
            Plateau du Kirchberg
            L-2929 Luxembourg
Telephone: 430 01
Telex: 3493 EUPARL LU; 2894 EUPARL LU
Fax: 436 972; 435 359

European Parliament
▲ Committee on Legal Affairs and Citizens' Rights

Address: 97–113, rue Belliard
            B-1040 Bruxelles
            Belgium
Telephone: 2/284 21 21; 2/284 33 45
Fax: 2/230 68 56; 2/231 12 57

▼ ━━━ ▼

Address: Palais de l'Europe
            F-67006 Strasbourg Cedex
            France
Telephone: 88/374 001; 88/374 164
Fax: 88/369 214; 88/256 516

Address: Centre Europeen
            Plateau du Kirchberg
            L-2929 Luxembourg
Telephone: 430 01
Telex: 3493 EUPARL LU; 2894 EUPARL LU
Fax: 436 972; 435 359

European Parliament

▲ Committee on Social Affairs, Employment, and the Working Environment

Address: 97–113, rue Belliard
            B-1040 Bruxelles
            Belgium
Telephone: 2/284 21 21; 2/284 35 04
Fax: 2/230 68 56; 2/231 12 57

Address: Palais de l'Europe
            F-67006 Strasbourg Cedex
            France
Telephone: 88/374 001; 88/374 037; 88/374 548
Fax: 88/369 214; 88/256 516

Address: Centre Europeen
            Plateau du Kirchberg
            L-2929 Luxembourg
Telephone: 430 01
Telex: 3493 EUPARL LU; 2894 EUPARL LU
Fax: 436 972; 435 359

Associations

▲ AIPC (International Association for Bridge and Structural Engineering IVBH)

Address: ETH-Honggerberg
            CH-8093 Zurich
            Switzerland
Telephone: 1/377 26 47
Telex: 822186 IABS CH

▲ European Committee of the Bureau of Engineers

Address: av. Louise 430 (Bte 12)
            B-1050 Bruxelles
            Belgium
Telephone: 2/646 06 95
Telex: 21591 CEBI B
Fax: 2/646 05 41

Table 36.1
CEC Subdirectorates—Engineering

Directorate and Subdirectorate Name	Directorate/ Subdirectorate Number	Directorate- General	Address
Internal Market and Industrial Affairs I			
Mechanical Engineering, Electrical Engineering, and Metrology	B/3	III	CEC HQ, Belgium Telephone: 2/236 30 12
Approximation of Laws, Freedom of Establishment, and Freedom to Provide Services			
Free Movement of Self-Employed Persons and Recognition of Diplomas	D/2	III	CEC HQ, Belgium Telephone: 2/236 30 12

▲ FEANI (European Federation of National Engineering Associations)

Address: 4, rue de la Mission Marchand
F-75016 Paris
France
Telephone: 1/42 24 91 43
Fax: 1/42 24 53 80

▲ ORGALIME (Liaison Group for the European Engineering Industries)

Address: rue de Stassart 99
B-1050 Bruxelles
Belgium
Telephone: 2/511 34 84/97
Telex: 21078 ORGALIME B
Fax: 2/510 23 01

Data Resources and Publications

Annual Review of Engineering Industries and Automation

Publisher: United Nations and the United Nations Economic Commission for Europe
Frequency of Publication: Annual
Scope: Analyzes data on production, investments, staffing levels, and price indexes

Bulletin of Statistics on World Trade in Engineering Products

Publisher: United Nations and the United Nations Economic Commission for Europe
Frequency of Publication: Annual
Scope: Statistics on the flow of machinery, transport, scientific, medical, optical and measuring equipment, watches, and clocks

Engineering Industries and Automation

Publisher: United Nations Economic Commission for Europe
Frequency of Publication: Annual
Scope: General developments of engineering industries, including computer, telecommunications, machine tool, industrial robot, and automotive industries; includes data on trade in engineering products

Engineering Industries: Dynamics of the Eighties

Publisher: United Nations Economic Commission for Europe
Frequency of Publication: One time
Scope: Study and assessment of the role and place of engineering industries in national and world economics over the period 1979–1986; reviews current trends and foreseeable developments in engineering industries

Panorama of EC Industry

Publisher: Office for Official Publications of the European Communities
Frequency of Publication: Annual
Scope: Description of 165 manufacturing and service industries, including the engineering profession, plus evaluations of the impact of the Single Market Program

Research on the "Cost of Non-Europe"—The Cost of Non-Europe in Business Services

Publisher: Office for Official Publications of the European Communities
Frequency of Publication: One time
Scope: Identifies barriers to providing engineering, architectural, management, legal, computing, marketing, public relations, research and development, accounting, and financial services throughout the EC; Volume 8 of the Cecchini study on the "cost of non-Europe"

Technical Engineering Services: Aiding Structural Adjustment and Competitiveness

Publisher: OECD
Frequency of Publication: One time
Scope: Report on current state of technical engineering services and their competitive future, including obstacles to the internationalization of these services

Related Topics and Industries

See *Part III—Sources on EC 1992 by Topic*

Accountants, Lawyers, and Notaries

EC Contacts

Table 36.2 lists official European Community directorates and subdirectorates that provide information about accountants, lawyers, and notaries. For the complete address of the Commission of the European Communities headquarters (CEC HQ in the table), refer to the Introduction to Part IV.

Commission of the European Communities
▲ Statistical Office

Directorate D/4—Business Statistics/Services and Transport

Address: Batiment Jean Monnet
             rue Alcide de Gasperi
             L-2920 Luxembourg
Telephone: 430 11
Telex: 3423/3446/3476 COMEUR LU

European Parliament
▲ Committee on Legal Affairs and Citizens' Rights

Address: 97–113, rue Belliard
             B-1040 Bruxelles
             Belgium
Telephone: 2/284 21 21; 2/284 33 45
Fax: 2/230 68 56; 2/231 12 57

Address: Palais de l'Europe
             F-67006 Strasbourg Cedex
             France
Telephone: 88/374 001; 88/374 164
Fax: 88/369 214; 88/256 516

Address: Centre Europeen
             Plateau du Kirchberg
             L-2929 Luxembourg
Telephone: 430 01
Telex: 3493 EUPARL LU; 2894 EUPARL LU
Fax: 436 972; 435 359

Table 36.2
CEC Subdirectorates—Accountants, Lawyers, and Notaries

Directorate and Subdirectorate Name	Directorate/ Subdirectorate Number	Directorate- General	Address
Approximation of Laws, Freedom of Establishment, and Freedom to Provide Services			
Free Movement of Self-Employed Persons and Recognition of Diplomas	D/2	III	CEC HQ, Belgium Telephone: 2/236 30 12
Restrictive Practices, Abuse of Dominant Positions, and Other Distortions of Competition I			
Banking and Insurance and Other Service Industries	B/3	IV	CEC HQ, Belgium
Company Law, Company and Capital Movements, Taxation/Company Law, Industrial Democracy and Accounting Standards	B/2	XV	CEC HQ, Belgium

European Parliament

▲ Committee on Social Affairs, Employment, and the Working Environment

Address: 97–113, rue Belliard
B-1040 Bruxelles
Belgium
Telephone: 2/284 21 21; 2/284 35 04
Fax: 2/230 68 56; 2/231 12 57

Address: Palais de l'Europe
F-67006 Strasbourg Cedex
France
Telephone: 88/374 001; 88/374 037; 88/374 548
Fax: 88/369 214; 88/256 516

Address: Centre Europeen
Plateau du Kirchberg
L-2929 Luxembourg
Telephone: 430 01
Telex: 3493 EUPARL LU; 2894 EUPARL LU
Fax: 436 972; 435 359

Associations

▲ CCBE (Council of the Bars and Law Societies of the European Community)

Address: rue Washington 40
B-1050 Bruxelles
Belgium
Telephone: 2/640 42 74
Telex: 65080 INAC
Fax: 2/649 32 69

▲ FEE (Federation of European Chartered Accountants)

Address: rue de la Loi 83
B-1040 Bruxelles
Belgium
Telephone: 2/231 05 55
Telex: 24105 B
Fax: 2/231 11 12

▲ IBA (International Bar Association)

Address: 2, Harewood Place
Hanover Square
GB-London W1R 9HB
Great Britain
Telephone: 71/629 1206
Telex: 8812664 INBAR G
Fax: 71/409 0456

▲ International Union of Notaries of the European Community

Address: 31, av. du General Foy
F-75008 Paris
France
Telephone: 1/42 93 06 45
Telex: 640059 F
Fax: 1/42 93 69 81

▲ Standing Conference of Notaries of the European Community

Address: Ruiz de Alarcon 3
E-28014 Madrid
Spain
Telephone: 1/531 49 05
Fax: 1/521 15 53

Data Resources and Publications

Conclusions on Accounting and Reporting by Transnational Corporations

Publisher: United Nations
Frequency of Publication: One time
Scope: Guide for preparers and users of financial statements of multinational businesses

Earnings: Industry and Services

Publisher: Office for Official Publications of the European Communities
Frequency of Publication: 2 times a year
Scope: Earnings of manual and nonmanual workers in industry and certain groups of activities in the service sector; prepared by the Statistical Office of the EC and also available online via the Cronos database

Panorama of EC Industry

Publisher: Office for Official Publications of the European Communities
Frequency of Publication: Annual
Scope: Description of 165 manufacturing and service industries, including the legal services, accounting and notarial professions, plus evaluations of the impact of the Single Market Program

Research on the "Cost of Non-Europe"—The Cost of Non-Europe in Business Services

Publisher: Office for Official Publications of the European Communities
Frequency of Publication: One time
Scope: Identification of barriers to providing engineering, architectural, management, legal, computing, marketing, public relations, research and development, accounting, and financial services throughout the EC; Volume 8 of the Cecchini study on the "cost of non-Europe"

Related Topics and Industries

Consumer Products and Services. See also *Part III—Sources on EC 1992 by Topic*

PRINTING AND PUBLISHING

EC Contacts

European Parliament

▲ Committee on Youth, Culture, Education, the Media, and Sport

Address: 97–113, rue Belliard
B-1040 Bruxelles
Belgium
Telephone: 2/284 21 21; 2/284 25 11
Fax: 2/230 68 56; 2/231 12 57

Address: Palais de l'Europe
F-67006 Strasbourg Cedex
France
Telephone: 88/374 001; 88/374 522
Fax: 88/369 214; 88/256 516

Address: Centre Europeen
Plateau du Kirchberg
L-2929 Luxembourg
Telephone: 430 01
Telex: 3493 EUPARL LU; 2894 EUPARL LU
Fax: 436 972; 435 359

Associations

▲ AEEA (European Association of Directory Publishers)

Address: sq. Marie-Louise 18 (Btes 25–27)
B-1040 Bruxelles
Belgium
Telephone: 2/230 26 72/78
Telex: 64393 EUROGF B
Fax: 2/231 14 64

▲ CEPE (European Committee of Paint, Printing Ink, and Artists Colours Manufacturers Associations)

Address: sq. Marie-Louise 49
B-1040 Bruxelles
Belgium
Telephone: 2/230 40 90 (ext. 179)
Telex: 23167
Fax: 2/230 14 09

▲ EUMAPRINT (European Committee of Printing and Paper Converting Machinery Manufacturers)

Address: 1899 Preston White Drive
Reston, VA 22091
USA
Telephone: 703/264 7200
Telex: 901753
Fax: 703/620 0994

▲ GEJ-FIJ (European Group of Journalists—International Federation of Journalists)

Address: bd. Charlemagne 1 (Bte 5)
B-1041 Bruxelles
Belgium
Telephone: 2/238 09 51
Telex: 61275 IPC B
Fax: 2/230 36 33

▲ GELC (Book Publishers Group of EEC)

Address: bd. Lambermont 140 (Bte 1)
B-1030 Bruxelles
Belgium
Telephone: 2/241 65 80
Fax: 2/216 71 31

▲ INTERGRAF (International Confederation for Printing and Allied Industries)

Address: sq. Marie-Louise 18 (Btes 25–27)
B-1040 Bruxelles
Belgium
Telephone: 2/230 86 46
Telex: 64 393 EUROGF B

Data Resources and Publications

Printing and Graphic Industry

Publisher: United Nations
Frequency of Publication: Periodically
Scope: Directory of basic industrial information
sources

Social Europe—Supplement: New Technologies in Printing and Publishing

Publisher: Office for Official Publications of
the European Communities
Frequency of Publication: One time
Scope: Summary of technological developments impacting printing and publishing industries, including impacts on employment; prepared by DG V

Related Topics and Industries

Communications and Information; Consumer Products and Services; Manufacturing. See also Part III—Sources on EC 1992 by Topic

▼

OTHER PROFESSIONS AND SERVICE INDUSTRIES

EC Contacts

Table 36.3 lists official European Community directorates and subdirectorates that provide information about other professions and service industries. For the complete address of the Commission of the European Communities headquarters (CEC HQ in the table), refer to the Introduction to Part IV.

Commission of the European Communities
▲ Statistical Office

Directorate D/4—Business Statistics/Services and Transport

Address: Batiment Jean Monnet
rue Alcide de Gasperi
L-2920 Luxembourg
Telephone: 430 11
Telex: 3423/3446/3476 COMEUR LU

European Parliament
▲ Committee on Legal Affairs and Citizens' Rights

Address: 97–113, rue Belliard
B-1040 Bruxelles
Belgium
Telephone: 2/284 21 21; 2/284 33 45
Fax: 2/230 68 56; 2/231 12 57

Address: Palais de l'Europe
F-67006 Strasbourg Cedex
France
Telephone: 88/374 001; 88/374 164
Fax: 88/369 214; 88/256 516

Address: Centre Europeen
Plateau du Kirchberg
L-2929 Luxembourg
Telephone: 430 01
Telex: 3493 EUPARL LU; 2894 EUPARL LU
Fax: 436 972; 435 359

European Parliament
▲ Committee on Social Affairs, Employment, and the Working Environment

Address: 97–113, rue Belliard
B-1040 Bruxelles
Belgium
Telephone: 2/284 21 21; 2/284 35 04
Fax: 2/230 68 56; 2/231 12 57

Address: Palais de l'Europe
F-67006 Strasbourg Cedex
France
Telephone: 88/374 001; 88/374 037; 88/374 548
Fax: 88/369 214; 88/256 516

Address: Centre Europeen
Plateau du Kirchberg
L-2929 Luxembourg
Telephone: 430 01
Telex: 3493 EUPARL LU; 2894 EUPARL LU
Fax: 436 972; 435 359

European Parliament
▲ Committee on Transport and Tourism

Address: 97-113, rue Belliard
B-1040 Bruxelles
Belgium
Telephone: 2/284 21 21; 2/284 35 02
Fax: 2/230 68 56; 2/231 12 57

Table 36.3
CEC Subdirectorates—Other Professions and Service Industries

Directorate and Subdirectorate Name	Directorate/ Subdirectorate Number	Directorate- General	Address
Industrial Economy, Service Industries, Non-Member Countries, and Raw Materials			
Services	A/4	III	CEC HQ, Belgium Telephone: 2/236 30 12
Internal Market and Industrial Affairs I			
Mechanical Engineering, Electrical Engineering, and Metrology	B/3	III	CEC HQ, Belgium Telephone: 2/236 30 12
Approximation of Laws, Freedom of Establishment, and Freedom to Provide Services			
Free Movement of Self-Employed Persons and Recognition of Diplomas	D/2	III	CEC HQ, Belgium Telephone: 2/236 30 12
Restrictive Practices, Abuse of Dominant Positions, and Other Distortions of Competition I			
Banking and Insurance and Other Service Industries	B/3	IV	CEC HQ, Belgium
Restrictive Practices, Abuse of Dominant Positions, and Other Distortions of Competition III			
Transport and Tourist Industries	D/3	IV	CEC HQ, Belgium

Address: Palais de l'Europe
F-67006 Strasbourg Cedex
France
Telephone: 88/374 001; 88/374 035
Fax: 88/369 214; 88/256 516

Address: Centre Europeen
Plateau du Kirchberg
L-2929 Luxembourg
Telephone: 430 01
Telex: 3493 EUPARL LU; 2894 EUPARL LU
Fax: 436 972; 435 359

Associations

▲ AIE (International Association of Electrical Contractors)

Address: 5, rue de Hamelin
F-75116 Paris
France
Telephone: 1/47 27 97 49
Telex: 620993 FELEC F
Fax: 1/47 55 00 47

▲ CEFEI (Committee of European Financial Executives Institutes)

Address: av. des Arts 56
B-1040 Bruxelles
Belgium
Telephone: 2/510 42 11
Telex: 21678 b

▲ CLAEU (Liaison Committee of the Architects of United Europe)

Address: rue de Livourne 158 (Bte 5)
B-1050 Bruxelles
Belgium
Telephone: 2/647 06 69

▲ COBCCEE (Butchers and Meatcutters)

Address: av. de Cortenbergh 116
B-1040 Bruxelles
Belgium
Telephone: 2/735 24 70
Fax: 2/736 64 93

▲ EDA (European Demolition Association)

Address: Wassenaarseweg 80
NL-2596 CZ's Gravenhage
The Netherlands
Telephone: 70/326 42 51
Telex: 32576 ECON NL
Fax: 70/324 51 18

▲ EFLA (European Foundation for Landscape Architecture)

Address: av. Brugmann 52
B-1060 Bruxelles
Belgium

▲ EURO-FIET (European Regional Organisation of the International Federation of Commercial, Clerical, Professional, and Technical Employees)

Address: 15 av. de Balexert
CH-1219 Chatelaine/Geneve
Switzerland
Telephone: 22/796 27 33
Telex: 418736 FIET CH
Fax: 22/796 53 21

▲ European Commission of the International Federation of Real Estate Valuers

Address: 23, av. Bosquet
F-75007 Paris
France
Telephone: 1/45 50 45 49
Telex: 201339 F
Fax: 1/45 50 42 00

▲ The European Group of Valuers of Fixed Assets

Address: 12, Great George Street
Parliament Square
GB-London SW1P 3AD
Great Britain
Telephone: 71/222 7000
Telex: 9155443 RICS G
Fax: 71/222 9430

▲ European Union of Practicing Veterinarians

Address: Dorpstraat 15
NL-3223 GZ Hellevoetsluis
The Netherlands

▲ FEACO (European Federation of Associations of Management Consultants)

Address: Maison de l'Ingenierie
3, rue Leon Bonnat
F-75016 Paris
France
Telephone: 1/45 24 43 53
Telex: 612938 SYNTEC F
Fax: 1/42 88 26 84

▲ FEUPF (European Federation of Professional Florists)

Address: c/o Federfiori
Via Massena 20
I-10128 Torino
Italy
Telephone: 11/54 70 51
Fax: 11/53 38 69

▲ FVE (Federation of Veterinarians of the EEC)

Address: av. Fonsny 41
B-1060 Bruxelles
Belgium
Telephone: 2/538 29 63
Fax: 2/537 28 28

▲ Groupement des Organisateurs de Ventes Publiques de la CEE {Auctions}

Address: rue du Parnasse 3
B-1040 Bruxelles
Belgium
Telephone: 2/5132 90 10
Fax: 2/511 99 40

▲ HOTREC (Confederation of the National Hotel and Restaurant Association in the European Community)

Address: 80, rue de la Roquette
F-75011 Paris
France
Telephone: 1/47 00 84 57
Telex: 216410 IHAAIH F
Fax: 1/47 00 64 55

▲ International Commission of Hairdressers of the Common Market

Address: Centre International Rogier
Residence Iris (Bte 10)
B-1210 Bruxelles
Belgium
Telephone: 2/217 85 09

▲ IUCAB (International Union of Commercial Agents and Brokers)

Address: Herengracht 376
NL-1016 CH Amsterdam
The Netherlands
Telephone: 20/22 19 44
Telex: 18313 GEBO NL
Fax: 20/26 0557

▲ Liaison Committee of European Surveyors

Address: 12, Great George Street
Parliament Square
GB-London SW1P 3AD
Great Britain
Telephone: 71/222 7000
Telex: 9155443 RICS G
Fax: 71/222 9430

Data Resources and Publications

Accounting Standards Harmonization: Operating Results of Insurance Companies
Publisher: OECD
Frequency of Publication: One time
Scope: Summary of current practices pertaining to insurance companies in OECD countries

Contract Research Organizations in the EEC
Publisher: Office for Official Publications of the European Communities
Frequency of Publication: One time
Scope: Directory of EEC contract research organizations; prepared by DG XIII

Earnings: Industry and Services

Publisher: Office for Official Publications of the European Communities

Frequency of Publication: 2 times a year

Scope: Earnings of manual and nonmanual workers in industry and certain groups of activities in the service sector; prepared by the Statistical Office of the EC and also available online via Cronos database ⊛

Erasmus—The Joint Study Programme Newsletter of the Commission

Publisher: Office for Official Publications of the European Communities

Frequency of Publication: 2 times a year

Scope: Newsletter about current activities of Erasmus (European Community Action Scheme for the Mobility of University Students)

Foreign Direct Investment and Transnational Corporations in Services

Publisher: United Nations

Frequency of Publication: One time

Scope: Review of established policy patterns of multinational businesses in direct investment in service industries

Freedom of Movement in the Community— Entry and Residence

Publisher: Office for Official Publications of the European Communities

Frequency of Publication: One time

Scope: Information on travel and residence throughout the EC

A Guide to Working in a Europe Without Frontiers

Publisher: Office for Official Publications of the European Communities

Frequency of Publication: One time

Scope: Handbook for employees on the impact of the Single Market Program on labor mobility

Health Care and Nursing Education in the 21st Century

Publisher: Office for Official Publications of the European Communities

Frequency of Publication: One time

Scope: Symposium proceedings

Occupational Hygiene Education in the EEC: A Survey of Existing Programs

Publisher: Office for Official Publications of the European Communities

Frequency of Publication: One time

Scope: Survey of national education programs on occupational hygiene; prepared by DG V

Panorama of EC Industry

Publisher: Office for Official Publications of the European Communities

Frequency of Publication: Annual

Scope: Description of 165 manufacturing and service industries, including information, software, computing and professional business services and the tourism industry, plus evaluations of the impact of the Single Market Program

Practical Guide to Legal Aspects of Industrial Sub-Contracting Within the European Community

Publisher: Office for Official Publications of the European Communities

Frequency of Publication: One time

Scope: Coverage of subcontracting practices in the EC

Research on the "Cost of Non-Europe"—The Benefits of Completing the Internal Market for Telecommunications Equipment and Services in the Community

Publisher: Office for Official Publications of the European Communities

Frequency of Publication: One time

Scope: Review of standards for telecommunications equipment and services in the EC and estimates the benefits of eliminating technical barriers throughout the EC; Volume 10 of the Cecchini study on the "cost of non-Europe"

Research on the "Cost of Non-Europe"—The Cost of Non-Europe in Business Services

Publisher: Office for Official Publications of the European Communities
Frequency of Publication: One time
Scope: Identification of barriers to providing engineering, architectural, management, legal, computing, marketing, public relations, research and development, accounting, and financial services throughout the EC; Volume 8 of the Cecchini study on the "cost of non-Europe"

Social Work Training in the European Community

Publisher: Office for Official Publications of the European Communities
Frequency of Publication: One time
Scope: Brief discussion of social work training

Tourism Policy and International Tourism in OECD Member Countries

Publisher: OECD
Frequency of Publication: Annual
Scope: Yearly developments in tourism and their impact on OECD members

Transnational Corporations in the Construction and Design Industry

Publisher: United Nations
Frequency of Publication: One time
Scope: Role of major multinational businesses in the construction and design industries, including investment, research, and development

Related Topics and Industries

Consumer Products and Services; Financial Services and Insurance; Health Care and Medicine. See also Part III—Sources on EC 1992 by Topic

37

Transportation

SECTIONS IN THIS CHAPTER

Aviation and Aerospace

Motor Vehicles

Ships and Trains

Other and Multiple Modes

ASSISTANCE

Appendix D contains a list of the Single Market measures dealing with transportation. For additional help on using the resources in this chapter, refer to the Introduction to Part IV.

AVIATION AND AEROSPACE

EC Contacts

Table 37.1 lists official European Community directorates and subdirectorates that provide information about aviation and aerospace transportation. For the complete address of the Commission of the European Communities headquarters (CEC HQ in the table), refer to the Introduction to Part IV.

▲ ESA (European Space Agency)

Address: 10, rue Mario Nikis
             F-75738, Paris
             France
Telephone: 1/45 63 82 85
Telex: 202746 ESA

European Parliament

▲ Committee on Economic and Monetary Affairs and Industrial Policy

Address: 97–113, rue Belliard
             B-1040 Bruxelles
             Belgium
Telephone: 2/284 21 21; 2/284 35 40
Fax: 2/230 68 56; 2/231 12 57

Address: Palais de l'Europe
             F-67006 Strasbourg Cedex
             France
Telephone: 88/374 001; 88/375 484
Fax: 88/369 214; 88/256 516

Address: Centre Europeen
             Plateau du Kirchberg
             L-2929 Luxembourg
Telephone: 430 01
Telex: 3493 EUPARL LU; 2894 EUPARL LU
Fax: 436 972; 435 359

Table 37.1
CEC Subdirectorates—Aviation and Aerospace

Directorate and Subdirectorate Name	Directorate/ Subdirectorate Number	Directorate- General	Address
Aeronautical and Aerospace Industries			
Internal Market and Industrial Affairs II	C/2	III	CEC HQ, Belgium Telephone: 2/236 30 12
Air Transport; Transport Infrastructure; Social and Ecological Aspects of Transport			
Air Transport	C/1	VII	CEC HQ, Belgium Telephone: 2/236 27 42
Science and Technology Support			
Espace (Strategy and Coordination)	H/5	XII	CEC HQ, Belgium
Telecommunications Policy, Technology Transfer and Innovation			
Space and Rural Telecommunications and Posts	D/3	XIII	CEC HQ, Belgium Telephone: 2/235 24 48

European Parliament

▲ Committee on Energy, Research, and Technology

Address: Palais de l'Europe
        F-67006 Strasbourg Cedex
        France
Telephone: 88/374 001; 88/375 485
Fax: 88/369 214; 88/256 516

Address: Centre Europeen
        Plateau du Kirchberg
        L-2929 Luxembourg
Telephone: 430 01
Telex: 3493 EUPARL LU; 2894 EUPARL LU
Fax: 436 972; 435 359

European Parliament

▲ Committee on Transport and Tourism

Address: 97–113, rue Belliard
        B-1040 Bruxelles
        Belgium
Telephone: 2/284 21 21; 2/284 35 02
Fax: 2/230 68 56; 2/231 12 57

Address: Palais de l'Europe
        F-67006 Strasbourg Cedex
        France
Telephone: 88/374 001; 88/374 035
Fax: 88/369 214; 88/256 516

Address: Centre Europeen
        Plateau du Kirchberg
        L-2929 Luxembourg
Telephone: 430 01
Telex: 3493 EUPARL LU; 2894 EUPARL LU
Fax: 436 972; 435 359

Associations

▲ AEA (Association of European Airlines)

Address: 350, av. Louise (Bte 4)
        B-1050 Bruxelles
        Belgium
Telephone: 2/43001
Telex: 22 918

▲ AECMA (Association of European Constructors of Aerospace Materials)

Address: 88, bd. Malesherbes
        F-75008 Paris
        France
Telephone: 1/45 63 82 85
Telex: 642701 AECMA F
Fax: 1/42 25 15 48

▲ EUROCAE (European Organization for Civil Aviation Electronics)

Address: 11, rue Hamelin
        F-75783 Paris Cedex 16
        France
Telephone: 1/45 05 71 88
Telex: 611045 sycelec f
Fax: 1/45 53 03 93

▲ EUROCONTROL (European Organization for the Safety of Air Navigation)

Address: rue de la Loi 72
        B-1040 Bruxelles
        Belgium
Telephone: 2/233 02 11
Fax: 2/233 03 53

▲ EUTELSAT (European Telecommunications Satellite Organization)

Address: Andrea Caruso, Tour Marie Montparnasse
        33, av. du Maine
        F-75755 Paris Cedex 15
        France

Data Resources and Publications

Deregulation and Airline Competition
Publisher: OECD
Frequency of Publication: One time
Scope: Summary of current policies in OECD member countries toward regulation and deregulation of competition in the airline industry

Monthly Traffic Statistics
Publisher: AEA (Association of European Airlines)
Frequency of Publication: Monthly
Scope: Summary of air traffic statistics

Panorama of EC Industry

Publisher: Office for Official Publications of the European Communities
Frequency of Publication: Annual
Scope: Description of 165 manufacturing and service industries, including airlines and air transport, plus evaluations of the impact of the Single Market Program

Related Topics and Industries

Housing and Infrastructure; Manufacturing. See also *Part III—Sources on EC 1992 by Topic*

▼

MOTOR VEHICLES

EC Contacts

Table 37.2 lists official European Community directorates and subdirectorates that provide information about motor vehicle transportation. For the complete address of the Commission of the European Communities headquarters (CEC HQ in the table), refer to the Introduction to Part IV.

European Parliament

▲ Committee on Energy, Research, and Technology

Address: Palais de l'Europe
F-67006 Strasbourg Cedex
France
Telephone: 88/374 001; 88/375 485
Fax: 88/369 214; 88/256 516

Table 37.2
CEC Subdirectorates—Motor Vehicles

Directorate and Subdirectorate Name	Directorate/ Subdirectorate Number	Directorate-General	Address
Internal Market and Industrial Affairs II			
Automobiles and Railways	C/1	III	CEC HQ, Belgium Telephone: 2/236 30 12
Restrictive Practices, Abuse of Dominant Positions, and Other Distortions of Competition III			
Motor Vehicles and Other Means of Transport, and Associated Mechanical Manufactured Products	D/4	IV	CEC HQ, Belgium
RACE Programme and Development of Advanced Telematics Services			
Information and Telecommunications Technologies Applied to Road Transport—Drive Programme	F/5	XIII	CEC HQ, Belgium Telephone: 2/235 24 48

▼ ▼

Address: Centre Europeen
Plateau du Kirchberg
L-2929 Luxembourg
Telephone: 430 01
Telex: 3493 EUPARL LU; 2894 EUPARL LU
Fax: 436 972; 435 359

European Parliament
▲ Committee on the Environment, Public
Health, and Consumer Protection

Address: 97–113, rue Belliard
B-1040 Bruxelles
Belgium
Telephone: 2/284 21 21; 2/284 28 48
Fax: 2/230 68 56; 2/231 12 57

Address: Palais de l'Europe
F-67006 Strasbourg Cedex
France
Telephone: 88/374 001; 88/374 418
Fax: 88/369 214; 88/256 516

Address: Centre Europeen
Plateau du Kirchberg
L-2929 Luxembourg
Telephone: 430 01
Telex: 3493 EUPARL LU; 2894 EUPARL LU
Fax: 436 972; 435 359

European Parliament
▲ Committee on Transport and Tourism

Address: 97–113, rue Belliard
B-1040 Bruxelles
Belgium
Telephone: 2/284 21 21; 2/284 35 02
Fax: 2/230 68 56; 2/231 12 57

Address: Palais de l'Europe
F-67006 Strasbourg Cedex
France
Telephone: 88/374 001; 88/374 035
Fax: 88/369 214; 88/256 516

Address: Centre Europeen
Plateau du Kirchberg
L-2929 Luxembourg
Telephone: 430 01
Telex: 3493 EUPARL LU; 2894 EUPARL LU
Fax: 436 972; 435 359

Associations

▲ CECRA (European Committee for Motor
Trades and Repairs)

Address: bd. de la Woluwe 46 (Bte 10)
B-1200 Bruxelles
Belgium
Telephone: 2/771 01 88
Telex: 26901 AUTOBE B
Fax: 2/771 20 13

▲ CLCA (Liaison Committee of Automobile
Manufacturers for the European Community)

Address: sq. de Meeus 5 (Bte 8)
B-1040 Bruxelles
Belgium
Telephone: 2/512 79 30
Telex: 62945 b
Fax: 2/512 60 44

▲ CLCCR (Liaison Committee of the Body and
Trailer Building Industry)

Address: Westendstrasse 61
D-6000 Frankfurt/Main 17
Germany
Telephone: 69/75 70 234
Telex: 411293 D
Fax: 69/75 70 261

▲ CLEDIPA (Liaison Committee for European
Manufacturers of Automobile Equipment)

Address: bd. de la Woluwe 46 (Bte 9)
B-1200 Bruxelles
Belgium
Telephone: 2/771 00 80
Fax: 2/771 16 55

▲ CLEPA (Liaison Committee for the Manufacturers of Automobile Parts)

Address: Forbes House
Halkin Street
London SW1X 7DS
Great Britain
Telephone: 71/235 7000
Telex: 21628 G
Fax: 71/235 7112

▲ ETRTO (European Tyre and Rim Technical Organization)

Address: av. Brugmann 32
         B-1060 Bruxelles
         Belgium
Telephone: 2/344 40 59
Telex: 63935 b
Fax: 2/344 12 34

▲ FIEA (International Federation of Automobile Experts)

Address: 48, rue Roymond Losserand
         F-75014 Paris
         France
Telephone: 1/43 20 86 50

▲ FIRM (International Federation of Engine Reconditioners)

Address: 5, rue Bellini
         F-92800 Puteaux
         France

▲ Liaison Committee for the International Union of European Buses and Coach

Address: rue d'Arlon 108 (Bte 6)
         B-1040 Bruxelles
         Belgium
Telephone: 2/230 29 80
Telex: 63338 B
Fax: 2/230 91 72

▲ Liaison Committee for the International Union of European Road Haulage

Address: rue d'Arlon 108 (Bte 6)
         B-1040 Bruxelles
         Belgium
Telephone: 2/230 29 80
Telex: 63338 B
Fax: 2/230 91 72

▲ Liaison Committee for the Motorcycle Industry of the European Community

Address: bd. de la Woluwe 46 (Bte 6)
         B-1200 Bruxelles
         Belgium
Telephone: 2/771 00 85
Telex: 63191 FEBIAC B
Fax: 2/762 81 71

▲ OICA (Organization Internationale des Constructeurs d'Automobiles {Automobile Construction})

Address: 4, rue de Berri
         F-75008 Paris
         France
Telephone: 1/43 59 00 13
Telex: 290012 BPICA F

▲ UEC (European Union of Vehicle Body Builders)

Address: bd. de la Woluwe 46 (Bte 14)
         B-1200 Bruxelles
         Belgium
Telephone: 2/770 17 89
Telex: 63253 AUTOBE
Fax: 2/770 20 42

Data Resources and Publications

Automobile Insurance and Road Accident Prevention

Publisher: OECD
Frequency of Publication: One time
Scope: Review of the existing and potential roles of automobile insurers in road accident prevention

Carriage of Goods—Road

Publisher: Office for Official Publications of the European Communities
Frequency of Publication: Annual
Scope: Data on movement of industrial goods and raw materials throughout the EC by trucks; prepared by the Statistical Office of the EC

Census of Motor Traffic on Main International Arteries (E-Roads)

Publisher: United Nations Economic Commission for Europe
Frequency of Publication: Every 5 years
Scope: Statistics on daily motor traffic on Europe's main roads

The Cost of Restricting Imports

Publisher: OECD
Frequency of Publication: One time
Scope: Analysis of the impact of import restrictions on the automobile industry

▼

Engineering Industries and Automation

Publisher: United Nations Economic Commission for Europe

Frequency of Publication: Annual

Scope: General developments of engineering industries, including computer, telecommunications, machine tool, industrial robot, and automotive industries; includes data on trade in engineering products

Innovation in the EC Automotive Industry

Publisher: Office for Official Publications of the European Communities

Frequency of Publication: One time

Scope: Analysis of state aid policy for the automotive industry

Research on the "Cost of Non-Europe"—Technical Trade Barriers in the EC: An Illustration in Six Industries—Some Case Studies on Technical Barriers

Publisher: Office for Official Publications of the European Communities

Frequency of Publication: One time

Scope: Identification of technical trade barriers, including standards, legal requirements, testing and certification procedures, and evaluation of their impact in the food stuffs, pharmaceuticals, automobile, building materials, telecommunications, and electrical products and machinery industries; Volume 6 of the Cecchini study on the "cost of non-Europe"

Research on the "Cost of Non-Europe"—The Cost of Non-Europe: Border Related Controls and Administrative Formalities—An Illustration of the Road Haulage Sector

Publisher: Office for Official Publications of the European Communities

Frequency of Publication: One time

Scope: Survey results on the costs of customs controls and formalities to businesses, including estimates of trade lost due to current customs barriers; Volume 4 of the Cecchini study on the "cost of non-Europe"

Research on the "Cost of Non-Europe"—The EC 92 Automobile Sector

Publisher: Office for Official Publications of the European Communities

Frequency of Publication: One time

Scope: Study of automobile industry in EC, including assessment of the impact of the removal of technical, fiscal, and physical barriers on design, engineering, production, and price; Volume 11 of the Cecchini study on the "cost of non-Europe"

Substitute Fuels for Road Transport: A Technology Assessment

Publisher: OECD

Frequency of Publication: One time

Scope: Assessment of the prospects of fuel that might substitute for gasoline in cars and trucks

Related Topics and Industries

Housing and Infrastructure, Manufacturing. See also *Part III—Sources on EC 1992 by Topic*

▼

SHIPS AND TRAINS

EC Contacts

Table 37.3 lists official European Community directorates and subdirectorates that provide information about shipping and train transportation. For the complete address of the Commission of the European Communities headquarters (CEC HQ in the table), refer to the Introduction to Part IV.

European Parliament

▲ Committee on Energy, Research, and Technology

Address: Palais de l'Europe
F-67006 Strasbourg Cedex
France

Telephone: 88/374 001; 88/375 485

Fax: 88/369 214; 88/256 516

Address: Centre Europeen
Plateau du Kirchberg
L-2929 Luxembourg
Telephone: 430 01
Telex: 3493 EUPARL LU; 2894 EUPARL LU
Fax: 436 972; 435 359

European Parliament
▲ Committee on External Economic Relations

Address: 97–113, rue Belliard
B-1040 Bruxelles
Belgium
Telephone: 2/284 21 21; 2/284 27 49
Fax: 2/230 68 56; 2/231 12 57

Address: Palais de l'Europe
F-67006 Strasbourg Cedex
France
Telephone: 88/374 001; 88/374 021
Fax: 88/369 214; 88/256 516

Address: Centre Europeen
Plateau du Kirchberg
L-2929 Luxembourg
Telephone: 430 01
Telex: 3493 EUPARL LU; 2894 EUPARL LU
Fax: 436 972; 435 359

European Parliament
▲ Committee on Transport and Tourism

Address: 97–113, rue Belliard
B-1040 Bruxelles
Belgium
Telephone: 2/284 21 21; 2/284 35 02
Fax: 2/230 68 56; 2/231 12 57

Address: Palais de l'Europe
F-67006 Strasbourg Cedex
France
Telephone: 88/374 001; 88/374 035
Fax: 88/369 214; 88/256 516

Table 37.3
CEC Subdirectorates—Ships and Trains

Directorate and Subdirectorate Name	Directorate/ Subdirectorate Number	Directorate- General	Address
Internal Market and Industrial Affairs II			
Automobiles and Railways	C/1	III	CEC HQ, Belgium
Shipbuilding, Wood, Leather, Paper, and Miscellaneous Industries	C/4	III	CEC HQ, Belgium Telephone: 2/236 30 12
Restrictive Practices, Abuse of Dominant Positions, and Other Distortions of Competition III			
Motor Vehicles and Other Means of Transport, and Associated Mechanical Manufactured Products	D/4	IV	CEC HQ, Belgium
Maritime Transport; Transport Economics; Legislation	A	VII	CEC HQ, Belgium Telephone: 2/236 27 42
Inland Transport; Market Analysis; Transport Safety; Research and Technology	B	VII	CEC HQ, Belgium Telephone: 2/236 27 42

Address: Centre Europeen
Plateau du Kirchberg
L-2929 Luxembourg
Telephone: 430 01
Telex: 3493 EUPARL LU; 2894 EUPARL LU
Fax: 436 972; 435 359

Associations

▲ AFEDEF (Association of European Railway Equipment Manufacturers)

Address: 12, rue Bixio
F-75007 Paris
France
Telephone: 1/47 05 36 62
Telex: 270105 TXFRA F
Fax: 1/47 05 29 17

▲ CESA (Committee of EEC Shipbuilders' Associations)

Address: An der Alster 1
D-2000 Hamburg 1
Germany
Telephone: 40/24 63 05
Telex: 2162496 VDS D
Fax: 40/24 62 87

▲ Community of European Railways

Address: rue de France 85
B-1070 Bruxelles
Belgium
Telephone: 2/525 30 50
Telex: 20424 BERAIL B
Fax: 2/520 76 04

▲ European Port Data Processing Association

Address: Stadhuis, Grote Markt
B-2000 Antwerpen
Belgium
Telephone: 31/220 82 11
Telex: 31807 b
Fax: 31/220 85 85

▲ ICOMIA (International Council of Marine Industry Associations)

Address: Boating Industry House
Vale Road
Weybridge
Surrey KT12 9NS
Great Britain
Telephone: 932/854 511
Telex: 885471 G
Fax: 932/852 874

▲ OCEAN (Organization of Ship Builders in EC-Countries)

Address: Prins Mauritsplein 29
NL-2582 ND's Gravenhage
The Netherlands
Telephone: 70/351 20 31
Fax: 70/350 35 31

▲ UNIFE (Union of European Railway Industries)

Address: 12, rue Bixio
F-75007 Paris
France
Telephone: 1/47 05 36 62
Telex: 270105 TCFRA F 110
Fax: 1/47 05 29 17

Data Resources and Publications

Carriage of Goods—Inland Waterways

Publisher: Office for Official Publications of the European Communities
Frequency of Publication: Annual
Scope: Data on movement of industrial goods and raw materials throughout the EC by river barges; prepared by the Statistical Office of the EC

Carriage of Goods—Railways

Publisher: Office for Official Publications of the European Communities
Frequency of Publication: Annual
Scope: Data on movement of industrial goods and raw materials throughout the EC by rail; prepared by the Statistical Office of the EC

Europe's Railway of the '90s: A White Paper

Publisher: United Nations Economic Commission for Europe

Frequency of Publication: One time

Scope: Position paper on the future of the railways in international transport in Europe, in competition and/or collaboration with other modes of transport

Inland Waterway Transport in ECMT Countries to the Year 2000: A New Dimension

Publisher: OECD

Frequency of Publication: One time

Scope: Discussion of inland waterway transport, particularly the Rhine-Main-Danube link; prepared by the ECMT

International Sea-Borne Trade Statistics Yearbook

Publisher: United Nations

Frequency of Publication: Annual

Scope: Statistics for each year about the international sea trade

Maritime Transport

Publisher: OECD

Frequency of Publication: Annual

Scope: Report on world shipping markets

Panorama of EC Industry

Publisher: Office for Official Publications of the European Communities

Frequency of Publication: Annual

Scope: Description of 165 manufacturing and service industries, including rail and water transport, plus evaluations of the impact of the Single Market Program

Related Topics and Industries

Housing and Infrastructure; Manufacturing. See also *Part III—Sources on EC 1992 by Topic*

OTHER AND MULTIPLE MODES

EC Contacts

Table 37.4 lists official European Community directorates and subdirectorates that provide information about multiple modes of transportation.

For the complete address of the Commission of the European Communities headquarters (CEC HQ in the table), refer to the Introduction to Part IV.

Table 37.4
CEC Subdirectorates—Other and Multiple Modes of Transportation

Directorate and Subdirectorate Name	Directorate/ Subdirectorate Number	Directorate-General	Address
Restrictive Practices, Abuse of Dominant Positions, and Other Distortions of Competition III			
Transport and Tourist Industries	D/3	IV	CEC HQ, Belgium
Air Transport; Transport Infrastructure; Social and Ecological Aspects of Transport			
Transport Infrastructure	C/2	VII	CEC HQ, Belgium Telephone: 2/236 27 42

▼ ▼

Commission of the European Communities
▲ Statistical Office

Directorate D/4—Business Statistics/Services and Transport

Address: Batiment Jean Monnet
   rue Alcide de Gasperi
   L-2920 Luxembourg
Telephone: 430 11
Telex: 3423/3446/3476 COMEUR LU

European Parliament
▲ Committee on Energy, Research, and Technology

Address: Palais de l'Europe
   F-67006 Strasbourg Cedex
   France
Telephone: 88/374 001; 88/375 485
Fax: 88/369 214; 88/256 516

Address: Centre Europeen
   Plateau du Kirchberg
   L-2929 Luxembourg
Telephone: 430 01
Telex: 3493 EUPARL LU; 2894 EUPARL LU
Fax: 436 972; 435 359

European Parliament
▲ Committee on External Economic Relations

Address: 97–113, rue Belliard
   B-1040 Bruxelles
   Belgium
Telephone: 2/284 21 21; 2/284 27 49
Fax: 2/230 68 56; 2/231 12 57

Address: Palais de l'Europe
   F-67006 Strasbourg Cedex
   France
Telephone: 88/374 001; 88/374 021
Fax: 88/369 214; 88/256 516

Address: Centre Europeen
   Plateau du Kirchberg
   L-2929 Luxembourg
Telephone: 430 01
Telex: 3493 EUPARL LU; 2894 EUPARL LU
Fax: 436 972; 435 359

European Parliament
▲ Committee on Transport and Tourism

Address: 97–113, rue Belliard
   B-1040 Bruxelles
   Belgium
Telephone: 2/284 21 21; 2/284 35 02
Fax: 2/230 68 56; 2/231 12 57

Address: Palais de l'Europe
   F-67006 Strasbourg Cedex
   France
Telephone: 88/374 001; 88/374 035
Fax: 88/369 214; 88/256 516

Address: Centre Europeen
   Plateau du Kirchberg
   L-2929 Luxembourg
Telephone: 430 01
Telex: 3493 EUPARL LU; 2894 EUPARL LU
Fax: 436 972; 435 359

Associations
▲ Action Committee of Public Transport of the European Communities

Address: av. de l'Uruguay 19
   B-1050 Bruxelles
   Belgium
Telephone: 2/673 33 25
Telex: 63916 B
Fax: 2/660 10 72

▲ CAACE (Committee of Associations of European Shippers)

Address: rue Ducale 45
   B-1000 Bruxelles
   Belgium
Telephone: 2/511 39 40
Telex: 26362 COMAR B
Fax: 2/511 80 92

▲ CLECAT (European Liaison Committee of Common Market Forwarders)

Address: CIR—Passage International 14
   Residence Palace (Bte 10)
   B-1000 Bruxelles
   Belgium
Telephone: 2/218 17 88
Telex: 64002 CLECAT B
Fax: 2/218 81 25

▲ ECMC (European Container Manufacturers' Committee)

Address: rue des Drapiers 21
B-1050 Bruxelles
Belgium
Telephone: 2/510 23 11
Telex: 21078 FABRIM B
Fax: 2/510 23 01

▲ EUROTRANS (European Committee of Associations of Manufacturers of Gears and Transmission Parts)

Address: 162, bd. Malesherbes
F-75017 Paris
France
Telephone: 1/43 80 04 09
Telex: 643788 f
Fax: 1/40 54 82 95

▲ Liaison Committee for the Union of European Freight Transporters

Address: rue d'Arlon 108 (Bte 6)
B-1040 Bruxelles
Belgium
Telephone: 2/230 29 80
Telex: 63338 b
Fax: 2/230 91 72

Data Resources and Publications

Annual Bulletin of Transport Statistics for Europe

Publisher: United Nations Economic Commission for Europe and the United Nations
Frequency of Publication: Annual
Scope: Statistics and brief studies on transport, plus tables on energy consumption for transport

Bulletin of Statistics on World Trade in Engineering Products

Publisher: United Nations and the United Nations Economic Commission for Europe
Frequency of Publication: Annual
Scope: Statistics about the flow of machinery, transport, scientific, medical, optical, and measuring equipment, watches and clocks

Cities and Transport

Publisher: OECD
Frequency of Publication: One time
Scope: Study of policies toward metropolitan transit issues in OECD countries

Containers—Towards a New Generation of Inland and Maritime Loading Units

Publisher: United Nations Economic Commission for Europe
Frequency of Publication: One time
Scope: Recent trends in shippers' demand for container transport services; also covers concepts for the interchangeability, intermodality, and modularity of maritime and inland transport equipment

COST 302—Prospects for Electrical Vehicles in Europe

Publisher: Office for Official Publications of the European Communities
Frequency of Publication: One time
Scope: Seminar proceedings under the COST program (European Co-operation on Scientific and Technical Research); prepared by DG VII and XII

COST 305—Data System for the Study of Demand for Interregional Passenger Transport

Publisher: Office for Official Publications of the European Communities
Frequency of Publication: One time
Scope: Discussion of systems for projecting demand for passenger transportation developed under the COST program (European Co-operation on Scientific and Technical Research); prepared by DG VII and XII

ECMT—Annual Report

Publisher: OECD
Frequency of Publication: Annual
Scope: Annual report of the European Conference of Ministers of Transport, including statistical trends in transport in European countries

Europa Transport

Publisher: Office for Official Publications of the European Communities
Frequency of Publication: 4 times a year
Scope: Developments in the intracommunity goods transport market, information broken down by mode of transport, plus an annual analysis and forecast; prepared by DG VII

Europa Transport: Observation of Transport Markets

Publisher: Office for Official Publications of the European Communities
Frequency of Publication: Annual
Scope: Overview of all EC transport markets; prepared by DG VII

Europe's Railway of the '90s: A White Paper

Publisher: United Nations Economic Commission for Europe
Frequency of Publication: One time
Scope: Position paper on the future of the railways in international transport in Europe, in competition and/or collaboration with other modes of transport

New Technologies in Commerce: The Potential and the Cost

Publisher: Office for Official Publications of the European Communities
Frequency of Publication: One time
Scope: Report on changes in commerce and distribution; prepared by DG III

Panorama of EC Industry

Publisher: Office for Official Publications of the European Communities
Frequency of Publication: Annual
Scope: Description of 165 manufacturing and service industries, including the tourism and transport industries, plus evaluations of the impact of the Single Market Program

Private and Public Investment in Transport

Publisher: OECD
Frequency of Publication: One time
Scope: Takes stock of problems and considers the contribution private capital could bring to funding transport infrastructure; prepared by the ECMT

Public Procurement in the Excluded Sectors

Publisher: Office for Official Publications of the European Communities
Frequency of Publication: One time
Scope: Official CEC communication, accompanied by proposals for Directives relating to water, energy, transport, and telecommunications procurement

Research on Transport Economics

Publisher: OECD
Frequency of Publication: Annual
Scope: General review of research activities undertaken by ECMT countries, as well as others in selected countries

Systems of Road Infrastructure Cost Coverage

Publisher: OECD
Frequency of Publication: One time
Scope: Examines the introduction of "road pricing" and compares approaches adopted in a number of countries; prepared by the ECMT

Tourism Policy and International Tourism in OECD Member Countries

Publisher: OECD
Frequency of Publication: One time
Scope: Review of impacts of tourist growth and transport deregulation and the impact of government policies toward tourism, as well as the impact of tourism on the environment

Transport for Disabled People. A Review of Provisions and Standards for Journey Planning and Pedestrian Access

Publisher: OECD
Frequency of Publication: One time
Scope: Examination of information available to and needed by elderly or disabled people during a voyage

Transport Information

Publisher: United Nations Economic Commission for Europe
Frequency of Publication: Annual
Scope: Broad picture of recent developments in the transport sector, including the status of international conventions and agreements covering international transport and the carriage of goods

Transport Policy and the Environment

Publisher: OECD

Frequency of Publication: One time

Scope: Analysis of problems in reducing adverse environmental effects of transportation; prepared by the ECMT

Transport Policy and the Environment: ECMT Ministerial Session

Publisher: OECD

Frequency of Publication: One time

Scope: Analysis of challenges of coordinating transport policies with environmental protection and examines how some Ministers of Transport are addressing them

Related Topics and Industries

Housing and Infrastructure; Manufacturing. See also *Part III—Sources on EC 1992 by Topic*

PART

V

Appendixes
and Indexes

INTRODUCTION

The material in the appendixes and indexes serves the following functions:

- Explains the selection criteria for the sources listed in Parts III and IV and ways to obtain the materials described

- Offers technical, detailed information supplementing the text in Parts I and II

- Provides ways to make connections between chapters in Parts III and IV

- Lists contacts in the United States, EC countries, Canada, and Japan that can further focus your data collection and assimilation about the Single Market Program.

How to Use the Appendixes and Indexes

Each appendix and index has its own purpose:

- *Appendix A. How Resources Were Selected for This Guide and How to Find Them:*
Provides additional technical information about the associations and organizations listed in Parts III and IV as well as the publications, databases, reports, and series included in the sourcebook. Helps you decide which report will be most helpful, by providing more information about its origins.

- *Appendix B. Glossary of Abbreviations and Acronyms:*
Provides a central list of the most commonly used names of EC programs, agencies, and political groups; helps you understand the coverage of a report or database mentioned in Parts III or IV.

- *Appendix C. EC Business Designations and Abbreviations:*
Lists all types of businesses described in Part II (the country profiles), plus the EEIG, described in Part I.

- *Appendix D. Single Market Measures by Topic and Industry:*
Groups the measures that make up the core of the Single Market Program. Start here if you know about a particular measure affecting your business. Find the measure in the lists and then turn to the chapter in Part III or Part IV that relates to it.

- *Appendix E. Where to Get Resources Described in This Book:*
Tells where to obtain copies of the reports and documents listed in Parts III and IV. Serves as a source for addresses of EC institutions mentioned in Part I but not directly listed as resources in Parts III and IV.

- *Appendix F. U.S. Government Contacts, Data Resources, and Publications on the Single Market:*
Presents a miniversion of Parts III and IV, focusing on U.S. resources. For U.S. business persons, many of the reports and contacts listed will be the resources used first, with those listed throughout Parts III and IV used after that.

- *Appendix G. Contacts in EC Member States on the Single Market Program:*
Provides a country-by-country breakdown of contacts in each EC Member State.

- *Appendix H. Contacts in Canada and Japan on the Single Market Program:*
Lists contacts inside and outside the Canadian and Japanese governments.

- *Index of Associations and Organizations:*
Lists the associations and organizations noted throughout the sourcebook with their pages of citation. A particular EC association involved in issues of importance to your business can be located here. If you find an association of interest in a chapter, you may wish to refer to this index to see whether that association is listed in another source chapter. If you do not know the name of a specific association, use the Subject Index to find a related product, service, or topic.

- *Subject Index:*
This traditional, general index covers topics other than resource names, databases, and publications, giving references throughout the book.

The appendixes are not intended to be your starting point for understanding the EC and the Single Market Program. Rather, the following approach may help you get the most from both the chapters and these appendixes:

1. Read the pertinent chapters about the country, topic, and industry you're considering for your business. In addition to the Subject Index that covers general topics, use the Index of Associations and Organizations and the Index of Databases and Publications to find other references to publications of interest to you.

2. To test whether the resources are likely to prove worthwhile, review the selection criteria used to assess them, which are described in Appendix A.

3. Check Appendixes B and C as necessary to find the meaning of unfamiliar terms as you read the chapters.

4. Use Appendix D to learn about directives related to your topic or industry as you read the chapters.

5. When you are ready to contact resources listed in the chapters, also refer to Appendixes E through H. Appendix E lists names and addresses for the data resources and publications given throughout the book. Appendixes F through H list Single Market Program contacts in the United States, EC countries, Canada, and Japan.

6. Turn to the steps indicated under the Assistance heading in each appendix as a last cross-reference to locate the related portions of the sourcebook you may not have checked yet.

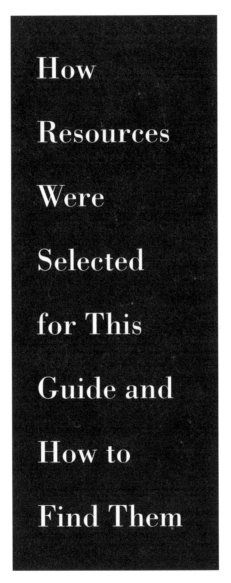

How Resources Were Selected for This Guide and How to Find Them

A

How to Use
This Appendix

This appendix contains detailed information on the resources in this sourcebook. It covers

- selection criteria used to select the resources,

- what organizations provide the resources,

- how to read and use the addresses listed in tables and text in each chapter.

Use this appendix to understand the reliability of the sources throughout the book and to help you prepare for contacting the services and organizations described and listed in Parts I through IV.

▼ ——————————————————————————————— ▼

Sections in This Appendix

Publications, Databases, and Subscription Services

Trade and Professional Associations and Organizations

Background on Non-EC Organizations Providing Data Resources and Publication

Proper Format and Use of Addresses and Telephone Numbers

Assistance

For an overall approach to using this sourcebook, see the general Introduction, as well as the part introductions.

———— ▼ ————

Publications, Databases, and Subscription Services

"Public" Resources

The data resources and publications identified throughout the sourcebook are primarily "public" data resources and publications, published by the EC itself or by other international organizations. Public sources have been included, for several reasons. They

- Usually reflect official views and actions
- Are the basis for many private sector subscription services, reports, and newsletters
- Usually cost less than similar private sector and secondary sources and may be free
- Are available throughout the industrial world, from either the agencies themselves or authorized distributors (see Appendix E)

Databases

The databases included in this book meet two criteria. They are:

- Produced or provided by the EC or its agencies
- Available to the public through commercial hosts and distributors, relay centers (European Documentation Centers and Euro Info Centres), as well as directly by subscription from the EC host and EC-approved distributors

Appendix E includes an extensive directory of the commercial hosts and distributors, as well as the EC's own hosts. For current information on the EC's databases, consult:

Dianeguide

Database Producer: ECHO
Distributors/Hosts: ECHO
Frequency of Update: Regularly
Scope: Databases and databanks, database producers, and host organizations available on Diane (Direct Information Access Network for Europe) ⊛

Timeliness of Resources

The following comments apply to the timeliness of the books, databases, or subscription services identified in this sourcebook:

- For the resources described as being updated, the frequency stated is that given by the publishers and may change. The titles of annual documents, such as agency reports, may vary slightly from year to year. The most common change is the inclusion of the year covered (not the year published) in the full title. This can be in the form of "1990 Annual Report . . . " or "Annual Report of . . . for 1990." In another variation, some institutions consecutively number their reports, such as "29th Report of the. . . ." The titles given in the sourcebook have removed these elements.

- The resources whose Frequency of Publication or Frequency of Update is noted as "one time," were published subsequent to 1988 and are included because they contain key information that is not available from other public sources.

———— 404 ————

TRADE AND PROFESSIONAL ASSOCIATIONS AND ORGANIZATIONS

The EC-specific trade and professional associations listed throughout this sourcebook (under the umbrella title "Associations") meet the following criteria:

- They have a permanent office at the European level.

- Their members are either national or Europe-wide associations, so federations whose membership consists of individual firms are not listed. A majority of these members (at least three in any case) must originate in EC countries.

- They are nonprofit.

- Their objectives are, according to the EC, "relevant to the development" of the EC.

Many associations and organizations are commonly identified by an official acronym, which is listed first, followed by the name of the association in parentheses. If no official acronym exists, only the association's name is listed.

Some associations have official names in several languages. The official English name (if one exists) is used in the sourcebook. If no official English name is provided, one of the other non-English official names is used, and the interests covered by the association are noted in { }.

All associations and organizations are indexed by both acronym and official name.

——— ▼ ———

BACKGROUND ON NON-EC ORGANIZATIONS PROVIDING DATA RESOURCES AND PUBLICATIONS

In addition to publications and data resources of the EC, this sourcebook provides information produced by the United Nations, the United Nations Economic Commission for Europe (UNECE), GATT, and the OECD and its constituent agencies.

The addresses of the outlets for their publications and other resources are listed in Appendix E.

GATT

GATT (The General Agreement on Tariffs and Trade) is a multinational forum for negotiating the removal of trade barriers throughout the world. The EC is a direct participant in these negotiations and negotiates on behalf of all Member States.

As a part of its activities, GATT operates a publishing program. Its reports cover a wide variety of issues, ranging from trade data on specific commodities to analyses of legislation affecting free international trade.

OECD

The OECD (Organization for Economic Cooperation and Development) was founded in 1961. It serves as a forum where government-level policy-makers meet and discuss mutual problems. It

maintains a substantial data collection and distribution center and annually produces more than 120 various publications.

Currently, GATT's member countries number over 90, including all 12 of the EC Member States. Thus, many OECD publications, studies, and data series provide significant assistance to those following the activities of the EC.

Four other organizations are affiliated, in one form or another, with the OECD: the International Energy Agency, Nuclear Energy Agency, Center for Educational Research and Innovation, and European Conference of Ministers of Transport. All produce reports, studies, and resources covering most (or all) of the Member States.

OECD manages each affiliated organization's publications program.

IEA

IEA, the International Energy Agency, was founded in 1974 to operate as an autonomous agency within the framework of the OECD. It serves as a forum to assist in developing a program of energy cooperation "designed to promote energy security." All members of the EC, with the exception of France, are also members of the IEA.

NEA

NEA, the OECD Nuclear Energy Agency, was organized in 1958 as a semiautonomous agency within the framework of the OECD. Its primary goal is to promote international cooperation for the development and application of nuclear energy for peaceful purposes. All members of the EC are members of NEA.

CERI

CERI, the Centre for Educational Research and Innovation, was set up in 1968. The organization assists the development of research activities in the field of education. All members of the EC are members of CERI.

ECMT

ECMT, the European Conference of Ministers of Transport, is an intergovernmental organization, concerned with monitoring and improving European transport. All members of the EC are members of ECMT. ECMT is administratively attached to the Secretariat of the OECD.

UNECE

Among the United Nations' specialized arms is UNECE, the United Nations Economic Commission for Europe, based in Switzerland. Created after World War II, it still collects basic economic data from throughout Europe.

Although many of its reports and data series are copublished by the United Nations itself, the UNECE also publishes many reports on its own. These cover all of Europe, including the EC.

▼

PROPER FORMAT AND USE OF ADDRESSES AND TELEPHONE NUMBERS

Directing Correspondence Through the Layers of EC Offices

EC and association addresses and telephone numbers are presented in this sourcebook in the style used in Europe. However, the convention chosen for this sourcebook is to omit the use of accents because many word processors and personal computers do not have special character generation capabilities.

In your correspondence with EC offices, whether by fax or letter, prominently note the directorate-general (DG), as well as directorate and subdirectorate with which you are corresponding. This can be done either of two ways:

- Using the numbers and letters referring to each office, such as DG XIX/A/3

- Using the key words from the title of each office, such as Budgets/Expenditure/Structural Funds

Machine-Readable Addresses Required by the U.S. Postal Service

Sourcebook users in the United States should be aware that the U.S. Postal Service's 1990 guidelines on machine-readable addresses also apply to mail to the EC. These users should make changes in the way they address mail to Europe. Specifically:

- Type all addresses, including return addresses, in all capital letters.

- Do not use any punctuation marks, such as accents or the comma (,), hyphen (-), or period (.).

- List any "attention" line first in the address.

- Follow the attention line with the organization's name and on the next line, its street address (with suite number if applicable).

- Place the name of the country separately on the last line.

Example:

ATTENTION: M LE BLANC

DIRECTORATE D 2

DG III

COMMISSION OF THE EUROPEAN
    COMMUNITIES

RUE DE LA LOI 200

B1049 BRUXELLES

BELGIUM

Addresses in Tables of EC Contacts

In tables throughout the sourcebook, key contacts in the CEC's directorates and subdirectorates are often presented in a tabular format.

The name of the directorate-general has been removed, leaving only the DG number. The names of all of the DGs are provided in Table 5.1 in Chapter 5.

Because many of these offices are located in the same complexes in Belgium and often use a common address and telephone, fax, or telex number, information is listed in an abbreviated form. In each table of EC contacts, "CEC HQ, Belgium" means:

▲ Commission of the European Communities

Address: rue de la Loi
             B-1049 Bruxelles
             Belgium
Telephone: 2/235 11 11
Telex: 21877 COMEU B

Any variation from the common telephone, fax, or telex number is specified separately in the table.

CITY AND COUNTRY TELEPHONE CODES

Throughout the sourcebook telephone and fax numbers are preceded by corresponding city codes (or in the United States, area codes). Luxembourg is the one exception, because it has no city code, only a country code.

The city codes used for London (71 and 81) throughout the sourcebook assume telephone calls will originate from outside Great Britain. When you are making intracountry calls, however, a zero should precede the designated city codes (071 and 081).

Although International Country Codes are necessary to place intercountry calls, these codes have not been included with the telephone and fax numbers listed in the sourcebook. Selected country codes, together with the time difference from Greenwich Mean Time (GMT) are shown in Table A.1.

Table A.1
EC Member States' Country Telephone Codes

Country	Code	Difference from GMT
Belgium	32	+1
Canada (Ottawa)	1	−5
Denmark	45	+1
France	33	+1
Germany, Federal Republic of	49/37 *	+1
Greece	30	+2
Ireland, Northern	44	0
Ireland, Republic of	353	0
Italy	39	+1
Japan	81	+9
Luxembourg	352	+1
The Netherlands	31	+1
Portugal	351	0
Spain	34	+1
Switzerland	41	+1
United Kingdom	44	0
USA (New York)	1	−5

* Use 37 when you dial the former German Democratic Republic.

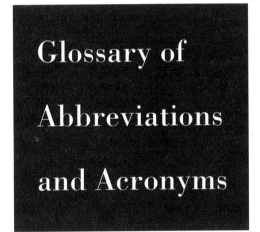

Glossary of

Abbreviations

and Acronyms

B

INTRODUCTION

This appendix collects in one place many of the abbreviations and acronyms used by official EC sources and the business press. These cover a wide variety of subjects:

- Agencies of the EC, such as the CEC
- EC-sponsored programs, such as Drive
- Transnational organizations and programs with which the EC deals, such as GATT
- Commercial concepts in the Single Market, such as VAT

In some cases, the acronym does not precisely parallel the name of the program. This is usually because the acronym reflects the program's name in a language other than English.

ASSISTANCE

Chapter 5 describes the EC Single Market Program and the agencies that make up the EC. Tables B.1 and B.2 list abbreviations and key terms used by the EC and non-EC sources, respectively, in this book.

Table B.1
CEC Acronyms and Abbreviations with Their Full Names

Acronym/ Abbreviation	Full Name
ACP	African, Caribbean, and Pacific countries that are parties to the Lome Convention
AIM	Advanced Informatics in Medicine
BAP	Biotechnology Action Program
BC-Net	Business Cooperation Network
BCC	Business Cooperation Center
BCR	Community Bureau of Reference, Directorate C/6, DG XII
BICs	Business and Innovation Centers
Bridge	Biotechnology Research for Innovation, Development, and Growth in Europe
Brite	Basic Research in Industrial Technologies in Europe
CAP	Common Agricultural Policy
CCT/CET	Common Customs Tariff/Common External Tariff
CEC	Commission of the European Communities
CEDEFOP	European Centre for the Development of Vocational Training
CEN	European Committee for Standardization
COM	Communication for the Commission of the European Communities
COM	Communication from the EC Commission
Comecon	Council for Mutual Economic Assistance
Comett	Community Program in Education and Training for Technology
COREPER	Committee of Permanent Representatives of the Member States
COST	European Cooperation on Scientific and Technical Research
CPC	Community Patent Convention
Crest	Scientific and Technical Research Committee
CUBE	Concertation Unit for Biotechnology in Europe
Delta	Development of European Learning Through Technological Advance
DFI	Direct Foreign Investment
DG or D-G	Directorate-General
Doses	Development of Statistical Expert Systems
Drive	Dedicated Road Infrastructure for Vehicle Safety in Europe
EAEC	European Atomic Energy Community (also Euratom)
EAGGF	European Agricultural Guidance and Guarantee Fund
EBRD	European Bank for Reconstruction and Development
EC	The European Community
ECJ	European Court of Justice
Eclair	European Collaborative Linkage of Agriculture and Industry Through Research

Acronym/ Abbreviation	Full Name
ECS	European Company Statute
ECSC	European Coal and Steel Community
ECTS	The European Community Course Credit Transfer System
ECU	European Currency Unit
EDF	European Development Fund
Edifact	Electronic Data Interchange for Administration, Commerce and Transport
EEA	European Economic Area
EEC	The European Economic Community
EEIG	European Economic Interest Grouping
EES	European Economic Space
EIB	European Investment Bank
EMCF	European Monetary Co-operation Fund
EMF	European Monetary Fund
EMS	European Monetary System
EMU	Economic and Monetary Union
EN	European Standards
EP	European Parliament
EPC	European Patent Convention
Epoch	European Program on Climatology and Natural Hazards
Erasmus	European Community Action Scheme for the Mobility of University Students
ERDF	European Regional Development Fund
ERM	Exchange Rate Mechanism
ESC	Economic and Social Committee
ESF	European Social Fund
Esprit	European Strategic Program for Research and Development in Information Technology
Euram	Research program on Raw Materials and Advanced Materials
Euratom	European Atomic Energy Community (Also EAEC)
Eureka	European Research Co-ordination Agency
Euret	European Research for Transport
EUROSTAT	Statistical Office of the European Community
FAST	Forecasting and Assessment in the Field of Science and Technology
Flair	Food-linked Agroindustrial Research
Green Paper	A discussion document or draft
Helios	Action Program to Promote Social and Economic Integration and an Independent Way of Life for Disabled People

Acronym/ Abbreviation	Full Name
IMP	Integrated Mediterranean Program
Impact	Information Market Policy Actions
ITAEGS	Information Technology Ad Hoc Expert Group on Standardization
ITSTC	Information Technology Steering Committee
Jessi	Joint European Submicron Silicon
Joule	Joint Opportunities for Unconventional or Long-Term Energy Supply
JRC	Joint Research Center
LDCs	Less-developed Countries
LEDA	Local Employment Development Action Program
Lingua	Program for the Promotion of Teaching and Learning Foreign Languages Within the Community
MAST	Marine Science and Technology
Media	Measures to Encourage the Development of the Audiovisual Industry
MEP	Member of the European Parliament
Misep	Mutual Information System on Employment Policies
Monitor	Research program on strategic analysis, forecasting, and assessment in research and technology
NACE	General Industrial Classification of Economic Activities within the EC
Naric	The EC network of National Academic Recognition Information Centers
NCI	New Community Instrument
NCPI	National Program of Community Interest
NICs	Newly Industrialized Countries
Nimexe	Nomenclature for Goods for the External Trade Statistics of the EC, a European commodity classification
NRSE	New and Renewable Sources of Energy
OCTs	Overseas Countries and Territories
OJ or OJEC	Official Journal of the European Communities
Pedip	Program to Modernize Portuguese Industry
Phare	Poland and Hungary Aid for Economic Restructuring
PIP	Priority Information Program
Poseidon	Program of Options Specific to the Remote and Insular Nature of the Overseas Departments
R&D	Research and Development

Acronym/ Abbreviation	Full Name
R&TD	Research and Technology Development
RACE	Research and Development in Advanced Communications Technology for Europe
Rechar	Program to Assist the Conversion of Coal Mining Areas
Renaval	Program to Assist the Conversion of Shipbuilding Areas
Reward	Program to Assist the Conversion of Steel Areas
RUE	Rational Uses of Energy
SAST	Strategic Analysis of Science and Technology
Scent	System for a Customs Enforcement Network
Science	Plan to Stimulate the International Cooperation and Interchange Necessary for European Researchers
SEA	Single European Act
SME	Small and medium-sized enterprises
Spear	Support Program for a European Assessment of Research
SPES	Stimulation Plan for Economic Science
Sprint	Strategic Program for Innovation and Technology Transfer
STAR	Community program for the development of certain less-favored regions of the EC by improving access to advanced telecommunications services
STEP	Science and Technology for Environmental Protection
Taric	Integrated Community Tariff
Tedis	Trade Electronic Data Interchange System
Teleman	Research and Training Program on Remote Handling in Hazardous or Disordered Nuclear Environments
Thermie	Program for the promotion of energy technology
Value	Program for the dissemination and use of research results
VAT	Value Added Tax

Table B.2
Non-EC Acronyms and Key Terms

Abbreviation/ Key Term	Full Name or Description
BENELUX	Belgium, The Netherlands, and Luxembourg
BLEU	Belgo-Luxembourg Economic Union
CSCE	Conference on Security and Cooperation in Europe
ECE	United Nations Economic Commission for Europe (also UNECE)
ECMT	The European Conference of Ministers of Transport
EFTA	European Free Trade Agreement or European Free Trade Association

Abbreviation/ Key Term	Full Name or Description
GATS	General Agreement on Trade in Services
GATT	General Agreement on Tariffs and Trade
GDP	Gross Domestic Product
GSP	Generalized System of Preferences
IEA	International Energy Agency
IMF	International Monetary Fund
IT	Information Technology
National Champion	A (private or state-owned) company designated to lead or "champion" development of a particular industry by the national government
NATO	North Atlantic Treaty Organization
NEA	OECD Nuclear Energy Agency
OECD	The Organization for Economic Cooperation and Development
SITC	Standard International Trade Classification, the UN International Commodity Classification for Foreign Trade
UN	United Nations
UNCTAD	United Nations Conference on Trade and Development
UNECE	United Nations Economic Commission for Europe (Also see ECE)
Warsaw Pact	Eastern European equivalent of NATO

EC Business
Designations
and
Abbreviations

C

INTRODUCTION

This appendix lists the abbreviations, names, and designations for the most common forms of businesses in the EC. Refer to the table in this appendix to associate specific business abbreviations with appropriate EC Member States.

ASSISTANCE

The country profiles featured in Chapters 7–18 discuss the general characteristics of each of the most important national forms of business (company, partnership, and so on), including key regulatory and tax issues. Chapter 2 discusses the characteristics of the new form of EC-wide business entity, the European Economic Interest Grouping.

Table C.1
CEC Business Designations and Abbreviations

Abbreviation	Name	Description
A/S	Aktieselskab	Danish public company
AE	Anonymos Eteria Eterorrythmos Eteria	Greek corporation Greek limited partnership
AG	Aktiengesellschaft	German limited company
ApS	Anpartsselskab	Danish private limited company
BV	Besloten Vennootschap	Netherlands private limited company
BVBA	Besloten Vennootschap met Beperkte Aansprakelijkheid	Belgium private limited liability company
CIA	Sociedad em nom colectif	Portuguese special partnership
CIA	Sociedad em nom colectivo	Portuguese special partnership
CIA	Sociedade em comandita simples	Portuguese limited partnership
CIA	Sociedade in comandita por accoes	Portuguese partnership limited by shares
Coop V	Cooperatieve Vennootschap	Belgium cooperative society
CV	Commanditaire Vennootschap	Netherlands partnership
CV	Cooperatieve Vennootschap Cooperatie; Samenwerkende Vennootschap	Belgium cooperative society
EEIG	European Economic Interest Grouping	A form of cross-border partnership created by EC regulation
EP	Empresa Publica	State-owned Portuguese company
EPE	Eteria Periorismenis Efthinis	Greek private company with limited liabilities
G.I.E.	Groupment d'interet economique	French type of partnership
GmbH & Co KG	Gesellschaft mit beschrankter Haftung Kommanditgesellschaft	German private limited company
GmbH	Gesellschaft mit beschrankter Haftung	German private limited liability company
I/S	Interessentskab	Danish general partnership
K/S	Kommanditselskab	Danish limited partnership
KGaA	Kommanditgesellschaft auf Aktien	German partnership limited by shares

Abbreviation	Name	Description
Lda	Sociedades por Quotas	Portuguese private limited liability company
Lda	Limited; Limited Company	British private limited company
Ltd	Limited Company	British or Irish private limited company
NV	Naamloze Vennootschap	Belgium or Netherlands limited company
OHG	Offene Handelsgesellschaft	German general partnership
Plc PLC	Public Limited Company	British or Irish public company
SA	Sociedad Anomina	Spanish limited company
SA	Sociedades Anonima	Portuguese limited company
SA	Societe anonyme	Belgium and French limited company
S.A.	Societe anonyme	Luxembourg joint stock company
SApA	Societa in Accomandita per Azioni	Italian partnership limited by shares
SARL	Societe a responsibilite limitee	French private limited liability company
S.a.r.l.	Societe a responsibilite limitee	Luxembourg limited liability company
SC	Societe cooperative	Belgium or Luxembourg cooperative society
SCA	Societe en commandite par actione	Belgium or French partnership limited by shares
SCS	Societe en commandite simple	Belgium limited partnership
S.E.C.A.	Societe en commandite par actions	Luxembourg partnership limited by shares
SECS	Societe en commandite simple	Luxembourg limited partnership
S.E.N.C.	Societe en nom collectif	Luxembourg general partnership
SL	Sociedad de Responsabilidad Limitada	Spanish private limited liability company
SNC	Societe en nom colectif	Belgium special partnership

Abbreviation	Name	Description
SpA	Societa per Azioni	Italian limited company
SPRL	Societe des personnes a responsibilite limitee	Belgium private limited liability company
SRL	Societa a responsibilita limitata	Italian private limited liability company
Teo	Teoranta	Irish private limited company
VGA	Vennootschap bij wijze van geldschieting op sandelen	Belgium partnership limited by shares
VOF	Vennootschap onder Firma	Netherlands partnership
VOF	Vennootschap onder Firms	Belgium partnership

Single Market Measures by Topic and Industry

INTRODUCTION

This appendix lists the core titles of several hundred Single Market measures, including directives, regulations, and other proposals that are generally considered a part of the Single Market Program. Eliminated from the titles were phrases such as *Directive Concerning . . ., Amendment to . . ., Revision Concerning . . ., Council Recommendation Concerning . . ., Proposal for. . . .*

The directives and other measures themselves range from the very general, such as "Product Safety," to the highly specific, such as "Spray Suppression Devices of Certain Categories of Motor Vehicles."

For convenience, within this appendix, these measures are *broadly* divided along the same lines as the resource chapters in Parts III and IV. This allows a direct connection between a specific measure and the EC and association contacts, as well as data resources and publications related to that topic. However, be advised that many of these measures, especially some of the more general ones, could have been listed under multiple resource chapters. Therefore, if you are seeking information on measures affecting, for example, Employment and Labor (Chapter 22), you should also see measures listed under Chapter 23, "Regulation of Business and Competition," and Chapter 25, "Social and Economic Policy."

Measures are of three types:

- Items that have been adopted by the Council of Ministers and are in the process of being imple-

mented by the Member States. These are known as "L" documents, because they have already been published in the "L" series of the *Official Journal.*

- Measures that are being considered by one or more institutions. These have not yet been adopted; thus, they are not yet binding on the Member States. The relevant documentation is known as "C" documents, as they were published by the EC in the "C" series of the *Official Journal.*

- Topics on which the EC has announced that it is committed to proposing measures but that do not yet have official published versions.

This appendix does not label the current status of each directive, for three reasons:

- The status of "C" documents changes rapidly and will continue to do so. A status list would be out of date as soon as it was printed.

- Although a measure is an "L" document, it may still change. Many "C" documents include proposed amendments to existing "L" documents.

- The topics on which the EC is committed to proposing regulations or directives will eventually be replaced with official published measures. Those will then become "C" documents.

To find out the status of a particular directive or measure, use the resources listed in Chapter 19, or contact the appropriate U.S. government office listed in Appendix F, or use the EC contacts listed in the parallel chapter.

Sections in This Appendix

Single Market Measures by Topic

Single Market Measures by Industry

Assistance

Chapter 19 describes the progress of the Single Market Program, and the goal of all of these measures. Chapter 6 describes the way in which Community legislation is adopted, the differences between directives and regulations, and the relationship between EC legislation and national law in the Community.

Chapter 19 and Appendix F identify EC and U.S. government resources, including the EC's *Official Journal*, which you can use to track the progress of these measures. Copies of individual measures can be obtained from the U.S. Department of Commerce's Single Market Information Service listed in Appendix F or other government agencies listed in Appendixes G and H.

Abbreviations and acronyms used by the EC are set out in Appendix B. The book's Introduction describes "Eurospeak," the EC's vocabulary of terms such as *harmonization* and *approximation*.

Single Market Measures by Topic

EC-Wide Macroeconomic, Population, and Census-Type Data (Chapter 20)

Statistics Relating to the Trading of Goods Between Member States

Economic and Business Development (Chapter 21)

Mutual Assistance between Member States' Authorities and the CEC to Ensure Application of the Law on Customs or Agricultural Matters

Special Schemes for Small Business

Employment and Labor (Chapter 22)

Comparability of Vocational Training Qualifications

Control of the Acquisition and Possession of Arms

Cooperation Between Higher Education and Industry for Advanced Training Relating to New Technologies (COMET)

Coordination of Provisions in Respect of Certain Activities in the Field of Pharmacy

Easing of Controls at Intra-Community Borders

Elimination of Cumbersome Administrative Procedures Relating to Residence Permits

Exemptions in International Travel—Increase to 350 ECUs

Freedom of Movements for Workers Within the Community

General System of Mutual Recognition of Higher Education Diplomas

Harmonization of Income Tax Provision

Minimum Health and Safety of Machine Equipment and Installations at the Workplace

Mutual Recognition of Diplomas in Pharmacy

Mutual Recognition of Higher Education Diplomas for Professional Training of at Least Three Years

Protection of Workers from Risks of Biological Agents at Work

Protection of Workers from Risks of Exposure to Carcinogens at Work

Recognition of Higher Education Diplomas Awarded on Completion of Professional Education and Training of Less than Three Years Duration

Right of Residence

Right of Residence for Nationals of Member States Not Yet or No Longer Employed

Right of Residence for Students

Safety Standards—Electrically Operated Lifts

Safety Standards—Mobile Machinery

Self Commercial Agents

Specific Training in General Medical Practice

Science and Technology (Chapter 24)

Access to Large-scale Scientific and Technical Facilities of European Interest

Advanced Informatics in Medicine—AIM

Biotechnology Research for Innovation, Development, and Growth in Europe—BRIDGE

Cooperation Between Higher Education and Industry for Advanced Training Relating to New Technologies (COMET)

European Collaborative Linkage of Agriculture and Industry Through Research—ECLAIR

European Strategic Program for R&D in Information Technologies—ESPRIT

Food-Linked Agro-Industrial Research—FLAIR

Framework Program for Research and Development

Framework Program for Research and Development (1987–1991)

International Scientific and Technological Cooperation and Interchange (1988–1992)

Marine Science and Technology—MAST

Multiannual R&D Programs in the Field of Biotechnology

Multiannual R&D Programs in the Field of the Environment (1986–1992)

Program for R&D of Statistical Expert Systems—DOSES

Program for the Dissemination and Utilization of R&D Results—VALUE

Promotion of Energy Technology in Europe—THERMIE

R&D in Advanced Communications Technologies in Europe—RACE

R&D in the Field of Industrial Manufacturing and Advanced Materials Applications—BRITE/EURAM

R&D Program in Technology, Particularly Controlling Harmful Organisms

R&D Program in the Field of Environment (1991–1994)

R&D Program in the Field of Nonnuclear Energies and Rational Use of Energy — JOULE

R&D Program in the Field of Raw Materials and Recycling (1990–1992)

R&D Program in the Field of Transport—EURET (1990–1993)

Reference Methods and List of National Laboratories for Detecting Residues

STEP (Science and Technology for Environmental Protection) and EPOCH (European Program on Climatology and Natural Hazards)

Stimulation Plan for Economic Science—SPES

Strategic Analysis Forecasting and Evaluation in Matters of Research and Technology—MONITOR

Strategic Program for Innovation and Technology Transfer—SPRINT

Social and Economic Policy (Chapter 25)

Abolition of Certain Derogations, Article 28 (3) of D. 77/388

Abolition of Controls Related to Transport

Abolition of Customs Presentation Charges

Abolition of Fiscal Frontiers

Abolition of Lodgment of the Transit Advice Note on Crossing an Internal Frontier of the Community

Abolition/Reduction of Excises Not Covered by the Common System and Giving Rise to Border Formalities

Accounts of Branches of Certain Types of Companies

Administrative Cooperation in Indirect Taxation

Amendment to 4th & 7th D. (Simplification for SMEs)

Amendment to the Scope of 4th & 7th Ds. (inclusion of PLCs)

Approximation of Indirect Taxes

Approximation of VAT Rates

Carryover of Losses of Permanent Establishments and Subsidiaries

Commercial Agents

Common Border Posts

Common Rate Bands for All Harmonized Duties on Alcoholic Beverages

Common Rate Bands for All Harmonized Excise Duties on Mineral Oils

Common System of Taxation Applicable to Parent Companies and Their Subsidiaries

Common System of Taxation of Mergers, Divisions, and Contribution of Assets

SINGLE MARKET MEASURES BY INDUSTRY

Agriculture and Food Stuffs (Chapter 26)

Acceptance for Breeding Purposes of Purebred Breeding Animals—Bovine

Additives to Animal Feedingstuffs

Alignment of National Standards and Intracommunity Standards in Plant Health

Animal Health Conditions Governing Intra-Community Trade in and Import from Third Countries of Fresh Poultrymeat and Fresh Meat of Reared Game Birds

Animal Health Conditions Governing the Placing of Rodents on the Community Market

Animal Health Conditions Governing the Placing on the Market of Aquaculture Animals and Products

Animal Health—Ovine and Caprine Species

Animal Health Problems Relating to Trade in Dogs and Cats

Animal Health Requirements—Intracommunity Trade in and Imports of Deep Frozen Semen—Bovine

Animal Health—Trade in Poultry and Hatching Eggs

Antibiotic Residues

Application of the Laws on Customs or Agricultural Matters

Application of Veterinary Rules

Aujesky Disease and Swine Vesicular Disease

Boar Meat

Calcium, Magnesium, Sodium, Sulphur Content of Fertilizer

Certification in Reproduction Materials for Decorative Plants

Coffee Extracts; Chicory Extracts

Compulsory Nutrition Labeling of Foodstuffs Intended for Sales to Consumers

Conditions for Granting Temporary and Limited Derogations from Specific Community Health Rules on the Production and Marketing of Products of Animal Origin

Control of Foot and Mouth Disease

Control of Residues

Controls of Harmful Organisms, Especially in Seed Potatoes and in Fruit Plant Reproductive Material

Definition of Spirituous Beverages and Aromatized Wines

Diseases Affecting Animals of the Ovine and Caprine Species

Disposal of Animal Waste and Prevention of Pathogens in Feedingstuffs

Echinococcosis

Emulsifiers

Entry into EC of Organisms Harmful to Plants/Plant Products

Entry into EC of Organisms Harmful to Plants/Plant Products—Rules of Liability

Equivalence of Field Inspection Carried Out in Third Countries on Seed-Producing Crops

Eradication of Brucellosis in Sheep and Goats

Eradication of Classical Swine Fever

Eradication of Infectious Hemopoietic Necrosis (IHN) of Salmonids

Established Inventory of Source Materials for Preparation of Flavorings

European Law on Plant Breeders

Expenditure in the Veterinary Field

Extraction Solvents

Financial Aid for the Eradication of African Swine Fever in Sardinia

Fixing of Guidelines for the Evaluation of Additives Used in Animal Foodstuffs

Flavorings for Use in Foodstuffs

Food Additives

Food for Particular Nutritional Use

Food Inspection

Foods and Food Ingredients Treated with Ionizing Radiation

Food Inspection

Foods and Food Ingredients Treated with Ionizing Radiation

Foodstuffs for Particular Nutritional Use

Frontier Controls Relating to the Welfare of Animals in International Transport

Fruit Juices

Further Proposals Concerning Classical Swine Fever

Game Meat and Rabbit Meat

Protective Measures Against the Introduction of Organisms Harmful to Plants or Plant Products

Pure Bred Breeding Sheep and Goats

Quick Frozen Foods

Reduction of Role of Phytosanitary Certificate in Intracommunity Trade

Residues of Pesticides in and on Fruit and Vegetables

Rules on Liability in Respect of Plant Health

Sampling and Methods of Analysis

Semen of Animals

Stimulants—Plastic Materials in Contact with Foodstuffs

Suppression of Plant Health Certificates

Suppression of Veterinary Certificate for Animal Products and Simplification of Certificates for Live Animals

Swine Fever

System of Certification of Reproductive Materials in Fruit Plants

Trade in Embryos of Domestic Animals—Bovine

Trade in Equidae Intended for Participation in Competitions

Trade in Fish and Fish Products

Trade in Fresh Poultry Meat and Fresh Meat of Reared Game Birds

Trade in Molluscs

Veterinary Checks in Intracommunity Trade

Veterinary Medical Products

Zoological and Genealogical Conditions for Intracommunity Trade in Equidae

Zootechnical and Pedigree Requirements for Marketing Purebred Animals

Zootechnical Standards Applicable to Breeding Animals—Porcine

Communications and Information (Chapter 27)

Approximation of Laws on Telecommunications Terminal Equipment, Including Mutual Recognition of Conformity

Broadcasting Activities

Community Action in the Field of Information Technology and Telecommunications in Health (AIM)

Community Action on Information Technology and Telecommunications in Health Care

Competition in the Markets for Telecommunications Services

Competition in the Markets for Telecommunications Terminal Equipment

Coordinated Introduction of ISDN

Coordinated Introduction of Pan-European Land-Based Public Radio Paging in the EC

Development of a Common Market on Telecommunications Services and Equipment

Establishing an Internal Market for Telecommunications Services with Open Network Provisions

Frequency Bands Reserved for Pan-European Public Radio Paging

Full Mutual Recognition of Type Approval of Terminal Equipment

Initial Stage of the Mutual Recognition of Type Approval for Telecommunications Terminal Equipment

Opening Up of Public Procurement in the Telecommunication Sector

Open Network Provision

Pan European Cellular Digital Land Based Mobile Communications

Plan of Action for Information Services Market

Policy and Plan of Priority Action for the Development of an Information Services Market

Pursuit of Television Broadcast Activities

Radio Interferences

Standardization in the Field of Information Technology and Telecommunications

Consumer Products and Services (Chapter 28)

Cosmetics

Definition of Spirit Drinks

European Agreement on Detergents

Exemptions in International Travel—Increase to 350 ECUs

Food for Particular Nutritional Use

Food Labeling

Fruit Juices

Furniture Flammability Safety Requirements

Harmonization of the Structure of Excise Duties on Alcoholic Beverages

Payment Systems, Particularly Relating Card-holders to Card Issuers

Pension Funds—Harmonization of Rules and Laws

Prospectus to Be Published When Securities Are Offered for Subscription or Sale to the Public

Published Accounts of Branches of Banks and Other Financial Institutions

Reorganization and Winding-Up of Credit Institutions

Services in the Field of Mortgage Credit

Solvency Ratio of Credit Institutions

Taxes on Transactions in Securities

UCITS Directive—Special Measure Concerning Certain Investments Like Mutual Bonds

UCITS: Jurisdictional Clause

Winding Up of Insurance Undertakings

Health Care and Medicine (Chapter 31)

Active Implantable Medical Devices

Active Medical Devices (Nonimplantable)

Advanced Informatics in Medicine (AIM)

Authorization and Administration System for the Free Movement of Medicinal Products, Including Establishing a European Agency for the Evaluation of Medicinal Products

Community Action in the Field of Information Technology and Telecommunications in Health (AIM)

Community Action on Information Technology and Telecommunications in Health Care

Coordination of Provisions with Respect to Pharmacy

Distribution of Medical Products for Human Use

Extension of Directives to Products Not Already Covered, Including Blood Products, Proprietary Medical Products, Radiopharmaceuticals, Serums, Toxins, and Vaccines

In Vitro Medical Diagnostic Products

Labeling Medicinal Products for Human Use, and Package Leaflets

Legal Status for Supply of Medicinal Products for Human Use

Medical Examination of Personnel

Medical Specialties

Membership of the European Pharmacopeia

Nonactive Medical Devices

Placing on the Market of High-Technology Medicinal Products, Including Those Derived from Biotechnology

Price Transparency in the Prices of Medicine and Social Security Refunds

Products Consisting of Vaccines, Toxins, or Serums and Allergens

Products Derived from Human Blood

Proprietary Medicinal Products

Radiopharmaceuticals

Specific Training in General Medical Practice

Test Relating to the Placing on the Market of Medicinal Products

Testing of Medical Specialties

Tolerance Levels for Residues of Veterinary Medicines

Transparency in the Prices of Medicines and Social Security Refunds

Vaccines for Veterinary Use

Veterinary Medicinal Products

Veterinary Medicines

Wholesale Distribution of Medicinal Products for Human Use

Housing and Infrastructure (Chapter 32)

Action Program for Transport Infrastructure to Complete an Integrated Transport Market

Community Railway Policy

Construction Products

Coordination of Procedures for the Award of Public Works Contracts

Interpretation of Standards for Construction Products

Municipal Waste Water Treatment

Protection of Hotels Against Fire

Tower Cranes—Permissible Sound Levels

Industrial Products (Chapter 33)

Calcium, Magnesium, Sodium, Sulphur Content of Fertilizer

Contained Use of Genetically Modified Microorganisms

Authorization of Scheduled Interregional Air Services for the Transport of Passengers, Mail, and Cargo Between Member States

Braking Devices of Motor Vehicles and Trailers

Civil Liability in Motor Vehicles

Code of Conduct for Computerized Reservation System

Community Railway Policy

Community Transit

Coordinated Action to Safeguard Free Access to Cargoes in Oceanic Trade

Drivers Seat on Wheeled Agricultural and Forestry Tractors

Duty-free Admission of Fuel in Motor Tanks of Commercial Motor Vehicles, Lorries, and Coaches

Earth Moving and Mobile Machines

Elimination of Controls and Formalities Applicable to Cabin and Checked Baggage of Passengers on Intra-Community Flights and Sea-Crossings

Elimination of Customs Formalities: TIR Convention and Common Border Posts

Engine Power of Motor Vehicles

Facilitation of Physical Inspections and Administrative Formalities in Respect of the Carriage of Goods Between Member States

Fares for Scheduled Air Services

Field of Vision of Motor Vehicle Drivers

Freedom to Provide Services Between Member States and Between Member States and Third Countries

Freedom to Provide Services Within Member States

Gaseous Emissions—Commercial Cars

Gaseous Emissions—Passenger Cars

Inland Waterways Goods and Passengers—Freedom to Provide Services by Nonresident Carriers Within a Member State

Installation of Lighting and Light Signaling on Motor Vehicles and Tractors

Limit Values for Gaseous Emissions of Cars

Maritime Transport—Goods and Passengers—Freedom to Provide Services in the Sea Transport Sector Within a Member State by Nonresident Carriers

Modification of Framework—Tractors

Mutual Acceptance of Personnel Licenses for the Exercise of Functions in Civil Aviation

Mutual Recognition of Diplomas, Certificates, and Qualifications of Goods Haulage Operators and Road Passenger Transport Operators

Opening Up of Public Procurement in the Energy, Water, and Transport Services

Package Travel, Including Package Holidays

Rear View Mirrors of Motor Vehicles

Road Transport—Common Rules for the International Carriage of Passengers by Road

Road Transport—Goods—Freedom to Provide Services by Nonresident Carriers Within a Member State

Roadworthiness Tests for Motor Vehicles and Their Trailers

Rollover Protection Structures

Safety Glass for Use in Motor Vehicles

Self-propelled Industrial Trucks

Shipment of Radioactive Wastes

Simplification of Community Transit Procedure

Single Administrative Document

Sound Levels and Exhaust Systems of Motorcycles

Spray Suppression Devices of Certain Categories of Motor Vehicles

Stores of Ships, Aircraft, and International Trains

Technical Standards for Civil Aviation

Tire Pressure Gauge [Standards]

Tractors—Weight and Dimensions, Driveshaft Engine Stopping Device, Windscreen Wipers, and Footrest

Type Approval of Motor Vehicles and Their Trailer

Unfair Pricing Practices

VAT and Excise Duty Applicable to Stores of Ships, Aircraft, and International Trains

VAT on Passenger Transport

Weights and Dimensions of Certain Road Vehicles

Weights, Dimensions, and Characteristics of Certain Road Vehicles

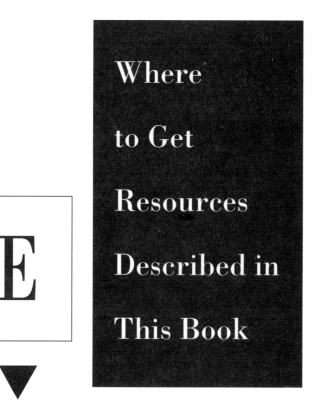

E

Where to Get Resources Described in This Book

INTRODUCTION

This appendix lists the names and addresses you can use to obtain copies of the data resources and publications mentioned throughout this sourcebook. You will also find information on accessing databases and subscriptions. The appendix includes the organizations listed throughout Parts III and IV as "Publisher" of books and periodicals, and "Distributors/Hosts" of online databases.

The list contains the headquarters address for each supplier and indicates the local office (or official agent) for that publisher in Canada, Japan, the United Kingdom, and the United States. Most of these publishers have other outlets throughout the world as well.

Some of these resources are free; some carry a nominal charge; a very few are relatively expensive. Because these prices occasionally change, inquire about the cost before placing any order.

Sections
in This Appendix

Official EC Resources

Resources Outside the EC

Official EC Resources

▲ Commission of the European Communities, Office for Official Publications of the European Community:

Address: Luxembourg: 2, rue Mercier
L-2986
Telephone: 49 92 81
Telex: 1324 PUBOF LU; 1322 PUBOF LU
Fax: 49 00 03; 49 57 19

United Kingdom:

Address: 8 Storey's Gate
GB-London SW1P 3AT
Great Britain
Telephone: 71/222 81 22

Address: 4 Cathedral Road
GB-Cardiff CF1 9SG
Wales
Telephone: 222/37 16 31

Address: 7 Alva Street
GB-Edinburgh EH2 4PH
Scotland
Telephone: 31/225 20 58

Address: Windsor House
9/15 Bedford Street
GB-Belfast BT2 7EG
Northern Ireland
Telephone: 232/407 08

United States:

Address: 2100 M Street, NW
Seventh Floor
Washington, DC 20037
Telephone: 202/862-9500
Telex: 64215 EURCOM UW
Fax: 202/429-1766

Assistance

For a description of the EC's principal institutions, see Chapter 5. Appendix A introduces the non-EC institutions, such as the UNECE and OECD, that are also sources for data and publications.

Address: 3 Dag Hammarskjold Plaza
305 East 47th Street
New York, NY 10017
Telephone: 212/371-3804

▲ Council of the European Communities

Address: Division IX-C-1
rue de la Loi 170
B-1048 Bruxelles
Belgium
Telephone: 2/235 61 11

▲ Court of Auditors of the European Community

Address: 12, rue Alcide de Gasperi
L-1615 Luxembourg
Telephone: 439 81

▲ Court of Justice

Address: Plateau du Kirchberg
L-2925 Luxembourg
Telephone: 430 31
Telex: 2510 LU

▲ ECHO (European Commission Host Organization)

Address: Boite Postale 2373
L-1023 Luxembourg
Telephone: 488 041
Telex: 2181 L
Fax: 488 040

▲ Economic and Social Committee

Address: Press, Information and Publications
rue Ravenstein 2
B-1000 Bruxelles
Belgium
Telephone: 2/519 90 11

▲ Eurobases (European Commission Host Organization)

Address: 200 rue de la Loi
B-1049 Bruxelles
Belgium
Telephone: 2/235 00 01

▲ EUR-OP. *See* Commission of the European Communities, Office for Official Publications of the European Community

▲ European Investment Bank

Address: Information/Public Relations Division
100, bd. Konrad Adenauer
L-2950 Luxembourg
Telephone: 437 91
Fax: 437 704

▲ European Parliament
Secretariat General

Address: Centre Europeen
Plateau du Kirchberg
L-2929 Luxembourg
Telephone: 430 01
Telex: 3493 EUPARL LU; 2894 EUPARL LU

▲ EUROSTAT. *See* Statistical Office of the EC

▲ Statistical Office of the European Communities

Address: Batiment Jean Monnet
rue Alcide de Gasperi
L-2920 Luxembourg
Telephone: 430 11
Telex: 3423/3446/3476 COMEUR LU

Sales Offices:

Japan:

Address: Kinokuniya Company Ltd.
17-7 Shinjuku 3-Chome,
Sinkiuku-ku
Tokyo 160-91
Telephone: 3/3439 0124

United Kingdom:

Address: HMSO Books (PC 16)
HMSO Publications Centre
51 Nine Elms Lane
GB-London SW8 5DR
Telephone: 71/873 9090

Subagent:

Address: Alan Armstrong Ltd
2 Arkwright Road
Reading
GB-Berks RG2 0SQ
Telephone: 734/75 18 55
Telex: 849937 AAALTD G

United States:

Address: UNIPUB
4661-F Assembly Drive
Lanham, MD 20706-4319
Telephone: 800/274-4888
Telex: 7108260418
Fax: 301/459-0056

▲ ECHO Customer Service

Address: 117 rue d'Esche
L-1741 Luxembourg

RESOURCES OUTSIDE THE EC ORGANIZATION

▲ Arthur Andersen & Co., S.C.

Address: 69 W. Washington St.
Chicago, IL 60602
USA
Telephone: 312/580-0069
Fax: 312/507-2548

▲ Arthur Andersen
EC Office

Address: Avenue des Arts, 56
B-1040 Brussels
Belgium
Telephone: 2/510 43 07
Fax: 2/510 43 08

▲ Bistel

Address: rue de la Loi, 16
             B-1000 Bruxelles
             Belgium
Telephone: 2/513 80 20

▲ Business and Trade Statistics

Address: Lancaster House
             Morelane
             Esher
             GB-Surrey, KT 108 AP
             Great Britain
Telephone: 372/63 121

▲ CEN (European Committee for Standardization)

Address: rue Brederode 2
             B-1000 Bruxelles
             Belgium
Telephone: 2/519 68 11
Fax: 2/519 68 19

▲ CENELEC (European Committee for Electrotechnical Standardization)

Address: rue Brederode 2
             B-1000 Bruxelles
             Belgium
Telephone: 2/519 68 11
Fax: 2/519 68 19

▲ Centre francais du commerce exterieur

Address: 10, avenue d'Iena
             F-75783 Paris Cedex 16
             France
Telephone   1/45 05 30 00
Fax: 1/45 05 39 79

▲ Cerved

Address: via Appia Nuova, 694
             I-00197 Roma
             Italy
Telephone: 6/5 90 35 28

▲ CITE (Commission Joint Research Centre—Centre for Information Technology and Electronics)

Address: I-21020 Ispra (VA)
             Italy
Telephone: 332/78 91 11

▲ Datacentralen, DC Host Centre

Address: Landlystvej 40
             DK-2650 Hvidovre (Kobenhavn)
             Denmark
Telephone: 1/75 81 22
Telex: 27122 D
Fax: 1/168 805

▲ Dimdi

Address: Weisshaustrasse, 27
             D-5000 Koln
             Germany
Telephone: 221/472 42 52

▲ DSI (Data Service and Information GmbH)

Address: Scholsstrasse 133
             D-4134 Rheinberg 1
             Germany
Telephone: 2843/602 73

▲ GATT:

Switzerland:

Address: GATT
             Centre William Rappard
             Rue de Lausanne
             CH-1211 Geneva 21
Telephone: 22/739 50 19
Telex: 412324 GATT CH
Fax: 22/731 42 06

United States:

Address: UNIPUB
             4661-F Assembly Drive
             Lanham, MD 20706-4319
Telephone: 800/274-4888
Telex: 7108260418
Fax: 301/459-0056

▲ GSI-ECO

Address: 45, rue de la Procession
             F-75015 Paris
             France
Telephone: 1/45 66 78 89

▲ ICEX (Instituto Espanol de Comercio Exterior)

Address: P. de la Castellana 14
Apartado 14 710
E-28046 Madrid
Spain
Telephone: 1/431 12 40
Telex: 44838
Fax: 1/431 6128

▲ Infotap

Address: 2 rue A. Borschette, BP 262
L-2012 Luxembourg
Telephone: 43 61 65
Telex: 60468

▲ Ministerie van Ekonomische Zaken

Address: Bezuidenhoutseweg 30
Postbus 20 101
NL-2500 's-Gravenhage
Netherlands
Telephone: 70/79 89 11
Telex: 31099
Fax: 70/47 40 81

▲ Normas Verlagsgesellschaft

Address: Waldseestrasse 305
D-7570 Baden-Baden
Germany
Telephone: 7221/21 040
Telex: 781 201
Fax: 7221/21 0427

▲ ODAV (Datenverarbeitung GmbH)

Address: Ernst-Heinkel-Strasse 11
D-8440 Straubing
Germany
Telephone: 9421/70 50

▲ Organization of Economic Cooperation and Development (OECD):

Canada:

Address: Federal Publications Inc.
301-303 King Street West
Toronto, ON M5V 1J5
Telephone: 416/581 1552

Address: Les Editions la Libertie Inc.
3020 Chemin
Sainte-Foy PQ G1X 3V6
Telephone: 418/658 3763

Address: Renouf Publishing Company Ltd
Editions Renouf Ltee
1294 Algoma Road
Ottawa, ON K1B 3W8
Telephone: 613/741 4333

France (Main Office):

Address: [Mail Orders]
OECD Publications Service
2, rue Andre-Pascal
F-75775 Paris Cedex 16
Telephone: 1/45 24 82 0

Address: OECD Bookshop
33, rue Octave-Feuillet
F-75016 Paris
Telephone: 1/45 24 81 67; 1/45 24 81 81
Telex: 620 160 OEDE
Fax: 1/45 24 85 00; 1/45 24 81 76

Japan:

Address: OECD Publications and
Information Centre
Landic Akasaka Building
2-3-4 Akasaka, Minato-ku
Tokyo 107
Telephone: 3/3586-2016
Fax: 3/3584-7929

United Kingdom:

Address: HMSO (Postal Orders Only)
P.O. Box 276
GB-London SW8 5DT
Telephone: 71/211 5656
Fax: 71/873 8463

United States:

Address: OECD Publications and
Information Center
2001 L Street NW, Suite 700
Washington, DC 20036-4095
Telephone: 202/785-6323
Telex: 440245
Fax: 202/785-0350

▲ OSEC

Address: Stampfenbachstrasse 85
CH-8035 Zurich
Switzerland
Telephone: 1/365 51 51
Telex: 817 272
Fax: 1/365 52 21

▲ Profile Information

Address: 79 Staines Road West
GB-Sunbury-on-Thames TW16 7AH
Great Britain
Telephone: 932/761 444
Telex: 8811720
Fax: 932/761 444, ext. 2615

▲ Saarbrucker Zeitung (Abteilung Informationssysteme)

Address: Gutenbergstrasse 11-23
D-6600 Saarbrucken 1
Germany
Telephone: 681/50 20
Telex: 4421262
Fax: 681/50 23 00

▲ Stjernquist Foretagskonsulter

Address: Magnus Ladulasgatn 53
S-11627 Stockholm
Sweden
Telephone: 8/720 03 21
Fax: 8/200 324

▲ TBD (Telematica e Bancos de Dados, LDA)

Address: rue Almeida Brandao, 24A
P-1200 Lisboa
Portugal
Telephone: 1/60 81 56
Telex: 15823
Fax: 1/66 70 12

▲ United Nations:

For Europe:

Address: Sales Section
Palais des Nations
CH-1211 Geneva 10
Switzerland
Telephone: 22/734 60 11,
extensions 2606/2612
Telex: 41 29 62
Fax: 22/733 98 79

For North America and Asia:
Address: Room DC2-0853
United Nations Building
New York, New York 10017
USA
Telephone: 212/963-8302

Agents:
Canada:
Address: Le Diffuser G. Vermette Inc.
Case Postale 85
1501 rue Ampere
Boucherville, Quebec PQ J4B 5E6

Address: Renouf Publishing Company
Mail Orders
1294 Algoma Road
Ottawa, Ontario K1B 3W8

Japan:
Address: Far Eastern Book Sellers
Kanda P.O. Box 72
Tokyo

Address: Hikari Book Trading Co. Ltd.
Nagatani Bldg.
Room 201
26 Sakamachi, Shinjuku-ku
Tokyo 16

Address: Kinokuniya Co. Ltd.
Book Import Department
38-1 Sakuragaoka 5-Chome,
Setagaya-ku
Tokyo

Address: Kitao Publications Trading Co.
Ltd.
Central P.O. Box 936
Osaka 530-91

Address: Maruzen Company Ltd.
P.O. Box 5050
Tokyo International 100-31

Address: Naigai Books Ltd.
Fukushima Bldg. 4-7
Nishikanda 2-Chome, Chiyoda-ku
Tokyo 101

▼ ── ▼

Address: Tokyo Publications Service Ltd.
             Dai-ichi Takiguchi Bldg. 20-7
             Ginz 1-Chome, Chuo-ku
             Tokyo 104

UnitedKingdom:
At retail through all HMSO bookshops

Address: HMSO Books
             P.O. Box 276
             London SW8 5DT
Telephone: 71/873 8372
Fax: 712/873 8463

▲ United Nations Economic Commission for
Europe

Address: UN Bookshop/Sales Unit
             Palais des Nations
             CH-1211 Geneva 10
             Switzerland
Telephone: 22/734 60 11, extensions 2606/2612
Telex: 41 29 62
Fax: 22/733 98 79

▲ Verlag Gluckauf GmbH

Address: Postfach 10 39 45
             D-4300 Essen 1
             Germany
Telex: 8 579 545 GAUF D

▲ WEFA

Belgium:
Address: WEFA Benelux SA
             52, avenue des Arts
             B-1040 Bruxelles
Telephone: 2/511 11 44

Canada:
Address: WEFA Canada Inc.
             777 Bay Street, Suite 2020
             Toronto, ON M5G 2C8
Telephone: 416/599-5700

United Kingdom:
Address: WEFA Ltd.
             Ebury Gate, 23, Lower Belgrave
             GB-London SW1W 0NW
             Great Britain
Telephone: 71/730 8171

United States:
Address: WEFA Inc.
             150 Monument Road
             Bala Cynwyd, PA 19004
Telephone: 215/667-6000

U.S.

Government

Contacts, Data

Resources, and

Publications on

the Single Market

F

How to Use This Appendix

The U.S. government can be a valuable source of information on the Single Market Program and how best to take advantage of the opportunities it provides. However, it can be difficult at times to get access to that information and to the people who have it.

In general, if you have the time, it is best to start with some of the publications listed in this Appendix. That will allow you to familiarize yourself with the issues and what data is available. It will also help in dealing with U.S. government contacts. Most will direct you to these publications to begin with, so reading them first will enable you to make better use of each person's expertise.

SECTIONS IN THIS APPENDIX:

HOW TO CONTACT AND WORK WITH U.S. GOVERNMENT AGENCIES

Writing Versus Calling for Assistance

Although the tips that follow apply to calling for information directly from the federal government in Washington, D.C., the same principles apply when you are dealing with the federal government's regional offices.

Writing for the information you want usually can take too long, or it may be impossible to do. Often you may not know *exactly* what you want or who has it, so you are guessing about both subject of the study or data collection efforts you want and the identity of the office or person who has it. Keep these points in mind:

- If your written inquiry for data is not directed to precisely the correct person or office, you may never get a reply.

- If the written inquiry does not specify what you are seeking in terms that are familiar to the agency to which you are writing, it can take weeks before your request gets to the proper person or office—if it ever gets there.

That means, in most cases, use the telephone to reach the right agency, office, and person. Before calling, be prepared to make notes so you can retrace your steps to your final contact person.

Know What You Are Looking For

Before you make any calls, jot down what you want in a single sentence, because you may need to repeat it to several people before you talk to the

right one. You will have to be able to elaborate on your request and eventually explain why the data you are seeking is important, but you should start with a summary of your needs. If you do not know exactly what you want, get as close as possible. In your single sentence, use key words like *data*, *reports*, *studies*, and *expert*.

The key to successful government telephone inquiries is to keep the statement of your needs very short but to include all of the most important concepts. Use the reporter's technique of expressing the most important concepts in the first few sentences and placing key words first in your sentences. The words that are important vary from agency to agency.

Starting

To learn what office to call, refer to the offices listed in this appendix. Each has a separate role with respect to the Single Market Program. In addition, each is in regular communication with other offices throughout the U.S. government, so that they can provide you with suggestions of where to call.

When to Call

- Avoid calling government offices on Monday or after a three-day weekend.

- Avoid calling on a Friday afternoon during the summer months. Just as with private businesses, there is always a lot of catching up on that day.

- Call before 3:00 P.M. in the agency's time zone.

- Avoid the period just around lunch time.

Etiquette in Government Calls

- Locating the data you want could take some time, so allow enough "search" time during your call.

- After you identify yourself, confirm where the representative works and his or her extension.

- Explain why you want the data as well as what you want, so the representative can determine where the data you want might be.

- Note buzzwords used by the representative. They may turn out to be your key to getting data. Revise your target question to incorporate or avoid some of the important buzzwords.

- If what the representative says does *not* apply or is not covered by an agency or unit of a

▼ ▼

department, take note so you will not get transferred back to that office by someone else.

- Get suggestions about where you can acquire new leads but don't rush off to call immediately. When you get the data from the representative, ask him or her for other suggestions about where to call, particularly other government agencies but also perhaps academics, consultants, experts, or trade associations. Even if these outsiders lack specific information, they may be able to direct you back to another part of the same agency or a different agency that can also help you.

- Ask for a name you can call for more help. Ask whether you can use the name of the person you are speaking to in contacting the names you are given. A referral like that can save time and speed up return telephone calls.

Transfers and Referrals

You will probably have to be transferred at least once when you call government offices. Before you are transferred, make sure you have the direct dial number (with area code for federal offices, because Washington, D.C., offices cover three area codes), as well as the name and office of the person to whom you are being transferred. Even if you are just referred to someone else, but not transferred on the telephone, you will need this. In addition, make sure that you know the same information about the office from which you are being transferred.

Getting Documents and Materials

When you have finished with your conversation, ask if there are any documents that can be sent to you. If so, how long will it take to get them out? Remember, at some agencies, copying may involve a long wait.

If you are referred to a report printed either by the United States Government Printing Office (USGPO) or the National Technical Information Service (NTIS), U.S. Department of Commerce, it is critical for you to get the full title, date, and most importantly the full access number before you hang up. You need this information to order copies of documents. Documents from these agencies take an especially long time to be delivered.

Make a note if someone is sending you literature so you can follow up if you do not get it. But allow a week before you do follow up. Even though U.S. government official materials are supposed to go by first class mail, they take longer than you might expect for first class.

Overnight Express Shipments

If you need the materials quickly, ask whether the person can have it sent by overnight air freight and charged to your account. Some agencies can and will do this. If you intend to ask for this service, have ready your account number, job number, and any other data the representative will enter on the freight bill. A federal employee can *only* do this if it is being charged to your account.

Faxing Materials

Sending data via facsimile machines is an increasingly popular option among businesses. Its popularity among government agencies varies. Some willingly fax materials; others have a limit—informal or formal—on the number of pages they can fax.

Still other government agencies can only fax materials at the end of the day (or later) to save on telephone charges. If that is the case, leave your fax on its automatic setting after business hours.

You may even find that some agencies, for cost reasons, do not fax any materials. If someone says he or she cannot use the fax, you might want to offer to absorb the charges by having the call made collect.

New U.S. Government Telephone Numbers

The U.S. government is in the process of a multi-year program that will upgrade its telephone system. One effect of the changeover will be to change some of the telephone numbers in Washington, D.C., over the next year. For some, the prefix will change, but for others, the entire number may change.

Contacts—General

These are the offices most directly concerned with the Single Market Program, its impact on the U.S. economy and trade, and with assisting U.S. businesses to take advantage of it.

▲ The Export-Import Bank of the United States

Europe and Canada Desk

Address: 811 Vermont Avenue, NW
Washington, DC 20571
Telephone: 202/566-8813; 800/424-5201
(Small Business Hotline)
Scope: Information and assistance on export credit

▲ U.S. Department of Commerce

Export Promotion Services

Address: U.S. Department of Commerce Building, Room H-2116
14th Street & Constitution Avenue, NW
Washington, DC 20230
Scope: Coordination of the Matchmaker Trade Delegations, bringing U.S. firms overseas to meet with prescreened agents and distributors, as well as numerous other programs, such as the comparison shopping service, foreign market research service, trade opportunities program

▲ U.S. Department of Commerce

International Trade Administration

Office of Western Europe

Address: U.S. Department of Commerce Building, Room 2106
14th Street & Constitution Avenue, NW
Washington, DC 20230
Telephone: Coverage of all of Europe, including the EC; callers can be referred to country experts within the Department of Commerce or at the Labor and State Departments

▲ U.S. Department of Commerce

NIST (National Institute of Standards and Technology)

Office of Standards Code and Information

Address: Room A629
Administration Building
Gaithersburg, MD 20899
Telephone: 301/975-4038, 975-4040
Scope: Information on EC standards development and organizations involved in the process; maintains on-site collection of materials on the subject

▲ U.S. Department of Commerce

SIMIS (Single Internal Market: 1992 Information Service)

Address: U.S. Department of Commerce Building, Room 3036
14th Street & Constitution Avenue, NW
Washington, DC 20230
Telephone: 202/377-5276
Fax: 202/377-2155
Scope: Central contact point within the U.S. Department of Commerce for information on the Single Market Program from the U.S. government's perspective, as well as for leads to U.S. government assistance

▲ U.S. Department of State

Europe/Regional, Political and Economic Affairs

Address: Main State Building
Room 6519
Washington, DC 20520
Telephone: 202/647-2395
Scope: Monitor of political and economic developments in the EC

▲ U.S. Mission to the European Communities (USEC)

Address: 40, Blvd. du Regent
B-1000 Brussels
Belgium
Telephone: 2/513 44 50
Fax: 2/511 20 92
Telex: 21336
Scope: U.S. government's "embassy" to the EC

▲ U.S. Small Business Administration

Office of International Trade

Address: Room 501-A
              1441 L Street, NW
              Washington, DC 20416
Telephone: 202/653-7794
Scope: Information on SBA international trade
           programs

▲ U.S. Trade Representative

Address: 600 17th Street, NW
              Washington, DC 20506
Telephone: 202/395-3320
Scope: Office that conducts trade negotiations
           with the EC; also chairs the 1992 Inter-
           agency Task Force

CONTACTS—BY INDUSTRY

These are the offices concerned with the Single
Market Program and its impact, from the perspective of particular U.S. industries.

▲ U.S. Department of Commerce

Office of Automotive Affairs and Consumer Goods

Address: U.S. Department of Commerce
              Building, Room 4324
              14th Street and Constitution
              Avenue, NW
              Washington, DC 20230
Telephone: 202/377-2762
Scope: Autos and consumer goods; assigned to
           Single Internal Market: 1992 Information
           Service (SIMIS) program

▲ U.S. Department of Commerce

Office of Basic Industries

Address: U.S. Department of Commerce
              Building, Room 4043
              14th Street & Constitution
              Avenue, NW
              Washington, DC 20230
Telephone: 202/377-0614
Scope: Chemicals, construction industry
           products, and basic industries; assigned
           to SIMIS program

▲ U.S. Department of Commerce

Office of Service Industries

Address: U.S. Department of Commerce
              Building, Room 1128
              14th Street & Constitution
              Avenue, NW
              Washington, DC 20230
Telephone: 202/377-3575
Scope: Service industries; assigned to SIMIS
           program

▲ U.S. Department of Commerce

Office of Telecommunications

Address: U.S. Department of Commerce
              Building, Room 1001A
              14th Street & Constitution
              Avenue, NW
              Washington, DC 20230
Telephone: 202/377-4466
Scope: Information technology, instrumenta-
           tion and electronics; assigned to SIMIS
           program

▲ U.S. Department of Commerce

Office of Textiles and Apparel

Address: U.S. Department of Commerce
              Building, Room 3109
              14th Street & Constitution
              Avenue, NW
              Washington, DC 20230
Telephone: 202/377-5153
Scope: Textiles and apparel; assigned to SIMIS
           program

▲ U.S. Department of Commerce

Office of the DAS for Capital Goods and International Construction

Address: U.S. Department of Commerce Building, Room 2001B 14th Street & Constitution Avenue, NW Washington, DC 20230

Telephone: 202/377-2474

Scope: Construction projects and industrial machinery; assigned to SIMIS program

▲ U.S. Department of Commerce

Outreach Program in Industry Trade Associations

Address: U.S. Department of Commerce Building, Room 2800 14th Street & Constitution Avenue, NW Washington, DC 20230

Telephone: 202/377-2474

Scope: Industrial trade; assigned to SIMIS program

▼

CONTACTS—BY COUNTRY

These are the offices most concerned with the Single Market Program and its impact, from the perspective of each EC Member Country. The International Trade Administration (ITA) desk officers can help develop information on current business conditions and opportunities. The U.S. and Foreign Commercial Service offices overseas can help when you need an answer to a very focused question about local business conditions.

Belgium

▲ U.S. and Foreign Commercial Service

American Embassy Brussels

Address: 27, bd. du Regent B-1000 Brussels Belgium

Telephone: 2/513 38 30

Fax: 2/511 27 25

Telex: 846 21336

▲ U.S. Department of Commerce

International Trade Administration

Belgium Desk

Address: U.S. Department of Commerce Building, Room 3043 14th Street & Constitution Avenue, NW Washington, DC 20230

Telephone: 202/377-5401

Denmark

▲ U.S. and Foreign Commercial Service

American Embassy Copenhagen

Address: Dag Hammarskjolds Alle 24 DK-2100 Copenhagen 0 Denmark

Telephone: 31/42 31 44

Fax: 35/43 02 23

Telex: 22216 AMEMB DK

▲ U.S. Department of Commerce

International Trade Administration

Denmark Desk

Address: U.S. Department of Commerce Building 14th Street & Constitution Avenue, NW Washington, DC 20230

Telephone: 202/377-3254

France

▲ U.S. and Foreign Commercial Service

U.S. Embassy Paris

Address: 2, av. Gabriel F-75382 Paris Cedex 08 France

Telephone: 1/4296 1202

Telex: 650221 AMEMB

▲ U.S. Department of Commerce

International Trade Administration

France Desk

Address: U.S. Department of Commerce
Building, Room H-3042
14th Street & Constitution
Avenue, NW
Washington, DC 20230
Telephone: 202/377-8008

Federal Republic of Germany

▲ Commercial Officer

American Consulate General Stuttgart

Address: Urbanstr. 7
D-7000 Stuttgart
Germany
Telephone: 711/210 221
Fax: 711/234 350

▲ U.S. and Foreign Commercial Service

American Embassy Bonn

Address: Deichmanns Aue. 29
D-5300 Bonn 2
Germany
Telephone: 228/339 2760
Fax: 228/334 649
Telex: 885 452

▲ U.S. Commercial Office

Address: Emmanuel-Leutze-Str. 1B
D-4000 Dusseldorf 11
Germany
Telephone: 211/596 790
Fax: 211/594 897
Telex: 8584246 FCS

▲ U.S. Department of Commerce

International Trade Administration

Germany Desk

Address: U.S. Department of Commerce
Building, Room H-3411
14th Street & Constitution
Avenue, NW
Washington, DC 20230
Telephone: 202/377-2434

Greece

▲ U.S. and Foreign Commercial Service

American Embassy Athens

Address: 91 Vasillissis Sophias Blvd.
GR-10160 Athens
Greece
Telephone: 1/721 2951
Fax: 1/646 3450
Telex: 21 5548

▲ U.S. Department of Commerce

International Trade Administration

Greece Desk

Address: U.S. Department of Commerce
Building
14th Street & Constitution
Avenue, NW
Washington, DC 20230
Telephone: 202/377-3945

Republic of Ireland

▲ U.S. and Foreign Commercial Service

American Embassy Dublin

Address: 42 Elgin Road
Dublin
Ireland
Telephone: 1/688 777
Fax: 1/689 946
Telex: 93684

▲ U.S. Department of Commerce

International Trade Administration

Ireland Desk

Address: U.S. Department of Commerce
Building
14th Street & Constitution
Avenue, NW
Washington, DC 20230
Telephone: 202/377-3748

Italy

▲ Commercial Officer

American Consulate General

Address: Centro Cooperazione Internazionale
Piazzale Guilo Cesare
I-20145 Milano
Italy
Telephone: 2/498 2241, 2242, 2243
Fax: 2/481 4161

▲ Commercial Officer

American Consulate General

Address: Piazza della Repubblica
I-80122 Naples
Italy
Telephone: 81/761 4303
Fax: 81/761 1869

▲ Commercial Officer

American Consulate General

Address: Via Vaccarini 1
I-90143 Palermo
Italy
Telephone: 91/346 036, 345 192
Fax: 91/343 546
Telex: 910313 USACON I

▲ U.S. and Foreign Commercial Service

American Embassy Rome

Address: Via Veneto 119/A
I-00187 Roma
Italy
Telephone: 6/4674 1
Fax: 6/4674 2113
Telex: 622322 AMBRMA

▲ U.S. Department of Commerce

International Trade Administration

Italy Desk

Address: U.S. Department of Commerce
Building, Room H-3043
14th Street & Constitution
Avenue, NW
Washington, DC 20230
Telephone: 202/377-2177

Luxembourg

▲ Economic/Commercial Officer

American Embassy Luxembourg

Address: 22, bd. Emmanuel-Servais
L-2535 Luxembourg
Telephone: 460 123
Fax: 461 401

▲ U.S. Department of Commerce

International Trade Administration

Luxembourg Desk

Address: U.S. Department of Commerce
Building
14th Street & Constitution
Avenue, NW
Washington, DC 20230
Telephone: 202/377-5401

The Netherlands

▲ Commercial Officer

American Consulate General

Address: Museumplein 19
NL-1017 DJ Amsterdam
The Netherlands
Telephone: 20/664 5661
Fax: 20/752 856
Telex: 044 16176 CGUSA NL

▲ U.S. and Foreign Commercial Service

American Embassy The Hague

Address: Lange Voorhout 102
NL-2514EJ The Hague
The Netherlands
Telephone: 70/62 4911
Fax: 70/63 2985

▲ U.S. Department of Commerce

International Trade Administration

Netherlands Desk

Address: U.S. Department of Commerce
Building, Room 3043
14th Street & Constitution
Avenue, NW
Washington, DC 20230
Telephone: 202/377-5401

Portugal

▲ U.S. and Foreign Commercial Service

American Embassy Lisbon

Address: Avenida das Forcas Armadas
P-1600 Lisbon
Portugal
Telephone: 1/726 6600
Fax: 1/726 8914
Telex: 12528 AMEMB

▲ U.S. Department of Commerce

International Trade Administration

Portugal Desk

Address: U.S. Department of Commerce
Building, Room H-3042
14th Street & Constitution
Avenue, NW
Washington, DC 20230
Telephone: 202/377-3945

Spain

▲ Commercial Officer

American Consulate General

Address: via Layetana, 33
E-08003 Barcelona
Spain
Telephone: 3/319 9550
Fax: 3/319 5621
Telex: 52672

▲ U.S. and Foreign Commercial Service

American Embassy Madrid

Address: Calle Serrano 75
E-28806 Madrid
Spain
Telephone: 1/577 4000
Fax: 1/577 5735
Telex: 27763

▲ U.S. Department of Commerce

International Trade Administration
Spain Desk

Address: U.S. Department of Commerce
Building, Room H-3042
14th Street & Constitution
Avenue, NW
Washington, DC 20230
Telephone: 202/377-4508

United Kingdom

▲ U.S. and Foreign Commercial Service

American Embassy London

Address: 24/31 Grosvenor Square
Box 33
GB-London W1A 1AE
England
Telephone: 71/499 9000
Fax: 71/491 4022
Telex: 266777

▲ U.S. Department of Commerce

International Trade Administration

United Kingdom Desk

Address: U.S. Department of Commerce
Building, Room H-3411
14th Street & Constitution
Avenue, NW
Washington, DC 20230
Telephone: 202/377-3748

DATA RESOURCES AND PUBLICATIONS

These are the U.S. government publications most directly concerned with the Single Market Program and its impact on U.S. businesses and the U.S. economy.

An Assessment of Economic Policy Issues Raised by the European Community's Single Market Program

Publisher: Office of the U.S. Trade Representative

Frequency of Publication: One time

Scope: Reviews a number of key issues in the Single Market Program from a U.S. perspective; prepared by the U.S. government Task Force on EC Internal Market

Background Notes on . . .

Publisher: Superintendent of Documents

Frequency of Publication: Periodically

Scope: Preparation of separate issues for each EC Member Country; provides basic information for U.S. citizens about political, cultural, and economic situations for the country; prepared by the U.S. Department of State

A Basic Guide to Exporting

Publisher: Superintendent of Documents and U.S. Department of Commerce Publication Sales Branch

Frequency of Publication: Periodically

Scope: Provides core information on exporting from the U.S. throughout the world; prepared by the U.S. Department of Commerce

Business America: The Magazine of International Trade

Publisher: U.S. Government Printing Office and U.S. Department of Commerce/ International Trade Administration Publication Sales Branch

Frequency of Publication: Biweekly

Scope: Covers all aspects of trade from a U.S. perspective; has annual issue (in January) dealing with the EC

Commercial News USA

Publisher: U.S. Department of Commerce, International Trade Administration

Frequency of Publication: 10 times a year

Scope: Catalog/magazine promoting products and services of U.S. firms seeking export sales; for additional information, call 800/343-4300 operator 940

Completion of the European Community Internal Market: An Initial Completion of Certain Economic Policy Issues Raised by Aspects of the E.C.'s Program

Publisher: U.S. Trade Representative

Frequency of Publication: One time

Scope: Reviews impact of Single Market Program as it impacts U.S. trade and related policies

EC 1992: A Commerce Department Analysis of European Community Directives—Volumes 1, 2, and 3

Publisher: U.S. Government Printing Office

Frequency of Publication: One time

Scope: Review EC directives—Volume 1 emphasizes manufactured goods, also touching on insurance, telecommunications, transportation, and broadcasting industries; Volume 2 emphasizes directives dealing with company law, trademarks, and processed food; Volume 3 emphasizes directives dealing with manufactured products, including capital goods, biotechnology products, and pharmaceuticals, and touching on financial services, telecommunications, travel, tourism, and public procurement; all three volumes are prepared by the U.S. Department of Commerce, International Trade Administration

EC 1992 Growth Markets

Publisher: U.S. Government Printing Office

Frequency of Publication: One time

Scope: Summarizes Single Market Program and its impact on trade, together with evaluations of the best prospects for U.S. exports and the market potential in the EC for selected products; prepared by the U.S. Department of Commerce, International Trade Administration

The Effects of Greater Economic Integration Within the European Community on the United States

Publisher: U.S. International Trade Commission

Frequency of Publication: One time

Scope: Summarizes major issues in Single Market Program from a trade perspective, including local content requirements and rules of origin, as well as the social dimension; consists of Report and First Follow-Up Report one year later

Europe Now

Publisher: U.S. Department of Commerce, International Trade Administration, U.S. and Foreign Commercial Service

Frequency of Publication: 4 times a year

Scope: Overview of activities of U.S. Department of Commerce with respect to the EC, and of developments in the EC impacting U.S. businesses; export-oriented

European Community: Issues Raised by 1992 Integration

Publisher: U.S. Congress, Congressional Research Service

Frequency of Publication: One time

Scope: Analysis of political and economic issues raised by the Single Market Program; prepared for U.S. Representatives and Senators

The European Community's Program for a Single Market in 1992

Publisher: U.S. Department of State, Bureau of Public Affairs

Frequency of Publication: One time

Scope: Brief review of the Single Market Program

The European Community's Program to Complete a Single Market by 1992

Publisher: U.S. Department of State, Bureau of European and Canadian Affairs

Frequency of Publication: One time

Scope: Brief review of the Single Market Program

European Single Market: Issues of Concern to U.S. Exporters

Publisher: Superintendent of Documents and the U.S. Government Accounting Office

Frequency of Publication: One time

Scope: Analysis of impact of Single Market Program on U.S. exporters, and U.S. government responses to it

Foreign Business Practices

Publisher: Superintendent of Documents and U.S. Department of Commerce Publication Sales Branch

Frequency of Publication: Periodically

Scope: Summarizes general U.S. laws applicable to U.S. firms doing business overseas; prepared by U.S. Department of Commerce

Foreign Economic Trends Reports for . . .

Publisher: Superintendent of Documents and U.S. Department of Commerce/ International Trade Administration Publication Sales Branch

Frequency of Publication: 1 or 2 times a year

Scope: Separate issues for each EC Member Country; provides basic information for U.S. firms about economic trends affecting the EC country

Foreign Labor Trends

Publisher: Superintendent of Documents

Frequency of Publication: Periodically

Scope: Separate issues for each EC Member Country; provides basic information for U.S. businesses about local labor markets and trends for the EC country; prepared by the U.S. Department of Labor

International Trade State and Local Resource Directory

Publisher: U.S. Small Business Administration

Frequency of Publication: Periodically

Scope: List of resources available on state-by-state basis for exports, including government agencies, international banks, and translation services

Letter from Brussels

Publisher: U.S. Mission to the EC
Frequency of Publication: Periodically
Scope: Newsletter on developments in the EC

List of European Community 1992 Directives and Proposals

Publisher: U.S. Department of Commerce— SIMIS
Frequency of Publication: Periodically
Scope: List of EC directives, regulations, and policies dealing with the Single Market Program, showing their current status; prepared by the U.S. Department of Commerce

Official U.S. and International Financing Institutions: A Guide for Exporters and Investors

Publisher: U.S. Department of Commerce/ International Trade Administration Publication Sales Branch
Frequency of Publication: Periodically
Scope: Analysis of U.S. exports and investment procurement sources

Overseas Business Report: Marketing in . . .

Publisher: Superintendent of Documents and U.S. Department of Commerce/ International Trade Administration Publication Sales Branch
Frequency of Publication: 3 to 5 years
Scope: Separate issues for each EC Member Country; provides basic information for U.S. firms about doing business in the EC country; prepared by the U.S. Department of Commerce

A Summary of the New European Community Approach to Standards Development

Publisher: National Technical Information Service
Frequency of Publication: Periodically
Scope: Brief review of the EC's standards-setting process; prepared by U.S. Department of Commerce, National Bureau of Standards (now known as NIST, the National Institute of Standards and Technology)

The World Is Your Market: An Export Guide for Small Business

Publisher: U.S. Small Business Administration
Frequency of Publication: One time
Scope: Handbook for small businesses, focusing on mechanics of exporting, as well as listing export assistance resources in the U.S. government, state governments, and the private sector

SOURCES OF INFORMATION

These are the sources from which you can obtain the U.S. government publications listed in the previous section.

▲ National Technical Information Service (NTIS)

Address: 5285 Port Royal Road
Springfield, VA 22161
Telephone: 703/487-4650; 800/336-4700 (rush orders)

▲ Superintendent of Documents

U.S. Government Printing Office
Address: Washington, DC 20402
Telephone: 202/783-3238

▲ U.S. Congress

Congressional Research Service
Address: 101 Independence Avenue, SE
Washington, DC 20540
Telephone: 202/707-5700

▲ U.S. Department of Commerce

International Trade Administration

Publications

Address: U.S. Department of Commerce
Building, Room 1617
14th Street & Constitution Avenue,
NW
Washington, DC 20230
Telephone: 202/377-5494

▲ U.S. Department of Commerce

Publications Sales Branch

Address: U.S. Department of Commerce
Building, Room H-1617
14th Street & Constitution Avenue,
NW
Washington, DC 20230
Telephone: 202/377-5494

▲ U.S. Department of Commerce

U.S. and Foreign Commercial Service

Publications—Sales

Address: U.S. Department of Commerce
Building, Room 2106
14th Street & Constitution Avenue,
NW
Washington, DC 20230

▲ U.S. Department of State

Bureau of European and Canadian Affairs

Address: Main State Building
Washington, DC 20520
Telephone: 202/647-6925

▲ U.S. Department of State

Bureau of Public Affairs

Address: Main State Building
Washington, DC 20520
Telephone: 202/647-6575; 647-6576

▲ U.S. General Accounting Office

Address: P.O. Box 6015
Gaithersburg, MD 20877
Telephone: 202/275 6241

▲ U.S. International Trade Commission

Address: 500 E Street, SW
Washington, DC 20436
Telephone: 202/252-1809

▲ U.S. Mission to the European Communities
(USEC)

Address: 40, bd. du Regent
B-1000 Brussels
Belgium
Telephone: 2/513 44 50
Fax: 2/511 20 92
Telex: 21336

▲ U.S. Small Business Administration

Office of International Trade

Address: Room 501-A
1441 L Street, NW
Washington, DC 20416
Telephone: 202/653-7794

▲ U.S. Trade Representative

Address: 600 17th Street, NW
Washington, DC 20506
Telephone: 202/395-3230

Contacts in EC Member States on the Single Market Program

G

HOW TO USE THIS APPENDIX

The EC has provided EC-based companies with a major resource to help them understand and use the Single Market Program: the Euro Info Centre (EIC). For any interested person, but in particular owners of small and medium-sized businesses, the EIC can be an important starting point for getting up-to-date information on the Single Market Program and its impact on business.

The Community set up the Euro Info Centre network (EICs) in 1987 to give European businesses better access to information on EC matters. Each EIC operates independently through a "host" organization that has established contacts with local firms. These typically include chambers of commerce, regional development offices, professional federations, and business consultants.

EICs provide customized information and advice services for business managers. Some of the EICs specialize in commerce, innovation, or finance; others have a broader expertise and outreach. Most of the questions handled by the EICs deal with EC policy and programs, such as the Single Market Program, R&D programs, and business financing. The EICs also provide feedback to the CEC on business concerns.

EIC personnel have been trained to use EC database information on ECHO and Eurobases. They are also familiar with other sources of Community information available from EC institutions and from commercial organizations.

Unless otherwise marked, all of the offices within this section are Euro Info Centre offices.

ASSISTANCE

For additional information on the EICs, see Chapter 2. Some of the EICs are also involved in the BC-Net program, described in Chapter 2. For additional information on Euro Info Centre offices, contact the central Euro Info Centre Office:

Commission of the European Communities

DGXXIII–Euro Info Centre

Address: rue d'Arlon 80
             B-1040 Brussels
             Belgium
Telephone: 2/236 11 74
Fax: 2/235 73 35

Belgium

▲ Bureau d'Etudes Economiques et Sociales de la Province de Hainaut

Euro Info Centre

Address: rue de Nimy, 50
             B-7000 Mons
Telephone: 65/31 93 10, 11, 12
Fax: 65/34 80 96

▲ C.D.P.—Idelux

Euro Info Centre

Address: av. Nothomb, 8
             B-6700 Arlon
Telephone: 63/22 72 46
Fax: 63/22 65 84

▲ Chambre de Commerce de Bruxelles/Fabrimetal

Euro Info Centre

Address: av. Louise, 500
             B-1050 Bruxelles
Telephone: 2/648 58 73
Fax: 2/640 93 28

▲ Chambre de Commerce et d'Industrie du Tournaisis

Address: rue Beyaert, 73-75
             B-7500 Tournai
Telephone: 69/22 11 21
Fax: 69/21 27 84

▲ Euroguichet Hainaut-Est

Euro Info Centre

Address: av. General Michel, 18
             B-6000 Charleroi
Telephone: 71/31 46 10
Fax: 71/32 86 76

▲ Euro Info Centre

Bureau Economique de la Province de Namur (BEPN)

Address: av. Sergent Vrithoff, 2
             B-5000 Namur
Telephone: 81/73 52 09
Fax: 81/23 09 45

▲ Euro Info Centrum

Kamer van Koophandel en Nijverheid van Antwerpen

Address: Markgravestraat, 12
             B-2000 Antwerpen
Telephone: 3/233 75 68
Fax: 3/233 64 42

▲ Euro Info Centrum

Ministerie van de Vlammse Gemeenschap Administratie voor Economoe en Werkgelengeheid

Address: Markiesstraat, 1-6e verdieping
             Batiment Marquise
             B-1000 Bruxelles
Telephone: 2/507 39 69
Fax: 2/507 31 30

▲ Gewestelijke

Ontwikkelingsmaatschappij voor Oost-Vlaanderen

Euro Info Centre

Address: Floraliapaleis, bus 6
             B-9000 Gent
Telephone: 91/21 55 11
Fax: 91/21 55 00

▲ Institute provincial des classes moyennes

Euro Info Centre

Address: bd. d'Avroy, 28-30
             B-4000 Liege
Telephone: 41/23 38 40
Fax: 41/22 19 76

▲ Kamer voor Handel en Nijverheid van het Arrondissement Halle-Vilvoorde en Arrondissement Leuven

Euro Info Centrum

Address: Brucargo Batiment 706
            1er etage—local 7127
            B-1931 Zaventem
Telephone: 2/751 96 32
Fax: 2/751 78 11

▲ Kamer voor Handel en Nijverheid van Limburg vzw.

Euro Info Centre Limburg

Address: Kunstalaan, 20
            B-3500 Hasselt
Telephone: 11/22 18 00
Fax: 11/24 16 20

▲ Nationaal Christelijk

Middenstandsverbond Kortrijk

Euro Info Centre

Address: Lang Steenstraat, 100
            B-8500 Kortrijk
Telephone: 56/22 41 23
Fax: 56/22 96 94

▲ Schulungs-und-Forschungszentrum SPK

Address: Gosperstrasse, 17
            B-4700 Eupen
Telephone: 87/74 22 12
Fax: 87/55 24 15

Denmark

▲ Dansk Teknisk Oplysningstjeneste

Euro Info Centre

Address: Rygaards Alle 131A
            Postbox 1992
            DK-2820
Telephone: 31/20 90 92
Fax: 31/18 58 04

▲ Det Danske Handelskammer

Euro Info Centre

Address: Borsen
            DK-1217 Kobenhaven K
Telephone: 33/91 23 23
Fax: 33/32 52 16

▲ EF-Radgivningskontoret for Fyn

Euro Info Centre

Address: Norregade 51
            DK-5000 Odense C.
Telephone: 66/14 60 30
Fax: 66/14 60 34

▲ EF-Radgivningskontoret Regionskontoret Arhus Amts-Kommune

Euro Info Centre

Address: Haslegaardsvaenget 18-20
            DK-Arhus
Telephone: 86/15 03 18
Fax: 86/15 43 22

▲ Handvaerksradet

Euro Info Centre

Address: Ll. Sct. Handsgade 20
            DK-8800 Viborg
Telephone: 86/62 92 99
Fax: 86/61 49 21

▲ Herning Erhvervsrad

Euro Info Centre

Address: Lykkesvej 18
            DK-7400 Herning
Telephone: 97/12 92 00
Fax: 97/12 92 44

▲ Sonderjyllands Erhvervsrad

Euro Info Centre

Address: Kirkeplads 4
            DK-6200 Aabenraa
Telephone: 74/62 23 84
Fax: 74/62 67 20

▲ Storstroms Erhvervscenter

Euro Info Centre

Address: Marienbergvej 80
            DK-4760 Vordinborg
Telephone: 55/34 01 55
Fax: 55/34 03 55

France

▲ Agence nationale de Valorisation de la Recherche

Euro Info Centre

Address: 43, rue Caumartin
F-75436 Paris Cedex 09
Telephone: 40/17 83 00
Fax: 42/66 02 20

▲ Aire Urbaine 2000

Address: Cours des Halles, 4
F-25200 Montbeliard
Telephone: 81/91 32 41
Fax: 81/91 24 76

▲ Alpes-Cotes d'Azur-Corse

Address: bd. Carabacel, 20
F-06005 Nice Cedex
Telephone: 93/13 73 05
Fax: 93/13 73 99

▲ Association Poitou-Charentes-Europe

Euro Info Centre

Address: 47, rue du Marche
BP 229
F-86006 Poitiers
Telephone: 49/41 46 61
Fax: 49/41 65 72

▲ CCI de Chalons-sur-Marne (Point Europe Champagne Ardenne)

Euro Info Centre

Address: 2, rue de Chastillon
BP 533
F-51010 Chalons-sur-Marne
Telephone: 26/21 11 33
Fax: 26/64 16 84

▲ Centre francais du Commerce Exterieur

Euro Info Centre

Address: 10, av. d'Iena
F-75783 Paris XVI
Telephone: 1/40 73 30 00
Fax: 1/40 73 39 79

▲ Chambre de Commerce et d'Industrie d'Annecy et de la Haute-Savoie

Address: rue du Lac, 2
BP 72
F-74011 Annecy Cedex
Telephone: 50/33 72 05
Fax: 50/52 89 95

▲ Chambre de Commerce et d'Industrie d'Avignon et de Vaucluse

Address: Cours Jean Jaures, 46—BP 158
F-84008 Avignon
Telephone: 90/82 40 00
Fax: 90/85 56 78

▲ Chambre de Commerce et d'Industrie de Clermont-Ferrand/Issoire

Euro Info Centre

Address: 148, bd. Lavoisier
F-63037 Clermont-Ferrand
Telephone: 73/43 43 43
Fax: 73/37 53 07

▲ Chambre de Commerce et d'Industrie de Guyane Francaise

Euro Info Centre

Address: place de l'Esplanade
BP 49
F-97321 Cayene Cedex
Guyane francaise
Telephone: 30/30 00
Fax: 30/23 09

▲ Chambre de Commerce et d'Industrie de La Reunion

Euro Info Centre

Address: 5bis, rue de Paris
BP 120
F-97463 Saint-Denis Cedex
Telephone: 21/53 66
Fax: 41/80 34

▲ Chambre de Commerce et d'Industrie de Lyon

Euro Info Centre

Address: rue de la Republique, 16
F-69289 Lyon Cedex 02
Telephone: 72/40 57 46
Fax: 78/37 94 00

▲ Chambre de Commerce et d'Industrie de la Martinique

Euro Info Centre

Address: 50, rue Ernest Deproge
             BP 478
             F-97241 Fort de France Cedex (La Martinique)
Telephone: 55/28 00
Fax: 60/66 68

▲ Chambre de Commerce et d'Industries de Nantes

Euro Info Centre

Address: Centres des Salorges—BP 718
             16, quai Ernest Renaud
             F-44027 Nantes Cedex 04
Telephone: 40/44 60 60
Fax: 40/44 60 90

▲ Chambre de Commerce et d'Industrie de Pointe-a-Pitre

Address: BP 64
             F-97152 Pointe-a-Pitre
             Cedex Guadeloupe
Telephone: 90/08 08
Fax: 90/21 87

▲ Chambre de Commerce et d'Industrie de Strasbourg et du Bas-Rhin

Euro Info Centre

Address: 10, place Gutenberg
             F-67081 Strasbourg Cedex
Telephone: 88/75 25 25
Fax: 88/22 31 20

▲ Chambre regionale de Commerce et d'Industrie de Bourgogne

Euro Info Centre

Address: rue Chevreul, 68
             BP 209
             F-21006 Dijon
Telephone: 80/63 52 63
Fax: 80/63 52 53

▲ Chambre regionale de Commerce et d'Industrie de Bretagne

Euro Info Centre

Address: 1, rue du General Guillaudot
             F-35044 Rennes
Telephone: 99/25 41 57
Fax: 99/25 41 10

▲ Chambre regionale de Commerce et d'Industrie du Centre/CRCE

Euro Info Centre

Address: 35, av. de Paris
             F-45000 Orleans
Telephone: 38/54 58 58
Fax: 38/54 09 09

▲ Chambre regionale de Commerce et d'Industrie de Franche-Comte

Euro Info Centre

Address: Immeuble Orion
             191, rue de Belfort
             F-25043 Besancon
Telephone: 81/80 41 11
Fax: 81/80 70 94

▲ Chambre regionale de Commerce et d'Industrie de Haute Normandie

Euro Info Centre

Address: 9, rue Robert Schuman
             BP 124
             F-76002 Rouen Cedex
Telephone: 35/88 44 42
Fax: 35/88 06 52

▲ Chambre regionale de Commerce et d'Industrie Limousin/Poitou/Charentes

Euro Info Centre

Address: place Jourdan, 15
             F-87038 Limoges
Telephone: 55/33 31 99
Fax: 55/32 07 87

▲ Chambre regionale de Commerce et d'Industrie Midi-Pyrenees

Euro Info Centre

Address: 5, rue Dieudonne Costes
             F-31701 Blagnac
Telephone: 61/71 11 71
Fax: 61/30 08 58

▲ Chambre regionale de Commerce et d'Industrie de Picardie

Euro Info Centre

Address: rue des Otages, 36
F-80037 Amiens Cedex
Telephone: 22/80 06 45
Fax: 22/91 29 04

▲ Comite de Liaison Chambres economiques Langedoc-Roussillon-Region

Euro Info Centre

Address: 254, rue Michel Teule
ZAC d'Alco
F-34030 Montpellier
Cedex 1
Telephone: 67/61 81 51
Fax: 67/61 81 59

▲ Comite d'Expansion Aquitaine

Euro Info Centre

Address: place de la Bourse, 2
F-33076 Bordeaux Cedex
Telephone: 56/52 65 47; 56/52 98 94
Fax: 56/44 32 69

▲ Counseil regionale de Guadeloupe

Euro Info Centre

Address: 5, rue Victor Hughes
F-97100 Basse Terre
La Guadeloupe
Telephone: 81/22 56
Fax: 81/85 09

▲ EUROGUICHET

Nord/Pas-de-Calais

Address: c/o Conseil regional ARD
Centre de Documentation
185, bd. de la Liberte
F-59013 Lille Cedex
Telephone: 20/40 02 77
Fax: 20/40 04 33

▲ GREX/Centre de Commerce International, Chambre de Commerce et d'Industrie de Grenoble

Address: place A. Malraux, 1
BP 297
F-38016 Grenoble
Telephone: 76/47 20 36
Fax: 76/87 73 11

▲ Ministere de l'industrie et de l'Amenagement du Territoire

Euro Info Centre

Address: 101, rue de Grenelle
F-75700 Paris
Telephone: 1/45 72 80 79
Fax: 1/45 72 87 57

▲ Region de Lorraine

Euro Info Centre
Address: place Gabriel Hocquard
BP 1004
F-57036 Metz Cedex 1
Telephone: 87/33 60 00
Fax: 87/32 89 33

▲ Reseau Point Europe—Ile-de-France

Euro Info Centre

Address: 2, rue de Viarmes
F-75001 Paris
Telephone: 1/45 08 35 90
Fax: 1/45 08 36 80

▲ SOMECIN

Euro Info Centre

Address: Mezzanine
F-13241 Marseille
Cedex 01
Telephone: 91/39 33 77
Fax: 91/39 33 60

Germany

▲ Berliner Absatz-Organisation GmbH

Euro Info Centre

Address: Hardenbergstrasse, 16-18
D-1000 Berlin 12
Telephone: 30/31 51 02 40
Fax: 30/31 51 03 16
Telex: 183663

▲ Bundesstelle fur Aussenhandelsinformation (BFAI)

Euro Info Centre

Address: Blaubach 13
Postfach 108007
D-5000 Koln 1
Telephone: 221/20 57 270
Fax: 221/20 57 212

▲ BZG-Unternehmensberatung

Euro Info Centre

Address: Breitenbachstrasse, 1
Postfach 930260
D-6000 Frankfurt a. M. 93
Telephone: 69/79 19 248
Fax: 69/79 19 245
Telex: 411627

▲ Deutsche Gesellschaft fur Mittelstandsberatung

Euro Info Centre

Address: Arabellastrasse, 11
D-8000 Munchen 81
Telephone: 89/9269 680
Fax: 89/9269 6839

▲ Deutscher Handwerkskammertag (D.H.K.T.)

Euro Info Centre

Address: Haus des Deutschen Handwerks
Johanniterstrasse, 1
Postfach 12 02 70
D-5300 Bonn
Telephone: 228/545 211
Fax: 228/545 205
Telex: 886338

▲ Deutsches Informationzentrum fur Technische Regein (DITR) im DIN e.v

Address: Burggrafenstrasse, 6
D-1000 Berlin 30
Telephone: 30/260 16 05
Fax: 30/262 81 25

▲ D.I.H.T. (Deutscher Industrie-und Handlestag)

Euro Info Centre

Address: Adenauer Allee, 148
Postfach 1446
D-5300 Bonn 1
Telephone: 228/10 45 44
Fax: 228/10 41 58
Telex: 886805

▲ EBZ—Europaisches Beratungs-Zentrum der Deutschem Wirtschaft

Address: Gustav Heinemann Ufer 84-88
D-5000 Koln 51
Telephone: 221/3708 491
Fax: 221/3708 730
Telex: 8882601

▲ EG-Beratungsstelle fur Unternehmen beim Deutschen Sparkassen und Giroverband

Address: Simrockstrasse, 4
D-5300 Bonn 1
Telephone: 228/20 43 15
Fax: 228/20 42 50

▲ EG-Beratungsstelle fur Unternehmen VDI/ VDE Technologiezentrum Informationstechnik GmbH

Geschaftsstelle Bremen

Address: Hanseatenhof, 8
D-2800 Bremen 1
Telephone: 421/18 503
Fax: 421/17 1686

▲ EG-Beratungsstelle IHK Aachen

Euro Info Centre

Address: Theaterstrasse 6-8
Postfach 650
D-5100 Aachen
Telephone: 241/438 223
Fax: 241/438 259

▲ Euro Info Centre

Bielefeld-Osnabruck

Address: Niederwall, 23
              Postfach 181
              D-4800 Bielefeld 1
Telephone: 521/51 67 02
Fax: 521/51 22 26
Telex: 823823

▲ Euro Info Centre

Bundesstelle fur Aussenhandelsinformation-BfAi

Address: Postfach 10 80 07
              Agrippastrasse 87-93
              D-5000 Koln 1
Telephone: 221/205 7270
Fax: 221/205 7212
Telex: 8882735

▲ Genossenschaftliche EG

Beratungs-unde Informationsgesellschaft GEBI mbH

Address: Rheinweg, 67
              D-5300 Bonn 1
Telephone: 228/23 75 44
Fax: 228/23 75 48

▲ Gesellschaft fur Witschaftsforderung Nordrhein-Westfalen mbH

Euro Info Centre

Address: Kavalleriestrasse, 8-10
              Postfach 20 03 09
              D-4000 Dusseldorf 1
Telephone: 211/13 00 0061
Fax: 211/13 00 064
Telex: 8587830

▲ Handwerkskammer Stuttgart

Euro Info Centre

Address: Heilbronnerstrasse, 43
              Postfach 102155
              D-7000 Stuttgart 1
Telephone: 711/2594 252
Fax: 711/2594 222

▲ Hessische Landsentwicklungs-und Treuhandgesellschaft mbH

Euro Info Centre

Address: Abraham Lincoln Strasse 38-42
              Postfach 31 07
              D-6200 Wiesbaden
Telephone: 611/774 287
Fax: 611/774 265
Telex: 4186127

▲ Industrie-und Handelskammer/ Handwerkskammer Trier EG-Beratungsstelle fur Rheinland-Pfalz

Address: Saarstrasse 137
              D-5500 Trier
Telephone: 651/3 55 49
Fax: 651/3 10 03

▲ Industrie-und Handelskammer Regensburg

Euro Info Centre

Address: D. Martin Luther Strasse, 12
              Postfach 110 355
              D-8400 Regensburg
Telephone: 941/569 41
Fax: 941/569 42 79

▲ Industrie-und Handelskammer Sudlicher Oberrhein

Euro Info Centre

Address: Lotzbechstrasse 31
              D-7630 Lahr
Telephone: 78/212 70 30
Fax: 78/21 27 03 22

▲ Kreis Steinfurt Amt fur Wirtschaft und Verkehr

Address: Tecklenbruger Strasse, 10
              D-4430 Steinfurt
Telephone: 25/51 69 20 18
Fax: 25/51 69 24 00

▲ Landesbank Schleswig-Holstein

RKW, Schleswig-Holstein

EG-Beratungstelle, EIC

Address: Martensdamm, 6
              Postfach 11 22
              D-2300 Kiel 1
Telephone: 431/900 14 84
Fax: 431/900 14 98

▲ Landesgewerbeanstalt Bayern

OTTI/WETTI/LGA

Euro Info Centre

Address: Karolinenstrasse 45
　　　　D-8500 Nurnberg 1
Telephone: 911/23 20 517
Fax: 911/23 20 511

▲ Landkreis Osnabruck Amt fur Wirtschaftsforderung

Address: Am Scholerberg 1
　　　　D-4500 Osnabruck
Telephone: 541/501 31 04
Fax: 541/501 31 30

▲ OMNIBERA

Address: Coburger Strasse, 10
　　　　D-5300 Bonn
Telephone: 228/23 80 78
Fax: 228/23 39 22

▲ R.K.W. (Rationaliserungs-Kuratorium der Deutschen Wirtschaft)

Euro Info Centre

Address: Heilwigstrasse, 33
　　　　D-2000 Hamburg 20
Telephone: 40/460 20 87
Fax: 40/48 20 32

▲ R.K.W. Rationaliserungs-Kuratorium der Deutschen Wirtschaft/Landesgruppe Baden

Euro Info Centre

Address: Konigstrasse 49
　　　　D-7000 Stuttgart 1
Telephone: 711/2299 80
Fax: 711/2299 810
Telex: 722274

▲ Technologie-Centrum Hannover GmbH

Euro Info Centre

Address: Vahrenwalder Strasse, 7
　　　　D-3000 Hannover 1
Telephone: 511/35 63 121
Fax: 511/35 63 100
Telex: 923798

▲ Verein Deutscher Ingenieure/Verein Deutscher Elektrotechniker

Address: Konigplatz 368
　　　　D-3500 Kassel
Telephone: 561/715 97
Fax: 561/171 61

▲ ZENIT (Zentrun in Nordrhein-Westfalen fur Innovation und Technik GmbH)

Euro Info Centre

Address: Dohne, 54
　　　　D-4330 Mulheim (Ruhr) 1
Telephone: 208/300 04 54
Fax: 208/300 04 29
Telex: 208363

▲ Zentrale fur Produktivitat und Technologie Saar

Euro Info Centre

Address: Franz Josef Roder Strasse 9
　　　　D-6600 Saarbrucken 1
Telephone: 681/508 289
Fax: 681/584 61 25

Greece

▲ Association of Industries in Thessaly and in Central Greece

Euro Info Centre

Address: 4, El. Venizelou Rd.
　　　　GR-38221 Volos
Telephone: 421/28 111; 421/32 622
Fax: 421/26 394

▲ Association of Industries of Northern Greece

Euro Info Centre

Address: Morihovou Square 1
　　　　GR-54625 Thessaloniki
Telephone: 31/53 98 17; 31/53 96 82
Fax: 31/54 14 91

▲ Chambre de Commerce et d'Industrie d'Athenes

Euro Info Centre

Address: 7, Akadimias Str.
　　　　GR-10671 Athina
Telephone: 1/362 73 37
Fax: 1/360 78 97

▲ Chambre de Commerce et d'Industrie du Piree

Euro Info Centre

Address: 1, rue Loudovicou
place Roosevelt
GR-18531 Piree
Telephone: 14/17 72 41
Fax: 14/17 86 80

▲ Chamber of Iraklion

Euro Info Centre

Address: 9 Koroneou Str.
GR-71202 Iraklion
Telephone: 81/22 90 13
Fax: 81/22 29 14

▲ Chamber of Kavala

Euro Info Centre

Address: 50 Omonias Street
GR-65302 Kavala
Telephone: 51/83 39 64
Fax: 51/83 59 46

▲ EOMMEX—Alexandroupolis

Euro Info Centre

Address: Miaouli 15
GR-68100
Alexandroupolis
Telephone: 551/33 565
Fax: 551/33 566

▲ EOMMEX—Larissa

Euro Info Centre

Address: Marinou Antipa & Kouma Str.
GR-41222 Larissa
Telephone: 41/22 60 77
Fax: 41/25 30 15

▲ EOMMEX—Mytilini

Euro Info Centre

Address: Iktinou 2
pl. Kyprion Agoniston
GR-81100 Mytilini
Telephone: 251/24 906
Fax: 251/41 501

▲ EOMMEX—Patras

Euro Info Centre

Address: 21 Aratou Str.
GR-26221 Patras
Telephone: 61/22 02 48
Fax: 61/22 34 96

▲ Hellenic Organization of Small and Medium-Sized Industries and Handicrafts (EOMMEX)

Euro Info Centre

Address: Xenias Str. 16
GR-11528 Athina
Telephone: 1/779 42 29
Fax: 1/777 86 94

▲ Panhellenic Exporters' Association

Euro Info Centre

Address: Kratinou 11
GR-10552 Athina
Telephone: 1/522 89 25
Fax: 1/524 25 68

Ireland

▲ Cork Chamber of Commerce

Euro Info Centre

Address: 67 South Mall
IRL—Cork
Telephone: 21/50 90 44
Fax: 21/27 13 47

▲ Galway Chamber of Commerce and Industry

Euro Info Centre

Address: Hynes Building
St. Augustine Street
IRL—Galway
Telephone: 91/62 624
Fax: 91/61 963

▲ The Irish Export Board

Euro Info Centre

Address: c/o Industrial Estate
The Cork Road
IRL—Waterford
Telephone: 51/78 577
Fax: 51/72 719

▲ Irish Export Board/Coras Trachtala

Euro Info Centre

Address: Merrion Hall, P.O. Box 203
            Strand Road Sandymount
            IRL—Dublin 4
Telephone: 1/69 50 11
Fax: 1/69 58 20

▲ Shannon Free Airport Development Company

Euro Info Centre

Address: The Granary
            Michael Street
            IRL—Limerick
Telephone: 61/40 77 7
Fax: 61/31 56 34

▲ SLIGO European Business Information Centre

Address: 16, Quay Street
            IRL—Sligo
Telephone: 71/61 274
Fax: 71/60 912

Italy

▲ Associazione "Compagnia delle Opere"

Eurosportello—EUROCDO

Address: Via V. Rossi
            I-61100 Pesaro
Telephone: 721/41 00 88
Fax: 721/41 41 74

▲ Associazione industriale

Lombarda
Euro Info Centre

Address: Via Pantano, 9
            I-20122 Milano
Telephone: 2/882 34 11
Fax: 2/882 43 6

▲ Associazione Industriali della Provincia di Vicenza

Euro Info Centre

Address: Piazza Castello, 3
            I-36100 Vicenza
Telephone: 444/54 22 11
Fax: 444/54 73 18

▲ Camera di Commercio, Industria, Artigianato, Agricoltura

Euro Info Centre

Address: Via Morpurgo, 4
            I-33100 Udine
Telephone: 432/273 222
Fax: 432/509 469

▲ C.C.I.A.A. di Ascoli Piceno—Eurosportello

Address: Via L. Mercantini, 23/25
            I-63100 Ascoli Piceno
Telephone: 736/27 92 55
Fax: 736/27 92 37

▲ C.C.I.A.A. Isernia

Euro Info Centre

Address: Corso Risorgimento, 302
            I-86170 Isernia
Telephone: 865/41 29 23
Fax: 865/23 50 24

▲ C.C.I.A.A. Ravenna

Euro Info Centre

Address: Viale L.C. Farini, 14
            I-48100 Ravenna
Telephone: 544/303 87
Fax: 544/396 72

▲ Centro Estero delle Camere di Commercio del Veneto

Euro Info Centre

Address: Via Guglielmo Pepe, 104
            I-30172 Venezia Mestre
Telephone: 41/98 93 44
Fax: 41/96 24 63

▲ Confederazione Generale dell'Agricoltura Italiana

Euro Info Centre

Address: Corso Vittorio Emanuele, 101
            I-00186 Roma
Telephone: 6/65 12 1
Fax: 6/65 48 578

▲ Confederazione Generale Italiana del Commercio e del Turismo

Euro Info Centre

Address: Piazza G.G. Belli, 2
I-00153 Roma
Telephone: 6/58 98 973; 6/58 97 613
Fax: 6/58 90 984

▲ Ente Economico Bresciano

Euro Info Centre

Address: Via Cipro, 1
I-25124 Brescia
Telephone: 30/22 63 82; 30/22 11 72
Fax: 30/22 56 82

▲ Euro Info Centre

Camera di Commercio, Industria, Artigianato, Agricoltura

Address: Via San Francesco da Paola, 24
I-10123 Torino
Telephone: 11/571 63 70
Fax: 11/571 65 33

▲ Euro Info Centre

Camera Commercio, Industria, Artigianato, Agricoltura Catania

Address: Salita Cappuccini, 2
I-95124 Catania
Telephone: 95/71 50 176
Fax: 95/71 50 265

▲ Euro Info Centre

Camera di Commercio, Industria, Artigianato, e Agricoltura di Milano

Address: Via delle Orsole, 4/B
I-20143 Milano
Telephone: 2/85 15 44 56
Fax: 2/85 15 47 22

▲ Euro Info Centre

Camera di Commercio, Industria, Artigianato, e Agricoltura di Napoli

Address: Corso Meridionale, 58
I-80143 Napoli
Telephone: 81/55 36 106; 81/28 42 17
Fax: 81/28 54 65

▲ Euro Info Centre

Centro estero Umbria

Address: c/o Camera di Commercio di Perugia
Via Cacciatori delle Alpi, 40
I-06100 Perugia
Telephone: 75/66 847; 75/298 206
Fax: 75/28 088

▲ Euro Info Centre

Confesercenti

Address: Piazza Pier Vettori, 8/10
I-50143 Firenze
Telephone: 55/27 05 247
Fax: 55/22 40 96

▲ Euro Info Centre

ME. SVIL. S.p.A.

Address: Via R. Wagner, 5
I-90109 Palermo
Telephone: 91/58 99 25
Fax: 91/61 11 121

▲ Eurosportello

Camera di Commercio di Firenze

Address: Piazza dei Giudici, 3
I-50122 Firenze
Telephone: 55/27 95 1
Fax: 55/27 95 259

▲ Eurosportello

Camera di Commercio di Genova

Address: Torre WTC—San Benigno
Via de Marini, 1
I-16149 Genova (Sampierdarena)
Telephone: 10/20 94 1
Fax: 10/20 94 200

▲ Eurosportello

Unioncamere/Mondimpresa/Cerved

Address: Piazza Sallustio, 21
I-00187 Roma
Telephone: 6/470 41
Fax: 6/470 24 240

▲ Eurosportello Assindustria Bologna—
Associazione degli Industriali della Provincia
di Bologna

Address: Via San Domenico, 4
I-40124 Bologna
Telephone: 51/52 96 11
Fax: 51/52 96 13

▲ Eurosportello Cagliari

Address: Viale Diaz, 221
c/o Centro Servizi
I-09126 Cagliari
Telephone: 70/30 68 77; 70/30 89 77
Fax: 70/34 03 28

▲ Eurosportello della Camera di Commercio,
Industria, Agricoltura, e Artigianato

Address: Piazza G.B. Vico, 3
I-66100 Chieti
Telephone: 871/65 750
Fax: 871/69 197

▲ Federpiemonte

Euro Info Centre

Address: Corso Stati Uniti, 38
I-10128 Torino
Telephone: 11/57 18 455
Fax: 11/55 75 204

▲ Institute for Development of Southern Italy
(I.A.S.M.)

Euro Info Centre

Address: Viale M. Pilsudski, 124
I-00197 Roma
Telephone: 6/84 72 230
Fax: 6/84 72 212

▲ Instituto Finanziario Regionale Pugliese—
Finpuglia

Euro Info Centre

Address: Via Lenin, 2
I-70125 Bari
Telephone: 80/41 67 35
Fax: 80/41 68 09

▲ Lega Nazionale delle Cooperative e Mutue—
Eurosportello Lega

Address: av. de la Joyeuse Entree, 1
B-1040 Bruxelles
Telephone: 2/231 10 05
Fax: 2/230 81 43

Luxembourg

▲ Chambre des Metiers du Grand-Duche de
Luxembourg

Euro Info Centre

Address: 41, rue Glesener
L-1631 Luxembourg
Telephone: 40/00 221
Fax: 49/23 80

▲ EUROGUICHET

Chambre de Commerce du Grand-Duche de Luxembourg

Address: 7, rue Alcide de Gasperi
BP 1503
L-2981 Luxembourg
Kirchberg
Telephone: 43/58 53
Fax: 43/83 26

The Netherlands

▲ Aktieprogramma Regionale Economie
(A.R.E.)

Euro Info Centre

Address: 271 Postbus
(Kasteellaan, 9 DA)
NL-6600 Wijchen
Telephone: 88/94 23 457
Fax: 88/94 24 305

▲ CIMK-RIMK

EG-Adviescentrum voor Ondernemingen-Insti-
tuut voor het Midden- en Kleinbedrijf

Euro Info Centre

Address: 9, Dalsteindreef—BP 112
NL-1110 AC Diemen-Zuid
Telephone: 20/90 10 71
Fax: 20/95 32 31

▲ EG-Adviescentrum

N.V. Induma/B.O.M.

Address: Prins Hendriklaan, 21a
             Postbus 211
             NL-5700 AE Helmond
Telephone: 49/20 48 468
Fax: 49/20 26 895

▲ Euro Info Centre

Zuid-Holland

The Hague Chamber of Commerce and Industry

Address: Alexander Gogelweg, 16
             PO Box 29718
             NL-2517 JH Den Haag
Telephone: 70/79 52 80
Fax: 70/45 76 00

▲ EVD, Economic Information and Export
   Promotion

Euro Info Centre

Address: Bezuidenhoutseweg, 151
             NL-2594 Den Haag
Telephone: 70/79 88 11
Fax: 70/79 78 78

▲ Kamer van Koophandel en Fabrieken voor
   Utrecht en Omstreken

Euro Info Centre

Address: Waterstraat, 47
             Postbus 48
             NL-3500 AA Utrecht
Telephone: 30/36 32 11
Fax: 30/31 28 04

▲ Noordelijke Ontwikkelingsmaatschappij

Euro Info Centre

NOORD-NEDERLAND

Address: Damport, 1
             PO Box 424
             NL-9700 AK Groningen
Telephone: 50/26 78 26
Fax: 50/26 14 75

▲ OOST Nederland

Euro Info Centre

Address: Postbus 545
             Institutenweg, 4
             NL-7500 AM Enschede
Telephone: 53/83 64 28
Fax: 53/83 63 80

Portugal

▲ Associacao Comercial e Industrial da Coimbra

Address: Av. Sa Da Bandeira, 90-92
             P-3000 Coimbra
Telephone: 39/22 843
Fax: 39/27 023

▲ Associacao industrial do Distrito de Aveiro

Euro Info Centre

Address: Av. Dr. Lourenco Peixinho, 146
             5° A
             P-3800 Aveiro
Telephone: 34/20 095
Fax: 34/24 093

▲ Camara do Comercio e Industria dos Acores

Address: Rua da Palha
             P-9700 Angra Do Heroismo (Acores)
Telephone: 95/2 34 70
Fax: 95/2 71 31

▲ Commissao de Coordenacao da Regiao do
   Algarve

Euro Info Centre

Address: Praca da Liberdade, 2
P-8000 Faro
Telephone: 89/80 27 09
Fax: 89/80 35 91

▲ EUROGABINETE

Associacao Industrial Portuguesa

Address: Avenida da Boavista, 2671
             Apartado 1092
             P-4102 Porto Codex
Telephone: 26/17 73 22
Fax: 26/17 68 40

▲ EUROGABINETE

Associacao Industrial Portuguesa

Address: Dept. de Associativsmo
Praca das Industrias
P-1399 Lisboa
Telephone: 1/362 01 00
Fax: 1/646 786

▲ EUROGABINETE

Banco de Fomento Nacional

Address: Av. Casal Ribeiro, 59
P-1000 Lisboa
Telephone: 1/56 10 71
Fax: 1/54 85 71

▲ EUROGABINETE

Caixa Geral de Depositos

Address: Av. da Republica, 31
P-1000 Lisboa
Telephone: 1/352 01 02
Fax: 1/352 02 97

▲ EUROGABINETE de Evora

Istituto de Apoio as Pequenas e Medias Empresas
e ao Investimento

Address: Rua do Valasco, 19C
P-7000 Evora
Telephone: 66/21 875
Fax: 66/29 781

▲ EUROGABINETE da Madeira

Associacao Comercial e Industrial do Funchal/
C.C.I. da Madeira

Address: Avenida Arriaga, 41
P-9000 Funchal (Madeira)
Telephone: 91/30/137; 91/30 138
Fax: 91/22 005

▲ EUROGABINETE para a Regiao Centre

Address: Rua Bernardim Ribeiro, 80
P-3000 Coimbra
Telephone: 39/71 14 36
Fax: 39/72 37 57

▲ Norma-Acores

Euro Info Centre

Address: Rua Antonio Joaquim Nunes da
Silva, 55
P-9500 Ponta Delgada (Acores)
Telephone: 96/26 808
Fax: 96/26 808

Spain

▲ Asociacion de la Industria Navarra

Euro Info Centre

Address: P.O. Box 430
E-31191 Cordovilla-Pamplona
Telephone: 48/101 110
Fax: 48/101 100

▲ Banco de Credito Industrial

Euro Info Centre

Address: Manila 56-58
E-08034 Barcelona
Telephone: 3/20 41 366
Fax: 3/20 57 335

▲ BANESTO—Cetro Europeo de Informacion

Address: Plaza de la Constitucion 9
E-29008 Malaga
Telephone: 52/22 09 59
Fax: 52/22 09 36

▲ Camera de Comercio e Industria de Madrid

Euro Info Centre

Address: Plaza de la Independencia, 1
E-28001 Madrid
Telephone: 1/429 31 93
Fax: 1/578 28 54

▲ Camera de Comercio e Industria de Toledo

Euro Info Centre

Address: Plaza San Vincente, 3
E-45001 Toledo
Telephone: 25/21 44 50
Fax: 25/21 39 00

▲ Camera Oficial de Comercio, Industria, y Navegacion

Euro Info Centre

Address: Avenida Diagonal, 452-454
E-08006 Barcelona
Telephone: 34/15 16 00
Fax: 32/18 68 57

▲ Camera Oficial de Comercio, Industria, y Navegacion de Bilbao

Euro Info Centre

Address: Alameda de Recalde, 50
E-48008 Bilbao (Viscaya)
Telephone: 4/444 40 54
Fax: 4/443 61 71

▲ Camera Oficial de Comercio, Industria, y Navegacion de Valencia

Euro Info Centre

Address: C/ Poeta Querol, 15
E-46002 Valencia
Telephone: 63/51 13 01
Fax: 63/51 63 49

▲ Centro Europeo de Informacion

CIDEM/FTN

Address: Av. Diagonal, 403 Ir
E-08008 Barcelona
Telephone: 3/238 21 68
Fax: 3/238 20 31

▲ Confederacion de Empresarios de Andalucia

Euro Info Centre

Address: Avda. San Francisco Javier 9
Edifico Sevilla 2-9a Planta
E-41018 Sevilla
Telephone: 5/465 05 11
Fax: 5/464 12 42

▲ Confederacion de Empresarios de Castilla La Mancha

Euro Info Centre

Address: Calle Rosario, 29
E-02001 Albacete
Telephone: 67/21 21 49
Fax: 67/24 02 02

▲ Confederacion de Empresarios de Galicia

Euro Info Centre

Address: C/ Romera Donallo 7a—Entesuelo
E-15706 Santiago de Compostela
Telephone: 81/59 76 54
Fax: 81/56 57 88

▲ Confederacion Espanola de Organizaciones de Empresarios

Euro Info Centre

Address: Diego de Leon, 50
E-28006 Madrid
Telephone: 1/563 96 41
Fax: 1/262 80 23

▲ Confederacion Regional de Empresarios de Aragon

Euro Info Centre

Address: Plaza Roma, F-1, 1a Planta
E-50010 Zaragoza
Telephone: 76/32 00 00
Fax: 76/32 29 56

▲ Consejeria de Economia y Comercio

Euro Info Centre

Address: Avda. Juan XXIII No. 2
E-35004 La Palmas de G. Canaria
Telephone: 28/23 11 44
Fax: 28/24 77 05

▲ Consorcio Centro de Documentacion Europe-as Islas Baleares

Address: Calle Patronato Obero, 30
E-07006 Palm de Mallorca (Baleares)
Telephone: 71/46 10 02
Fax: 71/46 30 70

▲ Euroventanilla del Pais Vasco

Address: C/Tomas Gros, No. 3 Bajo
E-20001 Donastia San Sebastian
Telephone: 43/27 22 88
Fax: 43/27 16 57

▲ Euroventanilla Grupo Banco Popular Espanil

Address: Rambla de Mendex Nunez, 12
E-03002 Alicante
Telephone: 65/21 62 91
Fax: 65/20 19 54

▲ Euroventanilla—Imade

Euro Info Centre

Address: Mariano Ron 1
           E-28900 Madrid (Getafe)
Telephone: 1/696 11 11
Fax: 1/695 61 74

▲ Federacion Asturiana de Empresarios

Address: Calle Doctor Alfredo Marinez,
           No. 6-2° pl.
           E-33005 Oviedo (Asturias)
Telephone: 85/23 21 05
Fax: 85/24 41 76

▲ Federacion de Empresarios de la Rioja

Euro Info Centre

Address: Calle Hermanos Moroy, 8-4
           E-28001 Logrono
Telephone: 41/25 70 22
Fax: 41/20 25 37

▲ IMPI-ICEX

Euro Info Centre

Address: Paeso de la Castellana, 141
           2a Planta
           E-28046 Madrid
Telephone: 1/571 46 40
Fax: 1/571 59 12

▲ Instituto de Fomento de la Region de Murcia

Euro Info Centre

Address: C/Garcia Alix, 17
           E-30005 Murcia
Telephone: 68/29 94 98
Fax: 68/29 95 48

▲ Instituto de Fomento Regional del Principado
   de Asturias

Euro Info Centre

Address: C/Cervantes, 27, 5° C
           E-33004 Oviedo
Telephone: 85/27 00 65
Fax: 87/27 18 53

▲ Sociedad para el Desarrollo Industrial de
   Extremadura (SODIEX)

Euro Info Centre

Address: C/Dr. Maranon, 2
           E-10002 Caceres
Telephone: 27/22 48 78
Fax: 27/24 33 04

▲ SODICAL

Euro Info Centre

Address: C/ Santiago, 9-2e
           E-47001 Valladolid
Telephone: 83/35 40 33
Fax: 83/35 47 38

United Kingdom

EURO INFO CENTRES

▲ Bristol Chamber of Commerce and Industry

Address: 16, Clifton Park
           GB-Bristol BS8 3BY
Telephone: 272/73 73 73
Fax: 272/74 53 65

▲ Centre for European Business Information

Small Firms Service

Address: 11, Belgrave Road
           GB-London SW1V 1RB
Telephone: 71/828 62 01
Fax: 71/834 84 16

▲ Euro Info Centre

Birmingham Chamber of Industry and Commerce

Address: 75, Harborne Road
           P.O. Box 360
           GB-Birmingham B15 3DH
Telephone: 21/454 61 71
Fax: 21/455 86 70

▲ Euro Info Centre

Northern Development Company

Address: Great North House
           Sandyford Road
           GB-Newcastle-Upon-Tyne
           NE1 8ND
Telephone: 91/261 00 26; 91/261 00 248
Fax: 91/222 17 79

▲ Euroteam

Euro Info Centre

The Business Advice Centre

Address: New Walk, 30
GB-Leicester LE1 6TF
Telephone: 533/55 44 64
Fax: 533/47 08 29

▲ Exeter Enterprises Limited

University of Exeter

Euro Info Centre

Address: Hailey Wing, Reed Hall
GB-Exeter EX4 4QR
Telephone: 392/21 40 85
Fax: 392/26 43 75

▲ Federation of Sussex Industries and Chamber of Commerce

Euro Info Centre

Address: Seven Dials
GB-Brighton BN1 3JS
East Sussex
Telephone: 273/26 282
Fax: 273/20 79 65

▲ Highland Opportunity Ltd.

Development Department

Address: Highland Regional Council
Regional Buildings
Glenurquhart Road
GB-Inverness IV3 5NX
Telephone: 463/23 41 21
Fax: 463/71 08 48

▲ Kent County Council

Euro Info Centre

Address: Springfield
GB-Maidstone ME14 2LL
Telephone: 622/69 61 30
Fax: 622/69 14 18

▲ Local Enterprise Development Unit

Euro Info Centre
Address: Ledu House Upper Galway
UK-Belfast BT8 4TB
Northern Ireland
Telephone: 232/49 10 31
Fax: 232/69 14 32

▲ London Chamber of Commerce and Industry

Address: 69, Cannon Street
GB-London EC4N 5AB
Telephone: 71/248 44 44
Fax: 71/489 03 91

▲ Manchester Chamber of Commerce and Industry

Euro InfoCentre

Address: Oxford Street, 56
GB-Manchester M60 7HJ
Telephone: 61/236 32 10
Fax: 61/236 41 60

▲ North West Euro Services Ltd.

Liverpool Central Libraries

Address: Will Brown Street
GB-Merseyside L3 8EW
Telephone: 51/298 19 28
Fax: 51/207 13 42

▲ Norwich and Norfolk Chamber of Commerce and Industry

Euro Info Centre

Address: 112 Barrack Street
GB-Norwich NR3 1UB
Telephone: 603/62 59 77
Fax: 603/63 30 32

▲ The Nottinghamshire Chamber of Commerce and Industry

Euro Info Centre

Address: Unit 14, Faraday Building
Highfields Science Park
GB-Nottingham NG7 2QP
Telephone: 602/22 24 14
Fax: 602/22 03 12

▲ Scottish Development Agency

Euro Info Centre

Address: 21, Bothwell Street
GB-Glasgow G2 6NR
Telephone: 41/221 09 99
Fax: 41/226 50 89

▲ Shropshire and Staffordshire

Euro Info Centre

Address: Industry House
Halesfield 20
Telford
GB-Shropshire TF7 4TA
Telephone: 952/58 87 66
Fax: 952/58 25 03

▲ The Southern Area European Information Centre

Address: Central Library
Civic Centre
Southampton
GB-Hampshire SO9 4XP
Telephone: 703/83 28 66
Fax: 703/23 17 14

▲ The Staffordshire Development Association

Address: Business Advice Centre
Martin Street, 3
GB-Stafford ST16 2LH
Telephone: 785/55/073
Fax: 785/21 52 86

▲ Thames Chiltern

Euro Info Centre

Address: Commerce House
2-6 Bath Road
Slough
GB-Berks SL1 3SB
Telephone: 753/77 877
Fax: 753/24 644

▲ Wales Euro Info Centre

Address: UWCC/Guest Building
P.O. Box 430
Cardiff
GB-South Glamorgan CF 1 3XT
Telephone: 222/22 95 25
Fax: 222/22 97 40

▲ West Yorkshire Network for European Business

Address: Bradford Enterprise Centre
Broadway
GB-Bradford BD1 1JF
Telephone: 274/75 42 62
Fax: 274/39 32 26

OTHER CONTACTS

▲ British Standards Institution

Address: 2 Park Street
GB-London W1A 2BS
Great Britain
Telephone: 1/629 9000
Scope: Contact point for preparation of standards required by the Single Market Program

▲ Department of Trade and Industry

Export Market Branch—Western Europe

Address: 1 Victoria Street
GB-London SW1W 0ET
Great Britain
Telephone: 71/215 4878; 71/215 5336
Scope: Provider of assistance to British exporters; produces a wide range of publications

▲ Department of Trade and Industry

Single European Market Unit

Address: Room 410
1-19 Victoria Street
GB-London SW1H 0ET
Great Britain
Telephone: 81/200 1992 [1992 Hotline];
71/215 4770
Fax: 71/215 5649
Scope: Involvement with all aspects of the Single Market Program; has information packs and factsheets available on many issues of interest to businesses, including the *Single Market Information Pack, A Guide for Business,* and *Guide to Practical Advice for Business;* provides referrals to other government departments with more detailed information on specific aspects of the Single Market Program

▲ EC Information Offices:

8 Storey's Gate
GB-London SW1P 3AT
Great Britain
Telephone: 71/222 81 22

4 Cathedral Road
GB-Cardiff CF1 9SG
Wales
Telephone: 222/37 16 31

7 Alva Street
GB-Edinburgh EH2 4PH
Scotland
Telephone: 31/225 20 58

Windsor House
9/15 Bedford Street
UK-Belfast BT2 7EG
Northern Ireland
Telephone: 232/407 08

H

Contacts in

Canada and Japan

on the Single

Market Program

HOW TO USE THIS APPENDIX

The EC's major trading partners have established contacts to help their businesses deal with the Single Market Program. This appendix lists the governmental and nongovernmental EC contacts for Canada and Japan.

SECTIONS IN THIS APPENDIX:

Canadian Contacts

Japanese Contacts

ASSISTANCE

Sources for U.S. businesses are provided in Appendix F.

▼

CANADIAN CONTACTS

Canadian Government

Note: Canadian Government services listed here are for the use of Canadian citizens and residents.

▲ External Affairs and International Trade Canada

European Community Trade Policy Division (REM)

Address: 125 Sussex Drive
          Ottawa, Ontario K1A 0G2
Telephone: 613/995-4017
Fax: 613/996-9103
Telex: 053 3745
Scope: Customs information

▲ External Affairs and International Trade Canada

Western Europe Trade and Investment Development Division (RWT)

Address: 125 Sussex Drive
          Ottawa, Ontario K1A 0G2
Telephone: 613/995-9402
Fax: 613/996-9103
Telex: 053-3745
Scope: Information about members of the EC as well as the EC as a whole

▲ International Trade Centres

Scope: Assistance to Canadian exports through publications, recruiting participants for trade fairs and missions, and other services related to export counseling, technology transfer, and foreign joint ventures

Alberta

Address: Room 540
          Canada Place
          9700 Jasper Avenue
          Edmonton, Alberta T5J 4C3
Telephone: 403/495-2944
Fax: 403/495-4507
Telex: 037-2762

Address: Suite 1100
          510 - 5th Street S.W.
          Calgary, Alberta T2P 3S2
Telephone: 403/292-6660
Fax: 403/292-4578

British Columbia

Address: P.O. Box 11610
          900 - 650 West Georgia Street
          Vancouver, British Columbia V6B 5H8
Telephone: 604/666-1444
Fax: 604/666-8330
Telex: 04-51191

Manitoba

Address: P.O. Box 981
          330 Portage Avenue, Suite 608
          Winnipeg, Manitoba R3C 2V2
Telephone: 204/983-8036
Fax: 204/983-2187
Telex: 07-57624

New Brunswick

Address: P.O. Box 1210
          Assumption Place
          770 Main Street
          Moncton, New Brunswick E1C 8P9
Telephone: 506/857-6452
Fax: 506/857-6429
Telex: 014-2200

Newfoundland

Address: P.O. Box 8950
Parson Building
90 O'Leary Avenue
St. John's, Newfoundland A1B 3R9
Telephone: 709/722-5511
Fax: 709/722-2373
Telex: 016-4749

Nova Scotia

Address: P.O. Box 940
Station M
1496 Lower Water Street
Halifax, Nova Scotia B3J 2V9
Telephone: 902/426-7540
Fax: 902/426-2624
Telex: 019-22525

Ontario

Address: Dominion Public Building
4th Floor
One Front Street West
Toronto, Ontario M5J 1A4
Telephone: 416/973-5053
Fax: 416/973-8161
Telex: 065-24378

Prince Edward Island

Address: P.O. Box 1115 Confederation
Court Mall
134 Kent Street, Suite 400
Charlottetown, Prince Edward
Island C1A 7M8
Telephone: 902/566-7400
Fax: 902/566-7450
Telex: 014-44129

Quebec

Address: P.O. Box 247
Stock Exchange Tower
800 Place Victoria, Suite 3800
Montreal, Quebec H4Z 1E8
Telephone: 514/283-8185
Fax: 514/283-3302
Telex: 055-60768

Saskatchewan

Address: 6th Floor
105 - 21st Street East
Saskatoon, Saskatchewan S7K 0B3
Telephone: 306/975-5925
Fax: 306/975-5334
Telex: 074-2742

▲ Mission of Canada to the European Communities

Address: 2, av. de Tervueren
B-1040 Brussels
Belgium
Telephone: 2/735-9125
Fax: 2/735-3383
Telex: 21613 DOMCAN B
Scope: Involved in market access issues and the development of industrial, economic and scientific cooperation between Canada and the EC; export market inquiries should be directed to the Canadian embassies and consulates in the Member States of the EC

Other Canadian Resources

▲ Delegation of the Commission of the European Communities

Address: Office Tower
Suite 1110
350 Sparks Street
Ottawa, Ontario K1R 7S8
Telephone: 613/238-6464; 613/741-0951
Fax: 613/238-5191
Telex: 0534544 EURCOM OTT

▲ Organization of Economic Cooperation and Development (OECD)—Sales Outlets:

Renouf Publishing Company Ltd.

Editions Renouf Ltee
1294 Algoma Road
Ottawa, Ontario K1B 3W8
Telephone: 613/741-4333

Federal Publications Inc.

301-303 King Street West
Toronto, Ontario M5V 1J5
Telephone: 416/581-1552

Les Editions la Libertie Inc.

3020 Chemin
Sainte-Foy, Quebec G1X 3V6
Telephone: 418/658-3763

▲ United Nations Publications—Sales Agents:

Le Diffuser G. Vermette Inc.

Case Postale 85
1501 rue Ampere
Boucherville, Quebec PQ J4B 5E6

Renouf Publishing Company

Mail Orders
1294 Algoma Road
Ottawa, Ontario K1B 3W8

▲ WEFA Canada Inc.

Address: 777 Bay Street, Suite 2020
Toronto, Ontario M5G 2C8
Telephone: 416/599-5700

JAPANESE CONTACTS

Japanese Government

▲ Japan External Trade Organization (JETRO)

Address: 2-5, Toranomon 2-Chome, Minato-ku
Tokyo 105
Telephone: 3/3583-5511
Fax: 3/3587-0219
Telex: J24378 (JETRO)
Scope: Development of information and
opportunities on trade throughout the
world; has offices in most EC countries,
many of which include offices of the
Center for Industrial and Technological
Cooperation (CITEC); business libraries
in Tokyo and Osaka provide access to
detailed trade and production statistics;
produces numerous publications and
special studies

Other Japanese Resources

▲ Delegation of the Commission of the European Communities

Address: Europa House
9-15 Sanbancho
Chiyoda-Ku
Tokyo 102
Telephone: 3/3239-04-41
Fax: 3/3261-51-94
Telex: 2391 DELEGEC

▲ OECD Publications and Information Centre

Address: Landic Akasaka Building
2-3-4 Akasaka, Minato-ku
Tokyo 107
Telephone: 3/3586-2016
Fax: 3/3584-7929

▲ Statistical Office of the European Communities—Sales Office

Kinokuniya Company Ltd.
Address: 17-7 Shinjuku 3-Chome
Sinkiuku-ku
Tokyo 160-91
Telephone: 3/3439-0124

▲ United Nations Publications—Sales Agents:

Far Eastern Book Sellers
Kanda P.O. Box 72
Tokyo
Hikari Book Trading Co. Ltd.

Nagatani Bldg.
Room 201
26 Sakamachi, Shinjuku-ku
Tokyo 16

Kinokuniya Co. Ltd.
Book Import Department
38-1 Sakuragaoka 5-Chome, Setagaya-ku
Tokyo

Kitao Publications Trading Co. Ltd.
Central P.O. Box 936
Osaka 530-91

Maruzen Company Ltd.

P.O. Box 5050
Tokyo International 100-31

Naigai Books Ltd.

Fukushima Bldg. 4-7,
Nishikanda 2-Chome, Chiyoda-ku
Tokyo 101

Tokyo Publications Service Ltd.

Dai-ichi Takiguchi Bldg. 20-7
Ginza 1-Chome, Chuo-ku
Tokyo 104

Index of Associations and Organizations

Name and Subject Index

D

E

❑   I want to order _____ copies of The Arthur Andersen European Community Sourcebook.

❑   I want information on Arthur Andersen's European Community Services.

❑   Send me information about future editions of the Sourcebook

Name_____ Telephone No. (   ) _____

Company_____Position _____

Street Address _____

City_____State_____Zip_____Country _____

❑ American Express   ❑ Visa   ❑ Mastercard   Account No._____

Signature_____Exp._____

Triumph Books
Phone (312) 939-3330   Fax (312) 663-3557

❑   I want to order _____ copies of The Arthur Andersen European Community Sourcebook.

❑   I want information on Arthur Andersen's European Community Services.

❑   Send me information about future editions of the Sourcebook

Name_____ Telephone No. (   ) _____

Company_____Position _____

Street Address _____

City_____State_____Zip_____Country _____

❑ American Express   ❑ Visa   ❑ Mastercard   Account No._____

Signature_____Exp._____

Triumph Books
Phone (312) 939-3330   Fax (312) 663-3557

❑   I want to order _____ copies of The Arthur Andersen European Community Sourcebook.

❑   I want information on Arthur Andersen's European Community Services.

❑   Send me information about future editions of the Sourcebook

Name_____ Telephone No. (   ) _____

Company_____Position _____

Street Address _____

City_____State_____Zip_____Country _____

❑ American Express   ❑ Visa   ❑ Mastercard   Account No._____

Signature_____Exp._____

Triumph Books
Phone (312) 939-3330   Fax (312) 663-3557